PERGAMON INTERNATIONAL LIBRARY
of Science, Technology, Engineering and Social Studies
The 1000-volume original paperback library in aid of education, industrial training and the enjoyment of leisure
Publisher: Robert Maxwell, M.C.

New Perspectives in Nonverbal Communication

D1552890

LUTHER COLLEGE

THE PERGAMON TEXTBOOK INSPECTION COPY SERVICE

An inspection copy of any book published in the Pergamon International Library will gladly be sent to academic staff without obligation for their consideration for course adoption or recommendation. Copies may be retained for a period of 60 days from receipt and returned if not suitable. When a particular title is adopted or recommended for adoption for class use and the recommendation results in a sale of 12 or more copies, the inspection copy may be retained with our compliments. The Publishers will be pleased to receive suggestions for revised editions and new titles to be published in this important International Library.

LANGUAGE & COMMUNICATION LIBRARY

Volume 5—*Series Editor:* Roy Harris, *University of Oxford*

Vol. 1. MORRIS—Saying and Meaning in Puerto Rico

Vol. 2. TAYLOR—Linguistic Theory and Structural Stylistics

Vol. 3. GAGNEPAIN—Du Vouloir Dire

Vol. 4. HARRIS—Approaches to Language

A Related Pergamon Journal

LANGUAGE & COMMUNICATION*

An Interdisciplinary Journal

Editor: Roy Harris, *University of Oxford*

The primary aim of the journal is to fill the need for a publicational forum devoted to the discussion of topics and issues in communication which are of interdisciplinary significance. It will publish contributions from researchers in all fields relevant to the study of verbal and non-verbal communication.
Emphasis will be placed on the implications of current research for establishing common theoretical frameworks within which findings from different areas of study may be accommodated and interrelated.
By focusing attention on the many ways in which language is integrated with other forms of communicational activity and interactional behaviour it is intended to explore ways of developing a science of communication which is not restricted by existing disciplinary boundaries.

* Free specimen copy available on request.

NOTICE TO READERS

Dear Reader

An invitation to Publish in and Recommend the Placing of a Standing Order to Volumes Published in this Valuable Series

If your library is not already a standing/continuation order customer to this series, may we recommend that you place a standing/continuation order to receive immediately upon publication all new volumes. Should you find that these volumes no longer serve your needs, your order can be cancelled at any time without notice.
The Editors and the Publisher will be glad to receive suggestions of outlines of suitable titles, reviews or symposia for editorial consideration: if found acceptable, rapid publication is guaranteed.

ROBERT MAXWELL
Publisher at Pergamon Press

New Perspectives in Nonverbal Communication

Studies in Cultural Anthropology, Social Psychology, Linguistics, Literature, and Semiotics

by

FERNANDO POYATOS

University of New Brunswick, Canada

PERGAMON PRESS

OXFORD · NEW YORK · TORONTO · SYDNEY · PARIS · FRANKFURT

U.K.	Pergamon Press Ltd., Headington Hill Hall, Oxford OX3 0BW, England
U.S.A.	Pergamon Press Inc., Maxwell House, Fairview Park, Elmsford, New York 10523, U.S.A.
CANADA	Pergamon Press Canada Ltd., Suite 104, 150 Consumers Road, Willowdale, Ontario M2J 1P9, Canada
AUSTRALIA	Pergamon Press (Aust.) Pty. Ltd., P.O. Box 544, Potts Point, N.S.W. 2011, Australia
FRANCE	Pergamon Press SARL, 24 rue des Ecoles, 75240 Paris, Cedex 05, France
FEDERAL REPUBLIC OF GERMANY	Pergamon Press GmbH, Hammerweg 6, D-6242 Kronberg-Taunus, Federal Republic of Germany

Copyright © 1983 Fernando Poyatos

All Rights Reserved. No part of this publication may be reproduced, stored in a retrieval system or transmitted in any form or by any means: electronic, electrostatic, magnetic tape, mechanical, photocopying, recording or otherwise, without permission in writing from the publishers.

First edition 1983

Library of Congress Cataloging in Publication Data

Poyatos, Fernando.
New perspectives in nonverbal communication.
(Language and communication library; 5)
Includes indexes.
1. Nonverbal communication. I. Title.
II. Series.
P99.5.P69 1983 001.56 83–2244

British Library Cataloguing in Publication Data

Poyatos, Fernando
New perspectives in nonverbal communication.
—— (Language and communication library; 5)
1. Nonverbal communication
I. Title
001.56 P99.5

ISBN 0-08-030203-3 (Hardcover)
ISBN 0-08-030204-1 (Flexicover)

LUTHER COLLEGE LIBRARY
University of Regina

Printed in Great Britain by A. Wheaton & Co. Ltd., Exeter

To Maria, my wife,
and Laura, my daughter,
for their love and understanding

Contents

List of Illustrations

Introduction

When I wrote my first book on nonverbal communication ten years ago I was already fascinated and disturbed by the scores of further theoretical and applied possibilities I could envisage which were suggested by the very topics I was dealing with. I was even more disturbed by the fact that, as I wrote in the Introduction, "In spite of the exactness achieved in many instances, nonverbal communication studies are still badly in need, in my opinion, of an integrative approach to *all* that is nonverbal, as well as of much preliminary theory and methodology."

Ten years later I find myself in the situation of having to make more or less the same statement. It is true that Nonverbal Communication Studies have made stupendous advances and that awareness of the need to look to the nonverbal in many disciplines has been awakened, yet my main complaint still is that most researchers continue to neglect each other's discipline and the many perspectives that true interdisciplinary fertilization could generate. In this book I attempt to show—much too often without being able to elaborate at length on many enticing topics which the reader will surely appreciate and hopefully heed—the interdisciplinary (not simply multidisciplinary) approach that can avoid the sort of shortsightedness one is liable to incur when keeping strictly within the traditional limits of each discipline. The realization that the study of human communication had to start at the level of the person's somatic system and then progress through extrasomatic, environmental and cultural ones, was the logical conclusion as soon as I had to face the multichannel reality of what we call discourse. I had set out to study what soon I acknowledged as the unquestionable *Basic Triple Structure* of human communication behavior, Language-Paralanguage-Kinesics, only to realize that an intended or unintended chemical reaction such as tear shedding could have on occasions as much semantic and syntactical value as any of those three basic systems based on *sound* and *movement* and *silence* and *stillness*, and that so could certain dermal and thermal unconscious signs, as well as shifts in interpersonal distance, during an interactive encounter. Only the fact that verbal language could not be unrealistically disassociated from paralanguage and kinesics—something easily demonstrable by a triple transcription—generated all sorts of new thoughts regarding traditional areas such as language development (as it is obviously the ontogeny of the three costructures from childhood to adulthood that psychologists and linguists must investigate), intercultural (and not only interlinguistic) translation, discourse analysis, foreign-language learning, universal and culture-specific verbal and nonverbal behaviors, psychotherapy analysis, and any areas in which normal or pathological interactive or noninteractive behaviors are dealt with.

But it was more than that, I soon found out. Any interactive encounter generates a great number of *direct and synesthesial sensory channels* for perceiving interbodily messages. Beyond that, those *extra-somatic systems* most immediately associated with the body—from clothes, food and drink, through adornment and cosmetics, to the objects we may manipulate during that encounter—can become as finely costructured in specific situations as language, paralanguage and kinesics are. This, in turn, led me to seek the relationships of the somatic and extrasomatic systems with the *objectual environment* (furniture, utensils, etc.), the *built environment* (architectural interior spaces, light, colors, etc.), the *modified environment* (landscaping, agricultural forms, etc.), and the *natural environment* (terrain, climate, color, flora, and fauna). I arrived in this way, therefore, at a definition of *nonverbal communication* as: the emissions of signs by all the nonlexical somatic, artifactual and environmental sensible signs contained in a culture, whether individually or in mutual costructuration, and whether or not those emissions constitute behavior or generate personal interaction. Communication was equated in that cultural context to the emission of information and its perception by humans and animals.

With this framework in mind, I pondered much over the semiotic-communicative nature of *culture*. I suggested in 1973 the unit I called *cultureme* and the progressive, systematic and exhaustive analysis of a culture—which Amos Rapoport (1976) deemed as probably the most useful attempt to apply structural anthropological and ethnoscientific methods. I discussed the *genetic and learned habits* of its members and their temporal and spatial dimensions, thus hinting at the true verbal and nonverbal intercultural barriers I would study later. I could envisage many more perspectives for an exhaustive and realistic study of communication, some of which are contained in this book, developed either from within specific disciplines or in a logically derived interdisciplinary fashion. Of these, the most crossdisciplinary endeavor, after having established the Basic Triple Structure, is that of classifying and defining, from a morphological and functional point of view, all the *nonverbal categories* by elaborating beyond those established fifteen years ago by Ekman and Friesen (1969) and earlier by Efrón (1941). I feel that this portion of the book can greatly facilitate the fieldwork and experimental study of normal or abnormal social behaviors, analyzed both culturally and crossculturally, thus shedding much light on, for instance, the interactive qualities of different personalities, the joint development of verbal and nonverbal interactive behaviors, the clinical and social sensible characteristics of medical team–patient or therapist–client relationships, the business encounter, man–woman relationships, the concept and judgement of esthetic or unesthetic behaviours (e.g., refined and unrefined, ladylike and gentlemanly, articulate and inarticulate), the culturally-defined conversational styles independently of linguistic differences (for instance, between English and Americans), and many more. All those nonverbal categories are susceptible of being displayed in the course of a *conversation*, and that is a topic to which I have given much attention over the years, concentrating on the structural organization, in good part inspired by and gradually elaborating on previous studies, mainly by Duncan, Kendon, and Scheflen, to mention only the most influential students of this aspect of interaction during the sixties.

I have tried so far to outline the basic interdisciplinary approaches to what I have subsumed under nonverbal communication, beyond which I have attempted to develop several other models which, though clearly within very specific disciplines, offer new interdisciplinary approaches and further avenues for research. The first one concerned *narrative literature*, best represented by the 1977 article which Kendon selected for his 1981 volume as what he considered one of the seminal articles published in *Semiotica*, one of the powerfully influential endeavours of Thomas Sebeok which has served as the disseminating channel of much nonverbal communication research. That analysis of nonverbal communication mainly in the novel has since then generated a number of studies which keep coming to my attention, as well as classroom discussions, as it opened new semiotic, literary and, in general, interdisciplinary perspectives. When later I was asked to write in a similar vein about the *theater*, I did so by outlining the implications of nonverbal systems as they are transmitted from the playwright to the reader, then to the director–actor team, and finally—going beyond the novel—to the spectator, the latter operating in a unique spatial relationship with the performer as regards the various nonverbal systems, which playwrights from the Euripides to Tennessee Williams have treated very differently. A logical development in my integrative approach to nonverbal communication while dealing with written narrative and dramaturgic texts was a reappraisal of the arbitrarily established *punctuation* systems to which both professional and lay writers have adhered religiously from centuries, even though a cursory review of that limited, often quite illogical and on occasions ambiguous symbols seemed to suggest a needed revision of such systems. To preach with my own example I have used in this book initial [¡] and [¿], instead of merely their closing forms, in all those instances in which clearly volume and interrogation features override the whole sentence and not only the last part of it.

After dealing for some years with the narrative literatures of different countries the initial cultural orientation of my work—which I consider a perspective that cannot be lacking in the analysis of whatever systems, from the reality of discourse to the psychotherapy client's background, or for a progressive exploration of so many nonverbal aspects of people's behaviors, attitudes and environment (in other words, their culture)—I began to probe into the anthropological but multidisciplinary nature of those national narratives, and the idea of *Literary Anthropology* as an area of study began to take shape. I tried to develop it in Calcutta in 1978 at a post-congress conference for the International Congress of Anthropological and Ethnological Sciences and, at this writing, as a more elaborate symposium in Québec City (from which a special volume is being planned) for the same congress in 1983. Hopefully it will offer anthropologists a systematic utilization of the national narratives as a unique source of multidisciplinary anthropological data and many research perspectives. People have, since their earliest epics to the contemporary novels, put in writing everything about themselves and their cultures, thus providing until recently in history the only way of recording their behaviors and their sensibly apprehended environment, except for representational painting, so akin to narrative literature in the advanced cultures.

The reader will find, of course, many more research implications (some of which, God willing, I hope to pursue in the future), even when certain topics are but touched upon. Take, for instance, the intimate situational costructuration of somatic and extrasomatic systems in, say, man–woman interaction; how language, paralanguage and kinesics condition each other and become further costructured with the form, color and material of clothes, perfume, food, drink, proxemic arrangement, and the color, light, and perhaps music, of the environment. Or an in-depth study of how often we judge the sensible qualities of people, objects, and food and drink, whether in their presence or in advertising, not through their direct perception but through indirect synesthial stimulation of senses other than the ones with which we normally perceive those qualities. Or the hierarchization of the sensible manifestations (visual, olfactory, gustatory, tactile) of each culture and its relation to people's dependence on sensory appreciation and their intercultural attitudes toward it. Or a detailed study of the nonverbal characteristics of good and bad acting both on the stage and in films (the latter from their beginnings) in order to offer the performer, the critic and the spectator a clear understanding of what is actually entailed in acting.

In spite, however, of the many areas and perspectives elaborated on or just outlined, or perhaps merely mentioned in passing, and in spite of being, to my knowledge, the most interdisciplinary and integrative treatment of nonverbal communication to date, I regard this book already as only a partial discussion of the many theoretical and applied perspectives it can lead to. Thus, while it attempts to provide the student and the researcher with a comprehensive set of much needed theoretical and methodological models (e.g., the 'cultureme' analysis, the study of nonverbal communication in literature, the structure of conversation), the sensitive reader will also find the leads for a number of further applications in the social and behavioral sciences as well as in literature and the representational arts.

A brief comment on the three nonverbal communication courses I teach in the Departments of Anthropology, Psychology, and Sociology (and whose 1982–3 outlines are shown on pages 369–375 as a possible model for similar courses elsewhere) might illustrate the interdisciplinary nature of Nonverbal Communication Studies as both a research area and an academic discipline. Forty per cent of the students come invariably from the School of *Nursing*, as there is much that sensitization to nonverbal communication can offer those in the helping professions (evidenced by the increasing, though still limited, attention it receives in the nursing literature) for the better approach to the physical, mental and spiritual needs of their patients. The rest are from: *Psychology*, as they realize the relevance of nonverbal issues for many of the established areas, such as social and developmental studies; *Sociology*, because they find that the realistic study of society demands that they understand the communicative nature of what we call nonverbal, from behaviors and attitudes to the very objectual and sensible environment people surround themselves with; *Business*, as nonverbal emission of intended or unintended messages and interactive fluency in general constitute the very foundation of business encounters and interviews, interecultural relationships, salesmanship, and television and magazine advertising; *Anthropology*, since the proper understanding of people's crosscultural differences and similarities in both sensible and intelligible systems is strongly based on their nonverbal ways of acting and defining themselves, their products, and their environments; *linguistics* and *foreign languages*, because verbal communication cannot be disassociated from its nonverbal costructures for an in-depth study not only of both one's or someone else's language but of language as a universal species-specific phenomenon; *Literature*, because they find that the true understanding of, say, a novel goes beyond the traditional 'stylistic' and 'technical' approaches, to include the semiotic-communicative transmission of the characters and their world from their creator to their recreator, the reader, by means of their nonverbal repertoires and surrounding nonverbal elements, which opens up a rich area of research and esthetic enjoyment; and *Education*, as they are becoming aware of the increasing literature on nonverbal communication in the classroom, both human and environmental. Beyond these main disciplines there are, of course, those from seemingly unrelated areas like *Physical Education*, where the athlete or player displays a great number of nonverbal facial and bodily attitudes, both as a competitor and audience-directed performer and as member of a team. There is occasionally the future *clergyman*, sensitive by nature and vocation to the added eloquence of sincerely and naturally displayed nonverbal behaviors from the pulpit or on a person-to-person basis. The student of *painting* finds, of course, a wealth of social kinesic behaviors in many different cultures and situations throughout the various historical periods, as well as clothes, artifacts and environmental cultural systems, for which often painting, as literature, provides the only documentation.

The academic experience is always very stimulating, as one has the opportunity every year of teaching face-to-face, and not just writing down on paper, that which constitutes one's major interest, and not for a one-time audience but for one with which it is possible to establish a deeper relationship. In addition, students become increasingly interested in nonverbal topics each from within their individual discipline, or out of a growing awareness outside the classroom that nonverbal communication pervades all our social activities from morning to night. Consequently, the majority of them are strongly motivated to do their papers or projects, which results in many interesting topics approached from different angles, for example: the much neglected olfactory messages in the hospital, the nurse–patient touching relationship, the nonverbal expressions of pain or fear in hospitalized children and adults, the first-hand studies of nonverbal behaviors of Canadian Maliseet and Micmac Indians and Alaska's Kotzebue Eskimos, bad manners across cultures, territorial definition and personal objectual environments in shared women's residence rooms, crying in men across cultures, the nonverbal aspects of hitchhiking discussed by a widely-travelled hitchhiker in three continents, nonverbal behaviors in transportation terminals, feminine stereotyping in magazine advertising, the objectual environments of living rooms (for which the students visit and photograph many homes), nonverbal behaviors of children during story-telling, and many more. I invariably profit a great deal and receive the great satisfaction of having taught something and have sensitized them to a field of study that makes us more sensitive to people and the world around us.

Other sources of much stimulation and incentive have been, first, the many contacts with colleagues from all over the world, not only by correspondence but personally when I lecture at institutions in disciplines like folklore, linguistics, business, or psychology. The contribution to my knowledge of and sensitization to other cultures on the part of an audience in Calcutta, Tokyo, Budapest, Leipzig, Copenhagen or Berlin has always had an indelible impact on my own intercultural understanding. Another source of continuing incentive has been my discussion of nonverbal communication issues at many international and national meetings, as well as my organization of sessions (with speakers from different disciplines) at those of anthropology, psychology, linguistics, phonetics, semiotics, communication, comparative literature, and languages.

On the other hand, along with the already impressive literature on nonverbal communication in many disciplines, other colleagues have contributed immensely to establishing Nonverbal Communication Studies as a strong research area. Witness the influential research programs (e.g., the psychologically and anthropologically oriented work centered around Paul Ekman in San Francisco, the semiotic, zoosemiotic and linguistic researches led by Sebeok at his Indiana University center, the Institute of Nonverbal Communication Research in New York), the equally influential publications too numerous to mention (but a good number of which will be found in the references), and special meetings such as the two Advanced Institutes of Nonverbal Research sponsored by NATO in 1969 and 1979 (the latter led by Paul Ekman and Klaus Scherer), and the 1983 International Conference on Nonverbal Behavior organized by Aaron Wolfgang in Toronto with many of the leading nonverbal communication scholars. These and other activities stem undoubtedly from seminal gatherings of some twenty years ago, most particularly the 1963 Indiana University Conference on Paralinguistics and Kinesics led by Sebeok, and the highly interdisciplinary meetings, during the late sixties, of the Royal Society of England, spurred by Sir Julian Huxley and chaired by W. H. Thorpe to define the nature of nonverbal communication, whose work was edited by Robert Hinde (1972). These are mentioned only as important milestones in the history of Nonverbal Communication Studies, without any intention to even outline the history of the field within the limits of this introduction.

Acknowledgements

Since all the main ideas I have developed in my work on nonverbal communication since the late sixties are contained in this volume, I feel that it would be unjust not to acknowledge those earlier researches from which I gratefully borrowed some seminal ideas. It is unfortunately quite easy for us to receive inspiration from others, whether from elaborate studies or an illuminating thought put in a few words—even though we may have developed it much further—and never express our gratitude. It is for this reason that I would like to thank, first of all, George Trager, Henry L. Smith, William Austin, Robert Pittinger, Kenneth Pike, David Crystal, Ray Birdwhistell, Edward Hall, Michael Argyle, and Thomas Sebeok.

Those who both personally or through their writings have since then incited me to seek ever newer perspectives in nonverbal communication, particularly Albert Scheflen, Adam Kendon, Starkey Duncan, David Efrón, Gordon Hewes, Amos Rapoport, Walburga von Raffler-Engel, Mary Key, Paul Bouissac, and very especially Thomas Sebeok for his many stimulating ideas and his kind encouragement.

Those whose invitations to lecture to audiences in various disciplines have provided me with unique opportunities to interact with colleagues and people of other cultures, besides the United States, Canada, and Spain, my native country: Mihály Hoppál, Vilmos Voigt, János Lászlo, and Ferenc Papp, in Hungary; Hand Tillman, Roland and Marlene Posner, and Manuel Muñoz-Cortés, in West Germany; Christian Heddesheimer and Philip Riley, in France; Hanne Martinet, Jens Klausen, and Oleg Wiberg, in Denmark; Prabodh Bwomick, in India and Frend Peng, in Japan. To discuss topics of my concern with colleagues in bodies or institutions such as the Linguistic Circle of Copenhagen, the Hungarian Linguistic Society, the Danish Export School, the Summer Language Sciences Institute of Tokyo, the University of Calcutta, the Institutes of Psychology, Ethnology, and Mass Communication in Budapest, etc., has invariably been most fruitful for me as I always received helpful ideas and comments.

Those institutions whose financial support have facilitated my mobility greatly by enabling me to visit and establish human contacts in four continents. First of all, the Canada Council, the Social Sciences and Humanities Research Council of Canada, the American Council of Learned Societies and, above all, the University of New Brunswick since I joined it in 1965, for its continuing support. Also the Centre de Recherches et d'Applications Pedagogiques en Langues at the University of Nancy, The Research Center for Language and Semiotic Studies at Indiana University, the Universidad Internacional de Santander, the Free University of Berlin, the University of Texas at Austin, Vanderbilt University, the New York State English Council, the Spanische Kultur Institut of Munich, the International Christian University in Tokyo and, in Denmark, the Copenhagen School of Economics and Business Administration, the Institute of International Economics and Management, the Danish Export School, and the Danish Merchant School.

The students in my three nonverbal communication courses, for their stimulating interest and their many illuminating observations and personal experiences, and for providing me every year with the classroom interaction I love so much, and very rewarding personal acquaintances.

In a very especial way, the Departments of Anthropology, Psychology, and Sociology, and their respective chairpersons, William Dalton, Mike Mikaelian and Peter McGahan, for having made possible the establishment of Nonverbal Communication Studies at the University of New Brunswick through the three courses offered.

To Roy Harris, of Oxford University, for his valuable support as Editor.

Finally, Patti Kirby, the secretary without whose generosity I would not have been able to have this and other manuscripts typed while attending to other writing and commitments.

FERNANDO POYATOS

1

Culture, Communication, and Cultural Fluency

1. The Nature of Culture

SINCE anthropology deals with culture, this book can certainly be said to be entirely about culture, for culture is the essence of every one of its interrelated parts. At a time when anthropology, like other sciences whose subject matter is People, seeks new perspectives on which to advance its studies (witness the emergence of visual anthropology, psychological anthropology, etc.), the integrative and interdisciplinary treatment offered in the present work attempts to provide a good number of mutually generated avenues of research, all of which can be subsumed under one label: *culture*. Whether dealing with the structuration of culture, nonverbal systems of human and animal communication, the coding processes of face-to-face interaction, the description of the objectual environment, or the communicative and historical aspects of punctuation systems in writing, the common denominator is still culture. In fact, one of the failures of different sciences, from literary theory, through clinical psychology and psychiatry, to the study of the dramatic performance, is that they often neglect the overwhelming importance of culture in the very topics they deal with.[1]*

Culture, therefore, must be understood in the full meaning of the term, without forgetting that each of the readers of these lines is a living part of a specific culture, a reality that, whether we want it or not, permeates our individual existence and our task with respect to this book—a much more conspicuous phenomenon when dealing with a literary text, as will be discussed—both as writer and reader or 'interpreter'. This ever present reality of culture demands a realistic definition that should not be exclusive of any one area of knowledge, as is usually the case, but valid for all of them; not a definition in which we take this and leave that according to our own disciplinary orientation, but one in which all concepts are equally applicable to whatever aims we may pursue in our study of man and his environment.

In a very basic but delightful little book, anthropologist Douglas Oliver

* Superscript numbers refer to Notes at end of chapter.

(1964) admits that it is confusing "that there should be such vagueness and such difference of opinion over what it [culture] means."

A good example of the uncertainty that typically dominates any interdisciplinary attempt to define culture was the 1973 international conference organized by the architect-anthropologist Amos Rapoport, of the University of Wisconsin-Milwaukee (Rapoport 1976) as part of the XIth International Congress of Anthropological and Ethnological Sciences. The invited participants (several anthropologists, sociologists, three architects, a demographer, a psychologist, an animal behaviorist, a psychiatrist, a social geographer, an ethnologist, and I) could not quite agree when it came to giving a straightforward definition of culture. The definition included in the paper I wrote for that occasion (Poyatos 1976e) met with the approval of such an heterogeneous group, perhaps because of the interdisciplinary orientation I was already trying to give to my work on human communication. Before quoting it, however, I will cite a few other authors in various disciplines.

The anthropologist-linguist Edward Sapir recognized three main connotations of the term culture: one, used by ethnologists and culture-historians, embodies "any socially inherited element in the life of man, material and spiritual," thus being "coterminus with man himself"; another one, referring to "a rather conventional ideal of individual refinement, built upon a certain modicum of assimilated knowledge and experience but made up chiefly of a set of typical reactions that have the sanction of a class and of tradition of long standing," concerns what we would call 'a cultured person'; the third conception embraces "those general attitudes, views of life, and specific manifestations of civilization that give a particular people its distinctive place in the world" (Sapir 1924; 402–405).

The anthropologist Edward Hall conceded that "though the concept of culture was first defined in print in 1871 by E. B. Tylor (*Primitive Culture*), after all these years it still lacks a rigorous specificity which characterizes many less revolutionary and useful ideas" (Hall 1959: 31).

A speech communicationalist, Richard Porter, uses the word culture as referring to "the cumulative deposit of knowledge, experience, meanings, beliefs, values, attitudes, religions, concepts of self, the universe, and self-universe relationships, hierarchies of status, role expectations, spatial relations and time concepts acquired by a large group of people in the course of generations through individual and group striving" (Porter 1972: 3), while his colleague K. S. Sitaram writes that culture is "the sum total of learned behaviors of a group of people living in a geographic area" (Sitaram 1972: 19).

Social psychologist Michael Argyle, interested as we are in social interaction, understands by "the culture of a group of people [. . .] their whole way of life—their shared patterns of behavior, their common ideas and beliefs, their technology, and their art, science, literature, and history (Argyle 1967: 77).

Finally, anthropologist-psychiatrist Robert LeVine uses the term to mean "an organized body of rules concerning the ways in which individuals in a population should communicate with one another, think about themselves and their environments, and behave toward one another and toward objects in their environments" (LeVine 1973: 4).

It is clear, then, that any definition of culture that may be offered tends to conform to the specific aims of a particular discipline. However, all students of culture, from whatever angle, agree on including as basic components: shared learned habits, ways of life, patterns of behavior, and material products.

Personally, since the complex area of communication studies draws from different interrelated fields, I prefer to offer a more comprehensive and realistic picture by offering the following definition of *culture*: A series of habits shared by members of a group living in a geographic area, learned but biologically conditioned, such as the means of communication (language being the basis of them all), social relations at different levels, the various activities of daily life, the products of that group and how they are utilized, the peculiar manifestations of both individual and national personalities, and their ideas concerning their own existence and their fellow people. Culture, then, is made up of a complex mesh of behaviors, and of the active or static results of those behaviors (cf. the table in Fig. 2.1). Naturally, a lengthier definition could specify even further, although every word of the present one encapsulates, if read closely, all the concepts and all the areas of human behavior that constitute the material of this book, and even more, for a culture will generate new topics of study as long as we seek beyond its surface.[2]

2. Active Culture vs. Passive Culture

It has been said many times, but perhaps without the necessary emphasis and without really explaining why, that *culture is communication*. A culture develops as an aggregate of people live according to certain common patterns of beliefs and behaviors, but they cannot fail to communicate about themselves and about those patterns and behaviors. Culture, from irrigation systems to the designing of dwellings or the elaboration of a monetary system, is unthinkable without the personal communicative exchanges that express ideas and attitudes about what is done and thought of. Since this book deals with communication in a progressive way, from basic forms of human interaction to the costructuration of those forms and their relationships with even further cultural manifestations, it will be necessary, first, to take a bird's-eye view of a culture as a series of basic blocks of controlled or uncontrolled ways of conveying certain messages, to later elaborate a detailed view of all the communicative systems in a live culture.

When I refer to live culture I try to emphasize the importance of differentiating an *active culture*, on which all theoretical and methodological ideas in this book are based, and a *passive culture*, when we speak, for instance, of artifacts, roadways, temples, and land distribution of a long-disappeared people. In the latter instance we are, of course, speaking of cultural traits, but not of culture in the dynamic sense of the word, for it is in a permanently static state, has no one to use those things and make them live, linking them to the human mind which devised them, prescribed specific roles for them, used them in a personal exchange of ideas and material goods, and assigned specific values to them. It is only dead material culture, suggesting an intellectual one, but lacking what would make it a dynamic continuum: people in constant interaction with members of their own species, with lower species, and with their environment. Interaction, the exchange of messages carried by signs with symbolic value (words, tone of voice variations, gestures, billboards, furniture shape and arrangement, clothes) requires a *transmitter* and a *receiver*, and the behaviors they display in their interaction are formed, or dictated, by the habits (learned but biologically conditioned, that is, inherited but culturally filtered) mentioned in the definition of culture, their meanings, as I will explain later, can be emitted and perceived in different ways in the interaction process.

3. Forms of Interactive and Noninteractive Culture

That interaction is the foundation and the maintaining element of an existing culture is illustrated in Fig. 1.1, 'Culture and Communication.' The two essential blocks that cannot exist without each other, as they are most of the time mutually conditioned, are: first, the one directly generated by human beings engaged in social interaction, their activities more than the by-products of those activities, in fact, the behaviors generated by the various somatic systems discussed later on; and then, the results of those activities, that is, nonsomatic and environmental elements, which reveal the culture-generating force of the former, including even the animal species associated with each culture. Following the table, then, the basic structure of culture appears, in a progressive approach that will be advancing throughout the book, as composed of:

Interaction, a two-way transaction between at least two socializing organisms, human–human, or human–animal, which sets in motion what we should understand by culture, as all the elements mentioned in its definition can be generated in those two situations. In fact, I have often argued whether one could legitimately speak of Robinson Crusoe's culture, in spite of the artifacts and personal habits and general life style developed by him in his deserted island before encountering another human being, Friday. It is, from a semiotic point of view, as soon as he discovers Friday's footprints that

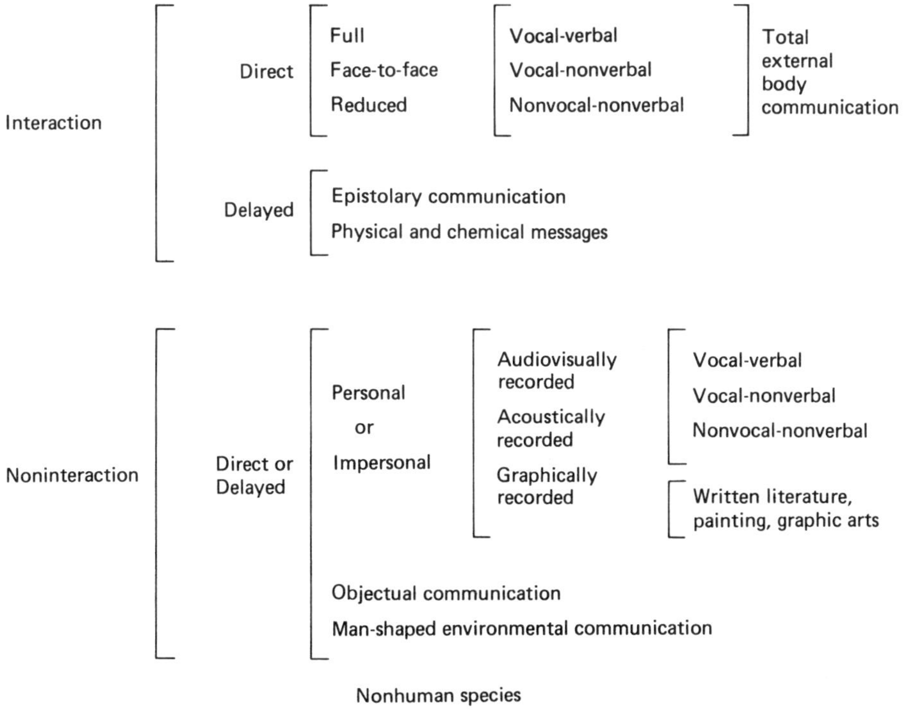

FIG. 1.1 Culture and Communication.

an interactive exchange, a true input–output of signs, is initiated, and a culture begins to develop. The footprints, marks on trees, a foghorn, or a personal perfume intentionally or unintentionally 'left' in a room, are forms of what in the table is indicated as *delayed interaction*, whether personal or impersonal, and the closest to graphic epistolary communication, with a conscious or unconscious encoding of messages, as the case may be. But *direct personal interaction* is activated by the *face-to-face* encounter of the two men, which will account for an already uninterrupted exchange (the cultural continuum discussed later) of material and intellectual tools. This face-to-face interaction, the most basic, most important and most complex of all forms of human communication, will already put in motion the various transmitting somatic channels that function consciously or out of awareness for the conveyance of intended or unintended messages. Thus, besides the two possible situations that can result from an encounter, namely, the *full direct interaction* and the *reduced interaction* (through physical or mental impairment, or because of environmental circumstances), the communication activity itself may adopt one of the three basic forms that constitute the foundation for the study of human communication: *vocal-verbal* (language), *vocal-nonverbal* (paralanguage), and *nonvocal-nonverbal* (kinesics, proxemics, and the rest of the bodily systems), in other words, what later is developed as Total External Somatic Communication (Fig. 3.3).

Noninteraction is, from the point of view of culture and direct social exchanges, as well as from a somatic standpoint—so far understanding interaction as a clear action–reaction process without yet considering, for instance, the semiotic interaction between the painter and the beholder of his work—a direct or delayed conveyance of information, originated or encoded by physical or intellectual activities that can be: *personal* or *impersonal*, according to whether it is meant to reach a given individual or individuals, or whoever may have access to it, as with *audiovisually* (film, videotape) and *acoustically* (tapes, records) recorded materials, both of which utilize the vocal-verbal, vocal-nonverbal and nonvocal-nonverbal modes; and *graphically* recorded material, such as written literature, painting and graphic arts, which only evoke the somatic interactive activities.

Objectual communication is what later on in Fig. 2.1 is represented as objectual systems, an extensive class of material products of universal or culture-specific nature, which in the latter case can define a culture and communicate even through time, though in a more passive way, a number of attitudes (e.g., cosmetics, clothes, food and drink) and conceptualizations (e.g., furniture, decorative elements in the home) that are conveyed by their characteristics and arrangement. Naturally, objects can play important functions in direct face-to-face interaction, either as randomly used props or as true instruments of aggression, argumentation, material evidence, and the like. By 'noninteractive' is meant only that they are detached from people and the mechanism of interaction. A perfume (a substance more than an object) or a piece of jewelry can act as an interactive instrument, but only as a cue representing a person or a specific culture when not used interactively.

Again, the *man-shaped environment*, as the landscaping around the homes, cultivation terraces in certain cultures, architecture, urban design, can also be considered as an element of interaction—the one-way interaction in which many behaviours are elicited and determined by such passive agents—as will be discussed later.

There is still another overlap which proves how futile it can be to assign absolute labels. *Animals* can be considered as part of the environment, but, far from qualifying merely as passive, manipulated or non-manipulated elements, they do engage in interactive exchanges with us humans, particularly the tamed and domesticated species, and our interaction with them constitutes an important topic in human communication.

4. Culture as a Dynamic Communication Continuum

If we acknowledge that culture is communication we must also acknowledge that communication, specifically the one based on interaction, constitutes a continuum of activities which is kept in motion as long as that culture is alive. This means that, independently of the exchanges that take place intermittently between individuals, *interaction* among the members of a culture is an ongoing multichannel and multipurpose activity thanks to which both sensible as well as intelligible systems are generated, kept active, transmitted from day to day, and also modified by use as time goes by; and which, furthermore, varies geographically.

Time and *space* are, therefore, the two basic dimensions of culture. In fact, the two basic dimensions of communication, most specifically acknowledged as proxemics and chronemics in Chapter 5. Thus, when the factor time is disrupted the communication exchanges are discontinued and we are faced with the sort of dead culture referred to earlier. The non-interactive part of a culture, the one in which face-to-face or other types of real interaction do not occur, does not represent a continuum and it can be there for us to experience, but only as either cultural remains or as a one-way information activity—if by information we understand now a non-intentional form of communication that does not require a volitive attitude.

The truly interactive activities, however, in which at least two participants engage in a back-and-forth transaction, occupy every second of a living culture. All such exchanges are not subject to time gaps and constitute, as they occur simultaneously to or alternating with each other, a *continuum*, year after year and century after century. With practically no bounds, the different cultures of the world are constantly linked today by direct forms of interaction, whether face-to-face, written or telephonic, and the resulting mutually conditioned behaviors keep the cultural continuum going. If the members of a clearly defined culture disappear and only some activities are perhaps adopted by other cultures (as may have happened to lost civilisations such as those of the Aztecs or Incas with relation to their conquerors), that culture ceases to be when its last two interactive members die.

This brings to mind how some people mistake culture for civilization and vice versa. If by *civilization* we understand, in a historical perspective, the sum of man's realizations, not only materially but socially, politically, ideologically, artistically, and scientifically, in his constant strife for improvement, then we see that the previous definition of culture falls within that of civilization.

It is a cultural continuum that Robinson Crusoe and Friday set in motion from the moment they start interacting and exchanging 'things,' 'actions,' and 'thoughts.' Both, however, carry with them the elements that will shape their own behaviors, while, in turn they are creating: the inherited idiosyncrasies which will typify many of their individual activities, on the one hand, and the ways of carrying out those and other activities learned from their kin and other members of their culture and later transmitted to others. Inherited or genetic habits and learned habits are, therefore, the two pivotal behavioral principles of any culture.

I am using the term *habit*, not just in a sense of controlled behavior, as we may initiate and terminate something which is habitual in us for a period of time, but as any kind of repetitive behavior, not arbitrary or random. The distinction just made between genetic habits and learned habits, the basis of so much ethological research today, is an important one that must be pondered as one considers any communicative (that is, cultural), behavior, for this sometimes ambiguous dichotomy permeates the attitudes and activities of each one of us, and is at the root of every personal-cultural manifestation, from discourse to dress or writing style.

5. Genetic Habits

Genetic habits are those of a biological origin, rooted at the very bottom of an individual's genetic configuration and determined by specific genes that produce a particular external feature; a characteristic pitch in laughter due to the shaping of the articulatory organs, a facial twitch gradually elicited by an existing propensity in the nervous system, a postural habit, say, sitting tailor-style, because it is elicited by the individual's anatomical configuration and bone structure, or a particular gait that may typify someone. Naturally, the fact that they are of a genetic origin appears obvious when they are clearly hereditary within one or two generations; which does not mean that they will necessarily remain as a peculiarity of a single individual, for we can make four clear distinctions:

a. It can be purely *idiosyncratic*, nonexistent before it is displayed by a particular individual, which would always remain a gratuitous assumption impossible to verify (e.g., a peculiar random behavior, a posture, a paralinguistic utterance, etc.).

b. It can be a *family-identifying* habit, that is, genetically inherited through a pervasive genotype that 'runs in the family.' Several members of the family, even in different generations, display similar gestures in similar situations, certain paralinguistic habits (e.g., an anatomically conditioned labial control of the voice), even some dermal reactions, such as blushing elicited by similar circumstances. That is recognized as part of the style of the family, whether among our personal friends or as observed in a family of actors or other public figures (e.g., the Kennedy brothers and their firm way of facial and hand gesturing, the film actor Kirk Douglas and his son, the actress Judy Garland and now her daughter Liza Minelli). Those features are not just conditioned by regular coexistence, by learning (although daily contact will establish them more emphatically in their personalities), but they are imbedded so deeply in the biopsychological configuration of a person that they cannot be concealed. Those habits, however, may always remain as typical of a specific family without ever reaching the status of group of cultural habits.

c. On the other hand, those habits may appear in *different families* of very different cultural and geographical backgrounds simply because the habit-forming genotype appears in them still without becoming a cultural habit if it is not spread to the rest of the community through learning. Again, we must think far beyond seemingly genetic habits which are only learned ones, such as certain kinesic behaviors observed in western royal families in formal situations or when acting in public. They are certainly not determined by their 'aristocratic genotypes' but by common norms of upbringing and social displays in keeping with their imposed status, noticeable even in many of the unconscious kinesic behaviors displayed during public events.

d. Finally, there are also perfectly *universally genetic habits*, that is, innate, due to biological mechanisms and genetic components characteristic of the species, which typify humans as such by their anthropomorphic somatic systems, whether linguistic, paralinguistic or kinesic, among their communicative ones (cf. Lenneberg 1964; and ethological studies [e.g., Eibl-Eibesfeldt 1979a, 1980]).

6. Learned Habits

Learned habits, then, require a biological foundation, since a way of laughing, a way of walking, or the quickness or pressure of a hand-shake are all, even if imitated or learned, rooted in that necessary propensity of the individual toward those behaviors. At any rate, it is learned habits that the whole interdisciplinary field of nonverbal communication studies (and therefore the subject of this book) is based on. But it is essential that we become trained in identifying the purely genetic or idiosyncratic habits of a person, lest we should interpret them as cultural and suffer the consequences of typical miscommunication. On the other hand, one must always keep in mind to what a great extent biologically conditioned behaviors may be in turn shaped by learning. Even purely physiological reflex reactions such as coughing, sneezing or stretching are performed differently by each person right after the onset of the behavior because they are, from that point on, controlled by 'display rules' that may vary mainly from culture to culture and among social strata (cf. Ekman 1977).

Learned habits are the ones that make up a culture. In the simplest form referred to before, Crusoe and Friday are both sharing habits they have learned previously from others, habits they have been developing based on previous (learned) experiences, and others they learn from each other. To them they may incorporate, not only the biologically conditioned ways of carrying out those habits, but their individual genetic habits, independently of a possible mutual borrowing through learning. It is clear, of course, that the main distinction genetic—biological and learned—cultural offered here to better understand this overlapping qualities of nonverbal behaviors, is at the very root of the universalists-culturalists (or relativists) controversy in human ethology, represented by Darwin (1865) and Eibl-Eibesfeldt (1979a, 1979b, 1980) on the one hand, and La Barre (1947), Leach (1972) and Birdwhistell (1970) on the other, while Ekman (1977, 1979) seems to take a conciliatory stand with his neurocultural theory of emotion.

Besides, it would be quite appropriate to cite Thorpe's (1972) reference to Dubos' (1970) discussion of the nature-nurture controversy to the effect that "genes do not actually determine the characteristics by which we know a person; they merely govern the responses to experience from which the personality is built" and that "almost everything we do, almost every response we make, results in the acquisition of memories that alter our subsequent responses to the same stimulus" (Thorpe 1972: 214–215).

7. Spatial and Temporal Aspects of Learned Habits

If we try to view learned habits as something not static but movable, as forming a cultural continuum, we see two different but complementary dimensions in them, a spatial or geographical one and a temporal one, a distinction we need to acknowledge when analyzing communicational behaviors and any kind of sensible or intelligible cultural forms.

Habits across space

From a *spatial* point of view, one has to be aware of a sort of behavioral geography, or behavioral territoriality, as a habit may be shared by only *two people*, perhaps a married couple; from there it can be transmitted to the *nuclear family*, later to the whole *extended family* and perhaps simultaneously to other individuals or other families, to an entire clan, and to larger *work groups*, and finally to an entire *community* closely knitted spatially; or, beyond that, to a whole *subculture* and to an entire *culture*, from which *intercultural borrowing* processes begin to develop. We have witnessed how the Latin gesture made by pressing the bunched fingers of one hand against the mouth, smacking the lips as the fingers open away from it and perhaps saying 'Delicious!' has become naturalized in Anglo-Saxon cultures even across the Atlantic, and we cannot imagine that it was ever a culture-wide kinesic behavior all at once without emerging first from a small group and even from an individual. Group habits are familiar to all of us: the way female students carry books against their chests, while men carry them against their hips; the higher-than-normal volume and pitch used by nurses while interacting with patients in many situations, particularly children and senile patients, etc. Culture-wide habits are, for example, holding a door for someone a little bit too long, as is done in North America, drinking coffee while eating one's meal, or shaking hands with one's own father, instead of kissing him as they do in other cultures.

We often observe the mutual influence between two married people, for instance, two business associates, or a secretary who borrows a verbal expression or a mannerism from his or her boss (easier, as will be discussed later, than it is for the higher-status person to adopt the habits of the subordinate one). When one is sensitized to nonverbal behaviors, it can become a pastime to match husband and wife at a gathering before one has met them as such. On the other hand, when we live in a foreign culture for a short while we also identify culture-wide habitual behaviors. For instance, in the United States and Canada a person holds a door for someone who comes behind, but if that person is a foreigner he will probably feel that the North American is holding it while he is still too far, and will judge ridiculous the typical situation in which one has to quicken his pace to get at the door; in many areas of North America a man and a woman do not shake hands when they are introduced, simultaneous speech is immediately avoided and the interactive equilibrium is reestablished by the formula: 'I'm sorry—,' 'No, go ahead!,' 'No, I was gonna say that—,'; father and son shake hands only instead of hugging and kissing as they do in Russia or in Latin and Arab cultures; the time spent talking around the table after a meal (which in Spanish is even linguistically labelled as *sobremesa*), or the time taken for a casual picnic, is comparatively much shorter in North America than in France or Spain; in Spain, male friends or simple acquaintances, while standing in conversation, usually touch each other briefly on the arm to convey warmth and a good mutual disposition; in India, after shaking hands, two men may keep holding each other's hand for several minutes while conversing, and a colleague at a congress in my first visit to the country took me by the hand through a crowded corridor to the very door of the washrooms when I asked where they were. But these are all easily identifiable habits by which we define a given culture. That is why it is so important to recognize the cultural quality of a particular behavior—which might otherwise be only a purely individual one—in order to avoid typical intercultural misunderstandings, or even borrow it in a mistaken act of acculturation.

Habits across time

That wider or narrower geography of specific behaviors, which we could trace in basic behavioral atlases similar to linguistic ones, is also subject to a *temporal dimension* which is essential for the study of a culture and communication systems; not only for serious cultural field work, but even for a deeper understanding of personality, whether normal or abnormal, or for the accurate evaluation of the social behaviors and thought patterns contained in a literary work. Learned habits have been consciously or unconsciously acquired through time, sometimes through successive generations. Others in a short period of time until they become part of a community or culture, either in a culture-specific way or panculturally. But the existence of any particular cultural learned habit implies a beginning, a certain life span, or a virtually permanent one, but always subject to a development and susceptible of ending, as many of them may disappear. Those aspects of the temporal dimension of habits are also crucial when we study the behavior of either individuals or social aggregates.

Any middle-aged person, or even younger, may witness the appearance of learned habits, whether in a group, culturally, or panculturally. The peculiar gait style, stance and hand posture (stuck in front pockets) determined by blue jeans in both sexes, particularly in women; the semantic modification undergone by, and the new use of, the word 'gay'; the beginning of the use of the Christmas tree in Spain in the late fifties; the many habits created by the consumption of tobacco by women; the postural changes also in women due to the evolution of social norms and to the breaking down of prejudices. We also observe through the years the development and modifications of habits, not so much directly as by combining the experience of live language usage with the literary sources. We find successive elaboration of similes such as 'As easy as falling off a log', '—as falling off a greasy log' (Erskine Caldwell, *Claudell Ingliss*), '—as falling off a log backwards', '—as rolling off a log' (*Green Bay Press Gazette*, 13-7-1948). The feminine habit of brushing aside the hair draping over one side of the face (which can be an unconscious or very conscious flirting behavior) changes according to the hairdo, and this is even observed in the same woman who, after changing from a bun or a hair tightly combed backwards to a loosely worn one, acquires that habit, performed with a delicate movement of the middle and third fingers, thus incorporating it into her repertoire of very effective and even stereotyped social behaviours, costructured facial expression, posture and orientation, and tone of voice. But we have also witnessed the conscious or unconscious gesture of men shaking their heads when they wear long hair.

On the one hand, habits can be born and developed and changes in life style can be brought about by evolving esthetic values regarding furniture[3] or dress, technological achievements such as those associated with TV watching or automobiles, from TV dinners to travelling by camper, intercultural borrowing in dress, gestures, food, or changing moral values reflected in dating patterns or in cohabitation; on the other, we can also see their disappearance in the course of several generations or just one: in North

America, saddle shoes worn by teenagers during the forties and fifties gave way to sneakers and other types of footwear, and smoked salmon virtually disappeared from the stores in certain areas of the country in the seventies, terminating the habit of using it at gatherings; ritualized gestures of greetings and goodbyes that we read about in the Spanish epic peom *El Cid* have never been known in Spain today, and mourning black is gradually disappearing in Spanish cities. We all remember children's games of different cultures that we cannot see any more. The old person has seen habits go by like we see the water on a river flow before our eyes, and this is truly live culture.

Culture, in sum, is a constant coexistence of simultaneous habits and succession of habits of many kinds and many origins, some displayed through bodily behaviors, others revealed by the environment as conditioned by both physical and intellectual activities of people, but all communicating in interactive or noninteractive situations and shaped by the life styles of social aggregates which differ in greater or lesser degree from other cultures across the world.

8. The Barriers of Intercultural Communication

When we view culture as such an infinitely complex mesh of intertwined behaviors projected into space and time in constant movement, and the results of those behaviors, and when we further realize that in today's rapidly shrinking world, due to a growing intercultural awareness and communication among countries, it is becoming more and more difficult to define individual cultures in themselves, we understand that the term communication can almost never represent an absolute concept. If we think of communication from a basic semiotic point of view, that is, in terms of the origin and transmission of signs—as will be done later on in this work—we immediately recognize the uncertainty inherent in the communication situation. Not only must we face another culture in its original geographic location or through some of its members elsewhere, but even within our own, as one may have to interact with people in different occupational groups, sex or age groups, or truly geographically-limited subcultures. For, once in that situation, we are automatically exposed to possible failure which, if it comes to worst, will take place without our being aware of it.

The realization of this latent problem, of this risk of miscommunication or lack of communication, entails a watchful attitude on our part while we are within a culture, subculture or group other than our own, when watching a foreign film (in which, unlike a pure documentary, we are not acknowledged as interpreters), seeing foreigners in our streets (a trousered old Chinese woman with her short steps, a turbaned Sikh, a strolling Mediterranean family in a rather deserted American street on a weekend), teaching a foreign novel (containing a culture which has not been translated, as its language was, if not totally so), or corresponding with a business relationship or an academic colleague from abroad, whose concept of time (handling an order or simply responding to a proposition, or a casual letter) might differ considerably from ours. In each of those instances our individual and cultural configuration (made up of beliefs, values, individual sensitiveness and inclinations) perceives different elements in the other culture; but, as a lens fitted with a photographic filter, it may let through whatever elements conform to our way of thinking about and dealing with the world around, while blocking off or at least altering all those culture-based phenomena which seem strange or elicit in us a negative reaction, from a dialectical encounter to a total mental or physical rejection.

Intercultural misunderstanding and clash is based on the disparate ways in which members of one culture conceptualize and give tangible form to somatic, objectual and environmental systems as well as to spiritual, intellectual and social intelligible ones, as compared to members of another culture. In broad but realistic terms we can say that cultural misunderstanding results from the different treatments given to the elements represented in the table 'Sensible and Intelligible Systems in a Culture' (Fig. 2.1). One can find ample literature on the subject, whether referring to biology (as with racial differences) geography (as with climate and our adaptation to it), history (as in the case of old feuds and relationships between nations), philosophy (as with western thought versus oriental one), religion (even within the same culture), or to customs and life style in general, all the growing concern of many anthropologists.

Edward Hall (1959, 1966, 1977) is perhaps the one who most enthusiastically and with more insight has devoted his efforts to analyze the sources of intercultural differences and their adverse effects upon our relationships with other cultures, particularly in the case of North Americans, whose mobility, facilitated by a higher economic status, exposes them to all the cultures of the world whether advanced or preliterate, in which they often assume serious responsibilities. Recently the most acute concern for the problems of intercultural communication, resulting in a painstaking elaboration of a systematic methodology, seems to be that of Lynn Tyler, Director of the Brigham Young University Language and Intercultural Research Center. This institution (aware of the main hidden units of meaning that are often the key to bridging the gap caused by cultural misunderstanding) has been developing the system of "languetics," for the development of individual "cultural grammars" for the analysis of international interactions. To this purpose, they have already prepared a voluminous *Codebook* (1978) of "intercultural communicative indicators", in which they propose an intercultural grammar system for handling culture-specific "miscues" (i.e., that which offends) and "missed cues" (i.e., those which confuse or are unintelligible) as well as for understanding what works best in new cultural settings.

As basic barriers that may impede intercultural perception and understanding, some authors (Porter 1972) have listed a series of overlapping and interacting factors, such as (a) *attitudes*, whether ethnocentrism (by which we tend to view and judge people according to our own standards) in religion, politics, customs, food, dress, or art; world view perspectives that may use different frames of reference; absolute values regarding good and bad, ugly and beautiful, true and false, etc.; or stereotypes by which we generalize about Blacks, Mexicans, or Italians, and prejudices which make us behave in certain ways toward those people; (b) *social organization*, as regards government, family, law, etc.; (c) *patterns of thought*, mainly between the Western and the Oriental worlds, but also between Anglo-Saxon and Latin ways of thinking about family ties, moral values, dating, etc., which cause so much confusion (as when an American friend of mine tried to date a young lady in New Delhi without understanding that that type of relationship between two unmarried persons practically does not exist, at least not while the girl is still living with the family, although, if she is working in another city, it would not face the criticism of relatives, friends and neighbors so much); (d) *role expectations*, obviously derived from patterns of thought, can also produce misunderstanding, as has traditionally happened between American girls attending Spanish schools and native males, since the role of moderating sex behavior in Spain has been traditionally assigned to men (although there is a strong tendency to equal roles among Spanish youth, mainly through American movies, literature and personal contacts) and the more unprejudiced attitude of the American women has always been taken for loose morals; (e) the *conceptualization of time* (discussed in Chapter 5) is also a most common source of clash between the two aforementioned cultures, since, in general, a half-hour delay is not so offensive in Spain as it would be in North America; (f) *the handling of space* (that is, proxemic behavior, dealt with in Chapter 5), whether in a man-environment relationship (architecture, furniture, etc.) or among people, is also a typical source of misunderstanding for Americans who, when in Spain, Italy or Morocco, feel their interlocutor's face about twelve inches from their own, while he grabs them by the arm or pats them on the shoulder; (g) the *language barrier*, which does not arise only with respect to correct or incorrect translation, but when the 'correct' translation, for instance, carries different semantic values deeply rooted in the cultural background; and (h) *nonverbal communication*, which some authors illustrate with comments on culture-specific gestures, but which is actually a much more complex series of systems, encompassing all bodily systems and the objectual and environmental ones, as discussed in this book.

Much could be elaborated on the topic of intercultural communication barriers and their own interrelationships and mutual conditioning, and a more accurate classification could be arrived at easily. I included the preceding comments simply to show the extent to which different disciplines must be aware of those problems.

9. Acculturation

As for *acculturation*, which for too many concerns only anthropological research, it is practically coterminous with intercultural communication, but actually comprising it, as it is the process to which we are exposed as soon as we become in contact with another culture; more specifically, in my opinion, the degree of adaptation achieved by a member of one culture when he is in contact with, or living in, another culture. Two cultures can communicate or fail to communicate in a personal encounter between two or more individuals, or through a film; but when we visit a foreign country, or decide to settle in it, either we strive to adapt our life style, our attitude toward people and situations and our gestures and mannerisms to what we see and feel as 'native', or we continue to display our own culture and then experience the inevitable misunderstandings. However, if we settle in a foreign country, or even during a short stay, we are, whether we want it or not, accommodating ourselves to its culture in one degree or another.

This process of adaptation to another culture, which may take place even without leaving our own (think of Eskimos taking up TV watching, or Spaniards introducing donuts, hamburgers, jeans and the sexual freedom of other countries since the early sixties), consists of the overcoming of each of the intercultural barriers just mentioned, the order in which it may happen varying with the individual disposition toward language, food, time handling, etc. We could say, then, that true intercultural communication is the result of proper acculturation.

Naturally, acculturation takes place also, as has been pointed out already, when confronted with subcultures or groups within our own culture. We might move from a Canadian Arctic community to the South of the province of New Brunswick, populated by families of English descent and people from quite a few cultures around the world who are going through acculturation processes themselves; or we might go from the Spanish Basque country to a southern province where the handling of time is perceived (even within the general chronemic laxitud of Spaniards as compared with Anglo-Saxons) as more relaxed, and where the kinesic repertoires of people are more illustrative and expressive, the paralinguistic features different, etc.

One thing becomes unquestionably clear, that in order for us to behave properly and effectively we must understand the degree to which the communication systems of others are typical only of their own group (or culture) or universal, the problems we ourselves could pose for them, and the behaviors we should modify or suppress altogether according to the interactive circumstances we find ourselves in.

Nonverbal intercultural clash illustrated

After having discussed at some length the composition of a culture, how a great number of learned habits succeed each other and cooccur with each other in the interactive continuum that generates and maintains that culture active, it seems appropriate—before dealing with the nature and components of verbal and nonverbal communication—to refer to an actual occurrence that illustrates quite eloquently the problems of intercultural miscommunication, the lack of *cultural fluency* (as discussed below), and the process of acculturation required to cope with them gradually. It was actually my first such experience, not as a foreigner in someone else's culture, but as a member of that culture, that is, the one to whose ways and behaviors a foreigner had to adapt himself.

It was during my student years at the University of Madrid and concerns my old friend Tom. After graduating from high school in Youngstown, Ohio, with a fairly good knowledge of Spanish, he decided to take some courses in Spain and be my roommate at a family home. What happened on the very first day of his 'acculturation process,' in different settings, was a most eloquent cultural true-life anecdote.

I met him at the railway station and, as soon as he saw me from the train window, he winked at me (not Spanish at all as a man-to-man greeting) and made an 'OK' hand gesture, known in Spain by some only through American movies and tourists. When he got off the train we greeted each other in Spanish and shook hands in a way common to our respective cultures, while I, as a Spaniard, added something: with my left hand I clasped his upper arm and then patted him on the shoulder blade, because a simple handshake in that situation would not be enough for a Spaniard, a Frenchman or an Arab. But when I tried to carry his suitcase, he translated his English '¡Oh, it's allright!' literally into Spanish, and said *¡Oh, está bien!*, thus telling me '¡Well done!'

Then we went to the home where we were to share a room, and when I introduced him to the landlady she stood there with her hand stretched out for a few second because Tom, a man from the American Midwest, was not thinking of shaking hands with a woman. 'Well, how was your trip?,' she asked in Spanish, and Tom, thinking of the English drawled 'Well—' (because it had not been too good at all), translated his English literally again and said *¡Bueno—!*, so she smiled and said she was so glad. Well, after that Tom sat on a chair and began to tell us about his trip with his hands clasped over his head while balancing his chair on its hind legs, and once he stretched his arms full width, yawned and said *¡Perdón!* (as if a Spaniard would stretch like that in front of others in the first place, apology or no apology).

Later, walking down the street, he was amused because men complimented attractive women verbally (a Spanish national habit with many), and he was quite surprised to see the window of any small grocery store filled with alcoholic beverages. When he bought me a beer at a bar counter he did not leave a tip, as is customary in Spain. Back in the street, he tried to hail a yellow car, thinking it was a Yellow Cab.

Once at the University, he admitted he never expected students to be able to drink anything they wanted at the well-supplied cafeteria-bar each school has within the campus, the meeting place between classes. We joined other students there and I introduced him to some girls, with whom he, of course, did not shake hands, and sat with them for a cup of coffee. However, I noticed that, after having been conversing with one of the girls for quite a while, he let her pay for her own coffee instead of doing it himself, as would be appropriate there. I also heard him ask why students in Spain did not work their way through college instead of living on and with their parents until they get married.

On the way home we took the subway, and Tom was about to hit a man who was pressing him on his ribs. I tried to explain to him that it was the rush hour, for one thing, that physical contact was much more common in Spain and not so emphatically avoided when it was hard to do so in such a situation, and that touching among men simply had different limitations than in North America.[4]

Back home again, the landlady was quite pleased when Tom held her chair as we were sitting for lunch (for that is not so common there among middle-class men), but then I noticed how she was looking at him through the corner of her eye as he kept crisscrossing his fork and knife from one hand to another, with his left hand on his lap (instead of keeping his fork in his left hand and using the right one only for his knife, as European do), when he kept biting from a slice of bread that would show his teethmarks (instead of taking a little piece at a time), and when he pushed something with his thumb and then licked two of his fingers (instead of at least wiping them in his napkin, which he never used anyway to wipe his lips before and after drinking instead of leaving their mark on the glass).

In sum, Tom was there with the sincere intention of behaving like a Spaniard and understanding Spaniards, and for that purpose he had attained some linguistic fluency. What he did not know was that he had carried his own culture with him, that he was displaying it all the time, and that he was in desparate need of a little 'cultural fluency.'

Although this illustration of intercultural communication refers only to a foreign culture, it would be wrong not to admit that our attitudes and behaviors in our native environment would be more efficient and successful if we were aware of the what's, the how's, the why's, the when's, and the with whom's of our own everyday behaviors, and the behaviors of those with whom we have to interact,[5] that culture is something formed not only of values, beliefs and artifacts, but of the many ways of communicating and establishing, or breaking, the flow of interaction, organically interrelated and mutually conditioned. Furthermore, whatever I included in the definition of culture earlier originates in man in contact with one or more congeners, with other animals species, and with the man-shaped or natural environment.

10. Cultural Fluency, Behavioral Choices, and the Fluency Quotient

We must agree, if only by considering the many pitfalls and barriers and misinterpretations that take place in the simple illustration I just offered, that no matter how much our world is shrinking, no matter how many goals are recognized, as personal and mass communication media develop, cultures are still different worlds in themselves, both physically and intellectually. In order to communicate we seek linguistic fluency, but around that core of language we need to build up other fluencies as well: paralinguistic, kinesic, proxemic, chronemic, to name only the most essential categories (Poyatos 1972a).[6] We need, in sum, to attain *cultural fluency*, and for this we must analyze a culture with a high degree of accuracy, decide what is universal and what culture-bound, contrast it with our own, and decide also which kind of observation (or acculturation) process we wish to go through, which type of communication we seek, how deep we want to probe into that culture, or whether we aim only at its general style. In fact, the strategies depend on the specific goals of each particular field, which actually converge in the study of culture, the interdisciplinary field where any attempt at conducting serious work through only one channel, say, social psychology, would prove most unrealistic.

Although I will elaborate further on this concept of fluency as I deal with the various systems of verbal and nonverbal communication, it should be clear now that a person can be said to be *fluent* in his own language, that is, his own culture, only when he is capable of functioning fluently among different types of cointeractants whose standards of usage we might not label (from our own biased point of view) standard, but 'extra-standard' (see Chapter 5), that portion of the communicative repertoires of each group which is not shared by the others, but of which those others may be perfectly aware. But even verbal behavior will occur in nonverbal contexts in specific cultural patterned situations (intelligibly, rather than sensibly apprehended) that will require our correct judgement, our 'cultural fluency.'

This implied possibility of more than one choice between two interactants in a given situation reveals the costructuration of systems which is basic to a culture (indicated by the lines joining the different systems in the advanced version of the chart 'Sensible and Intelligible Systems in a Culture,' Fig. 2.1) and what Pike (1954) called 'spots' in his theory of the structure of human behavior, which inspired some of my earlier thoughts on the complexity and structure of verbal–nonverbal communication situations (and incited me to search for and develop the concept of 'cultureme', the unit of culture discussed in Chapter 2). What immediately attracted me in Pike's thoughts was that he did not try to define an unchangeable minimal unit equivalent to the phoneme, as too many others have done in an attempt to apply structural linguistics to other fields. He understood clearly that in social interaction we are constantly coming to, or facing, certain behavioral junctions, or 'spots', at which point we can, according to circumstances and to our own judgement and capacity for fluency, adopt one of two or more behaviors, in other words, take one of several alternatives, which he called 'classes.' Later I shall return to these two concepts when dealing with culturemes and also when outlining the semiotic approach to culture I would like to suggest, but for now I only wish to relate it to the ideal of cultural fluency. In a very early paper (Poyatos 1969) written in Spanish, and still without speaking of 'fluency,' I nevertheless used a cultural situation typical of the Spanish culture with which I was trying to illustrate these *behavioral choices*, but which may serve to define cultural fluency as well.

The specific setting can be a home or middle-middle to low-middle class, or below, or a second-class train compartment (now a disappeared setting that was a more homogeneous social context than a first-class one), or a popular, trucker-type of roadside restaurant. A rather culturally refined person walks in and immediately faces two choices: (a) to say, as part of his greeting, *Que aproveche* (similar to French *Bon ap'tit!*) because certain signs in those who are eating (the situation would apply only to those at the table nearest to him) he takes as middle-middle or lower-class identifiers (clothes, eating manners, voice volume and other paralinguistic features, etc.); or (b) to maintain his own class patterns and simply nod and say good afternoon or evening (rarely remaining silent if the others are open to interaction by eye contact). The choice is between being fluent with those specific people, who would say *Que aproveche* themselves, or not to say it. The encounter serves as the behavioral choice or junction (spot). Were he the one who was eating at home, on the train or in the restaurant, and the lower-class people the ones who approached him, he would also have to choose between uttering any sort of greeting or, wanting to be fluent and observe the other people's etiquette norms, ask immediately *¿Ustedes gustan?* (Would you like [to join me]?), which they would automatically complete with *Gracias, que aproveche* ('Thanks, bon ap'tit'). But the 'refined' person (the one for whom etiquette means 'bourgeoise' etiquette) may choose not to be fluent in the other people's sense of fluency. That is our own choice according to our own sensitiveness towards others and toward the different styles of interaction we must face in our own culture. In fact, I shall elaborate further on fluency when dealing with interaction, for *interactive fluency* is our most important characteristic as members of a society and must be acknowledged, not only when we interact with normal persons, but with impaired ones as well, and in various forms of what I shall discuss as 'reduced interaction' situations.

In a later paper (Poyatos 1972a) I used a further example from the Spanish culture to illustrate these behaviors, the most typical 'kissing-or-not-kissing-her-hand situation', witnessed in the conventional social encounter of three married couples. In Spain kissing the hand of a married woman is common among the refined people, the high middle-class and, as a very conscious social control, among quite a few members of the middle-class in communities where these share a common ground with the higher class and feel the need to keep up with them. Now, in my example two 'refined' couples meet a 'non-refined' couple, and their encounter creates a tense situation in which the need to choose the right behavior or social technique plays a most important role, because it may happen, (a) that the refined husband kisses the hand of the refined wife, and then that of the unrefined one, producing either embarrassment or satisfaction on the part of the unrefined couple; (b) that he does not kiss the hand of the unrefined wife, therefore offending them; or (c) that he does not kiss the hand of either woman in order to avoid a very difficult situation. As for the unrefined husband, if made to choose a certain social technique, he may kiss the hand of the two refined wives, or may not do it at all, even if he feels certain embarrassment. In other words, the first husband's initial reaction offered a series of semantically different alternatives, there being a causative chain reaction. Furthermore, this causativeness is the product of a series of possible choices with marked distinctive characters, both of which aspects constitute, as we can see, important factors in the communication system from the point of view of culture. Kendon (1980) has illustrated this succession and interchangeability of behaviors within what he calls 'slots' in the sequential development of interaction, and his most didactic description can be most profitably understood in the context of *intracultural* as well as *intercultural* encounters.[7]

This simple instance (or not so simple from the point of view of costructured behaviors) proves also that cultural fluency starts at home, as we face a number of behavioural alternatives of which we may or may not be aware, hence the higher degree of adaptability; or as we might put it, the higher *fluency quotient* (FG) of the more culturally aware person, the one who can more easily modify his personal standard repertoire to include also behavior forms that are more characteristic of other persons or groups.

If we come out of our own culture—where the variety of geographical subcultures, work groups, etc., are, after all, hardly foreign to us, and where therefore we can act with a wider margin of safety—what I have referred to as fluency quotient is automatically diminished, as seen through my old friend's story, or what would have happened to me in the United States. However, the person with a higher FQ will fare much better when confronted for the first time with a foreign culture in an interactive situation, for instance. One must let himself be 'acculturated' and match the behaviors that, against his own 'foreign' views, seem natural in that cultural context, and at least try to mirror those behaviors as he is being introduced to them, and later practice them knowing that his cointeractants will expect them more when they are of a lower socioeconomic status precisely because they lack fluency. In India, for instance, we can easily adopt the greeting with vertical joint palms against the chest, which we learn from the time we board an Indian flight. Certain bodily-contact behaviors (studied later as alter-adaptor kinesic behaviors) are not so easy to adopt when they may carry other connotations in our own culture, thus when we ask for the secretariat office or the washrooms and our Indian colleague takes us there by the hand very solicitously, we will hardly adopt such behavior too soon; and when we shake hands and he retains our hand for one, two, even three and four minutes while we talk, we cannot concentrate fully on the conversation. Handshaking or hand contact will be discussed again, but it will suffice to indicate at this point that a man could easily escalate the handshake ladder by interacting consecutively in the United States (where often there is no handshake), in England (where it happens more often), in Spain (much more and with our co-interactant's left hand holding or patting our right arm), in France (very frequently with people we see every day at work), and then in India, and that he could gradually adapt his fluency to each individual culture. Some behaviors are easier to adopt than others, and there is host of factors in ourselves to condition our readiness, reluctance or simply degree of adaptation. But underlining all that is, above all, the principle of cultural fluency, to which anyone who must interact in a foreign culture must be acutely sensitized.

Intercultural fluency from within

On the other hand, cultural fluency in relation to a foreign culture without even leaving our own can be just as necessary. This is precisely the situation of the *literary translator*. He needs a fluent knowledge of the language in order to translate a novel or a play, and also of its paralanguage or, as will be seen, he will fail to perceive many semantic values of vocal nonverbal constructs and their cooccurrent kinesic constructs (in other words, he cannot ignore the Basic Triple Structure language-paralanguage-kinesics). He must also have a fairly good knowledge of other somatic, objectual and environmental systems as well as intelligible ones in order to carry out a truly intercultural translation, for there is no such thing as a purely linguistic translation, though that seems to be what most readers of literature in translation are exposed to unfortunately.

The second most important form of intercultural communication 'from within' involving also written language is *letter-writing*. The formality or informality in the tone we use when corresponding with members of other cultures does not depend, as within our own, on the status of the other person and our mutual relationship, but, most of all, on how (if we know at all) they interact face-to-face and in writing. I may write the same type of letter to not very close colleagues in the United States, France, Hungary, Japan, and India. But if I really wish to establish a good rapport, the one addressed to the American will be rather colloquial and informal, I may sign only my first name, and even address him by his first name (not so much hers usually unless she did it first); with the Frenchman it will take me a little longer to do that, as they "monsieur" each other more in their culture; with the Hungarian, I will naturally express myself in a warmer tone, after having interacted with Hungarians personally; with the Japanese I will certainly use a rather 'bowing' style, open yet respectful, because I know them to be that way; and the tone of my letter to the Indian colleague, will be, also naturally after having treated them in their own culture, warm, thoughtful, and pleased to enjoy his acquaintance.

Another way in which cultural fluency 'from within' can be extremely important is in situations in which we interact with members of other cultures who despite their own degree of fluency with relation to us, still act, perceive and judge through their own culture, by which they have been shaped. This problem is generally quite familiar to immigration officers, who so often fail to understand and behave properly with foreigners because they ignore their values and do not perceive or simply misinterpret their verbal and nonverbal attitudes—for instance, in an uncontrolled display of emotion by Arabs or Italians in the face of difficulties—but is not so familiar to doctors and nurses, particularly the latter, who actually live with the patients. In a country life Canada, for example, where there are so many first generation Latins, Slavics, Arabs, Indians, Chinese, etc., nurses would find it extremely useful if they included in their training a sensitization course on nonverbal communication and cross cultural differences in emotional displays, in the attitude toward death, nudity, privacy, etc. This would allow them to interpret without error, not only the verbal statements and remarks of many of their patients, but also their attitudes toward the hospital personnel, and as regards food, their own hospital clothes, isolation, ward rules and, of course, the exact significance of their gaze behaviors, their mannerisms and gestures, that is, the many intended or unintended nonverbal messages. The interactive fluency of nurses, in general quite good, would be enriched by their cultural fluency.[8]

Emitting and perceiving fluency

This concept of fluency, which transcends that of linguistic fluency to subsume our verbal as well as nonverbal capabilities, will be elaborated on in other chapters. In the next chapter it will be clearly implied that the fluency which is required to face a foreign culture is not only *emitting fluency*, illustrated by verbal and nonverbal behaviors as producer of signs mostly as we engage in social interaction. This is the type of fluency we would generally associate the term with, and that is why we are prone to fail in our communicative endeavors in spite of our linguistic, kinesic, even food-consuming abilities (our willingness to accept another culture's food) and dressing habits (according to another culture's social situations). However, it is beyond the level of how we conduct ourselves, what others perceive. It is precisely how we understand their behaviors and attitudes, our *perceiving fluency*, that must be spoused to the former type of fluency, and perception goes far beyond what we hear, see, touch, smell or taste, for it involves all the intelligible forms of the foreign culture, from religious ideas and their ramifications into that culture's ways of life, or the cultural values of certain verbal expressions, to the principles of child rearing. This is, then, the basis for the differentiation between sensible and intelligible systems and for the progressive approach to culture and communication problems.

Depending on a number of conditioning variables (suggested before in the very definition of cultural fluency), not only do our emitting and perceiving capabilities vary, but also, within the latter, our ability to decode more correctly sensible systems than intelligible ones. This thought is not a gratuitous one at all, nor, in my opinion, a negligible distinction. It is our perception of others, their behaviors, and all the immediate and farther-removed environmental messages that constantly (in the cultural continuum in which we live and which we maintain through generations) elicit our own subsequent behaviors. It is an ongoing eliciting process in which we relate to and interact with others, and the success or failure of our occasional or long-lasting relationships (from a short social encounter to a life acquaintanceship or a prolonged professional relationship) is heavily influenced by our understanding and acceptance of others and, first, by our perception of their behaviors. But it might happen that our perceptive fluency is rather limited, that through lack of social maturity due to age, because of a poor attention capacity or sensitiveness, or simply because of insufficient knowledge of all those social somatic, objectual and environmental systems, we do not perceive them and decode them properly, or that we do not perceive them at all. Someone may be quite conscious of the religious thoughts and beliefs of others, their role expectations, family and marriage structures, etc., and at the same time fail to perceive the true significance of the verbal paralinguistic, kinesic or proxemic behaviors of those very same persons he is relating to, or the social-identifying values of their clothes, interior decoration, patterns, food, and so on, and again fail in that relationship. The cultural concept of fluency, therefore, should distinguish within perceptive fluency between sensibly apprehended systems and those that are intellectually dealt with.

But in differentiating emitting and perceiving fluency one must not neglect the various conditioning factors that may increase or decrease the fluency quotient of an individual. The basic ones seem to be, succinctly outlined, the following:

Age. Just as one determines the development of verbal language and nonverbal systems in childhood, it is suggested later on that the ontogeny of paralinguistic, kinesic and proxemic behaviors should also be investigated. As the child's various communicative repertoires grow, then, his or her fluency capabilities will grow as well; not only as a producer of gradually more sophisticated gestures, manners, postures, distance behaviors, and of course, lexical messages, but in his or her perception of those activities in others. On the other hand, it is interesting to observe that the child's higher learning ability in a foreign language will be coupled, if he learns it in its own culture, to an 'accent-free' kinesic lexicon.

Psychological configuration. Fluency can be facilitated by higher learning ability, by an acute power of observation and imitation, by an ability to associate the various systems whether as an emitter or as an observer, just as any mental disorders or a low attention rate will affect it adversely. In fact, the fluency and lack of fluency of the psychologically handicapped should be investigated in depth because it is an important aspect of their interactive capabilities.

The *socioeducational level*, although it encompasses certain additional contextual elements, such as the geographical setting and its degree of accessibility to more complex social aggregates and the existence or lack of opportunities for social climbing, it affects perceptual, emitting, cultural and intercultural fluencies because the individual's contact with the more fluent circles is poor, as is his formal preparation for understanding and coping with all the different communication systems and their variations, and therefore his personal sensitiveness towards the behaviors of others. What in Chapter 5 is referred to as forms of usage is directly related to the degree of fluency, since a low fluency quotient betrays a conflict between the individual's shared standard (what is common to most members of his culture) and his extrastandard, that is, the standard peculiar to his own group, which can be appreciated and judged by the socioeducationally higher persons better usually than he himself could judge and adopt theirs. Again, the problems of fluency become apparent as we study each individual system of communication, since each system poses a different degree of difficulty (e.g., getting used to another culture's food is easier than mastering its paralinguistic nuances, adapting to its structuration and concept of time is easier than learnings its kinesics), a factor that should not be compartmentalized.

Notes

1. I first explored the cultural perspective of communicative behaviors in an article for *Linguistics* (Poyatos 1972a) where I offered a definition of cultureme, genetic and learned

habits, the Basic Triple Structure—without defining the concept—(Chapter 5), and the general Conditioning Background (Chapter 3), mainly. I regard that article as a modest start of all my later work, preceded by a brief behavioristic approach published in Spanish (Poyatos 1969). I was also discussing these topics in several papers presented at some national and international meeetings of Hispanists. My exposure to my adopted North American culture as a teacher of Spanish language and literature at that time was therefore revealing the semiotic-communicative implications that would soon change my academic orientation. Later I still offered an application of my work in Hispanic Studies at different meetings and in articles (Poyatos 1971, 1974a, 1974b, 1975a, 1975b, 1975c, 1978a) as well as another paper in Spanish (Poyatos 1974a).

2. For further discussion of the concept of culture see Johnson (1982), who follows Poyatos' (1976a) definition "in line with the tradition that treats language as itself a behavior, an intepretation . . . which underlies a great deal of the verbal versus nonverbal theory (Malinowski 1923; Sapir 1929; Kluchohn 1949; Pike 1967)" (see the same definition in Poyatos 1972a).

3. A typical example would be the change in furniture style since the eighteenth century, when curved, upholstered chairs and couches replaced the stiffness of previous times, conditioning more relaxed postures (cf. Hewes 1955, 1957) much in keeping with Versaillesque type of sensual habits, which illustrates the relationship furniture-kinesics indicated in Fig. 2.1, 'Sensible and Intelligible Systems in a Culture'.

4. I am rather fond of using the example of my old roommate, but I could easily illustrate the same problems profusely by simply quoting from the many happenings related by my students in such a multicultural campus as the University of New Brunswick, where, for instance, an ebullient Greek talks 'too loud' and 'too close' to me because he knows I am 'a Mediterranean'. Some Libyan men had to be advised not to walk around hand-in-hand, and a Canadian friend of my Greek student, while in Athens, thought the place was full of homosexual men because they touched each other 'so much' while conversing.

5. A good part of my students in my three nonverbal communication courses are from the School of Nursing. Most of the issues and problems addressed in this book and many more we discuss concern them so directly that I find them to be extremely receptive, a condition even more important in a multicultural country like Canada with truly multicultural hospitals.

6. I first began to develop the concept of cultural fluency—used by Johnson's (1982) book on nonverbal communication in language teaching, for which I served as consultant in 1976 and 1977—in much earlier papers (e.g., Poyatos 1974b [in Spanish], 1976a, 1977b, 1981a). Lately I discussed it in a paper read at the 1982 Internationa Congress of Linguists (Poyatos 1983c).

7. Returning to my friend Tom's incident with another passenger on the Madrid subway, it can serve as a perfect example of the intercultural use of 'slots'. It was the rush hour. The offender's behavior (intimate distance) was simply conditioned by two important circumstances: The crowding, in which we were all both actors and victims, and the fact that proxemic or spatial relation among people in those countries is such that certain ways of touching each other are not offensive at all, they are not taboos, they are very often a way to emphasize words and ideas in a friendly conversation between two or more men standing in front of each other. On the other hand, that portion of the stranger's behavior was considered by Tom as an indivisible unit, formed by a physical continuum that he obviously could not analyze. However, being a member of that culture myself, I could easily see a series of alternatives which would modify or give a special meaning—offensive or not—to the initial activity of that stranger, and also a contextual situation which, in this case, conditioned the whole behavioral activity. So my reaction would not have been such a violent one.

8. Recently I was invited to speak at a provincial nurses conference. Although the nursing literature is opening gradually to nonverbal communication issues, it was a mutually stimulating experience to discuss the crosscultural, somatic, objectual and environmental aspects of nonverbal communication, as well as the nonverbal side of the nurse's ministry of physical, psychological and spiritual care.

2

Toward a Systematic Analysis of Culture

1. Sensible and Intelligible Sign Systems[1]*

IT has been suggested in the preceding chapter that the study of communication systems within a cultural context is in itself a process of growing in awareness of the multifaceted composition of that culture. Once the two basic domains of the interactive and noninteractive cultural activities are clearly delineated in our minds, and once the preponderance of the noninteractive ones—and therefore the true nature of culture—is understood, we come to acknowledge in a logical progression the two overlapping ways in which we can perceive culture: through the senses (e.g., a gesture, the fragrance of a perfume, the interior decoration of a home) and through the mind (e.g., the husband–wife relationship in a Moslem country, a cultural system which is manifested through external signs and behaviors as well).

It is at this point, then, that the major distinction between *sensible* and *intelligible* systems must be introduced, as it constitutes the basis for the whole progressive and systematic approach to people's verbal and nonverbal systems of communication and to all the communication systems that surround them in their world, from vocally produced ones to environmental ones and from those which dictate and rule over words, such as morals or etiquette, to those which determine the sensible characteristics of the modified environment, such as social status and the varying concepts of esthetic values.

It is necessary to emphasize, however, that 'sensory' and 'intelligible' are, therefore, rather relative terms which overlap each other. Religious and moral values, for instance, or sex roles, are not just sociocultural concepts comprehended with our minds. They occur as sensorially perceived events manifested through linguistic, paralinguistic or kinesic constructs, proxemic (space) and chronemic (time) behaviors, dress habits, etc., in which we distinguish systems and other sign patterns. Consequently we will legiti-

* Superscript numbers refer to Notes at end of chapter.

mately discover intelligible systems through their sensory manifestations; or inversely, being aware of those intelligible cultural patterns, we will find their sensible characteristics within a given culture.

Thus, when speaking of sensible signs we must start by identifying the channel on which they travel between emitter and receiver when we deal with dynamic bodily-generated ones, or between environmental manifestations (static, as a building, or dynamic, as a roller coaster) and their decoder. When, on the other hand, we refer to intelligible signs we can also identify their carrying channels without believing that their perception is merely an 'intellectual' process just because we may 'think of,' for instance, the closely-knit family in certain cultures and decide that that is an intelligible category. Cultural characteristics, such as moral values, identify themselves precisely through 'behaviors' (language, kinesics, proxemics) and through static but still sensibly apprehended elements (e.g., an affectionate letter through which we may appreciate visually that the family ties are stronger than in other cultures).

It is therefore at this point that I would like to introduce, as a framework referred to throughout the book, the table in Fig. 2.1, 'Sensible and Intelligible Systems in a Culture.' All the different aspects of culture and communication that constitute this book can be said to be represented in this mapping of culture. The fact that later Literary Anthropology (Chapter 11) develops precisely from the same scheme and that the relationships among the different somatic, extrasomatic and environmental systems are also based on it illustrates the intended cohesion among the various parts of this approach and how it all stemmed from the study of verbal language and its immediate recognition as a non-autonomous system. Finally, what I try to illustrate with this and a few other tables is how every single aspect of communication, every system, and every application of the theoretical and methodological ideas developed here remains always within a *cultural context*.

One must then return for a moment to the first cultural chart, 'Culture and Communication' (Fig. 1.1) to see that the sensible-intelligible perspective was always contained in it and that it simply developed from it in a natural way. In fact, the first chart illustrated the conviction that verbal language had to be viewed in its total context and in relation to all forms of expression in a culture and that culture was by nature communication, while the second one built upon this view and emphasized the complexity of

(a) the *somatic complex*, a block in which verbal language is but one of the cosystems, though the one that surpasses the others in the average human communication situation,

(b) the *first objectual complex*, closer to the somatic one and intimately related to some of its activities, as the so-called body-adaptors (jewelry, food) and object-adaptors (an umbrella, a tool), for instance, may condition kinesic behavior,

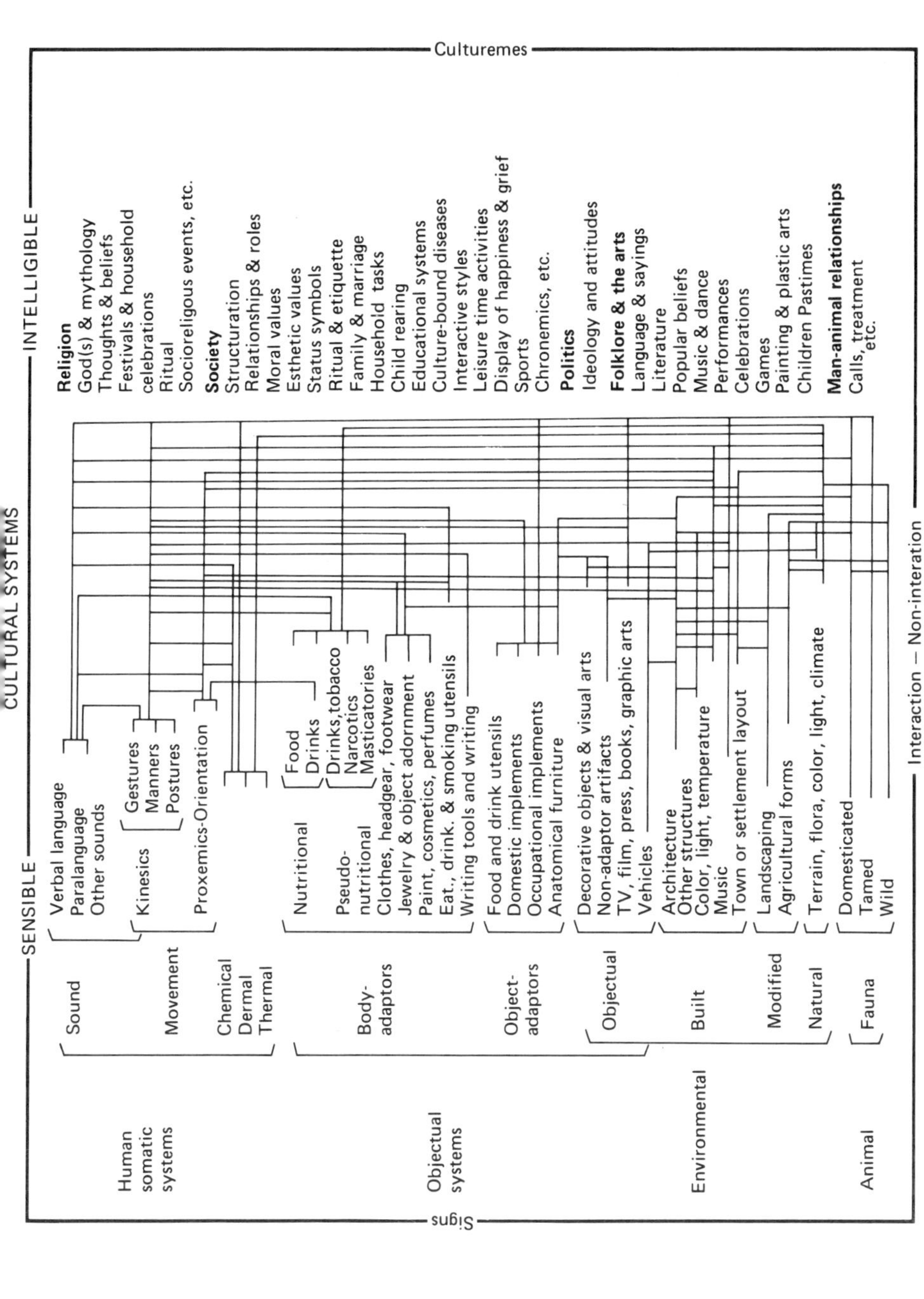

FIG. 2.1. Sensible and Intelligible Systems in a Culture.

(c) the *second objectual complex*, which contains already environmental systems whose relationships with the purely bodily ones is never direct, as they are physically farther removed from the body,

(d) the *environmental complex*, which in reality shows two forms: the static ones (utensils, architecture, landscaping) and the dynamic ones (moving billboards, vehicles, traffic signs)—hence the importance of movement as one of the two essential manifestations of social cultural-forming activities, the other being sound—and

(e) the *animal species*, which links again with the human somatic systems, as man and animals share a number of interactive situations which also define and may differentiate cultures.

Further stages in the differentiation between sensible and intelligible systems will be, first, their organization into somatic sign complexes and other coexisting complexes called 'culturemes'; then, the acknowledgement of the interactive and noninteractive forms of culture; and still farther, the costructuration of all systems and the behavioral results of those mutual relationships.

What this view of culture led me to, in what I believed to be quite a logically derived way, was the necessity not to plunge into seemingly refined analyses of individual cultural systems without first viewing all of them through a two fold approach: the basic semiotic understanding of what was being observed, described and studied, that is, their own internal structuration into signs and sign blocks, and the complementary anthropological perspective that recognizes all forms of culture as culturemes and components of culturemes.

2. Toward a Typology of Somatic Signs[2]

As a theoretical and methodological complement to the analysis of 'culturemes', developed later, one needs to be able to study human behavior, whether interactive or noninteractive, in a progressive fashion in order to understand the meaningful coarticulation of different parts of the body, and, on the other hand, the equally meaningful lack of coarticulation at times. Any general taxonomy of somatic signs, developed either through a specific strategy or discipline or in an all-encompassing approach, requires that we first take a broad view of the sign transmission processes that take place between its source and the receiver.

At the same time those somatic sign complexes reveal the intimate relationship betwen sensible and intelligible cultural forms and how a culture can be approached for as critical an analysis as we wish to undertake.

Sign systems, whether sensibly apprehended, such as proxemic behavior between cointerlocutors, or intelligibly perceived, such as the status or role relationships—revealed also sensorially by the very distance behavior in that same situation—appear in associations of varying complexity that ought to be recognized in order to have a systematic view of any type of cultural activity.

The semiotic parallels between somatic sign systems and 'culturemes' will be clear when the latter are discussed and both of them are understood as mutually complementary typologies, since they aim simply at fostering the much needed interdisciplinary study of culture and the communicative activities. Both, however, are perceived in a natural progression that normally follows our gradual knowledge of the people and their behaviors and the environment around them, in such a way that broader composites of signs define themselves without any apparent further internal structuration until experience reveals further possible distinctions. Take, for example, the greeting behaviors alluded to earlier. A handshake + smile + verbal salutation seems to be an indivisible block, and so we associate it with a number of different cultures. Our own experience, however, tells us later that even without considering other accompanying behaviors, such as the distance between the two cointeractants and the possible additional kinesic acts performed by the left arm, that handshake can be very firm or very limp, take the whole hand or just the fingers, shake once, twice, several times, or not shake at all, last for four seconds or thirty seconds, disengage quickly or slip slowly out of each other's hands, etc. Thus, even unrealistically dissociating it from the cooccurrent activities, a handshake must necessarily be located somewhere between what constitutes a sign system and a single type, or even a 'token' (each realization of type).

The chart in Fig. 2.2, 'Organization of Somatic Signs,' attempts to show how to locate and define sign types within the input–output process of human communication, and why we need to consider basic categories first; it also attempts to suggest the semiotic complexity of the last stage of the proposed analysis, that is, from the definition of a single specific sign type to the identification and definition of its various tokens, and what is termed 'subtype', since it is at that point that the uncertainty about which morphologically identical occurrences belong to the same type and which constitutes a different type becomes more apparent.

Channels

After differentiating the two major classes of signs, sensible and intelligible, one realizes that they both depend ultimately on a sensory input–output channel, observing, for instance: the kinetic-visual one within which we include kinesics, the dermal-visual one, which includes blushing, or the chemical-olfactory transmission of body odors, dictated by cultural and socioeconomic and personal 'intelligibly' perceived patterns.

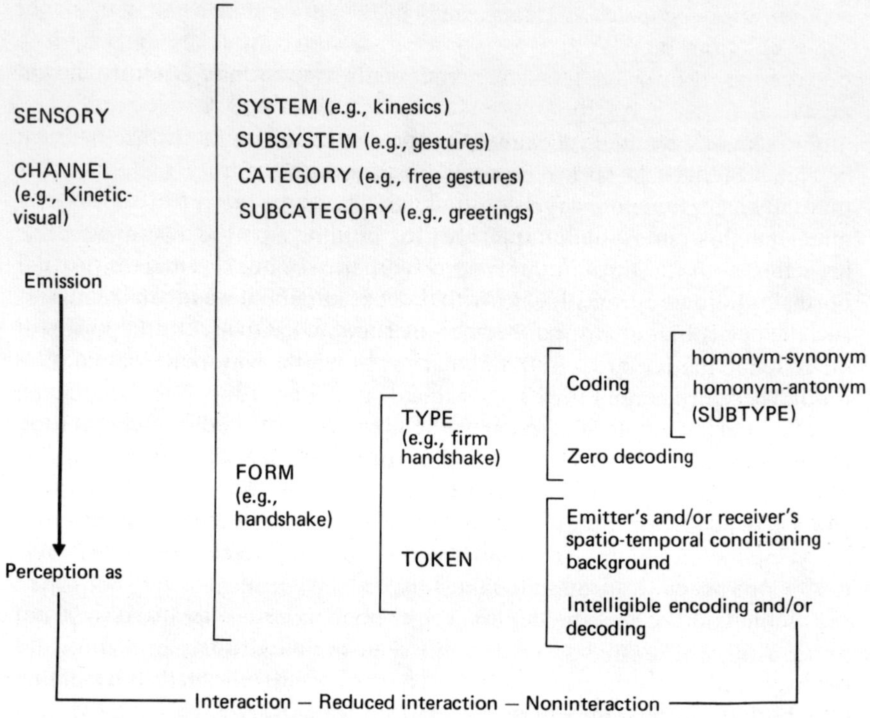

FIG.2.2. Organization of Somatic Signs.

Systems

Systems result from the input–output activities, whether in interaction or noninteraction, such as verbal language, paralanguage, kinesics and proxemics, and those for which labels have not been established yet, although they function as systematically as the others (e.g., dermal reactions), still without differentiating the various kinds of dermal reactions, as is done later.

Systems, therefore, can be equated to the broader types of 'culturemes' as discussed below, that is, the first general grouping of cultural signs. The handshake alluded to before would be classified later as part of kinesics, a system in itself.

Subsystems

Subsystems are still broad distinctions that have to be made within systems, such as gestures, manners and postures differentiated in kinesics; or, within skin phenomena, texture changes, coloration changes, and dermal-chemical reactions.

Categories

Within subsystems, categories would identify the free and bound modalities of gestures, manners and postures (without contacting ourselves, others or things, or establishing contact), while, within dermal coloration changes, one could now distinguish different coloration changes (e.g., blushing) meaningfully associated (i.e., bound) to various occurrences of language, or language-paralanguage-kinesics, and those which bear no apparent relationship (a virtually impossible instance, since silence and stillness are also acknowledged).

Subcategories

Subcategories may distinguish either motives or functions of free or bound gestures, manners and postures, that is, in greetings, goodbyes, bond-seeking, aggression, etc.; and, within dermal color reactions, shame, anger, fear, grief, etc.

Forms

Forms constitute the core of human behavior, and this is where we would now classify the handshake with no other qualifications as a bound manner involving the mutual engagement of the hand; and, within skin coloration changes, specific changes like blushing and blanching, and those caused by acute malfunctions.

Types

Having refined the distinctions from whole systems to concrete forms, types qualify those forms. The handshake can be limp or forceful, with or without shaking, with or without smiling, etc. Blushing can vary as to duration, intensity, area covered, amount of cooccurrent eye contact, etc.

Tokens

This suggested semiotic hierarchization shows the complexity of the deeper layers of analysis, that is, from a specific type, "the class of all occurrences of a type" (Sebeok 1974: 241), to a *token*, a single occurrence, as the differentiation between the two is not that obvious at all if one considers the many conditioning factors that affect both the emitter and the receiver.

One could rightfully argue that the various tokens of one given sign are not at all absolute concepts, since each occurrence does not happen simultaneously to, and with identical meaning that, another one of the same type (word tokens of the same work type in a poem, tears of the same chemical-semiotic type corresponding to a specific emotional context), but always, in a greater or lesser degree, temporally and spatially removed from that other one and from the rest of them. This entails of necessity a nonidentical contextual conditioning background, as has been pointed out. A careful study reveals a series of conspicuous and less conspicuous modifying elements in terms of the encoder's as well as the decoder's biopsychological, environmental, cultural, socioeconomic, etc., characteristics, whose complex costructuration becomes doubly intriguing when we view it in a diachronic or historical way, or in a synchronic one, either separately or combined, as they complement each other.

Several occurrences of, for instance, a slow wink (the one used as an example in the table among its kinesics cohierarchies)—or, for that matter, a written word, a paralinguistic click, or a limp handshake—can constitute a type when they are identically understood by both emitter and receiver (that is, when signifier and signified are the same at the input end in all the instances) and sensibly and intelligibly perceived in the same manner. But when either the coding or the decoding of a token (or both) vary, in other words, when it is understood differently by its emitter at the output end and/or interpreted differently by its receiver at the output end—in spite of being homomorphic (because the signified or denotatum, the other half of the sign, is different)—it can hardly be said to belong within the class that makes up one single sign type. In sum, I see it as a homonym-antonym, quite outside the supposedly matrix type, and any number of occurrences of that specific nature constitute a 'subtype.'

Subtypes

A subtype, then, would be defined as the deviating class or occurrences of an assumed type whose signified is sensibly and/or intelligibly emitted and/or perceived as different from another class of that type. It depends, therefore, on the receiver's and/or emitter's spatio-temporal conditioning background, as not only somatic and cultural differences will modify the meaning, but historical ones as well. A wink exactly performed fifty years from now, a written word that evoked a specific concept two centuries ago (when it was encoded and 'frozen' in its textual context) or a paralinguistic construct recorded on film, may be differently understood by its emitter and interpreted by its receiver as time goes by, even under virtually identical circumstances. This distinction between type and subtype, therefore, may help us in establishing a typology of signs, as it keeps us from dealing with different occurrences as if they were identical.

In addition, when the signified is not at all perceived by the receiver, and neither a correct or incorrect input–output takes place, we may refer to *zero decoding* to differentiate it from 'zero sign,' when a sign signifies "by its very absence" (Sebeok 1974: 241). Zero sign decoding is a semiotic blank that takes place much more often than one can imagine, not only in daily live interaction, but in every static sign manifestation of the arts, the environment, etc. In fact, much research could be devoted to seeking the rate between decoding (false or correct) and zero decoding in specific situations and by specific receivers across, for instance, socioeconomic and educational strata, age groups, cultures, etc.

3. The Analysis of a Culture Through Its Culturemes[3]

Every attempt to study human patterns of somatic behavior and thought and the end products of those physical and intellectual activities; or, to put it differently, every attempt to analyze culture in a systematic, progressive and exhaustive fashion, should seek a workable unit, without which such an analysis would prove quite problematic and precarious. Adopting a linguistic-like structure as has been done, or attempted, so many times in a number of research areas, would have unnecessarily encumbered the approach I proposed at the 1973 IXth International Congress of Anthropological and Ethnological Sciences (Poyatos 1976e, 1976f). Instead I sought a unit which I called *cultureme*, which I defined as any portion of cultural activity sensorially or intellectually apprehended in signs of symbolic value, which could be divided up into smaller units or amalgamated into larger ones.

The table in Fig. 2.3 'Analysis of a Culture Through Its Culturemes'[4] outlines the process of cultureme analysis and illustrates graphically its basic two-way progressive itinerary, that is, from the broadest units of culture, or culturemes (e.g., a given culture as perceived in its exterior settings, not within its buildings) to the simplest ones (e.g., eye contact at the table), or vice versa. I would like to point out that the table with which I tried to illustrate my theory of culturemes, as well as my explication of it, did not ignore that one could not make such dichotomy as 'urban-rural' universal, nor could one establish a clear-cut borderline between those two cultural settings; even though I included it at the beginning of the theory as two basic culturemes one would not resort to while studying, for instance, a preliterate culture. On the other hand, I am aware of the fact that within the urban physical setting we find, of course, the rural population drawn to the cities, not only as an outskirt belt, but mingled with the downtown urbanites. In that case we should decide whether we are interested, for instance, in the rural nonverbal communication repertoire, or in their urban behavior, regardless of social status. By the same token, we can study the life of urbanites residing in the rural areas for extended period of time. The very discussion of these differences would suggest a number of distinct culturemes, as will be apparent.

Phase One	Phase Two		Phase Three	Phase Four		Derived Phases		
Basic zones, Basic culturemes	Primary culturemes	Sensible-Intelligible / Visual-Acoustic-Tactile-Olfactory-Gustatory-Soc. Attitudes	Secondary culturemes	Tertiary culturemes	Cultural systems and Subcultures discernible here	Derived culturemes	Derived culturemes 1	Derived culturemes 2
Urban: 1 Exterior; 2 Interior Rural: 3 Exterior; 4 Interior	1 Environmental 2 Behavioral 3 Environmental 4 Behavioral 5 Environmental 6 Behavioral 7 Environmental 8 Behavioral		Settings: Home, School, Office, Class-room, Theatre, Restaurant, Bar, Park Church, Square, etc. (According to specific cultures)	Visual, Acoustic, Tactile, (Kinesthetic, Skin Senses), Olfactory, Chronemics, Social Atti-tudes		Clothing *Kinesics* Proxemics	Kinesics *at the table*	Kinesics at the table *according to social class* Derived culturemes 3: *Eye contact* at the table Derived culturemes 4 etc.
			PROGRESSIVE ANALYSIS Synchronic-Diachronic					

Conditioning background	
Biophysio-Psychological	Biological configuration; Sex; Age; Physiological state; Medical state; Nutritional habits; Psychological configuration; Emotional states
Environmental	Natural environment; Built or modified environment; Objectual environment; Socioeconomic environment
Sharing	Performer-spectator borrowing; Couple; Nuclear family/Extended family; Social/occupational group; Geographic/subcultural variety
Cultural patterns	Religious and moral values; Relationship and role expectations; Etiquette norms; Esthetic values
Socioeducational types	Superrefined; Average educated; Average middle-income employee; Low-income worker; Pseudo-educated; Rustic

FIG. 2.3. Analysis of a Culture Through Its Culturemes.

The analysis of a culture through its culturemes, then, consists of several phases or stages through which a progressive study is carried out, from a broader view of culture to an exhaustive and minute study of features.

Phase One

Any systematic observation of people must take into account their environment. Most cultural patterns are not the same in the URBAN society as they are in the RURAL one. Not only as social beings, but simply as socializing organisms, people function differently in each of those two environments, behave differently and, therefore, shape culture differently, communicating differently and displaying different *styles*. But, besides people themselves engaged in cultural interaction, what sets apart the urban and the rural worlds—both man-shaped—is the sensorial manifestations, the sometimes radically diverse ways in which the observers perceive them. Both these aspects, the living, organic one, people, and the static but highly communicative one, involving their total environment, offer the student and the observer of culture two principal domains, EXTERIOR and INTERIOR, the latter always more difficult to explore and scrutinize in a microanalytic way because it takes a high degree of familiarity never reached in the first stages of observation, study or acculturation, three activities after all complementary.

Phase one, then is carried out according to four BASIC ZONES: urban-exterior, urban-interior, rural-exterior, and rural-interior, which at the same time constitute the four *Basic Culturemes*.

Through them a given culture identifies itself, though in a rather impressionistic way and more sensibly than intelligibly, since patterns in social or religious attitudes, ideas concerning the handling of time in personal relationships or the deep cultural background of the display or restraint of emotions are not easily discerned at this early stage under normal circumstances. Unless, of course, the fieldworker has utilized the invaluable documentation of Literary Anthropology, by means of which he will be able to arrive in the new culture fairly well equipped to appreciate the basic culturemes in a much deeper way. But this scheme does not attempt to assume such a strategy.

In this phase we would distinguish in the *American culture*, for instance: *visually*, the general separation of business areas and residential zones in the cities, particularly the smaller ones, or the land distribution and the various styles of farm houses in the country; *acoustically*, the sirens of police cars, ambulances and fire engines, the chimes of some official buildings or college chapels, the sounds of cattle in the rural areas, or that of the lawnmowers in the residential ones; *olfactorily* (in spite of the typical American olfactory deprivation, in comparison with other cultures), the city bus exhaust gases in the urban areas, mixed with the smell of hamburger drugstore air and theater-lobby popcorn, or the newly-mowed lawns of residential areas and the newly-plowed fields of farm country; and one can feel, through *tactile and kinesthetic* perceptions, the pavement of highways and country roads, the carpeted halls of commercial buildings, or the spatial arrangement of classroom furniture.

The newly-arrived fieldworker in *Spain* will soon detect: *visually*, the blending of offices and homes in the same downtown buildings, the abundance of peculiar signs attached to windows and balconies calling the passers-by's attention to culture-specific concepts (*Venéreas, Gestoría, Oposiciones*),[5] gigantic film placards above theater entrances, sidewalk cafés with all sorts of alcoholic or nonalcoholic beverages and open-door bars, black taxis, heavy traffic, and male and female traffic officers, very busy sidewalks, proxemic behavior characterized by frequent elbow rubbing and even bumping in more crowded areas; through *olfaction*, side streets will offer him the old crafts and trades (the smell of leather, esparto and hemp, carpenter shops, wine *bodegas* and *tascas*, etc.), open door fish markets and butcher shops, bakeries, dairy shops, pastry shops, etc.

The traveller in *India*, in New Delhi, for instance, is immediately confronted with the *sights* of the Indian city: the white dhotis and women's saris with some peculiar combinations of Indian and Western garments, the crowded streets, heavy traffic of small 1940's-like cabs, scooter taxis driven by bearded Sikhs, and bicycle ones, competing with bullockcarts, peaceful beige-colored cows, jammed double-deckers, food stalls, newstands with no pornographic literature, *Suiting* signs, large film placards, etc., a whole new visual world; *acoustically*, the ubiquitous crows of India, the constant honking of cars and scooter rickshaws; *olfactorily*, the late afternoon and evening smog of kerosene and cow dung used for cooking, the incense aroma coming out of some merchant stores.

In socialist countries like Hungary and East Germany, one sees also the smaller cars in a gradually growing traffic, the abundance of bookstores and record and music stores, the typical lines formed in ice-cream parlors and at any counter-service place, and men carrying shopping-like bags (which, in Spain, for instance, identify the middle-class housewife), young men and women embracing and kissing among passers-by, middle-aged and older men sometimes arm-in-arm, etc.

These sensorial manifestations, however, when observed in an orderly way, will already prepare us for a deeper understanding of that culture by revealing basic features of a national personality and a specific life style, such as the concept of and the attitude towards bars and drinking (as when we see the sign about 'Dry Days' in an Indian establishment), or the definition of a 'contact culture' along the sidewalk, where people touch each other, greet with embraces and kisses, etc.

Phase Two

After differentiating these four basic zones by means of an approach that still takes a broad view of culture it becomes apparent that any culture that has reached a certain degree of complexity offers to the most novel observer two more broad domains in each of the four preestablished basic areas: on the one hand, the people's objectual and natural environments—which not only shape their behaviors but are in turn shaped, 'culturized', by those behaviors (becoming more and more complex as the number of social functions in a culture increase)—and, on the other, the people themselves, that is, the individuals functioning in their daily relationships as socializing beings, their sensible behaviors and their attitudes ('behaviors' subsuming, here, in a broad sense, physical and mental activities). Both are actually mingled in our first impressionistic view in Phase One, as they are in more specific observations; for even the study of, say, greeting behaviors between passers-by in the street, possesses a cultural environment that may have to be acknowledged (for instance, the wide or very narrow streets in which greetings take place). These two large subdivisions of each of the four basic zones or basic culturemes I have termed ENVIRONMENTAL and BEHAVIORAL, thus constituting *Primary Culturemes*.

An analysis in terms of these eight still basic categories allows for an intermediate level of study between the comprehensive basic zones and the progressively finer presentation of the more specifying stages, already offering a deeper understanding of culture; beyond which, depending on concrete strategies, certain studies may not have to proceed any further. We might want to deal with urban-interior culture in the United States or in Spain, without yet specifying the various settings (Phase Three), but just taking a general overview of all those cultural or pancultural characteristics displayed by the people themselves, that is, the more 'active' manifestations of a culture, as contrasted with the more 'static' man-shaped ones: proxemics in closed spaces, loudness of voice and other obvious paralinguistic features, the personal perfumed spaces, etc.

Here we feel the need to seek some kind of structural framework. We concentrate on people, but people utilize different communicative modalities, behave according to certain rules, and we can, for the sake of methodological organizations, classify those behavioral manifestations in several groups.

While it is true that we could apply the linguistic framework adopted by Hall (1959)—'isolates', 'sets', and 'patterns'—we would not require units below patterns (e.g., relationships between customer and waiter in sidewalk cafés, the social function of the porches in the Spanish small-town square), although we would recognize certain 'sets' (clapping or hissing as a beckoning signal for a waiter in the Spanish sidewalk café), but hardly any 'isolates' (the position of the hands in clapping for the waiter). In other words at this stage we do not want, nor are we prepared to focus on, individual cultural patterns, trying to categorize them and analyze them against the conditioning background (indicated at the bottom of the cultureme table). We simply make a broad distinction between behavioral and environmental elements. This stage can be experienced as part of the acculturation process, whether through systematic learning or through observation. However, we seem to have two alternatives in our methodology:

The first one is the *classification by topics*, either referring to settings (the street, the park, the bus stop, the sidewalk café), or to the social forms (general proxemic behavior, clothes, etc.).

The other one is the *sensible-intelligible approach*, which I favor myself. We perceive culture sensorially (smells, sounds, kinesthetic experiences) and intellectually (use of time, employer–employee relationship), as has been discussed earlier.

As soon as we initiate a process of acculturation—a term applicable not only to an immigrant or a diplomat, but to a traveller and the serious fieldworker—we are also starting a process of sensible-intelligible involvement—which, as we find in a finer analysis, may vary considerably from one culture to another. This is an involvement that may develop in this order: visual-acoustic-tactile(kinesthetic and skin senses)-olfactory-gustatory, although the first two may be perceived simultaneously as a visual-acoustic complex, depending on our initial cultural exposure. At first we do not acknowledge any hierarchy or classification of sensory perceptions, but we simply 'sense' them in a sort of cultural amalgam. At the same time, our culturally shaped intellect begins to discern *cultural patterns* (i.e., Hall's 'sets') such as the customer–waiter relationship mentioned earlier.

Phase Three

This stage offers a much more refined analysis by breaking down each primary cultureme into as many *settings* as we can find in a given culture, or as many as we need (as long as we do not ignore their interrelationships), such as the home, the church, the school, the bar, the restaurant, the square, the stadium, the park, some lacking in the less developed cultures. Each of them constitutes now a separate cultureme, called *Secondary Cultureme*, which, naturally, can also be approached, as long as it is feasible to do so, through the various sensible and intelligible channels. At this point, however, those areas of cultural perception are still viewed more impressionistically than analytically, that is, not as isolated provinces.

The idea is, therefore, to work in a systematic progression toward a finer and finer apprehension of various cultural systems (the home, the school, etc.), similar to the also progressive development of learning and observation in the acculturation process. To deal at the very start with smaller units not only would it be unrealistic, but it would hinder further analysis in many ways, because we would not consider broader areas first, and then, in a logical way, work through more specific compartments as our needs and particular strategies would demand.

Certain studies of, say, the home (within 'urban-interior-environmental') would outline the layout of the rooms, the proxemic arrangement of formal and informal space, etc. Later, of course, at the very end of 'visual perception', for instance, we could discriminate between foveal, macular and peripheral vision, should our research demand such detailed analysis, as perceptual modalities of one single cultureme, 'Visual Culture in the Home'; while still later, as a 'derived cultureme,' an even more critical study could deal exclusively with 'Peripheral Visual Perception as Related to Spatial Arrangement', also as a separate cultureme in itself.

One more example will suffice. Say we are studying 'Postural Behavior in the Living-room of a Laborer's Home.' We could hardly do it competently without first considering the general behavior of the laborer's class in the home as a setting (secondary cultureme); then the visually perceived patterns in that setting (tertiary cultureme), both behavioral (proxemic behavior, clothing, grooming, etc.) and environmental (furniture style and arrangement, temperature, music, etc.); later the kinesic repertoire (derived cultureme); and finally the kinesic repertoire in the same setting (derived cultureme 2); from which we can go into postures displayed by the same people in front of certain other people, and so on.

I would not recommend the type of fieldwork that would bypass secondary, tertiary, and derived culturemes, for instance, in order to carry out a minute analysis of 'Eye Contact at the Table Between Upper-Class Hosts and Middle-Class Guests,' without progressively studying first their kinesic behaviour in such a situation (derived cultureme 1), their general kinesic repertoires (derived cultureme), the other visually perceived systems, such as proxemics (tertiary cultureme), and the urban-interior human behavior of those two groups in the home as a setting (secondary cultureme).

It is at this level of secondary culturemes, however, that we begin to identify certain interrelationships among different *cultural systems* and *subsystems* (paralinguistic, kinesic, behavior in face-to-face interaction, proxemics and sex values, etc.) while some borderlines between various *subcultures* within the same culture, geographically as well as socially, begin to show themselves more distinctly. Both cultural systems and subcultures can be analyzed competently after Phase Four.

Phase Four

In this progressive probing of cultural layers in search of signs and sign complexes—whether or not the researcher in question regards his task as a semiotic exploration—there is a breakdown of each secondary cultureme into smaller units, or culturemes. Naturally, we are limiting the span of our analysis, but we are also gaining substantially in depth. Later on both span and depth will be combined in the regrouping of culturemes within each class.

Culturemes in this phase are *Tertiary Culturemes*, and here the sensible-intelligible approach allows for an even more systematic classification because each sensible or intelligible compartment is analyzed as a separate unit, e.g., 'Urban-Interior-Behavioral-Acoustic: the Home,' or 'Kinesic Behavior in the Urban American Home.' It is at this stage, when we have gone as far as isolating not only the various settings against which people develop a great number of behaviors at different levels, but also those behaviors—as we acquire more and more elements of judgement—that we, according to our specific aims, may identify with a reasonable amount of accuracy two important elements:

(a) *Cultural systems*. After observing, for instance, the urban-interior-human-*visual* culture as reflected in the home, the school, the church, the university, the theater, the funeral parlor, the barbershop, the supermarket, the bowling alley, and so forth, we have enough material to deal with systems such as furniture, or proxemic arrangement of interior spaces across one whole culture. But this knowledge comes *only* after working through Phases One, Two, and Three.

(b) *Subcultures*. Consequently, the recognition of certain systems allows us to differentiate some subcultures, both geographically (horizontally) and socially (vertically). After studying 'Urban-Interior-Environmental-Visual Culture in the Home' as one single cultureme in different areas of the country, the differences and similarities will usually stand out quite clearly. At the same time we will differentiate the interior of the upper-class home from that of the worker, or the richer and more articulate kinesic repertoire of the higher classes from that of the lower ones. If we acknowledge Hall's categorizations of cultural units we realize that 'sets' and 'patterns' become more obvious: the types of chairs, of pictures on the walls, etc. (sets) that constitute certain norms in upper- or middle-class homes (patterns), while 'isolates' (i.e., the material—brass, silver—of the typical "Last Supper" hanging in many Italian or Spanish middle- and lower-class dining rooms) would generally not be identified until later on.

Derived phases

Derived phases come after this point, when, pursuing our progressive analysis, we can once more break down the last unit we isolated, a tertiary cultureme, such as 'Urban-Interior-Environmental-Visual: The Home,' into smaller ones, focusing now on each manifestation of that communicative modality, that is, 'Visual.' Following the above example, we will break it down into: Clothes, Kinesics, Proxemics (previously included with a tertiary cultureme), each one being an individual *Derived Cultureme*. But Kinesics, for instance, would specify the behavior in the living room, at the table, etc., thus offering the possibility for finer further analysis.

Derived culturemes 1

These cultural units concentrate on specific areas of each derived cultureme, for instance, 'Kinesics at the Table,' which would refer to informal meals, or formal ones, according to the social status of both hosts and guests. So, should we require more critical distinctions, we would go into a more specific category.

Derived culturemes 2

'Kinesic Behavior of Upper-Class Hosts and Guests,' 'Upper-Class Hosts and Middle-Class Guests' (a most interesting situation) or 'Lower-Class Hosts and Middle Class Guests' would now be dealt with as derived culturemes 2. Formal and informal encounters around the table would also display characteristic social techniques: table manners; silverware; individual dishes or just a large one in the center, from which Spanish peasants, for instance, help themselves with spoon or fork; the use of glasses or, as among Spanish peasants, a single earthenware container that goes around without it being touched with your lips; the use of napkins (whose absence I have observed even in the privacy of some Canadian middle-class homes). In addition, within each of the situations mentioned, we may want (backed at this point by solid and systematic terms of reference), to concentrate on a further category.

Derived culturemes 3

'Upper-Class Eye Contact Behavior at the Table' would be a derived cultureme 3.

For the sake of orderliness, within the area of human behavior, all DC1s may deal with clothing, all DC2s with kinesics, all DC3s with proxemics, all DC4s with chronemics, and so on.

It was pointed out before that each time we deal with a different cultureme, such as 'eye contact,' it is possible to build up a whole *Class*, for instance, 'Eye-Contact Behavior in Exteriors as Well as Interiors in Urban and Rural Settings,' made up of carefully and progressively analyzed segments at different levels.

All systems and subcultures can be exhaustively described. In addition, the relationships between different systems, which began to appear after the analysis of tertiary culturemes, can now be studied in great detail, for instance: 'Relationship Between Eye Contact and Proxemic Behavior at the Table According to Social Status,' in a given culture; 'Relationship Between Proxemics and Architecture'; 'Relationship Between Kinesthetic Involvement and Architectural Style'; 'Relationship Between Peripheral Vision and Architectural Style,' etc.

Finally, any study of behavior and communication within the context of culture needs to consider at all times the Total Conditioning Background, that is, the biophysicopsychological and socioeconomic-educational variables one must consider when analyzing any type of behavior or cultural manifestation, for there will be several or many of those elements which have shaped things the way they are, and which will therefore offer a more solid basis for a critical analysis of features.

The cultureme scheme, in sum, can provide much exhaustiveness and an orderly method of dealing with all types of cultural manifestations, and I should hope that some anthropologists and other observers of culture have taken heed of these thoughts since we discussed them in 1973 and after they were published by Rapoport (1976) and McCormack and Wundt (1976).[3]

4. The Integration of Sign and Cultureme Analysis

Since a cultureme can be fragmented into smaller culturemes or incorporated into a more complex one, which is still analyzed as a cultureme—depending on our aims and the depth of the study we set out to conduct—it seems reasonable to assume that any relatively complex cultureme contains a homogeneous set of signs; the broader the cultureme, the broader the sign hierarchy contained in it. In other words, systems, subsystems, categories, etc., down to sign types, would have their correlates in the cultureme scale, from broader ones to as specific a type as the kinesic wink discussed earlier, or the firm handshake as a group characteristic. A semiotic analysis of culturemes, then, offers a double spatial and temporal perspective of human communication signs, since they are present in any cultureme based on communication, the number of types depending on the number of forms within a given cultureme, on the number of subcategories and categories, and on the number of systems displayed.

Signs are ultimately rooted in culture. An analysis of interactive signs must in itself seek their somatic intersystem costructuration (e.g., 'proxemic signs in lower-class women's greetings' must be related to language, paralanguage, kinesics, etc.), but it must also go beyond the boundaries of somatic activities, if a full understanding of sign constructs is sought, and assume their own costructuration with environmental (i.e., extrasomatic) cultural signs, such as clothes and jewelry, low-class greeting patterns, the specific setting (e.g., the home, the street). We may follow this progressive structural approach either from isolated signs to the broader and complex compounds or culturemes, or from primary culturemes to the smallest ones, which can be constituted by one form of behavior (e.g., kissing in a given culture), or even by a single type (represented by a specific way of kissing, or kissing among lower-class people in public place as a farewell behavior), after which different tokens or occurrences may or may not carry any difference in meaning according to the kind of analysis sought within specific areas or for specific strategies.

This application of cultureme analysis to the analysis of signs is not a gratuitous and contrived methodological framework that a radical semiotician can simply dismiss without further consideration, and it is suggested on this occasion precisely because of the advantages it offers, as well as for its multi- and interdisciplinary implications. These are obvious. Much too often one sets out to conduct a minute analysis of signs building up a complex net of relationships which a close look reveals insufficient.

Again, I am not ignoring the fact that the research areas and, within them, the strategies of each one, may differ in their objectives. Yet it is quite possible that someone engaged in, say 'diagnosis semiotics' (see Kahn 1977) referred to a particular ailment, fails to incorporate to this study the necessary cultural perspective, reflected not only in bodily signs (such as the ritualization of certain signs elicited by the ailment itself in, say women) but in extrasomatic ones that may take the researcher as far as the natural environment, where the presence of a specific local plant and its consumption, correlated with certain socioeconomic signs (revealed even in the local domestic architecture), would most appropriately complete the semiotic analysis, finally linking the particular vegetable in question to the medical symptoms. In like manner, a sign analysis of a given form of oral narrative—or a written one, for that matter—may require of the literary semiotician an escalation up the cultural ladder, through which oral (e.g., paralinguistic) features and the syntactical oral or written ones may be linked to the whole semiotic world of the narrator. Finally, the semiotic correlations of lexical or paralinguistic choice and the class-differentiating interior decoration of the character's settings may complete the semiotic configuration of the particular semiotic construct under study.

5. The Synchronic-Diachronic Approach to Culture

As suggested when discussing the spatial and temporal dimensions of cultural habits, space and time dominate all aspects of people's life and the culture in which they live. When we speak of communicative activities and of the various behaviors involved, of how they vary from culture to culture and of the fact that one can go through life hindered by a true communication handicap such as blindness or deafness, we are not referring to absolutely indispensable elements of human existence. We know that, in fact, certain species do not have any visual organs, while others are incapable of moving, and still others are not equipped to produce sounds or to hear them. All of them, however, are subject to *space* and *time*, not space and time merely as passive inherent elements that accompany our thoughts and activities, but truly as active factors that determine the course of our lives, of the very cultural context we produce and live in, and of our day-to-day activities and non-activities. Everything, to put it simply but factually, is shaped by the space it exists in and the time it goes through while it exists.

If I were to underline all those instances in which this book is dealing with space and time, I would probably be surprised beyond my own expectations, for it is space and time that is discussed with regard to intercultural communication, the composition and variations of culturemes, later the different bodily activities and how they are emitted and perceived, including verbal spoken language and any other form of truly human interaction, such as the nonactivities of silence and stillness. In order to undertake a serious study of any aspect of culture and communication, in sum, we need to recognize that it is, in an ongoing way, conditioned by its location in time and space, as well as by the space and time around it.

Having dealt with the basic structuration of cultural signs, then, it should follow that, if space and time dominate all aspects of communicative sign production and interpretation, one should deal with them—for a realistic view of their origin, development, propagation, costructuration, and perhaps disappearance—not simply with a here-and-now criterion because of the organismal quality of so many of them, but both diachronically and synchronically, as the two perspectives may prove to complement each other.

As was discussed with regard to learned habits, a sign, or sign type, once it is originated, may possess all the necessary qualities to become almost permanently established within certain communicative patterns whose general profile may even vary without affecting the semantic core of the sign. At the same time, a sign develops semantically and may acquire a wider (often in a truly geographic sense) range typically undergoing successive encoding and decoding modifications (and even splitting into new subtypes) and consequently constantly varying its costructuration with other sign types. Finally, signs may, as so often have in the never-ending continuum that constitutes culture, die away through biological, cultural and environmental modifications. Thus, the historical perspective may prove a much needed and enlightening one, along with the synchronic one through which we focus on a given time.

6. The Usefulness of the Pragmatic-Semantic-Syntactic Perspective

Just as space and time are such basic dimensions of any cultural and environmental systems we may study, there is an additional threefold approach that is actually present in any study of those systems in lesser or greater degree. It is the already classical distinction between pragmatic, semantic, and syntactic semiotic analyses. Since a book should not ignore the nonspecialists (as so many do) and because a book on communication is aimed at people in different disciplines (all of whom are not necessarily sensitized to certain basic semiotic principles) it will be in order perhaps to indicate that one must not lose sight of the basic composition of a cultural sign, that is, the *significant* (signans)—an uttered word, a gesture, a color—and the *signified* (signatum)—the meaning of that word, that gesture, or that color—both of which occur between the two ends of the transmission process, *input* and *output*; or thinking of their perception, *encoding* (at the producer/sender/emitter's end) and *decoding* (at the receiver's end). The thoughts offered so far regarding the structural and semiotic understanding of and approach to culture and Figs. 2.1 and 2.3 suggest quite clearly the three complementary perspectives.

(a) the *pragmatic*, that is, the forms and transmission processes of signs and sign systems of all kinds, including language and the nonverbal bodily systems of communication dealt with later; the forms and coding processes of all the objectual systems that somehow assist the somatic ones as their essential supporting elements and sometimes as true extensions of the organisms; and the forms and sign-coding of the environmental systems that surround us, including the systems that the animal species themselves originate;

(b) the *semantic*, that is, the meaning of those sign and sign systems, whether we deal with the intended messages put forth through words, proxemic behavior, orientation, gestures and postural shifts, choice of dress color, timing of specific activities, placement and characteristics of decorative objects, landscaping design, or the attitude toward domestic animals; the study of the functions of many of those messages given shape through those systems will in turn reveal their semantic values, thus complementing their pragmatic observation and presentation; and finally,

(c) the *syntactic* understanding of the same signs and sign systems, as suggested, for instance, by the joining lines in Fig. 2.1, that is, the universal or culture-specific combinations and structuration, in semantic complexes of those systems, made up of seemingly unrelated areas, such as olfactory perception and socioeconomic status, furniture design and postural kinesic behaviors, or lighting and male–female paralinguistic and proxemic behaviors.

That these three complementary perspectives do not constitute a separate chapter will not prevent even the nonspecialized curious reader from considering their implicit or explicit applications throughout the book, beyond their specific treatment at times.

7. Sign Sources and Directions Within a Culture

Trying to understand culture as communication one progresses from a panoramic view of a series of communicative manifestations generated by people, by animals, and by the environment that serves as setting for both, through a distinction of the two basic ways in which culture is perceived (through the senses and through the mind, both, however, subject to our sensible appreciation of cultural forms in either category), to the logical methodological and empirical differentiation of signs constructs of varying complexity and hierarchization.

As we do this, however, we must not, in our attempt to sound the depths of the countless semiotic microcosms, lose the necessary and realistic perspective of man's existence in this world by zeroing in on a minute vivisection of sign compounds of all sorts without first acknowledging the virtually inextricable complexity of the sign network of human interaction. Interaction is ultimately the basis of all human achievements and of any living culture. Although it is mainly understood as an exchange with our congeners, it also develops between us and members of other species, the environment, and even spiritual beings, not taking interaction, as will be later, in the strict sense of a behavior-eliciting transaction on the part of two co-interactants. A fragment of an interactive encounter contains such an elaborate system of sign exchanges (that are further and constantly subject to the modifying effects of the all-encompassing Conditioning Background) that even the more radical semioticians in specific areas other than human interaction would profit from an analysis of how signs are originated or elicited (that is, their sources) and then transmitted and decoded, or lost, in the course of interaction, from an ordinary conversational exchange to less usual cases of interspecific communication or extreme emotional circumstances. The need for this kind of approach was amply suggested to me by the existing literature, particularly in the always inspiring work of Sebeok (e.g., 1974, 1977a, 1977b). It has always been precisely his fruitful insistence on the integration of anthroposemiotic and zoosemiotic systems that has served as a clearly-aimed incentive to continue my interdisciplinary-oriented classification of interactive bodily systems.

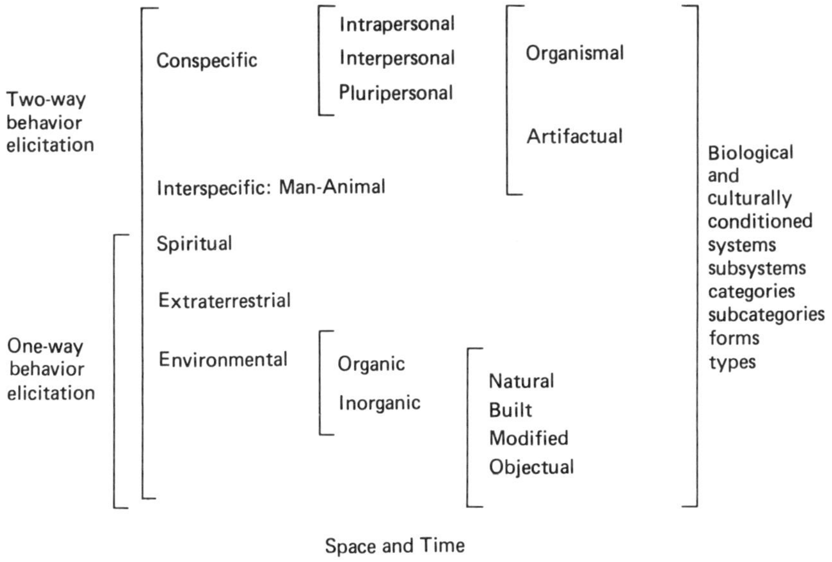

FIG. 2.4. Interactive Sign Processes Within a Culture.

The next stage of one's approach to cultural interaction—for that is the indispensable activity-generating dimension of a culture—is to determine the origin of messages and their direction in terms of the input–output process, as a step previous to the specification of the somatic channels along which interactive messages travel. The mapping of communication sketched in Fig. 1.1, containing the basic exchanges among members of a given culture (or crossculturally), between those people and animals, and, beyond strictly human activities, as generated by the environment of both, should at this point be elaborated on. It would include the distinction of the two different semiotic activities, emission and reception, that may take place between the two end-points, the source of the message and its destination, considered in this cultural context only insofar as it affects people and not, for instance, with respect to exchanges between sources and receivers that exclude humans. This is what the diagram in Fig. 2.4, 'Interactive Sign Processes Within a Culture'—inspired in part by Sebeok's classification of sign sources (Sebeok, 1974: 232–233)—attempts to illustrate, acknowledging the fact that the roles of both emitter and receiver are interchangeable. It suggests how every general domain in what constitutes a culture can be subject to the double synchronic-diachronic approach. Acknowledging Sebeok's 'supernatural' and 'extraterrestrial,' it indicates the sources from which we may expect to gather our experiences and research material.

A. ***Two-way behavior elicitation***

This is the exchange we regard as true interaction, in which humans not only act as emitters of messages that affect the behaviors of their receivers (eliciting further behaviors and message-producing activities on their part), but also receive messages, functioning as intended cointeractants on the part of other emitters. This type of relationship is far more preponderant than it may appear at first sight, as it includes:

(a) *Conspecific cointeractants*, which includes,

(i) *intrapersonal* situations, basically a monologic imagined exchange of the type illustrated, for instance, by the noninteractive kinesic activities mentioned in Fig. 2.2; in a strict sense, it seems as if this situation cannot possibly be included under interaction; however, not only does it assume a true interlocutor but it can elicit all sorts of conversational behaviors, such as turn-takings between speaker and listener, feedback verbal and nonverbal activities, pauses, etc., and even provoke the emission of sensible signs like gestures, body temperature raises, cutaneous reactions like blushing, chemical ones like tears; in sum, the exchanges of messages that would take place were the two interlocutors present;

(ii) *interpersonal*, the core of the present study and the subject of, but including also, the situation in which a single speaker remains as such for an indefinite time, as is the case with public speakers, lecturers and the like, in which the auditor's only behaviors are their feedback, usually nonverbal; and

(iii) *pluripersonal*, as cited by Sebeok (1974: 233) referring to the account of the Eskimo myth-teller (who speaks as many-to-many, not as person-to-person), but which is also eloquently illustrated by so many real-life situations, such as in public demonstrations, or when cheering at sport games;

(b) *interspecific cointeractants*, that is, man and animals, whether wild, tamed or domesticated, each group conditioned in varying degrees by their cultural environment.

(c) *spiritual* interaction, the exchange between man and God, or between man and other spirits, overlaps with one-way interaction; in the first instance, a person engaged in prayer, not only emits messages on faith without perceiving his cointeractant, but is also the receiver of God's answer; this answer can be either beyond his sensory and intellectual capabilities, or quite tangible and humanly understandable (whether instantaneously or in a delayed way), as exemplified by the "signs and wonders" announced in the New Testament (e.g., *Acts* 2: 22), associated, for instance, with physical, mental and spiritual healing—in itself a fascinating topic for semiotic research (not undergone as yet, to my knowledge), as the ultimate form of interaction.

(d) *extraterrestrial*, acknowledged by Sebeok's classification, is an emerging form (while the previous one is reported as the oldest in the history of humanity) of one-way/two-way interaction involving the possible communication of man with extraterrestrial beings, a situation of sign encoding from either end, without the sender being aware of whether or not his intended or unintended messages are being decoded, and with no form of feedback at this point.

Two-way behavior elicitation (except in its spiritual category) can take two forms: *organismal*, when the encoding-decoding process is carried out between and strictly by people, or people and animals, utilizing only their natural equipment, which is not always the most efficient means, as it is subject to many limitations (distance, noise, invisibility, physical impairment, etc.), but the most reliable one semiotically speaking; and *artifactual*, when man's natural means are boostered or replaced by his own technological ingenuity.

B. *One-way behavior elicitation*

This is not true interaction, in the sense that there is no exchange of messages that elicit predictable or unpredictable activities in the participants. The table shows how spiritual communication can be said to overlap one-way interaction, since it is beyond human understanding or scientific research.

One-way interaction (besides the seemingly 'unanswered' prayer encoding in certain humanly perceived situations) assumes one typical form, the *environment*, which provides that type of situation in our relationship with it. It is true that our behaviors can be conditioned by open or architectural space, and by metereological factors, and that our mental activities and our conceptualization processes can vary according to other people's landscaping; but there is actually no decoding by the environment, and we elicit no behavior on its part on the other hand, we could say that if we bend a branch and the branch hits us back, it has responded, but no active signs could possibly be generated by that branch as an agent; however, a plant like the popular Venus fly-trap functions as a perfect example of environment/animal two-way behavior elicitation, since it truly responds to a stimulus with emission of signs; thus environmental interaction can be

(i) *organic*, as in the example just cited, or the chemical reaction triggered by us in the common poison ivy; and

(ii) *inorganic*, either *natural*, as a rock, *built*, as a house, or *modified*, as the landscaping around the house, all of which give away signs and messages decoded by us.

As indicated in the table, since we deal with culture, we must investigate the ways in which a given culture affects the interactive characteristics of systems, subsystems, categories, subcategories, forms, and types of signs, viewed across both space and time.

8. A Preliminary Note on the Role of Literature as a Tool in a Semiotic-Cultural Analysis

Although semiotics and nonverbal communication in literature is discussed in the last three chapters, I wish to at least acknowledge at this point its relation with the discussion of signs just outlined, since literature is a powerful source of information which ought to be used more often to carry out the tasks dicussed here, namely, the analysis of signs, the definition and classification of culturemes, and the diachronic or synchronic study of people and their culture.

Such an important part of culture as narrative literature, from the early national epics to the contemporary novel, shows, both universally and culture-specifically, what is probably the richest abstract concepts and elements of the surrounding objectual world. But, on a deeper level, we find that they may evoke in turn whole cultural situations (together with a number of the writer's and the reader's own personal experiences) which contain a multitude of signs of virtually all types, whether described by the writer or implied 'between lines.' This occurs precisely because of that sort of chain reaction whereby the visually present signs in the written text, sensorially and intellectually perceived (though not identically by each reader, nor identically encoded by different writers), elicit many more according, again, to the conditioning background of each one of us.

Much more could be elaborated on this point. But I would also indicate that there is an important research subarea in the sign metamorphosis observed in the transmission of the narrative or dramaturgic character, as will be seen, from his creator, through the extremely limited text, to the reader's interpretation, as it affords a whole new perspective of the Writer–Character–Reader (or theatrical spectator) relationship. In this relationship, verbal, nonverbal, psychological, socioeconomic, historical and, in general, cultural features of the characters—besides important stylistic and technical functions—are revealed through signs conveyed by means of the written text.

But even limiting ourselves to the study of word types, we can consider the different decoding of signs in time and space, although the writer's exact encoding will always remain in the shadow. It would be only through a painstaking search for the writer's identity (cultural, physicopsychological, socioeconomic, etc.) that we might be able to approach his original sign creativity just a little closer. Occurrences of the same word may appear as tokens on the printed page, since they show the same dictionary definition; but this principle, already shaken by the inevitable plurality of the decoding carried out by the different readers, becomes even more doubtful in the light of a refined diachronic study of our lexicon. And thus, the thin borderline between tokens of a supposedly common class appears more conspicuously as certain unsuspected subsystems begin to show themselves in the sort of detailed typology I have tried to suggest.

The problem, of course, is further complicated in the case of an interlinguistic (therefore intercultural) translation, and a semiotic analysis of sign transmissions between writer and reader of different cultures and languages by the extremely complex process of translation would be a truly enlightening endeavor through a typological approach.

Notes

1. I first outlined this classification for my first approach to 'Literary Anthropology' (Chapter 11). Figure 2.3 is presented now and in that chapter because it actually contains all the issues addressed by this book and by any future work of mine on communication.
2. I suggested this scheme as well as the ideas in sections 4, 5 and 7 in a paper given at the 1977 Viennese Symposium on Semiotics, not published in the expected resulting volume (which I erroneously was instructed to give as a reference on some occasions), but in *Semiotic Inquiry* (Poyatos 1981f).
3. The cultureme approach—briefly suggested in an earlier paper (Poyatos 1972a), outlined in Spanish (Poyatos 1971, 1974b, 1978a), contained in another book (Poyatos 1976a), and now slightly elaborated on—was first discussed formally at the pre-Congress conference on 'The Mutual Interaction of People and Their Built Environment', organized by A. Rapoport (Dept. of Anthropology and School of Architecture) and J. Silverberg (Dept. of Anthropology), University of Wisconsin-Milwaukee, in the beautiful Frank Lloyd Wright's "Wingspread" home in Racine, a superb example of man–environment interaction. It was deemed by Rapoport "probably the most useful [attempt] to apply structural anthropological and ethnoscientific methods to the built environment" (Rapoport 1976: 258–259), and published in the volume edited by him (Poyatos 1976e) as well as in another one edited by William McCormack and Stephen Wurm from their session on 'Language and Man' (Poyatos 1976f). I also discussed it at the 1975 meeting of the International Communication Association.
4. Italicized words indicate sample culturemes broken down further into successive derived culturemes. Put together they would constitute a whole cultureme. The Total Conditioning Background, against which we must consider any type of cultural manifestation, whether static or dynamic and behavioral, is outlined in Chapter 3 when discussing external somatic communication.
5. *Venéreas*, 'Venereal Diseases', i.e., a specialist, a sign seen only in the more popular areas of a large city; *Gestoría*, an agency that speeds up beaurocratic procedures, a much needed national institution in a highly beaurocratic country; *Oposiciones*, indicating a private firm that prepares candidates for another fearful national institution, the extremely competitive ('oppositions') and complex examinations required for many positions.

3

Communication Between the Bodies: Forms and Coding of Messages

1. Intersomatic Communication in the Cultural Context

THE emission and perception of signs and sign compounds (as classified in the previous chapters and at the beginning of this one) presupposes the existence of a net of somatic channels into which the student of human communication must probe, enough at least to realize how much our social communication with others and the ways in which we conceptualize them depend on exchanges of signs and messages at the somatic level, that is, their encoding and decoding between at least two individuals. This discussion of bodily communication in a cultural context requires an intermediate consideration: the confrontation of two human bodies as socializing organisms, equipped by a unique highly cognitive and intellectual ability that combines their mutual sensorial and intelligible perception and that of their society and their world at large, operating in space and time, thus linking themselves to each other in each of those dimensions as well as to their congeners. The latter statement is not, of course, a gratuitous one, as will be indicated in the study of the various communicative activities. Suffice it to point out at this time that two human bodies relate to each other through physical distance and through time (e.g., the duration of interpersonal silences, the carrying of olfactory messages into the future).

After the general framework for the elaboration of a sign typology has been suggested, the diagram in Fig. 3.1 attempts to schematize some basic principles of intersomatic communication, acknowledging both organismal (e.g., kinesics) and artifactual (e.g., drumbeat messages) sign systems, since both have a somatic basis.

It does not include, however, what Sebeok (1974: 213) terms "endo-semiotics" to speak of cybernetic activities within the body, although those mechanisms which operate within an organism may, of course, determine the ones sensorially apprehended in the external world. Witness the laying on of hands by a doctor or a nurse on a patient with the true desire to heal,

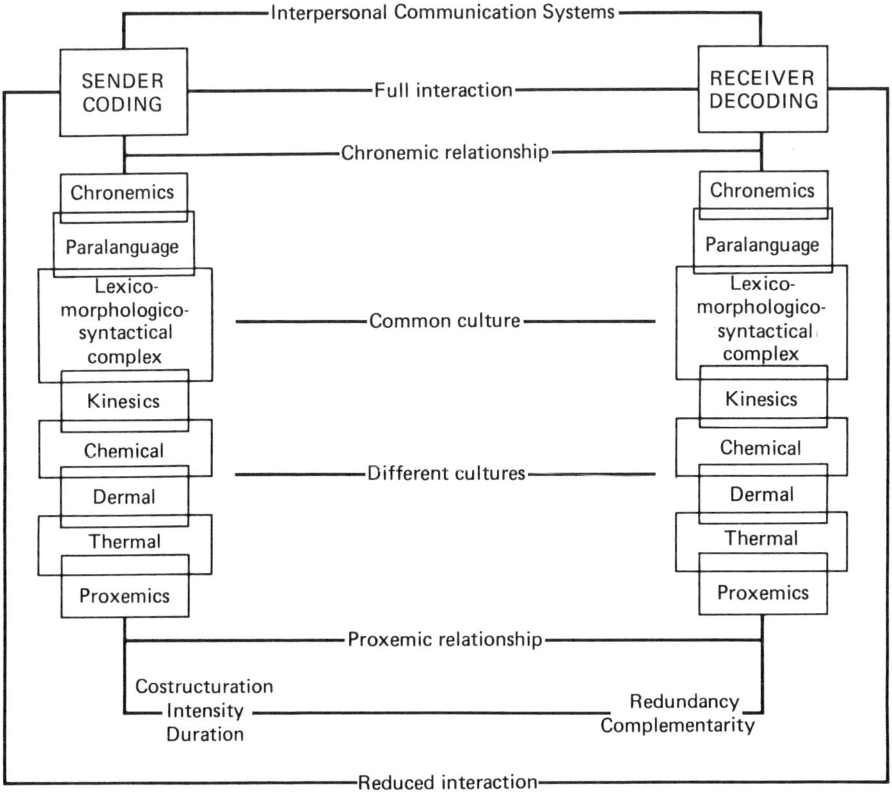

FIG. 3.1. Basic Intersomatic Communication.

as experimented by Krieger (1972, 1973, 1974, 1975) or reported by an already extensive literature on healing within the Christian churches (MacNutt 1974; Reed 1979; Sandford 1972, 1966, 1969; Shlemon 1976).

Signs, sensorially and intelligibly apprehended, reach their finest communicative structuration in the Basic Triple Structure (Chapter 5), the anthroposemiotic vehicle *par excellence* in human communication, to which any other systems are but secondary under normal circumstances. A typology of signs like the one suggested earlier can gain, I feel, by recognizing the sort of costructurations that take place within and between two or more human beings engaged in interaction as socializing organisms. As Sebeok (1977b) emphasizes, between the two polarities, the molecular code and the verbal code (completed in the diagram as the Basic Triple Structure) "there exist a whole array of other mechanisms, ranging from those located in the interior of organisms [. . .] to those linking them to the external 'physical world'" (1061). Furthermore, a typology of signs can aim at being exhaustive only when acknowledging the complex mechanism of human interaction, whether intraspecific, interspecific, or with the environment, as discussed before.

Once could very well concentrate, for a number of purposes, on the 'semiotics of conversation.' In the same paper by Sebeok just quoted, he refers to the "awesome entanglements of verbal responses with other kinds of acts [. . .] dealt with in Goffman's [. . .] paper (1975) on minimal dialogic units, and amply justify the research strategy [. . .] by workers like Duncan (1975) and Poyatos (1976: see his fig. 4, on p. 66), and others [. . .]". The mechanism of personal interaction based on intersomatic exchanges—without neglecting our exchanges with other species, such as tamed and domesticated animals—not only is the living foundation of all the social achievements in the history of the civilizations, but the basis of any behavioral analysis in psychotherapy interviews, in social work, in the kind of relationship established between actors and their audiences, as well as in the simplest encounters. The nature and interrelationships of the sign types generated in all of them deserve a critical and interdisciplinary semiotic study.

Two basic 'triple structures' (i.e., at least two sets of language-paralanguage-kinesics), are indispensable in full face-to-face communication between humans, and instances of only continuous paralanguage, kinesics, proxemics, or chemical communication, constitute cases of reduced interaction of different kinds. The more secondary interactional channels can function intermittently or by themselves in exceptional and generally brief dyadic or multiperson encounters. But the Basic Triple Structure stands by itself as a virtually self-sufficient, sign-producing block that determines major communicative differences among cultures and historical periods, as two basic dimensions, space and time, are in turn the major changing forces in man's experiences.

2. The Forty-one Sign-conveying Channels of Interbodily Communication: Direct Perception and Synethesial Assumption[1]*

It is apparent that what takes place as soon as the two bodies represented in the previous diagram begin to interact surpasses in complexity the mere linguistic social exchange. Even when verbal language seems to be the only message-containing behavior sustaining that interpersonal encounter, it is actually never dissociated from a more complex totality of cooccurrent hidden or explicit activities—neither biopsychologically on the part of the speaker, nor from the point of view of the conscious or unconscious

* Superscript numbers refer to Notes at end of chapter.

perception of his listener. This is the logically derived additional perspective opened to us as soon as we attempt to analyze a fragment of interaction, only to realize that we can be truly systematic and exhaustive only if we carry out at least an exploratory semiotic probing into the behavioral structure of that encounter. We are, in other words, recognizing that verbal language cannot be studied in isolation, as has been done for many years, and that the only realistic point of departure, after we locate language within its cultural context, is the integration of human intersomatic signalling systems whereby message-conveying activities must be assumed to be costructured in a number of universal, culture-specific, or individual-specific patterns.

That our starting point should always be verbal language is understandable, whether we are anthropologists, linguists, or psychologists. It is not long, however, before we become dissatisfied with our own simplistic stand and realize that the study of language is not even the study of what goes on within the vocal-auditory channel, for there are a series of other channels along which travel a complex net of bodily activities that affect even the very dictionary items we so respect. We soon become aware, in other words, of the existence of other input–output channels which develop between two human bodies engaged in interaction, and that, as receivers, we perceive our cointeractant's behaviors directly, or simply 'assume' them.

This discloses a new fascinating semiotic-communicative perspective of social communication, diagrammed in Fig. 3.2, which represents clearly enough the true location of verbal language and other forms of somatic communication as they operate in interaction between one sender and one or more receivers. While the receiver's perceptive systems are the activities of vision, audition, olfaction, gustation, and cutaneous and kinesthetic sensations, the sender's systems consist of both the active stimuli (kinetic, acoustic, chemical, thermal, and cutaneous) and the static characteristics of shape, color, size, consistency and weight, although the last two can be temporarily varied by autonomous (e.g., muscle tension) or externally applied movement and pressure. Naturally, under normal circumstances, the roles of sender and receiver, or emitter and perceiver, are alternately or simultaneously interchangeable (even language in simultaneous speeches).

The one-way relationship in which only the receiver is a real human being, the emitter being only a source of evocations triggered by the previously experienced reality, is the one established between the beholder and bidimensional representations in films, photography and painting, and the tridimensional one of sculpture.

The *solid lines*, joining the different sign-emitting activities and static characteristics and the receiving activities, stand for the input–output ends of the specific sensory avenues, that is, the process that takes place when a stimulus produced in one human body activates the receptors in the other body in a *direct* way: sound waves transduced into neural impulses within the

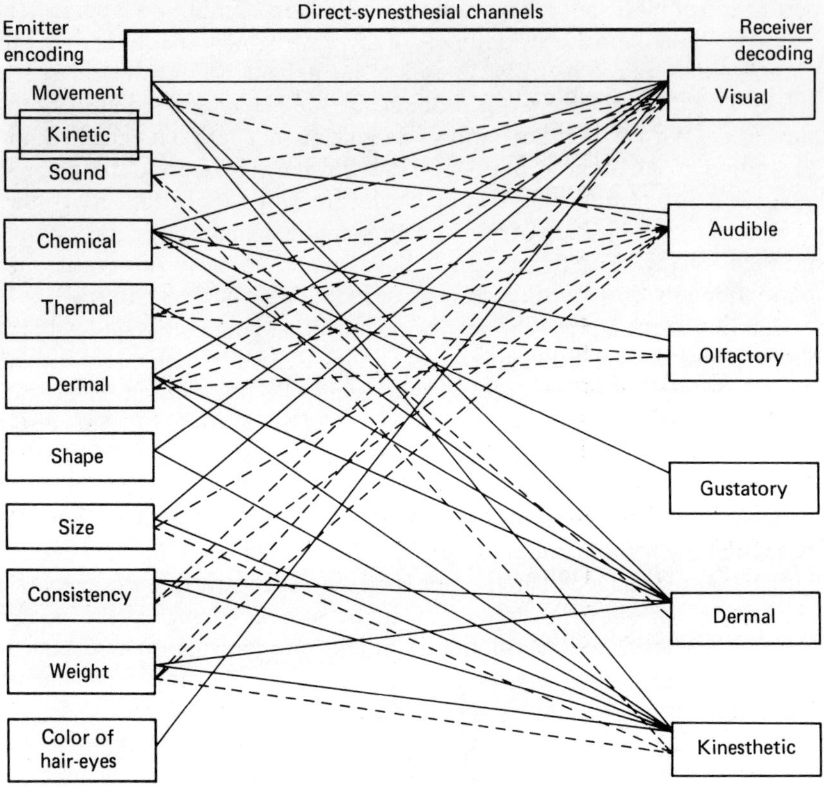

FIG. 3.2. Intersomatic Sensory Perception.

auditory system result in hearing; light energy associated with color and movement is transmitted through the eye; a chemical stimulus impinges upon the olfactory nerve and results in a smell sensation; another chemical stimulus is transmitted by the gustatory buds and sensed as a particular taste; changes in temperature in the body of one of the cointeractants are perceived as eloquent messages by the skin receptors of the other, as are varying degrees of applied pressure exercised by the former; a kinetic stimulus triggered by someone can be directly perceived by vision and by the kinesthetic receptors of our own joints, muscles and tendons, just as they transmit to our brain the sensations of our own movements and positions.

The *broken lines* between energy sources and sensory receptors represent, on the other hand, what is called *synesthesia*, which I believe to constitute the true complexity of sensory interaction or, in reality, of interpersonal communication. If we could decode an applause only by perceiving its sound, the odor of someone's perspiration stain by its actual olfactory perception, the warmth of a blush by its actual radiated temperature, the coarseness of a rough hand by its actual texture, or the consistency of another body's flesh by touching it only, our sensory and intelligible experiences of the people in our lives (whether really present or graphically represented in a photograph or painting) would be incredibly curtailed. We very often hear, smell, touch, taste, 'with our eyes', and a man can imagine the consistency of a woman's body by the sound of her footsteps or by his specific kinesthetic perception of her movements and her body weight mediated by a shared couch.

It is clear, then, that interaction, its complex sensory exchanges as well as the intellectualized interpretations of those exchanges, relies heavily on synesthesia, that is, the physiological sensation on a part of the body other than the stimulated one, and the psychological process whereby one type of sensorial stimulus produces a secondary subjective sensation from a different sense—from which derived the poetic image that ascribes to one sensory experience, e.g., color, characteristics of a different sense, e.g., softness. The interplay of stimuli and sensory perception of messages travelling over the various channels can then be outlined following Fig. 3.2.

Neurologically and muscularly controlled, *Kinetic activity* produces the two main communicative systems in people, *kinesics* and *linguistic* and *paralinguistic* sounds (after all, 'internal' kinesics).

1. *Movement*

A. Directly.

a. *Visually*: Silent movements,/¡Bye!/, a shrug, a sign of impatience, a shake of the hair.

b. *Dermally*: Contactual movements through the skin pressure and pain receptors: a kiss, a pat, a limp handshake, a crushing one, a blow on the face.

c. *Kinesthetically*: Through contactual kinesics, or transmitted by a physical mediator through receptors in the joints, muscles and tendons: someone's tense hand wringing sensed through a shared couch, or tense fidgeting with crumbs mediated by the dinner table.

B. Synesthesially.

a. *Audibly*. Unseen audible movements, that is, kinesics: an applause and its degree of tenseness, facial speech movements, the firmness of someone's gait assumed through the sound of footsteps.

b. *Visually*. We imagine the cutaneous pressure and pain reception caused by contactual movements applied to others: seeing another person being firmly held by someone, or hit by a blow or by objects, such as a knife, an invisible bullet, a lash.

2. *Sound*

A. Directly.

a. *Auditorily*. Language, paralanguage, and audible kinesics and other audible movements (bone cracking, finger snapping, an applause, tooth gnashing, clapping, slapping, flapping, thudding), and sounds which the body is capable of producing internally (heart beat, wheezing, intestinal rumbling).

B. Synesthesially.

a. *Visually*. Unheard but seen audible kinesics: lip reading, clapping, finger snapping.
b. *Dermally*. Contactual heard or unheard audible kinesics: slapping, clapping hands with someone else.
c. *Kinesthetically*. Through contactual or mediated perception of previously experienced audible kinesics: heard or unheard clapping, someone slapping his thigh in conversation, or convulsive or spasmodic laughter, all while sharing a couch.

3. *Chemical-glandular activities*

A. Directly.

a. *Olfactorily*. Depending on the specific distance travelled by odorous molecules and on external temperature, which increases odor reception as it rises: natural body odor, foot and axillary perspiration, breath, stomachic gases expelled through the mouth and intestinal ones let out through the anus, nasal mucus, urine, feces, blood, sperm, vaginal discharges, cutaneous supurations, blood, tears, and hair; pathological odors, whether due to tissue deterioration as in frostbite and gangrene, or due to kidney and liver failure; the reported smell of schizophrenic patients.[2]
b. *Visually*. The visual qualities of the chemical substances: tears, saliva, facial sweat, palmar sweat (which serves to measure emotional state).
c. *Dermally*. As perceived directly by the skin receptors of touch (sweat, tears, discharges) and temperature (sweat, tears, blood).
d. *Gustatorily*. When voluntarily or involuntarily tasted: tears, perspiration, etc.

B. Synesthesially.

a. *Visually*. Assuming (from past experience) olfactory, dermal, and gustatory qualities when seeing tears, perspiration, etc.

b. *Auditorily*. Assuming smell when hearing sound produced by belching and farting or smell or taste of tears when hearing intense weeping.

4. *Thermal activities*

The thermal state and changes of someone else's body are perceived:

A. Directly.

a. *Dermally*. Depending on distance, and as perceived by the skin receptors of warmth, cold, and pressure: raises and drops in body temperature, and the temperature of the chemical substances discussed.

B. Synesthesially.

a. *Visually*. Assuming the thermal qualities of certain visible chemical substances (perspiration, tears, etc.) and dermal reactions (flushing, reddening of the face due to exertion or temperature, pallor due to temperature or emotional reactions, etc.).
b. *Olfactorily*. Assuming the thermal quality of smelled substances (perspiration, urine, tears).
c. *Auditorily*. Assuming the warmth of the face by hearing intense crying.

5. *Dermal features and activities*

Dermal static signs and activities are perceived:

A. Directly.

a. *Dermally*. Through the skin touch, pressure, warmth, and cold receptors: the texture and irregularities of the skin (softness, smoothness, consistency, pimples, warts, scars), and skin reactions (papillary erection or 'goose flesh').
b. *Visually*. Ethnic or individual skin pigmentation, temporary pigmentation (sun tan), momentary reactions (blushing, goose flesh, blanching), irregularities (freckles, warts, scars, blotches), and pathological reactions (jaundice, hepatitis).
c. *Kinesthetically*. Sensing gross irregularities on the skin (warts, scars, inflammations).

B. Synesthesially.

a. *Visually*. Direct visual perception of kinesics may let us assume some dermal reactions when they are visually blocked or too far away: gestures of embarrassment suggest blushing, gestures indicating cold suggest goose flesh, violent kinesic activity suggests facial reddening.

b. *Auditorily*. The feminine voice of great embarrassment let us assume blushing, as do verbal aggressions and nonverbal behaviors associated with certain dermal changes.

c. *Olfactorily*. By smelling chemical reactions associated with certain dermal phenomena, as with severe frostbite.

6. *Shape*

A. Directly.

a. *Visually*. By looking at the external signs of the person's bone structure, proportions, and body topography (which clothes can hide or distort by emphasizing or de-emphasizing).

b. *Dermally-kinesthetically*. By palpation and appreciation of tridimensionality (stereognosis) through skin and joint, muscle and tendon exteroceptors of touch and pressure, and kinesthetic proprioception of spatial location: holding, stroking or exploring another body with various degrees of contactual continuity, that is, tracing the surface tactually-kinesthetically and simultaneously transferring shape to the brain as with a mechanical tracer, or just establishing brief contacts.

7. *Size*

A. Directly.

a. *Visually*. By looking at someone while having ourselves or others, or the environment, as a point of reference.

b. *Kinesthetically*. By discriminating the two-point spatial relationship through direct joint, muscle and tendon perception of someone's body: holding another body.

B. Synesthesially.

a. *Kinesthetically*. Assuming visible size through tactile perception of clothed parts of the body, or through its mediated movements: holding it or sharing a couch.

b. *Auditorily*. Assuming size and volume, correctly or incorrectly, by hearing a thin voice or a high and resonant one, or by 'hearing' the weight of the person's footsteps (if one mistakes tense walking for the actual effect of the person's weight).

8. *Consistency*

A. Directly.

a-b. *Dermally-kinesthetically*. By exerting varying pressure and perceiving the degree of firmness and/or softness through skin pressure exteroreceptors, and of suppleness through kinesthetic proprioceptors: holding firmly any part of the body, embracing it, etc.

B. Synesthesially.

a. *Visually*. We assume firmness or softness by looking at the body or seeing someone hold it firmly.
b. *Auditorily*. Through the contactual sound produced, for instance, by someone else's slapping of certain parts of another body.

9. *Weight*

A. Directly.

a. *Dermally*. Through pressure and/or main receptors.
b. *Kinesthetically*. Through muscles, joints, tendons: lifting another body, carrying it, holding parts of it.

B. Synesthesially.

a. *Visually*. Through perception of size of a body or parts of it.
b. *Kinesthetically*. Through mediated perception of body movements and pressure on mediator: sharing a couch, a bicycle.
c. *Auditorily*. Hearing the impact of a body moving against something: e.g., jumping.

10. *Color of hair and eyes*

A. Directly.

a. *Visually*. By looking at eyes, and at hair of scalp, face and body.

Although one would refer, for instance, to medical books to ensure a truly exhaustive taxonomy of the somatic signs transmitted along each of the direct channels, the above classification provides the total number of perceptual possibilities: 41 different modes of consciously or unconsciously receiving information in personal interaction, of which only 21 represent direct sensory perception between source stimulus and its corresponding sense, while 20 constitute indirect synesthesial assumption of the former.

The implications of this count are far from being just curiosities of communicative behavior or gratuitous semiotic thinking addressed to the encoding and decoding of bodily activities. When the distinction between full, unhindered face-to-face interaction and 'reduced interaction' is made later, the real significance of our perceptual capabilities will gain true value. Interaction should not be considered only from the point of view of totally unhindered, normal participants, but as concerns the blind and the deaf, mainly, and the various forms of physical disabilities that may curtail sensory reception of messages, such as lack of olfaction or a low threshold of cutaneous sensitiveness. It is precisely the highly combinatory properties of that array of systems that allow the sensitive interactant to step up certain signalling devices while stepping down others that may not be properly decoded by the receiver, thus seeking to acquire the interactive fluency necessary for each occasion. Beyond this desirable optimum combinations, the various systems will reach a specific order or hierarchization beyond our control due to emotional factors (e.g., blushing or sweating, overpowering words and movements), excessive distance (e.g., wide-range gestures and high-volume language, or no language), etc.

We see, therefore, how the strictly human (i.e. organismal) communicative potentials between two cointeractants rely on different bodily functions of emission and reception without the help of external agents, except when object-adaptors (e.g., a knife for aggression) are manipulated. But those are the least in face-to-face interaction. It is where humans lack the refinement of some animal systems that they may assist their bodies with extensions of their organisms, as when chemical-olfactory messages are conveyed with artificial products, wittingly or unwittingly utilized.

However, unlike his facility to interact in space, man's organismal emissions of messages fail to operate efficiently through time, as his only chemical messages disappear much sooner than among other species, and they lack the socializing properties of the animal ones. Here it is that the mind not only replaces but surpasses the communicative *temporal abilities* of animals by conceptualizing and remembering, and by having invented writing, the uniquely human and virtually limitless breaker of the time barrier.

But it is in the perceptual possibilities of the synesthesial 'assumption' of signs that one discovers the fascination of interbodily communication. Without trying at this point to elaborate on this subject, I might mention how my students in nonverbal communication gradually discover to what an extent we rely on synesthesial perception, which is never the genuine way of verifying the somatic features we are conceptualizing and yet provides the 'complete' appreciation of someone else's body through the subtlest trick of the human organism. And that trick dominates the decoding of messages in so many everyday-life situations that we can hardly discern between what we truly sense and what we think we sense: the flitting images of man–woman encounter, the erotic magazine advertisement and its commercial, multi-channel counterpart, the starvation victims reported in newspapers and television, the cold-beer billboard, the instantaneous photograph of a punch, the impressionistic paintings of bathers in full sunshine, and so on. They all fulfill their semiotic-communicative functions through synesthesial rather than direct sensory perception.

Returning briefly to the diagrams in Figs. 3.1 and 3.2, it is interesting to note the medium or channel of transmission of the various resulting systems operating between cointeractants, connecting their input and output ends. Sebeok dealt with this topic referring to animal species, indicating all the components of their existing channels of communication (Sebeok 1968 and 1974 [see his table 4, p. 234]) and advocating a systematic and comparative analysis of the various systems in terms of their specific design features, that is: whether the system in question requires tools or only the body, whether it can operate in darkness as in light, vary in intensity, fade instantaneously or remain in space for some time, and the like.

This otherwise incomplete discussion of intercorporeal sign systems spares the sort of zoosemiotic considerations so eloquently dealt with by Sebeok (1977), or the socializing implications of 'distal' systems (vision, hearing and, in lesser degree, olfaction) and 'proximal' ones (taste, touch, and kinesthesis), as well as the relations of movement and artifactual extensions of organismal stimuli (implied when discussing kinesics).

One is tempted, however, to incite fellow students of human interaction to ponder over one of the aspects of *verbal language* that makes it the unique anthroposemiotic and anthropomorphic social communication system far beyond the interactive possibilities of, for instance, chemical systems or gestures: that not only can words speak for themselves, but about the other intersomatic systems, either as those other activities take place or, what is more significant, long after they occurred. This otherwise obvious uniqueness of language makes it the moderator, judge and commentator of whatever kinesic, chemical, dermal or thermal behaviors we or our cointeractants may activate, thus enriching immensely the communicative possibilities of the encounter. This is, of course, directly related to the problem of false redundancy, dealt with later, for a verbal construct of any length that seems to duplicate what gestures are conveying, or the obvious message contained in the shedding of tears, is far from being redundant, as it enhances the semiotic contents of the nonverbal behaviors.

Another basic aspect of human communication that becomes apparent as soon as we try to establish a taxonomy of the transmitting channels and of the perceptual possibilities of man, is the *preponderance of sound and movement* over any other static or nonacoustic mode of emitting messages. They account for the transmission of verbal language and paralanguage as perceived on the vocal/narial-auditory channel, and of kinesics, on the visual one, that is, the components of the Basic Triple Structure (which is discussed in Chapter 5 as comprising also the message-conveying nonactivities of silence and stillness, as basic as sound and movement in social interaction.

Finally, this general view of human communication would not be complete without seeing it in the twofold inherent context of *space and time*—the two indispensable dimensions of culture and life—which, as communication modes themselves, have originated the areas of proxemics and the still developing area of chronemics, both discussed later on.

3. The Realms of 'Verbal' and 'Nonverbal' Communication

It seems to be mandatory at this stage in the development of nonverbal communication studies to consider whether in writing one more book in the field the term 'nonverbal' should be perpetuated or replaced by a more felicitous one that perhaps would not generate so much controversy. One would be amply justified, on the other hand, in trying to contribute to the field of nonverbal communication without questioning the term so much, but rather making another effort to advance that which it has come to represent. Whatever attempts we might make at this point to undo what has been done might prove quite futile. The literature of many disciplines has been displaying 'nonverbal communication' for years now, congresses and symposia in those fields, and their literature, have done likewise; the term has also gained ground in the academic world signifying very clearly that many of the things we utter beyond words, our 'body language' (to use the more superficial label) and whatever seems to form part of our corporeal or next-to-corporeal ways of emitting messages in daily interaction is, by excluding lexical language, nonverbal.

It might be appropriate to remember how not too long ago some argued over the term 'paralanguage', perhaps an even less fortunate one which we still feel we should so something about, but which has been accepted today at least as a perfectly workable term referring to the extremely complex series of highly significative sounds, voice modifications and silences produced in the vocal/narial-auditory channel beyond the recognized suprasegmental features of stress, pitch, and juncture in our western languages. Over twenty years ago, Hill (1952) used 'paralanguage' and then 'paralinguistic' (Hill 1958) as embodying both 'paralanguage' and body motion or kinesics, and other well known scholars did the same thing, among them Abercrombie (1968), backed in a way by Lyons (1972) and particularly by Laver and Hutcheson (1972), who distinguish "vocal paralinguistic features" ("tone of voice") and "nonvocal paralinguistic features" (kinesics). Most other scholars, however, agree in separating paralanguage and kinesics as two different although interrelated areas of research. Within paralanguage itself the controversy lies sometimes in the difficulty to draw a boundary line between language and paralanguage, as will be discussed.

Today those not satisfied with the all-encompassing label 'nonverbal' continue, we cannot say for how long, to voice their discontent with otherwise good arguments. Sebeok, whose perceptive arguments would succeed in shaking deep-rooted convictions in others, has offered the best criticisms of the term and reviews of other workers' thoughts on this matter. He feels that "the concept of nonverbal communication is one of the most ill-defined in all of semiotics" (Sebeok 1977b: 1065), mentioning for instance, the truly verbal value of many gestures, the nonvocal but verbal quality of American Sign Language, etc., and ends up by suggesting tongue-in-cheek that 'nonverbal' surpasses the sphere of bodily communication to subsume "the entire range of culture exclusive of language" (1067) but overlapping ethology. No one could disagree with him that "the formula, 'communication minus language = nonverbal communication' is clumsily negative, simplistic, and obscurantist" (Sebeok 1975: 10). In the first chapter of Johnson's (1982) pioneering handbook on nonverbal communication for language teachers, we find another incisive discussion of the term and what it has come to represent, and Kendon, in the excellent introduction to his recent compilation of papers on 'nonverbal communication' (which is part of the title of the volume) reviews the emergence of the term, its limits and consequences, since it served as the title of the book by Ruesch and Kees (1956) on communication, based on cybernetics and the mathematical theory of information (which regarded all behavior as informative, whether intended or unintended), and explains why behavior does not have to be intentional in order to communicate, as intentionality is not always possible to determine.

The work in 'nonverbal communication', leery of the term as we may be, goes on at an increasingly rapid pace, with some discrepancies regarding the behaviors included. While Ekman and Friesen in their very well known earlier paper (1969), included within nonverbal behavior only "any movement or position of the face and/or the body", thus not differentiating between nonverbal and nonvocal, Duncan (1969) includes paralanguage, kinesics, proxemics, olfaction, skin sensitiveness to touch and temperature, and even the use of artifacts, such as Ekman and Friesen's "object-adaptors"; and in body motion or kinesic behavior he includes facial expression, eye movement and postures.

Lyons (1972) distinguishes, in the first place, vocal and nonvocal signals, according to whether the signals are transmitted in the vocal-auditory "channel" or not (by this term implying the two end-points, sender and receiver), and then considers language as made up of verbal (extrictly lexical) and nonverbal (prosodic) components, the latter, of course, being still vocal; while he is inclined with Abercrombie to apply the controversial term 'paralinguistics' to features playing a supporting role, such as gestures and eye movements, and to include both prosodic and paralinguistic phenomena within nonsegmental ('linguistic,' therefore, subsuming for him verbal and prosodic).

Argyle (1972) comes the closest to the classification I shall propose by calling kinesics and proxemics nonverbal, as well as what he refers to as nonverbal aspects of speech, or paralanguage.

Laver and Hutcheson (1972), in the introduction to a volume of readings on face-to-face interaction, identify verbal with actual words, nonverbal with vocal or nonvocal conversational behavior (for them paralanguage) apart from words, thus distinguishing: vocal-verbal (words), vocal-nonverbal (intonation and paralanguage), nonvocal-verbal (written or printed language), nonvocal-nonverbal (kinesics: facial expression, gesture, and posture); four means of communicating that offer linguistic, paralinguistic (for them nonlinguistic, nonverbal phenomena, both vocal [tone of voice] and nonvocal [kinesics, proxemics and related modalities]), and extralinguistic features ("by definition non-verbal, non-linguistic and non-paralinguistic"; either vocal [biologically, psychologically and socially-based voice quality] or nonvocal [as the style of dress]) (12–13).

Laver and Hutcheson's definition of verbal, nonverbal-vocal and nonverbal-nonvocal coincides with the classification I have used within somatic communication, although in the case of nonverbal-nonvocal I have encompassed the rest of the communicative systems I study under 'external somatic communication' (Fig. 3.3), which comprises:

Somatic vocal-verbal communication, the acoustic nonautonomous bodily vocal system limited by the vocal-auditory channel and formed by segmental lexical structures and their essential suprasegmental patterns of stress, pitch and junctures.

Somatic vocal-nonverbal communication, the acoustic nonautonomous bodily system, whether respiratory or not, actually limited by the vocal/narial-auditory channel, formed by the extreme variations of the suprasegmental patterns of stress, pitch and juncture, and the series of audible phenomena and silences that constitute paralanguage.

Somatic nonvocal-nonverbal communication is the one conveyed by the rest of the bodily systems, namely, external movement and stillness, the chemical, dermal and thermal activities, and the static features of appearance, weight and consistency.

Beyond the strictly somatic modes of conveying and receiving messages two more 'blocks' mentioned earlier and represented in Fig. 1.1 can be defined: *objectual communication*, which includes systems gradually removed farther from the body, and *environmental communication*, which overlaps the latter and includes the rest of people's organic and inorganic environments. The last four groups together constitute *Nonverbal Communi-*

cation, obviously an 'all-inclusive' term on which I would like to add a word.

Explicitly or implicitly we recognize verbal language, words, as the ideal social means of communication, of conveying signs and messages and evoking a virtually infinite number of expressable as well as ineffable mental constructs. Precisely because of this, when anything else triggers in us sensible and mentally-extended sensible perceptions, that is, when anything from a gesture to the texture of an old wall (which may define a culture) communicates to us in that sort of silent one-way interaction, we call it 'nonverbal' because we know that it 'conveys' without words. Now, if we are going to perpetuate this futile controversy over the term 'nonverbal' because we all want to contribute our scholarly disquisitions on the matter, lest our fellow researchers should think us perfectly happy about an imperfect term, we may do so. However, I suspect that arguing over it will never stop now the use of 'nonverbal'. More and more researchers are devoted to the field and are providing increasingly solid foundations for it.

Verbal language is our unique means of communicating and building up relationships in a society, and whatever codes 'communicate'—a gesture, a billboard figure, a stone fence, an Indian dhoti—will be regarded as 'nonlanguage', 'nonverbal', 'beyond words'; and because of the intimate interrelationships of somatic verbal and extraverbal message-conveying systems (and of the latter and the objectual, animal, and natural environments), nonverbal communication' will be, I suspect, the only term prevailing over any other innovations.

The definition of *nonverbal communication* which I propose here would then be clearly suggested by the table in Fig. 2.1, 'Sensible and Intelligible Systems in a Culture':

The emissions of signs by all the nonlexical somatic, artifactual and environmental sensible sign systems contained in a culture, whether individually or in mutual costructuration, and whether or not those emissions constitute behavior or generate personal interaction. Communication is equated in that cultural context with the emission of information and its perception by humans or animals.

This interpretation of what constitutes 'nonverbal communication' attempts to establish a working framework without imposing limitations that would exclude personal objectual and environmental manifestations. Many, like Sebeok, feel that it includes too much and I could not agree more with their discontent over such a misnomer. Terms such as 'bodily communication' and 'environmental communication' would exclude each other; 'bodily and environmental' would seem to ambiguously exclude animal species, and so on. Thus, whether or not one agrees with it, the different areas must be researched today without awaiting the invention of the ideal term, and I must reluctantly continue to use it.

4. External Somatic Communication

If we still limit ourselves at this point to the systems that are developed only within the limits of our body, that is, those that include only the body and whatever elements of its immediate environment it can manipulate through movement (without yet trying to seek the relationships between the body and the rest of the systems that constitute each given culture), we can represent the various intercorporeal emission-reception exchanges classified earlier by grouping all the bodily behaviors as shown in Fig. 3.3, 'External Somatic Communication'.[3] This classification distinguishes the various sensory input–output modes (excluding synesthesial perception) and suggests the basic systems, subsystems, categories, subcategories, and forms (types falling beyond the behaviors classified here), although, naturally, not each of them is in each sensory mode of reception (shape, for instance, appears by itself, although it could be classified as a 'category' belonging to the 'subsystem' of slow-changing characteristics, and to the 'system' of static characteristics or appearance). As for the cultural or social functions common to all systems, the ones distinguished earlier as basic forms of a culture in Fig. 1.1 are shown here again as the four situations in which bodily behaviors may take place: full unhindered interaction, reduced interaction, noninteraction, and the sort of one-way interaction discussed before.

At first glance one sees the dominance of movement and how it determines, through linguistic and paralinguistic sound and kinesics, the greatest number of the higher-level interactional activities of which the body is capable as a socializing organism. Kinetic activity generates the two main blocks of human behaviors, which appear in the table as sensory experiences.

A. *Auditory perception*, which comprises one of the two main sensible complexes, as body sounds are produced mainly (a) by vocal modifications of respiratory air (as in language and most paralinguistic phenomena), or simply by its two phases of inspiration and expiration (as in some paralinguistic features); (b) by nonvocal-respiratory air (as in paralinguistic sounds emitted by ingressions and egressions of air through the nares); (c) by vocal-nonrespiratory air, as in paralinguistic clicking suctions or when expelling stomachic gases; (d) by nonvocal-nonrespiratory air, as when expelling intestinal gas, (e) by generally abrupt contact of various parts of the body, mainly the extremities, with itself (self-adaptors, producing sounds mentioned before, such as clapping, slapping, thudding, etc., and even suctions between the palms of the hands and by applying the palm of one hand against the ear), another body (alter-adaptors) or against objects (object-adaptors); and (f) by sounds produced in three bone joints: the first interphalangeals (as in knuckle-cracking), the femur-tibia one at the knee, and the talotibial one of the ankle (see Westcott's [1966] taxonomy of 'coenetics').

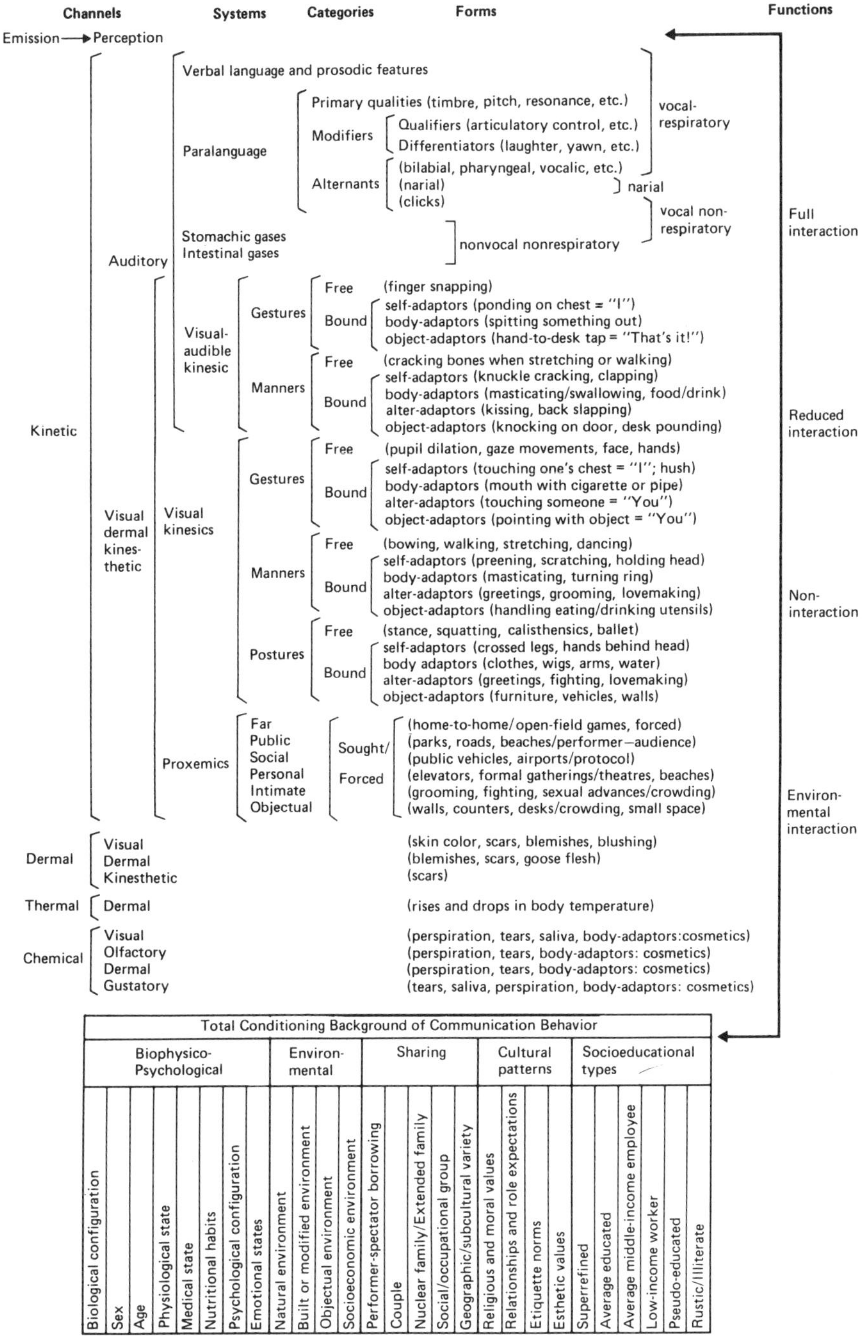

FIG. 3.3. External Somatic Communication.

The overlapping of the kinetic and acoustic modes results in visual perception of linguistic and paralinguistic sound-forming facial expressions, the other sounds mentioned above under (g) and all the interactive sound-producing kinesic behaviors, namely: free gestures (finger-snapping), self-adaptor gestures (slapping one's thigh), body-adaptor gestures (spitting something out signalling contempt), free manners (cracking bones while stretching), self-adaptor manners (applauding), alter-adaptor manners (kissing noisily), body-adaptor manners (chewing on something) and object-adaptor manners (knocking on a door).

B. *Visual perception*, besides the visually-perceived acoustic behaviors, consists almost entirely of kinesic activities divided into gestures, manners and postures, both free (e.g., frowning) and bound (e.g., handshaking); and, not precisely moving but visually perceived as motor-based results of previous activities, the six proxemic attitudes: far, public, social, personal, intimate, and objectual distances; the visual manifestations of dermal, thermal and chemical reactions; and the static visual signs of shape, size, consistency and color.

C. *Olfactory perception* of chemical substances.

D. *Gustatory perception* of the same chemical substances.

E. *Dermal perception* of touching movement and skin texture and temperature, and of chemical substances.

F. *Kinesthetic reception* of mediated contactual movement, skin, gross irregularities, shape, size, and weight.

The table excludes all types of synesthesial perception, as it acknowledges only direct sensorial reception of somatic signs.

5. Relationships Among Forms of External Somatic Communication

All forms of body communication activities, whether between interactants or within one's own repertoire (in what later I will refer to as self-regulatory function), are, we discover, interrelated and interconditioned in ways that even the student of his own language cannot ignore, as lexical, semantic, morphological and syntactical variations in his use of that language are tied to variations in the use of nonverbal communicative modalities.

While authors like Ekman and Friesen (1969) state that a nonverbal act can repeat, augment, illustrate, accent or contradict the words, and that it can anticipate, coincide with, substitute for or follow verbal behaviour (this part of communicative behavior, which is not autonomous, being the unquestionable core of human intellectual exchange and the truly anthropomorphic signalling system), one should consider that verbal behavior is not the only activity with which the nonverbal behaviors are related in the actual communication situation, and that all nonverbal acts can be mutually related, acting either as modifiers or as context. In fact, the issue of intersystem relationships beyond language is but touched upon in this book (e.g., when outlining the Conditioning Background in section 10 below and when mentioning the documentation of interrelationships in literature at the end of Chapter 10). I will simply suggest the following instances:

Paralanguage to kinesics. The apico-aveolar click ['tz'] + double head-shake is used to repeat negation; a loud and drawled '¡Well!' anticipates a firm handshake; an ironic '¡Sure!' + headnod contradicts the verbal affirmation; a paralinguistic growl while the hand advances forward like a tiger's head illustrate each other.

Paralanguage to proxemics. Whispery, breathy voice increases as intimate distance turns into erotic play; very open voice (pharyngeal control), high volume and tense articulation occur at public distance in oratory; if you whisper at someone while walking towards him, you anticipate personal or intimate distance.

Paralanguage to chronemics. Chronemics, discussed later, is the term I have proposed for the area of study that would deal with the conceptualization and handling of time, just as proxemics studies space. The pause and its structure (subject to duration, the two audible respiratory phases, kinesic markers, situational context, etc.) is a valid example of this type of relationship; another one is the kind of laughter and its duration according to upbringings, social status and situational context.

Paralanguage to dermal changes. Irregular rhythm of speech, slight glottalization, and use of hesitation vowels ('Uh'), clicks and pauses, may be concomitant to, or anticipate, blushing; a drawled ingressive labiodental fricative [$\underrightarrow{>}$f] may accompany goose flesh produced by cold.

Paralanguage to tactile perception. A spasmodic and ingressive labiodental fricative [>f̬] may illustrate the tactile perception of a hot object; lower pitch, whispering and rasp voice may be conditioned by kinesthetic perception of someone else's body in love play.

Paralanguage to olfactory perception. A drawled closed lip ingressive narial (nostril) friction [>$\underrightarrow{\text{Y}}$×] may signify the perception of a pleasant odor.

Kinesics to kinesics. Stretches or structural patterns within the same communicative type of behavior may condition each other. Two Latin friends who stop suddenly upon seeing each other, open their arms and display a happy facial expression are anticipating a mutual embrace with heavy slapping of each other's back.

Kinesics to proxemics. The embrace in the above example is anticipated while still at far personal, or even social, distance; his distance from the audience makes an actor emphasize his gestural behavior; kinesics replaces language as the distance between interactors makes it necessary.

Kinesics to chronemics. Depending, of course, on psychological, somatic and social variables, people in a waiting room or at a party change their postural behavior as time goes by, and it is possible for an observer to guess how long certain persons have been there.

Kinesics to body-adaptors. The special fitting of clothes on one's body and the use of cigarettes, pipes, glasses or jewelry gives certain characteristics to one's kinesic repertoire of gestures, postures and manners.

Kinesics to olfactory perception. You can tell by someone's gestures whether he is perceiving, or simply speaking of, bad or good odors.

Proxemics to olfactory perception. Certain body odors and some perfumes (body-adaptors) may induce shortening of distance between two bodies, just as odors considered offensive or carrying a negative sexual meaning for some, if not for all, make personal distance lengthen.

Proxemics to chronemics. The duration of a visit, whether formal, familiar or highly protocolarian, is directly related to the distance kept among the participants (the more informal, the longer it may last, and vice versa), unless unusual circumstances affect both the spatial and the chronemic behaviors; at an informal party, distances of flirtation, of sexual overtures or simply of common interests in conversation shorten as time passes, conditioned, of course, by drinking (as revealed by more relaxation, loss of certain inhibitions, etc.) and other factors.

6. Coding and Interrelationships of Verbal and Nonverbal Behaviors in Social Interactions

It is at this stage of inquiry, when the verbal and nonverbal bodily activities of people have been, I trust, clearly delineated, that the worker in communication must resort once more to basic semiotics, an approach still so foreign to many seeking (a) some fundamental principles that may enable him to establish the encoding–decoding processes by which those activities costructure themselves in the communicative continuum; (b) how the signs that are consciously or unconsciously emitted by their senders travel between them and their intended or unintended receivers; and (c) how they reach, or fail to reach, the decoding end.[4]

Conscious vs. unconscious coding

The first important basic aspect of personal interaction is that although the cointeractants (i.e., speaker and listener in true natural conversation, since otherwise unconscious gestures, for instance, can be controlled in a theatrical performance) may often be more conscious of their own verbal behaviors than of the nonverbal ones, it is a fact that the receiver is usually more conscious of the speaker's nonverbal behaviors than the speaker himself, because nonverbal activities, from a paralinguistic click of the tongue, to blushing, or momentarily interactive silence, may occur quite out of awareness. They may be, in other words, encoded and put in motion at a subconscious level, without the intellectual process required for the production of words (although one cannot ignore the many very lexical nonverbal constructs we may carefully 'think out' together with speech), but decoded nevertheless by the listener. Furthermore, they can play important functions and have a definite effect on the decoding process of even the verbal message when it is truly the central one (and not a secondary one, as will be seen), as diagrammed in Fig. 3.4.

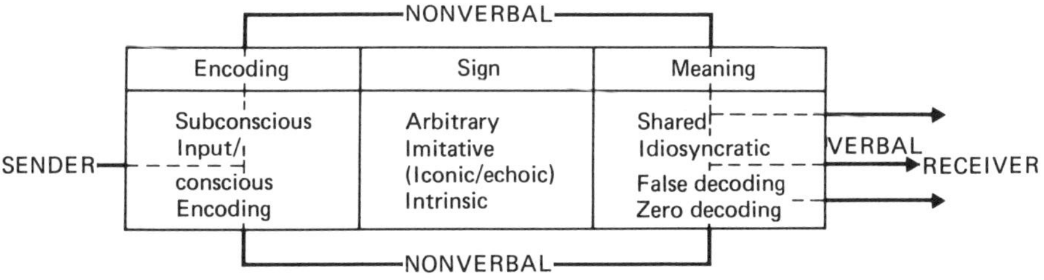

FIG. 3.4. Coding of Signs and Sign-meaning Relationships.

Two more relevant characteristics of the interactive encounter are suggested by the diagram when one considers the many different nonverbal activities that precede, cooccur, follow or replace verbal language among those shown in the table of external somatic communication.

One is that, given the inherent semantic limitation of words, the verbally encoded messages are fully decoded in natural conversation only when words are perceived and decoded along with their complementary nonverbal behaviors; which demonstrates how unrealistic it can be to analyze meaning in terms solely of the morphological and syntactical constructs of verbal discourse. One should not forget that encoding is not necessarily a conscious affair, and that the signs—let us say words—emitted, as far as the speaker is concerned, reach the decoding end of the process 'colored' in a way that may not have been meant by their sender.

This thought, which suggests an additional perspective through which we should study the production of communicative activities, has very specific applications in terms, for instance, of: crosscultural study of verbal and nonverbal signs; the specific effect that emotional states may have on the speaker-listener process, and which behaviors are more affected; and the different decoding capacity of socioeconomically lower persons.

Sign-meaning relationship

The other semiotic aspect of the encoding-decoding process is that of the *sign-meaning relationship*. Signs can be:

A. *Arbitrary*, that is, when the sign bears no resemblance to what it signifies, as happens with non-onomatopoeic words, an OK gesture, a perfume used for sexual attractiveness, etc., the bulk of interactive sign constructs being, therefore, made up of arbitrarily coded signs;

B. *Iconic or imitative*, when the sign resembles what it means, its signified. Lately, Kendon (1981: 34–36) has questioned the validity of the term 'iconic' and of the concept of 'resemblance', giving as an example the gesture for 'gun'. However, we can see that, in spite of its crosscultural variants (e.g., imitating the trigger action with the forefinger, or extending the first two fingers and shaking 'the gun' up and down), we certainly see that gestures (life signs travelling over other channels, such as chemical-olfactory ones) can "move up the scale of codedness" and become truly iconic when, because of previous experience, a particular sign is seen as the replica of a model. This is what may happen with, for instance, the arbitrarily coded perfume used for sexual attractiveness: it bears no resemblance to its signified, say, the desire to give a definite image of oneself; but after repeated occurrences, or because of repeated experience by the decoder, that perfume has become the replica of a model.

We might think—leaving aside the conceptual relationship of, for instance, seating arrangements and role relationships in small group ecology (which can also be regarded as iconic)—that admitting that 'iconicity' is possible along all channels of bodily sensorial communication (see Sebeok 1976), we might want to use the term 'imitative' to subsume the replica-model, or sign-referent, relationships (following the categorization of non-verbal behaviors offered in the next chapter) of:

(a) sound, as *echoic*, whether linguistically *onomatopoeic* ('a whirring noise'), *paralinguistic* (the whirring of an airplane engine), or *kinetic-paralinguistic* (a horse's galloping by tapping on a table and the vocal imitation of the sound of the hoofs);

(b) Movement, as *kinetographs*, imitating only movement (the galloping of the horse by running the hand across the table);

(c) movement + sound, as *kinephonographs*, combining movement and nonvocal sound imitations (running the hand across the table while rapping it to sound the hoofs);

(d) figures and volumes, as *pictographs*, to which the term 'iconic' would seem to correspond more appropriately than it does other sensory channels;

(e) *chemical, thermal*, and *dermal* properties as interpersonal messages, which contain no imitative relationship, can however acquire their iconicity through use, thus moving up the codedness scale suggested by Kendon;

nevertheless, apart from an artificially controlled system such as perfume, natural chemical, thermal or dermal messages cannot be considered 'icons', I feel, but 'symptoms'.

To the strictly somatic elements one can add, of course, body-adaptors (dress, jewelry, food and drink, etc.) and object-adaptors (tools, chairs, etc.), whose presence can constitute an iconic or imitative relationship signifying status, personality or culture.

One could hypothesize, with those who advocate the gestural theory of language origins—or, as I have suggested simply trying to adopt a realistic stand (Poyatos 1977a), the gestural-paralinguistic early stages—that in the early periods of vocal-kinesic human communication the greatest portion of interactive messages could have consisted mainly of imitative utterances and gestures, and that arbitrary lexical and paralinguistic messages and kinesic references to mental processes (defined later as 'identifiers', 'ideographs' and 'externalizers') could have developed as cognitive sophistication and more elaborate interpersonal social relationships and situations grew. I personally do not believe in biological language evolution, but I do believe in a logical historical elaboration of language-paralanguage-kinesics and the other systems of social communication.

C. *Intrinsic* proper, finally, is the sign-meaning relationship in which the sign does not resemble, but *is* its significant; that is, not a threatening fist, but the actual aggression, or the imitation of someone's gesture (a clear overlap of imitative and intrinsic).

Decoding

As for the capacity of the meaning itself to be agreed upon by a greater or smaller number of senders (encoding) and receivers (decoding) one must differentiate between:

A. *Shared*, when it is common to a series of individuals, to the members of an age or work group, to a whole culture, to several cultures in contact through direct interaction or through the media, or universal, as the expressions of emotion found to be universal (see Eibl-Eibesfeldt 1979a and Ekman 1977).

B. *Idiosyncratic*, whether recurrent or not, when the association of the sign and its meaning is peculiar only to a single individual. As idiosyncratic encoding, one person may perform a gesture, for instance, with a specific meaning only for himself; as idiosyncratic decoding, another gesture, or a paralinguistic feature, can be interpreted by one individual only, as happens, for instance, within the family, where only the wife may be able to understand some of her husband's gestures and other behaviors.

C. *False decoding* occurs more often than one can imagine. The message encoded at the input end of the emitter, that is, the sensible signs, is misinterpreted and, while the true meaning is lost, another one which was never wittingly encoded by the emitter takes its place. This interesting, though unintentional, semiotic trick, is illustrated, for instance, by intercultural homomorphic kinesic antonyms, by misinterpreted paralinguistic features, and even by misunderstood verbal constructs.

D. There are situations, however, when the signifier is not at all perceived by the receiver, and neither a correct or incorrect input–output occurs. In other words, they are acts which can be intentionally or unintentionally encoded but never decoded by anyone. I call this situation *zero decoding* to differentiate it from 'zero sign', when a sign signifies "by its very absence" (Sebeok 1974: 241). Zero decoding is a semiotic blank that takes place much more often than one can imagine, not only in daily live interaction, where so many messages go unnoticed, but in every static sign manifestation of the arts and the environment. In fact, much research is needed to seek the rate between decoding (false or correct) and zero decoding in specific situations and by specific receivers across, for instance, socioeconomic and educational strata, age or work groups, and whole cultures, as well as in pathological instances. There must be factors in each of those specific cases which condition the decoding capabilities of people, or what we might refer to as semiotic fluency, a concept intimately related to cultural fluency.

Those body behaviors with shared encoded and decoded meaning constitute, therefore, the accepted repertoire which typifies a group or culture. The degree of idiosyncrasy or sharing can be considerable, and it is clear that the ideally effective behavior in interaction is the one shared by as many individuals as possible, and that pancultural behaviors should be differentiated from national ones, since ignoring this differentiation may result, as already discussed, in cultural clash and in failure to communicate.

Interrelationships of behaviors

The fourth fundamental characteristic of interaction, and an additional perspective that affords a more exhaustive analysis of the roles and limitations of verbal and nonverbal behaviors, concerns, first, the *mutual relationships of the behaviors*, the basic functions of each activity in relation to each other and to both sender and receiver, and then the qualifying factors attached to all interactive activities. The diagram in Fig. 3.5 indicates those relationships.

All forms of body communication can be interrelated, either as they happen between interactants or within one's own verbal and nonverbal repertoire, in a way that cannot be ignored even if we want to analyze verbal language only, since phonetic, semantic, lexical, morphological and syntactical variations in the use of words and their prosodic features are tied to variations in the use of nonverbal modalities. Each activity can act either as

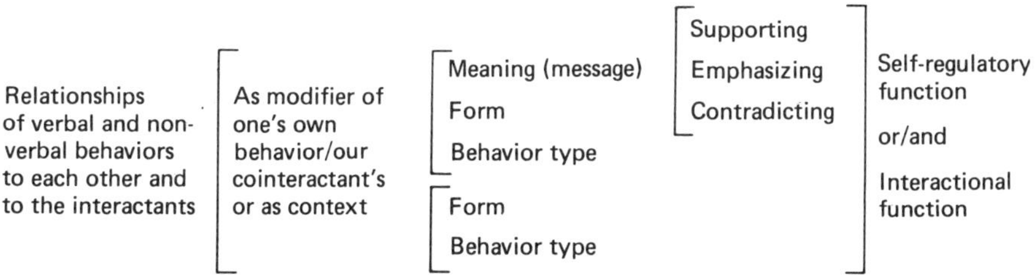

FIG. 3.5. Interrelationships of Behaviors.

modifier of one's own behavior or our cointeractant's, or simply as a *contextual* element. An apico-alveolar click, 'Tz' + pharyngeal ingression can elicit my own 'Well . . .', or slight frowning, or both, or it can make my interlocutor ask 'What is it?'; but it could be just a contextual behavior, as in 'Well, tz, I think I can do it.' Furthermore, that same click could modify the *meaning*, that is, the message (as when giving a following 'Yes' a rather negative tinge), the *form* (a hesitating sort of 'Yes') or the *behavior* itself (not eliciting a verbal expression but a shoulder shrug).

When modifying the meaning, a given behavior (a word, a click, a shoulder shrug or even a silence) can support, emphasize or contradict the basic message. On the other hand—and this happens in conversation more often than we can imagine, or elicit it purposely—my verbal or nonverbal behavior can modify my interactant's verbal or nonverbal behavior. My 'Please don't quote me, but—' can make him lean towards me, raise his eyebrows slightly, perhaps only blink slowly while staring at me; his blushing can (according to my interactive fluency and flexibility) give a new turn to my speech, or make me look away from him until his blush disappears, or smile. It can be observed that the behavior of one interactant can modify the form of the other interactant's behavior, or change it altogether, but not just the meaning of that behavior, as happens within one's own repertoire.

Finally, both modifiers and contextual elements perform either a self-regulatory function or an interactional one, or both. One of my verbal or nonverbal acts can regulate (and not exactly modify), not only the production of my other verbal and nonverbal activities—in terms of order of occurrence, amount displayed and beginning and end of the display (*self-regulatory function*)—but also my interlocutor's behavior—thus regulating the flow of our transaction, by means of cues (words, pitch changes, gestures, silences) which indicate my intention to conclude the conversation, change the subject, contradict or agree with him, etc. (*interactional function*).

It must be understood that, while an internal somatic activity (an endosemiotic one) cannot directly influence the other person's external (language, gestures) or internal (muscular tonus) behaviors, the opposite is possible, that is, one person's external activities can affect another person's internal activities, as has been experimented by Krieger (e.g., 1976) with regard to the hemoglobin level modified by the laying-on of hands with the intention of healing.

Of these two functions, self-regulatory and interactional, the first one plays the most important role. By regulating one's multiple repertoire, it conditions in turn the cointeractant's behaviors, and the smooth or irregular rhythm of the conversation.

The Qualifiers of Interactive Behaviors: Costructuration, Intensity, and Duration

These basic semiotic considerations would be completed by the triple measurable dimension inherent in the verbal and nonverbal behaviors of sender and receiver as they appear modified in various degrees by their costructuration, duration, and intensity. These three qualifiers of human interaction behavior—much less operative in other species, since the human intellect plays such an important function in predicting, judging and associating preceding behaviors with the present and succeeding ones—constitute its most complex aspect. They reveal the intricate mesh of intertwined behaviors that give shape to every fraction of the mechanism of human interaction, showing how unrealistic it can be to concentrate on a single message-conveying system, say, language, and attempt to discuss its communicative properties while neglecting its further relationships with the somatic and extrasomatic activities that may operate before, simultaneously to or after that system, closer or farther away from it, namely: somatic (physical/mental), environmental (subsuming living and objectual elements) and spiritual.

Costructuration refers, first, to that of the speaker's behaviors with his own most immediate behaviors, that is, preceding, simultaneous and succeeding, but also to the relationship with the verbal and nonverbal behaviors of his cointeractants. Apart from the more obvious effect of preceding activities, the simultaneous and succeeding ones are particularly interesting. As one of the aspects of the interactive functions, the speaker's silence can be, and generally is (if imperceptibly at times), accompanied by movement (kinesics), just as his stillness can be, but not as often, accompanied by speech, thus conditioning each other and being affected, in turn, by their respective intensity, location, and duration.

As for the speaker's own succeeding behaviors, they retroactively condition his other behaviors when he can predict them. For example, he prolongs his pause while intently looking at her, as he predicts the ensuing embrace. If he cannot predict that embrace, then the long, intense pause itself will elicit it (in fact, a blend of linguistic and/or paralinguistic, proxemic and kinesic complementary, and not redundant, messages). A similar process takes place for the costructuration of speaker and listener, except that the speaker cannot always accurately predict his cointeractant's behaviors. Apart, however, from this specific type of relationship, the behaviors of the two always condition or elicit each other in the course of a conversation (see Fig. 7.1). *Intensity*, which is measured as described below depends here also on the duration of the behavior in question, for the longer a pause is prolonged, the tenser the whole situation may grow. While intensity refers mainly to the cooccurring activities that truly fill the seemingly silent or motionless segment of behavior, it can certainly be enhanced by the effect of the preceding behaviors, which determines, in turn, the characteristics of those cooccurring with silence and stillness immediately after.

Duration, then, is ultimately related to both costructuration and intensity, as well as to what could be termed 'temporal signs' or chronemic attitudes.

8. Redundancy vs. Complementarity: Primary and Secondary Systems

One semiotic-communicative aspect of interactive human behaviors which I believe deserves the utmost attention, if some activities or systems are not to be neglected in the process of establishing their coding and interrelationships, entails a revision of the concept of redundancy.

That the concept of *redundancy* has been traditionally misused in everyday language as well as in serious research becomes obvious if we look at things with a semiotic eye. For what appears to be redundant is, most of the times, only *complementary*, that is, supporting, emphasizing or contradicting the essential message. Blushing, for instance, is not necessarily redundant after or before words of the same message, for it may act as a dermal means of expressing the degree of emotion contained, or perhaps controlled, in those words ('I think I love you'), or in their paralinguistic (a hesitant/affirmative closed-lips moan) or kinesic (a closed-eyes smile with averted gaze) equivalents. It could also betray a deceiving verbal or nonverbal statement. Likewise, a beckoning gesture is complementary to 'Come here' when it specifically denotes how we really mean it, since the kinesic act can be performed in different ways. A silence, even after having verbally stated that we cannot say anything, adds information, as a complementary message, by its duration and by its costructuration with our kinesic behavior (perhaps our very stillness). One could argue, then, that redunancy is a fallacy most of the time, as the blushing or the gesture always assist the verbal or nonverbal message. The complementary quality should be obvious enough, otherwise its unconspicuousness makes it a true redundancy.

But redundancy must not be given a negative connotation of purposelessness either. Gesticulation, frequent pauses in conversation, the adoption of still positions, could certainly be redundant, yet express a personal style characterized precisely by redundancy. Thus, we might speak of redundancy on the communicative or message level, since nothing is being added, but hardly on the social level of the cultural one when a crosscultural difference is being observed. I heard some refer to the redundant quality of Italian or Spanish gesticulation, ¡but that kinesic quality allowed them to identify those specific cultures!

This idea of redundancy *vs.* complementarity links with another needed differentiation in communication studies, that which exists between *primary systems* (or messages) and *secondary systems* (or messages), not to be confused with redundancy-complementarity. If we try to establish a hierarchization of systems in a given interactive situation—for each situation would entail a different organization of verbal and nonverbal behaviors—we soon discover that the verbal code, despite the claimed superiority of 'language' over any other systems, is not necessarily the main one. This is, in part, related to the differentiation between redundant and complementary. A rise in body temperature, the blushing in the former example, or a silence, may carry the main message when either language, paralanguage, kinesics or proxemics simply supports it as complementary information or duplicate it as a true redundancy. In this respect, what determines the hierarchization is the intensity of the various systems involved and their individual location in the communication stream.

Intensity is something we consciously or unconsciously measure by the degree of the qualifying features in each case, e.g.: light—deep blush, mild—energetic negative gesture, mid-volume, normally articulated, level-pitched—shouted, tensely articulated, high-pitched verbal expression. The same criterion can be applied to silence and stillness, discussed later, since they are both judged in themselves by their duration and by their modifiers, which are the cooccurrent and adjacent behaviors.

As for *location*, it refers literally to their physical position in the behavioral stream of the interactive situation. A seemingly clear handshake of agreement becomes secondary when it is followed by 'Okay, but I go first', for instance; tears can be the primary system (a chemical one) in relation to language if they give true shape to the main message. Silence and stillness may either precede or follow the most 'conspicuous' behavior, such as words or a gesture, but actually they may act as primary or secondary systems when judged by their location and by the characteristics of the related activities.

One could in human communication—not in zoosemiotics—refer to the criterion of *cognitive control* over the upcoming behaviors, which would modify all the factors just mentioned, and say that the controlled activities are primary ones while the uncontrolled ones are secondary, but this proves insufficient simply because an uncontrolled display of tears, or our dermal perception of someone's coarse hand on our forearm, can certainly constitute primary systems carrying the most significant cluster of signs.

It will be seen that the redundancy-complementary criterion, as well as the primary-secondary and controlled-uncontrolled ones, serve to enhance the internal costructuration of the Basic Triple Structure, language-paralanguage-kinesics, as does the revision of Hockett's (1960) scheme (Poyatos 1981e, elaborated on in Poyatos 1983d). In addition, the triple transcription of language-paralanguage-kinesics discussed later can be an excellent tool to observe the exact hierarchization of systems in a single sentence, for instance, or in a breath-semantic stretch of speech. But above all, it proves language as the purely anthroposemiotic system of communication.

Sebeok's (1974: 237) concept of symmetricality versus asymmetricality supports my view, except that two symmetrical signs (e.g., 'Yes' + nod) are not necessarily redundant in my definition, since I am not identifying synonymity with redundancy.

9. Interaction, Noninteraction, Full Interaction, Reduced Interaction, and Environmental Interaction

A serious study of the various bodily systems, whether from an anthropological, linguistic, psychological or semiotic point of view would require that we acknowledge not only their conditioning background, but the four different situations in which they can take place, namely, full interaction, reduced interaction, noninteraction and environmental interaction. What follows is a brief discussion that might hopefully generate as many thoughts and research topics as I feel it suggests, differentiating first the interactive situations from the noninteractive one.

A. *Interaction*

Interaction—apart from the various forms distinguishable within a culture as discussed in Chapter 2 and diagrammed in Fig. 2.4—is, from a social point of view, the situation that results from the conscious or unconscious, intended or unintended mutual message exchange and mental or physical activity elicitation between two or more individuals.

Interactional behaviors may take place with or without awareness on the part of both sender and receiver, even though they are engaged in a personal exchange. I may be carrying out a verbal dialogue and I may be aware of whatever words I or my interlocutor are saying to each other, and the tone in which they are said, just as I follow with my eyes his gestural illustration of the looping of an airplane or the heaping dish he put away last night. I reciprocate those linguistic, paralinguistic and kinesic acts with other words, other word modifications and nonspeech sounds, other kinesic acts, and probably some meaningful paralinguistic or kinesic pauses. They may all be perfectly conscious bits of behavior. On the other hand, during that same interactive continuum, when he indicated that he was going to tell me about the airplane and how it was flying, or about how much he ate, I might have shifted my posture slightly in readiness to hear what he had to say; or lifted my eyebrows, eyes wide open, while hearing about the airplane looping; or looked fixedly at his hands, which described the heaping dish. And yet the last three behaviors, elicited in me by his own, occurred most likely completely out of awareness of my part. Among out-of-awareness interactive behaviors are: posture shifts, eye contact, a great number of paralinguistic phenomena and proxemic variations, all of which, however, help maintain, or break, the flow of interaction.

The reaction to the emitter's behavior can also take the form of a mental behavior or activity, not necessarily a sensibly apprehensible one, although the 'externalizers' studied in Chapter 4 are precisely interactive reactions that can be micromomentary and virtually imperceptible. Furthermore, interaction can also occur when both emitter and receiver are unaware of each other, as often happens in the street among pedestrians regulating each other's routing quite unconsciously at times.

B. ***Noninteraction***

Noninteraction, on the other hand, is a situation in which, despite the lack of another interactant and of any external eliciting factors, bodily behaviors (that is, externalizers) are developed which reflect the effect of one's own mental and/or physical activities. Language and paralanguage may occur in dreaming, delirium, imagined interaction, or soliloquium. Still within acoustic behavior, intestinal sounds and bone sounds, which can be produced intentionally to communicate, happen in noninteraction too. Kinesic activity can be triggered by one's thoughts and conscious or unconscious feelings of restlessness, anxiety, fear, exhilaration, sexual arousal, physiological malfunction, etc. The same feelings can produce various types of secretions, as well as dermal changes, like papillary erection and blushing. On the other hand, those bodily behaviors can be elicited in interaction or in what I call below reduced interaction.

A more discriminating semiotic approach, however, clearly reveals that those behaviors elicited by an absent fearful agent, or the sexual arousal reactions triggered by a piece of erotic literature, for instance, differ quite definitely from the behaviors caused by a physiological malfunction, that they actually qualify as something between interaction and noninteraction, as a sort of *one-way interaction* (cf. Chapter 2, section 7) in which the sender cannot become the recipient of any feedback or response, yet he has had his messages encoded and decoded. In fact, some instances of what below is defined as reduced interaction are characterized precisely by that absence of true *inter*-action.

C. *Full interaction*

Ever since I have been preoccupied with the complexity of nonverbal communication in interaction I have felt the need to study separately what I see as a full unhindered exchange and a reduced one. Full unhindered interaction is the situation in which all interactants can make use of the vocal-auditory channel—that is, produce and perceive verbal language and paralanguage—and of the different nonverbal activities in the course of a face-to-face encounter. However, although we seem to think of social life and conversation as developed only among fully-equipped interlocutors, there are many people who constitute a series of subcategories I would subsume under reduced natural conversation, or reduced interaction, while any of the fully-equipped persons can be subject at one time or another to such hindered interactive situations.

D. *Reduced interaction*

By reduced interaction, to which I simply called attention before (Poyatos 1976a, 1980a), I understand the situation in which emission and/or perception of external body behavior, which may or may not take place face-to-face, is impeded in one or more channels by a somatic malfunction, external physical agents or mutual agreement between interactants. I have differentiated twelve forms of reduced interaction:

1. *A linguistic-cultural barrier*, which may totally or partially impede verbal communication without excluding the use of, and often successful coding of, the rest of vocal communication (paralanguage) and visual-tactile communication (kinesics). This does not constitute, however, the foreign language triple linguistic-paralinguistic-kinesic structure. Typically, it is a hybrid combination of three elements which, if observed in the sort of triple transcription suggested in Chapter 5, would reveal the abnormal costructuration of a simplified version of one's own language, and two compensatory elements: a stepped-up paralanguage, usually higher volume and pitch, slower tempo, and frequent laughter; and a stepped-up kinesics of wider movement range and higher movement intensity (parakinesic qualities), more frequent use of what in Chapter 4 are studied as emblems (word-replacing gestures), language markers, deictics, identifiers, and externalizers as well as more frequent eye contact. Thus, in spite of our possible nonverbal fluency with which we try to communicate, many messages are poorly encoded and incorrectly decoded (false decoding).

2. *A sound-carrying opaque obstacle*, which renders cointeractants blind

for communication purposes, language and paralanguage and audible kinesics being still available, plus perhaps olfactory signs. Stepped-up paralanguage is typical and some visual kinesics may also continue to operate in its usual costructuration with language and paralanguage. Or, not having to display kinesics, one may continue a manual task while producing only facial gestures. Synesthesial assumption of visual kinesics is typical. Examples: talking from both sides of a wall or door, from cell to cell in a jail, etc.

3. *A soundproof transparent obstacle*, which renders cointeractants deaf for communication purposes, kinesics (facial, manual, postural, gaze) being still available, plus perhaps olfactory signs. Stepped-up visual kinesics is typical, while language and paralanguage may be stepped-down, but still maintaining the triple structuration. Synesthesial assumption of audible kinesics occurs. Examples: from both sides of a glass.

4. *Excessive distance*, which renders cointeractants deaf or almost deaf, only visual kinesics being available, but with no gaze. Typically, visual kinesics is greatly stepped-up, hand movements are much more inefficient than arm movements, just as facial expression and gaze diminish as distance increases (cointeractants, however, maintaining constant facial orientation to compensate for lack of eye contact). Language and paralanguage, on the other hand, may quite typically not be interrupted just because we are not being heard, as we cannot easily control the natural costructuration of the Basic Triple Structure and at least whisper at a faraway interactant to accompany (this must be noted) mainly emblems (e.g., '¡Wait, I'll join you soon!', 'I'm coming') (cf. Sebeok 1977, in turn quoting Bateson, who corroborates this thought from a phylogenetic point of view [Poyatos 1980a: 239]). This is, of course, the situation for which various language surrogates have been used (e.g., smoke, flags, lights, walkie-talkies). Examples: in large construction sites, from the two fences at both ends of the neutral border space between Spain and Gibraltar, closed until recently.

5. *Excessive noise*, which renders cointeractants deaf for communicative purposes. Typically, kinesics is stepped-up; and, if distance allows it, touch and mutual eye contact are combined with facial and manual gesturing, otherwise hand-and-arm encoding being the only form used. Examples: at airport runways, factories, noisy taverns.

6. *Darkness*, which renders cointeractants blind for communicative purposes, language, paralanguage, audible kinesics (a curtailed Triple Structure), and (if proxemically possible) touch and olfactory 'presence' still available, plus synesthesial assumption of visual kinesics through sound. Naturally, speech-accompanying kinesics may typically continue as an inseparable part of discourse. Examples: when the lights go out, in a dark night.

7. *Social circumstances* which limit communication to whispering, gaze,

and normal or subdued visual kinesics, as when respect for someone else's privacy is prescribed, in situations when normal voice volume is felt incongruent (at a funeral, in church, in a waiting room, theater, restaurant), for secrecy, as interlisteners feedback cues during a group conversation or a performance, or when silence is necessary near a sleeping or ill person.

8. *Agreed-upon silence*, mostly in task-performing circumstances, such as among hunters, or as a prescribed characteristic of a life style, best illustrated by the centuries-old Cistercian sign language (see Barakat 1973).

9. *Blindness*, which blocks off visual kinesics and gaze from the Triple Structure, language, paralanguage and audible and tactual kinesics being still available, and perhaps olfactory signs. The blind person, therefore, misses: (a) visible gestures, manners and postures, (b) very specifically the cointeractant's gestures and eye behaviors with which interactive silences are filled (as discussed in Chapter 6), (c) the distance from his interactants, which cannot be appreciated by the voice or the odor coming from them, (d) social and psychological static cues, such as body-adaptors like clothes and jewelry, (e) signs of other people, and (f); whether they shed tears (unless short distance makes it perceptible either olfactorily or through touch). The most important loss is, of course, the kinesic behavior of his interactants, as it can emphasize, illustrate, contradict or repeat their words or replace them, displaying affects not given away verbally and revealing a number of cultural and personality characteristics. However, although blind persons cannot control the communicative consequences of dress style or the color of jewelry, for instance, they can develop an effective kinesic repertoire by using emotional-displays, illustrators, self-adaptors, alter-adaptors and object-adaptors, as in the case of the born blind person (see Eibl-Eibesfeldt's [1972, 1979a] study of universal expressions of emotion), who, however, can have no synesthesial assumption of visual kinesics, unless he has experienced it previously through active or passive touch.

10. *Deafness*, which blocks off language, paralanguage and audible kinesics, only visual and tactual kinesics remaining in severely curtailed Triple Structure. The loss of audible kinesics cannot compare with the deaf person's inability to perceive language and paralanguage. Not counting his own sign system, he relies (apart from lip reading) on the kinesic behaviors of his interactants, who usually make an effort to make themselves understood. Typically, the deaf person averts his gaze much less than the hearing one, maintaining almost constant eye contact with his cointeractant whose eye contact is also expected. He can properly interpret common emotional states (happiness, sadness, anger, horror), controlling gestures (stop, come, go, look), gestures describing ordinary objects, and manners and postures identifying certain social and personal relationships. However, gross misunderstandings also occur in the emission and reception of meaning between unimpaired people and deaf or deaf-mute people, that is, in the encoding

and decoding of the intended or unintended messages. On the other hand, the born deaf person can have no synesthesial assumption of sound.

Much research can be done, therefore, within nonverbal communication studies, on the perceptual world as well as on the emitting possibilities of both the blind and the deaf, and on how unimpaired people must adapt their interactive fluency when interacting with the blind and the deaf.

11. *Anosmia* and *ageusia* constitute the third pathological form of imposed reduced interaction,[7] as they entail the temporary or chronic absence of the sense of smell and taste respectively (the latter typically accompanying the former), due to various etiological factors (e.g., fracture of the cribiform plate at the base of the skull, through which nerves travel from nose to temporal lobe, nasal polyps, severe burns, after a stroke, or ear surgery, in hypothyroidism, smoking). While anosmia does not affect the emission and perception of language-paralanguage-kinesics (but it prevents their elicitation by chemical signs, say, a verbal comment about someone's perfume) it greatly affects personal and environmental interaction to a level which is not justly recognized, for it affects the perception of

(a) intrainteraction of self-awareness of one's natural or artificial (socially intended) chemical signs,

(b) interaction with others, not being able to perceive natural or artificial (socially intended) chemical signs and messages, the olfactory messages important in nurse/doctor–patient or mother–baby interaction, etc.

(c) the smell and taste of body-adaptors like food and drink (resulting in reported loss of appetite and weight, and even depression and anxiety), of 'morning coffee' (one of the anosmia sufferer's complaints, of such a semiotic-sociocultural significance), of one's or someone else's clothes, and of perfume and cosmetics.

(d) the smells of the objectual environment, such as newly acquired possessions, personal objects, books, magazines of different countries, etc.

(e) the built environment, such as different homes, public places in different cultures (markets, theaters, parks, etc.),

(f) the modified environment, as in residential landscaping (plants, freshly mowed grass that a foreigner in certain cultures may associate with them), and

(g) the natural environment, with the smells and tastes that determine our environmental interaction as defined below.

12. The *telephonic conversation* although similar in its limitations to the opaque-obstacle situation, deserves being set apart as a technologically imposed 'invisible dyad' in which two or more interactants still emphasize, support or contradict their verbal and paralinguistic messages with their kinesic behaviors (rather than disrupting the Basic Triple Structure) and acknowledge the possible lack of visual intermittent kinesic feedback cues by demanding: '¡Hello! ¿¡Are you there?!'

What this cursory view of the interactive consequences of anosmia suggests, what in fact I find its most fascinating aspect from a semiotic-psychological point of view, is the inability of the person to store olfactory and gustatory memories of people, animals, objects and places (not perceived before losing both senses and therefore not even associated synesthesially), thus missing the wonderful temporal dimension of smell and taste with all the deep emotional associations it carries.

E. *Environmental interaction*

Finally, I call environmental interaction the one-way active relationship between us and our environment in terms of the behaviors elicited in us by the mere presence and physical characteristics of nature's elements, the exterior and interior spaces we live in, the objects around us, and, in general, by the total surrounding, whether man-shaped or natural. It is a one-way dependence because, although we do not elicit any changes or behaviors with our behavior, our own behaviors or mental activities can be definitely affected by those seemingly passive elements. A landscape can induce man's exclamations of wonder, can make him open his arms, or run, in 'the great outdoors'; kinesic activity can also be elicited by the large empty room that makes the daydreaming girl dance around it; proxemic changes, by furniture arrangement, the size and shape of a beach or the location of trees in a park.

'Wingspread', the unique Wisconsin home by Frank Lloyd wright at which a 1973 conference on "The Mutual Interaction of People and Their Built Environment" was held, gave me an excellent opportunity to really live that man-environment relationship. As we stepped up or down to different levels on the same floor and walked through narrow, low-ceiling corridors, we were kinesthetically aware of space dimensionality, architectural style and the size of objects, and we could feel better our own comings and goings; intimately related to this kinesthetic involvement was the equally intense visual experience, since, from different locations in the living room, it was possible to actually look at places and objects upstairs and downstairs, while being aware of architectural design, decorative elements and outside landscaping by means of peripheral vision (the through-the-corner-of-an-eye covering of an angle of 90 degrees on each side). And just as that surrounding affected our walking, our looking around, or our sitting behavior, tactile experience was also elicited by the rough brick walls and by the smoothness of wood panels and large conference tables.

10. The Total Conditioning Background of Human Communicative Behavior

After outlining the different forms of bodily behaviors and their coding, interrelationships and qualifying features, the extremely multichannel complexity that may characterize a seemingly trivial social encounter—such as a customer–salesperson interaction supported mainly by the Basic Triple Structure—appears even greater when each behavior is considered against the Total Conditioning Background.[6] If one reads Dittman's excellent review of the application of information theory to personal interaction (Dittman 1972: 19–42) we realize once more that only by acknowledging the influence of the conditioning factors upon the interactive behaviors can we pretend to carry out an exact analysis of those activities and their true significance. Any realistic analysis of behavior, such as the structural work masterfully represented by Kendon (e.g., 1973, 1977, 1980a, 1980b) and Scheflen (1973a, 1973b), the microanalysis of facial expressions best represented by Ekman (1976a, 1977, 1978, 1979) or the sort of triple transcription-description just discussed, would always profit by at least acknowledging the possible influence of the conditioning background on the behaviors under study. The outline below is only a rather crude illustration of this background as we would apply it to kinesics, taken from a paper on kinesics (Poyatos 1977a) and sparing a more elaborate treatment for future work.

According to the biological configuration of people, of which racial characteristics constitute a basic part, postural habits, for instance, are partly determined by skeletal and muscular structures resulting in height, length and articulation of limbs, etc. *Sex*, a primary biological characteristic in itself, is normally identified in standing and sitting habits and in the general gestural behavior, partly conditioned in turn by evolving norms and taboos. *Age* appears as both a biological conditioner and a developmental factor in the gradual acquisition and enrichment of the kinesic repertoire (as well as the lexical and paralinguistic ones); a nine-year-old does not display the socially richer set of gestures, manners and postures a grownup does, although he is biologically endowed with a greater (but not more communicative) bodily articulation, and each one of them can recognize and mock the repertoire of the other. The *physiological state* of cold, heat, fatigue, pain or any momentary malfunction can be reflected in alterations of the usual kinesic habits. Similarly, the *medical state*, or state of health, influences facial expression and general kinesic behavior in varying degrees. *Nutritional habits*, "which may determine the amount of fat accumulated in posturally strategic parts of the body" (Hewes 1955: 1), may also have some traumatizing effects (see Howe 1977 on food cultures and the geography of diseases); in addition, they may result in socioeconomically and culturally different ways of eating postures and manners. As for the *psychological configuration*, not only are kinesic repertoires conditioned by pathological states, but by typical normal personality characteristics and, of course, in given emotional situations. Occasional *emotional states* should be regarded as important conditioners of verbal and nonverbal repertoires; not only in an individually idiosyncratic way, but as resulting in culturally institutionalized behaviors in critical situations, such as a funeral, at which both the grief of the relatives and the expressions of condolence on the part of friends and more distant acquaintances show peculiar patterns; or in passing states of fright, surprise, happiness, etc., also individually or culturally expressed.

There seem to be four basic environmental conditioners to be considered. The *natural environment* may not only determine postural habits according to terrain characteristics (e.g., grassy surfaces, sitting, squat or stance-conditioning terrain in wet or dry climates), by psychologically elicit relaxed postures (a meadow), movements of wonder (a grandiose view), etc. Even more so the *built environment*, such as architecture, landscaping, and town layout, which may condition walking postures (through narrow passages or steep stairs), or sitting habits (ledges, sidewalk curbs, stone benches). As a part, actually, of the built environment, the *objectual environment* conditions kinesic behavior even more noticeably, since it may result in socially-prescribed norms of etiquette, as with the use of chairs and sofas, eating utensils, even the way a pipe is interactionally used; and, of course, in the way tools and machinery are handled. As for the *socioeconomic environment*, it should be considered within this class as summing up different coexisting varieties of the natural, the built and the objectual types, as imposed by socioeconomic factors that certainly affect verbal and nonverbal repertoires in any culture.

Sharing refers to the degree of mutual borrowing (or inherited likeness) of behavior which develops and is socially observable in cohabiting people of either sex, from a couple through a family (whether the nuclear group formed by the two parents and their children, or the extended one composed of those children and their own families) or in specific groups within a society (teenagers, members of an association or a profession, deaf people), as well as within a regional or subcultural group with differentiating verbal and nonverbal peculiarities.

By *cultural patterns* I understand all the explicitly or tacitly prescribed, and consciously or unconsciously professed, evaluation rules and treatment of interpersonal as well as God–Man relationships. *Religious and moral values*, or their relaxation, have always resulted in stricter or looser postural behaviors, for instance (particularly in women, but also in men). So have *relationship and role expectations* with regard to heterosexual relations, relations between friends, employer–employee, doctor–patient, master–servant, husband–wife, etc., and what is expected from specific people of specific status in specific situations. Closely related to this are *etiquette norms*, a concept which should not be erroneously associated with middle and upper classes, since there are definite rules of etiquette among members of the lowest socioeconomic and educational strata, an interesting and revealing topic of cultural or crosscultural research. Due to a series of *esthetic values* rooted in individual sensitiveness and in cultural principles, one does not display certain kinesic behaviors because they are not considered to be in good taste, while certain manner and posture repertoires, for instance, are deemed elegant.

Finally, rather than a rigid class-oriented social classification, I would suggest the following socioeconomic one: the *superrefined* person, of clearly differentiated, even affected verbal and nonverbal repertoires; the *average educated*, whose standard behavior is considered proper by his peers as well as by those not far above or below his level; *the average middle-income employee*, who normally displays verbal, paralinguistic and kinesic repertoires of a 'louder tone', actually identifiable as higher vocal volume, higher vocal and kinesic tension, and greater range and velocity of conversational gestures (beyond cultural peculiarities); *the low-income worker*, who possesses a much more informal and inarticulte repertoire of gestures, manners and postures, congruent with a more limited vocabulary of frequent phonetic and semantic inaccuracies; the *pseudoeducated*, an intriguing subject of research, socioeconomically and educationally astride the educated groups and the rustic or less educated ones; a situation which can be observed as a tense one, as he or she tends to display verbal and nonverbal behaviors that are standard to higher-status people but obviously extrastandard to the user (revealed in mannerisms, in arrogant but poor handling of certain conversational topics, in clothing, etc.); and the *rustic*, diametrically opposite to the refined, and not only unaware of many social rules (although conscious of certain others) but actually conditioned against them, as in the case of the postural habits, related to his work and the type of furniture he uses.

Notes

1. I must confess to the oversimplified presentation of this topic, including a diagram, in two recent articles (Poyatos 1980b, 1982b), due to editorial limitations. For the same reason another article (Poyatos 1981f) contains only an outline of the topic (while the line joining "weight" and "audible" in the diagram is missing) (see a comprehensive discussion of language and nonverbal systems in interaction in Roy Harris' journal [Poyatos 1983a]).

2. One of the nurses in two of my nonverbal communication courses, Mrs. Anne Merrythew, wrote a very interesting exploration of odor discrimination. Besides quoting some well-known articles on olfaction (e.g., Wiener 1968a, 1968b), she interviewed other nurses and reported on their description of more than fifty odors given by as many medical disorders or offending substances to which the medical team is exposed. She described two intriguing phenomena reported to her: the smell of fever and the smell of impending death. She also reviewed some of the problems that hamper a wider use of professional olfactory identification: infrequency of some odors, inadequate labels, unavailability of the source in some areas (e.g., freshly-mowed clover, associated with liver failure), the professional's own condition (e.g., poor acuity), unawareness due to prolonged exposure to an odor, and the patient's use of perfume, breath lozenges, etc. (Merrythew 1982, unpublished).

3. Some authors have mentioned the earliest version of this chart (e.g., Harper *et al.*, 1978) from a paper read at the 1974 International Congress of Semiotics, of very delayed proceedings (Chatham, Eco, Klinkenberg 1979). It was perhaps the valuable incentive of the greatly missed Albert Scheflen, with whom I discussed the theoretical implications of an earlier version

(Poyatos 1972a, 1975e), that I continued to use it both in publications and as a lecture handout to illustrate at a glance the costructuration of bodily systems in the coding of messages. I heeded Sebeok's personal comments against its earlier title, 'Total Body Communication', since it represents only 'external', sensible signs. The chart does not include synesthesial decoding, and the examples are only the few space allowed.

4. I have offered the ideas in section 6 and 7 in earlier work (Poyatos 1976a, 1979b), as well as those in section 8 (Poyatos 1981f).

5. There are, of course, other pathological forms of reduced interaction that in the context, for instance, of doctor/nurse–patient relationships would warrant an interesting classification precisely because of the further risks involved in the improper management of situations like diabetic coma, unconsciousness due to anesthesia, to an overdose of sleeping pills or a cerebral vascular accident. Aside from the undoubtedly interesting semiotic aspect of the encoding (by the well person) and decoding (by the traumatized person) in such situations, there is a deep dimension in that relationship in which the person is unable to cerebrate and yet "it is possible [for the medical team] to implant negatives into the subconscious mind and conceivably into the spiritual being of the patient at the time of anesthesia or unconsciousness [. . .] affected by those things which occur while he is not conscious" (Reed 1979: 99).

6. Like the relationships indicated in Fig. 2.1, the conditioning variables against which any physical or mental activities must be viewed for a truly critical analysis would require a large piece of research by itself. Here I am once more using outlines included in some recent papers (Poyatos 1977a, 1980a), although the chart and/or comments (with slight changes) have been published since 1972).

4

Interactive and Noninteractive Verbal and Nonverbal Behaviors: Categories, Forms, and Functions

1. The Researcher's Need to Classify and Label Behaviors

AT this crucial point in the development of nonverbal communication studies within and across so many disciplines, there is still a great need to concretize which behaviors we are observing and analyzing, how those behaviors should be classified on a permanent basis (regardless of personality or culture) by means of reasonably identifiable groups to which the researcher could resort according to his own strategies, and how to refer verbally to each of those attitudes and activities when we need to describe them collectively and individually, talk or write about them, and isolate them for analysis.[1]*

If we consider the message-generating systems that are put in motion between sender and receiver on the somatic level, that is, strictly those originated in the body—particularly those outlined as external body communication in Fig. 3.3, or those which serve as its extensions immediately attached to it (e.g., clothes) or are manipulated by it (e.g., conversational props and tools); if, furthermore, we understand the ways in which the messages thus generated are encoded and decoded, it becomes necessary to establish a basic frame of reference that will acknowledge, along with the coding principles: the relationships of the systems to verbal language (after all, the core of human communication), the relationships among themselves, and the basic functions which each system can perform in everyday communication, or in noninteractive situations, beyond those of modifiers, contextual, and self-regulatory and interactional agents (Poyatos 1980a).

In a much cited and already classic paper, Ekman and Friesen (1969, 1981), inspired partly by Efrón (1941), established a series of categories within nonverbal behaviors, although by nonverbal they referred only to "any movement of position of the face and/or the body." However, it is my belief that the term nonverbal—given its doubtful legitimacy—should not be

* Superscript numbers refer to Notes at end of chapter.

exclusive of kinesics because many of the functions ascribed to their nonverbal categories in their scheme are perfectly common to other verbal and nonverbal systems.

Seeking a way of systematically calling each form of interactive or noninteractive behavior by its own name—even though in many instances a single act, say, a gesture, may show characteristics represented by two or more communicative systems—I gratefully borrowed Ekman and Friesen's terminology in such a way that it could be applied to all modes of external body communication, but with the following modifications:

(a) While some discourse illustrators (a pictographic description of a woman's body, a pointing gesture), and all self-adaptors (a hair-preening gesture, a cough-muffling one), alter-adaptors (a hug, a handshake), and object-adaptors (fidgeting with crumbs, clasping a chair's arm) are still recognized as exclusively kinesic behaviors, others, as will be seen, are acknowledged as being susceptible of multiple coding; in other words, not only kinesically, but by one or more of the other modes, namely paralanguage, proxemics, chemical, dermal, and thermal reactions, and immediately in contact with the body (or as extensions of it), by objectual expressions, that is, body-adaptors. This latter system reveals that the classification of the so-called nonverbal categories, as formulated by Ekman and Friesen, refers actually to *interactive functional categories*, to what nonverbal behaviors can do in the course of a social encounter, while the various forms or *systems* of somatic and extrasomatic nonverbal activities stand aside as the arsenal from which we draw in order to perform each or several of the possible functions. There is one point, however, at which the functional categories and the systems overlap completely, object-adaptors. An object-adaptor such as the handling of a pencil as we talk is in itself a 'function' in relation to the objects that can be used for such function, while the handling of the pencil belongs to the 'system' of object-adaptors we can resort to in order to give form to an affect-display, an illustrator or a conversational regulator. It can be pointed out at this point that all the nonverbal categories are represented, as illustrated in Fig. 4.1, by the contact with or manipulation of objects; thus, the category called object-adaptors overlaps with each of the others.

(b) As for their relationships with verbal language, I would like, first, to extend Ekman and Friesen's functions (which they sum up under "usage") to other nonverbal behaviors as well; secondly, use "contextual" to refer to an unrelated act not affecting verbal language, "anticipate" as 'predicting' the succeeding behavior, and "replace" as "substitute for".

(c) The shared, idiosyncratic or zero-decoding situations one may encounter in the interpretation of the message, and the arbitrary, imitative and intrinsic sign-meaning relationships, are identified for any systems and categories, as are their conscious or unconscious encoding.

(d) The *self-regulatory* function within the sender's own behavioral repertoire (conditioning his own activities) and the *interactional* one between the participants (regulating the flow of the transaction) are also applied to all categories.

(e) Their *costructuration* within the speaker's or the listener's behaviors, their intensity and their duration are emphasized as the ever-present qualifying features whenever interactive or noninteractive activities are triggered.

It should be clear that we must not necessarily refer to speaker and listener or auditor, as is customary in linguistic or linguistically oriented works, as we would be taking a rather unrealistic stand, but to 'sender' and 'receiver', or 'cointeractants' or 'participants', thus acknowledging all the communicative channels made possible, in various degrees, by the human body, as was outlined in the previous chapter. Any behaviors displayed consciously or unconsciously in co-presence, even random ones, play specific roles. They elicit or not subsequent behaviors from either interactor and, therefore, condition the structuration of that behavioral exchange.

The table in Fig. 4.1, 'Interactive and Noninteractive Categories of Bodily Nonverbal Behaviors,' schematizes the theoretical and methodological framework showing by which systems each behavioral category is displayed, and those combinations that do not seem to occur.

If we acknowledge verbal language as the main vehicle of social interaction, we must first consider (a) those behaviors that stand closer to it, *emblems*, as they truly substitute for words, followed by (b) those that are displayed as multichannel bodily accompaniments to discourse, *illustrators*, making it a rich behavioral complex far beyond just lexical expression; (c) those that reflect mental activities and reactions to external referents without accompanying words but reacting to them at the most, *externalizers*; (d) four formal categories: *self-adaptors, alter-adaptors, body-adaptors* and *object-adaptors*; (e) the category that actually may comprise or imbue all the others in greater or lesser degree, *emotional displays*, whether or not they accompany language; and finally (f) the ones that help carry out the back-and-forth flow of the interpersonal transaction, *regulators*, which in fact constitute an all-encompassing class, for they could very well include the previous ones as well as the other four interactive types of behaviors.

Within illustrators I have reached the following organization, in addition to having modified some of Ekman and Friesen's labels, and added a few new categories, as will be indicated: the behaviors that are truly inherent in discourse, *language markers*; those which point in space or time, *deictics*; the ones that refer the two basic dimensions of social life (in fact, of culture), space and time, *space markers* and *time markers*; those referring to the two basic activities, sound and movement, *echoics, kinetographs* and *kinephonographs*; those which represent the physical form of their referents, *pictographs*; those which have as referents concepts and qualities of both

INTERACTIVE CATEGORIES OF BODILY NONVERBAL BEHAVIORS

		Para-language	Kinesics	Proxemics	Chemical	Dermal	Thermal	Objectual	Non-interac.
	Emblems	X	X	(X)	(X)		(X)		X
Illustrators	Language markers	X	X	(X)	(X)	(X)		X	X
Illustrators	Space markers	X	X					X	X
Illustrators	Time markers	X	X					X	X
Illustrators	Deictics	X	X					X	X
Illustrators	Pictographs		X					X	X
Illustrators	Echoics	X	X					X	X
Illustrators	Kinetographs		X					X	X
Illustrators	Kinephonographs	X	X					X	X
Illustrators	Ideographs	X	X					X	X
Illustrators	Event tracers	(X)	X					X	X
Illustrators	Identifiers	X	X					(X)	X
	Externalizers	X	X	X	X	X	X	X	X
	Self-adaptors		X					X	X
	Alter-adaptors		X					X	
	Body-adaptors		X		X			X	X
	Object-adaptors		X					X	X
	Regulators	X	X	X	X	X	X	X	X
	Emotional-displays	X	X	X	X	X	X	X	X

Coding: Conscious – Unconscious
Sign-meaning relationship: Arbitrary – Iconic
Decoding: Shared – Idiosyncratic – False decoding – Zero decoding
Relationship to self and others: Modifier – Context – Self-regulatory

Relationships to verbal and nonverbal activities:
Contextual
Replacing
Confirming
Emphasizing
Repeating
Contradicting

Location:
Preceding
Simultaneous
Succeeding

Qualifying features:
Costructuration
Duration
Intensity

FIG. 4.1. Interactive and Noninteractive Categories of Bodily Nonverbal Behavior.

sensible and intelligible experiences, *identifiers*; references to thoughts, *ideographs*; and references to events, *event tracers*.

I have always chosen the terms keeping in mind—for it is not done often enough in research—foreign fellow researchers, readers, and translators, thus trying to minimize problems with which we are all too familiar. What follows, then, is a discussion of the nineteen categories of nonverbal behaviors that can be easily identified by the student of human behavior and social interaction.

2. Emblems

Emblems is the term used originally by Efrón (1941) to refer only to arbitrarily coded gestures, but lately it has been defined more widely by Ekman (1976b, 1977), Ekman and Friesen (1969, 1972), Johnson, Ekman and Friesen (1975), who include iconic gestures as well, and Scherer (1975), with whom I seem to coincide in referring also to paralinguistic emblems, called "paralinguistic emblems" by him, an example of which can be a narial ingression of impatience signifying '¡It's late!'. "Emblematic movements", differentiated by Ekman (1972) within illustrators as movements which illustrate and cooccur with verbal statements, are included here, since emblems are not the only behaviors that share the characteristics of other categories.

Although I refer the reader to the work on emblems by Ekman, I wish to add but a few thoughts and elaborate further on their inciting ideas in an attempt to foster the interdisciplinary fieldwork and theoretical possibilities suggesed by emblems.

Coding, complementarity, economy, and lexicality

Since emblems are individual, group, or culture-specific substitutes for words, their coding can be *arbitrary*, as most of them are (/Okay/, /Yes/, /No/; /Money/ by rubbing thumb and forefinger in many cultures; clicking the tongue + snapping the side of the ear and winking, to signify 'Let's drink' among Russian men),[2] *imitative*, mostly iconic (e.g., /The check, please/, by simulating writing on the palm of the hand; /I'll punch you/, by showing a fist); but possibly echoic (if a paralinguistic form like the whirring of an airplane replaces the verbal signifier), or *intrinsic* (punching something to signify punching, or swallowing by a nurse who cannot instruct a deaf patient audibly).

It would be interesting to investigate those seemingly intrinsic emblems (or other nonverbal categories, for that matter) which, only for those who are aware of their origin, may have a truly iconic value, already lost for many. Such is, for instance, the Caucasian greeting between two men in which they pat each other on both hips, a kinesic residue of a truly intrinsic ritual: checking each other for arms.[3]

As for the sign-meaning relationship, most of them have *shared* meaning because they are part of a true, mostly kinesic, lexicon typical of a group (longshoremen, hunters, doctors and nurses in the operating room), a culture (the single or double head tilt/rocking of agreement, equivalent to 'Uh-hu', used in India), or many cultures (/¡Stop!/). However, it is important to consider, when analyzing a culture, perhaps while collecting data, or simply while being exposed to it seeking true 'cultural fluency', that this sign-meaning relationship may be totally *idiosyncratic*, that is, the spur-of-the-moment creation of the inventive 'speaker-mover'; which in quite a few cases must account for the origin of certain emblems, gradually learned by others and borrowed by a growing number of people. Therefore, the idiosyncratic coding will usually result in 'zero-decoding', although, again, even a personal invention might be perfectly decoded by one or more receivers because of the specific quality of the emblem or because of their own perceptiveness. One must but agree with Ekman (cf. 1976b) on the necessary nonambiguity of emblems in order for them to qualify as such, even if we see (or hear) them out of context.

Emblems are used singly much more often than in groups, although one can use several emblems in situations when silence is necessary, or while communicating with someone because, as Kendon (1980a) puts it, the speech channel may be already occupied, as when trying to communicate kinesically with someone who approaches us while we are engaged in a telephonic conversation with someone else.

Emblems can precede words, coincide with them, replace them altogether or immediately follow them. When they replace verbal language they can be said to be *pure emblems* from a semiotic point of view, since the signified is not encoded through any other communicative systems, as contrasted with occasions in which we duplicate what is said verbally.

However, the combination of emblematic and verbal expressions of identical meaning are so typical of the more gesturing cultures, and of very extrovert, talkative and expressive persons, that what seems to be redundant is often precisely '*complementary*', as was discussed earlier, because it adds information about the speaker's personality, or about that specific culture, defining it as a very kinesic culture; and that is *not* redundant. On the other hand, if the kinesic abstraction does not have a verbal representation it would not qualify as an emblem, but only as an illustrator used while speaking.

Whether kinesic (a beckoning gesture) or paralinguistic ('¡Mmmmm!' with an intonation which can only mean '¡Delicious!'), emblems, out of *expressive economy*, avoid often a periphrastic expression, as, for instance, a shoulder shrug + raised brows + unilateral mouth distension, /¡Oh, well

. . . !/, or an obscene gesture of sexual invitation, which in so many cultures translate a whole sentence. In other words, a single emblematic gesture makes it possible to express something which is totally unacceptable in audible language, and even makes it possible 'to express something' difficult to put in words, yet perfectly understood by the interactants.

The tendency to emblematic communication reveals, therefore, for the linguist as much as for the semiotician, that economy of expression when the kinesic of kinesic-paralinguistic emblem is intended as an expedient substitute for a lengthy verbal construct. Maybe because of lack of time, or because we simply do not care to say things to someone.

These last thoughts link with the concept of *lexicality* (Poyatos 1977a: 201–202), that is, grammaticality, an inherent characteristic of emblems, and other nonverbal constructs which can also act as the subject of a sentence (/I/), its verb (/I ran/), its predicate when the emblem completes the sentence ('¡I am /up to here!/'), its circumstantial complement ('We can go on that icy road, but /slowly/'), and even as a conjunction (the magician raises his hand with forefinger pointing upward, /¡and!/, when he is about to produce the rabbit from his top hat).

Interactional modes

Emblems can be displayed either in *interaction* or, as any other nonverbal category, in *noninteraction* situations. In the latter case it would be only during inner speech, during soliloquy and in hallucinations, since emblems "are most often deliberately used with the conscious intent to send a particular message to other persons" (Ekman 1976b: 4)—and very characteristically during *reduced interactions* (see Chapter 3), which, briefly outlined here, are: when verbal language cannot be heard because it is impeded by excessive distance, which, however, may still allow visual emblematic communication; by excessive ambient noise (cf. Kendon 1980), which can be only a momentary channel blockage, immediately bringing into play the compensatory quality of kinesics, a characteristic associated to its lexicality; by various medical problems in doctor/nurse–patient interaction; by a soundproof transparent obstacle and by deafness or muteness, which allows only kinesic forms, just as a sound-carrying opaque obstacle transmits only language and paralinguistic emblems; when verbal language must not be used in order to accomplish a task, as in any agreed-upon situation (e.g., among hunters, in the operating room, in a game of charades) or when coping with certain circumstances. In the case of organic impairment in deaf and deafmute persons, serious research should be done which would determine their tendency to improvise emblematic movements and elaborate a lexicon of their own, as well as the tendency of those who interact with them to seek gestural expressions to substitute for verbal messages that would go undecoded otherwise.

As for the issue of emblem qualifiers, that is, costructuration, intensity and duration, besides those mentioned by Johnson, Ekman, and Friesen (1975), they have been discussed earlier.

Encoding channels

Following the table of nonverbal categories, the encoding of emblems can be:

(a) *Paralinguistic*, which include so many emblematic utterances among the so-called paralinguistic alternants (Chapter 5) that they deserve a separate paper. They can be classified according to their phonetic peculiarities and/or their meaning and interactive functions, and they share the same problems of other alternants, mainly the lack of verbal labels to refer to them and phonemic and written/orthographic representation. Among others are: beckoning alternants like the bilabial click (kiss sound) used with waiters in Mexico, or the bilabial stop + apico-alveolar fricative ('¡Pss!'), the apico-alveolar fricative ('¡Ss!'), and the apico-alveolar fricative + dental stop ('¡St!'), all used in Spain both to summon a waiter in unsophisticated places and to call a woman's attention in the street; the apico-alveolar click ('¡Tz!') of sympathy used in Spain, the same click followed by an audible pharyngeal ingression to indicate 'I wish to talk' instead of interrupting the speaker, and a double '¡Tz-tz!' as a negation; the latero-velar click equivalent to '¡Out!' when addressing a Spanish dog, but also, as in other cultures, to '¡Go!' when addressing a horse; '¡Uh-uh!' for negation and 'Uh-hu' for affirmation, etc.

(b) *Kinesic*, as are most emblems, either with the face (raised brows + wide-open eyes, for unexpected surprise; headnod for 'Yes' and headshake for 'No' in many cultures), with the hands, as most emblems are coded (/Okay/, /Stop/, /Finished/, /Victory/), the shoulders (the shrug + raised brows for 'I don't know' and the shrug+ pressed lips for 'I don't care'), or the whole body (/¡I'm beat!/), either in single 'action units' (Ekman 1976b) or in true emblematic constructs, as in the above examples.

(c) *Kinesic-paralinguistic*, such as the moaning sound accompanying fingertips-kiss, meaning '¡Superb!', '¡Delicious!'; the twist of the raised hand + eye contact + bilabial '¡Ps!' + head toss, used as a street distance greeting in New Guinea's Highland, Central, and coastal areas; the hand gesture for 'So-so' accompanied by a simultaneous 'Mmmm'; the French '¡Oh, la la!'; shaking of the hand accompanied by a whistling of the same length in Spain to indicate, for instance, an astronomical price; the very French throaty 'Ooh' with raised brows and open mouth, typical of the late Chevalier to signify '¡Magnifique!'; the 'Mmmm' alternant accompanied by frowning instead of verbal '¡I don't really know!'; the apico-alveolar click 'Tz' followed by the negation 'Uh-uh'.

(d) Beyond paralanguage and kinesics, which are, along with verbal language, the components of the Basic Triple Structure of human communication, *proxemics* may act as an emblem when, for instance, we quickly draw closer to someone to indicate 'We're together'.

(e) *Chemically*, the answer to '¿What did you eat?' can be offering one's breath; while, as an uncontrollable chemical emblem, tears might complete the sentence 'And then I ——' (cried), although according to the definition of emblem as unambiguous one could certainly argue that in this instance the possible emblem would not have a direct verbal translation.

(f) *Thermally* it is possible that a rapid raise in body temperature in response to a verbal or kinesic suggestion in an intimate situation might be the unequivocal emblem for an affirmative answer or an invitation to a still more intimate behavior, although this type can be ambiguous and require a context, which would then contradict the original definition.

Development and culture

As with some other nonverbal categories, the abundance of emblems may be due to the individual's lack of sufficient verbal facility, but this does not seem to have been investigated either. On the one hand, the tendency to expressive economy alluded to cannot be underestimated, since it can be an idiosyncratic gesture that must not be taken for a cultural one too hastily. Ekman's thoughts about the ontogeny of emblems (Ekman 1977: 46) should also incite researchers in child psychology, both normal and abnormal, as well as anthropologists. Ekman refers to the child's "limitations in capacity, needs, and problems in communicating with a caretaker", to the ages when emblems are obviously being incorporated into the child's repertoire, and to whether they are specifically taught. I would also suggest the cultural perspective, in order to observe whether the more articulate peoples possess also a wider lexicon of emblems at an earlier age. Then there is the social environment, for there must necessarily be interesting differences between the repertoires of slum children, who interact intensively, and those children who are, for instance, among schoolmates daily and who have fewer social contacts outside the school and the family. The difference, I would hypothesize, must not be necessarily in the volume of the repertoires but in the kinesic messages themselves. At any rate, emblems, as any other interactive nonverbal behavior, must be seen as part of the Basic Triple Structure language-paralanguage-kinesics. The topic of nonverbal developmental behavior—a crucial area headed within kinesics (the only one researched so far) by von Raffler-Engel (1981)—is, however, more relevant with regard to conversational illustrators, as they constitute the most important elements in the person's interactive fluency.

Apart from the more recent work on emblems by Ekman and his coworkers, in which they describe the method used with informants for establishing the emblem repertoire required for cultural or crosscultural research (Johnson, Ekman, and Friesen 1975; Ekman 1976b, and the resulting film), a number of descriptions referred to specific cultures can be found in the existing gestures inventories, such as those by Efrón (1941) on Jews and Italians in New York, Saitz and Cervenka (1962) for Colombia and the United States, some by Green (1968) for Spain, Barakat (1973) for the Arab world, Wylie (1977) for France, Creider for Kenia (1977), Sparhawk (1978) for Iran, Morris, Collett *et al.* (1979) for a number of European countries and Tunisia (in fact, the first rigorous attempt to draw a true kinesic atlas),[4] and Johnson (1982) for Japan.

The main aspects of emblems have been outlined, and yet a very substantial volume, to say the least, could be written as a worthy dissertation from one or many different points of view. Take, for instance, the intercultural communication functions of emblems, their relevance for the acquisition of cultural or crosscultural fluency, and the number of grave errors one can make, either by showing an emblem form from one's repertoire in another cultural context (e.g., displaying the hitchhiking upward thumb in Ghana, where it is an emblematic sexual invitation, and the subsequent understandable misinterpretation on the part of the Ghanaian) or by failing to decode another culture's emblems altogether (e.g., the salesgirl I saw recently in Canada who would not understand the Hispanic customer's index-finger-on-the-lower-eyelid gesture meaning 'Just looking' because he could not say it in English, a clear example of *remedial emblematic communication* in a situation of imposed reduced interaction).

What is certain is that, for whatever purpose in intercultural communication, foreign-language teaching should include basic lists (and not so basic at higher levels of instructions), that is, repertoires of emblems. The language teacher is not simply teaching the business person, for instance, to speak but to communicate, a much more complex and realistic endeavor, and to communicate is also 'to move' that foreign language. Other nonverbal categories would, of course, follow the teaching of emblems.

ILLUSTRATORS

Illustrators constitute another category, or rather, series of categories, defined by Ekman (1976b, 1977) and Ekman and Friesen (1969) as movements tied directly to speech, serving to illustrate what is being expressed verbally, or substitute for either or both, in other words, either making up for the limitations of verbal language or duplicating its message, as is culturally characteristic of Latin or Arab speakers. In my study of interactive illustrators I have constantly faced the fact that, as with emblems, they are not limited to the kinesic repertoire simultaneously, preceding or following speech, for although it is true that the majority of them are movements, they can actually be coded by other external bodily systems to illustrate tangible (a person, an object) or intangible (an idea) referents.

While Efrón (1941) distinguished five illustrators: 'batons' (here called language markers), 'ideographs', 'deictic movements', 'spatial movements', and 'kinetographs', Ekman and Friesen (1969) added 'pictographs', and later (1972) 'rhythmic movements' and 'emblematic movements'. To both classifications I found convenient to add time markers, echoics, kinephonographs, and identifiers. What follows is a survey of illustrators which could be much expanded, particularly as regards crosscultural differences and similarities.

The topic of language illustrators is, not only from the point of view of 'communication', but from that of 'language'—whether it be the language of the linguist, the foreigh-language teacher, the philosopher, the psychologist and the psychopathologist, the anthropologist, the student of narrative and dramaturgic literature, and the semiotician—a fascinating inter- and multidisciplinary subject of research. It is only by recognizing to what extent illustrators are integral elements of discourse that the 'living language' can be appreciated fully.

3. Language Markers

Language markers are conscious or unconscious behaviors which punctuate and emphasize the acoustic and grammatical succession of words and phrases according to their location and relevance in the speech stream and coincide with written punctuation symbols, which are grammatical and attitudinal themselves. They have a semantic function only inasmuch as they identify grammatical functions, not the conceptual or affective contents, which are identified by other nonverbal behaviors. While language markers have so far been observed and defined as kinesic only, close analysis of their occurrence reveals that other bodily behaviors simultaneous with speech truly mark language, particularly paralanguage, thus completing the basic language-paralanguage-kinesics communicative structure. Furthermore, discourse is also marked, although in a more limited way, by proxemics, and even certain chemical and dermal reactions at times, while object-adaptor behaviors are, of course, part of kinesics. I will outline the various forms of language markers.

A. *Kinesic language markers*

Kinesic language markers, called 'batóns' by Efrón (1941), include here Ekman and Friesen's (1977) 'underliners' and Birdwhistell's (1970) 'kinesic markers'. They are intended or out-of-awareness movements and positions which enhance the syntactical functions of words, punctuate them much as we do in writing (thus giving punctuation visual and audible form), and coincide with paralinguistic features of identical function. Their function, then, is primarily grammatical (i.e., syntactical and morphological), although the 'full' semantic value of a word or combination of words is given, of course, by their paralinguistic and kinesic coactivities and any other coocurrent behaviors—which only proves the coherence of the verbal and nonverbal channels. The following grammatical markers can be differentiated:

Pronominal markers—which, as will be seen, belong better among 'deictics'—are typically signalled by pointing with the hand(s), with a multiple head movement involving gaze (pointing even toward an absent human or nonhuman grammatical subject or object) and a tilt of the head, with a head tilt alone, or with a trunk-and-head orientation shift toward the referent. In many cultures chin-pointing toward another person for 'he', 'she', 'them', etc., is too familiar or low-class usage, never part of a more formal or refined interactive style. Head-pointing is accompanied by gaze-pointing when indicating our single cointeractant, but when two or more are present eye-contact may be (not necessarily but typically) maintained with the main addressee while the head points at a third party (cf. Jespersen's [1933] "pronouns of pointing").

In any case, it must be emphasized that kinesic pronominal markers, however subtle (from gaze shift to a head-and-orientation pointer) are practically always present as part of the verbal-paralinguistic-kinesic structure. A frame-by-frame study of speech reveals even almost imperceptible head nods coinciding with pronouns. However, the more conspicuous ones are those hand movements classified as another nonverbal category, deictics, which can point at both present and absent referents, an important quality apparently not noted by Birdwhistell. A typical instance of kinesic pronominal marker would be (John, Tom and Mary are conversing, and Tom addresses John): 'You should take her/slight head tilt toward Mary while looking at John/to the movies because I think she'll/head and gaze turned toward her/love that/very light head nod/movie'.

The preceding example serves to illustrate another function of the same markers, that of stress markers, since 'her' (Mary) and 'that' (movie) can carry also the two primary stresses which would be marked by the same object pronoun and demonstrative adjective.

One can classify pronominal markers, then, as deictics—that is, movements that seem to locate the referent in space, point, since many other nonpointing gestures should be understood as 'externalizers'—and as including 'pluralization markers' (cf. Jespersen's [1933] "pronouns of totality"), studied separately by Birdwhistell (1970) but which are included in the present classification subsuming both pronouns and adjectives.

Personal pronouns: we, they, you guys, we all, all of us, etc. (e.g., 'We can all/sweeping inclusive hand movement/contribute'); *demonstrative pronouns or adjectives*: those, these (e.g., 'These/inclusive glance and head sweep/are the best'); *identity pronouns or adjectives*: the same ('Two years later I went there and met the same man/short up-and-down hand movement, typically joining thumb and first finger in many cultures/'); *difference*: other, another /¿Another cup?/ without words, or accompanying the verbal expression; 'If he takes one glass, he'll take another and another/repeating the hand-circling movement away from the body/'); *totality pronouns or adjectives* (Jespersen [1933]); all, both, every, each, no ('Every girl/double hand up-and-down movement/he met fell in love with him'); *possessive pronouns or adjectives*: theirs, their, ours, our, yours, your (e.g., 'You can take our/sweeping pointing finger/bags now'); *indefinite pronouns or adjectives*: everybody, either, neither, someone, anyone, any (e.g., 'Either/pointing at two referents in succession/'; 'Any/head or hand pointing sweep/of them could do it') which could be only kinesic, thus qualifying as an emblem, in situations of impeded verbal expression, or as might happen in a depressed or paining hospital patient; *reflexive pronouns*: myself, yourself, ourselves, etc., performed like personal pronouns but often more emphatically; *reciprocal pronouns*: one another, each other (e.g., 'They did it to each/double pointing sweep/other'). It is clear, however, that if other elements of the sentence are not identified as kinesic markers (prepositions, conjunctions or adverbs), the inclusion of only these is not fully justified, for they would qualify as other types of nonverbal behaviors. Again, each of those pronoun markers can be stress markers as well, as was illustrated above.

On the other hand, the movement indicating *pluralization* is not determined by the plural pronoun or adjective, but by the spatial relationship described in the sentence. For instance, '/Several people spoke/' would be a hand-sweep movement, but '/There are several people in that car/' would not. So, we cannot classify 'several' as a pluralization marker in itself. However, if we include 'several' within another category, 'space markers', when it defines a spatial relationship, the other 'several', marked by other movements but not a hand-sweep, would be simply an 'identifier' expressing quantity. Thus, the sweep of the hand for plurals is actually a 'deictic', since it points at either present or absent referents.

I might add that Birdwhistell differentiated pronominal markers (which, as has been seen, are also adjectives), pluralization markers, verboid markers, area markers, and manner markers, while nouns, adjectives, adverbs, prepositions, and conjunctions do not appear in his classification. Yet, *nouns* appear under most 'illustrators', *adjectives* appear as 'identifiers' of quality and quantity, a great number of *adverbs* and adverbial constructions appear also as 'identifiers' of manner ('However' being an emphatically marked one, usually with a raised hand and typically dominated by its quality as 'identifier'), as 'time markers', as 'space markers', etc. *Prepositions* (mainly 'but') and *conjunctions* (mainly 'and') could have been clearly identified, since mainly facial and hand gestures (along with paralinguistic features) accent those linking words, quite typically coinciding with equally typical stress, pitch, volume and length features, enhancing their syntactical value and, naturally, functioning as syntactical language markers, the principal feature for a kinesic or paralinguistic act to qualify as a language marker.

The relevance of pronominal markers is still greater than it appears at first sight from a sociocultural point of view, for they determine not only cultural characteristics of pointing gestures (the North American head-points with a nod while the average Spaniard tosses the head back slightly, a trait more accentuated in lower-class speakers).

B. *Paralinguistic-kinesic stress markers*

In the sentence 'My *wife* doesn't think *he* did it, but *I* do', there is a secondary stress on *wife* and primary stresses on *he* and *I*. Stresses are characterized by higher pitch and volume and slightly tenser articulation and longer syllabic length. By themselves those paralinguistic features are truly markers that enhance the fact that 'my wife' (not everybody, nor the two of us) thinks that way, that she thinks he (among other possible suspects) did it, and that I myself (unlike her) think he did. One can speak the same words in an unspirited, monotone voice, devoid of markers, and one could also (e.g., in a deep depressive state) strip them of any kinesic accompaniments; or use paralinguistic markers but not any conspicuous kinesic behaviors. Under normal circumstances, however, there are kinesic stress markers, discussed first by Birdwhistell (1970), that would coincide with phonetic stresses on the same syllables, 'wife', 'he', and 'I', as an orientation head movement toward her (if she is present) or a brow raise with 'I'. The paralinguistic-kinesic compound appears, therefore, as the coherent construct perfectly costructured with verbal utterances as part of the Basic Triple Structure.

C. *Punctuation markers*

Both paralinguistic and kinesic markers truly punctuate the verbal sentence as clearly as we punctuate a written one. Again, a normal-speed or frame-by-frame analysis of a videotaped conversation reveals the precise correlation of paralinguistic and kinesic markers with written punctuation symbols, after all invented in an attempt to represent or evoke the reality of speech. Punctuation symbols represent audible features either overriding ([!] for volume, [" "] for emphasis) or momentary ([,] [:] [.] for juncture pitch registers), and they all have their corresponding kinesic markers. In the study of punctuation offered in Chapter 8, where I discuss, among other aspects of it, the advantages and limitations of the present systems as nonverbal communication (Poyatos 1981d), I have differentiated between syntactical ([,] [;] [:] [( )]), quantitative ([--] [. . .]), and qualitative ([!] [?]).

Although the realization of each punctuation marker can be said to belong in "a *range* of behaviors which are recognizable as the expected configuration" (Scheflen 1964: 317), within which range different speakers will act according to culture, gender, personality, status, health, and so on, it is a fact, nevertheless, that there are kinesic-paralinguistic markers, and that the written punctuation symbols evoke precisely nonverbal features. In other words, they have nonverbal functions. Therefore, both the silent reader of a novel or play or the enacting reader-performer face not only interesting semiotic-communicative problems (cf. Poyatos 1977b, 1981a, 1982a), but inter-cultural ones as well inherent in a translated text. The three types of punctuation elements are represented by language markers as follows:

Syntactical: [,] ('No, it's not important, but it has to be done', with momentary lower-register + head movement arrest with first comma, lower and sustained with the second comma), [:] ('The four rules are: first ——', falling-pitch + juncture + head-movement arrest and brow raise with colon), [,] [,] [,] [( )] or [- -] ('One day, before we knew each other, he ——', lower-volume-and-pitch juncture at commas + overriding lower pitch between them + lower-volume-and-pitch + movement arrest at interpolating symbols + overriding lower pitch between them).

Quantitative: [---] [. . .] ('But I thought . . .', lower/higher-pitch juncture and breathing pause + lower/higher brow raise + open mouth and eyes, all indicating suspension).

Qualitative: [" "] ('We said we "would think it over", you know?', slightly-raised pitch and head, with/without marking quotation with both hands), [!] ('¡I'm so glad you came!', overriding higher pitch and volume for loud voice; or lower volume and pitch when [!] indicates intensity, as in '¡I don't want you here!'), [?] ('¿Are you coming?', raising pitch, volume and brow toward interrogation end).

Again, even the 'expected configuration' mentioned earlier will be different for each semantic nuance and for each situation, and I do not pretend to give the above illustrations as a rigid classification, for the topic of punctuation markers would need much more elaborate investigation.

D. *Kinesic paralanguage markers*

The functions of kinesic 'marking' goes beyond the phonetic and syntactic characteristics of purely verbal utterances, as it also accompanies paralinguistic behaviors by themselves. This, again, illustrates the deep internal coherence of the Basic Triple Structure. Paralanguage follows the morphological and semantic nuances of verbal speech with congruent variations of the so-called primary qualities (volume, resonance, tempo, pitch, syllabic length, etc.), qualifiers (ingressive or egressive respiration, pharyngeal control, articulatory control, etc.), and differentiators (laughter, sighing, etc.). While our kinesic repertoire automatically matches both the linguistic and paralinguistic constructs, there are kinesic markers of paralinguistic features, such as drawling ('Weeell', with raised brows and open eyes), high pitch ('¡¿Whaat!?', with knit brows and lowered eyelids), husky voice matched with rather stiff head and face movements.

E. *Proxemic language markers*

Although paralanguage and kinesics provide the most important, ever-present markers of discourse as parts of the Basic Triple Structure, certain proxemic shifts (after all the result of kinesic behaviors) act also as markers, even as punctuators. Leaning forward toward one's cointeractant to coincide with the most pronounced stress and key word or words; leaning back at the end of a sentence marking its final junction and low-pitch ending; standing while facing each other or in a circle. Mediterranean men typically mark their language with very frequent proxemic shifts toward and away from each other, and postural shifts, both coinciding with peak syntactical and semantic elements in discourse. It is an easily observable cultural characteristic that strikes the foreign speaker if he comes from a culture where face-to-face interaction is a much more static affair.

F. *Chemical and dermal language markers*

One cannot neglect the thought that *tears*, particularly when they are controlled, may act as true markers of otherwise softly uttered words. The function of tear shedding as a marker is, of course, much more semantic than syntactical, being triggered by emotional reactions. It acts, therefore, as an emotional display as well as an externalizer of what is said or silenced, but felt, by us or someone else, or as reflections of the external world; although the key word that may carry the emphatic paralinguistic-kinesic construct may be the one to elicit the tears, usually immediately before or immediately after it is spoken. Two *dermal* reactions, blushing and skin papillary erection (goose flesh) can play the same function as tears and with the same type of structuration.

A further note on markers

Summing up, the distinction between nonverbal behaviors which truly mark the phonetic and grammatical parts of speech, and those which primarily identify its semantic and attitudinal elements, can be rather uncertain, since the marker of a parenthetical feature, for instance, or an interrogation, contains also a semantic change. If one decides, however, that the category of 'markers' as a label should be limited to phonetic and grammatical differentiations in speech, whatever accompanies the linguistic structure without adhering to those requirements must be placed, and in fact is found within, the other nonverbal categories.

Markers can relate exclusively to paralanguage when there is no verbal language involved, but only paralinguistic 'alternants' such as clicks, hissing sounds, moaning sounds, pharyngeal audible frictions, narial ingressions and egressions, and many more which form a veritable lexicon beyond words, yet with much lexical value. This subcategory of markers alone will merit future research and deserve much attention in nonverbal communication studies. It represents the exclusive costructuration of paralanguage and kinesics, a topic of relevance in the study of normal and pathological behaviors, as an identifier of cultural and socioeconomic characteristics, and as an important part of the craft of the actor and of its relationship with the audience.

If we were to classify language markers according to their anatomical location we would find that stress markers can be performed by the face, including brow and eye movements, head, shoulders, arms, hands, and even legs and feet (e.g., beating to stresses as we talk) as well as by postural shifts. Stress markers are the ones occurring with the highest frequency, as stresses are also more frequent than other grammatical features.[5]

4. Space Markers

Space markers (along with other categories that refer to spatial characteristics) and time markers represent the direct reference to the two basic dimensions of human life, which together with sound and movement dominate our experience of the world and of social life.

Space markers (Ekman 1977) illustrate size, that is, the space or area occupied by something—not its shape, which would be illustrated by a 'pictograph'—distance, and location (without pointing as deictics do): 'A box/this big around/' said with an inclusive gesture of both arms, '¡But, it is /so far away/!' said with a forward rising sweep of the hand, '¡He always sits right in the middle!', said with a down short-range inclusive gesture of both hands.

It is interesting to record the crosscultural differences in the morphology of spatial *size* markers and how their use is tied to certain etiquette norms. Among the Spanish rural class, for instance, the code of good manners prescribes that if one illustrates the size of the pig they killed, the scar on someone's abdomen after an operation or the watermelon they picked, before or after saying 'This big around' (*Así de grande/gorda*), or 'This long' (*Así de larga*), one must say *Perdone la manera de señalar*, or *Aunque esté mal señalar* (literally, 'Pardon the way I point/describe', or 'Even though pointing is not nice'). It is well known and a source of amusement that, while a Spaniard of American illustrates his little boy's height with the palm down and horizontal, a Colombian or Salvadorean, for instance, puts out his hand horizontal but perpendicular to the ground, since the former spatial marker is used only to refer to the height of animals, while a Mexican uses the palm-down gesture for an object, the second one for an animal, and the palm-up closed hand with the forefinger sticking upwards for a person.

It might be appropriate to point out that, as with other nonverbal categories, one cannot look only to the behavior that appears to be the only significant one, for it might be through the costructuration of that behavior and one or more cooccurrent ones that the complete message is conveyed. Take the exclamatory expression '¡A watermelon this big around!', in which we see not only a typical example of the Basic Triple Structure (the verbal utterance + the high volume and tenser articulation of '¡this big around!' + the kinesic act), but the kinesic illustrator complemented by what Ekman and Friesen (1976) call a facial action unit, specifically raised brows and wide-open eyes. There is, therefore, a synchronized movement of hands and brows in which the facial expression cannot be said to be just redundant, but complementary, as it provides additional emphasis. It will be seen that any nonverbal categories can have *complementary behaviors* coded by other systems. In some cases both systems will belong to the same category, say, a kinesic and audible emblem like a facial and paralinguistic sexual invitation, while in others, as in most of the space illustrators just discussed, only the kinesic construct qualifiers as illustrator. In crosscultural studies, as well as in studies of age, sex or personality groups, the single and multiple or complemented behaviors are significant indexes.

While illustrators of size are always kinesic—although we may utter a paralinguistic sound accompanying a puffed-up-cheeks facial expression along with or replacing the kinesic indication of 'fat'—those for *distance* (as for time, below), particularly a long or faraway one, are either kinesic (as when saying 'far away' with a sweeping hand movement at head height and away from the body) or paralinguistic (as when using a prolonged whistling sound accompanied or not by a hand gesture, the paralinguistic form being most common in Latin countries.

As for *location* markers, they do not point at present or absent referents, as has been clarified above, but only try to identify someone or something in space (either the actual present space of somewhere else, or an imaginary one) as we somehow refer to its size, usually using both hands to delimit the imaginary volume or the object or person, as in 'He came and sat/right there/', 'We could put one speaker there, and the other one over there'.

5. Time Markers

Markers of time must be added as an important category of illustrators together with markers of space. They refer to different points in the past and in the future, as well as to the present, and to the duration of events (which must not be confused with the occurrence and rhythm of an event, illustrated by even tracers), thus referring, like space markers, to the two basic dimensions of life. Time markers include, of course, what Birdwhistell (1970) calls 'manner markers', which comprise temporal adverbs.

Time relationships include not only the established adverbs of time and adverbial constructions such as 'tomorrow' or 'next year', but a number of colloquial expressions of time such as 'For ages', 'Ages ago' which can be accompanied by typical time markers, thus varying in word and gesture from language to language as part of the folklore of each culture. The standard time references are of five types:

A. References to the *past* can be made to:

Distant past, (a) Specific references: 'A hundred years ago', 'Last year'. (b) Vague references: 'A long time ago', 'Years ago', 'Eons ago', 'Ages ago', 'The following day'. *Immediate past*, (a) Specific references: 'An hour ago', '¡Five minutes ago!', 'Yesterday'. (b) Indefinite references: 'A little while ago', '¡Just now, just now!'.

B. References to the *present* can be made only in one relationship, *now*:

'Now', 'Right now', even when the present stretches behind and ahead of the true present now, as in 'This year', 'This week', 'Today'.

C. References to the *future* can be made to:

Distant future, (a) Specific references: 'A hundred years from now', 'Next year', and (b) Indefinite references: 'In a long time', 'Years from now', 'Next year', 'Next time'. *Immediate future*, (a) Specific references: 'Right now', 'Tomorrow', 'Next day', and (b) Indefinite references: 'Very soon', 'In a little while', 'Soon', 'One of these days'.

Kinesic and paralinguistic forms

Illustrations of time are mostly kinesic, using the hand alone, the hand and arm, and the head and brows, but also paralinguistic, using drawling and clipping mainly and alternants like whistling. However, some interesting characteristics are typical of specific time relationships in many cultures, as part of the culture's folklore, although proper research has not yet been conducted in this area. The nonverbal behaviors, based on the verbal time references given above can be outlined as follows:

References to the past are in general signalled *kinesically*, with a toss of the head usually accompanied by a congruent upward brow movement and/or with an arm-and-hand movement forward or backward (over the shoulder) away from the body at head height or even higher; and *paralinguistically*, by drawling of the word or words indicating the temporal extent of the referent; or with a preceding or succeeding alternant, such as a long whistle which usually accompanies the kinesic illustrator, both as part of the Basic Triple Structure even when words are lacking. Now, within references to the past, the *distant* past can be signified by a mid-range arm-and-hand forward or backward movement away from the body, either by itself or acompanied by congruent drawling ('A looong time') or simultaneously to or followed by whistling, with or without the verbal expression but always with the kinesic one; while the *immediate* past shows precisely the opposite feature, a short-range movement of the hand (hardly the arm) and congruent clipping of the time word, with no alternant (independent paralinguistic utterance) recorded in the cultures studied (¡Just now!).

References to the future, surprisingly enough, are signalled in many western cultures with illustrators similar to those used for the past, thus it being very difficult to display them without a verbal accompaniment or without a congruent situational context. For the *distant* future, the same kinesic and paralinguistic illustrators of distant past are used, but the hand, instead of describing a sort of dismissal movement with paralinguistic drawling, can also describe a single rotating one away from the body as if indicating the 'development' or 'passing' of time, without drawling, perhaps lowering the head without raised brows; while the *immediate* future, besides the short-range hand movement, is also signified by the forward half-circle hand rotation, sometimes with extended first finger.

Referents to the present logically need not go beyond the 'here' and 'now' of the time at which they are made, so they are on-the-spot movements that point at 'now' as the hand would point also at 'here' (compare 'Right here' with 'Right now'). Neither drawling nor clipping occurs, unless especial emphasis is attached, e.g., '¡You're gonna do it right now!' or '¡*Right* now!'.

It must be noted that the language markers used while displaying time markers are simply a coexistent feature, not to be labelled time markers, as in '¡Oh, but I did my Ph.D a long time ago!', for which one thing is the backward over-the-shoulder hand movement that signifies distant past, while the primary stress on "long" is marked by the added parakinesic intensity. At the same time a language marker, as any other behavior, might be emphasized as a true emotional expression.

We must recognize the emblematic value of certain time markers as true time emblems, such as /Right now/, /A long time ago/, as well as of some alternants, such as the prolonged whistling for 'A long time ago'. However, one could rightfully argue that a time marker like 'Right now' and a space marker like 'Right here' do not really qualify as emblems because they lack the nonambiguity that defines emblems.

Duration markers

As for duration markers, they correspond to adverbial lexical expressions ranging from slowness ('Slow', 'Very slowly', 'It took the whole day') to different degrees of fastness ('Quickly', 'In one second', 'Right away') and to a host of verbal colloquialisms at different levels of language usage ('In a jiffy', 'Like a shot', 'As slow as molasses'). The tendency is to use sharp, short-range hand movements (and lowered or raised brows) to accompany expressed rapidity, matched with higher pitch, or lower for adverse situations ('He hit and hit and hit'), while slowness is illustrated with slower and wider-range movements of the hand, and the whole trunk, lowered shoulders and lowered and even closed eyes, in expressions such as 'It'll take a looong time', 'Veery slowly'. Paralinguistically, clipping accompanies quickness, while drawling logically matches slowness. A whizzing or whistling alternant may accompany kinesic markers of quickness or stand by themselves as emblematic vocal utterances.

6. Deictics

Deictics are movements and sometimes utterances—by themselves or cooccurring with the movement—which indicate the location of a person, object or place in space, whether or not the referent is present, and an event in time. They seemingly overlap space and time markers, except that deictics truly point at their referents. As has been discussed, they include those pronominal markers which not only emphasize the word but actually point, while other markers only stress the word.

Kinesic deictics

Kinesic deictics or pointers are, first of all, performed with the whole hand, the forefinger or the thumb, but also with nods, tilts and tosses of the head. Typically, a North American nods to point at someone or something ('I'd like to buy that fridge'), while a Spaniard tosses his head back slightly (the lower the social status, the farther back and more forceful) because he actually uses his chin (as for pronominal markers), pointing with his eyes as well. Deictics with the extended hand palm up are used, for instance, in formal introductions, while the thumb (typically accompanied by a lateral head tilt) is used as a very informal way of pointing which would be utterly rude otherwise. The index finger is however the main pointer, as its name indicates, indispensable for locating small objects or referents not close by. Good manners in many cultures condemn it as a gesture used toward superiors or in formal situations. We use, however, 'an accusing wagging finger', or when we must single out someone in a situation of dominance, or pointing indiscriminately at objects or places. Pointing at someone in public places is also against the most elementary etiquette in many cultures. While engaged in a conversation one may use alter-adaptor *contactual deictics* by touching a cointeractant on the forearm, the shoulder or the knee.

The head tilt is typically combined with facial expression, either dissimulated and as subdued as possible or very pronounced, accompanied or not by the thumb pointer when it is meant to be a conspicuous behavior, unless our own body shields both the face and the hand because we refer to something or someone behind us. A typical combination is that of the head tilt, facial expression (a tense wink) and a preceding or simultaneous nudge on the other person's arm.

Kinesic-paralinguistic deictics

Kinesic-paralinguistically, it is quite common among Latin peoples (and more so in lower-class persons) to accompany the head toss—which seems to be slightly less accented than the Cuna's lip-pointing gesture studied by Sherzer (1973)—with a closed-lip slightly glottalized mid-central nasalized vowel [ˀə̃×], particularly in situations in which the hand cannot be used. In these situations the head movement certainly reaches the angle of the Cuna's gesture, as when carrying something, using also gaze direction, thus combining as effectively as possible head gesture, eye pointing and the closed-lip utterance which means 'there'.

Objectual deictics

Deictics that point at referents that are present can also be *objectual pointers* performed with any sort of conversational props or with tools one is handling at the moment. Conversational props such as a pencil, a letter opener, a pair of glasses or a pipe can be effectively (¡and annoyingly!) used to point at our interlocutor when we are or want to be in a position of superiority, for instance, advancing over the desk and pointing a pencil at someone, an attitude never adopted by a subordinate or a lower-status person.

Pointers of absent referents

Another class of deictics seems to be formed by those which point at referents that are not present, whether people, objects or places. The reason why it is so common to use a head tilt and the over-the-shoulder pointing thumb is that those referents exist already in the past, e.g., '¿Did you like that girl at the party?', '¿How did you like his apartment?', thus being both a time marker and a deictic. There is more subdued hand and head-tilt gesture cluster for which the hand may not leave our lap, or the thumb may point *at* the person we say we talked to, or the building in the campus we just came from, while both hands are still clasped around the knee, or while both arms are crossed, the thumb making a pointing motion. But when the gesture acquires a wider range it may characteristically make our interlocutor look at our hand and, what is worse, in the direction we are pointing where there is no referent to be seen. ¡There is always in me a sudden slight sense of guilt at cheating my interlocutor! Moreover, pointing at places not present, whether buildings or cities, is very typical of rather articulate speakers, but most of the time they are geographically inaccurate.

Pointers of events

A third class of deictics is that formed by *spatial references to events*, not only in the past but still to take place, with head tilt and the over-the-shoulder pointing thumb) and to something taking place right now, e.g., '¿This /pointing at the floor as for 'here' or 'now'/ is the best graduation ever, isn't it?' It is, in English, as if we always used the redundant adverb of place, as in the incorrect '¡This here wedding is just great!'.

7. Pictographs

Apart from emblems, which must replace words, the purest iconic behaviors in social interaction are: pictographs, which refer only to figures and volumes, echoics, which imitate sound, kinetographs, which imitate movement—therefore, the two basic activities of social life—and kinephonographs, which imitate both sound and movement simultaneously. Putting these four categories together proves the high level of iconicity in interactive behaviors. In fact, they can also qualify as other behaviors classified in this scheme, such as externalizers, space markers, regulators, and emotional expressions.

Pictographs (Ekman and Friesen 1969) are speech-accompanying movements, mostly manual, which draw a picture in the air, or on a surface, of the shape, contour or volume of the referent (either bidimensional or tridimensional): drawing the hour-glass profile of a curvaceous woman, illustrating the shape of a car, describing a piece of furniture, drawing on a table or on the ground an imaginary reproduction of a house blueprint. They always accompany their verbal reference, but this reference is not necessarily a lexical description parallel to the kinesic one, for it is precisely an unconscious principle of economy that often makes the speaker simply mention the referent and, simultaneously with the word that represents it (and perhaps any complementary verbal information, but not description), draw its figure with his hands: 'He bought one of those lamps/*a very elaborate chandelier*/, and a desk aall/*a richly carved desk*/, and you should see his new secretary/*the hour-glass woman figure*/and his new Alfa Romeo/*a sleek sports car*/'.

We can, of course, argue that the use of all those pictographs, save the 'woman' one, may also respond, at least partially, to verbal limitation on the part of the speaker, who just might not have the necessary fluency to explain what precisely the lamp, the desk and the car look like. That is why syllable drawling, hesitation vowels and silences accompany the pictographic illustration instead of a verbal description: 'He bought one of those lamps, uuuh/a very elaborate chandelier/(if the pictograph does not coincide with the sentence) and a desk aaall/a richly carved desk/, and you should see his neeew seeecretary/the hour-glass pictograph/, and his new Aalfa Romeeo/a sleek sports car/'. This, in fact, is a most common occurrence observed in two situations: one, when it is due simply to mental laziness and careless speech; the other one, because of sheer linguistic ignorance among the less educated. At any rate, *economy of expression, mental laziness*, and *verbal limitation* are the three main reasons for the use of pictographs, that is, kinesic iconic references, as are for the use of echoics, kinephonographs and, in a lesser degree, kinetographs, which illustrate simply how someone or something moves.

It must be noted, however, that drawling has also the function of emphasizing, even (in the example discussed) when the speaker, besides the pictographic illustrations, uses the correct lexical descriptions. In which case the pictographs make the evoked images even more vivid without redundancy. On the other hand, often the speaker has initiated the pictographic illustration before mentioning the referent, perhaps as a turn-claiming behavior which also ellicits interest.

If the woman figure were drawn with no verbal reference it would of course qualify as a pure emblem. Also, references that describe size, that is, space between two points only ('She is a big woman'), cannot be defined as pictographs, but rather as space markers.

As for the possibility of *paralinguistic pictographs*, one would be doubtful to assert that a 'curvaceous moaning' emitted while drawing her figure could be regarded also as pictographic, for it would not stand by itself with that precise meaning unless accompanied by the graphic kinesic illustration. The paralinguistic accompaniment would simply fall within the category defined later as 'identifiers'. But we may, for the sake of an orderly classification, speak of a *qualified pictograph or icon*. On the other hand, *objectual pictographs* are not uncommon, since any object held in the hand (a pen, a fork, a pipe) can also draw the figure of the referent as a simple extension of the arm.

8. Echoics

Beyond pictographs, the iconic group among nonverbal behaviors—apart from emblematic references to sounds, movements, persons, animals, objects or any other sensibly apprehended models—is formed by echoics, kinetographs, and kinephonographs, which represent the activities of sound and movement in different forms.

Echoics are iconic references to acoustic models performed by contacting objects (e.g., the Spanish guitarist's tapping on his instrument to imitate the religious procession's drum beats) or our own body (e.g., the imitation of a champagne bottle cork being popped out by distending one's cheek from inside with a finger), and by paralinguistic vocal utterances (e.g., imitating a hen's cackling). Their models, therefore, can be organic (e.g., animal cries or human voices), natural (e.g., the wind), mechanical (e.g., a steam locomotive), and mediated sounds (e.g., the squeaking of shoes, a tennis ball being hit by the rackets).

Onomatopeias

The vocal echoics can be of two kinds. First, *onomatopeic*, that is, linguistic sounds such as in 'The cat meowed', 'The drain gurgled', 'The motor was whirring', and the like. Onomatopeias, however their grammaticality, morphological flexibility (to gurgle, it gurgled, a gurgle) and, of course, dictionary status, are the least iconic of all echoics (as proved, for instance, by the absurdly different representations of the rooster's cry in different languages), due to the sometimes unnecessary limitations of orthographic forms, as is discussed when dealing with paralinguistic 'alternants' in Chapter 5. In other words, there could be more utterances of lexical nature (onomatopeic) had written forms been established.

Paralinguistic echoics

Those unwritten vocal echoics constitute the second type of vocal sound imitations, quite free *paralinguistic constructs*, actually 'alternants' which truly strive to imitate organic sounds, the most important of which are: the many imitations of animal cries and animal-directed human calls used by people of all cultures, mostly for deceptive purposes (deception being such an important function of nonverbal somatic and extrasomatic behaviors of all types), but addressed also to other humans; the sounds of nature (e.g., the howling of the wind or the roaring of an avalanche); mechanical sounds (e.g., the tic-tac of a clock or the clicking of a typewriter), and sounds that are mediated by different elements (e.g., someone's knocking on a door, a musical instrument). ¡But the paralinguistic imitation of the lion's roaring, for instance, is more faithful to its model than the onomatopeia with which I just referred to it! The howling and whistling of the wind have no realistic written representation either, nor do mechanical sounds like the whirring of an airplane, or mediated sounds like the gurgling of water in a drain pipe or the thump-thump of footsteps.

To say, on the other hand, that no conspicuous movements accompany the sounds we imitate paralinguistically or simply evoke linguistically, does not mean that we do not at times (depending entirely on our individual and cultural expressiveness) complement our own vocal utterances with, for instance, a hand movement, to explain the spiraling of the water gurgling in the pipe, the spinning of the whirring engine propeller, the swishing and rustling of long skirts as we evoke the swaying movements of the women (perhaps only with a slight sway of the head and eyes). These would already qualify as kinephonographs, defined below, by doubling the iconicity of the nonverbal construct. However, very often the movement accompanying the paralinguistic echoic bears no resemblance to the model, therefore qualifying only as a mere externalizer, identifier or emotional expression, of no iconic value.

Kinesic and kinetic echoics

On the other hand, the imitation of a horse's galloping by rapping with our fingers on a hard surface is only a *kinesic echoic*, as is the theatrical door knocking (since it imitates a model), the guitarist's drum imitation, or the imitating sounds produced by any two parts of the body. A subcategory might be differentiated as objectual or *instrumental echoics* by grouping all imitations performed by the handling of objects, such as sound-effect artifacts, whistles, etc.

Echoics can also be clearly *kinetic-kineparalinguistic* when we try to imitate a specific sound both kinetically (not kinesic, if it does not imitate the movement) and paralinguistically. The sound of the horse's galloping imitiated both by rapping the fingers on a table and uttering 'tu-ku-tuk, tu-ku-tuk', or the drum beating done both with the hands and vocally, are 'kinesic' only inasmuch as they require a 'kinetic' activity on the part of the performer which may develop into a specific style of carrying out the sound-producing movement, not because that movement imitates the sound-producing model (as does the airplane's looping, or the socially codified manner imitated by a kinesic echoic like door knocking). There is no *double iconicity* in a kinetic echoic, unless it is regarded as an imitation of a former performance of the imitation of the original model.

Echoics, on the other hand, may be accompanied by conspicuous movements which do not imitate any model, either because there is no movement simultaneous to the acoustic model (e.g., a radio monotonously repeating a tuning signal, both of which we imitate paralinguistically and also accompany, not imitate, kinesically) or because the existing movement is not visible anyway (e.g., an internal machine mechanism). They are instances of a *false iconicity*, since they fail to imitate the existing but hidden movement, yet they must be clearly differentiated both from the kinetic-paralinguistic constructs, which are based simply on a performance that involves movement, and from the pure echoic ones. In fact, they reveal an important tendency in us to associate sound to movement and movement to sound when there is no real relationship, depending very much on the personal or cultural expressiveness. These constructs can be identified as *pseudokinetographs*.

9. Kinetographs

Between echoics and kinephonographs one should differentiate *kinetographs*, which constitute an already established category referred to by Ekman and Friesen (1972: 360) as "movements which depict a bodily action or some non-human physical action." They would be better identified as containing kinesic iconicity only and not being accompanied by imitative vocal or nonvocal sounds, although they may produce or be accompanied by any other type of sound: the way someone ran, how the boat rocked, how the dolphin sprang out of the water, the flying bird, the soaring of an eagle, how the boxer hit his opponent. Responding to the associating tendency just mentioned, speakers may accompany these descriptions with nonimitative paralinguistic sounds. They still qualify as kinetographs, but must also be identified in nonverbal research as *pseudoechoics*.

On the other hand, any single or combined occurrence of paralinguistic or kinesic behaviors in which there is no iconicity of sound or movement fall within other nonimitative nonverbal categories, such as externalizers, identifiers and emotional expressions. And yet, the absence of iconicity must never be hastily assumed, for there are often clues to iconic sign relationships based, for instance, on culture, such as the Caucasian greeting alluded to earlier, which would escape the average foreigner as would many other similar behaviors in different cultures, many of which are often emblematic references. Similarly, a rather hidden or subdued kinesic iconicity can yield important clues in psychotherapy, in which the patient may be actually acting out unsuspected feelings and attitudes (cf., among others, Scheflen's [1965] 'quasi-courtship behaviors', Mahl's [1968] interpretations, or Ekman and Friesen's [1974] 'leakage').

10. Kinephonographs

Ekman and Friesen did not refer, to my knowledge, to the imitation of a model which is made up of both kinetic and acoustic activities, and which the replica represents by means of paralinguistic and/or objectual sound and kinesic behavior. The imitation of the horse's galloping by rapping our fingers on a table, a mere kinesic echoic, becomes part of a kinephonograph when its echoic iconicity is complemented by running our 'galloping' hand across the table, thus evoking the running of the horse by means of a true kinetograph. These are, therefore, instances of *double iconicity*.

This combination of iconic movement and equally iconic sound, that is, of an echoic and a kinetograph, is what I feel should be identified as a *kinephonograph*. Kinephonographs, then, can be variously formed. They can be performed, (a) through sound and movement produced by the same type of activity, as when we imitate the beating of drumsticks by hitting a surface with the hands; (b) by sound in one activity and movement in another, as with the paralinguistic imitation of the drum sound and the kinesic one of the drumstick, or the vocal imitation of a steam locomotive and the kinesic one of the wheel mechanism; (c) by sound in two activities and movement in another, as the paralinguistic-kinesic imitation of the horse's galloping by means of special-effect hoofs while running the hands over a surface in imitation of the galloping; which, of course, would constitute triple iconicity.

Echoics, kinetographs and kinephonographs reveal the human need to imitate the sounds and movements of nature, animals, man, and the very artifacts we create. But, of all these, we tend to imitate above all different animal species and our congeners, often identifying ourselves with the former, as when we roar like a tiger, walk and cry like a monkey, beg like a dog, cackle like a hen. All these iconic behaviors occur mainly in interaction, not only with other people but also with animals, as has been pointed out, by utilizing their own cries with the purpose of deceiving them in a true predatory behavior, or in the form of calls for true social interaction with tamed and domesticated species, and, in general, for what can be regarded perfectly well as survival purposes in many instances.

Developmental aspects

When elsewhere (Poyatos 1977a) I suggested, in connection with the theory of the gestural origin of language, the parallel development of vocal language and kinesics, I had iconicity in mind. Many linguistic constructs must have of necessity been preceded by paralinguistic and kinesic imitations, in other words, an essential preverbal iconic repertoire of such forms, because there would be no other signans to refer to certain tangible models just as many abstract, still ineffable concepts would have, for a time in the development of communication skills, no other references but 'identifiers'. Many of them could have been gradually replaced by lexically expressions syntactically arranged in grammatical constructions, but also succeeded by onomatopeic forms that developed true linguistic status, while others did not but could be referred to by means of elaborate periphrastic expressions. At the same time, however, the inevitable limitations of verbal language has always made speakers resort to kinetographs as well as pictographs, the closest iconic representation, although brief, of physical referents. On the other hand, a study of the ontogenetic development of iconicity would be but one of the many neglected interesting aspects of developmental studies, as it would probably reveal a wider repertoire in childhood, adolescence and young adulthood and a lesser tendency to paralinguistic and kinesic imitation in more mature persons. In fact, we tend to see it with amusement when a person in his middle or old age 'youthfully' makes 'funny' sounds and movements imitating animals, people, machines or nature's sounds. Although it can be, of course, part of the comedian's repertoire.

Crosscultural differences

But we must always look at the phenomenon of iconicity outside one single culture and consider that, for instance, just as Mediterraneans tend to refer to an abnormal sound in a car by imitating it with their mouths as best they can—instead of describing it verbally (with words that actually provide no truthful/accurate information about the malfunction) or with the correct onomatopoeia—they happen to be more articulate kinesically as well. I had many occasions not only to use established or improvised onomatopeic illustrations to explain a mechanical malfunction, for instance, but to observe the different ways in which my listeners accept those imitations. While I can with total confidence tell a mechanic in Spain, France, Morocco or India that my car goes —— (and here I skillfully imitate that abnormal sound), because he appreciates my vivid illustration and so he diagnoses accordingly, I have observed his American or Canadian counterpart smile uncontrollably when I consciously ignored this cultural difference and acted as I would in those other countries. My repeated experience is that the North American English-speaking mechanic seems to resort to a richer echoic repertoire of established lexical forms, and that even when a Spaniard would come closer to the English lexicalization by explaining that his engine *hace tic, tic, tic, tic*, the North American would use the construction 'a ticking noise', as he uses either this gerundial form or a true verb, like 'it whirrs'.

The fact is that a Latin, Arab or Indian speaker is more articulate kinesically, often accompanying with movements linguistically expressed ideas which an Anglo-Saxon hardly illustrates kinesically, and that he utilizes a wider range of iconic gestures which may result in some typical 'zero-decoding situation' when he interacts in certain foreign cultures. So, in spite of the greater abundance of onomatopoeic forms in English, it seems that speakers who are more articulate kinesically tend also to incorporate imitative phonetic movements into their speech in a more direct, spontaneous way.

On the other hand, we must also consider how the echoic lexicon of an individual or a whole culture goes beyond the onomatopoeic repertoire available to them in their dictionary; after which we must measure the facility to imitate sounds and integrate it into one's conversational expressive repertoire. This is another aspect of human communication intimately related to the concept of fluency that goes beyond the one traditionally understood as linguistic fluency, as discussed in Chapter 1, as well as the concept of redundancy *vs.* complementarity (Chapter 2), since the iconic repertoire of a speaker must not be regarded necessarily as redundant, for, at the very least, serves to identify a personality and a culture, therefore quite far from being 'redundant'.

11. Ideographs

Ideographs, which according to Ekman and Friesen (1969: 68, after Efron's definition) are movements "which sketch a path or direction of thought, tracing the itinerary of a logical journey," can also be paralinguistic utterances 'accompanied' by movement, or vice versa. They typically do not illustrate what is being said (although they may precede or follow words) but function by themselves without necessarily qualifying as emblems unless they are totally unambiguous, becoming, therefore, iconic references to what is being evoked.

It is important to clearly distinguish ideographs from externalizers, defined below as, in short, nonverbal reactions to verbalized or unverbalized thoughts, events, actions, or environmental referents. An ideograph is not a 'reaction to', as an externalizer is, but a 'tracing of' one's own thoughts only, a kinesic or kinesic-paralinguistic behavior that, therefore, runs parallel to those thoughts.

We all use ideographs, but it is easy to remember how eloquent ideographs are in the faces and hands of actors like Olivier, and, in a more flambuoyant fashion, de Sica and Mastroiani, following, for instance, in a very Latin style, the unworded or hardly worded recollections of a very pleasant experience, a great deed, a very difficult situation that unfolds fearful complications, or a beautiful woman; all, with slight variation, illustrated by raising one arm at face level while circling horizontally with the hand, looking upward or with blank gaze and uttering an all-expressing overdrawled central vowel-like paralinguistic alternant. In this particular example, such an Italian one, the expressiveness of the construct is shared equally by gesture and utterance, while in other instances either one may dominate. A rather pancultural ideograph is the illustration of doubtful thoughts by frowning and pouting, perhaps shaking the head slowly, and emitting a prolonged closed-lip mid-to-higher back vowel with rather high pitch, [ˀɔ̤³]. A kinesic ideograph, or a kineparalinguistic one for that matter, can also be an objectual (that is, kinesic-objectual) ideograph, as when actors like the Italian ones mentioned clutch a hat in their hands and turn it while following a pleasurable idea.

Iconicity in ideographs can be more or less conspicuous, as can be in a psychotherapy interview. The clutching of the hat can be the replica of an embrace, as the woman's spinning on her heels while tracing her romantic thoughts about her lover can contain the iconic reference to dancing.

12. Event Tracers

While an ideograph traces the itinerary of a thought, an *event tracer*, usually a longer behavior, is a kinesic or kinesic-paralinguistic activity which traces the occurrence of an event being described, that is, which follows "the rhythm or pacing of an event" (Ekman 1977: 49, where he uses the term "rhythmic"). Unlike the ideograph or the externalizer, therefore, the referent is being described in words as well: 'Well, it was good, but it went on and on for two hours and never seemed to end', the hand(s), head and eyes underlining the event from 'but' to 'end'; 'She was quite restless all day long, coming and going and touching this and that, until she finally saw the mailman approaching the house and ran to the door' (kinesically and paralinguistically modified verbal account following the occurrence from 'all day' to 'door'; 'We went to this little cozy restaurant, had a quiet dinner, and walked home', with gaze averted away from listener, tone of voice and hand gesture accompanying 'quiet dinner', and slow speech tempo underlining 'walked home').

It must be noted that iconicity appears in event tracers only when they overlap other categories, which they typically do, for instance: time markers, when the event involves movement ('during the conversation they kept walking down the alley'); time markers, if we refer to the duration of the event ('The lecture went on for, oooh, two hours'); pictographs, if someone or something is drawn kinesically ('The floor show was very elaborate, with these gorgeous girls dancing all over the place, then the guys came in, then the whole orchestra in the background, and more dancing . . .', drawling the main verbal descriptions and tracing the different parts with arm and head movements).

Independent paralinguistic event tracers, that is, when they do not simply cooccur with the kinesic forms, can be said to be nonexistent, since any tracing of things happening would entail kinesic illustrations. But the objectual modality, of course, is possible as long as something is held in the hand while illustrating the event.

13. Identifiers

Identifiers are more or less conspicuous kinesic behaviors or paralinguistic utterances (in reality forming kineparalinguistic constructs, slight as the movement might be) displayed mostly in interaction, simultaneously to or immediately alternating with verbal language to refer or, literally, give bodily form to and identify certain abstract concepts ('impossible', 'absurd'), moral and physical qualities of people and animals ('unfriendly', 'tough', 'hard', 'soft', 'cautious'), and qualities of objectual and environmental referents ('dirty', 'hard', 'soft', 'murky', 'crystal clear'). Identifiers, therefore, do not refer to our or someone else's feelings and our reactions to them, as externalizers do, but are direct nonverbal illustrations of the verbalized expressions, which externalizers are not.

Although the paralinguistic identifier normally cooccurs with the kinesic one, it can be an independent phenomenon. Not only an armless person—one of the many neglected aspects concerning the communicative possibilities of impaired people—but someone who for some other reason is not using his hands, can express physical or moral 'strength' by tense articulation and glottalization of the key word 'strength', 'softness' of character by slight drawling, slight nose wrinkling and nasalization, more relaxed articulation and lower volume, or 'smoothness' by prolonged drawling and 'smooth' articulation. As for objectual identifiers, they are, of course, possible, if, for instance, one has a pipe, a pencil or any other object in his hand while expressing the smoothness of a surface; but for many other qualities the object would have to be dropped first, since one would want to free the hands in order to shape them in many different subtle ways, as for signifying precisely 'subtle'.

Interchangeability with other categories

Depending on the emphasis placed on the verbal expression through kinesic and paralinguistic elements, some identifiers would qualify better as language markers, or could be used as language markers at the same time, or as emblems, and even pictographs, thus responding to the hierarchization among verbal and nonverbal systems according to their circumstantial mutual costructuration and to their intensity. Take, for instance, the expression 'It is so unnerving to face the inflexible/first gesture/personality barrier/single or double hand 'barrier'/over and over again/'progressing' hand movement/that in the end you are just exhausted/shoulder drooping/, completely/head movement/exhausted'. Said with moderate emphasis, but with accompanying face and hand gestures, 'inflexible', 'barrier', 'over and over', 'exhausted' and 'completely' are true identifiers. However, with a simple punctuating emphasis and no conspicuous or paralinguistic acts we would regard those word-accompanying nonverbal features more as language markers. Again, if, for instance, we use both hands to represent 'barrier' and then a collapsing shoulder movement to signify 'exhausted', with no verbal expression, we would have acted out a pictograph ('barrier') and an emblem ('exhausted').

We could perhaps trace the origin of some established emblems to their recurrent use as identifiers: the /fist/ we make for 'strength', the 'hand-rocking' gesture for /so-so/ or /wishy-washy/, the /face-and-hand/ construct to signify /just perfect/ in many cultures, and many more. But ¿what is the innate or inherited psychokinetic mechanism whereby the thoughts of 'strength', 'wishy-washy' and 'just perfect' are given their bodily expression in the first place? Apart, of course, from the variations determined by the different cultures and, lying even deeper, by the idiosyncratic ways of each person. For the factor dictating a specific identifier can be precisely the *cultural iconicity* (as when a Spaniard imitates a bullfighter's pass while saying that someone negotiated the situation very skillfully).

Iconicity

The last thoughts lead to another aspect of identifiers, namely, the basis for the iconicity of many of them. We see that their iconic quality is based, for instance, on physical elements that can be evoked through kinesic representations of form and movement, even when, in given context, the referent is not necessarily physical but totally abstract ('personality barrier', by putting up a wall with the hands; 'over and over', by a succession of hand movements suggesting a progressive happening), by kinesic activities associated with certain physical characteristics which perhaps are not physical in given connotations ('soft mannered' or 'soft music' with a horizontal palm-down movement as if caressing a smooth surface), or by anatomical association, or location of personality characteristics indicated with the hand directed toward self, usually in the heart and stomach regions ('troubled', 'intense', 'tortured', 'full of joy').

On the other hand, identifiers offer clear examples of what I have differentiated as *primary iconicity*, when the association is a direct one, as could be with 'barrier', 'soft' or 'exhausted', and *derived iconicity*, if it becomes established in an arbitrary way through usage simply because speakers imitate a model which in time acquires a true emblematic status. This happens with certain identifying behaviors initiated by well-known actors, such as the high-brow gesture displayed by movie stars of the thirties and imitated by young people as a gesture of sophistication, which we then see as both an identifier and an emblem.

At any rate, identifiers must form a separate category. They differ from emblems in that they are not agreed-upon symbolic, unambiguous behaviors. 'He's a very /rough/ person' accompanied by a facial (and perhaps manual) gesture is not as clear as 'He's a /strong/ person', by showing a fist or, for actual physical strength, by placing one hand over one's biceps; from pictographs in that they do not draw a concrete shape, as in 'She's a /big/ woman', with both hands in the air but no specific reference to her figure. From ideographs, in that they do not trace a thought, as in 'He is a little

/wishy-washy/', by combining slight nose wrinkling and frowning and a rocking hand movement, or 'He's quite /sneaky/', by frowning slightly; in other words, far from the thought-tracing quality of '¡Oh, those wonderful years!' said with dreamy eyes, drawled words and a vague gaze which seems to follow the path of the thought. From event tracers, in that they never trace the occurrence of a happening, as in 'It was a tiring lecture', by simply dropping head and shoulders, which is not like 'The lecture would never end, it went oon and on', trying to represent its undue length. From externalizers, the next category, in that they do not serve as clues to our reactions to what is being done, said or silenced by us or someone else, being only quite direct illustration intended as such; although there may be a degree of intensity, for instance, which may certainly act as the 'externalizing' quality of the identifier, according to the ever-present principle of nonexclusivity whereby verbal and nonverbal behaviors blend in the most subtle and intricate ways.

The performer's style and interpersonal borrowing

Another interesting aspect of identifiers is that, since they do not have the specificity and clear shared meaning of emblems, they depend very much on the performer's expressive style, as they do not require a rigid kinesic articulation as do representations like the /throat-cutting/ gesture, /Okay/, /Wait/, /Victory/, /A punch/, /A drink/, etc. Someone may refer to a soft surface by slowly sliding his hand over an imaginary surface (slowly for softness, but quickly and jerkily for coarseness), while someone else may use a similar gesture to indicate slow music or 'very carefully', but briefly rubbing both palms horizontally to refer to the soft surface, even with a drawling of the word 'soft', and a fist gesture to refer to a strong wine. Identifiers, besides, lend themselves ideally to much *individual inventiveness*, and they constitute a very important part of a person's style. When we speak of a person as refined, very articulate, lady-like, and so on, we are actually expressing a social view using a social label, of how he or she uses the nonverbal categories available. In the final analysis, this amounts, for the most part, to saying that that person uses and structures his or her Basic Triple Structure language-paralanguage-kinesics in such a way. In reality, the whole classification of nonverbal behaviors undertaken here—except for chemical, dermal and thermal modes and those involving the handling of objects and body-adaptors like clothes, food and cosmetics—is but a study of the interactive forms and functions of the Basic Triple Structure, of how verbal language can have a constantly varying communicative status within that structure and according to an equally varying hierarchization among all somatic and extrasomatic systems. To assert, therefore, that so-and-so is very lady-like simply suggests a multi-system style that would follow the present classification of interactive behaviors—all of which, except alter-adaptors, operate in noninteractive situations as well—until all systems have been related to each other and to each of the factors in what I outlined in the previous chapter as the Total Conditioning Background. Only when we have checked the various factors would we obtain the total picture of what being lady-like, rustic or natural involves. Even in a most impressionistic fashion we can see that the triple linguistic-paralinguistic-kinesic lexicon varies with age, sex, socioeducational status, personal sensitiveness, etc. If we go to extremes and observe the less educated people, we immediately notice their more limited triple structure in terms of vocabulary, that they operate with a shorter general dictionary repertoire (although they possess a wider one than ours in their own trade or occupation), that they do not display 'refined' paralinguistic voice modifications, nor do they perform, for instance, with the fingers to refer to something 'subtle', to 'a certain something' by rubbing slightly the first three fingers of one hand together, or to 'something you just feel' by bringing the two loosely cupped hands away from the chest as they slowly open like something that flows from inside, two typical identifiers among educated speakers.

Another most interesting aspect of identifiers is how they also lend themselves to *interpersonal borrowing*, something applicable in general to all nonverbal behaviors, but much more to those which, like identifiers, externalizers, ideographs and event tracers, are deeply rooted in the person. Depending on one's degree of influence on others or, on the other hand, vulnerability to the behaviors of those others, people who live together for a prolonged period of time, but above all married couples, are observed acquiring gradually each other's vocabulary, paralinguistic features, mannerisms and gestures displayed in similar contextual situation. In a different degree, many people betray the conscious or unconscious influence of actors and actresses and other public figures.

14. Externalizers

Externalizers are reactions to other people's past, present, anticipated or imagined reality, to what has been said, is being said or will be said, silenced, done or not done by us or someone else, to past, present, anticipated or imagined events, to our own somatic phenomena, to animal and environmental agents, to esthetic experiences, and to spiritual experiences.

This definition could be briefly paraphrased by referring, for instance, to facial expressions elicited in a man by a real present, remembered or imagined woman, to what someone told us, is telling us or we know will tell us, or so we imagine, as well as to what remained untold or undone, but which is felt nevertheless, or to an embrace or the lack of it; the verbal or nonverbal expression of affection toward animals; the tears shed at a funeral, remembering or anticipating it, or the sudden hand-rubbing gesture while imagining a forthcoming banquet, the patient's pained expression, the audible exhalation of a real or imagined romantic involvement, the ecstatic expression of a music listener or player, or the open-arms gesture of awe before a breathtaking view.

The importance of externalizers and identifiers is such that they constitute, along with language markers, by far the richest body of interactive and noninteractive nonverbal behaviors. Besides their very especial mutual relationships, the frequency of their occurrence is so high that the speakers can be said to communicate and identify themselves, both personally and culturally, mostly through these three categories of behaviors. In fact, any critical study of people in interaction, whether from an anthropological, sociological, psychological, clinical, semiotic or literary point of view, and even as depicted in painting, must acknowledge language markers, identifiers and externalizers because they constitute the very foundation of the expressive behaviors displayed during an interpersonal encounter.

And yet, there is a fundamental difference between externalizers and the other two categories, for externalizers do not illustrate the preceding, simultaneous or succeeding verbal expression; they are at the most reactions to them, and, more often than not, have no verbal referent to which we may relate them, as happens with other nonverbal categories. They must, therefore, stand as a separate category in themselves.

The definition of externalizers suggests the fascinating semiotic variety of the sign processes—whether real or imagined—that take place between the original sensible or intelligent referents and the final externalizing behaviors, through the reactions elicited by those referents and their sensory encoding channels. Furthermore, it hints at the great importance that externalizers have in social interaction and in clinical encounters. Those processes can be diagrammed as represented in Fig. 4.2, 'Semiotic Processes of Externalizers'.

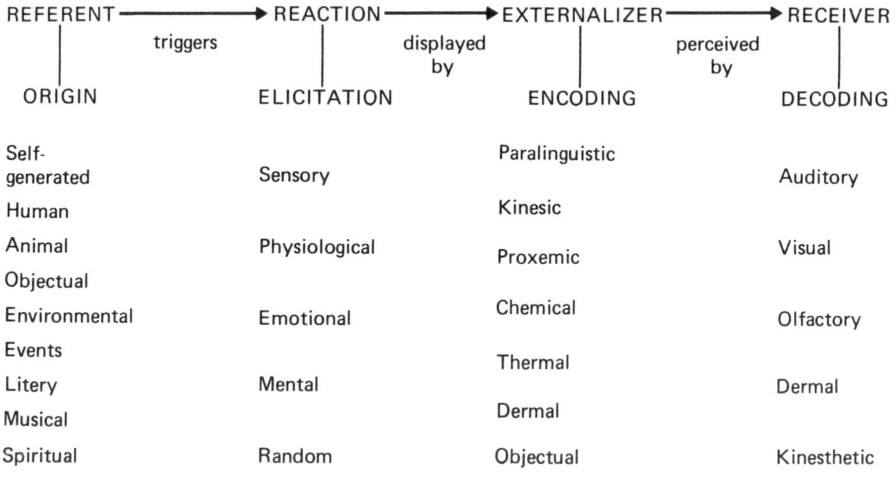

FIG. 4.2. Semiotic Processes of Externalizers.

Although an attempt at exemplifying all types of externalizers would be an endeavor beyond the limits of this chapter, I will at least expand on the diagram enough to outline and fully define their nature and forms, classifying them according to: *origin*, that is, their first referents of the externalizing behaviors, which triggers an elicitation in us, displayed through an *encoding somatic channel*, which constitutes the externalizer proper and finally perceived by the *decoding sensory channel* of the receiver. The original referents, then, are:

A. *Self-generated*

Some externalizers originate within one's own organism without apparent elicitation by any external agent although, naturally, we may at times trace their genesis to external causes—which are not the direct referents of the externalizers—such as the ambience cold that may trigger a bladder malfunction, which then causes the person's muscular tension. These include a host of what Kahn (1978) in her work on diagnostic semiotics, terms 'normo-signs', 'patho-signs' and 'neutro-signs', or the many nonverbal clinical signs discussed by a number of authors (e.g., Mahl 1968; Scheflen 1973; Ekman and Friesen 1974; etc.; see also Waxer 1978). On the other hand, the phenomenon of synesthsia plays a very important role, as it does in any social situation of personal copresence, whether or not it is an interactive one. A random list of examples (taking a few from Kahn) for the different encoding channels would show:

(a) *paralinguistic:* the lower pitch of boredom or sleepiness, the higher pitch of muscular contraction while experiencing pain, the slurred voice of intoxication, the esophageal one of laryngectomized patients, or a cleft-palate one;

(b) *kinesic:* facial palsies, limping, facial tenseness and general muscle tonus of bladder pressure, tremors, a nervous twitch, etc.

(c) *proxemic:* cowering in a corner, sitting farther than usual from the dinner table or too close to it, etc.

(d) *chemical:* the schizophrenic's odor perceived by some therapists and their abnormal urinary metabolites (Wiener 1966: 3157), body odors revealing lack of concern, the odor of the newborn's phenylketonuria urine, intestinal or stomachic gases, the odor of frostbite, the smell of impending death in the ward, reported by some nurses in my classes, etc.

(e) *thermal:* fever, erotic self-arousal, etc.

(f) *dermal:* the mental elicitation of skin papillary erection (goose flesh), blanching, flushing, pimples, itchiness synesthesially assumed through the person's scratching, etc.

(g) *objectual:* as mentioned by Kahn, body-soiled clothes that betray depression, use of wigs signifying hair loss due to cancer treatment, excessive makeup revealing mental disorder, etc.

B. *Human*

Human referents or elicitors, whether basically physical, such as touch, aggression, lacrimation, verbal expression of physical attractiveness, or verbal and nonverbal emotional expressions, such as hatred or love, are always manifested in ways sensibly perceived in direct interaction, for emotions can also be verbally expressed in writing or through the objects that communicate them, such as paintings, or in music. Those referents elicit *sensory reactions*, as the embrace prompted by the emotional facial expression, the fixed gaze and pupillary dilation through which a man may communicate his sexual attraction to a woman, the provocative gait of a female in the presence of the men she wishes to attract, the tear-shedding nervous female student anxiously awaiting her final mark, the sudden shout that makes us drop something or jump up in our chair, the facial expression of pain triggered by physical aggression, the thermal raise and perspiration caused by interpersonal crowding on a bus in New Delhi; *physiological reactions*, such as heart failure out of sheer panic caused by an aggressor, the urge to relieve one's bladder during a tense situation, bad breath caused by the same situation; *affective reactions* (though unverbalized) toward another person, such as suspicion, externalized through deep frowning, love that elicits words, gestures, tears, or objectually, engraving initials on a tree trunk; *mental processes*, such as memory searching, perhaps using frowning and/or a lip-biting gesture, etc., upon seeing someone, or word-searching; and *random behaviors*, seemingly non-purposive unconscious activities (whose importance in interaction cannot be stressed enough) that are true externalizations of subconscious attitudes and reactions elicited by others, whether present or absent, such as some of the typical self-adaptor behaviors (e.g., preening, fidgeting) displayed in social or clinical attitudes, but which, however unfocused they seem to be, we can assume to externalize truly not-so-hidden states and feelines: pencil-biting during writing pauses, lint-brushing during an interview, tongue-showing while performing something requiring visual and manual ability, etc.

C. *Animal*

Animal referents of human externalizers can be very similar to the human ones inasmuch as wild, tamed or domesticated animals elicit in us a variety of sensory reactions, emotions and feelings; those random behaviors can range from fear reaction to visual iconic reactions such as slapping oneself on the thigh with the hand or a twig while walking when one is used to using a crop on his horse, or slapping the back of the hand when bitten by an insect.

D. *Objectual*

Objectual referents of many types can trigger sensory, physiological, affective and mental activities that are externalized paralinguistically, kinesically, proxemically, chemically, thermally and dermally due to sensory, physiological, affective and mental activities: the reflex bilabial ingressive friction elicited by a prickling object, its accompanying facial gesture, or the face-and-handshaking gesture when hurting one's finger, the proxemic shift away from objects known as hazardous, the lacrimation triggered by pain or by proximity to an onion (a referent both objectual and chemical), the eye irritation produced by new contact lenses, the heat sensation produced by hot objects, direct gustatory perception of nutritional and pseudonutritional products (some being substances rather than objects but, in a broad sense, part of our objectual environment), etc. On the other hand, artistic objects like paintings, photographs, films and sculptures can elicit different affective reactions and mental processes, from the purely esthetic enjoyment of a painting's technical qualities, through the mental associations elicited by its subject, to an aversive physiological reaction provoked by a grim photographic document.

E. *Environmental*

Environmental referents, from the many different types of natural views, through the modified environment of residential landscaping, to the visual, tactile, kinesthetic—through spaces, volumes, colors, textures and light—or purely esthetic appreciation of a building, can elicit, besides those reactions, strong feelings of claustrophobia, admiration, mental associations of different sorts, fears, loneliness, etc., and random behaviors that can be viewed as overflows of those very feelings, not always within awareness. On the other hand, we tend to display reactions to sensory and physiological elicitations caused by heat, cold, dryness and humidity within architectural spaces as well as in the open, environmental pleasant or unpleasant odors, etc. (externalized paralinguistically and kinesically, mainly, from expressions like shivering '¡Brrr!' and nose-wrinkling '¡Eugh!' to retching as a reaction to a visual or olfactory stimulus).

F. *Events*

Events as referents, perceived both sensibly and intelligibly in their physical, spatial and temporal dimensions, can also produce—simultaneously with the externalizer or as thought-of past experiences and even as anticipated ones—sensory reactions (the Prince of Wales' tear-shedding at his wedding, ¡which he predicted!), physiological malfunctions (neuralgia due to the intenseness of a meeting, micturation due to much tension, etc.), affective reactions (happiness, boredom, fear, etc.), mental processes (memories, associations, etc.), and random behaviors triggered by the situation, such as a public figure's patting of his jacket pocket while entering a public place, or tucking at his cuffs, touching his tie, his ear lobe or the side of his nose while receiving his audience's feedback (all typically displayed, for instance, by TV hosts).

It is interesting—and a crosscultural comparative study would reveal cultural idiosyncrasies and personality and class characteristics—to observe on television the arrival of heads of state and other dignitaries at a meeting for the typical and recurrent kinesic externalizers displayed by each one of them: the buttoning of the jacket upon stepping off a car (this one, after all, a functional act), and then the single tap on one of its pockets; putting one hand into the jacket pocket; preening the side of the head with the palm of the hand over the hair; and then, as they approach others in the initial phase of the greeting ritual, the smile, the onset of a handshake or embrace, the completion of the greeting ritual; and back to pocket-patting, smiles, and behaviors of their individual repertoires. And yet there seems to be in all of them a situational type of familiar and well-managed tension, particularly during the brief transitional moments or gaps in the protocolarian activities, often the sort of unconscious tension which, again, is masterfully and naturally controlled through experience, self-training and self-assurance. Outside, again, of the circle of protocolarian situations, event externalizers can also be encoded objectually and thus communicate through time, as happens with very long or very short cigarette butts accumulated in an ashtray as a clear cue to the tension produced by the event, doodling patterns left on paper after a meeting, broken toothpicks and small balls of bread left on the table, etc.

G. *Literary*

The experience of literary reading (or listening to it) cannot be equated with the representational qualities of painting, film, television or photography, as it entails two things absent in those other media: the esthetic appreciation of the stylistic composition (which can very directly elicit facial expressions and even paralinguistic utterances and breathing sounds) and the multichannel metamorphoses whereby the reader brings back to life all the imagined and equally multichannel experiences of the writer that were reduced to the visible printed text (cf. Poyatos 1977a, 1981a) and which can also elicit kinesic, paralinguistic, dermal (goose flesh), and chemical (tears) reactions.

H. ***Musical***

So does the musical experience as a referent, whether the music is listened to, played or conducted. This experience relies solely on an interpretation by the listener infinitely more varied than that of literature or painting, no matter how 'descriptive' the music may be, although it is its esthetic enjoyment that can be equated to the imagined or real sound of narrative and poetry. However, the experience of music can also result in paralinguistic externalizers ('¡Mmmmmmmmm!, '¡Aaaaaaah!', vocal imitations of the orchestra, etc.), kinesic activities (lifting or lowering the head with closed eyes, 'conducting' frantically, beating the time with the feet or with the hands against something, and numerous facial expressions), proxemic shifts, chemical reactions like tear-shedding and sweating, body temperature rises (elicited by the mounting 'tempestuoso' of Mahler's Fifth Symphony, as it would be by some of D. H. Lawrence's more erotic passages), dermal reactions like skin papillary erection, and even, as objectual externalizers, the peculiar handling of object-adaptors (the arms of a chair or an improvised baton) and body-adaptors (the frantic ingestion of food and drink while listening to the same 'tempestuoso' movement, the simultaneous fidgeting with a necklace, etc.)

I. ***Spiritual***

Spiritual referents, however, appear as the ultimate referent as we escalate the ladder of the referent-externalizer relationship. Spiritual interaction between Man and God is, in terms of depth, the most intimate and profound experience and the least mediated of all behavior elicitations (save for the possible effect of the immediate environment, the company of specific persons, or the events that may prompt that spiritual communication). Elsewhere (Poyatos 1981f: 147) I have merely suggested in passing some of the sensible manifestations of direct or mediated (by another person) prayerful interaction, and I will not elaborate on it at this point either. It would represent, however, the ultimate semiotic investigation of sign processes, as those manifestations are profusedly documented not only in the lives of different holy men and women through history, who have described their mystical experiences, but even more today in the daily existence of an increasingly great number of Christians around the world who have experienced all the phenomena described in the *New Testament*, such as the typical fainting in the Spirit (cf. MacNutt 1977: 189–224; the University of Steubenville President Michael Scanlan 1979: 45–49; A. Sanford's [1972: 218–226] description of her own and MacNutt's experiences), the gift of unknown tongues, often recognized by modern native speakers or experts in ancient languages (cf. Scanlan 1979: 78–81; Flynn

1977: 179–190; du Plessis 1979: 81–91), and all the documented visible manifestations of supernatural healing (cf. MacNutt 1974; surgeon W. Reed 1979; psychiatric nurse B. Shlemon 1976; A. Sanford 1966, 1969, 1972; East 1977; Swiss Psychiatrist Tournier 1974). It has been in part my own interest in all aspects of interaction that has made me discover an endless field for the semiotician in the easily available gatherings of prayerful Christians, from private meetings within the different Christian denominations in several cities and towns in several countries to national and international conferences, at which I have observed closely all the scriptural phenomena in friends, acquaintances, strangers, and familiar well-known persons.

The topic of social random behaviors

Within the various types of behavior elicitations directly generated by the different referents, namely, sensory, physiological, emotional, mental, and random activities, this last group, within which my interest focuses on what may be termed *social random behaviors*—discussed extensively as "autistic gestures" by Krout (1935)—offers a very special incentive for the researcher in different disciplines.[6]

Although, as Dittman (1963: 155) puts it, "Every external movement in human beings is a source of information about the psychophysiological state of the person moving" (not just moving but uttering sounds, one should add), kinesic acts such as "playing with jewelry, clothing, scratching, rubbing, random touching of various parts of the body" (Mahl 1968: 301) during clinical encounters are not the social externalizers I wish to emphasize, nor are other similar behaviors discussed by Freud (1901, as "symptomatic acts"), Freedman (1972), or Scheflen (1972), although they are intimately related to the social occurrences of everyday life. In fact, all those externalizers (sometimes very difficult to interpret, if at all possible) of hidden states or past, present or anticipated motives, and of which our cointeractants are much more aware than ourselves, should be researched systematically in the various basic types of interactions in different cultures and subcultures, age groups, work groups, etc., without neglecting their pathological occurrences. Areas of psychological research, such as developmental behavior, should attempt to determine the gradual appearance and development of social random behaviors as an obvious part of the person's growing repertoire, specifically within the triple structure language-paralanguage-kinesics.

Social random behaviors (not necessarily 'interactive' but simply socially observable) can be channeled through *paralanguage*: some types of relief sighs, throat-clearings characteristically produced by many different kinds of social tension (after a passing greeting in a deserted corridor, joining strangers in the washrooms, during job interviews (etc.), some clicking sounds of the 'Tz' type, intermittent repeated humming of the same few notes of a tune (often clicking the notes), various forms of sniffs, coughs, sighs, etc.; *kinesics*, the most abundant type of social or clinical random externalizers, either free movements (foot shufflings, twitches, lip puckering, frowns, tongue-showing, shrugs) or adaptors, that is, self-adaptors (touching the chin, lips, nose, brows, both temples, hair, ear lobe, neck, pinching the nose or scratching different parts of the body, stroking arms, hands or legs, stroking the naked chest at the beach, preening, etc.), body-adaptors (touching, as in preening, cuffs, ties, lapels, slacks crease, belt, skirt, blouse, rings, necklaces, earrings, glasses, etc.) and object-adaptors (chair-arm-rubbing, tapping on chair arm or counter by oneself or while interacting, fidgeting with cutlery, glasses, crumbs, napkins, brushing off or flicking imaginary or real lint, doodling, etc.); proxemics: short-range advances and retreats while standing in conversation, when they are not used as language markers.

The iconicity of externalizers

As for the iconicity of externalizers, it is obvious that if one follows Sebeok's view on "multisensory iconic representations (no doubt insufficiently studied) that pervade human and other animal existence in everyday life" (Sebeok 1976: 1442) we find, at the encoding end of the process, that the activity represented by each of the somatic channels can be socially measured by degrees of the physical or chemical quality involved, that is, its intensity, and also by its duration. In other words, if we do not limit the concept of iconicity to visual resemblance, then we can speak of the iconic relationship of the degree of flushing to the fever it represents, the tenseness of someone's embrace at a funeral to the affection and grief felt, the amount of facial sweating to the environmental conditioning, the intensity of a woman's perfume to her courtship readiness, the amount of facial momentary movements to the interest of the book being read or the music being listened to, the odor perceived by some psychoanalysts in schizophrenics to the stage of the crisis, and so on.

ADAPTORS

The next set of nonverbal categories is that of *adaptors*, which can also be discussed as formal and functional categories of kinesic contactual behavior because they are codified only kinesically or as kinesically-based behaviors depending on objectual systems, but which constitute a very complex group on nonverbal behaviors.

Although Ekman has lately abandoned the term 'adaptor' because he feels the phrase is "too theoretically laden" (Ekman 1977: 46) and has used "manipulators" instead, I have preserved his original term 'adaptors' simply because they are all activities or positions in which parts of the body come in contact with other parts, with someone else, with certain animals or with the objectual environment, belonging therefore within bound kinesic activities or positions. Furthermore, the term 'manipulator' suggests, it seems to me, a kind of active association with the object of the behavior which is not always present, as in many instances it is only a static relationship (the hand consciously clutches a glove as the person walks, or slips into it with functional or affected mannerism; the socially effective necklace can be just worn stationary, or truly fidgeted with, 'manipulated'). These kinesic behaviors assume specific forms because our own anatomy becomes 'adapted' in lesser or greater degree, depending on its articulatory possibilities, to our own body (wringing the hands, picking the nose, biting the nails), to another person (an embrace, a handshake, a bodily confrontation), to an animal's (horse-riding, patting a cat, holding a bird), or to an object's shape (handling a pipe, holding a writing or eating utensil, or a rope in a tug-of-war), thus perfectly justifying the terms 'self-adaptors', 'alter-adaptors', and 'object-adaptors'; to which I have added, for methodology sake, 'body-adaptors' to include a most heterogeneous series of extrasomatic elements most intimately associated to our body and to which the body characteristically 'adapts' its movements and positions (the gloves of the previous example, a morsel of food, a bracelet).

While object-adaptors (e.g., handling a tool) and body-adaptors (e.g., food, jewelry), are the least interactional of the four—although, as will be seen, they can perform interactive functions if intended that way—self-adaptors and alter-adaptors, involving oneself and others, are the ones that contain by far the greatest variety of forms, in other words, kinesic behaviors, as well as the greatest number of interactive possibilities; particulary alter-adaptors, which are always interactive by their very interpersonal nature. Self-adaptors and alter-adaptor repertoires possess a great versatility, they constitute from a semiotic point of view the two most natural forms of bodily interaction with oneself and others, and they offer countless research possibilities, mainly developmental, psychological, social and cross-cultural perspectives.

15. Self-adaptors

Self-adaptors are movements or stationary positions in which some parts of the body come in contact with itself, of varying length and preceded and followed by onset and outset movements, among which we can distinguish the three basic kinesic categories of bound gestures, manners and postures (as opposed to 'free', without contact with anyone or anything).

While thc uncourth forearm jerk, the fingertip kissing or the nose thumb are emblematic gestures (see Morris, Collet, *et al.* 1979, whose crosscultural study of twenty gestures includes eleven self-adaptors), the flamenco dancer's or singer's clapping, the hair-preening movement, or the manual mouth-shielding act when coughing qualify as manners, and crossing the legs and keeping them crossed before uncrossing them, or clasping the hands behind while walking, are postures.

All parts of the body can be involved in alter-adaptor behaviors in a passive way, but only a few are anatomically capable of being active 'touchers' in the performance of self-adaptors, namely the hands, the feet, and much less, the legs (against each other), the head (actually only the region of the face and part of the occipital area touching a small part of the cervical area) and the chest (only against the thighs and knees), without acknowledging the more unusual flexibility of the professional contorsionist, the yogi or the double-jointed person, nor the ontogenetic development of self-adaptors due to the greater flexibility in early life. One could represent in a chart not only the articulatory possibilities of the human body with relation to itself, but also in interaction with another body, that is, in alter-adaptor behaviors. People touch themselves for a number of purposes, but also need to touch other bodies and, when deprived of those needed contacts, they may touch themselves in conscious or unconscious ways, whether normal or pathological.

But even from a cultural point of view, self-adaptors must surely have developed from basic somatic needs of the individual to more complex social needs, having to cope with increasingly sophisticated interpersonal relationships that would demand the conscious or unconscious performance of gestures, manners and postures in contact with the self.

Functions of self-adaptors

Sixteen basic functions can be differentiated within self-adaptors, susceptible, of course, of further classifications according to specific strategies.

a. *To adopt some of the universal or culture-specific postures:* standing or walking with hands clasped in front or behind, sitting cross-legged with hands holding the knees, sitting on the heels, deep-squatting with arms around knees, the stork-like Nilotic stance, the various ways of crossing arms, legs and feet, arms akimbo, etc. Postural habits vary not only with age (the infant brings one foot to the forehead most naturally while the adult props his head pensively with one hand), status (the superior may clasp his hands behind the neck in front of a subordinate while the latter might clasp them in front at waist level), socioeducational level (in many cultures the lower-status woman adopts the arms-akimbo posture or one arm across the abdomen and the hand of the other propping the face, while she will not cross her legs at the calves and clasp her hands limply over one side of the upper leg, as a refined woman does), situational context (the social-gathering cross-armed stance), etc.

b. *To facilitate or attend to some somatic needs:* resting the head on one hand out of fatigue, slapping oneself on the sides to fight the cold and rubbing both hands to warm up, scratching when itching, while males urinate, performing self-gratifying sexual activities, defecating in the deep-squat posture and holding the legs (the only one in many cultures without plumbing amenities), wiping the tears from the eyes; again, many of these acts vary with age: children wipe their tears off with the back of the hand or the knuckles, while normal adults do it with the fingertips, an infant sucks his thumb or toe.

c. *To conceal some somatic needs:* when men urinate near each other in advanced cultures (though they get exposed to each other in common showers or baths), shielding a cough, yawn or sneeze with the hand, etc., dissimulating behaviors all of them which can be assumed to develop both ontogenetically and culturally along with interpersonal relationships and the gradual etiquette ritualization of manners.

d. *To perform some body-adaptor activities*, that is, handling food (e.g., licking one's finger or fingers, putting food into the mouth in a childish, careless, or just normal way), drinks (drinking from one's cupped hands) or subnutritionals (e.g., taking snuff, handling chewing gum from the mouth), clothes (e.g., fitting, preening) and jewelry (e.g., turning a ring with thumb of the same hand, or earrings), all of them serving as identifiers of age and socioeconomic status.

e. *To facilitate or block sensorial reception or emission:* cupped hand against the ear to hear better, forming a visor over the eyes to see better, one or both hands around the mouth to speak louder, etc.

f. *To groom and cleanse the body:* washing, rubbing, cleaning the ear with the small finger, picking the nose with any finger or blowing it by pinching it with two fingers and releasing, as they do in many cultures (I have observed it in low-class people in India, Morocco, Spain and Canada, the more advanced the culture, the lower the status of the performer), dislodging food from between the teeth or from the gums with a finger or toothpick, wiping the corners of the mouth with thumb and forefinger, wiping the sleep off one's eyes, etc.

g. *To preen oneself*, whether alone or as true 'social preening'. This is a particularly significant type of self-adaptor. It includes different natural or learned, conscious or unconscious ways of touching ourselves to rearrange the position of the hair and stroke various parts of the body with rather rhythmic movements that may accompany speech and consciously or unconsciously qualify one's performance for the observer or interlocutor. In addition, preening behaviors serve as social identifiers as much as the grooming behaviors just discussed do. They include smoothing one's brows or the hair, pushing it or tossing it aside with a manner that differentiates, for instance, the lower-class older man (who brushes his bald head with a forward movement of the hand, often while resetting his cap) and the more refined man (who uses a backward movement or slides his right hand backwards along either side of the head), or the rustic lady (who pushes her hair with her whole hand or rake-shaped fingers) and the sophisticated woman (who delicately touches her carefully set hair with the upper part of the fingers, pushes it from over the forehead with the first and second fingers, or gathers her long hair behind her neck with both thumbs and then the fingers of both hands). Both men and women—but not so small children, who develop preening behaviors along with other verbal and nonverbal behaviors—display a number of preening activities that we all recognize in different social activities; some being very conscious and part of the person's communicative repertoire, while others are encoded out of awareness.

h. *To try to assuage physical pain or protect oneself from it:* holding the part that hurts (accompanied perhaps by characteristic paralinguistic utterances), sucking on a snake's bite, clutching the throat while choking (many of them being reflex activities) and shielding oneself against external agents.

i. *To cause oneself physical pain*, as when consciously hitting oneself in various emotional states, or as is done, for instance, by some autistic children, chastising oneself as ascetics have done in different periods of history, etc.

j. *To display emotional states and reactions:* holding one's head and pulling at the hair in bereavement (as documented in Egyptian paintings and witnessed crossculturally to this day), wringing the hands, biting the nails or the knuckles, clutching the arms or the knees while seated, hitting oneself in self-aggression, holding the head while seeing something; all of them abundantly stereotyped in the theater and in films (serving as a gauge for the actor's naturalness or lack of it); the Eipo women of New Guinea, when surprised, grasp their breasts from below with both hands, lift them, "and sometimes squeeze milk" (Eibl-Eibesfeldt 1979a: 27; reported by him for other parts of the world as well).

k. *To conceal or repress those very emotional states and reactions:* as dictated by crossculturally and socioeconomically-conditioned display rules: covering the face while laughing, crying or blushing, or when embarrassed, biting the knuckles to suppress weeping, covering the face and eyes in fear of looking at something.

1. *To engage in certain conscious or unconscious mental activities:* touching both temples with the hand, or forefinger and thumb, in an effort to remember, grabbing the chin or holding the front or back of the neck also during memory searching or word searching, scratching the head when in doubt, recollection or embarrassment, etc.; all of them behaviors that vary socioeconomically (the Spanish low-class man typically tries to remember

advancing one foot, one hand on his waist and the other holding the temples, while the educated one might grab his chin).

m. *To perform unconscious random acts*, both in interaction and noninteraction: hitting the sides of both fists with arms extended in front, or in front and back, several times in succession, patting one thigh while walking or standing (perhaps humming a tune), rubbing both hands together, biting the lower lip, or one finger (a more feminine form), stroking the shin of the upper leg when sitting cross-legged, pinching the nose, curling a hair; behaviors all of them that qualify also as externalizers (see many more in Krout 1935).

n. *To perform certain physical-fitness acts:* clasping hands behind neck, clasping one wrist while trying to flex the arm, touching the toes, standing arms akimbo.

o. *To perform certain folk, protocolarian and religious rituals:* clasping hands or putting them on hips while dancing, joining palms or intertwining fingers in prayer, washing in Hindu holy rivers; touching both cheeks with the back of the hands, forearms crossed, while making two or three curtsies in front of a shrine; kissing one's own hand in salutation to a superior as done in antiquity, or when handing or receiving an object to or from a person of quality (observed in seventeenth and eighteenth-century England); making the sign of the cross; putting one's right hand to the heart while listening to the national anthem, as Americans do, etc.

p. *To carry out a conversational or nonconversational interactive encounter* by serving as most of the NV categories discussed so far, that is: *emblems* (the Indian greeting by joining both palms vertically, the /superb/ or /delicious/ gesture with bunched fingers against the mouth, the /cuckold/ gesture imitating two horns in some cultures, /I'm full/ by tapping or rubbing the stomach in some cultures), *language markers* (/Me/ as a simple pronominal marker by touching one's chest or, in Japan, the tip of the nose with the forefinger; marking stresses by hitting the palm of the hand with the side of the other or with the forefinger), *time markers* (indicating /right now/ by hitting palm with forefinger), *deictics* (/I/, /You/, /This/, by touching the person or object), *pictographs* (tracing someone else's anatomy over one's own body), some *echoics* (imitating various musical instruments, a ship siren or a locomotive, by putting the hands to the mouth), some *kinetographs* (punching the palm of one hand to describe a fight), *identifiers* (rubbing both palms horizontally to describe a smooth surface, rubbing thumb and forefinger lightly to signify subtleness), and *externalizers* (/¡Good!/ by rubbing hands, /¡Eugh!/ by pinching nose, /¡Oh, no!/, by taking one hand to the head, resting the head on the knees while pensive).

Like other bodily behaviors, self-adaptors can be intimately related to language and paralanguage as well as to other nonverbal activities. While holding one's head in despair one may speak in a hoarse voice, breathe audibly, etc., covering one's mouth while yawning produces a special resonance, a woman may flirtatiously speak to a man in a moany type of voice while pushing her hair from her temple with a delicate movement of the middle and fourth fingers (thus being part of the Basic Triple Structure language-paralanguage-kinesics), which can be iconically measurable having become, in fact, a stereotype.

To the enlightening comments on self-adaptors by Ekman and Friesen (1969, 1972, 1974) I would simply add some thoughts that might entice others to further research.

Ethology, culture, age, gender, status, display rules, and personal characteristics of self-adaptors

Given the functional characteristics just mentioned we can hypothesize that in self-adaptors, as in alter-adaptors, it is possible to distinguish between the innate and the culturally-conditioned behaviors, and also recognize the cultural filtering through which many biologically determined acts, or innate motor habits, have evolved in different societies. Eibl-Eibesfeldt has studied, for instance, self-adaptor expressive patterns like hiding the mouth behind the hand and biting the fingers or nails as part of a display of the innate "releasing patterns" of coyness by a Southwest-African girl when he told her she was beautiful and he liked her (Eibl-Eibesfeldt 1979a). On the other hand, cultural modes have shaped self-adaptors like the typically feminine hair-preening behavior, or many gestures and manners in which we touch ourselves.

Another characteristic of self-adaptors worth studying in depth is that they reveal specific cultural, sex, age, status, normal and abnormal personality traits, medical state, sensitiveness, emotional states and chronic psychic conditions, all of them in turn decisive factors in their ontogenetic development, as they shape each individual's repertoire as well as the display rules governing their performance.

Cultural differences

Cultural differences in the display of self-adaptors are easily observable. Someone slapping himself on the sides with crisscrossed arm movements while standing in the cold might be regarded in Spain, for instance, as an 'American' behavior observed in films, since Spaniards tend rather to rub hands vigorously. Other 'American' self-adaptors that strike many foreigners in North America are, for instance, the interwoven hands over one's head around the occipital area while engaged in a conversation or the stretching of the arms with clasped hands as high as they can go, both considered quite rude in their own culture. Air India stewardesses greet their passengers with vertical joined palms perpendicular to the breastbone, thus identifying their culture, along with burnt incense and later some typical curry.

Age marks a sharp difference between childhood and later periods in the use of self-adaptors. Small children rub their eyes with their fist when they are sleepy, about to cry to crying (and clowns and other adults mock that behavior), which later they outgrow. Givens (1977) discussed his and other researchers' observations of the hand-behind-head position in children and adults, while the clasp-hands-on-the-head stance with one foot forward is observed among North American children and those of African cultures, for example.

As for *gender differences*, one can differentiate in the study of self-adaptors, as of other behaviors, the biologically conditioned movements and positions and the culturally learned ones; but beyond this broad dichotomy it is indispensable to distinguish also such important variables as age, the developmental aspect of self-adaptors, socioeducational level and personal sensitiveness, as well as the typical social 'techniques' employed by each of the sexes in goal-oriented situations such as courtship, for any of this conditioning factors may be the one informing the specific behavior under observation. We may consider, for instance: wiping tears away from the eye the 'feminine' (not the 'masculine') way, hair-preening, arm-preening and leg-preening, pressing the temples with the fingers of fisted hands in desperation or grief, putting the hand vertically over the face while laughing (as in Japan), crying, blushing, biting the lower lip while distending the mouth, wiping moisture from the corners of the lips with the ring finger or ring finger and thumb, sitting on the floor with legs at one side and hand-holding an angle, or on a chair with legs crossed at the calves, etc. Each of those behaviors offers variations within an articulatory margin due also to degrees of tenseness, range and velocity, which are socially deemed as within the range of the 'feminine' style. Any deviations are judged as 'mannish' and, in fact, they are quite ineffectual in many social situations that simply require the feminine style, from courtship encounters through stewardess–passenger relationship, to a job-applicant situation. A fact which, of course, applies to all the behaviors discussed in this paper.

Status is also betrayed by quite a few self-adaptors displayed in interaction. The less educated persons in most advanced cultures do not shield the mouth when coughing, sneezing or yawning (and even these self-adaptors can vary kinesically); the women peasants of Latin countries typically adopt the arm-across-waist-and-right-hand-propping-face posture, described earlier. Spanish males of not too high a sensitiveness, and those clearly unrefined, are in the habit of scratching themselves in the genital region in public while walking alone in the street or while standing with other men, to the extent that young teenagers pick up this 'manly' habit soon. Studying nonverbal communication in the novel (Poyatos 1977b, 1981a) I have quoted a description of this behavior to illustrate its technical use by the writer as a realistic social identifying feature, which suggests once more the value of the narrative literature of each country as a unique document in several disciplines.

The last observation links with the thought of the cultural variability of the *display rules* mentioned by Ekman and Friesen (1969), in this case for self-adaptors aimed at relieving physiological needs, such as scratching, or those involving the nose, ears, anus, and genital area, since they are not fully performed in the presence of others (less so, one might add, in interactive copresence than in noninteractive copresence, when one is not looked at) or in private. Their display certainly depends also on the person's sensitiveness and upbringing, and they are usually not looked at or commented upon, while some others are not tolerated in the company of others.

Some self-adaptors can also be associated with specific characteristics remembered as identifying features of the individual. The person who suffers from frequent abdominal discomfort tends to touch himself in that area, the one with painful arthritis in one arm will do the same often, while basic emotional states seem to be manifested by self-adaptor behaviors in many cultures, such as holding one's head between the hands in despair. LaBarre (1947: 63) mentioned "the back-of-the-hand-to-the-forehead and sideways stagger" of the early silent films to express intense emotion. A most interesting historical repertoire of self- and alter-adaptors could be elaborated tracing the development of the dramatic performance.

Within the literature on analysis of nonverbal behaviors in psychotherapy interviews quite a few self-adaptors have been reported by Ekman and Friesen (1968, 1974; rubbing, squeezing, scratching, picking, etc., specifying action and location), Scheflen (1965; discussing 'quasi-courtship behaviors' like preening and leg-caressing in women), and the valuable review by Waxer (1978) on his and other analysts' observations.

16. Alter-adaptors

Alter-adaptors, movements and positions in which we come in contact with others, constitute the only form of nonverbal communication that occurs always in interaction, whether intended or not and whether conversational or not, since there is bodily contact with at least one other body and that contact is reacted to, even if unconsciously so.

The tenser muscle tonus maintained in a crowded bus or elevator, and the much lower kinesic activity by fear of actively touching others instead of maintaining only a neutral attitude of forced intimacy are, nevertheless, *interactions*. When the interaction is conscious and intentional on the part of both partners an alter-adaptor can be performed simultaneously by two or more, as with two persons embracing; in a one-to-more-than-one relationship, as with a returning father hugging as many members of his family as he can hold with his arms; a more-than-one-to-more-than-one relationship, as in many folk dances in which partners hold each other by the shoulders, thus contacting two people on each side; and a many-to-one relationship, as when a sport player, a bullfighter or a rock star is overwhelmed by the crowd. But these are all still nonconversational alter-adaptors. The strictly *conversational* alter-adaptors, however, are the most engaging ones, although not the most abundant, as they form part of the communicative structure language-paralanguage-kinesics and complement other somatic systems and, beyond, the bodies themselves, objectual and environmental systems. The man-woman embrace, for instance, a discrete portion of their total encounter perhaps, is intimately associated with the cooccurring verbal messages exchanged, if any, and their paralinguistic voice modifications or independent sounds, their facial expressions, perhaps chemical reactions like tears, her cosmetics and perfume and his shaving lotion or cologne, and the characteristics of the place where the alter-adaptor behavior takes place. On the other hand, the semiotic intensity of the encounter can be enhanced by the nonconversational alter-adaptors, as they may betray precisely the ineffability of what one wishes to say but can only express by tactual messages, which may reach a high degree of iconicity through their measurable characteristics.

The semiotic experiences of alter-adaptor behaviors

From a semiotic-interactive point of view, the messages comprised in an alter-adaptor behavior, say, the embrace mentioned above, can be experienced in four distinct ways which affect the interaction greatly:

a. *As a single emitter*, by the person who generates the behavior, who has anticipated it for a varying length of time. Other behaviors by one of the cointeractants, or both, and/or mental associations and mental processes, and perhaps the psychophysiological reactions of one or the two of them, have prompted the embrace; which will in turn condition the further development of the encounter as a major interactive regulator.

b. *As a single receiver*, by the person who is being the object of the behavior, who may or may have not anticipated it, and who remains as a receiver only until such time as he or she becomes emitter of active or dynamic messages (as opposed to the signs from a mere receptor), thus betraying neither acceptance nor rejection of the embrace; unless the receiver never reciprocates, as happens in many alter-adaptor situations.

c. *As mutual emitters* of the simultaneous or successive encoding of similar messages, their emission being decoded both intelligibly and sensorially and experienced as such, that is, independently as receivers, until the embrace is experienced.

d. *As mutual receivers* of the embrace, which is then simultaneously encoded and decoded in its full signification, a situation of total interaction; in fact, a semiotically and socially optimum interaction we might call *symmetrical exchange*, since only one central behavior is being developed, even though the complementary behaviors (mental and physical ones) may not necessarily be the same in both of them.

In this exchange of messages the topographical possibilities of interbodily adaptors are virtually unlimited for the active toucher. Every inch of the other body can be contacted, but the receiver will normally not engage certain parts of the body, his or her anatomical possibilities being limited, unless he or she becomes the primary contacter even in the reciprocal situation I referred to as symmetrical exchange (symmetricality being a relative term only). In other words, symmetrical mirroring behavior is not always possible due to anatomical limitations.

However, the richness of indirect synesthesial assumption is such, as has been described in Chapter 3 (see a brief outline in Poyatos 1981f: 139–142) that the emitter, through direct contact with some parts of the body in a particular alter-adaptor act, will normally, consciously or unconsciously, register the consistency, shape and weight of the other person. The actual peception is then complemented by the synesthesial assumption, such as the firmness or softness of the rest of the body by the pressure exerted by one hand during a handshake. In this way a measurable iconic relationship may develop whereby the direct perception of a given characteristic becomes a gauge, not only for other sensible characteristics, but also for some personality traits. And yet, it is the joint direct and synesthesial message perception that will inform the present even as well as future social-semiotic interrelationships. On the other hand, it is the synesthesial perception of features that play the most powerful role in the visual decoding of alter-adaptors in, for instance, news photography and, even more, in the manipulated photo advertising of products; certain alter-adaptor situations, say, a man's hand feeling the softness of a woman's hair by inserting his hand between the hair and her neck, are depicted with a realism second only to the audiovisual ones offered by television, where we perceive, in addition, the triple structure language-paralanguage-kinesics as she says only '¡Touch me!', the message being then much more powerful for the viewer.

Functions of alter-adaptors

Assuming, then, as for self-adaptors but much more so, the double ontogenetic and cultural development of different social behaviors, one can easily differentiate the following functions:

a. *To initiate social encounters*, in itself a vast research topic, as it includes all the forms of contactual greetings used across society and across cultures, in other words, the opening of certain types of interactive encounters, including welcoming behaviors, as not all of them require a contactual salutation (cf., about the handshake, Morris 1972: 142–152; Schiffrin 1974; Henley 1977). But greetings must be researched also synchronically and diachronically (cf. J. Wildeblood 1965, for a historical account of greetings and other contactual behaviors) as highly distinct culturemes: the black handslap, the solidarity thumblink, the single-hand or two-hand clasp (with or without shaking), which may be very short or may linger for minutes into the conversation among, for instance, two standing men in India or New Guinea; hand-kissing, clearly prescribed across society in certain Western cultures; hand-to-foot, as done to a superior by a servant in India; cheek-kissing, as among females or female male friends in many Western countries; the Caucasian male greeting consisting of the highly iconic patting of each other's hips (from the old custom of checking for weapons); the adult-to-young child chucking under the chin, cheek-patting or cheek-pinching, hair-mussing or head-patting in Latin countries;

b. *To terminate social encounters*, from brief street presentations and social visits or gatherings, not necessarily initiated by contact greetings, to the type of single or repeated goodbyes performed at airports and stations or outside one's home before a prolonged absence.

c. *To learn about another person's anatomy* through topographic exploration, or scanning: the infant does it as part of its development, and so do many blind people, particularly in familiar or very informal situations. It can also be used when impeded visually by darkness, when testing musculature in informal situations, or palpating for dermal irregularities or anatomical deformations, thus approaching the professional ways of touching another body.

d. *As bond-seeking behaviors*, with which in the first place we can qualify any of the more informal greetings just mentioned, as when someone complements his handshake with clasping of the arm, a pat on the back or a calculated kiss, when he uses casual touching of the forearm, the knee, thigh, the back of the hand or the shoulder (some very restricted between men in certain cultures). These behaviors can be utilized either out of simple desire to establish a bond or for deceptive purposes and unselfish motives in order to ingratiate oneself with the person and attain a relationship not enjoyed as yet. There is, therefore, a visual-tactile intended iconicity as these behaviors strive to imitate the ones associated with that relationship. On the other hand, bond-seeking behaviors are not used only by lower- or equal-status persons, as is often generalized, but also by higher-status ones who wish to ingratiate themselves, either selfishly or unselfishly, with persons inferior to them whether socially or by age.

e. *To maintain social affiliation and intimacy*, in itself a whole research topic, as it involves many culturally-conditioned behaviors displayed between persons who already enjoy a mutual close relationship which must be affirmed by verbal statements ('Between the two of us', 'You are like me—', 'Look here, my dear—', etc.) and nonverbal cobehaviors that sometimes respond to lack of words: the full frontal embrace between same or different-sex relatives and close same-sex friends in Eastern and Southern Europeans, between male Arabs, and male African blacks, but not between the latter and their own mothers; the full side embrace used by children with relatives or when one consciously or unconsciously avoids the frontal form; the single-hand shoulder embrace and the mutual single-hand shoulder embrace, as between close friends; the two-hand shoulder-holding with eye contact, as when an important verbal statement is being made; the hand-on-shoulder, as when emphasizing something or pointing in the distance; the waist embrace, used among Southern European girls and young black African women; standing hand-in-hand, as seen done between males in India, Morocco, black Africa and New Guinea; walking hand-in-hand, done by male friends in the same cultures, but only by lovers and married people in western cultures; the Moroccan males walking down the street holding little fingers; walking arm-in-arm, typical of European and North American married couples, although the latter use the hand-in-hand posture more, as do middle- and lower-class Central and Eastern Europeans; older men, not only in Latin cultures, but in Eastern European ones like Hungary, can still be seen walking arm-in-arm; kissing, the multi-purpose alter-adaptor, which in this context will not assume any conspicuous sexual characteristics but will still vary kinesically (the embrace or shoulder-holding, the facial expression) and paralinguistically (smacking it for more conspicuous intimacy) and, of course, crossculturally (between friends in France or Russia, and seen recently between an American game-show's host and a close colleague, only between relatives and different-sex close friends in other western cultures, but never in Oriental ones); social dancing, often used to establish a close social relationship and even escalate a sexual one. There is, of course, a distinct iconic relationship between these behaviors and certain models, say sexual intercourse or sexual advances and perhaps, as Morris (1972: chapter 4) claims, some infancy intimacies that later in life are displayed only as formalized "fragments" of the original ones.

f. *To perform basic functions in mother/caretaker–infant/child interaction*, which begins with the unborn child's uterine experiences and then the grasp and Moro reflexes, the child's exploring of the mother's face and body, breasfeeding, kissfeeding in some cultures, tool-feeding, and the mother's fondling, kissing, patting, stroking, caressing, cleaning, rubbing, wiping, frictioning, and so on, accompanied by verbal and paralinguistic (cooing, clicking, kissing, crooning) sounds; and some acts that can be considered under alter-adaptors, such as hair-ruffling, slapping, holding vigorously by the wrist, etc.

g. *To escalate sexual contact and copulation*, in which the order in which the different parts of the body are reached does not seem to follow precisely the one proposed by Morris (1972: 73–97), as the process is subject to a host of cultural, socioeconomic, age, and simply circumstantial factors. Singly or mutually, the bodies can be kissed, squeezed, held, rubbed, stroked, caressed, etc., some actions being performed only in total privacy in some cultures. For instance, kissing, so far, is never seen in the streets of India or China (not even in their films), although a photograph in a recent issue of *National Geographic* (July 1980) shows two lovers on a street bench in Shanghai, he holding her hands with one hand and her shoulders with the other. In Western countries kissing in public has become quite familiar, very conspicuously so in Hungary, where lovers embrace and kiss in the middle of a crowded sidewalk. At the other extreme, kissing is a taboo in Ghana, and the only word in its Ashanti, Fanti, Wassaw, and Ga (in Accra) languages that would translate 'to kiss' is actually 'to suck someone's mouth', the idea being totally one of lust. The iconicity of sexual kinesics and proxemics is, of course, perfectly coded, and both behavioral taboos and permissible attitudes are based on a visual code which, on occasions, must be complemented by the contextual elements that may allow the same behavior to appear as sexual or nonsexual, as happens with the frontal embrace under very dramatic circumstances.

h. *For aggression and self-defense*, logically one of the most basic forms of encounter, shared with other species. The actions used are subject not only to age and sex differences but to certain social rules: slapping is more humiliating between men, but used more against and between women and children; kicking, apart from the more ritualized forms of self-defense, is used more by women and children, while a man repeatedly kicking another man in the shins would not be regarded as masculine; other aggressive behaviors could be recorded in many cultures as being applied only for child punishment in school, for instance: forcibly pulling and twisting the ear, hitting the head with the knuckles (or rubbing them hard upwards against the hair on the back of the head with a rubber band around them, ¡one of my memories of my primary school teacher!); while others, like buttock-spanking and slapping may await the child at home ¡after the school experience! Women and children also display self-defense alter-adaptors commonly not seen in men, as holding the aggressor's hands while turning the head away from him, as well as some typical aggressive behaviors like spitting on the face, a strongly humiliating act from childhood on in many cultures, a true extension of the body.

i. *To protect from physical harm and to soothe, cure, and nurse for physical or mental well-being*. The opposite of aggression, inflicting harm, is to protect from it, and the techniques range from those used by African medicine men, such as spitting on the patient, to the professional's techniques of tending wounds, palpating for abnormal symptoms, taking the pulse, straightening bones, working on teeth, tapping the chest, performing surgical operations, helping with physiotherapy methods, and, for mental health, establishing physical contact within certain therapy groups (cf. Argyle 1975: 297–298), elementary ones of shielding someone else's body from external harmful agents of whatever kind, etc. This is the context in which various professional forms of intimate touching are used which would be unthinkable outside the 'licensed' helping person-patient situation.

j. *To groom and condition the body*, displayed in various forms by primates and other mammals: the basic activities of washing, bathing, combing, scratching, and delousing (I have observed the latter in primates and in woman-to-child and woman-to-woman pairs in the lowest classes of some European cultures, sitting by the door of their homes, and in Arab cultures and in India) (cf., on delousing, Leach 1972); the professional techniques offered by barbers, hairdressers, manicurists and beauticians (who cut, pluck, etc.), on the one hand, and on the other gymnasium and athletes and prizefighter's attendants, and, with a wider variety of techniques, those in massage parlors, who knead, slap, stroke, rub, smooth and pull, offering all sorts of tactile and kinesthetic experiences warranted by their professional status.

k. *To handle and condition body-adaptors*, another way of providing and maintaining intimate distances, as done by valets, tailors and dressmakers, bullfighter and prizefighter attendants, or any other occupation consisting of assisting others to fit and handle different objects, from medieval armors to diver's gear. It is interesting, however, to see how the shoeshine has been disappearing in many places (I saw the last one in the Detroit Greyhound station, and I had one of the few shines of my life, and the best one, outside the New Delhi railway station in 1978), conspicuously so in socialist countries like Hungary, where they are occupations of the past.

l. *To express affection and nonsexual love* between parents and children of all ages, close friends, lovers, sharply differentiated between contact and noncontact cultures. Latin fathers and sons, or uncles and nephews, or first cousins, would never think of shaking hands, since they hug and kiss. While mothers and older sons in black African cultures do not touch even after a long absence, mothers in contact cultures grapple with and knead their younger and older children's faces.

Many of the behaviors used for initiating or closing encounters, to maintain intimacy, and to comfort, that is, embracing, patting, kissing, and so on, are also, when genuine, indicative of affection, although the true differentiation between sexually and nonsexually oriented will depend, not only on the circumstances, say, a crowd wanting to touch the Pope, but circumstances and individual attitudes, as happens with sports or music idols or as we can see today around the Prince of Wales when he is hugged and kissed by women. In these two situations there are at the same time a one-to-many relationship and a many-to-one, the latter conditioning individual behaviors. There is a unique occurrence of intimate contact, specifically embracing, seen between socially perfect strangers applying to greetings, affection and—the next functional group, when comforting someone—that does not cease to impress me (when I observe it in different cultures) if I look at it as a researcher: the genuine love not just developing but 'existing' among today's true Christians, who may in fact greet and relate to other Christians or those who would not reject it, and comfort others, with the warmest, sexually undifferentiated embrace.

m. *To comfort and reassure someone in distress or seeking comfort*, in different stressful situations such as bereavement, fright, disaster or any type of suffering or adverse situation. Different kinds of embracing, shoulder-holding, hand-holding, hair-stroking, back-patting, are instinctively used as they are some of them when there is a sexual attraction toward the person or a deep nonsexual affection; and yet, although there is a strong need to touch in all three situations, those contacts, except for mouth-to-mouth kissing and hand-to-breasts, buttocks or genitals (unless helping to hold the person), are permitted because of their total lack of ambiguity.

n. *To display emotions*, in situations of fear, happiness, unhappiness, hatred, surprise and those discussed under aggression and love, in which we hold others in ways very similar to emotional self-adaptors, that is, holding someone else's hands, shoulders, arms and head, as we do to ourselves, perhaps in an unconscious impulse to hold others. One of the most important situations is bereavement, in which according to the different cultural display rules and according to sexual and social differences, people hold each other and, particularly in Mediterranean and Arab cultures, embrace and kiss the deceased too; in fact, the Spanish middle-class widow, for instance, is expected to do it, just as her wailing measures the degree of her grief. Collective emotional displays are also important, not only in grief but in celebrations of a national victory, or a festive occasion such as the welcoming of the New Year in New York's Time Square, or the end of a war or a disaster. TV viewers can observe the most comical and even painful emotional displays in prize shows.

o. *To symbolize certain agreements*, a series of alter-adaptor behaviors that has undergone much change through the centuries, ranging from the handshake and the holding of the genitals recorded in the *Old Testament*, to the embrace seen today between heads of state, or the various ways of signifying a pact, a truce, the signing of a treaty, a challenge, etc.

p. *To perform certain religious, protocolarian and folk rituals* such as the Christian laying-on of hands since the early Church, kissing the bishop's ring or the hand of the priest (quickly vanishing as they began to wear lay clothes), the 'peace of Christ' handshake or embrace among members of different congregations; the embracing and kissing among monarchs in medieval times, and the kissing of the king's hand by the Spanish warrier El Cid, who in turn kisses one of his loyal friends in the face and in the mouth as a greeting; kissing on the face, as Arab leaders and French leaders do among themselves and when congratulating national heroes and winners; kissing in the mouth, as is still practiced quite forcefully by Soviet leaders; in the hand, done to some Moslem leaders by other politicians; the holding of each other in many folk dances of many cultures; the male dignitary's leading his counterpart's wife into the diningroom (cf. again Wildeblood 1965, for the history of protocolarian contacts); the holding of the deceased's hand before returning to the pew at a Kotzebue eskimo funeral, and the handshaking and kissing among women and different-sex close friends at a Latin funeral; the handshaking before some competitive sports; the ritualized handshaking of congratulation and well-wishing; and other like hand-kissing, etc.

q. *To participate in children's and adults' formally structured games*, a fascinating crosscultural research topic, in which there may be much bodily contact: leapfrog, American football, etc.

r. *To participate in children's and adults' informal play*, some of which seem to be quite universal, observed also in primates and other mammals: rough-and-tumble between youngsters, various forms of child and adult mock wrestling, running and catching each other, as when people gather at the beach, in which the males tend to show their physical prowess while the females struggle more awkwardly, laughing and giggling, a sort of 'horsing around' that enjoys much more freedom today in public in the Western cultures and which certainly may overlap sexual games.

s. *To assist others in performing a task*, whether professional or not: between two trapeze artists and in other circus acts, in certain sports, teaching how to handle different artifacts, or adopt certain dancing postures, for self-defense techniques, helping someone get off or on a vehicle, or mount or dismount a horse.

t. *Conducting momentary interpersonal social tasks* which may or may not require minimal contact: touching hands between cashier and customer, a security officer's checking at an airport, 'baby-kissing' and shaking hands during a political campaign, a policeman's frisking, during military training, helping a blind person across the street, a train conductor helping a passenger step off or on the train, someone assisting someone else in mounting or dismounting a horse, holding a woman's arm while she sets a shoe in place, etc.

u. *In situations of forced/inevitable contact*, whether interactive (friends conversing in a crowded bus, a crowded gathering, strangers talking in a waiting room) or, as is often the case, in noninteractive ones: a public conveyance in which lack of cultural fluency may cause serious misunderstandings on the part of foreigners (say, Americans in a Moroccan bus or a

Spanish subway) if verbal or kinesic apologies do not seem to be always required, in waiting rooms, in crowded sidewalks where pedestrian rules are observed in many different degrees according to culture (cf. Collett 1974; Ashcraft and Scheflen 1976: 27–28), at games in stadiums, in public celebrations and demonstrations, or in the proverbial elevator.

v. *Contacting animals* for various functions, in itself a body of alter-adaptors, as they involve individuals that are 'humanized' in different degrees by the relationship we establish with them, mainly the dog (patting, embracing, kissing, stroking, and even mouth-to-mouth kissing in some extreme out-of-the-ordinary cases), the cat (mainly caressing, what he or she seems to accept best), the horse (cheek-to-face, face-to-neck, flank-patting, and stroking of various parts), aside, of course, from laboratory animals, circus tamed animals, the stroking of fish or dolphins, the large farm animals, and the very especialized relationship established, for instance, by a bullfighter with a bull, or a rodeo man with a steer, whether accidental or showing off their prowess.

w. *As parts of the mechanism of conversation*, alter-adaptors, like self-adaptors, serve as most of the nonverbal categories discussed so far, namely: *emblems* (a pep-up pat on a player's back or buttocks), language *markers* (patting the listener's hand as we stress a word), *deictics* ('My friend here will tell you', touching someone), some *identifiers* ('you need strength', while grabbing someone's arm), *externalizers* (any of the expressions of love, hatred, happiness, etc.), and, of course, *regulators* proper (grabbing the listener's arm or forearm, various forms of contactual feedback messages, etc.).

The study of alter-adaptors

This review of alter-adaptors attempts to show their importance and the need to study them in an interdisciplinary fashion. Most of the literature on what here are called alter-adaptors deals with *touch*, and it can be gleaned from various disciplines. Hall, of course, refers to bodily contact in his classic book on proxemics (Hall 1966) and in his proxemic research handbook (Hall 1974), while Watson (1974) suggests areas of crosscultural interest better documented in recent nonverbal communication handbooks, such as the ones prepared at the Indian University Reserch Center for Language and Semiotic Studies (e.g., Sebeok, Johnson, and Hengst 1982, on Arab nonverbal communication) and Johnson's dissertation (1983 [chapter 7, on Japan]). Morris, from a rather ethological point of view, offers a detailed account of the different touching behaviors, mostly in dyads, classifying the activities according to the body parts involved. Montague (1971) discussed in depth our tactile experiences from birth and crossculturally. From a socio-psychological angle, Argyle (1975: chapter 15) discusses bodily contacts,

Ashcraft and Scheflen's (1976) work on crowding and other interpersonal spatial situations can inspire a great deal of sociocultural, psychological and ecological research, while Jourard (1966) studied the amount of touching and being touched among young Americans. Waxer (1978) reviews current views on touching during psychotherapy interviews. In nursing, most of the literature to date deals with the importance of touch in nurse-patient interaction. Other aspects of nonverbal communication which are just as important in that profession, such as paralanguage, general kinesics and gaze behavior, are being only discovered now as subject of serious research. One specific medical application of touching is the experiments conducted by Krieger (1972, 1974a, 1974b, 1975) on the effect of the nurse's strongly motivated therapeutic *laying on of hands* on the mean hemoglobin value of patients, which raised significantly as compared to patients not treated that way. This is intimately related to present-day Christian laying-on of hands while praying for physical, mental or spiritual healing, as described in the *New Testament* (MacNutt 1974, 1977; Shlemon, Linn, and Linn 1978). Finally, *etiquette* books from different cultures provide unique documentation on several forms of alter-adaptors, such as those dealing with American society (Vanderbilt 1956; Fenwick 1948; Bevans 1960; Page 1961; Sara 1963; Post 1965), Spain (Bauer 1967), etc. Of special interest are those of other historical periods, such as the ones reviewed in the very useful account of English manners (with references to other cultures and periods from the 13th to the 19th century) by Wildeblood (1965), although etiquette is always wrongly associated with the upper classes.

From the point of view of the *proxemic relationship* between the cointeractants, although alter-adaptor behaviors always occur in intimate and close-personal distances (Hall 1966) situations, we all in a number of occasions (elevators, subways, buses, waiting rooms) touch others without there being true intimacy, unless genital areas must be close to each other or the hands are forced into the area of another person's intimate space, and only if the proximity becomes conscious and perhaps elicites a reaction. Therefore, sought and forced alter-adaptors constitute in themelves important concepts and subjects of study, acknowledged in the present classification. Many references have been made to the elevator situation and the typical behaviors elicited in such a forced-adaptor situation. Other similar situations are created in the mutual rubbing of pedestrians, much more avoided by Anglo-Saxons than, for instance, Russians, Italians or Arabs (cf. Ashcraft and Scheflen 1976: 27–28). However, one must consider the crowded situation traditionally—that is, culturally—imposed on those peoples by their built environment, in other words, the layout of their towns since ancient or medieval times, with narrow streets and alleys, such as we can still observe today in the old districts of Spanish, French, Greek or Italian cities and towns, and much, much more in the medinas and suqs of Moroccan cities, or in the streets of Old Delhi's Urdu Bazaar, or across Calcutta's Howrah Bridge, or in Budapest's downtown Váci Street. And yet those same people would avoid touching others in the wider spaces of the modern quarters of the same cities, avoiding the same pedestrian rules they do not mind breaking otherwise. Driven to situations of imposed physical contact, they are much more tolerant toward touching, while I, being from Spain, a culture half-way between intense touching and nontouching cultures, can navigate in either situation and enjoy it too. But it is interesting to observe that those highly tactile peoples are also the more talkative and noisy ones in the street as well as more articulated kinesically and much more expressive emotionally and less restrained. The most impressionistic view of close-contact cultures suggests that the greater intensity in the occurrence of alter-adaptors of all kinds, based after all on kinesic behavior, corresponds to an equally higher intensity in the use of the Basic Triple Structure language-paralanguage-kinesics, which gives an Indian, an Arab or a Spaniard the interactive ebullience with which we associate him.

Some positive and negative aspects of alter-adaptors

It is interesting, obvious as it may seem, that the two extremes of the interpersonal affective parameter, *love and hatred* (with indifference in the middle) and their corresponding behaviors of affiliation and aggression, are expressed by bodily contact, and that the more intense both feelings are, the stronger the need for contact and the longer it is maintained.

But, at the same time, alter-adaptors are one of the more powerful behaviors of *deception*, precisely to feign feelings within the love scale when the actual feelings fall entirely within the opposite one. Alter-adaptors of deception are constantly utilized by the less sincere persons to gain the trust of others for a multitude of everyday life selfish purposes. Naturally, most of us at one time or another, and depending on our own sensitivity toward nonverbal behavior, become perfectly aware of the incongruity of someone else's verbal statements and touching behaviors, and his previous attitude, words, gestures, as well as the ongoing negative relationships between the two of us. A pat on the back accompanied by a forced (though seemingly natural) smile and some words of sympathy, promise, regret, etc., can deceive many and elicit behaviors that will benefit the deceiver. So does deceptive laughter, as discussed within paralanguage.

Aside from the phylogenetic and ontogenetic importance of interpersonal touch (because of its presence in primates and other mammals and because of the developmental characteristics from uterine life through infancy and childhood to old age), it is interesting to consider how alter-adaptors, directly or synesthesially experienced from the earliest stages of life through later social life, are gradually accumulated in the tractile and kinesthetic *memories* of a person. In addition, they undergo a cultural development through which people have overcome many noncontactual barriers, achieving a wider repertoire of alter-adaptors in public situations, for instance, as well as in private ones, from dancing since the appearance of the waltz to courtship in both public and private settings, or the highly intimate tactile practices at a doctor's office.

Reviewing the outline of tactual occurrences, it is easy, for instance, to justify all the issues raised by present-day studies on sex differences, and how the feminist movement has developed some rightful arguments on the tendency of researchers to recognize only the affectionate uses of touching over its use as a highly iconic status or dominance marker in a male-dominated society, in which a man, say, a doctor, may touch a woman, in this case a nurse, but hardly the opposite. This obviously appears as a negative use of touch, just as its deceptive uses do in everyday life between same or different-sex interactants, and Henley's (1977) plausible conclusions on heterosexual attitudes toward touch, such a basic human need, should also incite researchers to educate people in overcoming many existing culturally-conditioned barriers in the less tactile societies, showing the non-touchers how interactive touch can enrich social life.

Alter-adaptors, in sum, constitute a very important topic of research in themselves and a decisive touchstone for the understanding of interactive behaviors that define cultures and personalities as well as social, emotional and mental circumstances. One can affirm that Arabs are a close-contact people as are Indians, but social deprivation and alienation, such as we can witness in the streets of Calcutta or in the medinas of a Moroccan city, prevent social contact and affiliation. Likewise, the same person who may normally engage in alter-adaptor behaviors when interacting with others will be cowering in a corner to avoid physical contact if he or she is affected by depression.

17. Body-adaptors

As intermediate between self-adaptors and object-adaptors, body-adaptors can be defined both as the objects and substances most immediately attached to the body because they are aimed at protecting it, nurturing it and satisfying it, modifying its appearance or assisting it in various ways, and as the interactive or noninteractive movements and positions conditioned by them.

They are socially regarded as virtually inherent in the body, as part of its physical appearance and as anatomically 'adapted' to it, as happens with clothes, foot and head gear, jewels, and even objects such as pipes, glasses, sometimes to the extent that we may not recognize a person without those identifiers.

What differentiates body-adaptor and object-adaptor behaviors from all other behavioral categories is, first, that, although they are in greater or lesser degree kinesically manifested, they are, when performing their functions (e.g., as good, jewelry) primarily extrasomatic (in other words, they are defined as body-adaptors and object-adaptors by the objects and substances that qualify as such); and also that, while the others can acquire an objectual representation (say, an externalizer of impatience displayed by chair-arm rubbing) body- and object-adaptors have both a static and a dynamic semiotic realization, according to whether we consider them during their association with the body or at other times. This entails three distinct semiotic states or stages of deep significance in social life.

The three semiotic realizations of body-adaptors

The first semiotic-communicative stage is that of *static objects and substances*, such as a dress (body-adaptor), a perfume (body-adaptor), a piece of Indian betel (body-adaptor), or a chair (object-adaptor), which can stand by themselves, displaying physical and chemical qualities that result in sensible signs and messages.

And yet, those signs are so intimately associated in our minds to their somatic realization that they can evoke, through their static stage—and by means of different synesthesial associations generated by their visual, tactile and chemical perception—the behavioral body-adaptor and object-adaptor activities (e.g., the worn dress, the facial expression or gaze behavior associated with a perfume, the chewing facial movement and reddened tongue and gums of betel users, the postures and postural shifts conditioned by the chair).

This *synesthesial assumption of signs* constitutes the second semiotic-communicative stage, one of the hidden messages for the consumer who views a magazine advertisement. An armor in a museum, a dress in a shop window or a 'cold beer' in an ad are such static signs susceptible of a multiple sign evocation.

The third stage is, therefore, the one in which static and dynamic signs are blended into the actual *kinesic and multichannel realizations* of body- and object-adaptor behaviors, that is, the worn, 'live' dress (which is kinesically animated by the wearer, but visually, and perhaps tactually and kinesthetically, perceived by the cointeractant), the intimate distance and intimate paralinguistic voice modifications that may accompany the perfume, the kinesic-visual realization of the betel mouthful, or the 'humanized' chair.

Those realizations, in turn, will trigger further synesthesial associations, such as the consistency, shape, texture and weight of the body in the dress, when they are not directly perceived, through the visual perception of its kinesic activation.

The spatial-temporal dimensions of body-adaptors

On the other hand, body-adaptor and object-adaptor behaviors possess a double spatial and temporal dimension, not only because, as any other behaviors or sensible signs, they can be perceived in a spatial relationship and stored in the memory, but because specifically body-adaptors of olfactory and gustatory perception can also travel through time, as chemical messages do, while those of tactile perception remain, as alter-adaptors, in the skin organs proportionally to the duration and intensity of the contact experienced. Their iconicity, therefore, can be: chemical, as with the strength of the perfume measuring the intentions of the wearer, the evocations triggered by a garment worn by someone who has been dead for some time (triggered by the natural or synthetic odorous molecules still attached to it) or the flavor or nutritional and subnutritional products acting as identifiers of cultural, familial or personal characteristics; visual, as with the chromatic or morphological features of clothes associated with various cultural, socioeconomic or individual characteristics; and tactile and kinesthetic, as with the textural qualities and shape of body-adaptors in general measuring their origin, quality, and even some personal features of those to whom they are directly attached.

The functions of body-adaptors

This functional classification refers to the body-adaptor behaviors and the body-adaptors that condition them.

a. *To facilitate the oral ingestion of nutritional products*, that is, food and drink, by doing it directly with the mouth (as when drinking from a spring with various manners, biting from a large piece of bread or watermelon) or the hands (as with the right hand, the pure one in India and in Arab cultures, in which good and bad manners can be differentiated by the associated posture, the hand movements, etc.); by using utensils like fork, knife and wooden or metal spoons, with table manners that vary crossculturally and socioeconomically; by using culture-specific aids, such as Eastern chopsticks, bowls from which to eat and drink directly assisted by the former; glasses with and without stems, which condition manners, as do straws, containers from which to drink directly such as hollowed gourds and skins (sometimes observing nontouching rules, as with the Spanish *botijo*, *porrón* and wineskin), nearly universal tea and coffee cups, coexisting with, for instance, the delicate and tiny clay ones used only once at tea stalls along Calcutta's busy streets.

b. *To clothe the body*, protecting it, concealing it, enhancing it or modifying its natural visual characteristics by means of all the garments and other body coverings that have been used through history, from dress proper to footwear and headgear, whether for social, occupational or ceremonial purposes, ranging from bathing to fighting, diving or playing. This is the most important group of body-adaptors and, in turn, of body-adaptor behaviors, as the evolution of man's and woman's clothes—from infants swaddling, through underwear, to complementary body coverings such as hats, gloves, scarves and shawls—condition universal or culture-bound behaviors that are also influenced by economic, religious and psychological factors, Raffia, grass or leaf skirts, loin clothes, and present-day jeans, the Greek chiton and the Roman toga, the Japanese kimono and the Indian sari and dhoti, the South American poncho and the Eskimo anorak, the Arab haik, veil and turban, the Medieval and Renaissance codpiece, ruffs, head and chin scarves, the fighting armors and coats of mail, the apiarist's mask, the nineteenth-century crinoline and the space suit, they all have determined specific kinesic behaviors, some of which have naturally disappeared with the fashion while others have survived subject to formal changes in similar objects. How people put on and take off their clothes, how they manage a scarf or shawl, tip off a hat, hold an overcoat collar against the face, slip on gloves while conversing, and how they unconsciously tap pockets, fidget with buttons and hems, preen cuffs and ties, and straighten creases, hair ribbons, socks and blouses, constitutes a whole area of fruitful observation and research.

c. *To carry out child-rearing tasks*, whether facilitating the child's locomotion by means of baby walkers and straps, keeping track of them by attaching belts to their ankles as Burmese mothers do, pacify them with pacifiers, flatten the heads by pressing it between wooden boards (still practiced among certain African tribes), carry them in slings and back-bags, or the Kirghiz baby's small lamb-skin sack holding porridge which hangs from its cradle within reach.

d. *To display, conceal, enhance or modify the natural visual qualities of the body* by means of jewelry and other objectual adornments. Another vast area of crosscultural study that comprises all types of jewelry made of precious stones and different metals, feathers, bones and other materials, hairpins and combs, cufflinks, watches, charms and all types of adornments, for which the body can even be mutilated, as happens with earrings, noserings, African and Amazonian lip discs and neck rings.

e. *To enhance, conceal, add to or modify the visual and olfactory qualities of the body* by means of natural and manufactured chemical products, namely cosmetics, body paints of primitive and advanced cultures, perfumes and shaving lotions, deodorants, hair conditioners, the Hindu vermillion mark on the forehead, or the Hindu sadhu's ashes that cover his body. The social, religious, folkloric and sexual functions of these chemical products, which today account for a good part of the advertising industry, merit extensive research, not only in themselves (as with the human chemical messages versus animal ones) but, even more, as to their costructuration with all other verbal and nonverbal systems, a perspective that applies, of course, to all other body-adaptors.

f. *To enhance, modify or add to the visual qualities* of the body by using objects that act as extensions of it, such as artificial fingernails, eyelashes, hair pieces, the various 'falsies' used in different periods, the lip discs mentioned earlier, phallic extensions, etc.

g. *To facilitate the oral ingestion of pseudonutritional products or provide nutritional surrogates*, which condition specific behaviors besides identifying different cultures. They include, for instance, the various masticatories, such as the Western chewing gum and the betel used in India and adjacent countries, chewing tobacco, the various other forms of tobacco, such as cigarettes, cigars and snuff, tobacco and narcotics inhaled by means of various artifacts, from pipes and lady's cigarette holders to Indian hookah pipes, water pipes, or the Argentinian *mate* glass container.

h. *To cleanse and groom the body* by means of water applied in various ways with different objects such as soap, sponges, toothbrushes, towels, napkins (absent in the lower classes of napkin-using cultures), toothpicks (which some carry around in their mouths), handkerchiefs (versus nose-blowing by hand, observed in primitive cultures but also in persons of more advanced ones), bathroom paper (whose texture and quality varies between, for instance, highly capitalist cultures and socialist ones), and its surrogates (stones, newspapers, and leaves, etc.).

i. *To aid, complement or disguise the body's sensorial and motor functions* by using baby pacifiers, walkers, dentures, glasses and contact lenses, eighteenth and nineteenth-century lady's and gentlemen's eye-glass and lorgnette for social occasions, sunglasses (used today beyond their optical functions, as face-masks were in the eighteenth century), old and modern hearing aids, and the behaviors resulting from their use, mostly kinesic, as when using artificial limbs, wheelchairs, crutches, etc., but occasionally paralinguistic, as with the stereotyped speech behind dark glasses.

j. *To protect, soothe, and heal the body* by injection, ingestion or anatomical adaptation of natural or man-made objects and substances such as inhalers, oxygen masks, injections, i.v.s, postsurgical attachments, eye patches, medical or makeshift casts, slings, dressings, pads, and the many folk remedies of all cultures.

k. *To perform other functions involving objects carried on and manipulated by the person*. They may symbolize specific social status (e.g., scepters, crowns, shafts) or state (the Zulu bride's knife which symbolizes virginity, engagement and wedding rings, etc.), be part of the person's attire along with clothes and adornments such as festive, magical or criminal's masks, fans (used by both sexes in China and by Spanish older women in the summer and even younger ones until the nineteenth century, when there was a true fan sign code), pipes, walking sticks, umbrellas, etc.

1. *To perform unconscious random acts*, both in interaction and noninteraction: fidgeting with hems, creases, buttons and ruffles, sliding a medal along its chain, sliding the chain between parted lips, fidgeting with rings, the watch, bracelets, glasses, rubbing a pipe while in the mouth, etc.

Person-identifying body-adaptors

It has been indicated that, because some body-adaptors seem to be permanently 'adapted' to some persons, they are perceived as parts of them, even as personality-defining features, such as Chaplin's hat, pants, boots and stick, Churchill's cigar, or the cigar in the mouth of the American comedian George Burns. For years, many college professors in England and North America, particularly at the beginning of their academic careers, have made the pipe and the tweed jacket their identifying marks, much more than just a garment and a prop, since they are perfectly costructured with their other verbal and nonverbal systems as part of their total communicative repertoire. In fact, the very smell of pipe tobacco not only identifies the man, but delimits and announces his territory down the hall as part of his very personality, the odor iconically representing him, as does the specific perfume used by a woman.

Interactional and crosscultural dimensions

Some body-adaptors may act as emotional displays, or rather, as externalizers, mostly out of awareness or without the intention to communicate, e.g., by nervously handling a pipe, fidgeting with a ring or a necklace, pushing down bracelets, pulling out a collar, or pulling a glove over the hand in a contemptuous way.

While many objects like glasses or pipes can be handled as *illustrators* in a random, flitting fashion, that is, as object-adaptors that are not necessarily being used for that which they have been designed, they become body-adaptors when those glasses are worn and when the pipe is in our mouth, modifying our facial expression and even our speech articulation.

It is clear that body-adaptors, whether intentional or out of awareness, can always act as *regulators* of the interaction, influencing both the speaker's and the listener's behaviors, but less so than the other nonverbal categories because of the static quality of many of them. Their effect is more an overriding one, as with a pair of dark glasses that impede clear vision on the part of the cointeractant, a tight-fitting dress, a profusion of jewelry, or a noticeable makeup. This modifying, tone-setting quality of body-adaptors can be much less conscious than, for instance, manipulated conversational object-adaptors, ideographs or alter-adaptors. The dress habits, cosmetics and perfume of a woman can influence the interactive style and strategy of a man, as they may betray her own attitude toward the opposite sex, even though they may be displayed quite out of awareness at a given time, due perhaps to her own lack of interest in him.

On the other hand, body-adaptors may condition not only kinesic behavior, but even language and paralanguage, as when a woman speaks with a chosen vocabulary and a flirtatious tone of voice, fidgeting with her necklace and sliding it through her parted lips across a cocktail lounge table from a man, perhaps intently gazing at him, or when the man slowly blows the smoke of his cigarette and looks at her with a slight slow and intent smile and a forward posture.

Body-adaptors, like alter-adaptors, can function as strong *deceptors*, mainly clothes and cosmetics, as they may be designed to physically conceal undesirable imperfections or enhance some features and anatomical characteristics.

Even without wanting to deceive for one's ulterior benefit, women at a funeral may emphasize their makeup or use dark glasses, while many men will also wear sunglasses. Mourning black, on the other hand, could be aimed only at deceiving and feigning a false grief, just as would an alter-adaptor like an embrace.

This last observation links with the *ritualization of* body-adaptors even when presumably representing nonexisting feelings, as happens with the supressing display rules in time of bereavement or, at the other extreme, the professional mourners of some ancient and modern cultures. The process of cultural ritualization is undergone also by dress etiquette and habits, by prescribed tea time, table manners, religious practices, etc.

The *display rules* suggested, which are applied also to object-adaptors, refer to (a) age, prescribing dress style, amount (if not prohibition) of make-up used by women, the table manners in the use of implements, expected at a certain age but varying also according to social status, (b) sex, not only as regards dress but other body-adaptors such as pipes and perfumes, and (c) status, since the higher the status, the more lax the display rules of mourning black are in Italy, Spain or France, for instance.

Putting all the above factors together, that is, the various forms of body-adaptors, their interactive and modifying functions, their use for deception, their ritualization, and the rules governing their display, we can with confidence pursue a comparative *crosscultural* study. We would again establish the basic difference between primitive and modern cultures, since a data collecting of body-adaptors would provide us with a derth of determining elements in nonverbal behavior. Primitive body-adaptors are, for instance, the bracelets and necklaces of naked Wasúsu women of Brazil

Amazonia, leaf skirts, leaf loin pieces, and the bamboo lengths used to drink water from by Mindanao's Paleolithic-like Tasadays. But among modern cultures, we find culture-specific body-adaptors, such as the Western spoon and fork and the Eastern chopsticks, the coexisting Indian sari and blue jeans, the disappearing sash of older male peasants in Spain, the longer black skirts of the older women, and their *porrón*, or glass wine container from which to drink directly without touching it with one's lips.

18. Object-adaptors

Object-adaptors are the second group of interactive or noninteractive behaviors which comprise both the body itself and elements external to it which also give those behaviors special characteristics. They can be defined as cultural artifacts and organic or inorganic objects of the natural, modified and built environments, that is, further removed from the body than body-adaptors and closer to it than the rest of the objectual environment (see Fig. 3.3), and the resulting movements and positions.

The semiotic realizations of object-adaptors

The semiotic realizations observed in body-adaptors occur also in object-adaptors, including the olfactory perception, if secondary, of a number of them, besides the basic physical visual, tactile and kinesthetic modes. From their static perception, through the somatic activities they can evoke, to their actual realization, which may in turn generate still further synesthesial associations, object-adaptors occupy a relevant place in our daily interaction with the environment. Take, for instance, a car in a televison commercial or in a dealer's showroom. Its static perception, which in the latter context is accompanied by the smell of new upholstery, evokes the driving activity, with the kinesthetic appreciation of its driving characteristics and the consistency of the seats; while the actual experience of driving the car elicits yet new synesthesial associations still not present, such as the different kinds of pavements and terrain, the air-conditioning it is supposed to provide, and even the possible presence of an imagined or real driving companion and her (as is usually the case in the advertising situation) bodily characteristics.

Functions of object-adaptors

Although object-adaptors pervade so many activities in every culture, it is possible to distinguish a series of basic functions that determine specific personal and culture-identifying behaviors.

a. *Resting the body* on (i) *body-oriented furniture and other structures* which have developed through the various historical periods in the different cultures, thus determining in turn the evolution of postural habits because of their greater or lesser degree of anatomical design. The different forms of beds (ranging from the Indian wood-and-rope charpoy and the Namba banana-leaf one, through the four-post canopied bed, to the water bed), the Roman triclinium for reclined dining, the straight benches and chairs still in use, the executive swivel chair, the foot stool, the 'lazy-boy', the bar stool, and the Larsen chair of many public places (designed to discourage long sittings); they all elicit postural behaviors that a detailed study would classify not only crossculturally but within a given society, that is, the various ways of sitting on, say, an ordinary chair (stride and leaning on its back, balancing it, yogi-style, etc.) according to status and situational contexts. Some architectural body-resting forms would qualify quite legitimately as architectural furniture, the best example I know being the Spanish small-town *poyo* or stone bench attached like an appendix to the home façade by the main door, betraying its socializing function now threatened by street traffic; (ii) on *other structures* designed secondarily for resting, such as architectural ledges in public areas, the low walls around fountains and monuments, etc.; (iii) leaning against or sitting on nonanatomical furniture (e.g., tables) and railings, walls, steps, curbs, fences, and natural forms like trees and rocks.

b. *Performing household and occupational instrumental tasks*, involving rather universal or culture-specific objects which I will not attempt to classify here as they constitute the largest group of object-adaptors. To give a few examples: cooking utensils (clay pots, Indian brass pots, Chinese wok); food and drink containers (from fine china to the Filipino wild banana-leaf dish and the many forms of pitchers); cow dung or sheep manure, used as cooking fuel in India and Afghanistan respectively (the former giving New Delhi, along with kerosene, its characteristic early-evening smell); water-carrying and water-storing containers made of clay or metal (carried against the hip or balanced on the head on top of a doughnut-shaped cloth), and gourds and bamboo; cleaning tools, from the short Indian broom that cleaners typically handle squatting across public buildings and airports, to the various mechanical artifacts; mops and chimney sweeper's equipment; the tools of the different crafts, from the spinning-wheel (Gandhi's symbol of nonviolent revolution) to the shoemaker's, harness-maker's, tanner's, or carpenter's equipment), farming artifacts that have for centuries shaped the ontogenetic development of musculature, postural behavior and handling manners (reaping sickles, plows, hoes, etc.), creating mental images of soil-toilers, conditioning their time structuration (chronemics), and the hardening, weathering, and often early deterioriation of their bodies; the writing utensils used from the stylus era to the electric typewriter; the tools of artistic creation; and many more which can be classified and studied from the point of view of anthropology, psychology, and each of the areas of the objectual environment represented by the different artifacts.

c. *Self-adaptor tasks* involving mainly grooming tools, such as toothbrushes and its equivalents in certain cultures (e.g., India's neem-tree twig), sponges, combs, etc.

d. *Alter-adaptor tasks*, involving also grooming (household items, the barber's tools), surgical instruments or, at the other extreme of a positive-negative parameter, all the instruments invented to curtail the body's faculties through torture and even death (from all sorts of weapons and arms to artifacts like the guillotine), or others devised to punish minor infringements, as with the schoolmaster's feared ruler and strap.

e. *Interactive conversational tasks*, involving such 'props' as glasses, pencils or pens (when, for instance, glasses are not functioning as body-adaptors), objects on which to pound, tap, rap, etc., all of them susceptible of being used as kinesic language markers.

f. *Interactive nonconversational but communicative activities* using writing utensils, flags, batons, typewriters, oriental brushes, quill pens, etc.

g. *Interactive or noninteractive, conversational or nonconversational random acts* which, of course, may overlap other nonverbal categories and functions, such as doodling with pens, brushing or flicking lint or crumbs, twirling, rapping and tapping on objects, hitting one's leg with a twig while walking, kicking sand or rocks, rapping along a fence, turning a hat in one's hands, etc.

h. *Performing athletic, sport and physique-building tasks* involving discs, vaults, balls, gymnasium equipment, and all types of mechanical and powered instruments.

i. *Performing all kinds of children's and adults' games and entertainment activities*, using dolls and toys, dice, dominoes, cards, billiard's balls and cues, the magician's arsenal of props, etc.

j. *Producing music* by playing all types of ancient and modern instruments: India's sitar and Ireland's penny whistle, Scotland's bagpipe, the grand piano, the rural Spanish Christmas-time *zambomba* (a crude percussion piece) and the Australian Arnhem Land aboriginals' didgeridoo (a six-foot hollowed branch which produces a low, vibrating drone when blown), etc. Each represents deep cultural traditions, unique man-made sounds, and peculiar kinesic behaviors that can be judged through different esthetic conceptions.

k. *Animal-oriented tasks*, in training, taming, branding, riding, and hitching, plowing, grain threshing, etc., which would also fall within occupational and household chores, determining many typical behaviors, not only kinesic, but verbal and paralinguistic. This would constitute, in fact, a separate area of research, as it represents many forms of man–animal interaction which include culture-specific paralinguistic animal calls; in addition to naming, blasphemous speech among the peasants, and other vocal behaviors, such as "that hissing sound which hostlers are want to produce when engaged in rubbing down a horse", noted in Dickens's *Pickwick Papers*.

This nonexhaustive classification, which suggests the fascinating variety of object-adaptors, and, from a semiotic point of view, the intimate interaction of people with their natural and made objectual environment and their mutual conditioning, does not exclude Ekman and Friesen's (1972) "instrumental-task objects" because instrumental and noninstrumental may succeed each other and almost overlap. One can argue that if we are doodling with a pencil at a meeting in an intermittent way while taking notes with it, both the pencil and the actions performed with it are object-adaptors because by definition, the pencil is being manipulated. This, on the other hand, would exclude objects that are connected or truly adapted to the body, which qualify as body-adaptors.

Interactive, historical, and crosscultural dimensions

Object-adaptors are, like body-adaptors, kinetically based. A number of everyday interactive and noninteractive kinesic behaviors (see Fig. 4.1) are actually objectual displays which, first of all, may vary from culture to culture according to their own artifactual differences and ingenuity. Therefore, one of the most obvious research topics suggested by object-adaptors is their comparative study, which, if included within the behaviors recorded in the sort of kinesic atlases that need to be elaborated (cf. Morris, Collet *et al.* 1979), would trace the distribution of certain rather universal 'isokimes' along with other culture-specific ones.

At the same time, primitive cultures show the use of certain rudimentary object-adaptors as one of their characteristics, while many ancient artifacts still remain in use in modern cultures—along with the behaviors they condition in people—as vestiges of preindustrial and even premechanical periods, such as the foot-operated potter's wheel, the Roman plow and the stone slingshot still seen in Spain and other countries, etc. Other object-adaptors peculiar to specific modern cultures are, for instance: in India, the bells rang by worshippers in temples, the policeman's lathi-ring (stick), the public cigarette-lighting wick that hangs from power posts or curb railings in Calcutta, or the Chinese spitoon that we see in photographs of dignitaries sitting at both sides of it by the also typical tea set.

One of the aspects of the crosscultural study of object-adaptors is that it reveals their many interactive functions as truly communicative tools, as is the case with the conch blown in Southern India to call people, writing utensils, which allow people to bridge spatial and temporal gaps, the objects unconsciously or consciously handled and fidgeted with during a conversation, often serving as clues to state and personality characteristics. In turn, these functions suggest, because of their kinesic dimension, the inherent interchangeability of object-adaptors and body-adaptors, emotional expressions, emblems, illustrators and regulators, as discussed at different points.

Further, this interchangeability reveals the *grammaticality* ascribed to emblems earlier. The Spanish older woman who is handling a fan (not with a body-adaptor function) may say in a contemptuous tone *¡Pues a mí——!* filling the vocal pause with a closing movement of the fan—rather than completing the statement verbally, '*me da igual*' ('¡Well, I don't care!')—and a simultaneous eyelid closure, thus completing the sentence as accurately and effectively as words would, in fact, adding facial-objectual emphasis.

As will be seen within literary anthropology in Chapter 11, object-adaptors, even more than body-adaptors (because they cover a wider range of cultural and social manifestations) constitute a research area for which the narrative literatures of the different cultures are invaluable documents of diachronic and synchronic analysis, since object-adaptors and body-adaptors have been modified, replaced, preserved or created through the centuries. One of their historical aspects illustrated eloquently by literature is the documentation of the historical development of body-adaptors and object-adaptors—of importance in all the social sciences—through the behaviors described by the writer: table manners, linked to eating and drinking tools; the way a fictional character smokes as a cultural, sex, and social identifying feature; his or her dress style, the ways in which clothes are worn and the postures and manners associated with them through changing fashions as well as with furniture; the social, cultural and psychological information contained in those behaviors, the nonverbal kinesic behaviors linked to clothes and fighting gear of centuries ago (described not just in historical novels but in more authentic documents like the Spanish national epic poem *El Cid*), etc.

19. Regulators

Although all the bodily nonverbal categories can operate in interaction not all of them seem to have the specific function of regulating "the back-and-forth nature of speaking and listening between two or more interactants", as defined by Ekman and Friesen (1969: 82). This is not saying that they cannot in a given situation act as such regulators. The study of regulators is such an important aspect of the study of the mechanism of conversational or nonconversational interaction that all that can be done in this comprehensive review of nonverbal categories is to determine which somatic activities can perform regulatory functions.

It is essential to point out, however, that the regulatory functions are not designed solely to maintain the flow of a conversation between a speaker and a listener or listeners, for there are important forms of nonconversational yet interactive encounters in which regulators are as essential as they are in a face-to-face, mostly verbal, exchange. A man and a woman engaged in intimate interaction may not speak any words, but each of their behaviors, be it a flitting glance, a squeeze of the hand, a turning-away of the head, a tear or a kiss, may in each instance elicit the succeeding behavior by regulating the exchange. Likewise, two or more strangers actually interact in the street while walking toward each other along the sidewalk, although they will probably never exchange any words; but a shift in path by one of them may regulate the upcoming activities of the others, who will decide the outcome of the encounter by slightly modifying their path, perhaps looking at him in the eye and then averting their gaze and, in any case, performing the ritualized action known as "civil inattention" (Goffman 1963; cf. Collett's [1974] study of pedestrian behavior).

In a true conversation, whether a brief encounter while purchasing a ticket or asking for directions, or a truly topical social exchange, regardless of whether it takes place face to face or invisibly over the telephone, regulators must be used, and it is in these situations that we need a rather sophisticated arsenal of behavioral choices.

Regulatory behaviors

It is important, therefore, to see that such interactive activities as turn rules (claiming the speaker's turn, yielding it, taking it, closing it, etc.) and counterrules (interruptions, turn holdings), feedback, etc., can be achieved through more than one of the bodily codes, as can be illustrated with a few examples:

(a) *verbal language:* 'Excuse me, but—' (claiming the speaker's turn or interrupting him for different reasons), 'Go on' (extending the present speaker's turn);

(b) *paralanguage:* 'Uh-hu' (agreement feedback), '¡Mmmmmm!' (pleasurable moan that conditions the next cointeractant's behavior), 'Tz' (apico-alveolar click and audible pharyngeal ingression claiming the turn), breathing heavily as a reaction to the partner's behavior, etc.;

(c) *kinesics:* nodding (positive feedback), /Wait a minute/ (turn suppressing or turn holding by the speaker), /Go ahead/ (yielding the turn), postural shift (signifying attention, 'I have finished', or 'Let's deal with that point'), etc.;

(d) *silence/stillness:* terminating a topic, signifying acquiescence, refusal or tension, which will determine the succeeding behaviors;

(e) *proxemics:* getting closer may indicate the intention to develop intimate behavior, secrecy, threat, attack (regulating the behaviors accordingly), just as drawing away from the cointeractant would signify disinterest, intention to terminate the conversation, take leave, etc.;

(f) *chemical:* tears, strong regulator of the encounter, not only when they are being shed, but when they are anticipated and later remembered, nervous palmar or facial sweat, etc.;

(g) *dermal:* blushing, restraining verbal language, paralanguage and kinesics on the part of the blusher's cointeractant, or eliciting the escalation of a flirting strategy, among other regulatory functions;

(h) *thermal:* body heat radiated while in a public conveyance elicits withdrawal if it is at all possible, while a dancing partner may become aroused by it and change his or her linguistic and extralinguistic strategies;

(i) an *object-adaptor* can become part of a kinesic act in granting the speaker's turn, stopping it, negating it, etc.

The regulatory mechanism

Three important aspects of verbal and nonverbal behaviors that have been discussed in Chapter 3 must again be considered in order to understand the functioning of regulators: (a) their self-regulatory functions within the speaker's own behavioral repertoire, and their interactional functions between the participants coming from either speaker or listener (e.g. the speaker's verbal kinesic or chemical activities determine the listener's subsequent conscious or unconscious choice of behaviors, while the listener's own behaviors will also affect the speaker's by providing him with direct feedback or, as with a sudden scanning of the room while otherwise paying attention to him, with some additional information); (b) the fact that the regulating effect can be provided by behaviors (and, of course, events) that have taken place immediately prior to the present regulatory change, farther and farther back in the chronological development of the interactive stream or, thirdly, that have not taken place yet but are anticipated (e.g., tear-shedding, aggression); and (c) the intensity of the regulatory behaviors themselves, determining the degree of their momentary or overriding effect on the encounter.

It would be repetitious at this point to try to illustrate the obvious regulatory possibilities of the other nonverbal categories. I will only indicate that some have a low regulatory value, while others like externalizers, deictics and alter-adaptors can be intensively regulatory.

A note on the development and pathology of regulators

As happens when dealing with other nonverbal categories, even a cursory review reveals how relevant the matter of regulators of interaction is in developmental studies to determine how the child develops the total multi-repertoire of verbal and nonverbal behaviors, among which many of the regulatory ones are conspicuously absent before late childhood, as with certain verbal expressions ('Go ahead', for turn yielding), paralinguistic intermittent feedback cues, certain proxemic acts, as well as the sophisticated handling of conversational props. The systematic study of regulators can also throw light on the regulatory behaviors of impaired people, mainly deaf, deafmute and blind, and deaf persons, as well as those of disturbed interactants. This is a subject which, of course, falls within the study of the mechanism of conversation and its pathological variants, where, for instance, the response latency in Down-syndrome individuals must be intimately understood and met with the necessary 'interactional fluency', as it cannot be the same fluency displayed with other cointeractants.

20. Emotional Displays

It has been said much too often and quite wrongly that nonverbal communication expresses emotion, as if that were its only function in interaction, unless one concedes that various degrees of emotion or 'feeling' could be found in almost every single activity. There is certainly a clearly differentiated set of behaviors represented by every external somatic system which are consciously or unconsciously displayed for the 'expression' or 'communication' of feelings or emotional states (happiness, sadness, fear, anger, surprise, interest, tranquility, impatience, etc.). Since emotional expressions have been studied in depth by others, very especially by Ekman and by Ekman and his coworkers, I will only make three observations that I feel must be taken into account.

The ubiquity of emotional displays and their status as a category

While it is true that we can clearly differentiate a set of emotional expressions (the term with which Ekman [1977] seems to have replaced his earlier one of "affect-displays") encoded and decoded as such, this term actually overlaps all the others, and Ekman acknowledges the role of facial expression as emblems, abstractions, and regulators. An interactional *regulator* such as the typical apico-alveolar click, plus a pharyngeal audible ingression [tz′>†], used to claim the floor in a conversation and become speaker, can also be a conspicuous emotional display if given certain characteristics of intensity, loudness and duration; likewise, an *illustrator* like the pictographic representation of a female's body by an emotionally aroused man is also a clear emotional display modified, again, by its parakinesic qualifiers of intensity, range and duration; an *alter-adaptor* such as a highly emotional embrace of grief or happiness is also an emotional display; and so is an *object-adaptor* like grabbing something to threaten or attack someone.

So, ¿is an emotional display a behavioral category in itself or only a qualifier of any other category? For we know that we can perform an emblem, a deictic, a language marker or an event tracer 'with' emotion. The problem is, again, that we are mixing clearly morphological categories (kinetographs, adaptors, etc.) with motivational and functional ones (language markers, externalizers, etc.), and that some might deem the addition of emotional displays rather gratuitous. In which case, ¿what about externalizers and regulators? ¿Do they not also represent qualifying features of the other categories rather than legitimate categories? I feel, in the end, that since valid arguments are easily found for and against the inclusion of emotional displays, ¿why not classify them as a separate category, since in that way they could generate so much psychological (normal as well as pathological) and anthropological perspectives (e.g., crosscultural study of display rules) and therefore much needed research?

Anatomical distribution of emotional displays and emotional blends

Another characteristic of emotional displays is that, while Ekman rightly associates them principally with the face (cf. Ekman 1977, 1979a, 1969, 1972) and has produced the most specific body of literature on the subject, one can find a host of emotional displays performed by the hands (e.g., while wringing them in despair or making a tense fist) and eyes, which I prefer to study as part of facial expression in intimate costructuration with the neighboring areas of the face (e.g., an intense, unblinking look), the legs (e.g., rapid leg crossing and uncrossing, quick foot shuffling or dangling, tense stomping) and the whole trunk (e.g., shifting posture in uncontrollable expectancy). In fact, Ekman's *affect-blends*, or multiple-emotion displays, can be perfectly composed by the combination of emotions shown by different parts of the body, as well as by different somatic systems, and by using objects (e.g., nervously twirling a pencil against the desk), often through certain kinesic-paralinguistic constructs (e.g., grabbing the steering wheel convulsively while audibly exhaling air through the nostrils and gazing tensely at the dangerous traffic situation). We display such behaviors almost always out of awareness, unless we intend to communicate one of those emotions; while the cooccurrent ones are displayed, and even decoded, beyond our control. For instance, an apico-alveolar click 'Tz' linked to a sigh may reveal a complex and conflictive mixture of emotions which in fact appears duplicated by the concomitant facial expression. But, again, this category may overlap with the others. The click of regret or disappointment, an emblem with an agreed-upon meaning, is also an affect-display.

It is clear that words alone cannot constitute an emotional blend. '¿¡How could you?!' said 'with' anger and sadness means that 'with' implies at least the paralinguistic qualifiers of those emotions. But in reality (unless we try to imagine our decoding of that expression over the telephone) it will always be the uncontrollable display of the Basic Triple Structure, language-paralanguage-kinesics, that will give its specific form to that expression.

Forms of emotional displays

Emotional displays, then, can be unconsciously 'expressed' or intentionally 'communicated' by:

(a) *verbal language:* '¡Oh no!', '¡I love you so!' (necessarily accompanied by paralanguage);

(b) *paralanguage* alone: deep sighing, crying, laughter;

(c) *kinesics:* grabbing one's head in despair, or someone's arm;

(d) *silence and/or stillness:* the silent embrace, the stasis of emotional recollection;

(e) *proxemics:* drawing much closer to the cointeractant;

(f) *chemical reactions:* nervous perspiration, tears, palmar sweat, micturation;

(g) *dermal reactions:* an uncontrolled pallor, blushing, goose flesh, etc.;

(h) *thermal changes:* the heat radiated by an emotionally aroused person;

(i) *a body-adaptor:* fidgeting nervously with clothes or jewelry;

(j) *an object-adaptor:* clutching the arms of a chair in a heated dispute.

We can again easily observe the virtually infinite possible combinations among the various somatic systems, as one would never really occur alone. Breaking voice, for instance, would be congruent with holding one's head with both hands, just as paleness and sweat would in certain situations. Noninteractively, emotional displays are characteristic of any emotional state one is in when alone, and they can be linguistic, paralinguistic, chemical, dermal, thermal and objectual or artifactual, although not proxemic, as there is no present cointeractant.

As it is not within the scope of this chapter to review in detail, but only mention, the work of other researchers, I will only acknowledge the theoretical concepts put forth by Ekman and Friesen (1969) and Ekman (1977), namely the *evoking stimuli* (a personal insult, a situation of bereavement), which may or may not elicit the same emotion, and that, even when they do, the *display rules* dictated by culture and personality will then make people handle the emotional behavior differently by: *deintensifying* it (expected of upper-middle and upper-class members in many Western cultures at a funeral or in a hospital, where one is expected to check his own emotions), *looking neutral* (if, for instance, the relationship with the deceased must be concealed), *dissimulating it* with another emotion (as, for instance, in self-defense) or, at the other extreme, by *over intensifying* it (observed also at funerals in some Mediterranean or Arab cultures on the part of some distant relatives or friends, or even hired mourners). One should add the rule of displaying an emotion with sheer sincerity, which, regardless of its *behavioral consequences* (Ekman's and Friesen's term) for each individual, must not be interpreted as any of the other four controlled manifestations, and to which one could refer simply as 'looking natural'. The display rules, however, are applied to all the categories of nonverbal behaviors and not only to emotional displays, just as they are applied in verbal language usage.

Notes

1. My first work on nonverbal categories (e.g., Poyatos 1976a) adhered more closely to Ekman and Friesen's (1969), except that I introduced slight modifications and added 'body-adaptors'. I read a paper on the present one at the 1980 meeting of the Semiotic Society of America (Poyatos 1981g).

2. As was expertly illustrated by Professor Ferenc Pap, Chairman of the University of Debrecen Slavic Studies Department while discussing Russian kinesics at his home.

3. During a lecture I gave at the University of Debrecen in 1981 Professor Pap illustrated it with his typical and much appreciated vibrant style after politely asking me to stand up.

4. In an earlier paper on kinesics (Poyatos 1977a) I wrote: "one of the most enlightening applications of kinesic studies—from an anthropological point of view—would be the elaboration of *cultural kinesic atlases* whose *isokimes* (Hewes 1973b) could trace the distribution of basic conversational gestures, differentiate gestures, manners and postures, and deal separately (but within the total cultural and communicative context) with the first four functional categories: conversational, ritualistic, occupational, and task-performing." Morris, Collet and associates certainly created a model for much of the methodology that would be basic to such atlases. In a still earlier paper (Poyatos 1975d) I elaborated on the preparation of kinesic inventories in a systematic way that would include: the sources, the interactive or noninteractive types of live first-hand observation, the illustration of the inventory (sketches, still photographs, film), and the presentation of the material (classification, distribution, labelling, and description), avoiding the more common deficiencies and pitfalls one can observe in some existing inventories (e.g., ambiguity of usage, incomplete kinemorphemic or kinesyntactic constructs) and seeking the cultural and situational context, the frequency of occurrence, and the costructuration with language and other nonverbal systems. This paper has been edited later by Kendon (Poyatos 1981b).

5. The topic of language markers deserves much more research, very specifically on the crosscultural level. It does not cease to marvel me, as I visit many different cultures, how, beyond a few seemingly universal markers and a series of definitely Western forms, each language contains its own undeniable repertoire of markers which truly contribute to its unique kinesic and paralinguistic 'accent'.

6. I must voice my dissatisfaction with the label 'random', but also with such others as 'involuntary', 'unconscious', 'autistic', etc. Krout (1935), in a seminal paper, reviewed studies (Luria 1932; Allport and Vernon 1933; Freud 1914; Olson 1931; Koch 1933) that "were in favor of the assumption that the so-called sensory and affective processes, changes in attention, perception, thought, and even sleep, bear a definite, describable and measurable relation to involuntary motor movements" (2); such gestures, for example, as clearing one's throat, forced coughing, and convulsive spitting—present where there seems to be no specific or understandable objective stimulation which would throw light on their appearance—challenge the attention of the student of human behavior" (18), states that "when an individual, inhibiting his direct response to an external situation, responds to subsequent internal stimulation *explicitly*, we have what we may call *autistic gestures*" (18) differing, he adds, from the infant's reflex movements or the adult's talking to himself. As this note does not pretend to review Krout's study, I wish to emphasize only how difficult it can be sometimes to ascertain whether throat-clearing, tapping, a frown or a lint-flicking gesture is unconscious and random, conscious and random, unconscious and habitual, or conscious and habitual. Krout's list of 160 'autistic gestures' can in itself form a solid corpus to which we can add quite a few other kinesic and (not included by him) paralinguistic acts. I have been intently observing these gestures for many years, I have discussed their elusiveness with colleagues, and I find it impossible to assert with Krout, (a) that they have "no obvious relation to existing extraorganic stimuli", for which reason he defines them as "explicit responses to intraorganic stimuli" (119); and (b) that they

are not responded to by an observer, although it is true that by definition they are not consciously perceived by the actor (only when some are not truly voluntary) which, again, it is hard to determine. I agree, however, that they "tend to be consistent in their reappearance" and that, in cases consistently observed in their situational context, they "originate in conflict situations of which they become symbolic, as proved by the emotional freightage of their stimuli" (120). Krout adds that "The theory of autistic gestures is that, in the presence of conflict and blockage, there may be an escape of impulses into effector-systems which, were the impulses uninhibited, would provide normal outlets for them" (120). However, as I just pointed out, I find it extremely difficult to conclude in each specific occurrence whether the salesgirls's counter-tapping is conscious or unconscious, random or habitual, for there may be specific circumstances that make that behavior recur, in which case it cannot be termed random; while it may happen, in addition, in other specific or varied circumstances when those former circumstances are not present. At any rate, the reference to what I identify in this chapter as random behaviors aims at increasing in other the much needed sensitiveness in social interaction to those activities.

5

The Basic Triple Structure of Human Communication Behaviors: the Multichannel Reality of Discourse in Space and Time

1. Language Within Its Total Context: the Fallacy of the 'Linguistic' Approach

THERE is no need to emphasize that language, verbal language, is the unique anthroposemiotic, most elaborate and advantageous transactional tool and the backbone of human communication and culture. However, by blindly admitting this otherwise unquestionable truth, the very word language has been given a meaning which may seem either too broad or too limited in the light of a finer analysis of our communicative activities.

When we have given some attention to all that is generally not understood as language and yet communicates, the many forms of message-conveying systems which do not even have to cooccur with words, we may still speak of the superiority of verbal language, but could hardly separate it from all those activities.

We may, in the total communicative panorama of a culture, isolate what has been traditionally known as spoken language, but we realize that the treatment it deserves it not the one usually given it as an autonomous system, which it is not, that what gives shape to words, but not always simultaneously with them, is a series of elements other than the linguistic structure proper. It has been amply illustrated throughout the previous chapter that man, as he speaks, accompanying, altering or alternating with the purely linguistic core of his deliverance, supporting or contradicting the essential messages conveyed by words and sentences with their stress and intonation contours, develops other structured elements subtly interrelated which cannot be ignored. I am referring to the paralinguistic structure and to the kinesic one; and, from a cultural and interactive point of view, to all the other systems already mentioned whose analysis should never be disassociated from that of the main triple body of activities. Their combination and interdependence form the manifold communicative system of each culture and the subject of many different disciplines which thus contribute to give shape to the growing field of nonverbal communication studies (several branches of anthropology, social psychology, clinical psychiatry and psychotherapy, medicine, biology, semiotics and zoosemiotics, sociology, linguistics and psycholinguistics) which are gradually blending into a complex interdisciplinary area of research.

Many of the investigators, however, have in many instances resorted to the linguistic type of analogy when trying to analyze a portion of communicative behavior, which obviously poses serious problems. If they need to isolate a unit of communicative behavior on which to carry out that analysis, ¿what exactly must they regard as a unit, and which elements must they consider as its constituents? One immediately thinks of language, and inevitably tries to isolate a sentence which, we claim, represents a complete unit of meaning, distinguishing patterns of stress, pitch and pausal phenomena, but nothing else. And yet, that combination of phonemes and morphemes acoustically perceived appears quite lifeless if we only attach to it the intonational features of stress, pitch and juncture, for any stretch of speech under normal circumstances carries some extralinguistic elements (various voice modifications and independent sounds) which constitute what most of us agree more and more in calling paralanguage; and, if visually perceived, that sentence is accompanied by certain kinesic elements (gestures, manners, postures and postural shifts), perhaps hardly noticeable, but intimately intertwined with both the linguistic and the paralinguistic costructures.

This is what I began to develop over ten years ago as the *Basic Triple Structure of Human Communicative Behavior*[1]* which in turn became the basis for all my subsequent work on human communication. For I soon realized, perhaps more so because at that time I was teaching only language and literature courses, that the study of language, even if we think only of the communicative activities developed in the vocal-auditory channels, should not be limited any more to the traditional 'linguistic' approach that concentrates on an arbitrarily preestablished set of segmental and suprasegmental elements but ignores whatever seems to lie beyond 'our' accepted phonological system or, in a very western attitude, shunts it as 'nonspeech', even though it is part of the phonological systems of lesser known-languages. There are a great number of sounds perfectly normal from the physiological point of view, which as Pike (1943) complained, are traditionally considered either as marginal sounds because they do not seem to occur as phonemic norms in a given set of languages (whispered sounds, clicks, pharyngeal sounds, glottalized stops, ingressive sounds), or as nonspeech sounds,

* Superscript numbers refer to Notes at end of chapter.

equally normal from the anthropophonetic point of view—but further away from traditional "speech norms" (coughs, narial sounds, glottalized sighs, glottalized gliding vowels). Besides the fact that these sounds have been wrongly relegated to a status of abnormality and nonspeechness, and therefore excluded from phonemic charts, their semantic value within man's vocal communicative repertoire is such that a study of the functions they play and of their "lexical" value, would certainly enrich, not just the anthropolinguistic field, but the other areas referred to in this book.

It also became apparent to me, in a logical process of dissatisfaction with the traditional limited perspectives in language and communication studies, that one could not carry out an in-depth semiotic-communicative analysis of language, vocal or nonvocal, from within a single discipline without unrealistically dissociating it, first of all, from a given cultural context, and secondly, from the mechanism of personal interaction. In culture we find a series of conditioning factors (geographical, ethnic, socioeconomic, psychological) and other extralinguistic elements that complement the semantic contents of verbal language (nonverbal vocal acts, gestures, spatial and temporal behaviors). In the social interactive mechanism typical of a culture we find a set of rules and patterns that definitely affect verbal language, both morphologically and syntactically, and gives it the characteristics of a true living communicative system.

2. The Limitations of Spoken and Written Words and the Lexicality and Grammaticality of the Basic Triple Structure

I would like to illustrate the indivisible semantic values and grammaticality of the Basic Triple Structure as a unit in itself with a seemingly simple phrase like

¡Well, what did you think of that!

As I write it, it is inevitable to read it in my mind without elements besides those visually present in its simplest graphic representation. Without elaborating on the many possible paralinguistic and kinesic variations of which this lexical construct would be susceptible, the table on Fig. 5.1 attempts (for a paralinguistic-kinesic 'description' would never be totally accurate) to represent one of those forms.

As presented here, this 'linguistic' construct expresses a rather surprised reaction. Were we to shorten 'Well' and start with frowning brows and tightly-closed lips, the meaning would completely change. We could combine the linguistic, paralinguistic and kinesic pieces of an imaginary puzzle to convey all kinds of meanings and semantic nuances.

It is clear that *words*, whether coined and utilized as arbitrary signs ('house') or echoic signs ('swish) lack the capacity to carry the whole weight

LANGUAGE	PARALANGUAGE	KINESICS
Tz'st	Opening apico-alveolar click + pharyngeal ingression	brows begin to rise, direct eye contact
Weeell,	high volume, drawl, comma for falling junction and tone-group pause	raised brows, then facial stillness
what did	lower pitch and volume lower pitch and volume	lowering brows lowering brows
you	higher volume and pitch	slightly knit brows + narrow-angle head-nod deictic + gazing at cointeractant
think of	lower volume and pitch same	same same
that !	same volume, lower pitch + tone-group falling terminal juncture	lateral head-tilt deictic, then stillness with final lingering slight smile

FIG. 5.1. Basic Triple Structure.

of a conversation, that is, all the messages being exchanged in the course of it. Our verbal lexicons are extremely poor in comparison with the capacity of the human mind in encoding and decoding an infinitely wider gamut of meanings to which at times we must refer as ineffable. If a natural conversation were to be conducted by means of 'stripped words' only (a concept hard to imagine), there would be, not just an intermittent series of 'semiotic (but signless) gaps', but some overriding vacuums as well, which are actually filled by nonverbal activities, either segmental (i.e., a click of the tongue, a sigh or a meaningful silence) or stretching over varying portions of our speech, from single phonemes to sentences to a complete conversational turn.

An uttered word can act as an affect-display of anguish ('¡God!'), doubt ('Maybe'), fear '¡Oh!'), etc.—and even so it needs certain prosodic features and specific paralinguistic modifiers (implied in the context or described in written language)—but rarely as an emotional-blend conveying all three feelings. But such an affect-blend could not be expressed either by means of a morpholigico-syntactical arrangement of words—as one would not include in that sentence the lexemes 'anguish', 'doubt' and 'fear', to begin with—because it would entail an 'unnatural' complex periphrastic expression which just would not happen in such a state. What actually suffuses those words with life is a series of paralinguistic and kinesic elements subtly interrrelated which support, emphasize or contradict them.

As for *the written word*—which is mentally uttered as long as it is visually perceived—it is farther removed from the reality of the verbal-nonverbal construct, for which reason the narrative writer refuses to just let his characters speak in a printed language without commenting on that language himself and describing its paralinguistic features. Written words are not just printed symbols on a piece of paper, and even the snow-white paper, the smelly rough one or the grayish or time-yellowed one do become semiotically interrelated with both the events in the story and its readers' attitude and sensitivity. They are, in the first place, mentally (if not *sotto voce*) uttered by the reader, who must ascribe to them a series of linguistic, paralinguistic and kinesic elements—besides all the described, represented, evoked or between-lines situations which transcend the page and constitute an important part of the story. Besides, although it is true that writing and reading are predominantly intellectual activities, they are far from being limited to visual perception. Precisely because both writer and reader—in greater or lesser degree—attach to the verbal constructs they produce or interpret a series of nonverbal voice modifications and, if dealing with literary characters, speech-accompanying body movements and positions (plus any other somatic activities and contextual elements of the explicitly or implicitly described objectual world), the coding of signs in written language become an intricate and often ambiguous task, much more so when the written text is, in addition, an interlinguistic-intercultural translation.

As for *lexicality*, the Basic Triple Structure is the only communicative complex in which an object of the tangible world or an abstraction can be indistinctively denoted by a word from our established lexicon, a paralinguistic construct, or kinesically. A bad odor, for instance, after impinging on the olfactory epithelium and being decoded in the brain, can elicit a verbal reaction ('¡That stinks!'), a paralinguistic one ('¡Eeugh!'), or a hand-to-nose gesture. Furthermore, considering the capacity of these three systems for mutual substitution within a preserved syntactical order (altered only from a 'linguistic' point of view), we can argue that the sentence '¡Oh, I feel—!' can be completed, rather than verbally ('¡Oh, I feel like kissing you!'), proxemically, changing toward one's interactant while displaying an appropriate facial expression; or that blushing can act as a cutaneous predicate of '¡Oh, I'm so—(embarrassed)!', but this internal costructuration is never so deep as within the triple structure where verbal, paralinguistic and kinesic expressions combine invariably in a live sentence.

Thus, what makes language-paralanguage-kinesics a functionally cohesive structure—and therefore the true core of human communication—is, first of all, their common kinetic generator, and then their combined semanticity and lexicality and their capacity to operate simultaneously, alternate with or substitute for each other as needed in the interactive situation, as was just illustrated.

We cannot neglect the fact that the elements of the Basic Triple Structure can be seen in a complex of bodily articulation as it would be possible to draw a human body and indicate the various articulatory parts where specific movements are formed, and the way in which they can be formed (i.e., point and mode of articulation). The phonemic-kinemic representation of the head, for instance, would be particularly interesting, for it would show: internally, the speech organs (teeth, lips, tongue [tip, blade, front, back], etc.), and externaly, or anatomically, the facial moving parts (eyebrows [high, middle, low, knit], eyelids [raised, lowered], pupil [dilated, contracted], mouth [degrees of closeness and openness, of distension and contraction]), etc. The display of paralinguistic qualifiers like labial control, maxillary control or nasal control (referred to the nose and not only to actual velar position) demonstrates the intimate interrelatedness of vocal and kinesic communicative behaviors. The whining gesture of wrinkled nose is congruent with and conditions the heavy nasalization typical of such a behavior. This leads us to ponder on the parallel developmental characteristics of the actual morphological, anatomical and semantic interdependence of the speech and movement communicational streams.

When Kendon (1972: 451), one of the most perceptive and articulate students of nonverbal behavior today, expressed so rightly the obvious but neglected thought that "we must consider movement as well as speech if we are to understand what is entailed in what we somewhat loosely refer to as an act of speech"—and I would link this statement with those just made regarding the kinetic basis of communication—he confirmed the additional information provided by kinesics to what is being said (besides stress and grammatical markers). This shows that besides the very doubtful redundancy of kinesics in most situations, it is also an *economy device*, as it 'says' something else in the same length of time. On the other hand, there is still another way in which kinesics can operate, namely, when the same person addresses two receivers simultaneously, one verbally and nonverbally and another one kinesically only, as when giving directions to a waiter without interrupting our conversation with others (Key 1974), or when someone who is engaged in a telephone conversation with one cointeractant initiates a simultaneous exchange with a second one by using a string of kinesic emblems to say (move) to him '/Come in/, /I'll be with you in a minute/, /Good to see you/, /sit down/, /and look at this in the meantime/', while listening to his speaker on the phone.

3. Segmental and Nonsegmental Elements Within the Basic Triple Structure

As we try to probe deeper into the living communication situation, and the morphological, syntactical and semantic functions of nonverbal paralinguistic and kinesic activities show themselves beyond doubt, the more we tend to seriously question the heretofore uncertain dichotomy segmental-nonsegmental.[2] In fact, the study of paralanguage and kinesics—which, as discussed later, includes the nonactivities of silence and stillness respectively—lead us soon to the conclusion that certain nonverbal stretches of speech and body movement are perfectly segmental while others are clearly nonsegmental.

If we try to consider only a breath-semantic stretch of utterance—limited, that is, to the vocal-auditory channel involving language and paralanguage—as the most sensible division in speech, which disregards neither its physiological configuration nor its meaning or message, we soon come to the conclusion that it is possible to single out the vocal-auditory band, so to speak, and that we need to include kinesic behaviors as well, from both a semantic and syntactic point of view. That breath-semantic group (similar, for instance, to the one shown in Fig. 4.2 or one much more elaborate) allows us to recognize the segmental and nonsegmental levels of sign production, that is, two types of activities:

(a) some which precede or follow each other as discrete portions of a noncontinuous whole: *words* (i.e., phonemes), *paralinguistic alternants* (i.e., vocal/narial nonverbal constructs, e.g., 'Uh', 'Tz-tz', a narial egression of contempt), *silences* or breaks in that audible chain of segmentable events, conversational *kinesic constructs* (i.e., gestures, manners, postures) which coincide or alternate with the audible ones (although some movements can be heard as well) and which are also discrete semantic segments, and *still positions* of one or all the parts of the body which interrupt the kinesic chain;

(b) others which clearly change throughout that communicative stretch of sounds and movements and silences and still positions, with not so clear boundaries and overriding those other elements, from syllables and/or simple kinemic constructs to much longer portions of speech or whole kinesyntactic complexes, varying slightly but with a cumulative impression never given by the clearly discrete parts, therefore not being segmentable: the elements we subsume under *intonation*, *primary qualities* (e.g., volume, tempo), *qualifiers* (e.g., pharyngeal control) and *differentiators* (e.g., overriding laughter), and the *parakinesic qualities* of intensity, range and velocity.

It is interesting to note that while two segmental vocal constructs cannot go together (e.g., word with silence, silence with an apico-alveolar click), vocal segmental constructs and kinesic segmental ones can (e.g., a word with a gesture, silence with kinesics), just as vocal nonsegmental and kinesics (e.g., high pitch and gesture, low pitch and nonsegmental kinesics). Which further proves the semantic and somatic cohesion of the Basic Triple Structure—without ignoring other cooccurring and conditioning (not just contextual) systems (e.g., dermal)—and totally justifies the study of punctuation, not just on the basis of language but as involving language, paralanguage and kinesics.

This realistic view of a simple sentence poses two questions, besides showing how semanticity is both segmental and nonsegmental (which in turn reveals important problems with respect to written literature): the structural-semantic nature of intonation and that of silences and still positions. As silence and stillness are discussed more at length later on, I will only offer some thoughts on intonation with the Basic Triple Structure.

A practical thought on intonation and communication

We know that intonation, even if viewed as made up of stresses, pitches and junctures, cannot be broken into discrete units because it is a continuum formed, at any rate, by gradual elements (even if we acknowledge 'alotones') whose meaning is given by the whole contour and not by individual stresses or junctures, as is not given by single phonemes either. The fact that a number of nonvocalic, nonconsonantal, closed-lip or open-lip utterances are regarded by many as intonation ('intonation without words') leads some to the equivocation that intonation can be isolated, separated from a segmental stretch of speech and uttered alone, when in reality we are again producing the two levels referred to above, the segmental one (in this case a paralinguistic construct) and the nonsegmental or intonational one. Such is the case of a paralinguistic alternant like a glottalized gliding mid-to-higher-back vowel (segmental), with open or closed lips, overriden by a pitch contour 4-2, two stresses and a falling terminal juncture (nonsegmental), meaning, according to context and pitch variations, '¡Oh, I see!', '¡Good!', '¡Delicious!', etc.

The fact that intonation can be both grammatical and attitudinal (Crystal 1971: 200) does not mean that it can carry any more meaning than nasality or whispering would by themselves, unless they occur with words or with paralinguistic alternants (considered segmental) like '¡Eeugh!', '¡Hmm!'. One cannot speak with intonation alone. We can modulate a long stretch like 'Mmmmmmmmm', attaching to it the intonation contour which would correspond to '¿May I go with you?', for instance, or 'I don't know where she went'—and if done face to face, it would be doubly expressed by facial and other kinesic activities—but when we do that we are simply evoking an established and perfectly coded verbal or paralinguistic utterance, to both of which either a person or a domesticated animal will easily react. And if that person (a child, for instance) or that dog have only heard our 'Mmmmmm', that paralinguistic construct is a perfectly lexical item of that established repertoire.

This notion is, of course, compatible with the concept of 'entoneme' (see a very useful and comprehensive paper on intonation by Quilis [1975]), a meaningful unit comparable to the morpheme, as opposed to a meaningless phoneme. But, from a linguistic point of view, I believe that intonation operates as a permanent feature of speech however it may occur, that it is impossible to isolate it, and that it is not modified by other phonetic elements (but only by kinesic ones within the Basic Triple Structure), although it modifies those which are nonsegmental (itself being therefore nonsegmental), since segmental or nonsegmental elements of speech cannot modify themselves.

The cohesion of conscious and unconscious discourse

Returning to the breath-semantic group (cf. Lieberman's [1967] 'breath-group'), 'Tz, ¡Well, ¿what d'you think of that!?', a slightly different version of it would fare as follows (in a rather impressionistic fashion), showing the possible segmental and nonsegmental kinesic activities:

	3	2	4
Language	*well*	*what d'you think*	*of that*
Paralanguage			
segmental			
	Tz, pharyngeal ingression		
	pauses after 'tz'	junct. after 'think'	
	and 'well'	drawled 'what'	drawled 'that'
nonsegmental			
	drawled 'well'	clipped 'd'you'	
	high rising volume	same	same
	high pitch	lower pitch	higher pitch
Kinesics			
segmental			
	raised brows	same	same
	smile	same	same
	hand stretched out	same	same
nonsegmental			
	medium-tense movement	same	same
	wide-range brow raise	same	same
	med.-to-wide smile	widening smile	wide-range smile
	med.-speed movement		with last high pitch
			and primary stress
			still facial expression

Only in writing could we think exclusively of the vocal-auditory channel, since there is a cooccurrent kinesic (i.e., kinetic) activity formed by segmental linguistic-paralinguistic elements as well as (segmental) kinesic and parakinesic (suprasegmental) ones. Which suggests, of course, the ontogenetic costructuration of the Basic Triple Structure. Furthermore, its high cognitive capacity, not inferior in a beckoning sign than in its verbal counterpart, brings forth also the inevitable broadness of the concept of language, since it is clear that not only different messages, but a single one, can be—and most of the time is, if almost imperceptible—carried out in its totality only by the cooccurrence of verbal, paralinguistic and kinesic behaviors.

In consequence, the segmental and nonsegmental elements of the Basic Triple Structure, that is, of direct face-to-face interaction (in what later will be discussed as full, not impaired, interaction), can now be diagrammatically depicted like this:

<table>
<tr><td>SEGMENTAL</td><td>Words</td><td colspan="2">Paralinguistic alternants</td><td>Paralinguistic silences</td><td>Kinesic constructs</td><td>Still positions</td></tr>
<tr><td>NONSEGMENTAL</td><td colspan="2">Intonational features</td><td colspan="2">Paralinguistic Primary Qualities, Qualifiers, Differentiators</td><td colspan="2">Parakinesic Intensity, Range, Velocity</td></tr>
</table>

FIG. 5.2. Segmental and Nonsegmental Elements of the Basic Triple Structure.

Again, the extreme communicative limitations of written language, most significant in narrative and dramatic literature, becomes obvious when we realize that only words, some ambiguously represented alternants ('Tsk-tsk', 'Ugh'), a few paralinguistic features ([!], [?], [( )], [CAPITALS], etc.), and some unmeasurable silences ([, ,] [. . .], etc.) can be present in a written text.

To close this general comment on the Basic Triple Structure, two more points would be in order. One is that, while segmental is mostly controlled and conscious on the part of the emitter, the same cannot be said of the nonsegmental behaviors, which seem to belong to two categories: natural, that is, biological, either normal or pathological (e.g., a breath-intake pause, a spastic movement), and controlled, whether personal and idiosyncratic or culture-specific, according to status, occupation (e.g., the auctioneer, the preacher), and situational context (e.g., reading to children). The other one is that, unlike sound and movement, which show correlates of silence and stillness, signs of a chemical, thermal or dermal nature are opposed only by certain internal somatic non-activities which cannot be apprehended by a receiver. Besides, as I pointed out before, the absence of those signs is rarely as relevant in social interaction as that of language, paralanguage or kinesics.

4. A Basic Comparison of Language, Paralanguage, and Kinesics

Even a cursory comparison of language, paralanguage and kinesics demonstrates, as one seeks the true internal costructuration of the Basic Triple Structure, why none of them could be isolated in the actual occurrence of verbal language in whatever form of everyday conversation.

Language

Language, in the sense of the spoken string of words and sentences of human speech, shows, morphologically, (a) a *segmental* level or 'layer' formed by vowels and consonants made up of phonemes, or smallest distinctive units (with their alophones or variations), combined to form morphemes (words, suffixes), or smallest semantic units, which are themselves combined to form syntagms and syntactic costructurations; to that almost lifeless body we must attach (b) a *suprasegmental* layer formed by what is commonly referred to as intonation, consisting of about four degrees of relative loudness, or stress, four different pitches, and three terminal junctures (rising, falling, level). These intonation patterns have no referential meaning in themselves, unless they qualify the lexical construct; although, a paralinguistic inarticulated closed-lip expiration of air can convey different meanings simply by varying its most important component, intonation. We can say, however, that in a real communication situation a phrase with its intonation contour is 'colored' by certain paralinguistic and kinesic elements, and that it is only then that many semantic changes and many otherwise impossible nuances are expressed; in other words, when that phrase reaches the totality of the interrelation of the three communicative activities which are the basis of unobstructed human interaction.

Paralanguage

Taking into account all the ambiguities risked by a number of definitions I have discussed elsewhere (Poyatos 1976a), I have tried to delimit the boundaries of paralanguage by identifying it as: the nonverbal voice qualities, modifiers and sounds produced or conditioned in the areas covered by the supraglottal cavities (from the lips and the nares to the pharynx), the laryngeal cavity and the infraglottal cavities, down to the abdominal muscles, as well as the intervening silences of varying length, which we use consciously or unconsciously supporting or contradicting the linguistic, kinesic or proxemic messages mainly, either simultaneously or alternating with them.

Paralanguage, simultaneous or alternating with those essential segmental and suprasegmental elements, offers the observer a series of equally segmental elements, but many more segmental vocal and narial effects and sounds that cover a very wide range of acoustic phenomena determined, first of all, by the anatomy and the physiology of the individual's vocal tract, and secondly, by the idiosyncratic use he makes of those possibilities.

The problem with paralanguage, therefore, is that it does not always offer a 'unit' analogous to the phoneme, susceptible of being built up into larger structures. All we can do with paralinguistic nonsegmental voice modifiers is abstract a specific quality of the voice, say, syllabic duration, and establish a scalar series of degrees below and above a medium line, that is, overclipped—clipped—medium—drawled—overdrawled; or velar control, which makes voice very nasal—nasal—medium—oral—very oral. Other features, which override actual speech admit, (a) a scalar classification of, for instance, giggling (which, at any rate, would also depend upon other features such as the velar control just mentioned, or pitch, thus showing also as many as five degrees in each case), or (b) a sort of 'class' ranging, in the case of laughter, from closed-lip muffled snickering to uproarious guffawing. But there is a fourth group ('alternants') which is independent from 'words' and whose status must be elaborated on later, which shows actual phonemes (like the apico-alveolar click, although not from the point of view of the English language) and also certain inarticulated sounds that are difficult to measure according to a base line (unless we consider their modifying accompanying features) and whose variations may or may not produce a semantic change.

Kinesics

When applying to its analysis the methodology of linguistic structuralism, Birdwhistell (1952, 1970) found in conversational kinesics a smallest discrete element, the kineme (analogous to the phoneme), made up of various allokines (similar to allophones); kinemes combine into morphological constructs called kinemorphs (analogous to morphs), forming kinemorphemes (comparable to morphemes) and kinesyntactic constructions. What is more, some suprasegmental elements, namely, kinemes of stress and juncture, have been reported by Birdwhistell (1970) as appearing in the linguistic-kinesic stream (while the relationship between linguistic pitch and body movement is under study). In addition, parakinesic degrees of intensity, range and velocity (akin to stress and articulatory tension, syllabic duration and speech tempo) have also been identified, and they differentiate personal styles and in general all kinds of normal and abnormal visually-perceived behaviors as much as paralanguage differentiates audibly-perceived ones, therefore being as important to kinesics within the Basic Triple Structure as paralanguage is to verbal language. A foreign language, or a regional variety of the native one, can be spoken fluently, but usually with a certain accent which, under analysis, is revealed as inexact placement of stresses, pitches and junctures and incorrect articulation of some vocalic and consonantal sounds (that is, inaccurate internal movements). In a similar manner, a foreign kinesic repertoire, or a regional variety, can be imitated, learned and performed with more or less fluency, but perhaps with an inevitable alien 'accent' in many instances, consisting in inexact placement of kinesic stress and junctures and, more noticeably, in the incorrect use of the parakinesic qualities (intensity, range and velocity) and the misplacement of certain kinemes within kinemorphemic constructs.

5. Paralanguage

As I will be dealing with paralanguage in a separate volume (Poyatos 1983d, in preparation), I only summarize here the classification of paralinguistic phenomena I have offered before (Poyatos 1976a)[3] gratefully inspired by but drastically enlarging upon some pioneering work (mainly Pittinger and Smith 1957; Trager 1958; McQuown 1957; Pittinger, Hockett, and Danehy 1960; Austin 1965), on which I attempted to elaborate according to phonetic (i.e., phonological), semantic and functional criteria (in agreement with Crystal's [1974] excellent state-of-the-art paper). This classification acknowledges four well differentiated categories.

Primary qualities

Primary qualities are fundamental constituents of human speech which differentiate, first of all, a person from the others. Crystal (1971: 198) defines 'voice quality' as "the idiosyncratic, relatively permanent, vocal background of an individual, which allows us to recognize him . . . it may be both segmental and nonsegmental in character, but the latter is usually the dominant factor. It is a physiologically determined activity, over which most individuals have little or no measure of control" (others call it 'voice set', 'speaker identity', etc.). I have classified as primary qualities: timbre, resonance, volume, tempo, pitch register, pitch interval, pitch range, syllabic duration, intonation range, and rhythm, recognizing four basic factors: *biological*, that is, purely somatic (such as sex and age, conditioning, for instance, timbre), *physiological*, thus variable, whether due to temporary malfunctions or to traumatized states (nasal resonance due to catarrh, improper timing in aphasias), *cultural* (e.g., higher volume of Latins and Arabs, certain dialectal peculiarities), and *social*, such as status (the slow tempo of superiority), occupation (the orality of a preacher), or certain functions, like baby talk, story-telling, etc. In other words, primary qualities can also be based on nonpermanent factors that produce a sort of secondary or temporary voice set in a person, just as some qualifiers (next category) can become basic characteristics of a given individual, either as a permanent profile or in certain situations. I will comment only on volume, that is, loudness, due to the respiratory and articulatory muscular effort, referred both to utterance or speech and to single syllables (beyond stressed or unstressed ones, e.g., 'It was *aw*ful'). Like pitch or speed, it possesses syntactical and cognitive value—as in a speeded-up low-volume (and pitch) parenthetical observation—and its parameter can go from very high (fortisimo) to very low (pianisimo), either rising (crescendo) or falling (diminuendo). Volume has an important culture-identifying value, as Arabs and Latins, for instance, are louder in streets and public places than the average Anglo-Saxon. Elaborating later on punctuation, I discuss how there is no logical reason not to indicate with the exclamation point that a sentence is uttered with high volume, or very high, from beginning to end, or only part of it instead of having to find an unanticipated high volume at the very end of a long sentence, or being obliged to qualify a whole sentence with high volume when only part of it carries it. While Spanish makes it clear by using ¡——!, both English and Spanish could specify instances such as: ¡——, ——!, ¡¡——!, ——!!. The reader, for one thing, would be able to mentally synchronize himself with the text much better.

Modifiers

Modifiers, encompassing qualifiers and differentiators, are a series of vocal effects produced by factors like the direction and characteristics of respiratory air, by the way it is controlled in the vocal bands and how they vibrate, by certain changes in the pharynge, by the soft palate position, by how articulation is produced in terms of muscular tension and position of the organs, and by the anatomical configuration and shaping of the lips and the lower mandible. Some, of course, may appear as permanent traits of a person's voice, in which case they qualify words, differentiators and alternants as true primary qualities, while others may be due only to temporary states or contextual circumstances, such as the labializing effect of baby talk, the ingressive utterance of verbal expressions of terror or the traumatized nasality of certain malfunctions. Some are reported as being phonologically used in certain languages, and others only paraphonologically, and most of them modify from syllables to long portions of speech, while a few others modify the verbal utterance occasionally (e.g., laughter), or appear isolated from it, in which case they must be regarded as alternants, the next major category of paralinguistic phenomena.

Qualifiers

It is within qualifiers (respiratory-, glottis-, laryngeal-, velar-, pharyngeal-, articulatory-, labial-, and maxillary control, and articulatory tension) that we first encounter the typical ambiguity, from a phonetic point of view, of most of the descriptive or definitory labels employed, the utter lack of accurate physiological descriptions to refer to those effects, and the complete absence of orthographic forms to indicate at least impressionistically some important attitudinal features, just as we utilize exclamation marks or repetition of letters to symbolize drawling. Although they can also appear as primary qualities, they do not show clear parameters in which to identify different degrees of a continuum, as they usually involve more than one anatomical and/or physiological change in the laryngeal or pharyngeal areas, for instance. Ideally, each one ought to be analyzed in terms of: anatomical and/or physiological configuration (e.g., relaxed vocal band vibration, weak arytenoid closure); auditory effect (e.g., nasal twang); voice type it produces (e.g., nasopharyngeal, creaky, breathy); cooccurrent verbal and nonverbal behaviors, as some qualifiers may be part of a whole established construct (e.g., pursed lips + lowered brow with irritated '¡Oh, let me alone!'); phonological use (e.g., glottal stop in some West African languages); paralinguistic use (e.g., glottal stop for scorn, '¡Terrible!'); abnormal occurrences (e.g., hoarse voice of trachyphonia); and notation for phonetic purposes and because the core of the message may sometimes be carried by a qualifier.

Differentiators

Differentiators (laughing, crying, coughing, sighing, sneezing, belching, yawning, hiccoughing, snorting) characterize psychological and physiological states, and are closely costructured with kinesic behavior while being modified by primary qualities and qualifiers, since even reflexes like sneezes, belches and hiccoughs condition specific accompanying kinesic hand behaviors, for instance, according to cultural norms. Among them, laughter and crying deserve much research actually as paralinguistic-kinesic constructs, as regards: the biological foundation (age, sex, some sexual deviances); the influence of the psychological configuration on the frequency of occurrence, duration, acoustic characteristics and eliciting factors, as well as temporary emotional states and their relations to cultural display rules; pathological varieties; positive and negative social functions (e.g., affiliation, tension relief, comicality, grief, love, deception); the phonetic and kinesic variants according to the socioeconomic and cultural characteristics of the person; laughter and crying in noninteractive situations; their simultaneous or alternating costructuration with language, kinesics, proxemics, chemical (e.g., tears), dermal (e.g., blushing) and thermal (e.g., body temperature rise) messages; and the study of definitory references to and descriptions of laughter and crying in the narrative literatures of the various cultures.[4]

Alternants

Alternants, which I have discussed at length before (1975e,[5] 1976a), constitute the most controversial category, where the pretended "rigid dichotomy where certain semantic constructs are 'paralinguistic' and others are 'linguistic' " (Lieberman 1975: 279) appears to be totally unfounded. They are egressive and ingressive single or compound sounds, articulated or not, produced or shaped in the areas covered by the supraglottal cavities (nares, nasal chamber, nasopharynx, mouth, pharynx), the laryngeal cavity, the infraglottal cavities, the diaphragm, and the abdominal muscles, as well as communicative silences; they do not affect the verbal utterance, but are modified by primary qualities, qualifiers and kinesic activity, and occur either isolated or alternating with verbal language and kinesic constructs. In an impressionistic way, I would loosely describe them as sighs, throat clearings, clicks, pharyngeal ingressions and egressions, egressive frictions, hissing sounds, narial frictions, moaning sounds, closed- or open-lip sounds, meaningful silences, etc. Each language, each culture or social community possesses a great number of perfectly encoded and decoded alternants, as they constitute a true lexicon used constantly in personal interaction as systematically as dictionary items, which some are already. They deserve, therefore, a much higher status in linguistics as well as in any disciplines dealing with communication, and the following basic facts must be considered: (a) that they differ radically from other paralinguistic phenomena because of their lexical value, that is, their segmentality; (b) that they cannot be regarded any more as 'nonspeech' or 'marginal' sounds just because many are not constructed with phonemes from the best known languages; (c) that they play important roles in the mechanism of interaction, with as high a frequency rate as verbal items and often with an even clearer semantic and regulatory function (e.g., an apico-alveolar click + pharyngeal ingression as a turn-claiming cue, or signifying 'Don't say that'): (d) that they seem to form, more than 'words', the greater part of the communicative repertoire each culture utilizes for the interaction of people with mainly domesticated animals (see, e.g., Bynon 1976); (e) that they should be given serious thought with respect to the phylogeny of the Basic Triple Structure; and (f) that we need to increase drastically the present limited system of phonetic symbols, labels (i.e., verbs and nouns), and written forms, as we have for a few ('H'm', 'Psst', 'Er', 'Uh-hu'). While professional writers make their description of alternants a characteristic of their insight and literary style, they also, like the layman, try very hand to represent them.

It is obvious that many more dare treat the deceivingly easier field of kinesics (subject to all sorts of generalizations and conclusions inferred from one-shot controlled-situations and intuitive assumptions) than the extremely difficult one of paralanguage (in which the researcher avidly welcomes a masterful treatment of voice qualities like that by John Laver (1978) one of today's most insightful phoneticians and students of paralanguage.

6. Kinesics

Kinesics is, as part of the Basic Triple Structure, what truly differentiates man from other species, even the most advanced and human-like ones such as chimpanzees and baboons.[6]

Given all the definition discrepancies that one finds in the literature on kinesics, and in the light of the observations that follow, I will offer the following definition of kinesics: The systematic study of the conscious or unconscious psychomuscularly-based body movements and intervening or resulting still positions, either learned or somatogenic, of visual, visual-acoustic and tactile or kinesthetic perception, that, whether isolated or combined with the linguistic and paralinguistic structures and with other somatic and objectual behavioral systems, possess intended or unintended communicative value.

The least sensitive human being can display an infinitely richer repertoire of bodily kinetic articulations than any animal, through which not only can he carry out goal-attaining activities of survival, defence, procreation, leisure, etc., but also as has been illustrated in Chapter 4, use it as sensible externalizations of his unique mental and spiritual endowments. Lorenz (1966), for instance, illustrates the kinetic abilities of different species to display a number of ritualized actions of fight, of injure-preventing aggressive behaviors, the fallow deer's chivalrous antler fight, the superiority displays of fish, primate, canines, etc., the submissive attitudes of many species (even the need for forgiveness after mutual aggression), the bodily movements of passivity and the facial expressions elicited by deprivation and bereavement in geese or chimpanzees, etc. One could cite other ethologists and animal behaviorists to illustrate (without necessarily supporting the evolutionary hypothesis) the extent to which humans and animals share what following Sebeok's felicitous term 'zoosemiotics' (Sebeok 1972, 1977a) can be rightfully termed 'zookinesics'. Goodall (1971) has described how chimpanzees can use and even shape certain tools and handle them in human-like fashion. Eibl-Eibesfeldt (1979b, 1980) has amply discussed the behavioral similarities between people and animals in the ritualized motor patterns of both. Zookinesics, using the term to signify not only intended, visual, tactile or audible kinetic activity, but all goal-oriented or seemingly purposeless or random activities and positions, proves that movement constitutes by far the richest message-emission system, or rather, complex of systems. However, the need to differentiate 'anthropokinesics' from zoosemiotics becomes obvious as soon as we observe the communicative interactional functions of human movements and positions as an inherent part of the Basic Triple Structure, the point at which man departs from animals to become the sole user of Language, Paralanguage and Kinesics fused together in what is the most advanced socializing and communicating, culture-forming activity in the whole of creation.

If the comments and elaboration of Hockett's features I have presented elsewhere (Poyatos 1981e: 8–9) suffice to illustrate these thoughts, the discussion of man's interactive categories (which did not exclude noninteractive ones) in Chapter 4 proves beyond doubt the preponderance and indispensability of movement in any situation, under normal circumstances, and the curtailment of communication when it is impeded in various situations of reduced interaction. A new look at Fig. 4.1 shows that we can replace words with emblematic movements alone; punctuate them and emphasize their hierarchization in discourse with language markers; point at present or absent referents with deictics; refer to the two basic dimensions of life, space and time, with space and time markers, thus increasing the immediate spatial and temporal local by projecting our thoughts beyond their limits; evoke the shape of people, animals and things with pictographs; evoke the sounds and movements, the two basic activities of life's organic and inorganic agents, by means of onomatopoeias, kinetographs and kinephonographs; give bodily form to ideas, feelings, reactions to external and internal stimuli, and to real or imaginary events and emotions, through ideographs, identifiers, externalizers, event tracers, and emotional displays, thus establishing with our congeners a virtually limitless range of mutual expressive possibilities; structure the back-and-forth flow of our daily encounters with others by means of regulators; satisfy our need for physical proximity and bodily contacts, which convey the nature of our relationships, by means of variously regulated alter-adaptors; and consciously or unconsciously feel our own body to externalize a great number of thoughts and sensations, and satisfy its many needs, through self-adaptors and body-adaptors; and, finally, handle the objectual world around us, and far beyond the possibilities of other species, extend our body to achieve a limitless number of tasks by the kinetic display of object-adaptors.

Kinesics as total-body articulation

It is an unquestionable principle that social interaction depends on sound and movement, and when either of those dimensions is lacking in man's emission or perception capabilities, normal life is severely hampered. That lexicality, based on verbal language, is however increased by the conceptual possibilities of the joint language-paralanguage-kinesics structure. On the other hand, it has been seen how both sound and movement can not only be perceived directly, and the signs conveyed by them decoded audibly and visually, but also interpreted through other channels by our intellectualized synesthesial abilities that greatly enlarge our relationship with other human beings and the whole universe.

Even considering only the emitting capabilities of anthropokinesics and, in a broader frame, its anatomical possibilities, one could very well prove once more the preponderance of movement over all other systems by representing in an anatomy-chart fashion (as was suggested earlier) the total articulatory possibilities of people, or more specifically, of a culture, as one represents—so poorly—the phonemic system of a language, for one definitely 'speaks' and 'moves' that language. It would be possible to draw a kinemic chart of the human body (which some would want to compare to that of a chimpanzee and, going lower in the animal scale, of a dog, a bird, and so on) and indicate the various articulatory parts where movements are formed (as those in the head, suggested earlier), all subject to intensity, range and velocity. What such a chart would illustrate, in the first place, would be the mutual inherence of sound and movement and the relevance not only of Birdwhistell's (1970) kinesic-linguistic analogy, but of the actual morphological, anatomical and semantic interdependence of the speech and movement communication streams. In normal interactants the previous experience of such interdependence in their social life allows them to interpret language and paralanguage, when they cannot be heard, through the accompanying movements, not only of the face because they condition vocal production directly, but of other parts of the body as well, thanks to the already discussed phenomenon of synesthesia.

A more workable anthropokinesic chart showing the universal articulatory possibilities—including not only different culture-specific behaviors but the cultural modifications of similar ones—would represent the basic characteristics of anthropokinesics, against which the limitations of any other kinetic systems in the animal world would become apparent. From this general mapping of bodily articulations more refined charts would be derived. One, for instance, would deal exclusively with facial expressions—in a way similar to Ekman's (1972, 1975, 1979, 1982)—showing the different areas of the face, the muscles involved, and the semantic or message-conveying possibilities of the resulting movements, both in interaction and non-interaction, and whether conscious or out of awareness or randomly.

What no study of kinesic behaviors of any one part of the body must overlook is that the relationships between, for instance, the face and other parts of the body must be established at all times. One can set out to observe, analyze and describe the different expressions of the face in a given situation (cf. Kendon 1975), but the concomitant movements and positions of the legs, hands and arms and the whole trunk must not be judged solely as independent 'contextual' elements, for it is the whole body that becomes articulated along with the face in that particular situation. It is possible, for instance, that we might record someone's brow raising + smile of surprise as someone else enters the scene, but it is hard to believe that a person under normal circumstances would not uncross his arms or legs if they were crossed, or lean forward at least slightly, in which case the articulation that constitutes the construct 'happy surprise' engages face, trunk, legs and/or arms and hands. This would be the truly complete 'kinesic phrase' that will precede words of greeting or act by itself. In the same situation the lack of body movement, except for the face, may convey physical impairment or true absence of happy surprise, the passive attitude of the limbs and trunk betraying indifference at the very least.

It is this total-body articulatory complex that illustrates the unparalleled possibilities and semantic nuances of anthropokinesics over zookinesics.

The development of kinesics with the Basic Triple Structure

Among all intersystem costructurations, the cohesion of external body articulations (kinesics) and internal or phonetic ones is a fascinating phenomenon that should be fully investigated from the point of view of ontogenetic development. But even if one decided to join the interesting series of phylogenetic evolutionary hypotheses, one would have to suggest that communicative kinesic behavior developed as an inherent part of the Basic Triple Structure, or at least of a primitive protolinguistic double structure made up of sounds possible in the vocal (kinetic)-auditory channel, many of which would fall within paralinguistic alternants (Poyatos 1975e). However, in an article by Hewes (1973a) that includes his as well as his commentators' thoughts on the gestural origin of language, I find no concern for the fact that both vocal language and kinesic language should have been felt as necessary to each other, not just because of the cognitive demands of a life constantly becoming more sophisticated and dependent upon social communication—which can be considered a conditioning factor for a larger lexicon of whatever kind—but simply for natural reasons. While communicative movements could be decoded in the distance, or when silence was necessary, sound should have been indispensable to overcome physical obstacles; but, above all, to communicate in the dark (especially before the use of fire, which must have increased the opportunities for social contact), without forgetting that deaf people would perceive only kinesics, and blind people only sound and contactual kinesics. Thus, what is defended as adaptive development and cognitive sophistication should be applied, I feel, to both acoustic and gestural communication, without disregarding that perhaps audible kinesics would have lost status as the vocal-tract repertoire increased. Even accepting Glenn McBride's (1973) theory (summed up in his comments to Hewes' text) of communication progression from mime, or acting out of an event, through signs, to speech—facilitated by important changes in the brain, vocal and auditory systems—kinesics and paralinguistic behaviors must have always coexisted, as he himself believes, to later remain as an inseparable complement to verbal language.

By these brief comments on the 'primitive' nature of kinesics and paralanguage I did not intend at all to join the evolutionists, but simply suggest the coexistence of sound and movement, as they are both based on kinetic articulations. Furthermore, by acknowledging the biological and cognitive development of the vocal-auditory channel, I wish to point out the kinesiological-symbolic development of kinesic behavior, from rough, broad movements—of the whole body, the head, the arm or the whole hand, to signify basic situations of danger, agression-affiliation, protection-rejection, hunger, happiness, anger, etc.—to subtle and sophisticated articulations (akin to the ones progressively achieved in the vocal tract) of the fingers of both hands, of various types of eyelid closures and eye movements, and their mutual coarticulation.

The fact that cultural advancement and technology have enriched the repertoires of gestures, manners and postures through the evolution of the dwellings, of furniture, utensils, clothes, etc. (which also betray the progress of social and intellectual life), can be attested today by systematically observing the kinesic repertoires of the urban and/or educated groups with those of the less educated peasants. The repertoire of the rural class is much more limited in gestures, manners and postures, as well as in paralinguistic expressive means (as it lacks the versatility of subtly different types of laughter, of meaningful narial egressions, or closed-lip vocalic sounds) and vocabulary. In fact, this seems to emphasize the cohesiveness of the Basic Triple Structure from a functional, interactive and historical point of view, and the assumption that not just verbal language, but the three cosystems, have evolved along with the different cultures, since, the more primitive the culture, the more limited those repertoires seem to be.

On the other hand, what Raffler-Engel (1978, 1980, 1981) and Hoffer and St. Clair (1981) are currently studying as 'developmental kinesics' ought to be applied to the total linguistic-paralinguistic-kinesic complex and, very specifically, to the acquisition of paralanguage, particularly alternants.

From a semiotic-communicative point of view, even the direct visual perception of movements, without considering any type of synesthesial interpretation, appears far more advanced as a message system in anthropokinesics than it is in any other species. We cannot underestimate, however, the ability of many animals for retaining olfactory, acoustic, visual and dermal sensations and react to them accordingly, both as short and long-term memory. Which proves how even those messages that suffer from 'rapid fading' (Hockett 1960), such as sound and movement, 'come back' later in many species to condition their behaviors. Without going into the nature of consciousness in humans as compared to animals (cf. Thorpe 1972) we must consider how in humans, in spite of the also rapid fading, visually perceived movement can be said to travel through time. A derisive smile or an intent static look can linger and linger and truly regulate our subsequent behaviors and thoughts as the stored visual image is replayed over and over in our memory. We can also reconstruct the physical appearance of a person by gradually fitting together language, paralanguage and kinesics until that triple structure brings the person to life in our minds (a process central to the existence of the fictional character, as described in Chapter 9). And, with no mental effort whatsoever, one may easily renew the physical presence of someone else by carefully seeing and hearing with the eyes and ears of the memory as has been described so many times in literature.

The morphological-perceptual characteristics of kinesics

It is very important in kinesic research to make a clear distinction, which is often neglected, between: *gestures*, conscious or unconscious body movements made mainly with the head, the face alone or the limbs, learned or somatogenic, and serving as a primary communicative tool, dependent or independent from verbal language, either simultaneous or alternating with it and modified by the conditioning background (e.g., smiles, eye movements, a gesture of beckoning and other emblems, a tic); *manners*, although similar to gestures, more or less dynamic body attitudes that, while somatogenically modified, are mainly learned and socially codified according to specific situations, either simultaneous or alternating with verbal language (e.g., the way one eats, greets others, coughs, crosses arms or legs to adopt those postures); and *postures* (conscious or unconscious positions of the body, more static than gestures (although the still posture proper is preceded by an important dynamic forming manner),[7] learned or somatogenic, either simultaneous or alternating with verbal language, modified by social norms and by the rest of the conditioning background and used less as a communicative tool, although they may reveal affective states and social status (e.g., sitting, standing). Unfortunately the existing kinesic inventories still neglect this basic differentiation that proves indispensable for systematic research, as they do another morphological distinction that carries important sociopsychological, cultural and historical implications, that between free and bound movements and still positions, which occur both in interactive and non-interactive situations.

By *free* I understand a kinetic act or position performed by one or more parts of the body or limbs in space, that is, by themselves, without contacting other parts nor assisting themselves in any props provided by the objectual world. Free gestures (in interaction) are, therefore, the movements of the eyes, eyelids and the different parts of the face, head nods, shakes and tilts, and the gestures made with hands, arms and legs. Free manners are, in interaction, the way we bow in greetings, or stretch our hands; and in noninteraction, the way we walk (without trying to elicit someone else's behavior, as a female may typically do), yawn, or stretch. Free postures are stance, squatting, and any position in which only the feet are touching the sustaining surface.

By *bound* I understand any movement or position in which the hands come in contact with other parts of the body or with each other, or in which any part of it comes in contact with other bodies or, mainly, with objects. Bound gestures, in interaction, are self-adaptors like touching one's temple to indicate 'He's crazy', and object-adaptors like pointing with a pencil. Bound manners are, in interaction, self-adaptors, like preening, scratching or rubbing one's eyes; object adaptors, as when handling fork and knife, jewelry, pipes and glasses, or when knocking on a door; alter-adaptors, as in grooming, protecting, punishing; in noninteraction they are self-adaptors, as in preening, object-adaptors, as in handling tools or playing an instrument, and body-adaptors, as in chewing gum, masticating food or drinking. Bound postures in interaction are, apart from standing, sitting and lying, the ones assumed mainly as alter-adaptors of aggressive or affiliative nature, of sexual behavior, etc.; and as object-adaptors, as a female's provocative way of leaning against a table toward her male interlocutor; and, in noninteraction, the object-adaptor positions of stance (against a wall), sitting and recumbence (on furniture, on natural objects, or as conditioned by clothes or by the characteristics of a vehicle), and those adopted in certain occupational activities in which desks, counters, mechanical artifacts and tools are engaged.

This distinction between free and bound activities whose importance has been amply illustrated when discussing self-adaptors, alter-adaptors, body-adaptors and object-adaptors, should be extended actually beyond kinesics to, as it applies to any occurrence of any bodily activity and its costructuration with one or more other body parts or activities, say, a facial gesture combined with a postural shift, blushing, cigarette smoking, a paralinguistic alternant, a verbal expression or tear-shedding.

Although the discussion of nonverbal categories covers all possible forms of kinesic behaviors, the table in Fig. 5.3, 'Morphological-Perceptual Classification of Anthropokinesics' attempts to present at a glance the interactive and noninteractive forms of gestures, manners and postures both in their free and bound modalities.

Conditioning Background: Biophysicopsychological — cultural — socioeconomic

		FULL INTERACTION Visual/audible/tactile-kinesthetic	REDUCED INTERACTION Audible/tactile-kinesthetic (unseen)	REDUCED INTERACTION Visual/tactile-kinesthetic (unheard)	NON-INTERACTION
GESTURES	Free	Head, hair Face: eyes, eye-contact, brows, nares, mouth, lips, tongue, verbal & paralinguistic movements Shoulders, arms Hands, fingers Trunk, legs, feet	Verbal and paralinguistic production movements Synesthesial assumption of gestures by association with verbal and paralinguistic signs	Head, hair Face: eyes, eye-contact, brows, nares, mouth, lips, tongue, verbal and paralinguistic movements Shoulders, arms; Hands, fingers; Trunk, legs, feet. Assumption of sound through vision	Random acts Imagined (monologic) interaction Emotional displays Mental activities
GESTURES	Bound	Self-adaptors: hand(s)-to-body Object-adaptors: gesturing with cultural or pancultural conversational props (pipes, cigarettes, glasses, canes, sticks, tools, hats, gloves, etc.) Alter-adaptors: deictics	Self-adaptors: finger-snapping clapping & slapping gestures Object-adaptors: hitting cultural or pancultural conversational props against self, objects, or ground Synethesial assumption of gestures through their sound	Self-adaptors: hand(s)-to-body Object-adaptors: gesturing with cultural or pancultural conversational props Synesthesial assumption of sound through visual signs	Random acts Imagined (monologic) interaction Mental activities
MANNERS	Free	Emotional displays: face, arms, etc. Greetings and goodbyes Eating & drinking (chewing, swallowing), masticatories Gait, dancing, acrobatics, sports Physiological: sneezing, belching, stretching, spitting Posture-forming manners	Eating & drinking (chewing, swallowing) Physiological: sneezing, belching, spitting, coughing, throat-clearing Laughing, crying Synethesial assumption of manners through their sound	Emotional displays Greetings & goodbyes Eating, drinking, masticatories Gait, dancing, acrobatics, sports Physiological, posture-forming Synesthesial assumption of sound through visual signs	Emotional-displays: unconscious imagined (monologic) interaction Eacting, drinking, masticatories Gait, solo dancing Physiological (coughing, etc.) Posture-forming
MANNERS	Bound	Self-adaptors: affect-displays grooming, preening, scratching picking, rubbing Body-adaptors: clothes, hats, jewelry, food, drink, eating & drinking tools, pipes, glasses Object-adaptors: tools, furniture Alter-adaptors: sexual behaviors, aggression	Self-adaptors: applauding, slapping Body-adaptors: jewelry, eating & drinking tools Object-adaptors: tools, knocking against objects, furniture Alter-adaptors: kissing, clapping, handshakes, patting, aggression	Emotional displays Greetings and goodbyes Eating & drinking, masticatories Gait, dancing, acrobatics, sports Physiological, posture-forming Alter-adaptors: kissing, wrestling Synesthesial assumption of sound through visual signs	Self-adaptors: mental activities random acts, preens Body-adaptors: clothes, etc. Object-adaptors: tools, etc. Alter-adaptors (imagined interaction) with self or objects Surrogate alter-adaptors
POSTURES	Free	Ground-based: standing, squatting, sitting, kneeling Air-based: jumping, acrobatics sports Water-based: swimming	Synethesial assumption of postures through associated sounds as secondary sign systems	Self-adaptors: arms/legs cross Body-adaptors Object-adaptors: furniture Alter-adaptors: arm-in-arm Synesthesial assumption of sound through visual signs	Ground-based: standing, squatting Air-based: jumping Water-based: swimming
POSTURES	Bound	Self-adaptors: clasping crossed arms & legs Object-adaptors: with furniture, objects, etc. Alter-adaptors: affect-displays, sexual behaviors, aggression, etc.	Synesthesial assumption of postures through associated sounds or tactile/kinesthetic perception as secondary sign systems	Self-adaptors Body-adaptors Object-adaptors Alter-adaptors Synesthesial assumption of sound through visual/tactile signs	Self-adaptors:random,mental activities Body-adaptors:clothes Object-adaptors:furniture Alter-adaptors(imagined interaction)with self or objects Surrogate alter-adaptors

Parakinesic qualities: Intensity — Range — Velocity

Costructuration with [Verbal language-Paralanguage (& silence) — Kinesics (& stillness)
Proxemics, Chemical, Dermal, Thermal systems, Chronemics

FIG. 5.3. Morphological-Perceptual Classification of Anthropokinesics.

Finally, this brief introduction to kinesics as part of the Basic Triple Structure shows (a) that kinesic acts are not only visual or silent, as there is visual-acoustic kinesics (e.g., finger-snapping, desk-tapping), perceived only as sound when vision is blocked, or by the blind interactant, (b) that they can constitute contactual kinesics, also important in the interaction with the blind, who can in this way perceive variously encoded alter-adaptor behaviors, (c) that whatever external movement in someone's body can be detected visually or tactually-kinesthetically perceived qualifies as kinesics, as with eye movements or unconscious jerks and twitches, for there is no difference (from a kinetic point of view) between a brow raise and a gaze raise or between an intended smile and a facial tic, as they all make up the visual image of the person as perceived by his cointeractant, and (d) that the intervening still positions within the interactive linguistic-paralinguistic-kinesic stream qualify also as kinesic behaviors, as they are costructured with movement as much as postures do.

7. The Triple Transcription-Description

The transcription I would like to simply suggest here (as it seems to derive naturally from the comments made about the Triple Structure), was first used by a joint team from the Universities of Birmingham and Nancy in 1976.[8] It was inspired to me in the late sixties by the classic in the field, *The First Five Minutes*, the pioneering work of the psychiatrists Pittinger and Danehy and the linguist-anthropologist Hockett (1960) on a five-minute segment of a psychiatric interview, where, mainly by means of arbitrary graphic symbols, they represented the linguistic and paralinguistic behaviors of the patient, adding to it a minute analysis of what goes on during the interview. To that I added the third element of the Triple Structure, kinesics, for a realistic depiction of the speech-and-movement occurrence.

The characteristics of the transcription are indicated in Fig. 5.4, in what is actually the beginning of a blank transcription sheet showing the order in which the different features are incorporated from top to bottom, this first sheet being followed by successive ones.

1. *Orthographic transcript* that can be read quickly by turning the pages of the transcription.

2. *Paralinguistic transcription*, comprising four types of speech phenomena: (a) *primary qualities*, or overriding person-identifying features with three degrees above and below a base line: general timbre, volume, resonance, tempo, pitch level, intonation range, syllabic length, and rhythm, plus any of the qualifiers listed as the next paralinguistic category which might also be part of the person's permanent voice set (e.g., poor articulatory control or creaky voice due to laryngealization); any of these overriding features can be indicated by a capital initial and degree (e.g., Rn3 for very

Orthographic transcript			A
			B
Primary qualities	A. Speaker/listener B. Listener/speaker	Qualifiers	A
			B
		Differentiators	
		Alternants	A
			B
Phonemic transcription			A
			B
Parakinesic qualities	A. Speaker/listener B. Listener/speaker	Face: eyes brows, forehead nose, cheeks mouth	A
			B
		Head trunk legs, feet	A
			B
		Shoulders arms, hands fingers	A
			B
Body-adaptors Object-adaptors			A
			B
Proxemic behavior			A
			B
Contextual description			A
			B

FIG. 5.4. Triple Transcription-Description (chronemic features added to each behavior).

nasal resonance), (b) *qualifiers*, as nonpermanent features among: respiratory control, glottis control, laryngeal-, velar-, pharyngeal-, articulatory-, labial-, and maxillary controls, and articulatory tension; and, within the same band of the transcription, (c) *differentiators*, when they override words (otherwise included within segmental alternants below): laughter, crying, sighing, yawning, sneezing, belching, hiccoughing and extremes of whispering and loud voice; and (d) independent segmental *alternants*, such as clicks, moans, hesitation vowels, narial ingressions and egressions, etc., and including pauses.

For the paralinguistic part of the transcription the researcher may resort to what symbols may seem best among the International Phonetic Alphabet, those used by Trager (1958), Pittinger *et al.* (1960), Crystal and Quirk (1964), Austin (1965), McQuown *et al.* (1971), or Poyatos (1975e).

3. *Phonemic transcription*, including intonational features, using mainly the IPA (International Phonetic Alphabet).

4. *Kinegraphic and parakinegraphic transcription*, completing the Basic Triple Structure, using either Birdwhistell's (1970) kinegraphs, or from a more practical point of view, the abbreviated system suggested by Kendon (1969), consisting of: eyes, brows and forehead, mouth, head, hand and arms, shoulders and trunk, and direction of gaze. Based on these two systems, one could simplify the recording of body movements and positions by differentiating, as shown in the table, three principal areas: face (eyes, brows, cheek, nose, mouth), head-trunk-legs-feet, and shoulders-arms-hands (arms, forearms, wrists, angle, whole hand, fingers). *Parakinesic* nonsegmental features, that is, intensity, range, and velocity of movements, are recorded for specific activities but they can also appear as the permanent person-identifying features of an individual's body set, indicated, like voice set, at the beginning of the kinesic transcription.

5. *Adaptors*, that is, body-adaptor behaviors (mainly clothes and jewelry, masticatories, etc.) and object-adaptor ones (occurring either throughout the speaker's deliverance or momentarily, must be indicated at this level closest to kinesics (fidgeting, tapping, chewing, etc.).

6. *Proxemic notation*, for spatial features and shifts that are intimately built in the interaction and associated with language, paralanguage and kinesics, can follow Hall's (1974) technique or one's own according to the aims of the study, so that the roles played in the interaction by interpersonal intimate or personal distance are clearly acknowledged.

7. *Chronemic notation*, added to each of the other sections of the triple and proxemic notations, indicates the significant temporal feature of the activities registered in all the other sections after primary qualities, that is: the duration of qualifiers like labial control and whispering, of differentiators like laughter, of alternants like independent laughter, moaning sounds and pauses; then the length of certain gestures, manners and postures (manners

constituting the 'formative' and 'releasing' phases of postures) and of the various parts of the speaker's turn, of the turn itself and of the whole speaker-listener exchange.

8. *The contextual description* implies that, regardless of the aims of the research, the transcription cannot be limited to a symbolization of physical events in a rather 'desocialized' or 'deculturized' way, and so we must also indicate, among other conditioning factors, the cultural environment as well as the cultural background of the participants, the nature of the encounter, the personal characteristics of the participants, both physically (appearance, dress and grooming, etc.) and psychologically, their socioeconomics and socioeducational status and, of course, the type of relationship that determines the encounter. One characteristic of the proposed transcription is that both the speaker's and the listener's behaviors should be recorded simultaneously, since the interaction is at all moments a two-way affair. The listener's feedback and the speaker's simultaneous turns and interruptions, among other behaviors within the mechanism of conversation (discussed in Chapter 7) must be recorded for a proper understanding of the encounter.

8. On the Concept of Usage

Inherent in this basic study of the Basic Triple Structure behaviors displayed within a culture—but necessary for the understanding of crosscultural differences—is the concept of *usage*, which should be applied to nonverbal behaviors and not only to verbal language; not in terms of "standard", "colloquial", "slang" or "vulgar" (although there are undoubtedly features that are characteristic of specific socioeconomic strata), but bearing in mind: first, that groups next to each other overlap as an ever-shifting and self-renovating part of their members and are socioeconomically and culturally astride the two; and secondly, that there is in the more developed cultures today a constant borrowing of verbal and nonverbal habits, mainly by the higher-up groups from the lower ones. Therefore, rather than resorting to a vertical classification of linguistic, paralinguistic, and kinesic usage, I would briefly suggest the horizontal one I proposed earlier (Poyatos 1972a, 1976a, 1980a) in which the following categories or 'forms' are differentiated:

A. *Standard*, which consists of the verbal repertoires, paralinguistic expressive constructs and accompanying phenomena, kinesic activity and, in fact, any social attitudes sensibly apprehensible common to the refined and the rustic, the educated and the pseudoeducated, as the national or 'cultural' standard used by everybody and observed in everybody.

B. At the same time, each socioeconomic group and each occupational group possesses a portion of its standard communicative repertoire which is not shared by the others, but of which those others are perfectly aware, and for whom that portion is felt and judged as *extrastandard*. Each individual, from his own level or group, can easily identify that extrastandard and, according to his or her capacity, adopt it under special circumstances as a functional variety for the sake of adaptability to a particular group and/or situation. One interesting fact about this capacity for adaptation to another group is that it seems to decrease in direct proportion to the socioeconomic and educational status of the individual, while the tendency to criticize extrastandard behaviors increases in direct proportion to it. Clearly enough, the average uneducated person does not have the capacity to use the same words, the same paralinguistic features and the same gestures, manners and postures used by the educated one. This is so because uneducated people lack the proper sensitiveness for judging the different ways in which other people speak and move (something which is acquired only through daily contact with the educated groups) and a conscious and unconscious appreciation of the values related to the dominant norms and tastes in other groups. But a person with a much larger cultural capacity, who is often in close contact with people in other strata, is prepared to appreciate and judge those differences and, when necessary, to adopt them if he so wishes. For the same reason, the rustics will not find as many faults with the behavior of the educated people as the latter will find with them, even if they mock the 'fine manners' of the higher-up for fun, not for the sake of criticism.

C. But below the standard and the extrastandard, and regardless of social class, there is definitely an *infrastandard*, unacceptable for most people under normal circumstances, as it happens with repeated blasphemy, habitual yelling, certain obscene gestures, physical contact in ways that should be avoided, excessive unpunctuality, etc.

D. Naturally, an overdisplay of lexical sophistication, of gestural expressions, excessively refined manners and affected postures, and excessive politeness or a situationally improper sweet voice are also felt as outside the standard forms, whether we traditionally consider them good or bad, and they represent a typical *ultracorrectness* that deserves special research.

E. What I would subsume as *technical or group usage*, for lack of a more adequate term, is an independent category which on occasions, can be shared by individuals of different socioeconomic levels, and which includes religious and sport ritualistic behaviors, the verbal and nonverbal codes of certain professions, teen-age verbal and kinesic slang, certain sex-differentiated repertoires, etc.

9. Proxemics and Chronemics: the Spatial and Temporal Dimensions of Behaviors and Relationships

As space and time constitute the two basic dimensions of any of the activities that we may carry out in a living culture, whether interactive or noninteractive, the discussion of proxemics and chronemics the two areas to which I always need to refer—and which future work will hopefully develop much more in depth in the context of this intersystem, interdisciplinary approach to communication—could be at least briefly outlined at this point. The spatial and temporal aspects of culture-maintaining activities has been apparent as soon as the situation of Crusoe and Friday engaged in mutual interaction has been pondered in the first chapter. From that moment on the duration of their individual actions and the location of their bodies in space lent specific significance to their relationship. Instead of two men alone on an island one could imagine the proverbial castaway boy and girl and their very different progressive spatial relationship as well as their specific costructuration of their time, or the also proverbial split group of castaways equally characterized by their mutual nearness-farness situation and the temporal shortness and abruptness-uniformity and continuity of their relationships. In every instance, as in every situation of our own daily existence in society, not only are our relationships characterized by different interbody distances but by the different duration of each activity as well as by our conceptualization of both the space and the time that surrounds us. It is obvious, then, that even the inclusion of a proxemic and chronemic identification of the situation depicted in a triple transcription as the one suggested in this chapter is far from being a gratuitous one, and that it amply justifies the presentation of at least an outline of the basic principles of proxemics and chronemics to provide better cohesion among the various areas discussed in the book. Although at this point the emphasis will be on interpersonal relationships it must be pointed out that I am using the term interpersonal in a broad but realistic way, as it must be associated, for instance, with the writer–reader spatial and temporal relationship discussed in Chapter 9, as much as with the spatial and temporal aspects of face-to-face interaction, clearly implicit in the study of the structure of conversation undergone in Chapter 7.

Proxemics

Proxemics, developed by the anthropologist Edward T. Hall (1959, but above all, 1966) with great insight, will be defined here as: people's conception, use and structuration of space, from their built or natural surrounding to the distances consciously or unconsciously maintained in personal interaction; a definition that, wanting to deal exhaustively with spatial behavior, should include many other animal species, which throws much light upon man's own behavior.

Proxemic behavior covers a very wide range of manifestations, both culture-specific and universal, but, first of all, biological, that is, shown by human beings as living organisms claiming, delimiting and maintaining their own territory or occupying someone else's, as practised in personal interaction, in the layout of their towns and buildings, in the arrangement and spacing of their furniture and in the distances kept from the inanimate environment and its objects as well as from their fellow men. Neither our objectual proxemic behavior nor our similarities with other species in the handling of time are, however, the specific concern of this chapter. Instead, I will concentrate on how we use space as a system within external body communication (as indicated in Fig. 3.3) closely associated with the rest of the verbal and nonverbal activities of which the Basic Triple Structure is the very core.

As a body-originated system of communication in personal interaction, proxemic behaviour appears as patterned along with other message-conveying activities, whether consciously or unconsciously displayed, as a motor-based modality (not necessarily moving, but resulting from movement shifts, thus intimately related to kinesics), visually, olfactorily and kinesthetically perceived, and displayed through kinesic activity as interactants space themselves during a conversation, walking down the street, watching a game, or at the beach. In whatever situation, the basic stage of each proxemic distance is, from a strict point of view, a static one, until a new spacing behavior (e.g., in the back-and-forth stepping of two standing interlocutors) takes place. It is interesting, therefore, to consider the various intersystem relationships and observe how language and other verbal and nonverbal systems are modified by proxemic behavior, and vice versa.

I will refer once more to the chart 'External Somatic Communication' (Fig. 3.3) to suggest the more typical relationships of the various communicative systems with each of the four basic distances differentiated by Hall (1966), obviously for his American subjects: *public* (far phase, 25 feet or more; close phase, 12 to 25), *social* (far phase, 7 to 12; close phase, 4 to 7), *personal* (far phase, 2.5 to 4; close phase, 1.5 to 2.5), and *intimate* (far phase, 6 to 18 inches; close phase, total contact between bodies); to which I felt the need to add *far distance* at one end and *objectual distance* at the other.

Far distance is an extreme but not untypical distance in actual interaction. Light and smoke signals are common at such a distance, and two people trying to communicate between two hills, from the street to a tenth floor, etc., must increase enormously the range of their emblematic (message-conveying) gestures. If hearing it not impossible, they will use their hands as a megaphone and shout, but if it is, as when someone is waving at a rescue helicopter, one tends to actually speak at normal volume while violently moving. As a rule governing communicative behavior, as distance between interactants shortens (from an air pilot waving at his girl friend on the ground to the two of them cuddled on a couch), the richer their nonverbal repertoires become, while verbal expression diminishes.

At *public distance* the visually and acoustically perceived ways of communicating become the only means of establishing contact, but they are heavily modified in comparison with the more common situations, those occurring at social and personal distances. An orator, although boosted by extensions of our organism, such as loudspeakers, uses his full voice volume and clear and tense articulation, while occasionally banging his lectern (object-adaptor) and using various self-adaptor gestures and self-adaptor manners, like clapping hands or hitting the palm with the first of the other hand. I must point out that the greater the distance between a speaker and his audience, the more obvious the kinesic and paralinguistic repertoires should be, since, as well all have experienced at one time or another, an otherwise good text can be a failure if delivered by a poor speaker who hardly moves and hardly changes his tone of voice and the rhythm of his deliverance, although we may have enjoyed him earlier at close range distance. Stage actors are, of course, sensitive to the linguistic, paralinguistic and kinesic means of reaching the balcony, from where the audience needs their nonverbal conveyance of situations and affects more than from a first row; while a movie actor or actress is considered 'theatrical' if he or she cannot display the paralinguistic and kinesic subtleties of personal and intimate distances, made possible by the camera. In any proxemic situation the speakers need to keep the proper equilibrium among the vocal, proxemic and kinesic systems, but mainly between the first two, as reflected in the '¡¡Louder!!' heard at the back of an audience when the equilibrium is missing, just as someone may tell us 'You don't have to shout, I'm right here'; and, most typically, in the inevitable, almost unconscious full-volume voice during a long-distance call, always invariably so when carried out by the less educated people.

Social distance is the distance normally kept among people during a formal introduction (first they approach each other to shake hands, then retreat to their former locations), in a waiting room (if lack of sitting space does not make it personal), or even while walking around in a department store. It is obvious that social, personal and intimate distances cannot always be defined in terms of specific situations. There are too many variables to be considered. While walking around in a department store, or moving inside a bus depot, or at a cocktail party, interpersonal spaces shrink and stretch quite frequently, and the same people who are keeping a close-phase social distance one minute find themselves three or four feet from others the next. One could elaborate a great deal on the widening and narrowing of interpersonal distances and, above all, on the very different implications found in specific distances according to the different situational contexts in which they may occur. For example, waiting in a box-office line two strangers are one or two feet apart probably, which, according to Hall's classification, corresponds to personal, even intimate distance, although we know very well that those two people may not even look at each other and that the situation is entirely 'social', that is, representing a social context. The same thing happens aboard a crowded subway car. In all those forced, falsely personal-intimate situations the protagonists try to avoid eye contact as much as possible, and occasional smiles or movements tell each other that they would not be that close if they could avoid it.

Returning to the emission and perception of communicative signals through the various bodily channels, it is interesting to note that at both phases of the so-called social distance (from 4 to 7 feet, and from 7 to 12), the volume of the voice, for instance, requires a culturally dictated control. Regardless of the topic being discussed, people try to keep their voices down when surrounded at social distance by people they are not directly interacting with (indirectly, they do condition each other's volume control, to begin with, and that is definitely interaction), although we find exceptions everywhere in North America. Voice volume at social distance distinguishes several cultures. Spanish, Italians and Arabs, for instance, talk loudly in public places like ordinary restaurants and side-walk cafés, as well as at social and family gatherings. At social distance, the kinesic repertoire can be more subtle and expressive. Some hand gestures usually performed about one foot from the body would be acted closer to it when interacting at personal distance; that is, kinesic range is shortened, just as voice volume can be lowered. Visual contact becomes very important since movements of the eyes can be perfectly seen and decoded. Postural shifts and object-adaptor manners (tapping the desk, fidgeting with a pen) can be detected as feedback better than at public distance (at which they may pass unnoticed by an actor or a lecturer in a large room). Also, it is at social far-phase distance that body-adaptors (wigs, jewelry, clothes), grooming signs, dermal changes (blushing, goose flesh) and secretions (tears, heavy perspiration) become perceptible and meaningful; while at its close phase, as when sharing, joining a group at a party or occupying a vehicle with someone else, olfactory communication begins to work, increased by rising temperature (since a shaving lotion, feminine cosmetics or perspiration are more noticeable at high skin temperature). Even bad breath and body odor can be detected at this distance, being more so at the next proxemic stage, far-phase personal distance.

At *personal distance*, not only olfactory perception is increased, but complexion, hidden marks of aging and the true quality of body-adaptors can be valued as indices to physiological and socioeconomic states, which in many instances can be corroborated by paralinguistic features (as with the socially inferior person trying to 'talk natural' with upper-class interlocutors), and by kinesic behavior (gestures, manners and postures). But, most important, even at the far phase of 2.5 to 4 feet, interactants are within physical reach of each other. Arabs and Latins jump easily from social to personal distance. I can remember the expression on the face of an Anglo-Saxon tourist walking through a Marrakesh market when being literally grabbed by a persuasive merchant and pulled into the shop. It is a highly cultural characteristic that

Spanish men, for instance, touch each other much from the waist up when engaged in friendly conversation. So, being a native of Spain myself, while I unconsciously keep my tactual repertoire under control among Anglo-Saxons, can act most 'fluently' with Arab merchants and farmers because I grasp them by the neck and by the arm and pat them while conversing with them. Although I would not hold hands with another man (as many of them do going down the street or standing by a door) because it is a taboo in my own culture to which I have been conditioned. However, at personal distance, paralanguage and contact kinesics are intimately related in my native culture, as they are in other western cultures. When two good Latin friends motion towards each other anticipating a firm handshake with a broad smile (or a stern countenance if expressing condolence) at personal distance, the loud, high-pitched and drawled '¡¡Well!!' gives way to a lower-pitched '¿How are you?' at close personal distance, their paralanguage will correspond to their tactual involvement and the kinesic stress of each handshake and each syllable will regulate each other. A cold person is thought cold when he, in spite of a close personal distance, keeps his paralanguage inadequately adjusted to the situation.

Through tactile perception, available at personal distance, one can learn about a person from a loose handshake, a callous hand, a kinesthetic appreciation of physical strength or weakness, and various emotional states are revealed by language and paralanguage, by kinesic behavior, by trembling and perspiration, by heat and by cold. A new look at the elements constituting the biophysicopsychological and sociogeographical-economic background (Chapter 3) and at the interrelationships among sensible systems (Fig. 2.1) reveals countless research possibilities regarding the interrelationships of the different body communicative activities, including the Basic Triple Structure, language-paralanguage-kinesics, at the various distances being discussed.

Finally, *intimate distance* provides also a wealth of possibilities for study in each of the areas discussed in this book which even someone interested 'only' (quite an unrealistic attitude) in language should not overlook. At intimate distance visual communication is not so important any more, except for long deep glances carrying basic emotional states (love, anger, aggression, sexual arousal), in which different 'allokines' of an eyelid closure, for instance, and pupil size are far more eloquent and subtle than conventional verbal constructs in a given language can ever be.

But it is, above all, kinesthetic, tactile and olfactory inputs and outputs that are incredibly stepped-up when intimate distance between two persons is reached. And two things may happen:

(a) that such a proxemic situation is not at all sought by participants, not even direct interaction, as happens in a crowded elevator: one stands still, hands kept alongside the body, or against the chest if really crowded by others (lest one's position should be misinterpreted); the longer the trip, the more tension builds up, even if unconsciously; eye contact is avoided beyond an initial glance when stepping in, receiving another passenger or asking to be let out, many look insistently, but quite unnecessarily most of the times, at the jumping floor numbers above the door, look down or whisper-whistle; the company of a friend is appreciated, while the others go through their own 'ordeals', and a funny remark from a good-humored elevator attendant is always welcome and elaborated on;

(b) that proxemic behavior gradually progresses from the far and close stages of personal range to the intimate one, as in wrestling, rescuing, helping someone in moments of moral and physical stress, at which language is kept to a minimum while bodies communicate kinesthetically mostly and through paralinguistic features such as whispering, coarse voice, heavy respiration, etc.

Sexual involvement is perhaps the best example of intimate proxemic behavior. Intimate distance, at which hands, faces, lips, legs and abdominal areas (usually in this order) come into contact, develops an intense, ever-mounting multisensory involvement unparalleled in any other animal species, since the intellect plays an important role in valuing shape, texture, color, consistency, temperature, eye contact and tone of voice. Effective vision, is impeded, and verbal messages (conveyed only by whispery, hoarse, breathy, arhythmic voice, heavily dependent on paralinguistic alternants) may even be lacking, as other channels carry out a continuous display of sensorial communication. Since proxemic and kinesic behavior are kept at very close range, kinesthetic perception plays the most important role of all, as the whole body of the other person is perceived through muscles, tendons and dermic contact through the skin's temperature and pressure receptors. In this type of involvement, the most intense one in personal interaction, not only body-adaptors like lotions and cosmetics, but the bodies themselves, communicate their specific odorous molecules to the olfactory epithelium inside the nasal passage, and odors of which more molecules would be necessary at greater distances, are transmitted at two or three inches by the olfactory nerve to the olfactory bulb of the brain, where smell is 'thought of', just as other sensorially perceived body features are conceptualized in different degrees and according to different types of sensitiveness. On the other hand, synesthesial appreciation of bodily features plays a very important role as visual characteristics must be assumed only through toponimical exploration.

Objectual distance is the distance people keep from their objectual world, specifically from elements of the built environment like walls and fences (which we touch as we walk by, lean on, keep closer or farther apart from), the natural environment, like trees and rocks (which we sit on, lean against, climb, and touch for their texture), or furniture, which determines an important part of our environmental interaction, as with desks (behind which we take positions of defence, superiority or aggressiveness, and on which we tap, scribble, flick off imaginary lint, lean on or collapse out of exhaustion). Objectual proxemics, thus revealing personality, cultural and circumstantial variables, includes also other artifacts, such as steering wheels, and, in sum, any objects from which we may consciously or unconsciously keep different distances for obvious and not so obvious reasons.

Chronemics

After realizing the relevance of the spatial dimension in the production of the Triple Structure and any other interactive systems within a culture, I felt the need to never dissociate it from the temporal dimension. Consequently, I began to explore a systematic way of speaking about time in a manner analogous to the way proxemics dealt with space, and suggested on several occasions what I soon came to regard as an indispensable tool for the scientific analysis of human behavior.

The proposed term for it was *chronemics* (Poyatos 1972a [acknowledged in Key 1980, and in her December 1973 Newsletter])[9] and its subject matter: our conceptualization and handling of time as a biopsychological and cultural element lending specific characteristics to social relationships and to the many events contained within the communicative stream, from linguistic syllables and flitting gestures to meaningful glances and silences.

Edward T. Hall (1959, 1966) has expressed deep concern for the cultural miscommunication resulting from the different ways of understanding time and has written some very interesting pages on the American structuration and conceptualization of time, which the readers ought to be acquainted with in order to comprehend better the cultural background of what here I refer to as *interactive chronemics*. Hall's observations deal mostly with the characteristics of what he calls informal time, that is, the conceptualization of culturally-based and flexible units like 'a while', and the idea about punctuality and promptness, the 'apology period' and the 'insult period' when waiting and making others wait (much shorter and harder to understand by American standards), the American 'monochronism' (doing one thing at a time) as clashing with Latin or Arab 'polychronism' (performing several small tasks at the same time) and, in general, the 'feeling' of time in different cultures. Just by mentioning some of Hall's topics concerning time one would amply justify the necessity to develop a theoretical and methodological scheme for chronemics, more or less as it has been developed for proxemics.

Although other writers have borrowed the term *chronemics* and have been trying to develop the area in certain directions different from mine (cf. Bruneau 1980) at this writing, however, my own ideas about chronemic analysis, clear as they may be at times, have not as yet crystallized in a full-grown schema, although I have attempted to set some realistic cultural and interactional principles with respect to the conceptualization and use of time. The preparation of such schema will be based, of course, on the principle that time communicates. Whether passively engraved in a recent footprint and in a crumbling medieval wall, or actively expressing something in a pause between verbal sentences and kinesic constructs, in the duration of a wink or in the lingering of a handshake, time, that is, temporal length of activities and the gaps between them, must be acknowledged as a measurable constituent of behavior, and the result of behavior, and as a communicative system in itself.

Chronemic behavior, then, must be analyzed as a structured overriding 'supraactivity', a continuum that can bc coded in universal as well as in culture-specific ways, and whose meaning serves to differentiate situational contexts, cultural backgrounds and personality and biological configurations.

As a still very preliminary (but hopefully useful) framework, I will differentiate three types of time equally valid in any culture: conceptual time, social time, and interactive time.

Conceptual time as a research subarea is a prerequisite for the study of the social and interactive categories. Acknowledging the cultural background as in any other study of communication, it must define the conceptualization of time, not only of what Hall calls formal time (the year, the month, the fortnight, etc.), and how far into the future life is planned, or how far back into the past one's behavior is still 'operative', but as regards basic concepts like promptness—tardiness, punctuality—unpunctuality, on which I must not try to elaborate here.

Social time, directly depending on conceptualized time, is time as handled in social relations at all levels within a culture as well as interculturally (that is, by people from different cultural backgrounds coming into contact on one setting or another).

If as a field-work project we have to study social time among, say, Arabs, or Japanese or Spaniards, it would obviously constitute a cultureme, and this cultureme could be broken down into other culturemes according to the system proposed for the analysis of a given culture in Chapter 2, e.g.: 'Duration of informal gatherings among middle-class Americans according to situational factors'; 'Chronemics of employer–employee relationship'; 'Time handling among academics'; 'Chronemic relations between doctors and patients'. Each of these culturemes includes what I define below as 'interactive time'. On the other hand, chronemic behavior in each case varies from the urban center, where time pressure reaches the point of what Hall refers to as 'the obsessional handling of time in the U.S.', to the small-town, country-style setting.

It is, then, in *interactive time* that we find the interrelationship among the various communicative modalities (paralanguage to chronemics, kinesics to chronemics, proxemics to chronemics, etc.). Below this level is the duration of each individual meaningful activity in a conversation as has just been discussed, and that is the basic level in the handling of time upon which all communicational behaviors are built. Besides speech tempo, syllabis duration, paralinguistic duration, I would call the first level *inter-system timing* (or chronemics), and the second level *primary timing* (or chronemics).

Notes

1. After submitting a paper for the 1970 meeting of the Northeast Modern Language Association, Professor Mahmud Okby suggested that I elaborate on "the basic triple structure of human communication behavior", which term, embarrased at my ignorance, I tried to find in vain, ¡until I read it discussed in my own paper! Since the Basic Triple Structure formed the foundation of most of my work to date I must dedicate this brief discussion of it to Professor Okby with deep gratitude for his very wise incentive of thirteen years ago. Lately I have discussed the Basic Triple Structure and the multichannel reality of discourse at the 1982 International Conference on the Language Sciences ('Language in a Semiotic Perspective') held at the International Christian University in Tokyo (Poyatos 1983b).

2. I have discussed the segmentality of certain paralinguistic and kinesic elements (which in fact could be applied to certain other somatic activities when they function with truly syntactical value in the stream of discourse) at the 1977 International Congress of Linguists, the session on paralanguage I organized for the 1977 International Congress of Phonetic Sciences (Poyatos 1979a), and the 1979 International Congress of Semiotic Studies (Poyatos 1981e).

3. After introducing *paralenguaje* and *kinésica* as costructures at the 1968 International Congress of Hispanists (Poyatos 1970a) I wrote my first paper on paralanguage in Spanish (Poyatos 1970b), offering the same basic classification as I do now and tracing its development since the coinage of the term by Hill (1952) and the greatly inspiring observations in Pike's *Phonetics* (1943), through the pioneering work by Trager (1955, 1958, 1960), Trager and Smith (1956), Smith (1953), the psychiatrist Pittinger and Smith (1957), Pittinger (1956), McQuown (1957), the psychiatric-linguistic team of Pittinger, Hockett and Danehy (1960), Birdwhistell's (1952, 1961) paralinguistic-kinesic association, Crystal and Quirk (1964), Catford (1968), the interdisciplinary conference organized by Sebeok on paralanguage and kinesics (Sebeok, Hayes, and Bateson 1964), and Austin (1965). Later I profited from more recent work of Crystal (1974), Lieberman (1975)—who participated in the first paralinguistic session, which I organized for the 1973 meeting of the Northeast Modern Language Association—and Laver (1978). I have discussed my taxonomy of paralanguage at several meetings, among them, the 1977 International Congress of Linguists (Poyatos 1979a), the 1977 International Congress of Phonetic Sciences, and the 1982 International Congress of Linguists, for which I organized a session on 'New Interdisciplinary Perspective in Linguistics Through Nonverbal Communication Studies', aside from my first book on nonverbal communication (Poyatos 1976a) and several papers (Poyatos 1970a, 1972a, 1974b, 1975e).

4. Differentiators, if used independently of language, that is, alternating with it or by themselves, must be regarded as alternants.

5. I first discussed alternants in detail at the 1973 pre-congress conference on the organization of 'Behavior in Face-to-Face Interaction' organized at the University of Chicago Linguistics Department for the Ninth International Congress of Anthropological and Ethnological Sciences.

6. Besides discussing kinesics in another book (1976a) and in other articles and at numerous meetings, I wrote a paper in Spanish (1970c) and the one on gestures inventories mentioned earlier (Poyatos 1975d), reedited (Poyatos 1981b) by Kendon, himself one of the most incisive and inspiring students of interactive kinesics (Kendon 1970, 1971, 1973, 1975, 1980a, 1980b).

This brief discussion of kinesics as one of the components of the Basic Triple Structure spares any detailed elaboration of the main principles of kinesics. I will summarize them, however, for the more unfamiliar reader as I did in my earlier book (Poyatos 1976a).

Just as there are a bewildering number of sounds that are anthropokinetically possible, of which we use only a limited portion in each language, there are also a staggering number of anthropokinetically possible bits of body motion of which only a specific number seem to constitute the distinctive kinemic system of each culture. Each of those semantically distinctive movements (a wink eye-closure, a skeptical brow knit, an affirmative head nod) that make up our kinesic, or rather, kinemic, system, is a *kineme*, just as each unreplaceable sound (*p*it, *k*it, *n*it, *s*it) that makes up our phonetic system is called a phoneme.

However, a phoneme is not a single sound, although we treat it as such when we speak or hear others speak, no matter where they come from. A cup of tea said with unaspirated [t] is just as good a cup of tea said with aspirated [t'], because aspiration/nonaspiration is not a distinctive feature in English speech and they are not different phonemes; just as the various realizable positional degrees of the eye-lid closure continuum of a wink (not counting additional modifiers, like cheek, brow, etc.) are not different kinemes, being understood by us (at least in our own culture) as 'a wink', without differentiating between so-and-so's type of eye-lid closure and so-and-so's slight variation from it. Thus, that series of similar movements are called *allokines*, or kine variations, that make up a kineme, just as the several sounds that make up a phoneme are called *allophones*. And just as a phoneme cannot be 'pronounced' because it is not a single sound but an abstract unit, so a kineme is not 'movable' but realized only through one of its allokines (Hayes 1964: 157).

Next, going up the morphological linguistic-kinesic analogy, one finds that, just as a pronounceable series of phonemes, or *morph*, form a minimal unit of speech called *morpheme* (friend [free morpheme], un-friend-ly [bound morphemes]), the combination of movable particles of body motion, or *kinemorphs*, are joined into *kinemorphemes* (a wink eye-closure by itself [free kinemorpheme], the same closure + raised cheek + unilateral upward mouth-distension [bound kinemorpheme]).

Beyond this point, Birdwhistell (1970) tells us: "Until we become much more secure as to the morphology and syntactics of kinesics (even for American English movers) our emic assignments must be registered as tentative." One should expect, however, the kinesicist's further kinemorphological and kinesyntactical constructs similar to sentences and paragraphs, and that is suggested in this chapter.

Besides these segmental units, Birdwhistell (1968) explained how certain body motion features apart from kinemes, kinemorphemes and complex kinemorphic constructions, which were at first dismissed as muscular, skeletal or skin phenomena in speech production, were later given the status of suprasegmental stress kinemes when the correlation of spoken and moved behaviors were analyzed in sound-filmed sequences of interaction. As a result, his kinesic analysis could show four degrees of stress (primary, secondary, tertiary or unstressed, and destressed) and, according to earlier research four kinesic terminal junctures, as well as "one and perhaps two" internal kinesic junctures.

As for the other subarea of kinesic analysis, Birdwhistell (1970) distinguished four *parakinesic* "motion qualifiers" which I will reduce to three and define as follows: *intensity*, or muscular tension (akin to stress and articulatory tension): movement overtense—tense—medium—lax—overlax; *range*, or extent of the movement (similar to syllabic duration): overwide—wide—medium—narrow—overnarrow; *velocity*, or temporal length of the movement (similar tempo of speech): overfast—fast—medium—slow—overslow.

Birdwhistell, who published the principles of 'kinesics' over thirty years ago (Birdwhistell 1952), later put together his different researches in a rather difficult but valuable volume (Birdwhistell 1970). In sections 16 and 18 of this book, for instance, he explained his progress towards analyzing the American movement system, specifying that, among the more than twenty thousand different facial expressions that are somatically possible, they had been able to isolate thirty-two kinemes (smallest significant units, described above) in the face and head area (three types of head nods, four kinemes of brow behavior, four degrees of lid closure, four nose behaviors, etc.), but that they vary "dialectically", just as speech does, throughout the country. He also identified a number of "kinesic markers" (which are "particular movements that occur regularly in association with or in substitution for certain syntactical arrangements in speech"), four degrees of "kinesic stress", and parakinesic qualities of intensity, frequency, extent of movement, and duration. In sections 26 and 27, written as chapters and extensive microanalytical (structural) work for *The Natural History of an Interview* (McQuown *et al.*, 1971), Birdwhistell presents the current state of kinesics in its relationship to language, giving us a detailed account of the theory and methodology of kinesic research to that date, and showing an eighteen-minute interactional sequence, its analysis and the problems involved in it. Finally, he presents his original 1952 kinegraphic transcription system of symbols and pictographs according to his division of the body into eight sections (differing from Kendon's [1969] abbreviated one): total head, face, trunk, shoulder, arm and wrist, hand and finger activity hip, leg and ankle, foot activity and walking, and neck (each one showing a number of distinctive kinemes. Finally, the book contains an earlier example of conversation linguistically, paralinguistically and kinesically transcribed (Birdwhistell 1960); and, confusingly enough, another selection from Birdwhistell's contribution to the *Natural History of an Interview* with a more advanced microkinesic system for recording and notation. For a better reading of this very valuable but not too organized book see two reviews of it: Dittman's (1971), in which he disagreees with the kinesic-linguistic analogy, and a more extensive one, with an important personal contribution, by Adam Kendon (1972).

Other researchers, of course, have taken different directions, concentrating on specific body areas, the best known being today Kendon (cited here often) and Ekman, the latter particularly on the face (Ekman 1972, 1973, 1976a, 1976b, 1977, 1978, 1979, 1980, 1982) and the hands (Ekman and Friesen 1972; Johnson, Ekman and Friesen 1975; Ekman 1976; Friesen, Ekman and Walbott 1979), but there have been quite a few others after Birdwhistell's introduction of kinesics, recently reviewed in a book (Waxer 1977), himself a clinical researcher (Waxer 1978). Earlier the role of kinesic behavior in psychiatric interviews had been painstakingly analyzed in minute analyses of a few-minute slices of therapist–patient transactions, of which two excellent models are the still unpublished, but available, *The Natural History of an Interview* and Scheflen's (1973a) *Communicational Structure: Analysis of a Psychotherapy Transaction*. He was intensively interested also in kinesics and language in relation to culture and social organization, and examined "facial expression, posture, body movement and touch in relation to larger contexts of group processes and the social order as a whole" (Scheflen 1972: xiii).

7. I would say more static, and not just static, as there is movement involved in postural behavior. In fact, we can distinguish three stages in the display of any given gesture, manner or posture: a *formative* phase, which we would define as manner, e.g., the way we pass from a standing position to sitting, the act of crossing our legs, or the way we move our arms for crossing them, in which parakinesic qualities of intensity, range and duration vary according to individual and cultural characteristics; then a *basic* or central phase, which we perceive as the gesture, manner or posture itself; and a *releasing* phase, again subject to parakinesic modifiers.

8. I was invited to join the research team working on the interrelationships between the linguistic, paralinguistic and kinesic components of speech (under the auspices of the Centre National de la Recherche Scientifique), which included the elaboration of a triple-structure transcription as I had already discussed it at meetings.

9. Mary Ritchie Key, of the University of California at Irvine, herself an avid and inspiring student of nonverbal communication phenomena (Key 1975a, 1975b, 1980, 1982) generously distributed a typed newsletter, *Nonverbal Components of Communication: Paralanguage, Kinesics, Proxemics*, for years, keeping scholars informed of the publications and ongoing projects in the five continents and serving as personal liaison for many researchers.

6

Silence and Stillness as Message-conveying Processes

1. Silence and Stillness in Culture and the Environment

AT this point in the development of nonverbal communication studies, when so much is being investigated about their morphological and functional characteristics within various disciplines, and above all, when semiotics is gradually permeating any approach that seeks to carry out a critical analysis of man's communicative activities, one thing is conspicuously lacking which ought to be at least initiated and explored by semioticians: the acknowledgement of communicative values, and therefore the semiotic nature of the two basic nonactivities in our lives, silence and stillness. The recognition of this fact is but the logical conclusion at which one arrives in a gradual way while studying communication systems in an integrating, comprehensive and realistic way.

At the 1977 Viennese Symposium on Semiotics I tried (Poyatos 1981e) to suggest the status of silence and stillness as the nonactivities resulting from the absence of sound and movement in the sensible exchange between two human beings as socializing organisms.[1]* In the present chapter I wish to elaborate on the premises set forth on that occasion and offer a basic framework for a more systematic investigation of silence and stillness, establishing their basic forms and functions in human relations, as well as in man–environment and man–God interaction, and trying to prove their deserved status as communication systems in themselves, costructured with the other modes of expression.

Any in-depth analysis of silence and stillness must derive from the realization of their frequency in the daily happening of living things and their environment, if only in an impressionistic fashion at first. Deriving from the chart, 'Sensible and Intelligible Systems in a Culture' (Fig. 2.1), the semiotic nature of the basic forms of silence and stillness can be diagrammed as shown in Fig. 6.1, "Semiotic Forms of Silence and Stillness".

* Superscript numbers refer to Notes at end of chapter.

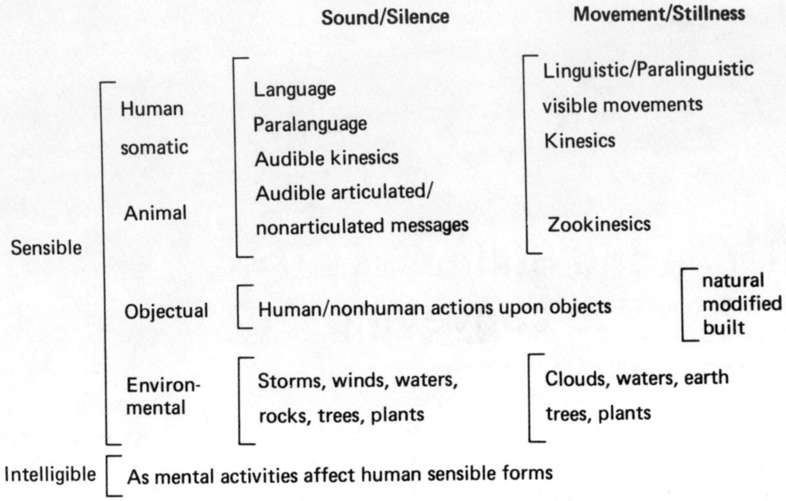

FIG. 6.1. Semiotic Forms of Silence and Stillness.

Beyond any doubt, human existence as well as the existence of other organisms, if imperfectibly in some instances, is based on and shaped by the mutual succession of sound and movement and their passive opposites, silence and stillness. While alive in his world man survives by constant interaction with his congeners, or other species, and with his natural, modified or built environment, and that interaction is characterized by the production of sounds and movements and also by their very absence.

In similar manner, the other organisms interact cospecifically or interspecifically in order to survive in their environment. The research area developed by Sebeok (1972) as zoosemiotics investigates the sign coding mechanisms typical of the simpler species. On the other hand, it has been proven that, far from the complexity of human interactive or noninteractive activities of social life, "animal movement . . . is fundamental to their whole appearance, their whole biology, life history, their brain and 'mental development', in short to their very nature" (Thorpe 1974: 43). Thus, between the periodical contractions of the sea anemone, the change of pace of the woodlouse, the light-conditioned turning of the flatworm or the vibrations of the spider's web, on the one hand, and the flying of birds, the ritualized greeting movements of chimpanzees or the human smile, on the other, lies one of the most fascinating topics in the whole of creation, namely, the movements of life, whose very nature is defined by the fact that they alternate with periods of stillness.

Second only to living movement is the living sound of many species, though not all, for no sounds seem to have been observed in the animals just mentioned. But, again, between the tapping and bubbling of certain crabs, the cracking of the Snapping shrimp and the songs of birds, the calls of elephants or chimpanzees and man's linguistic-paralinguistic repertoires, there is a vast gamut of communicating or noncommunicating sounds that the semioticians can try to classify within a sign typology in the wider context of systems, forms, etc., as I suggested in Chapter 2.

Some of the species referred to combine either sound or movement, or both, with other systems such as chemical and luminous signals, but those which emit certain specific scents through the olfactory molecules called pheremones, such as the fire ant, or light emissions, like the firefly, are endowed with movement and/or acoustic abilities as well.

Between all those sounds and movements characteristic of very simple or very complex organisms and the natural ones that are mostly beyond our control, we can produce a virtually infinite number of sounds by coming into contact with: our congeners, mainly through actions of aggression (e.g., slapping), affiliation (e.g., slapping, patting) and affection (kissing, patting); the natural environment (e.g., the sounds of foot-steps on various types of terrain and flooring, the splashing in the water); natural objects, and man-made objects and artifacts, some of which are built precisely to produce sound (e.g., musical instruments, bells, signalling devices).

Both man and the other species are, in greater or lesser degree, surrounded by the noncontinuous sounds and movements of their environment, as indicated in Fig. 6.1, and their behaviors may at times be conditioned by those activities and their contextual circumstances. Even plants display chemically-elicited movements of growth, for instance, not perceived by the human eye as they take place, but acknowledged by the mind, just as the absence of it is acknowledged both visually and intelligibly.

I have discussed when dealing with echoics in Chapter 4 how man tries to imitate the movements of people, of animals and even of the environment and his own built artifacts, but, above all, the sounds of all those surrounding elements, some universal, others especifically cultural, some somatic and many purely mechanical, and the crosscultural differences in the conversational use of sound imitations.

Sound and movement, in sum, are the preponderant sensible activities in people and nature, which we also appreciate intelligibly. In addition, man's mental activities condition his own production of sounds and movements and their absence, as well as those of other animal species, particularly the tamed and domesticated ones; and, naturally, the sounds and movements of his objectual environment as it is handled by him.

2. Silence and Stillness as an Affirmation of Culture

If we now concentrate on man as a God-endowed socializing organism, we will recognize that sound and movement, and silence and stillness, constitute the very pillars of culture, since it is an unquestionable fact that culture is communication and that most of the relevant occurrences of sound/silence and movement/stillness are of a communicative nature, that is, they take place as interactive behaviors. On the other hand, since a culture is an immensely intricate series of sign complexes, sound and silence and movement and stillness are the most important complexes of all in a live culture. In Chapter 1 I suggested Robinson Crusoe and Friday as the minimal social aggregate that could be termed culture. Their main communicative activities were sound and movement and the existence of those activities, their importance as culture, a live culture, was confirmed by their intermittent absence, by the silences and times of stillness produced by the two beings that constituted that culture.

Once the sounds and movements of a culture are permanently turned into silence and stillness the very concepts 'sound' and 'stillness' become questionable because, if we project them into the future as permanent, they cannot be said any more to represent the temporary absence of activities, that is, what precisely makes them be, by opposition, what they are, silence and stillness. ¿Are they, really? Once humans are not present any longer and there is no interaction, sound and movement cease as cultural activities, and only static material products of that culture, of that disappeared interactive exchanges, remain. However, as these considerations would lead one into the sort of semiotic inquiry which is not the main purpose of this discussion, I shall concentrate on the semiotic aspects of silence and stillness in everyday social interaction, mentioning only in passing their noninteractive aspects.

I should point out perhaps that the relevance of silence and stillness was gradually becoming more apparent to me in view, first of all, of the rather negative treatment given traditionally to the so-called 'unfilled pauses' in speech, as they seemed to be loaded with meaning; and also because of the concept of 'zero sign', developed in semiotics as the "very absence" of a given sign (Sebeok 1974: 241), which also appeared to me as being full of meaning, neither of them lacking a significant nor, therefore, a signified when subject to analysis. As I studied sound and movement as language, paralanguage and kinesics I had to acknowledge more and more the ability of silence and stillness to perform structural and communicative functions, as well as their importance as sign-producing nonactivities in social interaction, consciously or unconsciously encoded and decoded and, at the very least, acting either as redundant or complementary information, as discussed below. In fact, 'nonactivity' might be thought of as a questionable negative term, unless it is understood only as the absence of sensibly perceived actions, for if we affirm that they produce signs, that is also an activity Finally, I realized that the absence in man of his few sensible chemical signs (e.g., tears, sweat), thermal signs (body temperature rises and falls) or dermal signs (e.g., blushing) could never be as significant as the absence of sound or movement—except perhaps in specific situations, such as moments of intense grief, in a sexual encounter, in medical diagnostics or during a psychotherapy session—for they are most of the time secondary systems, and they are not so predictable as the activities that constitute language-paralanguage and kinesics.

3. The True Status of Silence and Stillness in Interaction

In the investigation of the nonactivities, once we acknowledge the preponderance of sound and movement in our lives and that of our environment, as well as the resulting alternatives of silence and stillness—which, first of all, serve to confirm them through their absence—the next step in a progressive approach that would later afford refined analyses in specific areas is to study the interactive forms and functions of silence and stillness. That they act as systems in their own right, subject even to the rules and coding mechanisms that govern speech and kinesics, the most elaborate communicative systems, is quite obvious. Based, then, on social interaction, silence and stillness must be viewed, first, in the context of the exclusively anthropomorphic Basic Triple Structure of human communicative behavior, after which would follow their semiotic identification as signs and sign processes, and their coding, and finally the specific functions they perform in the various forms of interaction as well as their costructuration with other interactive somatic systems of signs. This approach is schematized in the chart 'Semiotic and Interactive Forms and Functions of Silence and Stillness', in Fig. 6.2.

What further support the specific nature of silence and stillness within a communication situation would be the also discussed dichotomy segmental-nonsegmental, including also paralanguage and kinesics and, therefore, silence and stillness.

I have purposely postponed offering a workable definition of silence and stillness in order to show how we must understand them as important anthroponemic elements of interaction inherent in the Basic Triple Structure, and why we must seek their status as message-conveying systems essential to sound and movement.

Silence is, along with stillness, one of the two basic nonactivities of social interaction in a living culture, resulting from the absence of sound and limiting communicative segments of audible utterances transmitted over the vocal/narial-auditory channel, whose beginning, duration and end it marks, linking them to each other and putting a stop to them; it does not override any audible vocal/narial activity, but only audible-visual and silent-visual kinesic constructs, and it possesses communicative properties in costructuration with sound and movement and, secondarily, with other somatic and extrasomatic systems.

Stillness is, along with silence, one of the two basic nonactivities of social

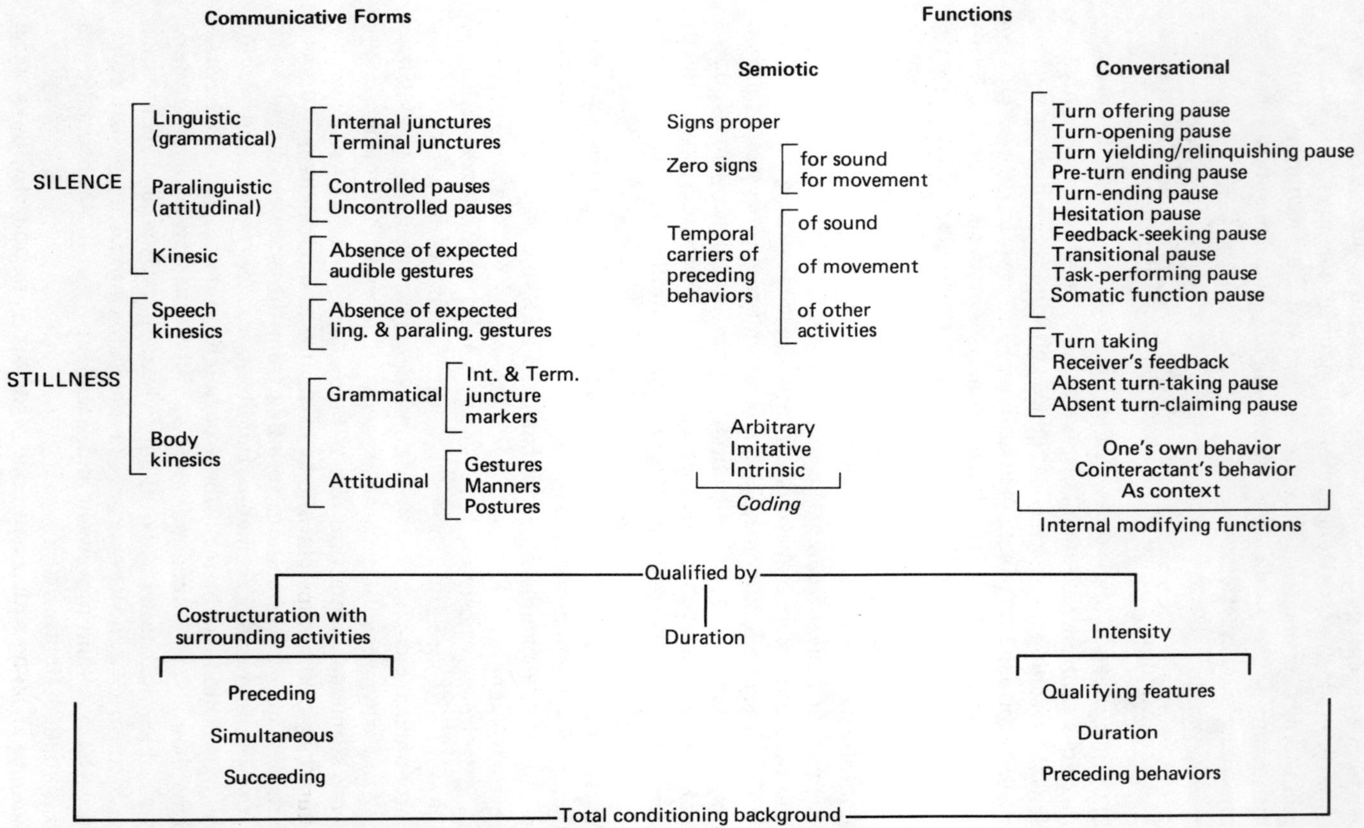

FIG. 6.2. Semiotic and Interactive Forms and Functions of Silence and Stillness.

interaction in a living culture, resulting from the absence of body movement and limiting communicative (or just informative segments) of visual and visual-audible kinesic constructs transmitted over the kinetic-visual and kinetic-auditory channels, whose beginning, duration and end it marks, linking them to each other and putting a stop to them; it does not override any kinetic visual activity, but only audible vocal/narial constructs, and it possesses communicative properties in costructuration with movement and sound and, secondarily, with other somatic and extrasomatic systems.

Even though we could offer similar definitions and still see no differences that would make us underrate the semiotic and communicative significance of stillness in favor of silence, the fact remains that stillness has received very little attention, if any. This is not surprising at all, when the more basic aspects of communication and human interaction have been neglected for such a long time; and it certainly warrants every effort one might make in trying to bring the research status of stillness to that of silence—just as we have tried to study movement as seriously as sound in the last twenty years—for one cannot be conceived of without the other. Both sound and movement appear intimately costructured within the same communicative constructs as complementary systems that are equally encoded and decoded, whether consciously or out of awareness. To do otherwise would be to perpetuate a very narrowminded attitude as regards communication, from which linguists, first of all, must free themselves by recognizing that the study of language is, by definition, the study of communication, and that communication is far more than what the majority of them still understand by language. Silences have received more attention at the 'linguistic' level because they give a specific dimension to the sounds they limit, whether language, a mechanical signal code or a musical score.

4. The Traditional Study of Pauses and the Realistic Approach

Linguists have wasted many of the research possibilities the study of silence offers by directing all their attention at a very limited number of otherwise perfectly segmental, syntactical silences, the so-called internal and terminal junctures in tone groups (as affected by intonation, lengthening of the preceding phoneme, and intonation), and a few attitudinal ones that fall better within the study of silence proposed here, as they involve personality, cultural, and circumstantial characteristics in given situations. Rarely, however, have they referred to silence as an element of interaction, thus missing the true relationship between language and interaction. They have invariably ignored the important fact that when speech is interrupted by a 'pause', at least one of the other two cooccurrent activities, that is, paralanguage or kinesics, or both, still fill that apparent gap, which once more proves the semantic and structural characteristics of language, paralanguage and kinesics among themselves as well as with relation to silence and stillness.

Interestingly enough, however, the punctuation system inherited through the centuries from various sources—and a proof of the traditional lack of interest on the part of linguists and writers for contributing some improvements and additions to the very limited repertoire of symbols—provides the researcher with more indispensable information about the communicative and social forms and functions of silence and stillness than the fields of linguistics and phonetics put together, particularly through the descriptions of their occurrences offered by narrative fiction and, in a lesser degree, by the theater.

As for the inaccuracy (specially from a semiotic or communicative point of view) of the poorly studied dichotomy *filled pause* (e.g., 'Er—') *vs. unfilled pause* it simply leads many into disregarding the communication values of nonverbal paralinguistic and kinesic messages, for 'Er—' is, in the first place, a very lexical paralinguistic alternant and it is difficult, besides, to imagine it orally displayed without an accompanying kinesic gesture of hesitation, or at least a purely contextual kinesic behavior which also fills that communicative segment. But even the so-called 'unfilled pause' is not unfilled at all either, since any breaks in speech are actually filled by paralanguage (e.g., a narial egression of contempt, a turn-claiming prespeech pharyngeal ingression) or by kinesics (e.g., a smile, a beckoning gesture), or both, and on some occasions by proxemic, dermal, thermal or chemical activities that may very well convey certain messages as effectually or more than words; which compels one to defend the true continuity that exists between the beginning and end of an interactive encounter, as we should obviously not consider solely the behaviors that we might, perhaps incorrectly so, regard as the principal ones, but all the somatic activities discussed in Chapter 2. In fact, they may perform important interactive, and even (in combination with verbal language) syntactical functions within different types of pauses.

In other words, there are no pauses that can be truly called unfilled; or to put it differently, a truly 'unfilled' space would not be a 'pause', for a pause is, by definition, an interactive segment with a very specific structure determined by the cooccurrent behaviors and the varying intensity of those behaviors, and by its duration, affecting in turn the preceding (in its decoding) and succeeding (both in encoding and decoding) behaviors. A silence, in sum, or a still position, which is not limited at both ends by interrelated behaviors, and which is not related to those behaviors itself, is not a pause, and it occurs only as *noninteractive silence or stillness* that occur only before, between and after interactive encounters (and not 'turns' within each encounter, as shown in Fig. 6.2 discussed later). It is, then, interactive silences and still positions that semioticians and other investigators alike should study in depth, seeking to understand their coding processes, their functions within the mechanism of interaction (mainly in what is called natural conversation) and their relationships with the somatic and extrasomatic sign systems engaged in a particular situation.

5. Coding of Silence and Stillness

Once we have a clear idea of what exactly we should understand by 'pause' in interaction and dismiss the notion of a vacuum traditionally associated with it, we can attempt to establish, not only the interactive functions of the various forms of silence and stillness that give a true structure to those deceptive communication gaps, but their basic semiotic foundation, that is, their transmission from emitter to receiver, as well as the specific characteristics of the encoding-decoding process between the two. Here, however, I acknowledge only the average normal member of a society, leaving for the time being the pathologically or artificially impaired person as well as the other agents that generate sound and movement and their nonactivities, as shown in Fig. 6.1.

There are three basic aspects of nonverbal messages (discussed in Chapter 3) one must be aware of in order to comprehend the complex functioning of silence and stillness. One is that the receiver is usually more conscious of the speaker's nonverbal behaviors than the speaker himself. The second one is the acknowledgement of the *complementary quality* of behaviors in situations in which they may be hastily dismissed as redundant. A silence, even after having verbally stated that we cannot say anything, adds information, as a complementary message, by its duration and by its costructuration with our kinesic behavior (perhaps our very stillness), and although gesticulation, frequent pauses in conversation or the adoption of still positions could certainly be redundant, they might, even then, express a personal style characterized precisely by redundancy. Thirdly, we also recognize that the verbal code, despite the claimed superiority of language over any other systems, is not necessarily the *primary system*, but perhaps quite secondary, and that a silence or a still may carry the main message when either system in the Basic Triple Structure, or proxemics, simply supports it as complementary information, or duplicate it as a true redundancy. And this happens precisely because of their *intensity* (consciously or unconsciously measured by the degree of the qualifying features) and their *location* (the physical position in the behavioral continuum of the interactive situation, preceding, coinciding with, if possible, or following the most 'conspicuous' behavior), actually acting as primary or secondary systems when judged by that location and by the characteristics of the related activities.

In addition, as we experience silence and stillness in the light of the discussion of their coding process and the sign-meaning relationship of nonverbal behaviors (Chapter 3), it is easy to see that they are almost always arbitrary, as the signification must be sought in the preceding or succeeding behaviors and not in the two nonactivities themselves. They could only be iconic if by silence or stillness we wished to convey precisely that, the absence of sound (e.g., Question: 'What did he tell you then?' Answer: [Silence]) or the absence of movement (e.g., 'If you see the mouse, [stillness]). This incidentally, shows again the *syntactical* and even lexical value of nonverbal communication, since the stillness that follows the verbal 'If you see the mouse' acts as the principal clause of the sentence. But they could also be intrinsic sign constructs at times, as when we give silence or stillness for an answer, or as an indication that our cointeractant (as in a hunting party) must be silent or still.

6. Decoding Functions of Silence and Stillness

Central to the understanding of the semiotic and communicative significance of silence and stillness, or any communication systems, is their very functioning as signs, the decoding of their meaning, and the factors that underlie that operation at the receiving end of the communication process. In my first discussion of silence and stillness I illustrated this with a table which I use here with some formal changes.

As could be concluded from the previous discussion of the semiotic status of silence and stillness, from their segmental qualities within the Basic Triple Structure to their hierarchization as sign systems and the sign-meaning relationship of their occurrences, both nonactivities perform three very specific functions as they are interpreted by the receiver, which are not necessarily encoded in the same way, for which reason I refer to them as decoding functions only:

A. *As signs proper*

Silence and stillness can be decoded as signs proper, with various designata, as when we read in a novel that "there was in her silence/stillness all the anguish of the situation". In this occurrence the nonactivities are not understood as 'absence' of sound or movement (in which case we would speak of zero signs), nor as replacement for sound or movement, just as the static pose of a ballet dancer is not. The meaning, the true message, is not given by the 'lack' of expected signs, but by the silence itself or the still position, without reference to anything else. In this way they are encoded as sign clusters in their own right, in fact, as segmental elements, which are shaped by certain specific qualifiers (discussed below) as words or gestures are shaped by paralinguistic and parakinesic features respectively.

The obvious thought here is, ¿can more than one silence or more than one motionless position occur side by side as sounds and movements, succeed each other without necessarily being delimited by pauses? Speech, for instance, or kinesic behavior, can change without any intermediate nonactivities or interruptions, but their modifying elements do change and are sensibly perceived as volume, pitch or nasality in speech, as intensity of kinetic articulation or range are in movement.

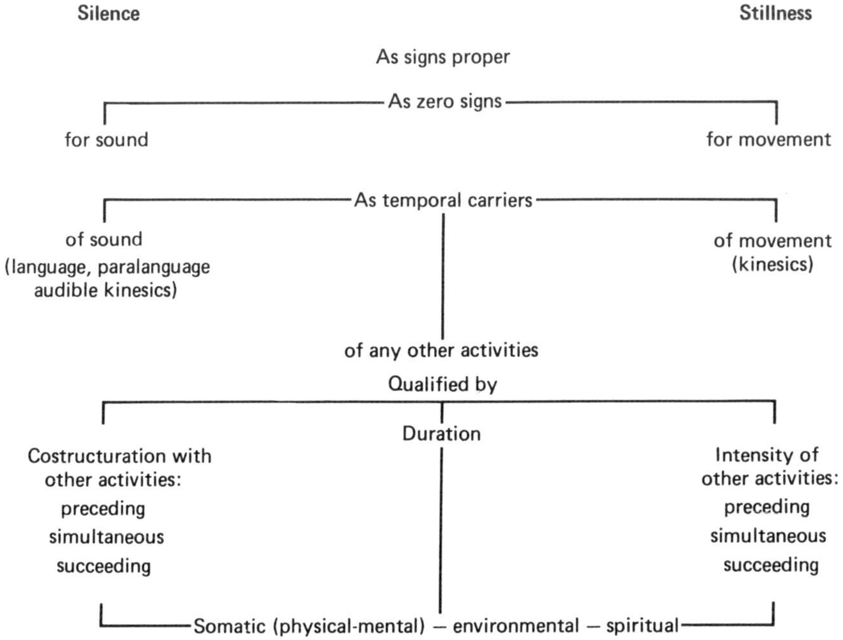

FIG. 6.3. Decoding Functions of Silence and Stillness.

Silence and stillness, however, cannot vary in a sensible way, since they are nonactivities from a physical point of view. It should be clear by now, I trust, that the nature of silence and stillness is a negative one only in a physical way, but as we study or conceptualize it, that is, from a semiotic point of view. One silence, then, or one still position can be differently interpreted only by virtue of the cooccurrent activities and, in a lesser degree, by the preceding and succeeding ones, as seen earlier. With sound and movement it is what makes them be what they are that changes, but with silence and stillness it is what surrounds them.

B. ***As zero signs***

Silence and stillness can also act as zero signs and signify precisely "by their very absence" (Sebeok 1977a: 118), that is, by the lack of sound or the lack of movement when those activities could be expected: the silence with which someone responds to our greeting unwilling to answer verbally or kinesically, or because we have not been heard (e.g., with a deaf person, or in the 'Anybody home?——' situation), the witting silence with which we avoid saying something, the motionless stance of expectancy or shock, the comedian's sudden feedback-seeking pause mentioned below, the sudden halt of someone who is walking, they all convey messages through the absence of the very activities they replace.

One could elaborate on the further distinction between zero signs whose messages we know and those which we decode as absence of sound and movement only. I would, tentatively only, suggest the terms *positive* and *negative* zero signs respectively.

C. *As carriers*

The most interesting semiotic aspect of silence and stillness in interaction, though totally neglected to my knowledge, is perhaps their capacity to act as carriers of the activity just perceived, a topic that should generate a great deal of thought, not only in semiotics, but in linguistics, communication, psychology, and philosophy as well. If a long pause follows a rotund '¡Stop it!', that verbal negation prolongs itself more intensively in our minds, carried over and enlarged by the silence which makes it more conspicuous and better defined in a sort of mental replay, its effect being quite greater than if our interlocutor continued to speak. The same holds true for a grotesque shout, a stentorian guffaw or a simple statement uttered in a normal voice. As for movement, a threatening gesture, a smile, a static look without averting our gaze from the other person's eyes, a hug or a kiss, are greatly magnified and intensified by the stillness that may follow, the nonactivity which, like silence, is dominated by the 're-echoing' sensations of the gradually vanishing signs (which can still re-echo back through memory).

One of the many applications of the carrying function of silence is, for instance, in story-telling and story-reading to children (or for that matter, reading or, as with medieval minstrels, narrating orally). It is a very important part of the imagined development of the story in the child's mind to give him appropriately and sensitively timed silences after significant events so that he may recreate them and give them shape even beyond the narrator's description.

It is important to emphasize that the carrying effect of silence is intensified when simultaneously accompanied by stillness, and that of stillness when accompanied by silence. This is a situation, on the other hand, that occurs quite often, since they are two basic physical activities which we tend to cease at the same time—thus causing a double nonactivity—for the same reason gesticulation usually accompanies speech, one more proof of the internal cohesion of the Basic Triple Structure.

7. Qualifiers of Silence and Stillness

To complete this basic semiotic discussion of silence and stillness, before considering their specific conversational functions, I will comment on the triple measurable dimension they possess, as they appear modified in different degrees by their costructuration, their duration and their intensity. These qualifiers constitute the most complex aspect of the functioning of silence and stillness, or any other communicative behaviors, in communication. They have been discussed in Chapter 3 with relation to somatic (physical/mental), environmental (subsuming living and objectual elements) and spiritual activities. Noninteractive activities, therefore (in the social sense, not a semiotic one), affect also our behaviors, as does the general conditioning background.

Costructuration, refers to the relation of the speaker's silences and stills to his own most immediate behaviors, that is, preceding, simultaneous and succeeding, as well as to the verbal and nonverbal behaviors of his cointeractants, considering also that silence can be accompanied by kinesics, as stillness can be accompanied by speech, thus conditioning each other while being affected, in turn, by their respective intensity, location and duration; their *intensity* depends also on the duration of the silence or the still position (the longer a pause or a static position in speech are prolonged, the tenser the whole situation may grow); and their *duration* is related to both costructuration and intensity.

As shown in Fig. 6.1, silence and stillness, or any other interactive behaviors, are affected, not only by somatic activities and extrasomatic ones (whether human, animal or environmental), but by mental activities, such as the tense evocation of a preceding emotional outburst, the confused thoughts about a tragic event, or the hesitation that may lengthen a pause and/or a still position; and, one step further, by the spiritual interaction that can take place between man and God, during which the person, truly touched by an irresistible divine power, experiences either a true union with God (the mystical ecstasy described by Saint Teresa de Jesús, for instance, or related by Saint Paul in 2 *Corinthians* 12:34) or a much more common heightened inner awareness of God's presence referred to as 'resting in the Spirit'. The latter spiritual phenomenon, which results in the most elevated form of silence and stillness, is reported by thousands of Christians around the world in special circumstances I would not elaborate on here, and I personally have seen it happen to both strangers and some perfectly 'normal' friends and acquaintances exactly as described by scholars like the professor and theologian Francis MacNutt (1977: chapter 15).

8. The Costructuration of Silence and Stillness with Surrounding Activities

As I have not elaborated at any length on the costructuration of silence and stillness with the surrounding activities, I offer here a diagram showing, besides the various relationships mentioned, other obvious points of one-way or reciprocal behavioral conditioning which would certainly merit

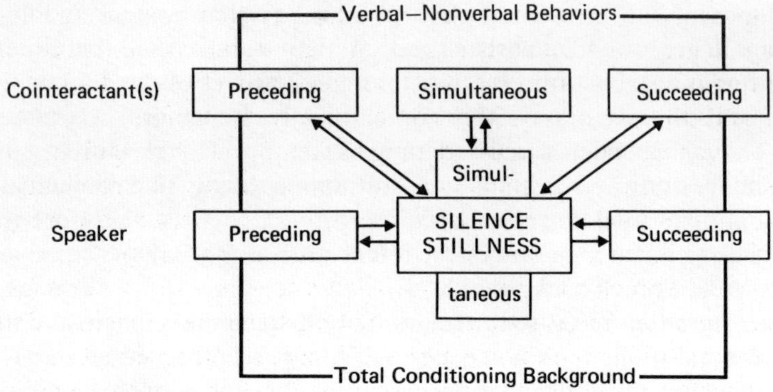

FIG. 6.4. Costructuration of Silence and Stillness with Surrounding Activities.

extensive investigation, and whose study has been suggested already when discussing the qualifiers of interactive behaviors (Chapter 3) and externalizers (Chapter 4).

What this diagram attempts to illustrate at a glance is that any given silence or still, of whatever duration, that occurs in whatever type of interactive encounter, is far from standing as a semantically (and therefore semiotic) independent event, for it is affected in every instance not only by the verbal and nonverbal activities of our cointeractants, whether preceding, simultaneous with or succeeding it, but by our own.

Sometimes our cointeractant is unexpectedly silent and/or still. '¿What *did* I say?', or '¿Is it something I *said*?' are more common questions than '¿What *am* I saying/doing?' or '¿What *will* I say/do?'; and yet his silence or stillness, or both (although sometimes he might attempt to fill the acoustic gap with movements like fidgeting, preening, smoking, scanning, etc.) may be a simultaneous or anticipating externalizer as a reaction to what I am in the process of saying, or to what he knows I am going to say or may say or do. Still the semiotic process is more complex than that because what I said, am saying, or will say can be conditioned by his own preceding, simultaneous or succeeding behavior, such as the very silence or stillness I am using in this example.

We have only assumed two basic types of activities as conditioners of our cointeractant's silent or still reaction. However, not only can silence and stillness be elicited by language, paralanguage and kinesics, but by any one or more of the controlled or uncontrolled bodily activities (since I am referring strictly to interpersonal, interbodily encounters), as diagrammed in Fig. 3.2 when dealing with intersomatic perception in Chapter 3. In other words, my interactive silences and stills, of varying duration, can be determined by two different elicitors, myself and someone else.

They can be elicited by my own words, paralanguage (e.g., laughter, crying, a pleasurable moan) or kinesics (e.g., a tense gesture of contempt, a threatening sway of the hand + intent gaze against my cointeractant), and by my chemical reactions (e.g., tear shedding) and dermal reactions (e.g., deep, embarrassed and embarrassing blushing), all immediately preceding the silence and the static position; but they (except language and paralanguage) might precisely override, fill, that silence ('fill' used here in a consciously erroneous way, since silence is not a void just because of the absence of speech). In other words, the gesture can be communicating during the silence, as can the tears or the blushing that elicit it; and they can also, from language, paralanguage and kinesics to tears or blushing, follow the silence or the still, in which case my anticipation of those activities of mine will elicit the silence or stillness. It is a sort of *a priori* or anticipating reaction, which my cointeractant may or may not perceive as such. If he does he may wish to behave accordingly, either trying to deemphasize my upcoming behavior if he does not deem it advantageous for either of us, or precisely taking advantage of it and reinforcing it (e.g., by staring at me or emotionally touching me when my silence or stillness make him anticipate my blushing or tear shedding, which he wants to suppress.

This sort of everyday interactive deep structures (implied by Fig. 3.5 when discussing the interrelationships of behaviors in Chapter 3) are then, operative between two or more cointeractants. In fact, the last reference in the previous paragraph to my cointeractant's *a priori* response to the anticipated silence or stillness illustrates the mutual speaker-listener behavioral structuration indicated in Fig. 6.4. Since it is a conditioning by succeeding behaviors, we can easily illustrate how our silence or stillness can also be dictated by our cointeractant's simultaneous behaviors, e.g.: the look in his face that keeps us speechless and/or static while mumbling something or breathing audibly, his/her tears, with which we do not know how to cope, the blushing that makes us halt in our speech, or the words that keep us silent and/or motionless without daring even to shift posture.

It is clear that this mechanism which, again, applies to any behaviors, is also intimately related to extrasomatic factors such as body-adaptors (e.g., the thinking silences elicited in a man by a woman's clothes or perfume, the interactive longer-than-usual silences of someone who is chewing gum, which may in turn affect our behavior as cointeractants), object-adaptors (e.g., the silent attitude while manipulating a machine that may require concentration, or facilitated by the table where I can recline my head and make my listening silence longer). And there are still the different elements that constitute the Total Conditioning Background, that is, sex, age, psychological configuration, medical state, cultural patterns, socioeconomic status, and so on (see Chapter 3).

9. The Functions of Silence and Stillness in the Mechanism of Conversation

It is not my intention to review in this chapter all the behaviors that take place in the course of a conversation, as I outline them more fully later in Chapter 8, but only mention some instances in which silence and stillness perform clearly interactive functions.

I might point out that one of the characteristics of *contrived conversation* (as opposed to natural conversation, discussed in the next chapter), represented mainly by the theatrical or cinematic performance, in which the possible failure of the participants in achieving the desired naturalness is actually due to the fact that verbal and nonverbal activities are not properly costructured sometimes, is precisely the way in which quite typically amateur performers deal with silence. The interactive silences that must occur on the stage are not properly integrated in the actor's own repertoire, who may treat his or someone else's silences as though they were nonacting voids during which he actually 'drops out of character', as they call it in the theater.

Of all the activities that take place to initiate, maintain and terminate, or disrupt, the normal succession of turns and the flow of the conversation, the following are among those displayed through controlled or uncontrolled silences and still positions; besides language, paralanguage, kinesic activities and other nonverbal behaviors. The rest (see Fig. 6.2) are discussed in Chapter 7.

As speakers we engage in: *turn offering* to the listener: '¿What d'you think?', '¿Right?'; '¿Mm?', silence + hand-offering gesture, or stillness; *turn yielding*, after the listener's claiming: 'Yes', 'Go ahead', 'Uh-hm', silence, nod + raised brows + smile, stillness.

As listeners we engage in: *turn taking*: 'Well, but [pause]'; 'Uh [pause]', lip moistening, posture shift, taking cigarette puff and blowing smoke, all while being silent; as *listener's feedback*, silence is what generally cooccurs with the speaker's deliverance, accompanied by nods, smiles, eye contact with him or other listeners, or by attentive stillness and blinking, although silence can also signify disinterest, inattention, hesitance, etc.

A special category is formed by the *interactional pauses*, mainly uncontrolled silences that correspond to some of the typical activities in conversation, such as: *absent turn-taking pause*, in which the silence occurs when the speaker has yielded his turn but it is not taken by his listener at the appropriate moment, or as a consequence of simultaneous turn yielding and failure to take it by all the cointeractants; absent *turn-claiming pause*, when the speaker has to terminate the silence and resume his already closed turn upon noticing his listener's failure to claim it; *turn-ending pause*, following perhaps a 'That's all' gesture and/or postural shift, mainly leaning back on one's seat; *transitional pause* between different topics, or between turns, differently regulated according to the interactant's socioeconomic status, educational level, conversational fluency and socializing competence, etc., and managed with different behaviors besides or together with, silence and stillness: various types of laughter, 'Tz', postural shifts, proxemic shifts, use of object-adaptors (e.g., a drink, a pipe, imaginary lint, a necklace), self-adaptors (e.g., preening behaviors, hand rubbing), dermal changes (e.g., blushing), etc.; *task-performing pause*, which can be intentionally produced to stall for time, during word-searching or memory-searching, or as any of the other pauses just mentioned, and during which we may pick up the cup of coffee, the drink, light a pipe or cigarette, straighten our clothes, etc.; *feedback-seeking pause*, displayed mainly by static staring at the cointeractant, perhaps with lips parted, smiling, etc.; and *hesitation pauses*, practically the only ones that have received some attention as 'filled pauses' ('Uh . . .', 'Well . . .', 'Actually . . .', 'Er . . . yes', 'I . . . think so', 'Tz + pharyngeal ingression'; raising index and second fingers to lips, gaze vaguely fixed on floor, ceiling or infinity, scratching one's head, arms akimbo while looking down, etc.), in all of which silences and still positions (often cooccurring) of varying length are typically displayed, once more confirming the cohesion of the Basic Triple Structure.

Apart from the semiotic aspects of silence and stillness, the central topic of this discussion, much more could be elaborated on silence and stillness in conversation, investigating, not only their interactional functions, but mainly, as suggested here: their semanticity, their truly segmental and grammatical qualities, their hierarchization among other surrounding conversational behaviors, and their costructuration with those behaviors. Even within the area of social interaction there are a number of unexplored perspectives that could be generated by the thoughts offered in this chapter and developed by others. An inciting paper is the one by Bruneau (1973), whose work, then and more recently (e.g., Bruneau 1979, where he already adds "stills" to silence) contains always a copious body of references, and one by Johannesen (1974) also with a number of suggestions for the study of "positive" and "negative silences" (Baker 1955).[2]

Stemming perhaps from the concept of fluency, silence and stillness should be seen as elements that can maintain or break the normal flow of conversation, which would in turn assist in determining what precisely is conversational fluency. But the cultural setting could not be overlooked (witness the many accounts of the interactive use of silences much longer than ours among, for instance, the Alaskan Kotzebue Eskimos,[3] the Western Apache Indians [Basso 1972], and the Asians [Oliver 1971]), as could not the other factors included in the Total Conditioning Background, for even a clinical study must acknowledge them as important behavioral conditioners.

From a pathological point of view, the structuration of silence and stillness within the patient's own behaviors, as well as with those of his cointeractants, would help in assessing his interactive style and his general state.

Finally, one topic on which I hope to elaborate soon is that of silence and stillness as represented or evoked in narrative literature (as well as in the theater as part of the character's personality and portrayal by the actor) and the degree in which the writer uses them.

In the area of man-environment interaction, there is also much to be investigated within semiotics, anthropology and sociology as regards the environmental elements shown in Fig. 2.1, as well as architecture and, for instance, the different ways of experiencing silence according to the dimensions of the spaces determined by architecture, landscaping, light, and color.

Notes

1. After having touched upon silence and stillness at different times both in articles and in presented papers (e.g., on paralanguage for the 1977 International Congress of Phonetic Sciences [Poyatos 1979a] and with sign typology at the 1977 Viennese Symposium on Semiotics [Poyatos 1981f]), I elaborated further in a paper for the 1979 International Congress of Linguistics, published fully in *Kodikas/Code* (Poyatos 1981e).
2. Bruneau and Mihaila-Cova (cf. Mihaila-Cova [1973]) presented also papers at the 1979 Congress of Linguistics.
3. Reported in a 1980 term paper by my student Janet Murphy, who has lived for long periods of time with them.

7

The Structure of Conversation

1. The Study of the Mechanism of Conversation: Natural vs. Contrived

IN spite of the existing studies of various aspects of conversation, not only those by Duncan (1972a, 1972b, 1973, 1974a, 1974b, 1975a, 1975b), Duncan and Fiske (1977), Scheflen (1964, 1973), Kendon (1973a, 1973b, 1977, 1980a, 1980b, 1982) and Dittman (1972b), but by other very exacting researchers,[1]* we still lack a theoretical comprehensive schema that may show the basic internal structuration of conversation and serve at least as a solid frame of reference. I have attempted to design such basic schema on several occasions, both in writing and in public discussions, always providing the earlier version of the table in Fig. 7.1, 'The Structure of Conversation'.[2] My intention was that investigators who might otherwise have different (yet complementary) aims, such as the social phychologist, the crosscultural comparatist or the student of narrative literature and the theatrical script, be provided with a comprehensive tool that might afford them a systematic approach to what constitutes the most essential but also the most important and complex event in social interaction, or rather, its very foundation.

What must be understood as conversation, ranges from the *brief encounter*, actually a short, generally dyadic encounter, such as when ordering food, purchasing a ticket, asking for directions, etc., to the truly *topical conversation*, the interactive transaction, whether face-to-face and unhindered (full interaction) or reduced, formed by a series of participatory sequences between one speaker and one or more listeners, who must at varying intervals exchange their respective roles for the encounter to qualify as conversational. As compared, then, with the brief encounter, a true conversation (which may very well develop from it) is the average living-room or business encounter centering around at least one topic during which several 'presentations', 'positions' and 'points', to use Scheflen's (1964) useful terms, are displayed, speaker and listeners taking *turns* (Duncan 1972a) to hold the floor.

* Superscript numbers refer to Notes at end of chapter.

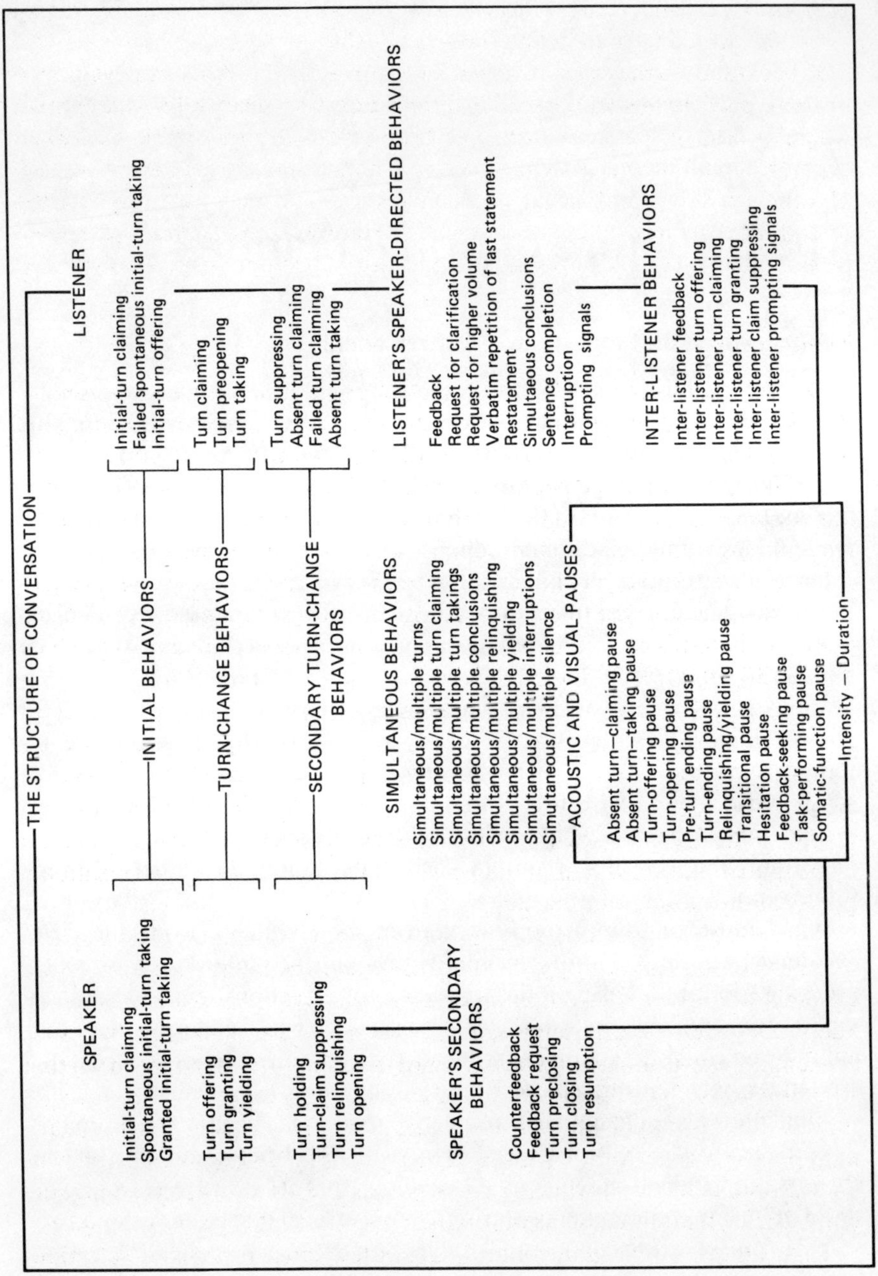
THE STRUCTURE OF CONVERSATION
SPEAKER
LISTENER
INITIAL BEHAVIORS
Initial-turn claiming
Spontaneous initial-turn taking
Granted initial-turn taking
Initial-turn claiming
Failed spontaneous initial-turn taking
Initial-turn offering
TURN-CHANGE BEHAVIORS
Turn offering
Turn granting
Turn yielding
Turn claiming
Turn preopening
Turn taking
SECONDARY TURN-CHANGE BEHAVIORS
Turn holding
Turn-claim suppressing
Turn relinquishing
Turn opening
Turn suppressing
Absent turn claiming
Failed turn claiming
Absent turn taking
SPEAKER'S SECONDARY BEHAVIORS
Counterfeedback
Feedback request
Turn preclosing
Turn closing
Turn resumption
SIMULTANEOUS BEHAVIORS
Simultaneous/multiple turns
Simultaneous/multiple turn claiming
Simultaneous/multiple turn takings
Simultaneous/multiple conclusions
Simultaneous/multiple relinquishing
Simultaneous/multiple yielding
Simultaneous/multiple interruptions
Simultaneous/multiple silence
LISTENER'S SPEAKER-DIRECTED BEHAVIORS
Feedback
Request for clarification
Request for higher volume
Verbatim repetition of last statement
Restatement
Simultaeous conclusions
Sentence completion
Interruption
Prompting signals
ACOUSTIC AND VISUAL PAUSES
Absent turn—claiming pause
Absent turn—taking pause
Turn-offering pause
Turn-opening pause
Pre-turn ending pause
Turn-ending pause
Relinquishing/yielding pause
Transitional pause
Hesitation pause
Feedback-seeking pause
Task-performing pause
Somatic-function pause
Intensity – Duration
INTER-LISTENER BEHAVIORS
Inter-listener feedback
Inter-listener turn offering
Inter-listener turn claiming
Inter-listener turn granting
Inter-listener claim suppressing
Inter-listener prompting signals

FIG. 7.1. The Structure of Conversation.

A truly realistic view, which would suggest the typical conversational structure, would have to define *conversation* as:

A back-and-forth series of verbal and nonverbal exchanges between two or more participants who observe certain rules and also violate them in an irregular flow of speaker's turns and listener's turns, acceptable and unacceptable simultaneous activities, acoustic and visual pauses, and a number of other positive and negative behaviors within each turn, differently oriented between speaker and listeners or among listeners, and conditioned by personality, situational context, and cultural background.

Natural conversation

Having established in Chapter 3 the differentiation between full unhindered interaction and reduced interaction, a further important distinction must be that between natural conversation and contrived conversation.

I would give a minimal definition of natural conversation as the spontaneous communicative exchange of verbal and nonverbal signs between at least two cointeractants, qualifying such definition with the more elaborate one offered above. However, I am deliberately using the term natural throughout this paper, not just to refer to natural languages as opposed to artificial ones, but in terms of *naturalness* as opposed to contrived situations in which there is no spontaneity of thought and deliverance.

While it is true that nonhuman primates, for instance, engage in a rather elaborate display of nonverbal vocal utterances (relatively close to some human paralinguistic constructs) and a definitely symbolic kinesic behavior (see van Lavick-Goodall 1971), their limited cognitive capacity places their type of communication within zoosemiotics (Sebeok 1972, 1977b) and far from the truly intellectual affair which makes our kind of conversation a purely anthroposemiotic exchange.

On the other hand, one is tempted to hastily limit the term natural to members of the same culture, arguing that members of different cultures are exposed to miscommunication and misinterpretations due to their lack of fluency in each other's language as well as in paralanguage, kinesics, proxemics, etc. But in would be naive not to call natural (if not normal) that situation in which two persons try hard to convey different types of messages to each other without being able to speak a common language, but displaying a stepped-up repertoire of intonation patterns, paralinguistic constructs and kinesic behaviors, while as efficiently as possible complementing and emphasizing their thoughts as well as their uncontrollable verbal utterances.

That situation reveals a sophisticated intellectual process of selection, substitution and/or duplication or triplication not decoded as redundant. In terms of the spontaneity of the signs utilized, the messages that are encoded and the ones that do not reach the decoding end of the transaction, such exchange is not less a conversation than the one carried out between or with impaired interactants. It has already been considered as a form of reduced interaction, but that certainly does not make it an artificial one. While there is no fluency in the intended use of a foreign language and its complementary nonverbal behaviors by a mediocre speaker—who, however, is totally fluent in the production of his native verbal and nonverbal repertoires—the ingenuity of his motives, the originality of his own sign encoding, and the unpredictiveness of his cointeractants' feedback behaviors and general response make their conversation an entirely natural affair.

Contrived conversation

It is a lack of naturalness and a self-betraying nonverbal lack of fluency that differentiate a real-life conversational encounter, that is, natural conversation, from the contrived conversation of the theatrical 'multiple recreations' of characters carried out by performers who memorize, rehearse and represent 'someone else's' words, paralanguage and kinesics. They endeavor to feign a natural situation by complementing that Basic Triple Structure with the supposedly appropriate proxemic and chronemic behaviors—thus simulating, in addition, the two essential spatial and temporal dimensions of any human activity in real life—plus any other nonverbal cues that may be required by a specific character belonging to a specific culture in a specific situation.

This type of 'theatrical' conversation, whether performed on the stage, as part of a secret agent's memorized repertoire or as an artifically elicited topic previously agreed upon, cannot be natural, and if it requires a foreign cultural background, as in a play, always gives away the performers' own culture, particularly in the kinesic behaviors displayed, for their motives are not original, nor are the artifically coded messages for which only a limited number of predictable behaviors can be expected. Summing up, the failure of many actors to achieve the ultimate goal of naturalness can be cursorily explained (as suggested when discussing the theater in Chapter 10) by their inability to pretend that what is not natural conversation appears as natural, but a careful analysis of this situation deserves attention. In the first place, verbal language and nonverbal activities are not properly costructured in a contrived conversation: intonation patterns do not always correspond to the memorized verbal utterances, paralinguistic features such as volume, rhythm, glottalic control, specific types of laughter, etc., do not seem to agree with the type being portrayed, the situational context, and the cultural background. The otherwise rich and flexible repertoire of paralinguistic alternants in their own real-lives gives them away, since, for example, prespeech clicks and pharyngeal ingressions are almost lacking in the mechanism of their interaction, subtle narial egressions are often replaced by conspicuous verbal expressions or coarse gestures, and so forth.

In narrative literature, what in Chapter 9 is defined as interactive realism concerns precisely an inevitable type of contrived conversation and, in the more traditional fashion, a series of contextual comments about a supposedly natural one. But the more realistic writers, such as Dickens, Hardy, Dostoevsky, Dreiser or Huxley, make a conscious effort to achieve naturalness in their fictional written conversations, granting nonverbal systems—particularly paralanguage and kinesics, and even silences—a very important communicative value, aside from their stylistic and technical ones. And yet their characters engage most of the time in unrealistically flowless types of conversations in which quite a few of the rules, counterrules, and cues typical of interaction just do not occur.

The present study

Given the general characteristics of conversation and some specific ones, such as the costructuration of verbal and nonverbal behaviors (mainly those within the Basic Triple Structure) and the influence of situational context and culture, the topic appears as one intimately related to almost every other topic discussed in this book and, therefore, as an indispensable part of it if a comprehensive panorama of social interaction is to be unfolded. The present discussion, however, does not pretend to be an exhaustive one, even though the new version of the table showing the mechanism of conversation is a decisive improvement over the previous one. Extensive analytical observation of real-life encounters, as well as of filmed real-life or fictional ones, has prompted me to acknowledge quite a few behaviors finely co-articulated with the ones already studied.

The table in Fig. 7.1 'The Structure of Conversation' attempts to show at a glance the six basic types of conversational behaviors: (a) the essential rules that must be displayed by the speaker, on the one hand, and (b) the essential rules that must be displayed by a single listener, on the other, both types including the activities that establish the roles of speaker and listener as well as those which aim at abolishing them, (c) the activities displayed by the speaker within his turn proper beyond the basic rules, and (d) those which are displayed by his listener or listeners towards him or among themselves, (e) the behaviors of both speaker and listeners that occur simultaneously and even with identical form, and (f) the different forms and functions of paralinguistic and kinesic (i.e., acoustic and visual) pauses that are wittingly or unwittingly produced by the participants. An orderly discussion, however, must try to maintain a realistic sequential arrangement of at least the basic speaker's and listener's activities as they succeed each other in actual conversation.

What follows, then, is a succinct comprehensive description of those behaviors, as represented by language (Lg), paralanguage (Pg), kinesics (K) and the resulting proxemics (Px) only, although a more detailed future study would acknowledge the possible conversational functions of, for instance, a chemical message like tears or a dermal one like blushing, and the role of possible external agents, such as interruption by noise.

Also, an exhaustive presentation would have to describe not only linguistic, paralinguistic, kinesic, etc., activities individually, as is done here most of the time, but the typical multichannel blends. The reader, then, must be aware of possible blends at all times, something which his own experience will suggest as he reads the sample behaviors.

2. Speaker's and Listener's Initial Behaviors

Initial-turn claiming by one or more of the gathered candidates to the conversational encounter, displayed perhaps while taking places, pulling up chairs, still removing coats, etc.

Lg: 'Well . . .' or any expression that anticipates a possible speaker. *Pg:* Prespeech click 'Tz' + pharyngeal ingression, laughter, throat clearing, etc. *K:* Orienting oneself toward a possible listener or listeners, smiling, prespeech lip-parting and eye contact with one participant or rapid scanning of several participants. *Px:* Approaching a possible listener or listeners, in combination with any of the other behaviors.

Spontaneous initial-turn taking, a typical situation on the part of one or more participants in which, unless simultaneous turns occur after two or more successful attempts at taking the floor, only one individual becomes the speaker, the attempts of the others having resulted in 'failed spontaneous initial-turn taking'.

Lg: 'Well . . .' or any verbal sentence opener. *Pg:* 'Tz' + prespeech pharyngeal ingression. *K:* According to the type of verbal or kinesic message to be conveyed, e.g., negating with head movement and thus initiating the first statement, which develops verbally after that. *Px:* Reorienting oneself toward a chosen listener, holding his forearm, etc.

Failed spontaneous initial turn taking is characterized by a first phase containing the spontaneous turn-taking behaviors followed by the actual failure phase in which the aborted verbal, paralinguistic and kinesic interventions come to a halt, the kinesic ones typically losing strength until they disappear into a listener's state.

Initial-turn offering, with or without an existing initial-turn claiming, is made by one of the candidates in the gathering willing to become a listener, and it grants a more legitimate status to the first speaker.

Lg: '¿Well . . .?', 'Go ahead'. *Pg:* uncommon. *K:* Smiling and pointing at future speaker with palm-up extended hand. *Px:* Leaning back as a sign of attention and gazing and/or smiling at future speaker.

Granted initial-turn taking is, therefore, the logical next behavior (unless failed turn taking takes place), the speaker acquiring his turn according to the prescribed ritual.

Lg: 'Well . . .', 'Yes, well . . .'. *Pg:* 'Tz', 'Tz + throat clearing'. *K;* Nod, postural shift if seated.

Following these initial-turn activities, the participants engage in a series of turn-changing activities in the course of the encounter which form a new group.

3. Speaker-Listener Turn-Change Behaviors

To simply list the various turn-changing behaviors as has been done so far may result in quite a simplified way of defining turn taking, for what can be loosely called turn taking is actually an umbrella term for a family of behaviors, or rather, a series of structural alternatives. While the term taking may rightfully signify the straightforward beginning of the new speaker's speech, it should also be understood as a different phenomenon, a gradual taking that can be broken down into several stages preferably alternating with some complementary speaker's behaviors. What earlier, following mainly Duncan, I simply classified as turn taking (Poyatos 1976a, 1980a), a continuing and deeper structural analysis of conversation revealed to be a whole finely structured series of events, that turn-taking must be viewed in the context of the variable behavioral complex of *turn-changing*, of which the earliest possible activity is turn-offering and the last one turn-taking, and that this established new speaker's state or last turn-changing stage could be reached through any of these alternate turn-taking structures:

(a) offering—claiming—granting—preopening—yielding—opening
(b) offering—claiming—preopening—yielding—opening
(c) offering—claiming—yielding—opening
(d) offering—preopening—yielding—opening
(e) offering—claiming—yielding—taking
(f) offering—opening (suppressing)
(g) offering—taking (suppressing)
(h) claiming—granting—preopening—yielding—opening
(i) claiming—granting—opening (suppressing)
(j) claiming—granting—taking (suppressing)
(k) claiming—opening (suppressing)
(l) claiming—yielding—opening
(m) claiming—yielding—taking
(n) claiming—taking (suppressing)
(o) yielding—opening
(p) yielding—taking
(q) suppressing

Turn claiming, shown, under normal circumstances, (a) when the listener thinks that he wants or must say something, that the speaker held the floor long enough, (b) when the latter indicates that he is willing to relinquish his turn through 'turn offering', or (c) when the speaker displays a 'turn preclosing' behavior. We must distinguish speaker-directed turn claiming from 'interlistener turn claiming', which may succeed the former either because it seems to fail (due to the speaker's 'turn holding' or even 'turn suppressing') or because support is sought from the other listeners).

Lg: 'Well—', 'Yeah', 'but—'. *Pg:* Prespeech click + prespeech inspiration (and/or out-in tongue-tip movement). *K:* Raised brows (low for disappointment, sadness, etc.) and/or raised hand, forward postural shift, prolonged eye contact with speaker, slight smile, lip moistening, out-in tongue-tip movement. *Px:* social-to-personal/personal-to-intimate shift, or reorientation, toward the speaker.

Turn offering on the part of the speaker may avoid the claim and elicit the listener's 'turn taking':

Lg: '¿Right?', '¿What d'you think?'. *Pg:* '¿Mmh?', '¿Uh?', giving language a questioning tone + pause. *K:* Intent eye contact, raised brows, stillness + eye contact. *Px:* reorientation toward invited speaker.

Turn preopening, not always present, is however a distinct listener's intermediate step between his turn claiming (preceded perhaps by offering and followed by granting) and the speaker's yielding, the latter followed by the actual opening, instead of the other structural alternative (i.e., listener's claiming, speaker's yielding, and listener's direct turn taking), the claiming in both instances being preceded perhaps by speaker's turn offering as indicated.[3]

Turn granting is a very brief signal emitted by the speaker to acknowledge the listener's turn claiming prior to the actual yielding. It is hardly ever verbal, but rather signified by a smile, raised brows, a slight 'wait' hand gesture + affirmative nod, etc., which permits him to conclude his turn while 'reserving' the future speaker's turn. It can appear in several structures, as indicated earlier, but it should be followed by the speaker's yielding later on instead of the listener taking the turn right after this granting cue, as often happens.

Lg: 'Yes'. *Pg:* Affirmative 'Mm'. *K:* Affirmative nod, smile, raised brows, etc.

Turn yielding is the step previous to the listener becoming speaker, as is turn offering, if the turn has not already been given through turn offering, thus precluding any yielding, and often after turn granting. The turn is 'yielded' and 'taken' also in a typical answer–question sequence.

Lg: 'Yes', 'Go ahead', self-interrupted sentence, falling/rising terminal juncture. *Pg:* Clipping final syllable, or drawling it emphatically, long conclusive pharyngeal ingression. *K:* Nod, raised brows, offering hand palm up and/or smiling, crossing arms and/or sitting back, relaxing posture. *Px:* Retreating slightly if standing, changing orientation.

Turn taking, however, is the expected fluent and legitimate way of acquiring the turn, and it occurs (a) when the listener takes the floor after the speaker shows his willingness to relinquish his turn through turn offering, granting or yielding, (b) when (perhaps because his turn claiming failed) he just decides to take it through turn suppressing or (c) by claiming and taking the turn rapidly in succession without medieating turn yielding. When the turn is taken by the new speaker in the most appropriate manner the actual turn taking consists of a turn-opening signal establishing the new listener(s) state followed by the development of his speaker's topic. The typical openers are:

Lg: 'No, I was gonna say that—', 'Yeah', 'Well', 'Uh—'. *Pg:* Prespeech click, throat clearing and/or prespeech pharyngeal ingression. *K:* Lip moistening + 'Tz', posture shift, thankful nod, taking off glasses, blowing smoke quickly before speaking. *Px:* Approaching interactant (personal-to-intimate), holding his arm.

4. Secondary Turn-Change Behaviors

What here I call speaker's secondary behaviors and listener's secondary behaviors are part of what I first termed 'within-turn behaviors' (Poyatos 1967a, 1980a) borrowing the term from Duncan (1973) to subsume a series of activities which further complement the turn mechanism by providing information on the development of the encounter, that is, on its smooth or irregular flow and on the success or failure of the intentionally or unintentionally emitted behaviors on the part of both speaker and listener or listeners. I am not using the term 'within-turn behaviors' now because some of the main rules and counterrules are obviously 'within' the speaker's or the listener's turns as well. Instead, I call them 'secondary' because they are not among the essential turn-taking activities. But I am differentiating a third group of behaviors as 'secondary' which are still part of the turn-changing complex as activities that modify its structure if the basic ones (claiming, offering, preopening, granting, yielding, taking) are not used properly.

Turn holding (Duncan's [1970] 'attempt suppressing') can however be displayed as a counterrule by the speaker after the listener's claim beyond what is felt to be the limit of his turn (according to the situation):

Lg: 'On the other hand—' or any similar continuation cues. *Pg:* Pharyngeal ingression (of air to be used in speaking more), quickening of tempo to overpower listener's claim and avoid turn yielding. *K:* Quickening of gestures, forward leaning. *Px:* Getting closer to listener if possible.

Turn-claim suppressing (Duncan 1973) is the second counterrule that should be analyzed as an important element in conversation, since it differs from turn holding in that it can be displayed (a) by the speaker or (b) by any of the auditors other than the one claiming the turn:

Lg: By speaker: 'Wait', 'Let me finish', 'Yes, but'. By listener: 'Wait', 'Let him finish'. *Pg:* By speaker: 'Tz + quite audible pharyngeal ingression. By listener: 'Uuuh' + suppressing kinesics. *K:* By speaker: overpowering postural shift and gesturing, 'stop' gestures, holding the listener's forearm/arm (more in contact cultures). By listener: 'wait' facial gesture, 'stop' hand gestures, holding the claimer's arm. *Px:* By speaker: invading the listener's intimate space.

Turn suppressing, a third unacceptable way of taking the speaker's turn, a counterrule that can be used by the listener taking the floor through actual interruption without waiting for the speaker's turn offering or his own turn claiming and the subsequent speaker's yielding. It should be noted that turn opening and turn taking constitute turn suppressing when they are not preceded by the speaker's yielding of his turn.

Lg: 'Yes, but' and continued verbal invasion, straight interruption unpreambled talking. *Pg:* Overpowering volume, volume and quick tempo. *K:* Postural shift, domineering gesticulation, standing up, holding the speaker's arm. *Px:* Approaching the speaker's intimate zone.

Turn relinquishing must be differentiated from turn yielding (i.e., after it has been claimed) to define the situation in which the speaker just stops his turn. His listeners then can take the floor with no prescribed preambles, offer it to each other, or still claim it.

Turn opening, after the turn has been relinquished or yielded to claim by the previous speaker, simply granted, or right after having claimed it (which is a disguised but unacceptable form of speaker's turn suppressing).

Lg: 'Well . . .' *Pg:* 'Tz' + prespeech inspiration, throat clearing, etc., the degree and recurrence of which are subject throughout the interactive mechanism to different psychological variables. *K:* Postural shift, reorientation and, in specific cases, blushing blended with hesitation behaviors.

Absent turn claiming is not an unusual situation, in which the speaker, arriving at a point at which he feels his listener should or could claim the turn but does not, might make a brief pause and continue his turn.

Failed turn claiming, on the other hand, occurs often when the speaker holds his turn beyond what is felt as his appropriate intervention, typically paying little attention to his listeners' possible claiming cues.

Absent turn taking after having been claimed, even preopened, may occur for several reasons and cause an interruption in the conversation, after which the original speaker resorts to turn resumption or another listener takes the turn.

5. Listener's Speaker-directed Behaviors: Feedback and Secondary Activities

It becomes apparent as soon as one probes into the mechanism of conversation that, after the initial and turn-changing activities, the listener's behaviors are more numerous than those of the speaker's, since the speaker is engaged in the main activity of the conversation, while his cointeractants remain free to use different channels of communication simultaneously to his speech. Most of the listener's behaviors are oriented toward the speaker, but some can be aimed at the other listener or listeners.

Among those that are addressed to the speaker, some constitute what is called feedback, while the others, which are not essential, serve a series of either positive or negative functions.

Feedback

Listener's feedback constitutes a whole family of activities travelling over the various bodily channels and must necessarily be displayed intermittently if the mechanism of conversation is to develop normally, as they serve to provide evidence that the listeners are actually listening, that they agree or disagree, like it or dislike it, but that they react in some way or another. Nobody can take utter silence and utter stillness for too long, as it creates anxiety, and if the speaker-listener relationship allows it, the latter will sooner or later demand some sort of feedback: '¡Well, say something!', '¡Well, don't just stand there!'. This is typical in what I discussed within reduced interaction as the invisible dyad resulting from a telephonic conversation, in which the listener, who is perceived only acoustically, must time his silences and provide his cointeractant with feedback cues such as 'Uh-huh', 'Yeah', 'Sure', 'Okay', 'Right', 'I see', '¡Mmm!', and the like at regular intervals, or he will provoke the *speaker's feedback request*: '¿¡Hello!?', '¿¡Are you there!?'. In other words, feedback behaviors serve to communicate about the speaker's performance and the listener's response to it, and thus the success or failure of the transaction depends not only upon the topic and the speaker's correct or incorrect use of certain rules and cues but upon the listener's exclusive feedback behaviors. Besides 'feedback' (Argyle 1967, 1969, 1972, 1975; Poyatos 1976a), it has also been called 'accompaniment behavior' (Kendon 1967), 'back-channel communication' (Yngve 1970: Duncan 1972b, 1973, 1974a, 1975a, 1975b, 1977), and 'listener's response' (Dittman 1973).

It will be understood when reviewing the other listener's behaviors that feedback is the only truly permissible and desirable type of simultaneous activity on his part, whether verbal or nonverbal. But besides the basic expected feedback responses of attention, interest and approval, there can be many others that are elicited by a speaker as what in Chapter 4 has been discussed as externalizers, that is, reactions (in the context of conversation) to what has been said, is being said, or will be said, silenced, done or not done by the speaker. This definition of feedback reveals a complexity that is generally not recognized in the existing studies of conversation. Any of the listener's conscious or unconscious feedback reactions may respond not only to the speaker's simultaneous (or virtually simultaneous) verbal or nonverbal behavior, but to a behavior he has already produced, or as an anticipation to something he may or may not say or do in the most immediate future within that segment of the conversation (his point, position, or presentation, to use Scheflen's terminology once more). Thus, by a series of directly elicited reactions or *a posteriori* and *a priori* mental associations, the listener will respond to the speaker's performance by means of activities channeled through the following bodily systems: language, paralanguage and silence, kinesics and stillness, proxemics, chemical messages (tears, perspiration, etc.), dermal messages (goose flesh, blushing, etc.), and thermal messages (rises and falls in body temperature). It should be noted, however, that the *a posteriori* and *a priori* feedback responses normally include attitudes other than the basic ones of attention-inattention, interest-disinterest, and appproval-disapproval, as these three pairs must be qualified precisely by simultaneity. These three and some others, some of them also in pairs of alternates, are shown in the table in Fig. 7.2, 'Forms and Functions of Feedback Behaviors'.

I will comment on just a few responses.

Attention–Inattention is the first reaction a speaker looks for and perceives in his auditors, the indispensable feedback expected in a business or diplomatic encounter, in a classroom, in the family living room, and even from a public audience, although, depending on etiquette rules and other circumstances, not all of its forms are permissible in every context:

Lg: 'Sure', '¡Oh!' with rising pitch for attention; 'Oh' with falling pitch, an unspirited '¿What?' for inattention. *Pg:* 'Uh-hu' and its closed-lip variant. 'Mm-hm' for attention, a congruent type of laughter; an unspirited single-pitched '¿Mm?' for inattention, besides the pitch variations mentioned above. *Silence:* Filled wth fixed gaze, directed either at the speaker or at no specific point, for both attention and inattention; although the auditor gives away his inattention by fixing his look in mid-air between his eyes and the speaker's or by scanning the room, averting his gaze while performing a task (smoking, drinking, etc.) instead of keeping his eyes on the speaker's while doing it, etc. *K:* The only type of forms permitted in certain situations, as when one is part of an audience: headnods, raised brows, forward postural shifts, smiles, eye contact, hand-to-chin, leaning back while crossing arms, for attention; a blank gaze revealingly added to headnods and smiles, slouching or using object-adaptors and self-adaptors without other attentive behaviors, for inattention. *Stillness:* Filled with appropriate paralinguistic cues ('Uh-hu', '¡Mm!', laughter) or verbal reactions ('Sure', 'I see') it signifies attention, while utter silence + stillness can definitely be ambiguous, depending on variables such as the intensity of the situation and, of course, on additional somatic signs like tense (expressive) facial muscle tonus, tearful eyes, and blushing. *Proxemics:* Leaning forward on one's seat + positive facial expression, pulling up a chair closer to the speaker,

Basic expected feedback behaviors				Other behaviors
	Attention Inattention	Interest Disinterest	Approval Disapproval	Pleasure – Displeasure Surprise Anticipation Happiness – Unhappiness Anger Disappointment Disgust Fear Doubt Realization Embarrassment Dissimulation etc.
Language Paralanguage (Silence) Kinesics (Stillness) Chemical Dermal Thermal				

FIG. 7.2. Forms and Functions of Feedback Behaviors.

reorientation towards him, indicates attention; leaning back, or shifting distance or orientation away from the speaker without any other positive behaviors contains the opposite message.

Interest–Disinterest are equally sought by some speakers, and they are, in general, variations of attention-inattention cues. *Pg:* Drawled and high-pitched final syllables: '¡Oh!', 'Is that so?', '¡I see!', for interest, or by pronouncing the same utterances rather unspiritedly. *K:* More frequent nodding than for attention cues, perhaps accompanied by intermittent blinking and frequent and more prolonged eye contact, and by a posture shift at the beginning of the speaker's turn and at important points in his speech, for interest; restlessness, or quite unchanged posture behavior, for disinterest, or open negative gesturing in some contexts, for disinterest.

Other somatic channels have been exemplified along with silence and, of course, can be finely costructured with the rest of the feedback conscious or unconscious activities. The conscious or unconscious quality of the basic forms of feedback must be stressed for its value in the analysis of conversation.

Listener's secondary behaviors

Request for clarification is permissible in most small group contexts other than very formal ones or from any type of audience.

Lg: '¿I beg your pardon?', '¿Richard who?', '¿What's that?'. *Pg:* '¿Mm?', '¿Uh?'. *K:* Frowning while gazing and/or talking to the speaker (frowning and brow-raising typically, though not always, indicate negative and positive attitudes respectively), cupping one hand against the ear as for higher volume request. *Px:* Leaning forward toward the speaker with raised or knit brows.

Request for higher volume is also permissible in most contexts but much less during performances, in which context it depends on the audience's social status.

Lg: '¡¡Louder!!', '¡¡We can't hear you!!'. *K:* The hand-to-ear gesture and, in other cultures, an upward palm-up movement of the arm.

Verbatim repetition of the speaker's last statement is the auditor's termination of the speaker's turn or turn segment in an echoing fashion, but perhaps with different paralanguage that indicates the listener's attitude (amusement, mockery, adulation). It is a socioculturally relevant behavior which I have always observed as a basic reaction of the uneducated rural listener toward his educated or uneducated speaker, as is the case in Spain, therefore something interesting to note in a crosscultural study of interaction.

Restatement, reported by Duncan as 'brief restatement', as the case in which "the auditor restates in a few words an immediately preceding thought expressed by the speaker" (1973: 39).

Simultaneous conclusion, also mentioned under 'simultaneous behaviors', refers to what in some people constitutes the bad and perhaps uncontrollable habit of saying with you in a duo your last word, words, sentence and even more of each portion of your own speech (with identical or almost identical words), which they anticipate but cannot keep for themselves.

Sentence completion (Yngve 1970; Duncan 1973), which earlier I equated to simultaneous conclusion (Poyatos 1980a) later I have repeatedly observed to be quite different. It does not involve simultaneous speech as in the true simultaneous conclusion, but simply the termination of the sentence begun by the speaker but not finished, because his listener finishes it, even if he continues to speak as if uninterrupted; for, as will be seen, sentence completion does not really constitute an interruption.

Interruptions are, strictly speaking from a communicative point of view, those behaviors which truly break the flow of the speaker's deliverance, (a) because of their disruptive quality (even if they are very brief), as happens with disturbing comments that will make the speaker halt in his speech, hesitate before continuing and even provoke other listeners' comments, or (b) because the listener's intervention lasts long enough to constitute a new turn (if only a sort of short-lived aborted one) or a true suppressing of the speaker's turn, which can take place precisely through an interruption.

Prompting signals form the last group of speaker-oriented behaviors within the listener's turn which I have analyzed to date. They are aimed at monitoring or controlling the speaker's performance by instructing him, linguistically, paralinguistically or kinesically, to (a) say something he is forgetting to say or the listeners want him to say: *Lg:* 'Tell us about . . .', *Pg:* Throat clearing and eye contact, *K:* Eye contact, headnod, raised brows; (b) prevent him (usually paralinguistically) from saying something: *Pg:* Throat clearing and eye contact, *K:* Intent eye contact, raised or knit brows; and (c) introduce someone he was supposed to introduce: *Pg:* Throat clearing and eye contact, *K:* Unconspicuously pointing at the person with one's gaze only.

6. Interlistener Behaviors

The common characteristic of these behaviors is their low-key quality. When they are verbal or paralinguistic they are whispered. The kinesic ones are of equally subdued parakinesic nature, although a look can be highly tense and so can a gesture as long as it is a narrow-range one. The material analyzed to date reveals six of these activities.

Interlistener feedback is the one conveyed through various verbal and nonverbal expressions not addressed directly *to* the speaker but to one or more of the other listeners *about* the speaker, which he may or may not perceive.[4]

Lg: Usually whispered during a performance or lecture, but perhaps at half-volume otherwise. *Pg:* Laughter + eye contact with other listeners, or, at a performance, leaning toward a seatmate while still looking at the performer. *K:* Nodding in approval, rolling the eyes in disapproval. *Stillness:* Gazing at colistener.

Interlistener turn offering is a form of becoming the speaker without having claimed the turn, when the other listeners feel the speaker has spoken long enough, or inappropriately, or want their fellow listener to intervene.

Lg: *o ahead', 'You tell him'. *Pg:* Tz + headnod deictic and raised brows toward the speaker. *K:* Headnod deictic + raised brows (or knit signifying, for instance, '¡Come on, show him!'), hand deictic.

Interlistener turn claiming, mentioned earlier, is the request for the floor addressed to the other listeners, not to the present speaker, either because the speaker holds his turn or because he suppresses the speaker-directed claim.

K: Looking at the other listener or listeners, perhaps with prespeech lip-parting gesture, slightly raised brows, etc., rather than in an audible way.

Interlistener turn granting, also defined when first discussing turn claiming, responds, then, either to interlistener claiming or to speaker-directed claiming if the latter fails.

Lg: Whispered '¿Why don't you . . .?', 'Go ahead', '¿Why don't you tell him?'. *K:* Nodding alone or acompanying language.

Interlistener claim suppressing occurs often when the other listeners do not wish the speaker to stop talking or the claimer to speak.

Lg: Whispered 'Wait', '¡Quiet!'. *Pg:* '¡Sss!', 'Tz' + ingression as if to stop him verbally. *K:* Low-key facial gesture for 'Quiet', headshake, hand palm-down extended near body to signify 'Stop'. *Stillness:* While giving appropriate gestures or paralinguistic signals.

Interlistener prompting signals, similar to the speaker-directed ones, are used among his listeners to monitor each other's behaviors by instructing each other to pay attention, to keep quiet, not to say the wrong thing, to wait before speaking, and to intervene, the latter being more of a turn offering. While verbal prompting signals are usually whispered, unless the situation is very informal, paralinguistic and kinesic ones are equally subdued.

7. Speaker's Secondary Behaviors

Once the speaker's turn is under way there are still a few behaviors on his part that may or may not occur, as happens with several types of pauses. They serve to maintain the proper back-channel communication on the ongoing conversation, to gradually announce the end of his turn, and to regain it if something has interrupted it.

Sender's counterfeedback, which is conveyed by cues that serve as feedback to the auditor's own feedback, is an important complement to the analysis of the receiver's basic feedback. For the formal study of the sender's counterfeedback one could expand the table offered in Fig. 7.1, adding to each form of feedback channel (i.e., silence, language, etc.) and to each different cue the corresponding forms and cues on the part of the sender.

Counterfeedback for interest, for example, can be expressed through repetition of a successful statement and/or a brief pause, in which case the auditor's (or audience's) interest is confirmed by silence (therefore another type of pause). Slight or broad smiles and a whole repertoire of conscious signals are a most effective part of the politician's campaign. In any case, proper counterfeedback may elicit still more auditor's feedback and achieve mounting results.

Counterfeedback for anger at what the speaker said or did may reveal more anger, or perhaps fear, which in turn will elicit other auditor's reactions (i.e. feedback), and so on. In fact, a detailed analysis of a complex encounter will show the specific points at which, and the specific cues with which, the outcome of that encounter was anticipated and developed. On the other hand, some interesting conclusions would be arrived at by studying the many verbal and nonverbal counterfeedback cues and how they correspond to the same channels used by the receiver or to different ones.

Feedback request, observed often in conversation (besides the feedback-seeking pause discussed below) are secondary activities that may or may not be used by the speaker. Although they appear more often in situations in which the speaker is not sure about the success of his communication, when approval is sought or when one must ascertain that the listener is understanding properly, feedback-request cues can be performed even quite out of awareness. Verbal requests for feedback are the least.

Lg: '¿You know?' (and not just 'You know'), '¿'nd'stand?'. *Pg:* '¿Mm?', '¿Uh?'; the intonational curve may qualify a statement as with an additional feedback-request tone, as in 'We went to that little restaurant in that square?'. *K:* Nodding with verbal and paralinguistic requests, using illustrators of size (space markers), shape (pictographs), movement (kinetographs) and quality (identifiers) with verbal, paralinguistic or kinesic questioning features.

Turn preclosing, indicated, after having technically relinquished the floor or using it as a preyielding signal.

Lg: 'So . . .'. *Pg:* Accelerated tempo. *K:* Postural shift, and gaze directed to the auditor.

Turn closing, indicated by relaxation of the posture, lip moistening, and other idiosyncratic or cultural behaviors.

Lg: Simply ending speech. *Pg:* 'Tz' + pharyngeal ingression and egression. *K:* Out-in tongue movement, smile, leaning back, engaging in some task (lighting cigarette, drinking).

The matter of closing and opening can be analyzed, not just in relation to turns, but to the different topics within the same encounter and to the conversation as a whole. What earlier has been defined as spontaneous initial turn taking is one of the typical behaviors complementary to certain preopening activities, such as furniture arrangement ('Pull up a chair'), postural patterning, eye contact, mutual offering of cigarettes or drinks, etc.; and what Schegloff and Sacks (1973) have studied as 'opening up closings' offers new insights into the terminating structure of encounters.

Turn resumption is the continuation of the speaker's state after having been momentarily disrupted through actual interruption and not just by permissible listener's behaviors (turn claiming, preopening, etc.) or through the listener's failure to take the turn.

Lg: 'And . . .', 'Well, as I was saying . . .', or unpreambled continuation of even the interrupted sentence, which seems to freeze linguistically and kinesically through silence and stillness.

8. Simultaneous Behaviors

If the turn-changing rules and counterrules occurred always in an orderly fashion, that is, if participants claimed, yielded and took their turns at the appropriate moment—from the structural point of view—a conversation would be unrealistically smooth—from the sociopsychological point of view—possible only in a very protocolarian encounter. However, it seems that in all cultures and social contexts certain situations occur in the course of a conversational encounter in which at least two participants become engaged in the same activity at the same time. Besides simultaneous speaking about the topic, other simultaneous behaviors should be analyzed if one is to achieve an exhaustive knowledge of the linguistic and nonlinguistic inner structuration of conversation.

If we consider that the speaker's deliverance and his listener's feedback take place at the same time, that one participant's silence may be accompanied by another participant's gaze, or that the next speaker's turn-claiming prespeech click cooccurs with the present speaker's speech, we realize the ambiguity of the term simultaneous. It seems necessary, therefore, to differentiate mere 'simultaneity' of actions which may be of the same or different type, and the 'coincidence' of activities that are truly identical in both type and structure. I will call the latter *symmetrical* and the nonidentical one *simultaneous*. Furthermore, I am using the term *multiple* to refer to the cooccurrence of more than two participants, and 'simultaneous' only to refer to two active participants.

Simultaneous turns (Duncan 1973)—a more accurate term than simultaneous speech, if we think of the simultaneous signalling of deafmutes or of some other forms of reduced interaction—is a peculiar situation that deserves much investigation from the linguistic, sociopsychological and cultural points of view. It is certainly one of the causes of intercultural clash between Anglo-Saxons and Latins, for instance (but not between Latins and Arabs, both of whom possess the same tendency to simultaneous floor-holding behaviors), and it is characterized—from the linguistic point of view—by syntactical disorder and word repetition, when speaker B does not address speaker A necessarily, but speaker A's listener(s), until the latter stops paying attention to his interlocutor, who then gives up and relinquishes his turn.

Although, in general, this situation is not acceptable and cannot be maintained for too long, it can be treated quite differently according to the culture of the participants (something to be measured by its duration and the intensity of the activities involved, as I will indicate below). While in the Anglo-Saxon world we try to avoid simultaneous talking from the moment this situation is initiated, by apologizing for the intrusion ('Sorry', 'No, go ahead'), speaker A then accepting perhaps the interruption ('Go ahead', 'That's all right', while smiling), and speaker B justifying it once more ('No, I was just gonna say—')—in which case simultaneous talking lasts no more than a few seconds—Spaniards, for instance, break the turn-taking rules much more conspicuously.

Multiple turns are not uncommon among the kind of speakers and in the type of situations in which simultaneous turns occur, three or more participants speaking and gesticulating at the same time. In addition, a differentiation must be made within this type of interaction between *parallel multiple turns* and *crisscrossed multiple turns* to define the sort of turn configuration in which speakers and listeners who are in an ordinary small group gathering establish lines of communication that are felt comfortable or, on the other hand, uncomfortable because their gazes (and therefore their audible and visual speeches) cross in the center of the group. The diagrams in Fig. 7.3

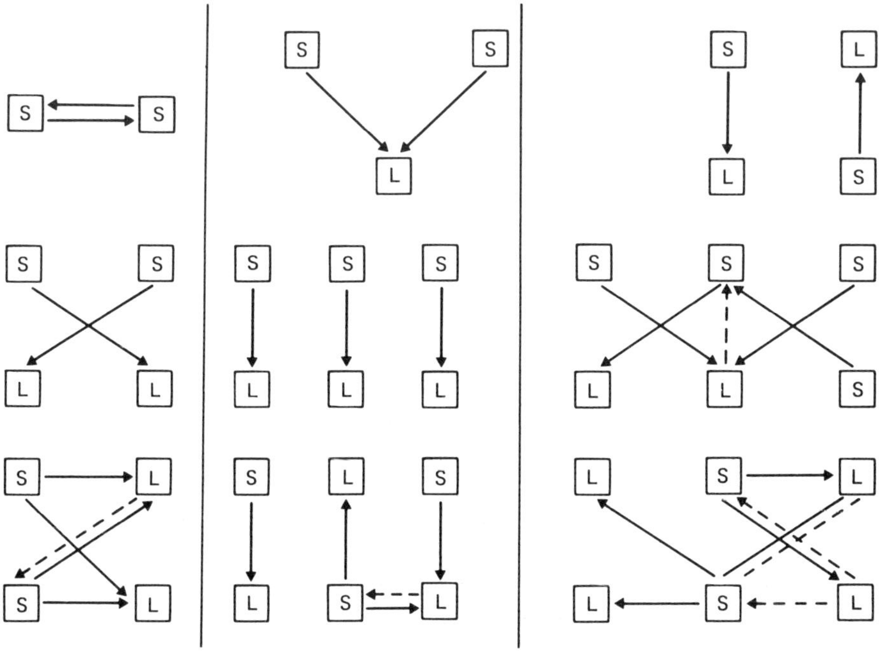

FIG. 7.3. Simultaneous and Multiple Turns.

attempt to define only some of the most typical simultaneous- and multiple-turn situations observed as well as parallel and crisscrossed ones, showing how in the multiple-turn situation speakers address themselves to listeners, usually not to other speakers, as a listener's turn is much easier to disrupt than a speaker's turn. On the other hand, the axes of each of the interactions are not formed only by one speaker and his listener or listeners, but by him and another's speaker's listeners, who try to pay attention to both speakers mostly either out of politeness or interest. The reader can easily form many other combinations of parallel and crisscrossed turns (or interactions), considering proxemics, orientation, status, personality and culture as important variables (see also the broken lines indicating other listener's behaviors).

Simultaneous turn claiming may occur without hardly causing any simultaneous turns. Two or more interactants may gaze at each other, while perhaps inhaling and/or clicking, seeking acknowledgement of their claims, until only one of them manages to overpower both the speaker and the other claimers, which results, therefore, in a sort of undue turn taking or abrupt interruption, anticipated by clipped words and paralinguistic and kinesic signals.

Simultaneous/Multiple turn taking occur either through simultaneous/ multiple interruptions or when the speaker yields the turn to one listener but two or more listeners open their turns.

Simultaneous/Multiple conclusion, defined earlier as the situation in which a listener or listeners complete the speaker's statement because they anticipate it.

Simultaneous/Multiple turn relinquishing may originate within simultaneous or multiple floor holding when two or more conversants suddenly try to control their rule-breaking behavior at the same time and come to a stop, producing one of the interactive pauses, resolved with the usual linguistic and nonlinguistic yielding cues.

Simultaneous/Multiple turn yielding is similar to the previous situation, except that the turn is yielded by all the speakers when a new speaker claims it or one of them overpowers the others.

Simultaneous and multiple interruptions are of course possible as soon as the speaker has two or more listeners. It sometimes results in one of the interruptors prolonging his intervention into what is actually a brief simultaneous turn, which, if maintained beyond a single statement, may become a new turn that has been taken through interruption and suppression because the lawful speaker may yield the floor.

Simultaneous/Multiple silences may result in a situation similar to that produced by simultaneous or multiple relinquishing, when all the speakers suddenly come to a halt because they have said what they had to say, not because they were relinquishing or yielding their turns. In North America an easy familiar expression by one of the participants is '¡Don't everybody speak at once!', while in England someone may say 'An angel is passing'.

Much more should be investigated as regards simultaneous and multiple behaviors in conversation. *Symmetrical interventions*, for instance, can be a double simultaneous conclusion of the speaker's last sentence by two of his listeners, multiple silences, identical prompting signals by two or more listeners, a number of feedback behaviors, etc. Symmetrical behaviors, of course, can occur between speaker and listener or between two listeners.

9. Acoustic and Visual Pauses

The matter of conversational pauses has been outlined already when dealing with silence in the previous chapter. However, it will not be exhausted even here, as many more could be analyzed which do not appear in the table of the mechanism of conversation. The failure of many discussions of pauses to date lies in their typical neglect of the kinesic pause; a flow, on the other hand, easy to understand if one considers the also typical dissociation in the study of language between verbal expression, paralanguage and kinesics. It is precisely the intimate costructuration of paralinguistic pauses (whose paralinguistic nature has been defined when discussing segmental and nonsegmental elements of discourse within the Basic Triple Structure) or, to put it better, the cohesion between the silent *and* still parts of a pause in discourse, that must incite deeper research into the structure of what much too often is defined as pause without a strong semiotic basis.

There are several aspects to the issue of pauses that could be listed as follows:

(a) the cooccurring silence and stillness within a pause, (b) the onset of the acoustic gap with the parallel slowdown of movement, and then how both sound and movement are resumed at the offset, (c) the costructuration of a paralinguistic-kinesic pause with the immediately preceding, simultaneous and succeeding activities (the studied aspects of silence and stillness), (d) the intensity of pauses (determined by their duration and their costructuration with preceding, simultaneous and succeeding activities) and their duration (in turn related to both costructuration and intensity), (e) how a pause which is not at all a semiotic vacuum, can be occupied by activities other than sound and movement, such as tears, blushing or goose flesh, (f) how the pause can be only paralinguistic or only kinesic, one of the systems still operating while the other one ceases to operate, but still communicates either by its very absence (zero sign) or precisely through the meaningful characteristics of silence, stillness, or both, and (g) the conversational functions of each occurrence of a single (silence) or double (silence and stillness) pause.

Only the essential conversational pauses are outlined here and shown in the table in Fig. 7.1 merely to indicate the more typical situations in which they occur. It must be noted that some pauses are produced consciously on the part of the participants, thus having an intended interactive function, while others are uncontrollable pauses that happen when some interactive activity fails to function; which would also allow us to distinguish *attitudinal pauses* and *uncontrolled pauses*.

Absent turn-claiming pause may also occur if the speaker closes his turn or has to continue upon noticing his auditor's failure to claim the floor (due to shyness, bewilderment, etc.), and then resumes his speech, even changing his topic. It is more paralinguistic than kinesic, as various movements can be performed during the gap in speech.

Absent turn taking, either as a consequence of simultaneous yielding, during which mutual gazing and verbal ('Well—', 'I—'), paralinguistic ('Tz', ingression, throat clearing), kinesic (posture shifts), and proxemic behaviors (reorientation) take place, or because the listener fails to become speaker after the turn has been yielded to him.

Turn-offering pause occurs often between the perhaps unexpected offering of the turn by the speaker and the listener's response.

Turn-opening pause is the one contained between the turn-taking 'Well—', 'Tz' + ingression, postural shift or momentary stillness, and the actual beginning of the speaker state.

Pre-turn-ending pause occurs sometimes before and anticipates the actual turn-closing sentence, for example; '—so we left that same day—. And that was it', after which someone else takes the floor either as the new speaker or just to ask a question.

Turn-ending pause is the one shown by a postspeech click ('Tz', as the prespeech one), a pharyngeal ingression, the visually perceived intake of breath, a 'that's-all' gesture followed by stillness, a posture shift, etc.

Relinquishing or yielding pause is the one caused either by the unexpected speaker's relinquishing of his turn or when he yields it but it is not taken immediately.

The *transitional pause* (apart from the also transitional syntactic breaks) may occur between different topics (or simply between turns) and, although it may also be due to psychological variables, it seems to be differently regulated according to the interactants' socioeconomic status (educational level, socializing capacity, etc.):

Lg: 'Well—', 'So—'. *Pg:* Different types of laughter, lip smacking or moistening, 'Tz'. *K:* Posture shift, slapping one's knees, joining both hands. *Px:* Slow distance shifting. *Others:* Object-adaptors (a drink, a pipe, imaginary lint, a necklace), self-adaptors (preening behaviors, hand rubbing), dermal changes (blushing).

Hesitation pause, due to a break in one's train of thought, to negative and disturbing auditor's feedback, etc., takes different forms according to sex, personality and other factors, and is shown by a number of characteristic verbal and nonverbal cues:

Lg: 'and uh—', 'Well—', curtailed words, 'Er—yes'. *Pg:* Stammering, 'Tz', audible pharyngeal ingression, throat clearing. *Silence:* Filled with eye contact or with gaze aversion, both usually accompanied by stillness. *K:* Raising index and middle fingers to lips, pinching the nose bridge, gazing vaguely at floor, at the ceiling or at a point in infinity, touching one's brows with thumb and middle finger, scratching one's head, arms akimbo while looking down, crossing arms tightly while looking down. The hesitation or gap can be also kinesic in the stilling of a movement which is interrupted as are words, thus appearing as true *kinesic stuttering*.

Feedback-seeking pause is the one shown mainly kinesically by staring at the other interactant(s), lips parted perhaps, perhaps smiling, or frowning at suspected failure; out-in tongue-tip movement; or the more showy pause displayed as part of his repertoire by a comedian, who does it more consciously: both hands on his chest sometime, or arms akimbo or loosely flexed and hanging over the sides, or open as in a come-on gesture. This pause, although a form of feedback request, is more important than the verbal or paralinguistic type of request, for speech is replaced by a type of pause which is closely related to the carrying silence and stillness (it is often formed by both silence and stillness) discussed earlier. The listeners must replay the speaker's linguistic-paralinguistic-kinesic structures (the three systems being hierarchized differently according to their semiotic relevance) during the break. In fact, the professional comedian knows how to give his audience a second such pause, knowing he will get their laugh once more.

Task-performing pause, as the term indicates, is a very important kind of paralinguistic silence or break in speech which has also been neglected. Although it seems to be produced with the sole purpose of performing tasks such as puffing at the cigarette, picking up the cup of coffee or a drink, drinking and setting it down, changing eyeglasses, producing a pen, shifting posture, arranging one's clothes, looking at a pocket watch, opening a book or newspaper, serving food or pouring tea, putting on a coat or a pair of gloves, etc. However, as has been pointed out discussing body-adaptors and object-adaptors in Chapter 4, these tasks can be consciously used to manipulate the flow of the interaction, thus acting as strong regulators. Whether a tense man–woman conversation or a delicate business meeting, the silence of the task-performing pause will acquire all the significance of silence, subject to costructuration with preceding, simultaneous and succeeding activities, as well as their duration and intensity.

Somatic-function pause, with which this discussion of conversational pauses is far from being exhausted, is another kind of silence very similar to the previous one, as in fact allows the speaker to carry out usually brief bodily tasks such as physiological reflexes (coughing, yawning, sneezing, and belching), engage in scratching, stretching, spitting, nose-blowing, preening, hand-rubbing, etc. But that these activities can also be manipulated and performed quite unnecessarily (e.g., throat-clearing) is quite obvious, and their functions in the mechanism of conversation cannot be underestimated.

10. The Functioning of Somatic Systems in Conversation

In addition to the ideas offered in Chapter 3 concerning the various forms of reduced interaction according to somatic states or to external circumstances, I would suggest the need to be fully aware, not just of the expressive repertoires of impaired people, but of their perceptual capabilities as well. We realize, usually as unimpaired interactants, that deaf interlocutors do not perceive the semantic nuances or words and subtle paralinguistic constructs, or the audible interactive use of object-adaptors. In sum, our own extremely articulate and flexible multirepertoire can never be fully appreciated by them. This should indeed compel us to try to achieve the kind of interactive fluency specifically appropriate for each impaired situation, in which they are still dealing with natural conversation. Which comes to prove once more why the concept of *fluency* ought to be revised in terms of the perceptual capabilities of our cointeractants and not of our own repertoires only. There can be no fluency in a conversation that lacks the necessary *equilibrium* among the communicative activities of its participants. By the same token—aside from impaired conversants—members of higher socioeconomic and educational levels, who are generally equipped with a greater ability to adapt themselves to the communicative styles of lower-status people, can achieve more fluency if they adopt their linguistic, paralinguistic and kinesic repertoires; and in a greater scale, natural conversation among members of different cultures requires not only linguistic fluency, but cultural fluency as well.

If we search our data for the type of behaviors that perform specific functions in the mechanism of conversation, we soon discover, first of all, the preponderance of the Basic Triple Structure—plus kinesically-based proxemic behavior—within that mechanism; that is, the turn rules (claiming, yielding, taking, etc.) and counterrules (holding, suppressing, etc.) that are consciously displayed in the course of natural conversation. In addition, turn suppressing, feedback, counterfeedback, etc., can also be displayed through the Basic Triple Structure and through proxemics. However, this last group of behaviors and the different types of pauses that have just been discussed can also be indicated by activities developed in the dermal-visual channel (by unintended blushing or perspiration), the thermal-dermal channel (in an intimate-distance situation, by unintentional loss or gain of body temperature), or the chemical-visual channel (through intentional or unintentional shedding of tears or through perspiration).

This obvious limitation of what appears as secondary human channels seems to strengthen the thoughts about the phylogenetic and ontogenetic codevelopment and costructuration of language-paralanguage-kinesics as the typically anthroposemiotic complex, although paralanguage and kinesics are also zoosemiotic systems. However, the encoding and decoding of *olfactory signals* in natural interaction should not be underestimated. Although they are not controllable as the Basic Triple Structure is—at least not in the degree they are in other species for communicative purposes—body odors can be produced in the course of a conversation which, being triggered by specific and easily identifiable emotional stimuli (e.g., axillary perspiration), cannot only act as the emitter's self-regulators, but as regulator of his interlocutor's repertoire, as in a heated conversation or in a flirting encounter. On the other hand, perspiration is visually perceived too, thus doubling its decoding phase. But we are forced to acknowledge lotions and cosmetics (intimate extensions of body communication) as true body-adaptors with which humans compensate, in gender-specific ways, for their almost total lack of natural controllable olfactory systems. They can play definite roles in interaction, as they are overriding elements during, for instance, a man–woman encounter, provoking specific changes in that encounter, not only as they become costructured with verbal and nonverbal activities, but even providing an additional important dimension to verbal silences (which may not be kinesic, paralinguistic or proxemic pauses).

As for the *dermal-dermal channel*, that is, the cutaneous perception of our cointeractant's dermal signs—apart from the intervention of the thermal receptors for temperature changes—it contains an important kind of information about skin texture. Between the smoothness of a well-cared feminine hand and the coarseness of a country-woman's or a farmer's lie a number of sensations associated to certain socioeconomic factors as well as to the receiver's sensitiveness and expectations; but above all, those sensations, or rather, the uncontrollable signs on the part of the emitter, may act as regulators of the encounter, which can also be associated to chemical signals. At the same time our skin possesses pressure receptors which, through kinesic contactual behaviors, elicit our intellectual appreciation, besides the physical one, of a firm handshake and a limp one, of a tense embrace of grief, of the differently decoded degrees of pressure in a crowded public vehicle, etc., in ways that will regulate our verbal and nonverbal behaviors accordingly.

11. A Further Note on the Total Conditioning Background

If we now consider the mechanism of conversation in the light of the Total Conditioning Background outlined in Chapter 3, it should be pointed out, first of all, that the conditioning factors may affect two things: the rate of the display of the various systems during an encounter and the capacity of those systems for the display of the different behaviors. But the mutual intertwining of the conditioning factors themselves is so intricate that I will merely indicate some instances of these relationships, trying to cover both their capacity for the production of specific behaviors and their capacity for their display in the interactive mechanism.

We observe that the difference between childhood and adulthood (biological configuration) affects the interactive repertoires of children. Still, in the more conspicuous developmental stages of their linguistic-paralinguistic-kinesic complex, they hardly display any turn claiming (except for crying or shouting), turn taking (except for suppressing behaviors) or turn yielding signals, very few intermittent feedback cues (e.g., the adult's double closed-lip mid-central vowel [$\overset{2}{ə} - \overset{3}{ə}$×] for attention, the drawled double glottalized mid-central nasalized vowel [ˀ$\overset{2\,1}{\tilde{ə}}$ᵓ] for agreement, etc., so untypical in children), and practically no sender's within-turn behaviors (counterfeedback, turn preclosing cues). Rules and counterrules are treated differently according to the person's psychological configuration (very extrovert and/or excitable people tend to use simultaneous speech more often than introvert and/or relaxed people), to emotional states (pathological conditions, as in some of Scheflen's reported schizophrenic patients [1973], or in occasional critical states of depression, fear, etc.), or to the proxemics imposed by furniture arrangement (objectual built environment), which may block off subtle paralinguistic cues at an improper far social distance and thus increase the use of some receiver's within-turn behaviors. The mechanism of conversation definitely varies from a formal setting (role expectations, etiquette norms) to a family living-room, where simultaneous behaviors are most typical, just as they are in Latin or Arab countries (cultural background), and certainly in the lower socioeconomic strata, along with fewer polite turn-yielding and feedback cues.

Notes

1. E.g., Argyle and Ingham (1972), Dittman (1972), Duncan (1972a, 1972b, 1973, 1974a, 1974b, 1975a, 1975b, 1977), Gallois and Markel (1975), Jefferson (1973), Kendon (1971, 1976), Lindenfeld (1971, 1973, 1974), Markel (1975), Rochester (1973), Sacks, Schegloff, and Jefferson (1974), Schegloff (1972), Scherloff and Sacks (1973), Wiemann and Knapp (1975).
2. I first discussed it at the 1975 International Congress of Applied Linguistics (Poyatos 1976g), and outlined it often elsewhere (Poyatos 1975c, 1976a, 1979c, 1980a, 1981c), besides a recent article on the subject (Poyatos 1982c).
3. As with turn preopening, we cannot naively believe that each behavior, say, turn closing or turn taking, is delimited in such a way that its boundaries appear perfectly clear to the observer, even in a frame-by-frame film analysis. Future refinement of this chapter will be to recognize that virtually all the behaviours included in the chart in Fig. 7.1 consist actually of three phases: a pre-, anticipating or leading act, a central activity that constitutes the truly regulatory behavior, and a post- or residual act which is but a tail. Take, for instance, turn claiming. The listener does not always make his claim passing abruptly from a state of total listening to the claiming behavior, but rather goes through a preparatory phase, a *pre-claiming*, during which he may show lip-moistening, slight postural shift, raised brows, or parted lips. At this point he may still abort his claim, resulting in *abandoned turn claiming*, otherwise he will then display the appropriate *turn-claim behavior.* But even if the speaker has granted him the turn, the listener's claim will still be noticeable until his actual preopening or taking behavior, through his muscle tonus, eye contact, posture, in other words, his *post-claiming*.
4. An exhaustive study of feedback behaviors would have to make the distinction between interlistener feedback and *shared speaker-directed feedback*.

8

Punctuation as Nonverbal Communication Toward a Revision of the System

1. The Need for a New Approach to Punctuation[1]*

IT is an obvious though neglected fact that written language is always alienated, in a lesser or greater degree, from the reality of the living, organized, psychosomatic activity of speech, let alone cooccurrent movement.

It is also a fact that, in spite of the overwhelming growth and propagation of written thoughts and the manifest desire to express so many vocally produced messages that are part of our real-life system of communication, we have been using for centuries a most limited repertoire of punctuation symbols. We must face the unquestionable need for a revision of our very concept of what written communication should be like. Furthermore, it is necessary to at least explore the possibility of improving the expressiveness of punctuation by modifying and adding to the present system.

It seems apparent that the various aspects and problems of punctuation fall naturally under the domain of nonverbal communication studies, and that it is nonverbal communication that man has historically strived to represent, therefore acknowledging its use as an essential part of the human message-conveying activities of speech and movement. As will be pointed out below, although punctuation reveals a conscious effort to symbolize speech for the better evocation of its semantic variations and the avoidance of too conspicuous ambiguities, it simultaneously, and quite unwittingly too, evokes and marks the cooccurrent body movements and still positions that are an integral part of the kinetic-acoustic continuum of human and animal communication. In fact, from a strictly anthropophonetic viewpoint, we would affirm that punctuation attempts to convey as closely as possible the structural-semantic forms of the Basic Triple Structure language-paralanguage-kinesics. It has been discussed already that it is the true core of human communication behavior, both from an ontogenetic and a phylogenetic point of view—as differentiated from the communicative systems of other

* Superscript numbers refer to Notes at end of chapter.

species—and that its main characteristic is the combined cognitive and lexical properties of the three cosystems and their capacity to operate simultaneously, alternate with or substitute for each other as needed in an interactive situation.

A handwritten or printed text can symbolize only sounds and silences, that is, audible language with its pauses and its very absence (silence being regarded as segmental, as discussed below). But a large proportion of acoustic or silent constructs remain still unrepresentable (and most of them will always be so), although their semiotic values are not inferior to those of the written ones; in fact, they can be central to the conveying of messages, which betrays once more the illogical limitations of written language. Semiotically speaking, sound and movement are the basis of communication. So are they culturally. But punctuation, along with words, represents, or more exactly, evokes movement and, as a counterpart of silence, stillness, as was pointed out in the previous chapter, and it is a rich source of signs and sign transmission and a legitimate concern of semiotics.

Certain paralinguistic features like high volume ([!]), pitch ([?]), articulatory tension (CAPITALS, [!]), or silence ([. . .]) act as *primary sign systems*, because of their intensity and location in the communicative stream, in relation to words, which on occasions can be just secondary systems. This is one of the proofs of the relevance of punctuation, of what it represents as well as what it fails to represent in a written text, because it also evokes cooccurrent or alternating movements which can also be primary systems.

Punctuation can represent silences directly through established symbols (from grammatical pauses to emotional ones), and stillness indirectly by the evocation of lack of movement. They are both conditioned—as other communicative elements—by culture in different degrees, an important context so often, if not regularly, neglected in reading and in serious research.

What is apparent then is that a purely semiotic analysis of the signs and sign types involved in punctuation can afford the investigator a much deeper study of written language and, therefore, of a written work, and not just a superficial and rather mechanical series of observations of a purely technical nature, as is often done in so-called literary analysis. This perspective would reach very deep layers in the artist's written text, behind which lies the whole process of creativity and transmission to the reader between the two end points, input–output, both subject to their own spatial and temporal conditioning factors, as discussed in the two previous chapters.

That punctuation is the concern of phonetics (as it is of grammar and literature) appears, on the other hand, clear enough; and yet many phoneticians dismiss the unavoidable relationship between phonetics and nonverbal communication, of which punctuation is but a part! Applied phonetics, then, must serious undertake the analysis of paralanguage, kinesics and whatever nonverbal system may be consciously or unconsciously evoked by the writer through the use of punctuation symbols, and establish a very clear concept of what exactly punctuation aims at.

The arguments for a deeper and revisional approach to punctuation are soon found to be multidisciplinary and, still better, interdisciplinary, as they should easily elicit action from within various disciplines and research areas. As an exclusively phonetic and linguistic posture would not take us far enough at a time when man's communication activities occupy such a central place in the world of research, we should try to analyze punctuation through at least:

(a) semiotic probings into the sign types and forms contained in and symbolized by punctuation, in itself an interdisciplinary pursuit;

(b) the anthropological interest in the development of writing, as man's greatest communicative endeavor, and of reading habits, from three different but complementary viewpoints: psychological (psychological anthropology), physiological (visual anthropology) and intellectual (literary anthropology);

(c) the literary-sociocultural concern (literature being the highest form of communication and interaction in time and space) about the forms and achievements of punctuation devices; and

(d) the equally integrative linguistic study (quite explicit throughout this paper) of the interrelationships between verbal language, semantics, grammar and punctuation.

2. The Story of Punctuation

The evolution of punctuation until the eighteenth century, when the system became definitely established, can be briefly outlined:[2]

Before VII B.C.	No word or sentence separation in Greek inscriptions, but phrases were separated by [:] or [⋮] in some. For over fifteen centuries only majuscules are used.
IV B.C.	Paragraphs, periods and clauses appear separated in two papyri. Greek literary texts on papyrus divide *paragraphos* with a dash under the beginning of the line for each new topic. This is the only feature mentioned by Aristotles (384–322 B.C.), who initiated the study of grammar, developed about 180 B.C. with Dionysious de Max's grammar.
III B.C.	Aristophanes of Byzantium, the museum librarian, is credited with the punctuation system used later by Greek grammarians in the Alexandrian schools, dividing discourse into sections by means of: [·] at the end of a short

	section or clause; ('comma'), equal to modern [,]; [.] at the end of a longer clause; ('colon'), equal to [;]; and [·] at the end of the longest section or sentence ('periodos'), equal to modern [.].
I B.C.–II A.D.	Roman documents and books had words separated by points, and first letter or two of first paragraph indicating new topic were projected into the margin (not indented as from XVII on).
IV–VI	The grammarian Donatus (IV) and Cassiodorus (VI) recommended Aristophanes' three-point system, still possible with Latin scripts in majuscules, but books were actually written continuously, at most separating sentences by a gap or an occasional point. Copies of St. Jerome's Vulgate Bible (V) had phrases separated (after Demosthenes and Cicero) to help reading aloud, with first letter projected out.
VII–VIII	Transition from majuscule to minuscule handwriting. Words, sentences and paragraphs were separated, and high or low points were still used for sentences.
VIII–IX	Under the influence of Charlemagne and his adviser, Alcuin, a new system appears, perfected in XII. Besides points and commas, Gregorian chant prompted the inflectional 'punctus elevatus' [·⁄] and the 'punctus interrogativus' [.ᴐ].
X	A hyphen [-] is used to divide words at end of line.
XII	'Punctus circumflexus' [.>] for raising inflection at end of subordinate clause, always for reading aloud in churches and refectories.
XIII–XIV	Virgule [′] as a light stop ('punctus elevatus' before), then replaced by [:]. The virgula sank to bottom of line and became a comma.
1455	Gutenberg's Vulgate Bible has stops, colons, and middle points [·] as commas. Words are separated, and sentences begin with a capital.
late XIV	Caxton (in Westminster) used punctuation very irregularly: [:], [′], and a lozenge-shaped period, and sometimes [‖] instead of virgule.

c. 1490	Aldus Manutius, founder of the Aldine Press in Venice, used italic and roman types reversing our present practice, and replaced the Greek system with a new and lasting one that included [,], [;], [:], [.], and [?] for syntactical purposes.
XVII–XVIII	[!], [" "], [-], and ['], with modern names.
mid-XVIII	Spanish [¡] and [¿].

In view of the arbitrary development of the punctuation system we should see no logical reason why we could not try to increase its representational and evocative capabilities to better suit some expressive needs that are strongly felt by anyone who is a little sensitive to the fascinating human gift of written language.

3. Punctuation as the Joint Anthropological Concern Within Physiology, Psychology, and Literature

It would be exceptional if punctuation, one of man's tools for communication with his congeners, and an eloquent proof of his effort to transmit information and make it last through both time and space, were not within the interest of anthropology as so many other aspects and products of civilization are. From the emergence of writing to the most highly intellectual texts of our days the gradual invention of punctuation has, in a rather casual fashion, put in man's hands certain means of complementing the reading aloud of those writings, until those and still other devices were disseminated for the one-to-one relationship between writer and reader. This process must be viewed by anthropology as one of man's achievements, and certainly as one of his strongest attempts to convey to others the elements in his speech which were felt to be indispensable for the transmission of certain messages and the completion of others.

From a multiple physiological, psychological, literary and, of course, semiotic point of view, the development of the differently directed scripts of the world (namely, left-to-right, right-to-left, boustrophedon (as oxen in plowing, lines running alternately left to right and right to left), vertical-downward, and vertical-upward), allows for an approach to punctuation that shows reading both as the activity undertaken by a socializing intelligent organism that projects itself into time and space and as a motor skill. As Hewes (1948: 237) observed, basket weaving lacks "the complex intellectual and emotional involvement of reading." Anthropology could deepen further into the correlations of visual (motor skill) perception of words and their cooccurent or simultaneous features conveyed by punctuation, in other words, the intellectual *a posteriori perception* and the *a priori perception* or anticipation of those features and their associations, the former as an intellectual operation, the latter also as a physical one through macular and even peripheral vision when catching the still distant [!], [. . .], or [*italics*], for emphasis.

It is interesting to note how macular vision (operating 12 to 15 degress in the horizontal plane, but only 3 in the vertical one, therefore not so fit for vertical scripts) and peripheral vision (through the corner of one'e eye, covering 90 degrees) must have become more important and genetically adapted as man had to pay attention not only to distant punctuation but to so many elaborate mechanical and artistic visually perceived structures that demanded the joint collaboration of foveal, macular and peripheral visions. From a literary point of view, it is true—and this could be the concern of literary historians preoccupied with the evolution of reading—that punctuation may have contributed to a higher intellectual ability in us, as it facilitates the mental reconstruction of real-life speech and movement and also richer poetic, psychological and cultural associations. This seems to be more elaborate in the advanced stages of horizontal writing systems that have incorporated all the known devices of punctuation.

Which in turn allows us to consider how narrative literature, particularly the novel, develops, as is discussed in the next chapter, the richest evocations of the writer's own world of physical and intellectual experiences, changed through a sort of sign metamorphosis into the reader's own world through a complex web of decoded images and ideas and complementary associations. The role of punctuation reaches its greatest functional complexity in a novel, both in dialogs and in the author's own comments, as it can symbolize and/or indirectly suggest subtle psychological and physical reactions which reveal not only universal and culture-specific patterns of human thought and behavior, but an intricate series of associations on the part of both writer and reader.

Although the literary implications of punctuation have been suggested in the preceding paragraphs, the traditional differentiation between the 'elocutionary' (i.e., rhetorical, dramatic) system of punctuation and the 'grammatical' (i.e., logical, constructional) one would warrant the specific literary approach to the evoking and reconstruction exercise of reading in which consciously or unconsciously we bring a character (or a known or unknown correspondent) back to life. It is actually by imagining the person's paralanguage coupled to his kinesic repertoire that we undertake that task. But paralanguage, more directly symbolized than kinesics, is culturally conditioned in many instances and, while members of different cultures may use the same punctuation marks with identical connotation, say, [!] for high volume, the behavior represented by those marks may be differently used and interpreted in different cultures.

That the literary rendering of a fictional character has an important phonetic aspect to it has already been indicated. We only have to look at a novel by Dickens, Dostoevsky or Huxley to see how the writer's 'literary' descriptions of paralinguistic phenomena are almost rich enough to make us dismiss the idea of a richer punctuation repertoire; and yet there are certain features for which new marks could well be added.

If we review the devices that a novelist has at hand to indicate the paralinguistic repertoires of his characters we realize that the more 'structural' aspects of punctuation do not matter as much as the more 'elocutionary' ones. The absence of [,], [;], [:] or [.] cannot be so confusing, and does not demand so much attention, as the absence of [!], [?], or [. . .]. One cannot help but wondering, first, whether the average narrator ever considers how his punctuation will fare now and in a hundred years, here and in a faraway culture, and secondly, to what extent the spatially and temporally distant reader is aware of his handicap, and the professional or nonprofessional translator of his intercultural task. As for the innovations that modern narrators have introduced occasionally by adopting typographical changes, original uses of different quantities of suspension dots, or large blank spaces and geometrical arrangements of the text, they are not the specific concern of this chapter.

4. Segmental and Nonsegmental Elements in Punctuation

I have discussed in Chapter 5 the dichotomy segmental-nonsegmental referred to linguistic, paralinguistic and kinesic features within the Basic Triple Structure and their cognitive capacity. This realistic view of speech shows that while kinesic acts can be only evoked by a secondary type of association through punctuation marks as well as verbal and paralinguistic representations, syntactical and communicative silences (which override only movement) are represented by [,], [;], [:], [.], [( )], [- -], and [. . .], and these are segmental, although paralinguistic in nature.

In addition, the different punctuation symbols that correspond to the various forms and functions of silence (evoking also certain types of kinesic behaviors) could be added to the diagram in Fig. 5.6. As for the capacity of punctuation to evoke kinesic behavior, a sentence like 'Well, what did *you* think of that!' used to illustrate the structure language-paralanguage-kinesics in Fig. 5.1 could also be given here to demonstrate the functions of the punctuation symbols. In this case, paralanguage was conveyed by vowel repetition for drawling, a comma for a juncture pause, *italics* (underlined in handwriting) for emphasis, (['] proposed below for major stress), and the exclamation mark (which could be complemented by a question mark) for high volume and higher pitch. As will be discussed below, however, the lack of opening [!] prevents us from correctly indicating that high volume actually overrides the whole sentence.

5. Forms and Functions of Punctuation

After discussing punctuation from different but complementary points of view, it is important to see—without duplicating the functional and normative explanations offered in the existing books on the subject—what exactly is involved in nonverbal language and what in punctuation; in other words, the voice modifications and silences we produce and the morphological and functional classification of the representational devices afforded by the present punctuation system, what is and what is not representable when we wish to express attitudes that are perfectly clear in our minds. The basis for this discussion is the chart 'Morphological and Functional Classification of Features in Punctuation' (Fig. 8.1), which contains in round brackets the new or modified symbols with which I feel we could improve our repertoire. But a cursory glance at the chart suggests two considerations which help to understand further the true nature of punctuation, concerning both the duration of the phenomena symbolized and the functional objective of the symbols involved.

Overriding and momentary features

The first of these considerations is the basic differentiation between features which override whole stretches of speech from those which cover only momentary portions—although the former may occur very briefly as well—and whether they are directly represented or simply evoked by association with more complex features of which they may be just components. The features included in Fig. 8.1 are, according to this criterion, distributed in the following way in the existing punctuation system (see the classification of paralanguage in Chapter 5).

Overriding

volume	represented by exclamation (high), quotation (higher), emphasis (higher), interpolations (lower)
tempo	evoked by exclamation (faster), interpolation (faster), emphasis (slower)
pitch level	represented by interrogation (higher/level), exclamation (higher/lower), emphasis (higher/lower), quotation (higher), interpolation (lower)
pitch range	evoked by interrogation (narrow/wide), exclamation (narrow), quotation (wider), interpolation (narrower)
all qualifiers	only precise articulation (by quotation, emphasis) and tension (by high volume features and emphasis) are evoked
all differentiators	neither represented nor evoked

Functions	Syntactical							Quantitative							Qualitative											
	pauses			stop	interpolations			duration —omission			silences				emphasis						voice volume		interro-gation	basic affects		respira-tion
labels	comma	semi-colon	colon	period	commas	paren-thesis	hyphens	quicken-ing	drawling	clipping	dash	double dash	suspen-sion	silence	quota-tion	major stress	italics	hyphen-ation	capitals	ve-hemence	exclam-ation	whisper	interro-gation	laugh-ing	crying	ingres-sion
paralinguistic features	[,]	[;]	[:]	[.]	[, ,]	[( )]	[- -]	[.] [. .]	[repeti-tion]	['] [deletion]	[–]	[—]	[. . .]	[. . . . . .]	[" "]	(')	[*italics*]	[- - -]	[CAPITALS]	(¡ !]	(¡¡ !!]	(+ +)	(¿ ?]	(^ ^)	(˜ ˜)	(› ‹)
silence	tone group juncture	larger juncture	similar duration	longer pause or stop	tone group juncture	tone group juncture	tone group juncture				brief	longer	brief	long												
volume					lower	lower	lower								slightly higher	higher	slightly higher	higher/ lower	higher	slightly higher	high	very low		variable	variable	
tempo					faster	faster	faster	fast	slow	fast						slower	slower	slower	slower	slower	faster					
pitch-level					lower	lower	lower								higher/ lower	higher	variable				higher/ lower		higher/ lower			
pitch register	raising/ falling	level/ falling	raising/ falling	falling												raising							high/ low			
pitch interval	variable				variable	variable	variable								variable											
pitch range					narrower	narrower	narrower														narrow		wide/ narrow			
syllabic length	longer				longer bef & aft.	longer bef & aft.	longer bef & aft.	short	long	very short			long	long		longer		longer	long	slightly longer						
intonation range																wider										
rhythm								stacatto	glissando	stacatto														irregu-lar	irregu-lar	
respiratory control																										ingres-sion
glottis control																						whisper				
articulatory control																	more precise	precise								
articulatory tension																	slightly tenser	tense	tenser	slightly tenser	very tense					
laughter																								variable	variable	
crying																										
movement								faster	slower			possibly slow	possibly slow	possibly slow		possibly slow				possibly slow						
stillness									possible		possible	possible	possible	possible												

	capitals	vehemence	exclamation	whisper	interrogation	laughing	crying	ingression
Possible combinations	(!CAPIT!]	(¿¡ !!?]	[¡¡ !!?]	(¿ ?)	('¿ ?,)	(¿̂ ?̂)	(›̆ ‹̆)	(¡› ‹!)
	(¿CAPI?]	(↑ ↓)	(¡¡ !!)	(+̂ +̂)		(› ‹)		(¡¡› ‹!!)
	(+CAPI+)	(¡̂ !̂)	(¡̂¡ !̂!)	(+̆ +̆)				(+› ‹+)
		(¡̆ !̆)	(¡̆¡ !̆!)					

1. Punctuation here is understood as representing speech only, disregarding other uses.
2. Symbols between round brackets or besides one round bracket are new.
3. Paralinguistic clusters of features neither represented nor evoked are: timbre, resonance, laryngeal control, velar control, pharyngeal control, labial control, and maxillary control.
4. Movement and stillness are only evoked, not represented, as co-occurent with or contextual to words and paralanguage.
5. Possible combinations of symbols at right can be expanded to suit the purpose.

FIG. 8.1. Morphological and Functional Classification of Features in Punctuation.

Momentary

pitch register	represented by juncture marks (higher/level/lower)
syllabic length	evoked by clipping (shorter), ellipsis (drawling), hesitation (drawling)
all qualifiers	only articulatory control (by emphasis) and tension (by exclamation and emphasis) are evoked
all differentiators	neither represented nor evoked.

One could add to that outline two more features within the Basic Triple Structure that appear also in the chart: movement, evoked, but more ambiguously, by drawling (slower), silences (possibly slower), and emphasis (possibly slower); and stillness, also ambiguously evoked by drawling (possible), and silences (possible).

Representation, not only evocation, is inevitably ambiguous and, not being susceptible of improvement due to the very nature of writing, will always depend upon other adjacent attitudinal elements and certain culture-bound speech features (circumstantial degree of high volume, the pitch of interrogation, etc.). Evocation, then, seems to be removed from reality one step further and depends even more than representation upon the reader's cultural and intellectual competence, and his fluency in a foreign culture in the case of an original or translated foreign text. It is precisely all those paralinguistic features that the foreign reader so imperfectly may attach to the verbal written language when reading aloud. These are, in sum, the shortcomings inherent in a secondary system like writing, and any attempts at 'enriching' the present punctuation system should be made with great caution. A statement that does not contradict the very purpose of this paper, but rather warns one while carrying out the task of weighing the merits and limitations of the existing system, with a view to considering some possible modifications and additions without going to the absurd extreme of developing a cumbersome and unpractical system.

Regulatory, quantitative, and qualitative features

A second look at the chart reveals four main functional categories of phenomena further subdivided into six others, under which each symbol performs a more specific function: (a) *syntactical or regulatory*, that is, serving to indicate the limits of syntactical structures (thus avoiding semantic ambiguities), to integrate interpolated thoughts and to make and measure silences; (b) *quantitative*, either omitting or lengthening utterances in the normal flow of speech; and (c) *qualitative*, the most attitudinal of the three, as it involves paralinguistic primary qualities and qualifiers, to which a few modifiers (both qualifiers and differentiators) could be added. This functional classification can be schematized (with proposed symbols, discussed later, in round brackets) like this:

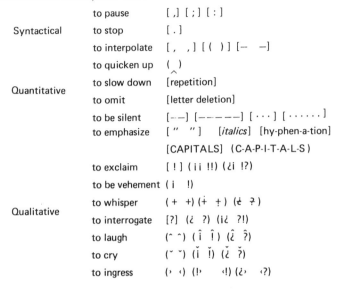

	to pause	[,] [;] [:]
Syntactical	to stop	[.]
	to interpolate	[, ,] [( )] [– –]
	to quicken up	(‸)
Quantitative	to slow down	[repetition]
	to omit	[letter deletion]
	to be silent	[––] [–––––] [· · ·] [· · · · · ·]
	to emphasize	[" "] [*italics*] [hy-phen-a-tion] [CAPITALS] (C-A-P-I-T-A-L-S)
	to exclaim	[!] (¡ ¡ !!) (¿¡ !?)
	to be vehement	(¡ !)
Qualitative	to whisper	(+ +) (+̇ +̣) (¿̶ ?̶)
	to interrogate	[?] (¿ ?) (¡¿ ?!)
	to laugh	(ˆ ˆ) (¡̂ !̂) (¿̂ ?̂)
	to cry	(˘ ˘) (¡̆ !̆) (¿̆ ?̆)
	to ingress	(› ‹) (!› ‹!) (¿› ‹?)

FIG. 8.2. Functional Classification of Punctuation Symbols.

6. Limitations and Possibilities in the Present Punctuation System

All the comments made so far point at the very nature of the written text and also at its inherent limitations, what can or cannot be expressed or suggested, and consequently at the nature of reading as the visual-evocative intellectual experience pointed out earlier. The inadequacy of words (the basis of the interdisciplinary development of nonverbal communication studies) without the support of sign-conveying nonverbal systems becomes most acute when we attempt to transcribe speech on paper. Written language barely bridges the gap between the two, and certainly more nonverbal elements are grasped through evocation than through actual symbolization.

Further, it has been made clear that punctuation evokes kinesic behavior simply because kinesics is part of the Basic Triple Structure, but that this association takes place only on an intellectual-associative level and not on a visual one.

It is at this point, then, following Figs. 8.1 and 8.2, that one may arrive at certain otherwise obvious conclusions concerning some of the current symbols, whose forms and/or functions could be modified, and those new ones which I am proposing below as additions to the system.

Interpolation

Using only one dash [—] to interpolate in narrative literature before the final stop can cause the uncertainty of whether it is a silence or the equivalent of a bracket, therefore either round brackets [( )] or two hyphens [- -] would make interpolation clear enough.

Omission, length, and tempo

The term 'clipping' is often used quite ambiguously to refer both to quickening of tempo and to actual clipping or curtailment of the word.

Clipping is indicated by apostrophe ['] for either apocopated (mos', an', foun') or syncopated speech (ma'am, catt'l, can't), in which there is a phoneme loss.

The modification of the length of a word, but preserving all its phonemes, consists of: *quickening* of tempo, which could be represented by an angular circumflex [$_\wedge$] under a syllable, or at both ends of a stretch of speech [$_\wedge$ $_\wedge$] when it is conspicuously shortened in tempo (not in the number of sounds); and *drawling*, when phonemes are stretched in one or more syllables, which usually we represent by repeating vowels and consonants ('Grreeat!,' 'Ooooh, yees!'); better than dashes, which symbolize silences more accurately. Drawling does not necessarily coincide with the tensely articulated marked emphasis represented by hy-phen-a-tion.

Silences

A careful yet not at all exhaustive study of the various silences that writers attempt to represent in literature with the very limited means at their disposal, reveals at least ten well differentiated categories of absence of speech, apart from the normative syntactical pauses and stops marked by [,], [;], [:], and [.].

The following are literary examples, gleaned from some personal readings, of the silences referred to, in which a rather heterogenous and at times ambiguous use of punctuation is observed. Each type could, of course, be subdivided (as hinted by the italicized functional labels) and the topic would deserve an elaborate paper by itself.[3]

a. *Understood lexical ellipsis* either to avoid saying something or when verbal completion is superfluous: "—Is there any . . . no trouble I hope? I see you are . . . (Joyce, *U*)," "[. . .] et, si vous aviez des commisions à me donner . . ." (Balzac, *EG*). *Self-imposed ellipsis*: "—¿Es que te parece bien que a mis hijos . . .? [. . .]/—¿Qué quieres que se le haga? A su edad . . ." (Hortelano, *TV*), " 'It's laying there, watching Cash whittle on that damn . . .' Jewel says. He says it harshly, savagely, but he does not say the word" (Faulkner, *ALD*).

b. *Introductory pause* after one or two words, generally for questioning: "—Dis-moi, Gertrude . . . t'a-t-il dit qu'il t'aimait?" (Gide, *SP*).

c. *Post-interrogation pause*: "—Vous m'aimez? . . . dit-elle" (Balzac, *EG*).

d. *Emotional pause*: " 'Jewel,' ma said, looking at him. 'I'll give—I'll give—give—' Then she began to cry" (Faulkner, *ALD*), "Elle s'agenouilla près de lui /«Antoine . . . Antoine . . .»" (Sagan, *CH*), "Vous savez bien que c'est vous que j'aime, pasteur . . . Oh! pourquoi retirez-vous votre main?" (Gide, *SP*).

e. *Lexical hesitance*: "Je voudrai savoir si je ne . . . comment dites-vous cela? . . . si je ne . . . [. . .]" (Gide, *SP*), "—Si, unos bombones . . . La Filo es como una criatura, es igual que un . . ." (Cela, *LC*).

f. *Thought hesitance*: ". . . et je viendrai prendre vos dernieres instructions a . . . a quelle heure?" (Balzac, *EG*).

g. *Insecurity*: " 'O—how stupid this is! I thought my visitor was—your friend—your husband—Mrs. Fowley, as I suppose you call yourself?" (Hardy, *JO*).

h. *Concealment*: " "Yes—yes, I do. But . . ." Herzog hesitated." (Bellow, *H*), " 'I know,' she said. 'I'—Then she stopped, and I said, / 'Know what?' / 'Nothing,' she said." (Faulkner, *ALD*).

i. *Carrying or thinking pause* or indefinite silence, after one or several words which elicit a series of memories or associations: ". . . how nice it's gonna be, in California. Never cold. An' fruit ever'place [. . .] I wonder—that is, if we all get jobs an' all work—maybe [. . .]," Steinbeck, *GW*), "[. . .] avec un petit sourire complice:/«Les hommes sont si desordennés . . .»" (Sagan, *CH*).

j. *Interpolative pause*: "[. . .] to have to limp around on one short leg for the balance of your life—if you walk at all again." (Faulkner, *ALD*).

k. *Interruption by someone else* overlapping speech or action: "[. . .] he is my boy. He was sent to get the coal. He—" / "We don't mind what they pick around the yard," interrupted the detective [. . .]" (Dreiser, *JG*), "—No, Mr. Bloom said, the son himself. . . . / Martin Cunningham thwarted his speech rudely." (Joyce, *U*), "[. . .] je voulais vous prier ce matin de . . . / —De vous acheter cela? di Grandet en l'interrompant." (Balzac, *EG*).

l. *Action-filled interruption*, a break during which a bodily activity can be carried out: " "That you Ed? . . . Why Ed they are jacks. How extravagant of you." [Her hair was over her face] (Dos Passos, *MT*), "—Ecoutez, ma chère cousine, j'ai lá . . . Il s'interrompit pour montrer [. . .] [Balzac, *EG*).

m. *Impaired speech*: "—C'es bien di . . . di . . . di . . . différent, si çâââ ne coû . . . ou . . . ou . . . ou . . . oûte pas . . . pas . . . pas plus cher, di Grandet" (Balzac, *EG*).

For all these silences writers use only [—], [——], [. . .] and [. . . . . .], often with the same symbol for different types of silences. However, considering that adding any more symbols for silence not only would be cumbersome, but would even interfere with the writer's stylistic freedom and with the intellectual intepretative nuances of the very task of reading, I feel that a first major differentiation could be made between *controlled or voluntary silences* (ellipsis, introductory, post-interrogation, emotional, hesitation, carrying or thinking, and interpolative), for which a variable number of *dots* could be used consistently, and *imposed silences* (interruptions and impaired speech), for which short dash [—] and long dash [——] respectively could also be used consistently. Thus we can choose between shortening or lengthening these symbols, but trying to legislate on specific uses, not only would be absurd but would mean trespassing the writer's own inviolable territory.

Only a sensible suggestion could be made: that shorter and longer silences of the types just mentioned be consistently represented by shorter and longer symbols. Such ambiguity as between an interruption and an ending pause should and could be easily avoided, since the context does not necessarily make it clear.

Major stress

The highly semantic function of the major stress accompanied by higher pitch is totally lost in written language, when such a distinct attitudinal phenomenon is so significant in English, as it distinguishes two different occurrences of identical verbal expressions. An accent [´] placed over the vowel could easily differentiate 'Excuse me!' (pardon me) from 'Excuse mé!' (as used by some pseudorefined persons after belching as part of their etiquette), 'Oh, yes!' ('I know', 'Of course') from 'Óh, yes!' ('I see!'), 'I'll be there' ('I plan to be') from 'Í'll be there' ('I certainly will, if not the others'). This is the major stress that modifies meaning, and not only emphasis, and the systematic use of the accent (or a mark that would not conflict with the use of [´] in other languages) would help not only the native reader but even more the foreign one as well as the professional translator, since this stress reveals marked emotional, cultural, and even socioeconomic features and situations.

Emphasis

On the other hand, the emphasis placed on words and sentences in different degrees and independently of volume modifications, is currently symbolized (apart, possibly, from single quotation marks) by quotation marks, italics, capitals, and hyphenation, which in context seem to correspond to: *mild emphasis* (*italics*), *marked emphasis* (hy-phen-a-tion) and *high emphasis* (CAPITALS), through which more precise and tenser articulation gradually increases independently of high volume; volume, then, symbolized by the current exclamation marks, would accompany only capitals, while *high marked emphasis* would be conveyed by placing major-stress accents on each syllable of capitalized speech, i.e., Í DÓN'T WÁNT YOÚ TÓ GÓ, without shouting.

Loud voice, vehemence, and whispering

Voice volume, such a strong attitudinal manifestation, is basic in actual speech, but not in writing, because of the perpetuation of two illogical limitations: the failure to accurately represent its overriding quality (as pointed out when discussing the reading process earlier) and the lack of a low-volume symbol as opposed to high volume.

The single final exclamation mark [!] stands today as the only symbol for four different speech phonemena: (a) all degrees and types of ordinary loud voice ('Hello!', 'Hey, look!'); (b) tense affective low-volume utterances (Don't let me see you again, you scoundrel!); (c) the also strongly attitudinal use of pitch, more important than volume in expressions like 'Really!' with high pitch (It's true) and 'Really!' with low pitch (Shame on you); and, as if it were not enough, (d) tense, subdued loud whisper; so the novelist must add that "he whispered earnestly in his ear while grabbing his arm", or something of the sort.

In sum, the confusing versatility of the exclamation mark only shows its great ambiguity. But this ambiguity is most apparent in the fact that [!] stands for an overriding feature which often the reader's eyes cannot possibly detect on time. Since he decodes the text through a primary visual channel, his macular vision cannot read the far end of the wholly exclamatory sentence (where the exclamation mark is placed!), much less so if that end is on the next line; consequently the effect of [!] is not triggered in the mind and attached to the printed words before the eyes hit the end of that sentence, or very near it, for it may be semantically relevant, but that is not necessarily (grammatically or otherwise) conveyed by the context.

If punctuation attempts to reflect the reality of speech, but [!] is only one end of an overriding feature, it seems clear that an opening exclamation mark [¡] (as is used in Spanish) should be proposed as the most logical addition to the current system. We cannot readily accept the argument that the exclamatory quality is indicated in English by the syntactical order, for we do not always have a relative like 'What a—!' or an adverb like 'How—!', and even these do not necessarily lead to an exclamatory sentence, e.g., 'How mistaken I was when I did it, anyone could see'.

On the other hand, in actual speech the exclamatory or high-volume feature begins only near the end of the sentence in many instances, and the initial or opening [¡] can then be as misleading as is its absence on other occasions. This would seem to warrant the only justified use of the final or closing [!] to indicate the gradual built-up volume of the voice towards the end.

Another very serious limitation of the exclamation mark one should try to solve is, as has just been indicated, that 'exclamation' does not always necessarily imply 'high volume' but only *vehement expression* of thought, for which emphatic punctuation, up to accented capitals, has already been suggested. This causes in narrative literature (and certainly, for the actor, in a play) another typical ambiguity. Countless times a character's voice is not being raised at all, on the contrary, it is even low, though tense and vehement; but the writer's only recourse is the exclamation [!], as in: 'Phillotson smiled sadly. "You are an odd creature!" he murmured as the sun glowed in his eyes. "The idea of your coming to see me after what has passed!" ' (Hardy, *JO*). It is clear that the person is murmuring and definitely not shouting or even elevating his voice. In the same manner many tender, subdued love scenes are copiously punctuated in literature with exclamation marks, for lack of a more precise mark. This obvious paralinguistic difference in speech would amply justify its corresponding differentiation in the punctuation system. If we look at all the symbols for emphasis, we realize how difficult it would be to replace [!] for vehement speech with, for instance, italics or capitals. Therefore, without deviating much from the practice of so many years, the only sensible solution would be perhaps to duplicate the exclamation mark [¡¡ !!] for actual shouting, and leave the simple [¡ !] for vehement voice, as *vehemence mark*, or more colloquially, 'intensity mark'.

Now, in addition to high volume, we use very low volume too in situations in which its use is as natural as shouting is in others, and yet, for no logical reasons whatsoever, we have no means of representing any degree of overriding whispering as opposed to loud voice. In other words, a writer can always spare any comments on his character's high-volume speech if he so wishes because he can resort to [!], but he must necessarily explain that those words are going to be or were whispered. Again, there is no reason to blindly accept the historical limitations of our punctuation systems, and I am proposing the introduction of opening and closing *whisper marks* [+ +], combined with [¡ !] for tense (false high volume) whisper, [$\dot{+}$ $\dot{\top}$], as well as with the interrogation mark, as suggested below, [$\dot{ c}$?], although I would not necessarily quarrel over the choice of one mark or another.

Interrogation

As with high volume, the interrogation [?] is not all clear in a long written sentence which does not begin, in English, with an auxiliary verb ('Do you—') or inverted syntactical order ('Where were you—'), and relatives do not necessarily initiate a questioning sentence. We read, 'Which one went there when the house was empty nobody knows', but it is only when we get to 'nobody' that we know it is not an interrogation so we may or may not have to make our mental rereading of the sentence. As with exclamation, this momentary ambiguity when reading can be sensibly solved by using opening and closing interrogations [¿ ?], combined when needed with exclamations [¡¿ ?!] and with whisper [¿̵ ?̵]. If, as Husband and Husband (1905: 71) noted, "In speech tone helps to get closer to sense than does grammar alone," let us then indicate tone as the overriding feature it is. Skelton's (1933: 38) statement that any questions demanding yes/no answers have rising inflection is not exactly true, since questions ending in '—, would you?' or '—, isn't it?' are most attitudinal and can be spoken with rising or falling pitch.

Crying and laughter

If punctuation strives to convey as basic an emotional paralinguistic attitude as shouting, which in turn justifies the representation of whispering, written language could most logically adopt the symbolization of two equally basic and overriding features, *crying* and *laughter*, easily conveyed by two downward and two upward limiting circumflexes respectively, [ˆ ˆ] and [ˇ ˇ], which can be further combined with exclamations [¡¡̂ !̂!], [¡¡̌ !̌!], and interrogations, [¿̂ ?̂], [¿̌ ?̌].

I would not speak for these as strongly as for the four previous features, but we must admit that the communicative value of overriding crying and laughter would also warrant the use of representational marks as legitimately as some other features did in the past.

The idea of incorporating crying and laughter into the paralinguistic repertoire of written language is not gratuitous at all. While a narrative writer or a playwright could still describe the particular characteristics of his character's weeping or guffawing, before or after using the punctuation marks, the letter writer would also be able (only we simply are not used to this possibility) to attach to his handwritten (but imagined or even real) speech a tone of sincere grief or sadness, or the sarcasm or happiness of laughter running through the words. As with loud voice, whisper and interrogation, laughter and crying are basic displays of human nature, elicited in both interactive and noninteractive situation, and if they had invented written symbols to represent them along with other affect displays, we would use them today as casually as we use the established ones.

Ingressive speech

Finally, it seems to me that if speech can be produced both with egressive air (as is usually the case) and with *ingressive air*, the latter (very rare indeed but most significative) could be indicated with two inward horizontal circumflexes, [›   ‹]. Ingressive speech, besides being a feature of English in the 'Yeah' used in the Atlantic Provinces of Canada (often as a duplication of an immediately preceding egressive 'Yes') and of Swedish in the feminine *Ja*!, it occurs in various lengths in situations of terror, surprise, indignation and acute physical pain.

In conclusion, I feel that this attempt to grant our punctuation system, so arbitrarily limited, greater paralinguistic possibilities has been justified. I feel further that the proposal of six new symbols for quick tempo, stress, whisper, laughing, crying, and ingression, plus the modification of emphasis, loud voice and interrogation, can only enrich written language, interferring neither with the literary aspect of writing nor with the visual-intellectual process of reading.

Speaking on a piece of paper will never approach the physical complexity of oral speech, but its possibilities can no doubt be enhanced. And while the forms of the new symbols respond to my personal criterion of availability (when possible) from the typewriter and their combinatory features, they could certainly be different, and their specific adoption could be open to discussion. No other alternatives, however, would lack their own drawbacks, and their purpose would still remain the same.

Notes

1. Although I discussed briefly some of the problems posed by punctuation, mainly when dealing with nonverbal communication in narrative literature (Poyatos 1976a, 1977b, 1981a), I wrote my first full-length paper on the subject for the 1977 International Congress of Phonetic Sciences (Poyatos 1981d).
2. A comprehensive work dealing with the development of punctuation systems in at least European cultures is, to my knowledge, lacking. More or less detailed references are found in *Encyclopaedia Britannica* (vol. 19, 1971, 520–523), *Enciclopedia Italiana* (vol. 28, 1949, 546–548) for Italian punctuation, and in the books of Husband and Husband (1905), Partridge (1953, 1966), Skelton (1933) and others.
3. The works quoted, with the initials used above in titles are:
   Balzac, Honoré: *Eugénie Grandet* (1833) *EG*
   Bellow, Saul: *Herzog* (1964) *H*
   Cela, Camilo José: *La colmena* (1951) *LC*
   Dos Passos, John: *Manhattan Transfer* (1925) *MH*
   Dreiser, Theodore: *Jennie Gerhardt* (1911) *JG*
   Faulkner, William: *As I Lay Dying* (1930) *ALD*
   Gide, André: *La symphonie pastorale* (1919) *SP*
   Hardy, Thomas: *Jude the Obscure* (1895) *JO*
   Hortelano, Juan García: *Tormenta de verano* (1962) *TV*
   Joyce, James: *Ulysses* (1922) *U*
   Sagan, Francoise: *La chamade* (1965) *LC*
   Steinbeck, John: *Grapes of Wrath* (1939) *GW*

9

Nonverbal Communication in the Novel: the Author–Character–Reader Relationship[1] *

The rank on his rounce him ruched in his sadel,
And runischly his reden he reled aboute,
Bende his bresed browes, blicande grene,
Wayved his berde for to waite whoso wolde rise.

(*Sir Gawayne and the Grene Knight*, vv. 303–6)

Mr. Weller, the elder, gave vent to an extraordinary sound, which being neither a groan, nor a grunt, nor a gasp, nor a growl, seemed to partake in some degree of the character of all four.

(Dickens, *Pickwick Papers*, LII)[2]

1. Nonverbal Communication in the Printed Narrative Text

A cursory reading of a page in a novel, where both the writer and his characters speak (they among themselves, he to us), that is, where an interactive conversational encounter takes place alternating with the author's own observations about it, shows that if we were to rely exclusively on what words those characters say—depicted on paper as printed lexemes—and on a few punctuation marks, plus some instances of extralinguistic communicative features, a good part (perhaps the most important one) of the total human message would be simply lost, even though not so in the mind of the novelist.

A page picked at random from the end of chapter eight in Huxley's *Point Counterpoint*, for instance, in which a dialog is carried out among Spandrell, George Rampion and Mary Rampion,[3] appears to be constructed of the following elements:

(a) a printed morphologico-syntactical exchange whose morphemes and lexemes express a present situation with evocations of the last fifteen years, and a series of intellectual concepts and of references to the social relationship of marriage; to which the author added a few structural punctuation

* Superscript numbers refer to Notes at end of chapter.

marks, some quotation marks to indicate direct speech, periods that limit complete sentences, and commas that suggest juncture points and pauses;

(b) two exclamation marks, one question mark, suspension points in two places and commas, all of them trying to symbolize—but unsatisfactorily representing—certain suprasegmental elements with which to complement the reader's imagined paralinguistic features concomitant with the linguistic ones;

(c) three paralinguistic descriptions concerning: Spandrell's peculiar way of laughing on two occasions (later used as a recurrent identification) and George Rampion's way of interrupting "with impatience" (a cultural, and not necessarily universal, quickening of the speech rhythm, and pitch raising);

(d) eleven descriptions of the kinesic behavior of the three participants in their face-to-face conversation, of which: two describe the way Spandrell throws back his head before laughing, and one the way he looks from Mary to Rampion "almost triumphantly"; two more, Rampion's frowning at what is being said, one his "staring into his coffee cup," and one his looking at Spandrell "distastefully"; and two, Mary's glancing at her husband, once "enquiringly," one her lighting a cigarette, and one her shutting her eyes to think of her youth.

(e) the author's exclusive comments on the characters' interrelationships, on their feelings towards each other, now and at other times, and on their very thoughts.

Another passage might have had fewer, or more, elements to be broken into. This example will suffice. It was meant simply to show the limited number of devices available to a novelist, and ultimately to a printer, for the readable conveyance of people's physical and intellectual activities, and this we can grasp at first sight.

A second look at the same page, however, will tell us:

(a) that a substantial part of the printed text is aimed at describing nonverbal activities which are produced either simultaneously with words or alternating with them;

(b) that the author, by so doing, openly acknowledges the limitations of his written-typographical presentation of verbal behavior to portray vividly the physical and psychological configurations of his characters;

(c) that the ratio between verbal and nonverbal activities must be an indication of certain stylistic characteristics more accentuated in some novelists than in others, and therefore an important touchstone for the analysis of the novel; and

(d) that, as I will specify later, the repertoire of nonverbal communication symbols is much more limited than the one symbolizing verbal language, that is, what traditionally—but perhaps not one hundred percent accurately—we call words.

Once the basic observations about a printed narrative text are made, the logical question is which human nonverbal communicative activities are acknowledged by novelists in general as elements complementary to their characters' verbal ones. The answer is those produced by the human body as a socializing organism, which, although psychomuscularly and chemically originated, we can contrast against the intellectual ones, and thus subsume under what has been discussed as *external somatic communication* (Chapter 3), since most of the semantic content of face-to-face interaction is conveyed by the body through motor, respiratory, dermal, thermal and chemical channels, which includes four basic categories: acoustic (verbal language, paralanguage, and audible gestures, mainly), visual (gestures and postures, use of space, body appearance, dermal changes, and secretions), olfactory (body odors and perfumes), and tactile (contact movements and kinesthetic perception of others); which are distributed among vocal-verbal, vocal-nonverbal and nonvocal-nonverbal forms of communication.

All bodily activities within those categories are present in narrative fiction—not only the direct perception of someone else's body but its synesthesial appreciation—and writers, in greater or lesser degree, try to convey to their readers the perception of blushing and goose flesh, of perspiration and tears, of soft skin and body scents. Naturally, the degree in which bodily phenomena are granted true literary and intellectual values depends entirely on the artistry of the narrator, and this quality plus the activities themselves deserve serious attention.

Etiemble, in his novel *Blason d'un corps* (1961) exalts bodily messages and carries to extremes the appreciation of the type of bodily messages that are usually not talked or written about in connection with the feeling of love, but rejected by the average sensitivity. His narrator, besides his childhood enjoyment of the smell of his own sweat, relives in the letters to his dead lover: "je te vis, ma sirène, plonger dans l'écume incertaine, et t'enfouir le visage dans mes chemises. Les yeux clos, tu respirais fort, fort, fort" (115), and her smelling his armpits and taking the hair with her teeth (116); but above all his tactile and olefactory enjoyment of her body, "le plaisir olfactif s'ajoutant au tactile" (155), explaining that "C'est par les poiles qu'on aime, et pour la sueur; par et pour les odeurs des diverses parties du corps" (155).

In addition, the secondary perceptual processes that take place through the synesthesial associations discussed in Chapter 2 play an important role, of which the narrator is conscious in greater or lesser degree, in the reader's decoding stage of the text.

The present perspective of nonverbal communication applied to narration concentrates only on the Basic Triple Structure of Human Communication Behavior, language-paralanguage-kinesics, other systems being discussed under literary anthropology in Chapter 10. I have argued before how it is unrealistic to try to isolate any of them in a serious study of the actual communication situation—either from a structural point of view or from a semantic one—for even the reader of narrative literature will consciously or unconsciously reconstruct, according to his sensitiveness and to the elements provided by the writer, words, 'tone of voice' and 'gestures'.

It is those three elements, jointly or independently, that the reader appreciates, above all others, in the fictional characters, and that is why I have so far excluded even proxemic behavior when analyzing nonverbal communication in the narrative text, in spite of its sociopsychological and cultural values. Proxemic behavior can actually be absent when language, paralanguage and kinesics cooccur, even though imperceptibly at times, as when only the eyes or a single muscle move. As for chronemic behavior, although time—including the duration of silences—plays an important structural function in the interactive encounter being depicted in the text, and on some occasions defines certain social and cultural characteristics, it is not an essential element by which to judge the stylistic and technical qualities of a narrator, as are language, paralanguage and kinesics.

A further note on the role of punctuation

After identifying nonverbal communication in the written text and acknowledging its preponderance among other forms of communication (just as happens in real life), I would like to point out how writers and printers have managed heretofore to represent nonverbal elements (implied already in Chapter 7), so that I may later discuss how the message is transmitted from the original author, or creator of characters, to the ultimate, but multiple, recreator, the reader. Although a semiotic discussion of the encoding and decoding of nonverbal communication since the first printed narrative texts would probably deserve a volume by itself, I will just refer in passing to the relatively simple and most arbitrary development of punctuation marks, originated in the Greek and Roman rhetorical signs deviced for the reading aloud of texts, in medieval biblical and liturgical manuscripts read in churches and refectories, in the French and Italian printing shops of the Renaissance, and in some seventeenth-century additions.

As for the role of the writers themselves, little or no attempt seems to have been made on their part to enrich the very poor repertoire at their disposal, although a reasonable number of additional symbols for representing certain features of human interactive behavior would simply be feasible. However, neither printers nor writers during the great periods of the modern novel—so concerned with physical and psychological realism—have shown much initiative for trying to represent many of the nonverbal qualities of speech and voice modifications that play such an important role in personal interaction, which would assist readers in their silent or audible reading of the characters' communicative peculiarities. Apart from some individual efforts to transcribe a few paralinguistic alternants ('Er—', 'Ugh!'), exclamation and interrogation marks can be doubled, tripled, or combined. Ambiguity would be avoided in English, German, French, etc., in cases in which syntactical order does not indicate the interrogative or exclamative inflections, if the marks were placed also at the beginning of the sentence, as I do in this book when I punctuate examples of the different topics discussed. A long dash [——], or suspension or ellipsis points [. . .], are used to represent direct speech, and indistinctively to suggest the level juncture typical of hesitation and the true ellipsis caused by interruption or by the cutting-in of an interlocutor; a parenthesis suggests the lower pitch of an insertion; *italics* indicate emphasis, and hy-phen-a-ted words indicate emphasis and also the breathless rhythm of accelerated speech. But no new symbols have been introduced in the traditional repertoire, and writers have gone as far only as changing the size of the letters (to indicate VERY HIGH VOLUME or INDIGNATION) or using apostrophes to represent syncopated and apocopated rural speech. I would not just say that "writers are not linguists and have other needs and interests than that of making their writing a perfect image of their speech" (Bolinger 1968: 158), because the fact is that linguists do not seem to express serious concern about the limitations of written language, nor about a possible revision of the system itself.

2. Paralanguage: Literary Description and Transcription

Although some of the voice inflections represented by thc established punctuation symbols discussed before would be visually perceived as gestures as well, that is, audible gestures, it is actually in paralanguage—the closest to audible verbal segmental and suprasegmental language—and not in kinesics, that we can trace an effort to transcribe certain speech qualities not revealed by written words. It is also in that area that we can foresee certain ways to enrich the written and printed rendering of spoken language by means of both direct orthographic transcriptions similar to 'Pst' or the ambiguous 'Tsk-tsk', and indirect voice quality indicators for whispering (as opposed to the exclamation mark), sighing speech, panting speech, etc. It is quite obvious that if a few signs exist in written language to which authors resort in a true effort to represent, and not describe, certain sounds and paralinguistic features, but only a very small number of them, there is no reason why some additional ones could not be incorporated into the existing repertoire without interfering with the stylistic aims of literary works.

Thus, knowing that both the average letter-writing layman and the professional novelist strive, in different degrees, to achieve a certain paralinguistic realism, and that a few solutions have been used for centuries while others reflect today's concern, I would like to suggest the possible objectives in this endeavor by simply outlining the classification of paralinguistic phenomena I have differentiated. The challenge it presents for the written representation of nonverbal-vocal interpersonal communicative behavior could generate much research on the part of linguists, and certainly some interest for a minimum of experimentation on the part of novelists.

What follows is only a series of examples illustrating the various paralinguistic phenomena (dealt with in Chapter 3) as used by the narrator.

A. *Primary qualities:* timbre, pitch level, pitch registers, pitch interval, intonation range, resonance, volume, syllabic duration, overall tempo, and general rhythm of speech.

> "You're revolting," said Daisy. She turned to me, and her voice, dropping an octave lower, filled the room with thrilling scorn. (Fitzgerald, *GG*, VII, 100)

B. *Qualifiers:* glottalic control, velar control, articulatory control, articulatory tension, pharyngeal control, laryngeal control, labial control, and respiratory control.

> "You don't know what it is to be a cripple. Of course you don't like me. I can't expect you to." / "Philip, I didn't mean that," she answered quickly, with a sudden break of pity in her voice [. . .] / He was beginning to act now, and his voice was husky and low. (Maugham, *HB*, LXI, 367)

C. *Differentiators:* forms and degrees of whispering, of loud voice, of crying, of laughing, etc., when they override words.

> "Go away," she cried through her tears, "go away." (Huxley, *PC*, XIII, 185)

D. *Alternants:* consonantal (bilabial, labiodental, whistling, clicking, velar), vocalic (mainly glottalized voiced central vowel-like sounds, with up to five pitch levels and varying nasalization, each of which has a closed-lip variant with identical or almost identical meaning), inarticulated (pharyngeal, nasopharyngeal, and nareal frictions), and pausal (modified speech pauses with different meanings).

> Her round eyes started and her mild mouth gaped. "A gentleman?" she gasped [. . .] She broke into a breathless affirmative groan. (James, *TS*, V, 44)

> "Hmph!" he murmured, with a movement of his head to one side [. . .] It was totally unassured. / Mrs. Hurstwood noticed the lack of colour in it. (Dreiser, *SC*, XXII, 217)

It is within alternants that we find most of the existing forms of written paralanguage ('Ssh', 'Hm', 'Mh-hm', 'Ha-ha', 'Grr', 'Pshoo') and also most of the nonverbal sounds which writers must describe with literary ability as the only way to include them in their narrative, thus lacking in the theater. The situation is rather absurd and merits serious investigation. Those sounds, although traditionally regarded as abnormal and nonspeech sounds from the point of view of our western languages, possess a perfectly 'normal' semantic value within our vocal communicative repertoire, form constructs that have as much lexical value as words, and are perfectly encoded and decoded by members of a culture as well as crossculturally. Therefore, there is no reason to believe that, if they were consistently represented by the existing orthographic signs, complemented by some additional ones, they could not appear as dictionary entries and be used in literary as well as in nonliterary writing. ¿Why should not the novelist or the playwrite be able to resort to a richer repertoire of vocally produced signs which actually exist in their minds when they are at work, which they have learned to use and perceive in their proper context, but which, due to restricting spelling and linguistic taboos, they cannot represent vividly on paper?

That writers acknowledge the semantic importance of paralinguistic features in their characters' speech, and how their description contributes to convey their vitality as individuals, is amply demonstrated in their efforts, not only to represent, but failing this, to describe how they speak, and not only quote what they say in words. The study of alternants in literature, whether described or transcribed, would cover perhaps the most important part of the paralinguistic repertoires of the characters, apart from the overriding qualities of their voices.

> "I'll tell 'ee what—you [Sue] ought not to marry this man again!" said Mrs. Eldin indignantly [. . .] / "Pshoo! You be t'other man's." (Hardy, *JO*, VI, v, 372)

> She breathed a vague relief. (James, *TS*, V, 41)

> "H'm!" said Gerald, in disapproval. (Lawrence, *WL*, II, 33)

> "Would you like to dine with me and my wife sometime?" / "Why . . . er . . . I'd be delighted." (Dos Passos, *MT*, III, 58)

> "He's talkin' red, agitating trouble." / "Hm-m-m." The deputy moved slowly around to see Floyd's profile [. . .] "Ever see 'im before?" the contractor insisted. / "Hmm, seems like I have." (Steinbeck, *GW*, XX, 235)

> "You wouldn't want them nice molars all smashed, would you?" / "Aw-haw. Big talk [. . .]" (O'Hara, *AS*, VI, 105)

> "Wagh! Whoo!" howled Remi in the evening streets of Frisco [. . .] "Aaah-how!" he wrapped himself around a pole to laugh. (Kerouac, *OR*, XI, 63)

As for silences (discussed in Chapter 6 and, as represented by punctuation, in Chapter 8), they are indicated in the novel as breaks in speech, which the author may fill by describing the still continuing paralinguistic (signs, hesitation ingressions), kinesic (gestures, postural shifts) or proxemic (distance shortening, orientation shift) behaviors. If he does not indicate silence verbally ('he gave a long sigh', 'she paused', 'there was a long pause/silence'), he can resort to a varying and eloquent series of suspension points that may take up to several lines.

Only from an acoustic point of view is silence the opposite of speech, but it is not complete as long as it is filled with consciously or unconsciously displayed paralinguistic sounds (hesitation clicks, narial egressions of contempt) that simply replace verbal expression. If there is a total absence of sound, however, the semantic content of that silence is then built up and defined by its duration and by the concomitant kinesic and/or proxemic behaviors; and those interactive breaks can carry many meanings, from the minimal pause of surprise or hesitation to the prolonged one that can become unbearable, or the infinitely expressive silences between Anna Karenina and her lover; in which case there is acoustic silence, but not communicative one, since Tolstoy tells us that they speak with "the flash of glances and smiles". We could refer to nonacoustic, nonvisual silence (in a telephone conversation, or from adjoining rooms), and yet time would grant that silence its meaning, and we would respond to our interlocutor according to our decoding of it. The incisive narrator recognizes the semantic importance of silences and uses them as interactive elements; in fact, as part of the repertoires of certain characters—and differentiates what we might call paralinguistically-filled silences, kinesically-filled silences, and proxemically-filled ones. In addition, the decoding functions of silence, as well as stillness and their costructuration with the surrounding activities are also profusely documented in the novel.

> "There is a space between us" he [Gudrun] said [. . .] / "But I'm very near," she [Gudrun] said caressively, gaily. / "Yet, distant", he said. / Again she was silent with pleasure before she answered speaking with a ready, thrilled voice. (Lawrence, *WL*, XII, 201)
>
> A hush fell on the class. Mr. Tate didn't break it but dug with his hands between his crossed thighs [. . .] A short loud laugh from Mr. Tate set the class more at ease. (Joyce, *PAYM*, 79)
>
> A moment of listening silence. (Malamud, *T*, 36)

One can observe that the narrator sometimes exaggerates the duration of interactive silences: "The insinuating gentleman sighed deeply, fixed his eyes on the spinster aunt's face for a couple of minutes [. . .]" (Dickens, *PP*, VIII, 144).

The writer's paralinguistic ability

Summing up this brief discussion of paralanguage in the novel, if we think, for instance, of Aldous Huxley's almost clinical descriptions of paralinguistic features, we realize that he is so conscious of their semantic and lexical properties that he makes a point of exercising his linguistic-stylistic ability, coupled to his acute perception of others, to describe how a person speaks and the 'nonwords' that person utters. In fact, he seems to develop more than many others a rich linguistic style to write about his characters' paralinguistic one. One cannot help wondering how his style would have been affected had he been able to resort to established written forms of such message-conveying sounds as "a brief and snorting laugh", or "a rueful little laugh". But most of our paralinguistic utterances having no written form, nor a label (a verb and a noun) to refer to them in a standard way, Huxley appears as extremely conscious of the role played by them in personal interaction:

> "Do you *really*?" It was an intense, emphatic voice, and the words came out in gushes, explosively, as though they were being forced through a narrow aperture under emotional pressure. (*PC*, IV, 53)

> "Poor man!" repeated Lucy, and the words came out on a puff of explosive mirth. "He could hardly speak for terror". Suddenly changing her tone, she mimicked Lord Edward's deep blurred voice bidding her sit down, telling her (stammering and with painful hesitations) that he had something to talk about. (*PC*, XI, 146)

> Polly pronounced the words in a sonorous monotone, as though she were reciting to an audience. She lingered lovingly over them, rolling the r's, hissing on the s's, humming like a bee on the m's, drawing out the long vowels and making them round and pure. "Ghost rattle of ghost rifles, in-fin-it-es-imal ghost cannonade". Lovely words! It gave her a peculiar satisfaction to be able to roll them out, to listen with an appreciative, a positively gluttonous ear to the rumble of the syllables as they were absorbed into silence. (*PC*, XI, 150)

For the extensive research could be done about paralanguage in narrative literature for instance: the voice qualities that seem to appear more often; those associated with specific cultures or specific socioeconomic strata; how far novelists can go in the realistic portrayal of the people they create; and which literary tendencies are apt to give more weight to nonverbal communication. From a semantic point of view, we find, for instance, how the same paralinguistic alternants, identically transcribed, reflect the variety of meanings and contextual situations found in real life.

3. Kinesics: the Character Through Gestures, Manners, and Postures

Kinegraphic representation vs. literary description

As for kinesics, its possible written representation would certainly be a controversial subject which does not fall within the aims of this chapter, although it seems incredible that at least some attempts to transcribe movements—other than Birdwhistell's (1970) and Kendon's (1969) kinegraphs—should be, as far as I know, totally absent among those interested in written communication and its historical development.

If we widen the concept of language without limiting it to the signs emitted and perceived in the human vocal-auditory channel, but acknowledging the semantic value of those produced in the kinetic-visual one—which constitutes an essential element of the Basic Triple Structure—we know that in real-life interaction the total message between sender and receiver is perceived fully only when nonverbal activities can be decoded along with verbal ones. Furthermore, there are countless situations, usually critical ones, in which messages are encoded only through nonverbal channels, particularly through kinesic behavior; and even when words are used, it may be in gestures and glances, in manners and in conscious or unconscious positions of the body that we find the real meaning of those words, because, as Merezhkovsky wrote in connection with *Anna Karenina*'s descriptions of kinesic behavior:

> The language of body gestures, while it may be less variable, is nevertheless more unmediated and expressive, endowed with a greater force of *suggestion* than the language of words. It is easier to lie with words than with body gestures and facial expressions . . . One glance, one frown, one quiver of a facial muscle, one movement of the body can express that which cannot be expressed with words. (Merezhkovsky, in Gibian 1970: 804)[4]

And referring to both paralanguage and kinesics, he notes:

> But Anna and Vronsky speak not with words, but only with "the flash of glances and smiles", with the tone of their voices, their expressions, and the movements of their bodies, like animals in love. And how much deeper than all human words is this element and animal, wordless language of love! (Ibid.: 804)

It is true that a written sign symbolizing 'standing', or 'sitting', or 'raised eyebrows', would still need a complementary verbal specification, unless a very refined transcription of kinesic activity were devised. In other words, such a system would require kinemes (see Chapter 5), and not just broad kinemorphemes and kinesyntactic constructs, in order to indicate with some accuracy the formation and development of the movement in question. Naturally, it is hard to imagine a kinealphabet side by side with the orthographic one on which we have built up a whole rhetorical and esthetic system and based our national literatures. The mere thought of it, we feel now, seems to destroy the concept of literary style as conceived today, by means of which a gesture can be described in many ways by speaking about it, and not writing it.

We could also argue that while a verb, an adjective, or an adverb can stand by itself and suggest a very specific idea—although the counterargument would be that an adverb like 'mildly' contains a gamut of degrees differently perceived by readers or listeners—a kinegraphic construct would be a rougher representation. Again, if an ancient rebus broadly depicted certain kinesic activities, we can wonder why that system could have not gradually become more and more refined until it would have been able to represent kinemorphemes and kinemes, just as the representation of phonemes followed that of syllables, and syllables succeeded whole words in writing. After all, just as phonemic elements are determined by phonetic articulations, we can refer to kinesic constructs as formed by kinesiological articulations, and even draw up an acoustic-kinetic chart of the head, as suggested earlier, in which the relationships sound-movement, verbal language-gestural language would be clearly demonstrated.

In spite of the fact, however, that language or paralanguage are not always more important than eye contacts and other body movements—since a subtle gesture can modify a whole linguistic-paralinguistic compound—no kinegraphic symbols were devised after alphabets were used, not even (as one might desire at times) to indicate a basic overriding posture, or a facial affect display that may accompany a stretch of speech as exclamation does. The advantage of using a few basic kinegraphic markers would be that the reader would perceive the kinesic behavior of the characters, not before or after their linguistic one, as happens with the author's descriptions, but actually synchronized with it.

At any rate, one must concede that whatever kinegraphs one could introduce in a literary text would undoubtedly replace the literary process itself (by which reality can be rendered in subtly varying forms), and that the artistic difference between two writers, based on their individual description and evocation through words, would be seriously curtailed. We only have to read the narrative production of various national literatures, from their epics to their contemporary novels, to realize the extreme importance of the kinesic descriptions with which authors, in different degrees, endeavor to achieve, not only physical realism but psychological one as well.

As I admitted before, to reach any definite conclusions as to the notable differences among authors in their depiction of the characters' kinesic (or nonverbal) repertoires would take much research. The tendency to let the character define himself through his linguistic, paralinguistic or kinesic behaviors seems quite understandable in behavioristic type of novels like Dos Passos', or in those of great realists and naturalists such as Dickens, Galdós, Dostoevsky, Mann or Dreiser. But one cannot hastily decide what prevents Salinger from showing the personality-revealing gestures and manners that the reader tends to attach to Holden Cauldfield's most realistic language; or why Lawrence insists so much on the slowness of glances and gait of *Women in Love*'s Hermione, Gerald, Birkin, etc., without extending this apparently defining quality to other characteristics.

As with paralanguage, the three basic types of kinesic behaviors, gestures, manners and postures, should be illustrated separately in a more elaborate research of literary kinesics. In the example below, as in others given so far, the three of them appear often side by side.

> by the way he opened his eyes, staring down at the ground without batting a lash for quite a while, and how other times he closed them, compressing his lips and arching his eyebrows, we easily know that some kind of madness had come upon him. (Cervantes, *DQ*, I, xxiii, 223, translation mine) (1)[5]

> Mr. Weller planted his hands on his knees, and looked full in Mr. Winkle's face [. . .] having accompanied this last sentiment with an emphatic slap on each knee, folded his arms with a look of great disgust, and threw himself back in his chair, as if awaiting the criminal's defence. (Dickens, *PP*, XXXV, 575)

> She exerted all the powers of her mind to say what she ought; but instead she fixed on him her eyes filled with love and did not answer at all. (Tolstoy, *AK*, II, vii, 127)

> That officer [policeman] yawned, stretched out his elbows, elevated himself an inch and a half on the balls of his toes, smiled and looked humorously at Jude [. . .] (Hardy, *JO*, II, vi, 123)

> She was well primed with a good load of Delahunt's port [. . .] Every jolt the bloody car gave I had her bumping up against me [. . .] She has a fine pair [. . .] Like that. / He held his caved hands a cubit from him, frowning: / I was tucking the rug under her and settling her boa all the time. Know what I mean? / His hands moulded ample curves of air. He shut his eyes tight in delight, his body shrinking, and blew a sweet chirp from his lips. (Joyce, *U*, 235)

Lady Edward hailed her over the heads of the intervening crowd with a wave of her long feather and a smile. The late arrival smiled back, blew a kiss, laid a finger to her lips, pointed to an empty chair at the other side of the room, threw out both hands in a little gesture that was meant to express apologies for being late and despairing regret at being unable in the circumstance to come and speak to Lady Edwards, then, shrugging up her shoulders and shrinking into herself so as to occupy the smallest possible amount of space, tiptoed with extraordinary precautions down the gangway toward the vacant seat. (Huxley, *PC*, II, 29)

"Sure I et all right", said Bud and ran his tongue round his teeth dislodging a sliver of salt meat that he mashed against his palate with his tongue. (Dos Passos, *MT*, II, 34)

The proprietress, her hands in the pockets of her apron, her shoulders thrown back and her legs apart, calls him [Pepe, the waiter] in a dry, cracked voice [. . .] [Cela, *LC*, I, 53, translation mine) (2)

4. The Communication Process Between Author and Reader: Transmission of the Character in Narrative Literature

The fact that verbal communication in its written or printed forms has reached such a degree of refinement and versatility—in spite of its limitations as a surrogate of speech—forces us to recognize the communicative superiority of words over gestures and their unlimited possibilities for symbolizing, and reduce to visual signs, all existing signs, that is, for writing down things and ideas. Although, as I have just shown, a great amount of words are used to speak about gestures and about other nonlexical behaviors.

In written literature, spoken language (or vocal-auditory signs in general) and movements are evoked by means of written signs we call words and punctuation marks. In fact, the whole sensorial world which surrounds us in real life is transmitted to us through writing and printing, which in turn will elicit images of it in our intellect, according to the writer's skill. In a novel, acoustic, visual, tactile and kinesthetic, olfactory and gustatory signs are all reduced to visually perceived ones. This is the limitation and wonder of the written word. A film may show physical images, sounds and colors, thus avoiding their description, but will not reach—in spite of the lenses' play with angles, focus, colors and light—the lexical combination which is available to the writer. And yet, a cinematic or musical construct might express, we could argue, the ineffable.

From a semiotic point of view—not perhaps a literary one, unless the very concept 'literary' is revised—any novel, even a poorly written one, appears as a fascinating display of communicative power and of transmitting devices.

Even if we concentrate only on how nonverbal communication is conveyed and perceived in the novel (as the subject of this chapter), we must first delineate the process by which the character (along with his contextual elements) is transmitted to and perceived by the reader (also subject to his own circumstance). That creative-recreative process—some of whose aspects will be discussed here—are outlined in Fig. 9.1 'The Communication Process Between Author and Reader: Transmission of the Narrative Character'. It develops through three main stages, as indicated in the chart.

Stage One

The process is initiated when the writer, drawing from his own world of physical and intellectual experiences, begins to decode and select as his material all the signs related to those experiences. This he can do in two ways:

(a) directly, that is, sensorially, almost as he lives them, as with the narrator's own sensations, which he simultaneously grants his character, whether consciously or unconsciously, shaping him in a way similar to the artist who works in front of his model, or facing a landscape that will elicit peculiar reactions in that fictional human being; or

(b) in a delayed way, including whatever was directly experienced in the past or is recreated through other verbal and written stories, that is, in an intellectual and more selective manner.

It is in this phase that the writer, by accumulating signs of different origins, carries out a selection of linguistic, paralinguistic, kinesic, proxemic and other nonverbal behaviors (more or less conscious of their technical and stylistic functions), besides psychological and ideological characteristics. In other words, he gives shape to his character, both physically and intellectually.

Stage Two

As that character acquires life in the mind of the narrator through somatic and intellectual features, codified now for the future reader, the second stage of his transmission to the latter takes place. It consists of a *channel reduction*, made possible only by words, since the whole multisensory and intellectual world directly experienced by the writer is going to be reduced to the morphologico-syntactical representation (supplemented by a few punctuations signs) which is the written text, that is, a visual form of expression. We could say that it is a sign metamorphosis, which the reader will later trigger again so that the inverse may take place in the decoding process of his reading.

In this phase the nonverbal repertoires, mainly paralanguage and kinesics—very often so important in narrative literature—are revealed as

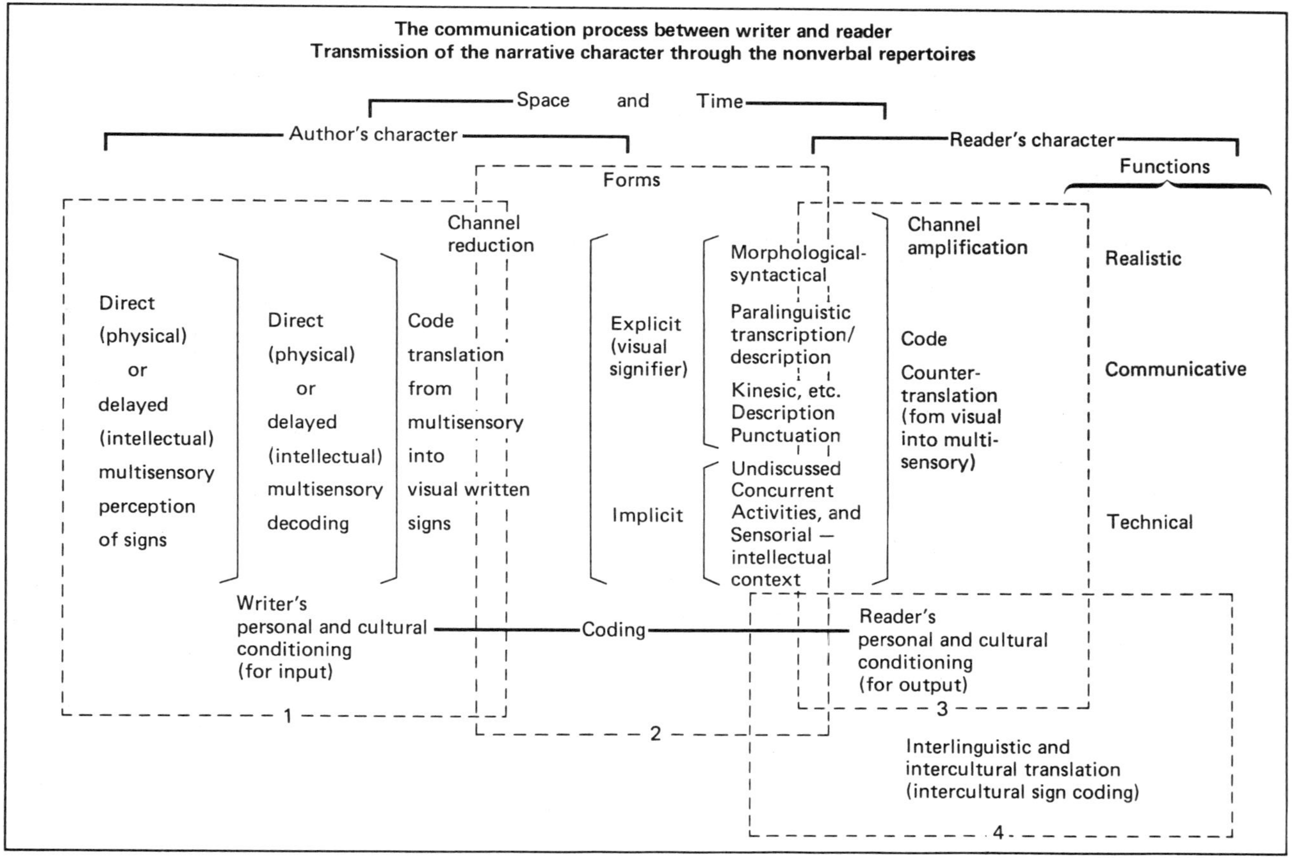

FIG. 9.1. The Communication Process Between Author and Reader: Transmission of the Narrative Character.

factors which must be considered in the analysis of the work because of the power of the written word for describing and evoking those repertoires in spite of the imposed sensory limitations. We, as readers, find the character's behaviors in two forms:

(a) *explicit*, in other words, the visual printed signs: morphologically and syntactically modified words, verbal descriptions of nonverbal activities, and punctuation marks; and

(b) *implicit*, not even visually present in the written or printed text, but rather latent 'between lines' and intellectually perceived, in which way they will, in a hidden dimension, complement the author's implicit repertoires, and also enrich the reader's own sensations according to his own sensitiveness: the paralinguistic modifications that correspond to certain linguistic constructs, the gestures, manners and postures equally costructured with language and paralanguage in real life, the spaces that separate people in their interactive encounters according to the contextual situation, the types of silences dictated by that situation, etc.; all of which are, in greater or lesser degree, grasped by the reader, thanks to those printed words, in what is actually the next stage. But the first two actually overlap at the point in which the writer's real world is changing into his created, transformed or imagined one through the necessary channel reduction.

My concern for the reader's decoding and recreating end of the communication process is corroborated (I found after elaborating my own ideas) in the already cited study of Tolstoy by Merezhkovsky:

> we experience in the muscles and nerves directing the expressive gestures of our own bodies, upon reading similar descriptions, the beginning of those movements which the artist describes in the external appearance of his characters. And, by means of this sympathetic experience involuntarily going on in our own bodies, that is, by means of the most realistic and shortest path, we enter into their internal world. We begin to live with them and in them. (Merezhkovsky, in Gibian 1970: 804)

Stage Three

In what can be the last stage in the literary process between author and reader, a reverse sign metamorphosis takes place when the reader begins to act as such by transforming the printed visual signs, and those which he can intuit further through them—an indefinite series of secondary, tertiary, etc., signs mutually elicited according to certain semiotic patterns that deserve attention—into their original sources, that is, by mentally bringing them back to life and turning the written words into intimate imagined sensations of optical, auditive, tactile, olfactory, kinesthetic, and dermal experiences.

The reader, in sum, recreates the author's flesh-and-bone character, thus completing the intended cycle, or rather, the literary recycling of signs. This duality, the author's character and the reader's character, spans between the two end points, output and input, of the coding process, at both of which the individual's own personal and cultural conditioning background affects the entire process. From a literary point of view, I will discuss later the important communicative and technical functions that the character's verbal and nonverbal repertoires, thus transmitted, plays in the narrative work.

The narrator–listener situation

Another angle from which to consider the process just outlined would be that of *interaction*. Although the silently read narration does not elicit actual personal interaction, we can easily imagine a speaker–listener relationship in the case of the medieval poems whose characters and events we must appreciate today only through their printed evocation. But the living, direct audiences of the medieval minstrel or the local entertainer surely must have displayed a rich repertoire of verbal, and mostly nonverbal, feedback (approval–disapproval, surprise, disappointment, etc.) and listener's behaviors (mainly completion of key sentences or expected expressions, and anticipation of the character's gestures).

The minstrel–audience encounter certainly deserves an anthropological and sociopsychological type of approach, which would include today's oral literature, transmitted in a similar fashion mostly. In an interactive encounter, even if it is not a typical conversational one, the listener displays a series of activities: mostly *feedback* verbal or nonverbal cues (words, smiles, hand gestures, laughter, postural shifts that may indicate attention or boredom, but something); and, in a lesser degree, *listener's secondary activities*, such as the ones outlined in Chapter 7. In terms of the decoding process, one must consider the fact that individuals within the collectivity that constitutes the audience can be mutually influenced into a sort of collective decoding, quite different from the isolated private reading. Which implies that certain activities (mainly linguistic, paralinguistic and kinesic) did not have to be decoded through the visually perceived text of the poem, as we must do today, but directly from the minstrel's own performance of those behaviors.

After all, this is the situation generated during story-reading and story-telling to children, in which one has to make the narrative come alive by enacting the paralanguage and kinesics of the characters and, very important, by allowing for strategically placed silences during which the child replays in his imagination (assisted perhaps by the book's illustrations) the most relevant episodes.

5. Vitality, Plurality, Culture, and Time of the Narrative Character

One can conclude from these thoughts that the creation, transmission and perception of the people in the fictional world of the novel is a process based on the author's own exclusive circumstances in the real world, at one end, and the individual reader's own exclusive circumstances, also in the real world, at the other; each of them occurring in a specific spatial and temporal situation.

From the literary as well as from the psychological point of view, this would deserve much elaboration if we were to probe as deep as possible into the most hidden layers of the creative process, on the one hand, and of the recreative process, on the other; that is, if we were to analyze the motivations, sensitiveness and general contextual circumstances of both writer and reader. The exclusiveness that defines each of them as individual human beings is, I feel, an unfathomable abyss in which the relationship Author(real world)–Character(fictional world)–Reader(real world) lies partly hidden to our curiosity. It is, therefore, the basis for the three premises which constitute the backbone of the analysis of nonverbal communication as a new perspective of narrative technique, namely: the vitality of both writer and reader, and the in-between position of the character, whose own vitality, confirmed by each reading, confirms in turn his inherent plurality.

The flesh-and-bone character

When we acknowledge the human attributes of the characters in a novel—in this chapter mostly their nonverbal repertoires—it is imperative to acknowledge also the novelist's own vitality, his contact with the real world, his cultural locus. Robbe-Grillet (1963: 149), referring to the inevitable subjectivity of objectivism and to the fact that only God can be objective, says about the author that "c'est *un homme* qui voit, qui sent, qui imagine, un homme situé dans l'espace et le temps, conditionné par ses passions [and by his culture, with whatever that implies, I would add], un homme comme vous et moi"; and, among many other similar statements, Mendilow (1965: 89) asserts: "The most original mind does not work in a vacuum". Therefore, an imagined human being, created by a real human being and later recreated by still another human being, will offer the literary critic at least a double image (the original character and the 'read' one), perhaps a triple one (when identifying the author's own personality and communicative repertoires, as it happens sometimes), and actually an infinitely multiple one as 'lived' by each reader, here and there, now and in a hundred years.

A character may have been given life mainly as a highly intellectual vehicle for the conveyance of the writer's philosophy, as in the case of Sartre's

Roquentin in *La Nausée*, Unamuno's Augusto Pérez in *Niebla*, or Gregor Samsa in Kafka's *Die Verwandlung*; as the tool for a satire, like Swift's Gulliver, or Voltaire's Candide; as a sort of intermittent lecturer for encyclopedic novels like Huxley's *Point Counterpoint* (whose people are, however, highly individualized and deeply rooted in a mimetic world); or as a fictional individual being drawn from and depicted in the author's daily environment, like Richardson's Pamela, Dostoevsky's Raskolnikov, Zola's bourgeois, Mann's *Buddenbrooks* family, Dreiser's self-made men, or Dos Passos' city dwellers. But, in each case, no matter how intellectualized he is, a character is, or has been, a flesh-and-bone individual in his author's mind, and his vitality is always confirmed.

The multiple decoding of the character

It is important to recognize, however, that this undisputed vitality appears at the completion of the semiotic process I have outlined before, that is, when the reader decodes the explicit and implicit signs in the literary text, bringing back to life the dormant, awaiting human being left in the pages of the narrative by his creator; and furthermore, that this process that begins as a consequence of the synchrony between the writer and his time, reflects in the end the disynchrony between the reader and the character's first version. In other words, the reader, conditioned by a new circumstance in a new time in his culture, will not reconstruct Cervantes' Don Quijote, Dickens's Pickwick, or Malamud's Yakob Bok exactly as their authors lived them during the creative process, not even as they lived them in the subsequent readings of their own work, for those readings would take place at an already different time, conditioned by a new set of circumstances.

On the other hand, we can suspect, in some cases, that the nonverbal repertoires of the characters are a reflection of the author's own behavior; and this, along with his whole personality, is certainly an important asset for the true understanding of his work and the people in it. I believe that direct acquaintance with a writer or, failing this, careful attention to his biography, may help us, to a certain degree, to understand better the behaviors of his characters. In the nineteenth-century Spanish masterpiece *La Regenta*, for instance, the frail and timid, yet much sensitive toward women, provincial intellectual reveals much of Alas himself; and so does, in a sort of dreamed anti-Alas, the physically strong and sensuous, yet frustrated and repressed, male protagonist, whose nonverbal behaviors and reactions are most carefully described. In a similar fashion, Theodore Dreiser reveals himself through the passionate and ambitious Eugene Witla, of *The Genius*, and through other typical men in his novels.

I hope that this brief discussion of the creative-recreative multiple process, as part of the semiotic process outlined in Fig. 9.1, will have clearly suggested the existence of two basic intellectual forms: *the author's character* and *the reader's character*.

We have seen that whatever characters say and do can be determined, first of all, by the author's own vitality, for which reason the linguistic-paralinguistic-kinesic style of the character, and that of his author, become in themselves both tools and subjects of complementary scholarly endeavors. This close relationship suggests the need to consider what are actually the two basic dimensions of any human activity: space and time.

Space and time of the character

There is a *cultural setting* for a fictional character. Whether his creator wants it or not, he will almost always, if we look for it, give away a specific culture (even above a possible intended plurality of cultures), either his own or another one. This poses one more problem for the reader, since he might not need to interpret those cultural characteristics properly in order to fully understand (and we might questions this) the character's ideas and general personality, but he would certainly need to if he is to relive that character as closely as possible to the original one.

On the other hand, there is also a *temporal setting* the novelist draws from during his creative process. It can be his own present time, in which case he is using first-hand material. He can project us into the future, as in Utopian and science-fiction works. Or he can be trying to bring the past back to life, as in the historical novel. But even in the case of a historical novel, he will inevitably draw from his own time locus. In other words, he will dress his own contemporaries in sixteenth century clothes, and will see them move in those clothes, but that will not make their movements the true kinesics of the sixteenth century, as it was Cervantes' while making Don Quijote and Sancho display their magnificent repertoire of gestures, manners and postures.

Human kinesic behavior has been modified through history by changes in furniture style (the series of more relaxed postures and accompanying manners determined by the eighteenth-century trend toward curved and softer sitting furniture), in clothes and hairdo (men's stockings and tight pants, jeans for both men and women, long or short hair in women, and long hair in men, all have produced conscious and unconscious gestures, manners and postures), etc., and just as actors must make an effort to move naturally in the clothes of the past, so the non-contemporary writer must make an effort to make his characters move in strange clothes.

The problem of recreation, therefore, and the probability of minimizing the plurality of the characters will depend much on those two dimensions, time and space (indicated in the chart), as much as the creative process does.

Signs (the spoken word, the accompanying voice modifications and paralinguistic sounds, the movements of the body, the proxemic behavior displayed in the novel) vary with time, but also through space, due to geographical differences, cultural settings and racial differences. The author's time and space relationship with his readers needs much research, and a semiotic approach to this relationship, in terms of the encoding and decoding of the many messages contained in the narrative work, could be a very fruitful one.

We must not forget, however, that a number of signs decoded by the readers of a novel might have never been intentionally encoded by the writer, and that a very valid argument in favor of the literary work is precisely the plurality of interpretations and appreciations to which a piece of narrative, for instance, is subject once it is released by its author. But this is not a new subject. I am referring to the *plurality* of the character, not, in fact, as a virtue on the part of his creator, but as something he himself would like to avoid if he could in many cases. A writer can say, of course, that his readers will bring his characters to life as he created them, but we know only too well that this is not true, that each new reading is like a genetic act in which a new person comes to life. Or to put it more mildly, another Don Quijote in the endless series of Don Quijotes.

Finally, I would add that this unavoidable characteristic of the narrative or dramaturgic character is determined, as I have tried to show, by the vitality of both author and reader and, in sum, because the written text is so dissociated from the sensory world it tries to depict.

The medieval character–narrator–listener relationship

This basic problem, the central one to my topic, made me think many times of the advantageous position of the characters in the medieval poems, as I hinted earlier. The plurality of the epic heroes and their surrounding personages in pre-Gutenberg times must have been greatly minimized, as I implied in the former reference to the medieval character, since each minstrel, each time, would act the same Green Knight or the same Cid for many people, conveying a very similar image for which tone of voice and body movements, particularly in important passages, would be not only almost automatically displayed, but much closer to reality; as in the case of El Cid (a living contemporary Spaniard in those days), or to the original Green Knight, or Sir Orfeo, as imagined by their authors.

Authors, characters, minstrels and audiences were dealing in those days with the same, or very similar, space and time settings. What would not we give today to be able to see and hear the real-life *Poem of El Cid* as sang by its minstrels, when El Cid and his mean leave Vivar and, upon seeing the raven fly on their right hand side and then on the other, he makes the then prescribed head-and-shoulder movements to cast off the ill omen; or how

Pedro Bermúdez and the Infante Don Fernando get ready to charge against each other. Likewise, although not based on real events, the minstrel would enact Sir Orfeo's gestures and tone of voice, as described in the poem, when he faces the demented queen, and the dramatic dialog that ensues in *Sir Orfeo*; or the appearance, in *Sir Gawain and the Grene Knight*, of the Green Knight at Camelot, his challenge, and how, after Sir Gawain severs his head, he gropes for it, remounts his horse and leaves with a final fierce jerk on the reins.

6. The Fate of Nonverbal Communication in the Translated Text

A serious and fascinating aspect of translation, although hardly acknowledged in the scholarly literature, is that of the problems encountered by the translator (whether a professional one who produces a text in the target language or the common reader who, inadvertedly perhaps, tries to translate and interpret) when confronted with the nonverbal behaviors of the characters, not only the explicit ones, but those hidden beyond the words of the written text.

Since I plan to elaborate on this topic elsewhere with the appropriate documentation, I will simply outline here what in the chart is indicatd by *interlinguistic and intercultural translation*, which can be a fourth stage beyond the basic recreation of the original character by a reader who is not a member of the author's (or the character's) culture.

Referring to foreign-language students, diplomats and serious travelers. I have already elaborated on the need to seek, not merely linguistic fluency, but *cultural fluency* as well, implying, among other things, an ability to understand and/or produce the nonverbal behaviors that must be displayed along with verbal language, and that are rooted in ethnic, geographical and socioeconomic factors. In the case of the novel, it is important for the translator to acknowledge his responsibility as mediator between author and reader and, therefore, as the conveyor or the literary character; but the author himself, who writes for an audience here and there, now and tomorrow, should perhaps be able to predict the fate of the nonverbal repertoires he grants his characters, for those repertoires may be conditioned by elements which vary through space (climate, race, clothes) and time (clothes, furniture, etiquette norms, moral values).

The concept of translation should not be applied only to the rendering of a text into another language, but also to the intellectual process of *intracultural translation*. A reader can appreciate his own language in a novel whose characters belong to a subculture which is not his subculture; but that does not mean that he is equipped to fully understand the explicit and implicit nonverbal behaviors (without counting the linguistic localisms) contained, for instance, in a regionalistic novel dealing with rural life and all its human and emotional elements, from paralanguage and kinesics through proxemic behavior to chronemic behavior, unexplained furniture arrangement, and local customs.

Even if we concentrate on explicit nonverbal communication as described in a foreign culture's literature, I would offer some tentative suggestions just to elicit scholarly interest as to:

(a) how the foreign reader decodes certain paralinguistic, kinesic and proxemic behaviors which do not correspond to the behaviors displayed in his own culture in similar situations;

(b) how often he misses certain important nuances of meaning attached to some nonverbal activities, and whether or not these could be clarified by a translator's note when it might cause a gross misunderstanding (after all, practiced already by some translators occasionally);

(c) how to transcribe paralinguistic alternants for which there is an orthographic representation in the source language but not in the target one (English 'Tsk-Tsk', 'Whew!', 'Hm', and 'Uh-uh', for instance, are not written in Spanish); the greater or lesser capability of different languages to accommodate paralinguistic sounds into their established phonemic-orthographic system is in itself an important subject of study, closely related to the problems and methodology of literary translation; and

(d) how to internationalize the orthographic representation of some basic pancultural paralinguistic alternants.

A few more comments about nonverbal communication and translation could be made which would suggest the interrelationships of the elements mentioned so far. They would prove further how the subject of literary translation, particularly of the novel, is necessarily related to the study of nonverbal communication and communication in general; and that, as long as the nonverbal elements of human interaction are not studied in depth, and the professional translator and the student of literature do not strive to deal with a written text in an exhaustive way, we will not understand fully what is involved in translation; in fact, what translation is all about.

7. Nonverbal Communication and Narrative Realism

From the discussion of how nonverbal communication in narrative literature reveals the semiotic (or communicative) process which in turn shows the author–character–reader relationship, and of how the character's repertoires affect the literary text itself both in its original version and in translation, we could conclude that the use of those repertoires is a necessity inherent in the author. It is, in different degrees, a mimetic goal which, disguised in ephemeral artistic currents at times, always pervaded the fictional narration, from *Satyricon* to the work of our contemporaries. To decide, however, why some 'realists' give so much weight to the nonverbal behavior of their characters while others do not, would not be simply an easy cataloguing task. We can, for sure, associate the specification of paralinguistic and kinesic behaviors with the great figures of nineteenth-century realism or with the authenticity of Dreiser's world, but it would take a very deep analysis of the most hidden layers of literary, esthetic and personal characteristics to even attempt anything like a taxonomy of narrative literature based on the use of the representation and description of nonverbal communication.

Poetic narrative and functional narrative

Trying to come closer to the understanding of the forms and functions of this tendency, however, I would like to point out that the morphologico-syntactical-orthographical vehicle used by the writer for that purpose can be either *poetic*, that is, deliberately esthetic (sometimes evoking more than saying), or merely *functional*, as a significant stripped of any artistic intentions, expressing with the most indispensable elements the physical behaviors of the characters. And yet, because of the writer's basic poetic vein, we may find both forms side by side, giving us a straightforward but artistic image of the world:

> Uncle Jeff leaned towards him across the table with bulging gray eyes. / Jimmy chokes on a piece of bread, blushes, at last stammers weakly, "Whatever you say Uncle Jeff." [. . .] he stands back against the wall with his hands in his pockets, watching people elbow their way through the perpetually revolving doors; softcheeked girls chewing gum, hatchetfaced girls with bangs, creamfaced boys his own age, young toughs with their hats on one side [. . .] fed in two endless tapes through the revolving doors out into Broadway, in off Broadway. (Dos Passos, *MT*, V, 94)

But the literary fusion of the two forms, the 'poetization' of the functional description and the 'functionalization' of the poetic, is felt by the sensitive reader as the truly artistic form of realism, as in the following description of Lucy Tantamount's kinesic style in *Point Counterpoint*:

> The cigarette between her thin lips, she leaned forward to drink the flame. He had seen her leaning like this, with the same swift, graceful, and ravenous movement, leaning toward him to drink his kisses. And the face that approached him now was focussed and intent on that flame, as he had seen it focussed and intent upon the inner illumination of approaching pleasure. (Huxley, *PC*, XII, 160)

From indifferentiation to behaviorism

Touching again upon the difficult subject of the inclusion or exclusion of nonverbal repertoires, we can observe—from a stricter communicative point of view—that, regardless of which linguistic style is used, poetic or functional, in the physical and psychological descriptions of the characters, there exists in narrative literature a clear-cut dichotomy between total verbal and nonverbal indifferentiation of the characters, on the one hand, and extreme behaviorism on the other. But extreme behaviorism, yielding to a high degree of objectivism and objectualism, fails to really define the individual's behavior (nor perhaps the behavior of the group), as in *Manhattan Transfer*, where the author does not take full advantage of his constant verbal and nonverbal descriptions to help us identify his many recurrent characters (an important technical function, as I will mention later); or as in the internationally-prized *Tormenta de verano*, by the Spanish social realist García Hortelano (1962), who certainly defines a specific social group, but hardly so the individuals, except for two who do not belong to that group.

Of these two tendencies, *indifferentiation* seems to be a permanent characteristic of some authors through different currents of narrative literature, even of some of those who call themselves 'realists', but whose characters seem to use all the same language, which, in fact, is the language of the narrator himself. To consider nonverbal communication as a touchstone for the analysis of true realism offers, therefore, some interesting possibilities.

On the other hand, we also find, as with poetic and functional styles, an eclectic, integrative *selectivism* that relates the physical and psychological activities of the people to the meaningful objectual observations of the environment, as in Steinbeck's *The Grapes of Wrath*, or Sánchez Ferlosio's *El Jarama*, the most celebrated Spanish social novel of the fifties.

Considering then, the literary possibilities of poetic language and functional language, of differentiation and selectivism, a close look at what the narrator achieves through the use of verbal and nonverbal personal repertoires, reveals, not only six important types of realism, but, in all, the three classes of functions that the verbal-nonverbal compound language-paralanguage-kinesics can play in narrative literature: realistic, communicative, and technical.

8. The Realistic Functions of Nonverbal Communication

In all periods of narrative literature, from the national epics on, the depiction of the linguistic-paralinguistic-kinesic structure of the people involved in the story has conveyed a feeling of authenticity we could call *human realism*, which is usually, but not always, complemented by the *objectual* or environmental kind of realism.

A close analysis of what the authors achieve by letting us know what their characters say and how they say it, and how they move their bodies as they say it, or in their silences, reveals an interesting perspective, since we can differentiate six types of realism, that is, six *realistic functions* of nonverbal communication: physical, distorting, individualizing, psychological, interactive, and documentary.

Physical realism

This form of realism, as differentiated from the psychological one, conveys the sensorial perception of people's behavior and, therefore, their intended authenticity:

> They [the pilgrims] began to eat with the greatest gusto and very slowly, savoring each mouthful, which they took on the end of their knives, and very little of each thing, and then [. . .] they raised their arms and winebags in the air; the mouths of the winebags on their mouths, their eyes nailed on the sky [. . .] wagging their heads from side to side [. . .] (Cervantes, *DQ*, II, liv, 931, translation mine) (3)

> "[. . .] and that's my sister, Miss Rachel Wardle. She's a Miss, she is; and yet she ain't a Miss—eh, sir, eh?" And the stout gentleman playfully inserted his elbow between the ribs of Mr. Pickwick, and laughed heartily. (Dickens, *PP*, IV, 89)

> Spandrell uttered a brief and snorting laugh, and letting his chair fall back on its four legs, leaned forward across the table. Pushing aside his coffee-cup and his half-emptied liqueur glass, he planted his elbows on the table and his chin in his hands. (Huxley, *PC*, VIII, 103)

> "I never see the dawn," said Marco, his voice rattling in his throat, "that I don't say to myself perhaps . . . perhaps today." He cleared his throat and spat against the base of a lamppost; then he moved away from them with his waddling step, taking hard short sniffs of the cool air. (Dos Passos, *MT*, II, 31)

As a variety within physical realism, it is interesting how the description of task-performing behaviors contribute to what I have classified as documentary or historical realism:

> To ladies and gentlemen who are not in the habit of devoting themselves practically to the science of penmanship, writing a letter is no very easy task; it being always considered necessary in such cases for the writer to recline his head on his left arm, so as to place his eyes as nearly as

> possible on a level with the paper, while glancing sideways at the letters he is constructing, to form with his tongue imaginary characters to correspond. These motions, although unquestionably of the greatest assistance to original composition, retard in some degree the progress of the writer. (Dickens, *PP*, XXXIII, 485)

Dickens' most realistic description of such a common yet unthought of habit reminds one of Mateo Alemán's identical type of realism in his sixteenth-century picaresque novel *Guzmán de Alfarache*, in which he proposes the different types of penalty for the correction of various *necedades*, or 'foolish acts':

> Those who, while bowling, if the ball goes to one side, twist their bodies in the same direction, thinking that the ball will do what they do [. . .] and those who make odd faces when an object is knocked down [. . .] Those who make patterns with their urine while urinating, painting on the walls or sketching on the ground (Alemán, *GA*, II, iii, i, 188–189)

Whether meant to attack human follies or simply to humorously call the reader's attention toward such acts, the systematic and perhaps comparative or intercultural study of those descriptions would contribute to what in the original version of this text (Poyatos 1977b) I suggested as literary anthropology or historical social psychology.

> He took the wineglass and put his nose into it, slowly smelling the wine. Then he raised it to eye level and, with a turn of his hand, he made the liquid slide toward the glass brim. He wetted his lips by taking a little sip, tasting the thick coolness of that vintage. He finished the glass with short swallows. (Cabellero Bonald, *TDS*, VII, 84, translation mine) (4)

The preceding description poses a problem of what earlier I called cultural translation, since it refers specifically to the ritualistic wine tasting as performed by any connoisseur in the wine region of southern Spain. Many similar culture-specific actions can go unnoticed by the foreign reader when the writer offers no indication of their being customary and characteristic of certain social groups or individuals. It seems to me that a translator's note, as is sometimes done, would be in order.

Distorting realism

This is the literary, or artistic, expressionistic rendering of physico-psychological reality, meant to ridicule, to offer a caricature of reality, to gratuitously exaggerate it or truly to show what the eyes cannot see.

> When Sancho saw that he could not find the book, his face turned deadly pale; and feeling all over his body in great haste, he once more

realized he could not find it, and suddenly he threw his fists to his beard and tore off half of it, and, hastily and without stopping, he gave himself half a dozen blows on the face and on the nose, until it was all drenched in blood. (Cervantes, *DQ*, I, xxvi, 255, translation mine) (5)

Individualizing realism

Many narrators show a conscious effort to differentiate the characters, as to their physical and psychological characteristics, by means of their verbal repertoires and, in the best cases, by their nonverbal ones as well:

> The eloquent Pickwick, with one hand gracefully concealed behind his coat tails, and the other waving in air, to assist his glowing declamation [. . .] (Dickens, *PP*, I, 41) His nostrils dilated, and his fists clenched involuntarily, as he heard himself addressed by the villain. But he restrained himself again—and did *not* pulverize him [. . .] He panted for breath, and looked benignantly round upon his friends. (Ibid, X, 170)

> But Jude's mind seemed to grow confused soon, and he could not get on [declaiming the Nicene's creed]. He put his hand to his forehead, and his face assumed an expression of pain. (Hardy, *JO*, II, vii, 127). He [Jude] was leaning with his elbows on the table and his chin on his hands, looking into a futurity which seemed to be sketched out on the tablecloth. (Ibid., III, vii, 171). 'It is horrible how we are circumstanced, Sue—horrible!' he [Jude] said abruptly, with his eyes bent to the floor. (Ibid., IV, ii, 216). He [Jude] shook his head hopelessly, his eyes wet. (VI, iv, 367)

> "My dear Betsy! [. . .] I really must ask you if you understand our financial position? [. . .] Well, I can tell you in a few words", the Consul said. He sat up straight on the sofa, with one knee crossed over the other, puffed at his cigar, knit his brows a little, and marshalled his figures with wonderful fluency . . . The Consul puffed at his cigar until it glowed, threw back his head and blew at the smoke, and then went on" [. . .] (Mann, *B*, I, v. 58)

> The preacher began to speak in a quiet, friendly tone. His face was kind and he joined gently the fingers of each hand, forming a frail cage by the union of their tips (Joyce, *PAYM*, 127)

I would add, just in passing, that a careful analysis of the nonverbal repertoires may reveal sometimes, behind an apparent individualization, a rather intriguing commonness among the main characters in a novel, as, for instance, in Lawrence's *Women in Love*.

Psychological realism

This is, of course, the conscious ultimate aim of individualizing realism, and includes also the sensorial world (as the perception of it may let us probe deeper into subtle inner reactions):

> "But it was the devil who killed the old hag, not I. [Raskolnikov] [. . .] Leave me alone!" he exclaimed in a sudden convulsion of anguish [. . .] He propped his elbows on his knees, and clutched his head tightly in his hands [. . .] "Well, tell me what to do now," he begged, raising his head and gazing at her with a face monstrously distorted with despair. (Dostoevsky, *CP*, V, iv, 355)

> Willie flicked his nail along the part in his hair. After a while he scratched both pink palms with hard brown nails and blew into his stubby-fingered fist. He shuffled one foot, then the other (Malamud, *T*, 50–51)

> Maslova said nothing in her defence. When the president told her she might do so, she only lifted her eyes to him, cast a look round the room like a hunted animal, and dropping her head, began to cry, sobbing aloud. / "What's the matter?" the merchant asked Nekhlyudov, hearing him utter a strange sound. This was a forcibly suppressed sob. Nekhlyudov had not yet understood the significance of his present position, and attributed the sobs he could hardly keep back and the tears that filled his eyes to the weakness of his nerves. He put on his pinz-nez in order to hide the tears, then got out his handkerchief and began blowing his nose [. . .] He was still keeping up his courage and sat on his chair in the first row in his usual self-possessed pose, one leg carelessly thrown over the other, and playing with his pinz-nez. (Tolstoy, *R*, XXI–XXII)

> "Tst! tst! Tst!," was the only sound he [Asa] made at first, a sucking sound of the tongue and the palate—most weak and inadequate, it seemed to Clyde. Next there was another "Tst! Tst! Tst!," his head beginning to shake from side to side. Then, "What do you suppose could have caused her to do that?" Then he turned and gazed at his wife, who gazed blankly in return. Then, walking to and fro, his hands behind him, his short legs taking unconscious and queerly long steps, his head moving again, he gave vent to another ineffectual "Tst! Tst! Tst!" (Dreiser, *AT*, III, 35)

> "I was hoping now for a man to come along," Gudrun said, suddenly catching her underlip between her teeth, and making a strange grimace, half sly smiling, half anguish. Ursula was afraid. (Lawrence, *WL*, I, 8)

"Do you love me, Walter?" she [Marjorie] suddenly asked. / Walter turned his brown eyes for a moment from the reflected tie and looked into the image of her sad, intently gazing grey ones. He smiled, "But if only," he was thinking, "she would leave me in peace!" He pursed his lips and parted them again in the suggestion of a kiss. But Marjorie did not return his smile. Her eyes took on a tremulous brightness, and suddenly there were tears on her lashes [. . .] Through her closed eyelids the tears were welling out, drop by drop. Her face was trembling into the grimace of agony. (Huxley, *PC*, 1, 9–10)

Interactive realism

This kind of realism is always a thoughtful depiction of the mechanism of conversation, mainly in face-to-face encounters, and its study offers an interesting sociopsychological angle of narration, as we observe whether that mechanism reflects reality or seems rather improbable. The latter is often the case, since the flow of conversation is falsely smooth, its participants taking turns in an orderly manner, not even showing feedback cues or turn-requesting signals. Therefore, if the less obvious structural elements of interaction are indicated, suggested, or implied in a novel in a way the average reader can appreciate, it should be valued as much as the other types of realism outlined so far.

Documentary realism

Finally, documentary (or historical) realism through nonverbal behaviors is a logical result of physical realism, mostly, another rich source of research material, and certainly a fundamental part of the area discussed in the last chapter as *literary anthropology*, which would not seek its material in narratives only, but in different types of nonfiction works, such as the ones investigated by Hewes (1974: 1) in connection with his thoughts on glottogenesis and gestural communication, for which he gathered data (to prove that "gestural communication is the regular counterpart, for cross-linguistic, cross-cultural communication, of vocal language or speech") from many logs and journals of different voyagers, from Columbus to James Cook and others in the eighteenth century.

As far as narrative is concerned, however, it is important to note that, although the documentary-historical value of certain descriptions increases in direct proportion to the aging of the work, the student of literature can also search in today's production for the documentary elements whose value will increase through the years. In addition, I should refer again to the problems of translation, since the value of documentary realism is subject, not just to time, but to space as well, that is, to cultural differences; in which case the nonverbal documentary descriptions in the narrative production of cultures other than our own would constitute an interesting topic for a comparative study.

A serious study of documentary realism would require a classification of the various types of descriptions found according to the functions played by those activities, for example: ritualistic and etiquette behaviors, occupational activities, general task-performing activities, and activities conditioned by clothes, hairdo, furniture, etc. The following quotations illustrate ritualistic and etiquette prescribed kinesic behaviors, from the eleventh century to the late nineteenth century:

> [When El Cid and his men meet the King upon their return from exile] he fell to the ground on his hands and knees, / the grass of the fields he took with his teeth, / welling his eyes from the great happiness [. . .] (*Poema del Cid*, v. 3031, translation mine) (6)

> He [the gentleman] put his sword back in and fixed it in place, along with a string of large beads as belt. And with calm gait and erect, rocking his body and head very elegantly, throwing the end of his cloak over the shoulder, sometimes under his arm, and resting his right hand on his side, he left [. . .] (*Lazarillo der Tormes*, III, 99, translation mine) (7)

> [Don Quijote to Sancho] Do not eat garlic or onions, lest they should discover your rusticity by the smell. Walk slowly; speak calmly, but not in such a manner as to appear as if you were listening to yourself, for all affectation is bad [. . .] not to stuff your mouth with food, nor eruct in front of anyone [. . .] when riding, do not bend your body over the back of the saddle, nor carry your legs stiffly and straight, away from the horse's belly; but do not ride so limply that it may seem as if you were astride your donkey, for riding makes gentlemen of some and grooms of others. (Cervantes, *DQ*, II, xliii, 843–845, translation mine) (8)

> Their daughters, who remembering the maternal injunction to make the best use of their youth, had already commenced incipient flirtations in the mislaying of scarves, putting on gloves, setting down cups, and so forth; slight matters apparently, but which may be turned to surprisingly good account by expert practitioners. (Dickens, *PP*, XXXV, 534)

> When Ana stretched out her hand at him, she was afraid he might dare to press it a little, but nothing like that happened; he gave it that firm jerk he always used, according to what in Madrid was beginning to be fashionable. (Alas, *LR*, XVI, 345, translation mine) (9)

> Sappho Stolz entered with a short, brisk step, in shoes with high French heels, and shook hands with the ladies with a firm grip like a man [. . .] the extravagant fashion of her costume [. . .] the boldness of her

manners [. . .] well-developed and much-exposed bust. At each strenuous step as she advanced the shape of her knees and thighs was distinctly visible under her dress, and one involuntarily wondered just where, behind, under her heaped and swaying bustle, the real, graceful little body ended which was so exposed at the top and so hidden at the back and below (Tolstoy, *AK*, III, xviii, 273)

Serpukhovskoy kissed the smart-looking sargeant-major on his moist fresh lips and, wiping his mouth on his handkerchief [. . .] (Tolstoy, *AK*, III, xxi, 281)

"But, Huzoor!" said Hari, touching the foreman's black boots with his hand and taking the touch of the beef hide to his forehead. "Be kind . . ." (M. R. Anand, *C*, 199)

9. Communicative Functions of Nonverbal Repertoires in Narrative Literature

After having considered all other aspects of nonverbal communication in narrative literature—and before discussing the specific technical functions of the description and/or representation of nonverbal communication—I would like to discuss briefly what exactly the nonverbal behaviors of the characters communicate to the reader.

We are faced again, first of all, with the two basic dimensions of time and space, in that order. Mostly through the objectual world of the narrative, the time locus is revealed—in an anthropological way, first—in works whose stories take place in other periods of history; and that sense of the past diminishes until it reaches the uncertain boundary felt as the transitional years before today's world, namely in the works of the twenties and thirties. Naturally, as the narrative becomes more a thing of the past its documentary value increases, as I pointed out earlier.

Secondly, there is a more difficult aspect of the novel that sometimes needs the assistance of the author: the space setting, or cultural context.

As for the characters themselves, what the average writer gives us about them is: their physical portrait and their psychological one, the latter either through their own behaviors and thoughts or straight from the creator, or both; their clothes, which so many disregard in spite of their communicative value; their linguistic-paralinguistic-kinesic activities, discussed earlier; and, subsuming some of those behaviors, and clothes as well, their cultural differentiating behaviors, but perhaps not as specified.

Those are, therefore, the basic elements for the individualization of the character, some of which could be absent. But through them, and by what we may know of their geographical location, we will gradually be able to complete the character as we learn about their whole conditioning background (or some of its constituent elements).

Concentrating on sensorially perceived nonverbal activities—but leaving aside some of the anthropoliterary elements, such as descriptions of interiors and the rest of their objectual environment—I will summarize and illustrate the four ways in which the author usually transmits the nonverbal behaviors through the narrative text.

(a) *By describing the behaviour and explaining its meaning* (signifier and signified), obviously the most traditional method:

> Now, although this question was put in the most careless tone imaginable, Mr. Job Trotter plainly showed by gestures that he perceived his new friend's anxiety to draw forth an answer to his question. He emptied his glass, looked mysteriously at his companion, winked both of his small eyes, one after the other, and finally made a motion with his arm, as if he were working an imaginary pump-handle: thereby intimating that he [Mr. Trotter] considered himself as undergoing the process of being pumped, by Mr. Samuel Weller [his master] [. . .] he turned his glass upside down, as a means of reminding his companion that he had nothing left wherewith to slake his thirst. Sam observed the hint and feeling the delicate manner in which it was conveyed, ordered the pewter vessel to be refilled, whereat the small eyes of the mulberry man glistened. (Dickens, *PP*, XVI, 251–252)

> "Such an old magician!" Polly spoke in a thrilling whisper, leaning forward and opening her eyes very wide, as though to express in dramatic pantomime as well as words the mysteriousness of the magical old man. (Huxley, *PC*, III, 42)

(b) *By describing the behavior without explaining the meaning* (signifier, but not signified), as in the prescribed kinesic behaviors described in the *Poema del Cid* (8.6), meant for a contemporary audience familiar with their meanings; or in the following brief mention of the kinesic behavior of the cynical and cold-blooded man who is the seducer of his interlocutor's sister, and his mortal enemy:

> The other man [during a tense conversation] kept hitting the thyme plants with little strokes of his stick. (Cela, *PD*, III, 50, translation mine) (10)

(c) *By explaining the meaning without describing the behavior* (signifier, but not signifier), which may or may not be fully understood by the reader, at least as meant by the author:

> "Bidlake? The man who . . . who painted the pictures?" Polly spoke hesitatingly, in the tone of one who is conscious of a hole in her education and is afraid of making a ridiculous mistake. (Huxley, *PC*, IV, 51)

(d) *By providing a verbal expression always concurrent with the nonverbal one*, which is important, but not referred to at all; as in the following very specific variant of the expression *It goes in one ear and out the other*, which does not mention *ear* because the gesture describes it:

> "Me? It goes in this way and out the other." (Sánchez Ferlosio, *EJ*, 214, translation mine) (11)

10. Technical Functions of Nonverbal Repertoires in Narrative Literature

Finally, but most important from the point of view of the craft of fiction, there is another interesting perspective of the narrative: the analysis of the technical functions played by the nonverbal behaviors represented or described in the text.

When the author creates a character, if he wants to make him live as a well differentiated individual, he has at his disposal an array of psychobiological and culture-based characteristics with which to make him *that* character and no other. But those personal features, which are not at all difficult to invent and handle throughout the story, must be put to good use in two ways that represent some of the writer's most important responsibilities towards the readers.

First, those features must reflect, not a random inventory of easily replaceable linguistic, paralinguistic or kinesic characteristics, but a conscious selection that may give the characters the necessary consistency as credible people. To say that a character *must* look real to us may be the personal view of many, and not of many others, but when the author himself wants the character to seem real and unique we should expect him to maintain that unique personality from the beginning to the end of the story in a progressive, logical way, just as we become gradually acquainted with real-life people.

With these otherwise commonplace aforethoughts I merely tried to bring home one point: that the nonverbal repertoires of the characters can play, and do play, in the novel—though not as widely as they ought to—four definite and important functions in narrative technique, which I will only outline here, but which certainly merit more attention when discussing a novel.

(a) *Initial definition* of the character, by means of an idiosyncratic linguistic, paralinguistic or kinesic feature: a verbal expletive or personal choice of words, a particular tone of voice in certain situations, a gesture, a socially but individually conditioned way of greeting others or eating (that may agree with what we will know about that person later) a typical posture we can identify as a recurrent behavior, etc.

> Friederich Wilhelm Marcus, for years the dead Consul's confidential clerk, was a tall man [. . .] He spoke softly, hesitatingly stammering a little and considering each word before he uttered it. He had a habit of slowly and cautiously stroking the red-brown moustache that grew over his mouth with the extended index and middle fingers of his left hand; or he would rub his hands together and let his round brown eyes wander so aimlessly [. . .] (Mann, *B*, V, i, 198)

(b) *Progressive definition*, by means of still new additional features made noticeable gradually, as in real life, and not hastily at the onset of the story: a feature adds to another feature previously observed, complements it, builds up the physical as well as psychological or cultural portrait, and assists the reader in the progressive total appreciation of the narration. For instance, in *Buddenbrooks*, after Herr Grunlich is introduced in III, i, 72, we are still completing his physical portrait, many pages later:

> "What are you looking at? Why are you staring like that?" he [Herr Grunlich] said to her. He showed his teeth, and made vague movements in the air with his hands, and wiggled his body from side to side. His rosy face could not become actually pale; but it was spotted red and white like a scarlet-fever patient's. (Mann, *B*, IV, iv, 163)

(c) *Subsequent identification*, by means of a feature or features repeated for the first time. Its technical importance is that not only does it bring back that image (the verbal expletive, the gesture, the peculiar tone of voice), but that it does it precisely at a point in the story when the author knows that the readers need to identify some characters, as they may begin to confuse them or forget their external personalities. For this reason, this function and the next one, recurrent identification, are specially useful in saga series, in voluminous epic novels peopled by many characters, such as Mann's *Buddenbrooks*, and in the panoramic type of novel, like Dos Passos' *Manhattan Transfer* or Cela's *The Hive*; or any other type of narration whose author may insist on certain defining, individualizing features, such as Hardy's, e.g.:"Friederich Wilhelm Marcus rubbed his hands circumspectly [. . .]" (Mann, *B*, V, i, 201, i.e., after he was identified by that behavior).

(d) *Recurrent identification*, by means of a known feature repeated as many times as necessary at varying intervals in the narration. In *The Hive*, for instance, the enormous amount of characters makes it technically advisable, or rather, indispensable for the novelist to save us from becoming absolutely lost, at least in a first reading and without a true effort on our part; But Cela, for one thing, wisely presents Martín Marco, for instance, leaning his head on his hands on pages 24 and 44, walking in a peculiar way on pages 98, 148 and 315, etc. The following is an example of some of the technical functions (which are also communicative) played by the implicit paralanguage and the explicit kinesics of Hardy's Arabella Donn, in *Jude the Obscure*, which define her throughout the novel as Jude's sensuous part of his personality, in opposition to the fragile and physically inferior Sue Bridehead:

> she [Arabella] gave, without Jude perceiving it, an adroit little suck to the interior of each of her cheeks in succession, by which curious and original manoeuvre she brought as by magic upon its smooth and rotund surface a perfect dimple, which she was able to retain there as long as she continued to smile. [*Initial definition*] This production of dimples at will was a not unknown operation, which many attempted, but only a few succeeded in accomplishing. (I, vi, 45)

> by artificially producing in each cheek the dimple before alluded to, a curious accomplishment of which she was mistress, effecting it by a momentary suction. [*Subsequent identification*] (I, ix, 66)

> "O—how stupid this is! I thought my visitor was—your friend—your husband—Mrs. Fowley, as I suppose you call yourself?" said Arabella, flinging her head back to retain the dimple she had just taken the trouble to retain. [*Recurrent identification*] (V, ii, 274)

> Arabella smiled grimly as she resumed her way, and practised dimple-making all along the road from where the pollard willows begin to the old almhouses [. . .] [*Recurrent identification*] (VI, iv, 364)

In Arabella's case, her repeated behavior serves as a recurrent definition rather than true identification for the reader, a common function of nonverbal descriptions. So does Karenin's peculiar habit in *Anna Karenina*:

> "First the important of public opinion and propriety [. . .] thirdly [. . .] the harm that may result to our son [. . .]" And interlacing his fingers, palms downwards, he stretched them and the joints cracked. / That movement—a bad habit of cracking his fingers—always tranquillized him and brought him back to that precision of mind he now so needed [. . .] A woman's steps were heard ascending the stairs. Karenin, ready to deliver his speech, stood pressing his interlaced fingers together, trying whether some of them would not crack again. One of his joints did crack. (II, viii, 131) Karenin started and bent his hands to crack his fingers. / "Oh, please don't crack your fingers! I dislike it so!" she Anna said. (II, ix, 133)

Notes

1. Some of the ideas in sections 5, 7, 8 and 9 (applied only to the Spanish novel) were read at the 1971 International Congress of Hispanists and at the 1972 University of Toronto International Symposium on the Hispanic Novel (Poyatos 1972b, 1972c). Reduced versions of the

present text were read at the 1975 joint meeting of the Canadian Associations of Semiotic Research and Comparative Literature (Poyatos 1976c), the 1976 Carleton University 'Colloque d'automme de littérature comparée', and within the Canadian Association of Hispanists (Poyatos 1976h), which awarded its 1977 prize to a slightly reduced Spanish translation of the present text (Poyatos 1976b). This text, with some fewer examples, was published in *Semiotica* (Poyatos 1977b) and reedited by Kendon (Poyatos 1981a) in a volume of "articles that have proved to be particularly seminal over the years" (Kendon 1981).

2. Works quoted and publication dates after these two examples are indicated by initials only. Where translations are offered the original texts are given in note 4 below, numbered as throughout the chapter.

Alas, Leopoldo, *La Regenta*, 1884–5 *LR*.
Alemán, Mateo, *Guzmán de Alfarache*, 1599–1604 *GA*.
Anand, Mulk Raj, *Coolie*, 1972.
Caballero Bonald, José, *Dos días de setiembre*, 1962 *TDS*.
Cela, Camilo José, *La colmena*, 1951 *LC*.
Cela, Camilo José, *La familia de Pascual Duarte*, 1942 *PD*.
Cervantes, Miguel de, *Don Quijote de la Mancha*, 1605–15 *DQ*.
Dickens, Charles, *Pickwick Papers*, 1836–7 *PP*.
Dos Passos, John, *Manhattan Transfer*, 1925 *MT*.
Dostoevsky, Feodor, *Crime and Punishment*, 1866 *CP*.
Dreiser, Theodore, *An American Tragedy*, 1925 *AT*.
Dreiser, Theodore, *Sister Carrie*, 1900 *SC*.
Etiemble, *Blason d'un corps*, 1961.
Fitzgerald, F. Scott, *The Great Gatsby*, 1925 *GG*.
Hardy, Thomas, *Jude the Obscure*, 1885 *JO*.
Huxley, Aldous, *Point Counterpoint*, 1928 *PC*.
James, Henry, *The Turn of the Screw*, 1898 *TS*.
Joyce, James, *A Portrait of the Artist as a Young Man*, 1916 *PAYM*.
Joyce, James, *Ulysses*, 1922 *U*.
Kerouac, Jack, *On the Road*, 1958 *OR*.
Lawrence, D. H., *Women in Love*, 1921 *WL*.
Lazarillo de Tormes, in *La novela picaresca española*, 1554 *LT*.
Malamud, Bernard, *The Tenants*, 1971 *TT*.
Mann, Thomas, *Buddenbrook*, 1901 *B*.
Maugham, W. Somerset, *Of Human Bondage*, 1915 *HB*.
O'Hara, John, *Appointment in Samarra*, 1934 *AS*.
Poema de Mio Cid, 1140, ed. R. Menéndez Pidal *PC*.
Sánchez Ferlosio, Rafael, *El Jarama*, 1958 *EJ*.
Sir Gawain and the Grene Knight, 14th c.
Sir Orfeo.
Steinbeck, John, *The Grapes of Wrath*, 1939 *GW*.
Tolstoy, Leo, *Anna Karenina*, 1873–7 *AK*.
Tolstoy, Leo, *Resurrection*, 1889–99 *R*.

3. Spandrell threw back his head and laughed, profoundly but, as was his custom, almost inaudibly, a muted explosion. "Admirable!" he said. "Admirable! The first really good argument in favour of matrimony I ever heard. Almost thou persuadest me, Rampion. I've never actually carried it as far as marriage."

"Carried what?" asked Rampion, frowning a little. He disliked the other's rather melodrammatically cynical way of talking. So damned pleased with his naughtinesses. Like a stupid child, really.

"The process of infection. I've always stopped this side of the registry office. But I'll cross the threshold next time." He drank some more brandy. "I'm like Socrates", he went on. "I'm divinely appointed to corrupt the youth, the female youth more particularly. I have a mission to educate them in the way they shouldn't go." He threw back his head to emit that voiceless laugh of his. Rampion looked at him distastefully. So theatrical. It was as though the man was overacting in order to convince himself he was there at all.

"But if you only knew what marriage would mean", Mary earnestly put in. "If you only knew . . ."

"But, my dear woman, of course he knows", Rampion interrupted with impatience.

"We've been married more than fifteen years now", she went on, the missionary spirit strong within her. "And I assure you . . ."

"I wouldn't waste my breath, if I were you."

Mary glanced enquiringly at her husband. Wherever human relationships were concerned, she had an absolute trust in Rampion's judgement. Through those labyrinths he threaded his way with a sure tact which she could only envy, not imitate. "He can smell people's souls", she used to say of him. She herself had but an indifferent nose for souls. Wisely then, she allowed herself to be guided by him. She glanced at him. Rampion was staring into his coffee cup. His forehead was puckered into a frown; he had evidently spoken in earnest. "Oh, very well", she said, and lit another cigarette.

Spandrell looked from one to the other almost triumphantly. "I have a regular technique with the young ones", he went on in the same too cynical manner. Mary shut her eyes and thought of the time when she and Rampion had been young.

4. Dimitri S. Merezhkovsky, *L. Tolstoi i Dostoevsky: zhizn,' tvortchesvo, i religiia* (St. Petersburg-Moscow, 1912), M. O. Volf Edition of Merezhkovsky's *Collected Works*, Vol. VII, pp. 154–7 and 193–201, as cited (with the title "Tolstoy's Physical Descriptions") by G. Gibian in his edition of *Anna Karenina*, Norton Critical Editions (New York: W. W. Norton, 1970), p. 804.

5. (1) por lo que hacía de abrir los ojos, estar fijo mirando al suelo sin mover pestaña gran rato, y otras veces cerrarlos, apretando los labios y enarcando las cejas, fácilmente conocimos que algún accidente de locura le había sobrevenido.

(2) La dueña, que tiene las manos en los bolsillos del mandil, los hombros echados para atrás y las piernas separadas, lo llama [. . .].

(3) [los peregrinos] comenzaron a comer con grandisimo gusto y muy de espacio, saboreándose con cada bocado, que le tomaban con la punta del cuchillo, y muy poquito de cada cosa, y luego [. . .] levantaron los brazos y las botas en el aire; puestas las bocas en su boca, clavados los ojos en el cielo [. . .] meneando las cabezas a un lado y a otro [. . .].

(4) Cogió la copa y metió la nariz dentro, oliendo despaciosamente el vino. Luego la levantó a la altura de los ojos e hizo resbalar el líquido hacia los bordes del cristal, girando la mano. Se mojó los labios, dando un sorbito y paladeando la pastosa frialdad de la solera. Terminó la copa a pequeños tragos.

(5) Cuando Sancho vio que no hallaba el libro, fuésele parando mortal el rostro; y tornándose a tentar todo el cuerpo muy apriesa, tornó a echar de ver que no le hallaba, y sin más ni más, se echó entrambos puños a las barbas, y se arrancó la mitad de ellas, y luego, apriesa y sin cesar, si dio media docena de puñadas en el rostro y en las narices, que se las baño todas en sangre.

(6) los inojos e las manos en tierra los fincó, / las yerbas del campo a dientes las tomó, / llorando de los ojos, tanto avíe el gozo mayor.

(7) [el escudero] Tornóla a meter la espada y ciñósela, y un sartal de cuentas gruesas de talabarte. Y con un paso sosegado y el cuerpo derecho, haciendo con él y con la cabeza muy gentiles meneos, echando el cabo de la capa sobre el hombro y a veces so el brazo, y poniendo la mano derecha en el costado, salió [. . .]

(8) No comas ajos y cebollas, porque no saquen por el olor tu villanería. Anda despacio; habla con reposo; pero no de manera que parezca que te escuchas a tí mismo; que toda afactación es mala [. . .] no mascar a dos carrillos, ni de eructar delante de nadie [. . .] a caballo, no vayas echando el cuerpo sobre el arzón postrero, ni lleves las piernas tiesas y tiradas y desviadas de la barriga del caballo, ni tampoco vayas tan flojo que parezca que vas sobre el rucio; que el andar a caballo a unos hace caballeros; a otros caballerizos.

(9) Ana, al darle la mano, tuvo miedo de que él se atreviera a apretarla un poco; pero no hubo tal; dio aquel tirón enérgico que él siempre daba, siguiendo la moda que en Madrid empezaba entonces.

(10) El otro daba golpecitos con la vara sobre las matas de tomillo.

(11) ¿A mí? Por aquí me entra y por aquí me sale.

(12) Los que jugando a los bolos, cuando acaso se les tuerce la bola, tuercen el cuerpo juntamente, pareciéndoles que, así como ellos lo hacen, lo hará ella [. . .] y los que semajantes visajes hacen, derribándose alguna cosa [. . .] Los que orinando hacen señales con la orina, pintando en las paredes o dibujando en el suelo.

10

Nonverbal Communication in the Theater: the Playwright–Actor–Spectator Relationship

CYRANO, *Surgissant du parterre, debout sur une chaise, les bras croisés, le feutre en bataille, la moustache hérissée, la nez terrible* (Rostand, *Cyrano de Bergerac*, I, iii)

ABBIE (*both her arms around him—with wild passion*) I'll sing fur ye! I'll die fur ye! (*In spite of her overwhelming desire for him, there is a sincere maternal love in her manner and voice—a horribly frank mixture of lust and mother love*) Don't cry, Eben! I'll take yer Maw's place! (O'Neill, *Desire Under the Elms*, II, iii)

1. The Unwritten Messages of the Script and the Need for Nonverbal Communication Studies in the Theater

THIS study of the theater in the light of semiotics and nonverbal communication reflects still the editorial limitations of a recent paper (Poyatos 1982a) on a topic upon which I will expand much further in future work. It attempts to establish the basic relationship between narrative and dramatic literature, based on my earlier study of the novel (Poyatos 1977b, 1981a) and thus studies (a) the semiotic transmission of the character from the playwright to his reader, the director or actor, and finally his potential audience, and (b) the nature and problems of the conveyance of somatic communicational systems, mainly paralanguage and kinesics. Given the complexity of the subject, I have not as yet focussed on all the important nonverbal aspects of the performance put together, that is, somatic, objectual and environmental.

The two introductory quotations illustrate the much needed systematic study of the forms and functions of nonverbal behavior in the theater, both in the written text and on the stage, and reveal the complex field of nonverbal communication studies, with which playwright, director and actor must be familiarized beyond their natural sensitiveness, as it is central to their craft.

Except for experimental plays such as Beckett's *Act Without Words* (1957), the theater, like narrative literature, is based on the conveyance of abstract concepts and the evocation of images and experiences of the sensible world through the medium of the written and printed words. Essential as the playwright's lexical repertoire is, however, words are much too limited, even at the reading stage of the play, to transmit ideas and evoke sensible experiences, or give form in our minds to unexperienced elements of the tangible world. It has been amply discussed in the previous chapters how limited words are for carrying the weight of a conversation and how different emotional reactions, for instance, could not be expressed either by a periphrastic combination of lexemes representing each of the emotions or by any of them individually, as purely 'linguistic' constructs or dictionary items. And yet, our deepest and most ineffable messages are conveyed precisely by such emotional-blends, and even the read play, as the read novel, will be decoded in a conscious or unconscious way, with certain often indescribable voice modifications, with cooccurrent facial and body movements, however subtle; and, whether or not specified by the author, with certain congruent chemical reactions such as tears or perspiration, dermal signs like blushing, and thermal changes, all costructured to convey precisely a given intentional or unintentional unique message.

The unwritten messages, in the text, therefore, are as numerous as the ones emitted without words in real life, and, as has also been discussed, both novelists and playwrights, depending on the degree of physical and psychological individualization with which they wish to endow their characters, refuse to just let them speak in a printed language without resorting to both additional words and an illogical but traditionally limited repertoire of punctuation symbols, in an effort to awaken their own sensorial experiences in the reader's imagination. In sum, the creator of flesh-and-bone characters is striving to put in motion two main sign-emitting complexes: first, the mutually inherent bodily message-conveying systems, the core of which constitutes the Basic Triple Structure of human communication, language-paralanguage-kinesics, the basic of nonverbal research; and secondly, the rest of the bodily systems, all of which transmit information between sender and receiver through kinetic (generating language, paralanguage and kinesics), chemical, dermal, olfactory, gustatory, thermal and kinesthetic receptors, either simultaneously or individually. This complexity of systems and the basic requirements for their reception suggest immediately the essential difference between the novel and the play, what is or is not possible on the stage. While the novelist can choose to describe and evoke all somatic activities, leaving it to the reader to recreate them in his imagination, the playwright must limit himself to only those activities that can play a function in the actor–audience relationship—which depends on what can be perceived visually and auditorilly by the latter—while, on the other hand, he can go much farther than his narrative counterpart; for beyond the reading there is always the possibility of the sensorial realization of his characters on the stage, at least through language, paralanguage, kinesics, and proxemics.

2. The Verbal and Nonverbal Components of the Dramaturgic Text

A cursory reading of both a page from a novel, where the writer and his characters speak (they among themselves, he to us), and a page from a play, where the author (not as clearly omniscient) is also addressing us in stage directions, reveals the limitations of written language and the fact that we would never rely solely on what words the characters say. Take, for instance, the last part of the fourth scene in Part I of O'Neill's *Desire Under the Elms* (1924)[1]* (actually a self-contained scene), in which Abbie, old Cabot's new woman, confronts Eben, one of her future stepsons and soon lover in their doomed desire, and then Eben expresses his resentment against his father's betrayal of the family and his mother's memory. Just as was illustrated in the previous chapter with regard to the novel, the reader, perhaps also director and actor, should recognize this text as being constructed solely by the following elements:

(a) a printed morphological-syntactical exchange whose morphemes and lexemes express mainly two conversational exchanges, Abbie–Eben and Eben–Cabot, revealing the women's attempt to win Eben's affection through deceitful means, his equivocal hatred and already hidden lust for her, the story of her life, and the father's harshness toward his children and his also equivocal claim of God's support;

(b) two kinds of symbolizations of silences (apart from the normative syntactical pauses and stops marked by [,] and [.], the dash [–] used twenty times to indicate short breaks, and four suspension points [. . . .] used twice to convey longer pauses that act in one's mind as carriers of the previous statement ("Yer Paw's spoke a lot of yew . . . .", "an' then your Paw come . . . ."), eight question marks, and eighteen closing exclamation marks which, given the historical limitations of the symbol [!] (see Chapter 8), serve two different purposes, high volume and tense emphasis;

(c) twenty-four descriptions (stage directions) or paralinguistic features concerning: Abbie's laughter of "seduction" and then of "confidence", her tone of "admiration", "a scornful sense of power", "calm", "strength", "defiance", slow speech of sexual desire, the "mouthing" of certain words, and a long pause; Eben, who speaks viciously, "with bitter scorn", "in forced stilted tones of emotion and desire", "harshly", "furiously", "maliciously", "stupidly and as hypnotized", "violently", and "mockingly" at his father; and Cabot's "fury", "contempt", "obliviousness", "summoning God", "harshly", "quickly", and "matter-of-factly";

(d) twenty-one descriptions of the kinesic behaviors of the three particip-ants in their face-to-face encounters: Abbie's "eyes gloating on the house", looking at Eben "penetratingly" and then "watching him carefully", and

* Superscript numbers refer to Notes at end of chapter. The extract from Part I, Scene iv of *Desire under the Elms* is reprinted from *The Plays of Eugene O'Neill* by permission of Random House Inc., copyright © 1924 and renewed 1952 by Eugene O'Neill.

looking "proudly" at her new table, smiling queerly and then "satisfiedly", her "queer coarse expression of desire in her face and body" for Eben, putting her hand on his arm, but being "stung" by his calling her a harlot; Eben's leaping to his feet and "glowering at her speechlessly", shuddering when she talks to him, then "as if he were to attack her" furiously "flinging off her arm" when she touches him, "slamming the door behind him", "breaking in violently", staring at his father "with hate", and glowering at him; and Cabot's "glowering" at his sons' voices off-stage with "his fist clenched" and "his face grim with rage", "raising his arms to heaven" in fury, glowering at Eben, and "shaking his finger threateningly at him";

(e) one instance of Abbie flushing, which in the proxemic actor–audience relationship can only be interpreted as a glowing facial expression rather than as an otherwise perfectly congruent dermal reaction in a situation in which she is called a harlot;

(f) seven indications of the movements of the characters about the stage: Cabot returning from the barn; Eben rushing out the door, coming around the corner, and stopping at seeing his father; and Abbie coming into the kitchen, a specifically proxemic behavior when she walks up to Eben, and later washing her dishes;

(g) finally, we could single out the playwright's exclusive comments on the character's mutual feelings, given as qualifying elements of some of their paralinguistic and kinesic behaviors: Abbie's "appraisal of his strength as against hers", her desire "timely awakened by his youth and good looks", her "sense of power", her "confidence" and "pride"; Eben's "fighting against his growing attraction and sympathy", and his hate for his father; and Cabot's "fury", "contempt", and claim for God's help and justice.

3. The Development of Stage Directions on Nonverbal Communication

We must conclude that a substantial part of O'Neill's written scene consists of descriptions of nonverbal activities which are produced either simultaneously or alternating with what they express verbally, supporting, repeating, emphasizing or contradicting those words. The author, therefore, openly acknowledged the limitations of his written-typographical conveyance of verbal behaviors to portray vividly the physical and psychological configurations of his characters, and resorted to the few means available to him and to what Hess-Lüttich (1979) has studied incisively as 'grapho-stylistics'.

Another passage from another author might contain more or fewer indications of nonverbal behaviors, which at this point I still do not refer to as stage directions, since they actually become such when the text is treated as a script to be performed on the stage. Thus, it becomes evident that the ratio between verbal and nonverbal activities is an indication of certain stylistic characteristics of individual writers as well as of specific tendencies and periods.

Classical Greek tragedies such as Aeschylus' *Agamemnon* (458 B.C.), Sophocles' *Oedipus Rex* (430 B.C.) and Euripides' *The Bacchae* (*ca.* 406 B.C.) bear almost no stage directions on the characters' nonverbal behaviors, while a comedy like Aristophanes' bawdy *Lysistrata* (411 B.C.) has specific basic paralinguistic, kinesic and even objectual behaviors.

Elizabethan dramatists, including Shakespeare, provide only a few essential directions for the performance and, therefore, almost no help for the reader's recreation of the character and his cultural and social setting. Later, Restoration comedies such as Wycherley's *The Country Wife* (1675) include already occasional descriptions of paralanguage: "surlily", "whispers", "sighs", only; and kinesics: "salutes her", without the modern reader knowing exactly how, "drawing near", "walks carelessly to and fro", "clapping his hand in his breast" in love, "rubbing his forehead" signifying his thoughts, "offers to draw" (leave), "holds up the penknife", "looking about her", "pulls him by the cravat", "alone, leaning on his elbow", "draws his sword", "pulls aside her handkerchief", "lays his hand on his sword", "makes signs with her hand for Pinchwife to be gone", something which changes culturally, "she claps him on the back", "offers to whisper", and the final undescribed "dance to cuckolds".

A century later, Sheridan's comedy *The Rivals* (1775) offers very unevenly distributed directions on paralanguage: "speaking simply", "aloud", "whimpering", "in a low hoarse tone", softly, "peevishly", "sobbing", and "softening"; and kinesics: "exeunt severally", "kissing his hand to Lydia", "practicing a dancing step", "makes signs [. . .] to leave them together", "looking round by degrees, then starts up", "sits sullenly in her chair", "walking about in heart, bowing, muffles up his face, and takes a circle to go off", and "puts himself in attitude" (of being shot at).

Finally, from early nineteenth century on the theater explodes with realism, much as it happened in the novel. Contrary to one's expectations, Fielding's picaresque *Tom Jones* (1749) contains almost no descriptions of paralanguage or kinesics, although Cervantes' *Don Quixote* (1605–15), the model for the modern realistic novel, offers wonderful instances of that type of physical and psychological realism which develops even further with Dickens, Dostoevsky, Galdós and other nineteenth-century realists. In the theater, from stormy romantic dramas like Hugo's *Hernani* (1830) and Rivas' *Don Alvaro* (1835), Wagner's operas, and the post-romantic anti-prose reaction of Rostand's *Cyrano* (1897) (of otherwise extremely realistic scenery and nonverbal stage direction, incarnated by the great actor Coquelin), to the naturalistic characterizations by Chekhov, Ibsen, Strindberg or Hauptman, the audience can immerse itself in the play through a linguistic, paralinguistic, kinesic and environmental recreation of the playwright's creation (see Hess-Lüttich 1982).

In America this stage 'authenticity' grows with Belasco's painstaking film-like realism in Broadway and the social-psychological plays of O'Neill, Rice, Saroyan, Tennessee Williams and Arthur Miller, while social realism develops in Europe as well. The playwright's comments not only provide stage directions for a better understanding of the 'mis-en-scene' and the character's personality, but intervene very much like the omniscient narrative author's. His specifications of verbal and nonverbal behaviors would not suffice, in their opinion, for us to define them as true-to-life persons, while the characters themselves would not elaborate on their own past or present circumstances either.

This has some complementary effects on the play and on the reader or spectator. On the other hand, the specification of the character's behavior diminishes the *plurality* of interpretation by each reader, in each reading and in each performance, as much as the novelist's descriptions do. While some could argue in favor of the actor's freedom of choice and interpretation and say that the lack of stage directions of this type is precisely an important requirement from an artistic-intellectual-semiotic point of view, others, of course, would easily take the contrary opinion and consider the writer's responsibility to convey the reality of his characters as he created them in his imagination. Therefore, the theater can reach that degree of 'originality' in passages like the tense silent encounter between Amanda and her son, Tom, in *The Glass Menagerie* (1945), in which Tennessee Williams gives the reader, and then the actor, as many as six paralinguistic cues and fourteen kinesic ones:

> (Tom glances sheepishly but sullenly at her averted figure and slumps at the table. The coffee is scalding hot; he sips it and gasps and spits it back in the cup. At his gasp, Amanda catches her breath and half turns. Then she catches herself and turns back to the window. Tom blows on his coffee, glancing sideways at his mother. She clears her throat, Tom clears his. He starts to rise, sinks back down again, scratches his head, clears his throat again. Amanda coughs. Tom raises his cup in both hands to blow on it, his eyes staring over the rim of it at his mother for several moments. Then he slowly sets the cup down and awkwardly and hesitantly rises from the chair). (Scene Four)

As for the omniscient attitude of today's realistic playwrights, very much like the one traditionally exercised by the novelist, it provides an added dimension, as they tell us about the mutual inner feelings of the characters, not only now but before the staged present. Again, one could argue against this attitude, but it is nevertheless part of the modern play, which is to be read by a much larger public than the earlier dramatists could have ever dreamed of. On the other hand, as *Death of a Salesman* (1949), for instance, develops before an audience the sensitive spectator can interpret in the dialogues Linda's personality and attitude toward her husband, Willy, unaware of the author's comments on the two of them:

> (LINDA, his wife [. . .] Most often jovial, she has developed an iron repression of her exceptions to WILLY's behaviors—she more than loves him, admires him, as though his mercurial nature, his temper, his massive dreams and little cruelties, served her only as sharp reminders of the turbulent longings within him, longings which she shares but lacks the temperament to utter and follow to their end) (Act I)

4. The Semiotic Itineraries of the Character Between Playwright and Reader, Actor, and Spectator

As one ponders on the many semiotic limitations of the written word, he sees that spoken language (vocal-auditory signs) and movements are evoked by means of signs we call words and punctuation marks, that the sensorial world is transmitted to us through writing and printing, which in turn elicit images of it in our minds according to the writer's skills and our own capabilities. In both the novel and the theater, acoustic, visual, tactile and kinesthetic, olfactory, and gustatory signs are all reduced to visually apprehended ones. From a semiotic point of view, which naturally includes the very craft of play writing and its ultimate realization on stage, it is interesting for the actor, as much as for the critic and the writer himself, to consider the itinerary followed by the characters and their environment—but mainly the characters—from the time they are created by the playwright to the time when they are either recreated by a reader, by a reader who then becomes actor or director, or by a spectator who is only part of an audience and has not read the play in most cases. The semiotic sign processes observed in narrative literature (Poyatos 1977a) are therefore much more complex in the theater, since the characters can be subject to those mediating agents, and not simply a reader. The various possible itineraries followed by the character between playwright and audience are outlined in the chart 'Playwright–Reader–Actor–Audience Relationship, represented in Fig. 10.1.

Stage One

The writer, drawing from his own world of physical and intellectual experiences, selects as his material verbal and nonverbal signs of different origins (perceived directly as he creates his characters, through memories of experiences, or from other literary or artistic sources), thus giving shape to

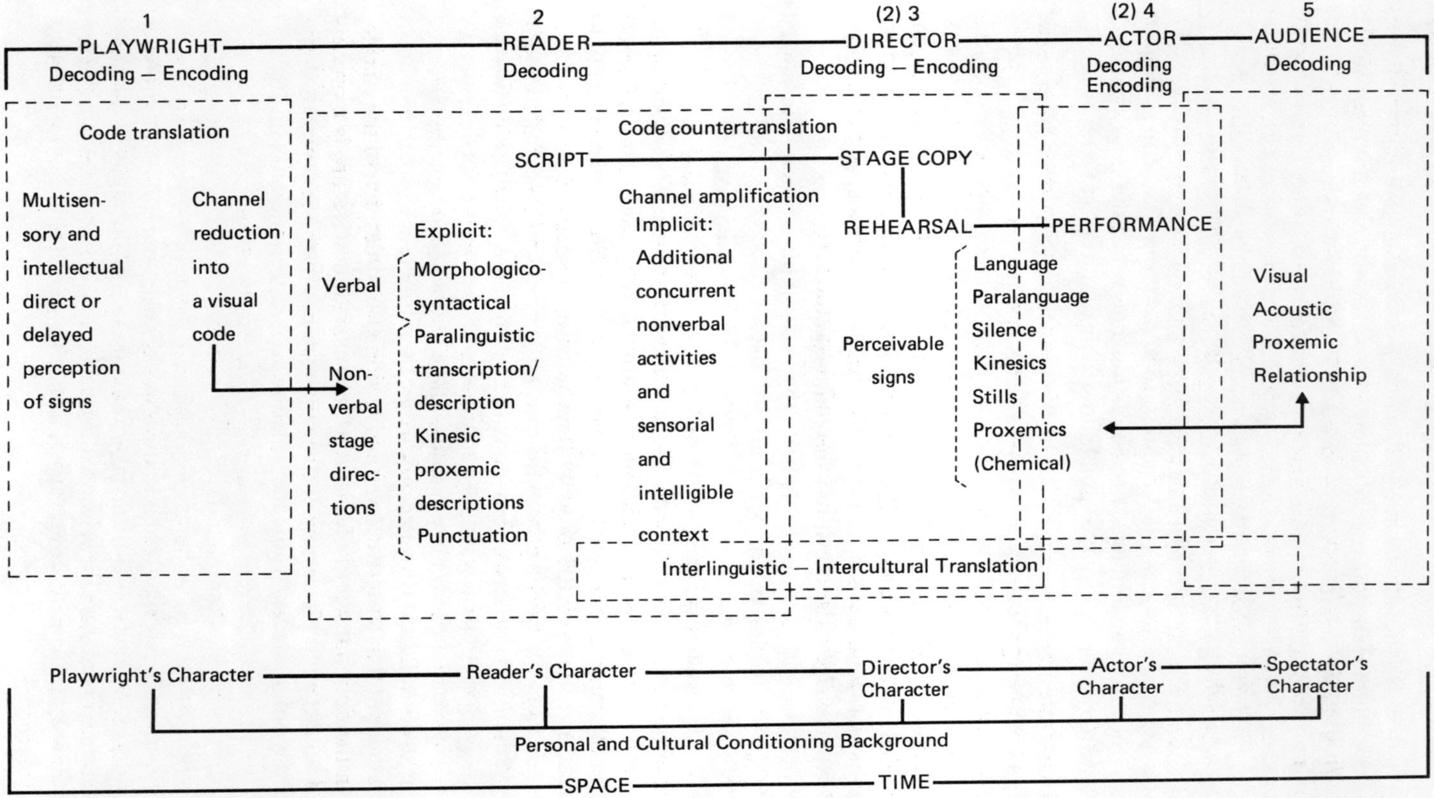

FIG. 10.1. The Playwright–Reader–Actor–Audience Relationship.

the physical and psychological peculiarities of his characters. But, unlike the novelist, these characters must define themselves and consistently develop as individuals through their verbal and nonverbal behaviors, as in real life. The omniscient author's considerations and shortcuts offered to the narrative reader must be absent, except for the stage directions. We know, of course, that nonverbal behaviors, mainly paralanguage and kinesics, are not given only by stage directions, but much more through their written speech, which implicitly carries them as cooccurrent activities.

Stage Two

At any rate, this is the reduction of all channels to the printed page, a sort of sign metamorphosis, the silencing of the playwright's experience, with all its living details, into the visual medium of the written page, with its words and punctuation symbols, the latter unnecessarily limited since their invention (Poyatos 1981d). And it is in this form that the Greek tragedies, the comedies of Aristophanes, Plautus and Terence, and the plays of the Renaissance were transmitted from their author's infinitely richer intellectual experiences to the inevitably limited story, the text.

Stage Three

Next comes what for the novel (see Fig. 9.1) is the third and last stage in the transmission of the character and his world, the reader's decoding of the text, a fascinating counter-metamorphosis whereby the author's mental images of sensorial and intellectual experiences are brought back to life as we interpret the printed page. There are two inherent problems here, however, as this semiotic process of recreation is inescapably subject to the basic dimensions of space and time. Any character, whether or not his creator intends it that way, responds in lesser or greater degree to the writer's own spatial and temporal settings, as he later responds to the reader's cultural and historical background.

It is evident that the creation, transmission and perception of the characters in the fictional world of narrative and dramatic literature is a process based on the author's own exclusive circumstance in the real world, at the encoding or input end, and the individual reader's own exclusive circumstance, also in the real world, at the decoding or output end.

It is at this point, then, that the infinite possibilities in the decoding of the character as portrayed in the script reveal, as in the novel, his flesh-and-bone vitality, since he is shaped from real-life experiences and then brought back to life shaped again by real-life experiences. This problem, which constitutes the ultimate consequence for narrative literature, is not at all the last one for the 'dramatis personae', except when their reader is their last intellectual manipulator.

Stage Four

It is beyond the reading of the play, however, that one finds the 'raison d'etre' of the theater and the intellectual, social and physical fascination of the verbal, but even more nonverbal, theatrical experience. A fourth stage is reached by the play when its story, that is, the logical (except for the theater of the absurd) succession of messages exchanged through verbal and nonverbal activities, far from remaining in one's mind as an intellectual exercise, acquires a sensible reality again when the dormant creations of the playwright are finally brought to life by the persons who embody them and who are looked at as if through the keyhole by a not always silent witness called the audience. This is the stage at which the verbal and nonverbal behaviors of the characters must be carefully put together in the rehearsals in order to give that audience the illusion of a pretended reality, the ultimate goal of the actor, above any other scenic means.

The Basic Triple Structure language-paralanguage-kinesics is what makes the play come to life on the stage. Pirandello can show us an empty stage in *Six Characters in Search of an Author* (1921), and the audience will recognize it as such, just as Arthur Miller, in *Death of a Salesman*, asks us to construct an unreal scenery made up of different rooms, "imaginary wall-lines" and "one-dimensional" roof-like, yet both made the utmost effort to convey the reality of their flesh-and-bone human beings by carefully specifying as often as necessary, not just what they say (language) but how exactly they say it (paralanguage) and how exactly they move (kinesics) about their make-belief settings. By doing this they, consciously or not, minimize the plurality of their creations. Miller knows that Willy Loman's complex feelings and profound and yet common personality must be externalized the way he is in his creator's mind, the same way as Tennessee Williams' Laura, in *The Glass Menagerie*, must speak like herself, "breathlessly at him", despairingly, frightened and shyly, and look and walk and handle her figurines all like herself, anything else being a deviation from the original reality.

This is the basic craft of the stage, to act as real-life people without being so, to develop further that counter-metamorphosis of sensible signs that were reduced to just a visual medium, the text, and later given life in the reader's mind, and infuse them with life, thus generating an additional and ultimate process of sign encoding and decoding. At this point, *the rehearsal*, that is, the director and his cast, bring together each of the individual readings of the play with their individual interpretations and try, not only to "discover a 'person' who could mean something by the sum of the expressions which compromise his part" (Miller 1972: 362), but 'the person' whom the playwright shaped verbally and nonverbally into a personality which for him has no other form. Granted that between the author's character and the reader-actor/director's one there exists a *behavioral margin* which makes it possible for both to see Willy Loman, Laura, Hedda Gabbler or Hamlet slightly different as to their paralanguage and kinesics, just as people in real life may naturally vary due to certain circumstances. It is precisely this narrow personality margin, skilfully contained in the director's stage copy of the script, that betrays the fictional nature of the dramatic character.

Yet both director and actor must possess an acute sensitiveness toward the playwright's own life and personality, which might be portrayed in a character and revealed in both verbal and nonverbal behaviors—as well as the cultural and historical settings of the story. It is through true 'cultural fluency' (Chapter 1) that they must try to embody and preserve the subtle cultural attitudes shown, for instance, by Chekhov's characters in *Uncle Vanya* (1897) as closely as possible, we might say, to Chekhov's contemporary recreation done by the Moscow Art Theater's famous director Stanislavsky in 1898, when the sign universe of both writer and company were closer to each other than they would ever be afterward. But our semiotic process of recreation is hopelessly removed from the play's first reality, and the need for deep insight and true knowledge of the man Chekhov and his Russia becomes much more acute for us because we may be treading the dangerous domain of the translated play, always an 'intercultural translation'. This is not just a mere linguistic rendering into another language, but a whole substitution of codes, which in fact affects all the decoding stages, from the reader to the spectator.

Stage Five

The last possible sign-transmission in the semiotic itinerary of a play is that which develops between the cast 'living' the script with all of the author's and director's directions—complemented by an objectual environment and by the use of sound and light effects—and its audience. An audience, however, is in itself a conglomerate of playgoers each having in common only an interest in decoding the world of the play and judging both the creator and the recreators, yet possessing different capabilities for such a task. The spectators are the ultimate decoders of the playwright's characters and only infrequently have they been readers of his text with its own 'grapho-stylistics', stage directions on nonverbal behaviors and on the scenery, and the comments on the characters' lives and interrelationships.

What the spectator sees and hears is the performance, that is, the conveyance of the characters as the product of the actor-director team's decoding of the text (in turn the encoding of the writer's experience) and their own sensorial verbal-nonverbal encoding. This actor–audience relationship is a visual-acoustic-proxemic one and comprises a sensible and intelligible stage reality which is the focal point of the wider reality of the house. Those two realities are linked by the interplay of human factors, such as the collective presence of the audience, the spatial relationship among its members, and the further spatial and structural relationships determined by the architectural environment and its acoustic and visual properties, all topics for further semiotic-social research. It is, then, in this context that one, either as reader, director or actor, must judge the sensible elements of the performance and the forms and functions of its nonverbal behaviors.

5. Nonverbal Communication Systems of the Characters

It is clear, then, that nonverbal communication constitutes a very important part of the interactions depicted in the play and that its decoding takes place at several levels, author–reader, author–actor, author–director, author–spectator, and actor–spectator. One realizes that while the behaviors of the narrative characters are controlled by the writer, those in the theater come under the influence of the director–actor team in such a way that the playwright can lose a great deal of control over his characters while the script is being handled by the company.

In addition, we must also differentiate between the *explicit* nonverbal behaviors, that is, the ones verbally described by stage directions (together with the few paralinguistic features represented by punctuation) and the *implicit* ones, which our previous experience of human behavior tells us cooccur with specific verbal constructs without the need for stage directions. Both performers and director can interpret these implicit behaviors accurately, without unnecessarily 'inventing', since certain paralinguistic and kinesic acts just 'go with' certain words and phrases.

Again, a major cultural problem arises in the translated play, and we face a dilemma: we can 'translate' certain gestures, for instance—since this problem concerns particularly kinesics and proxemics, varying much more conspicuously across cultures than paralanguage—as we translate from the original language, for one speaks and moves in his own language; or, for the sake of cultural accuracy, we can translate the foreign script preserving certain typical gestures and trying to look American, for instance, while embodying Jimmy, of *The Glass Menagerie*, or the characters in *Desire Under the Elms*. But this is also a central problem to be elaborated on in the future.

At any rate, while the novel, as I pointed out earlier, is meant to be read and contains descriptions of every somatic system, from a faint gasp or a pupillary reaction to tense emotional gestures or stentorian shouting, the play must depend only on paralanguage, kinesics and kinesically-based proxemic shifts about the stage, and only in their higher-key manifestations (within certain limits and without 'overacting') because of the spatial relationship between the performers and the spectators across the whole house.

6. Paralanguage

As discussed in Chapter 5, paralanguage is today a very complex field of interdisciplinary research. It should be more systematically acknowledged by theater people, as it deals with nonverbal voice qualities, modifiers and alternants or independent sounds that cooccur or alternate with verbal language, kinesics and other somatic systems, determined by anatomical, physiological, psychological, social and cultural factors. Here I will simply review the paralinguistic phenomena included in each of the four categories discussed before, indicating some instances of the playwright's labels or descriptions and giving the context only occasionally. I would urge the reader, however, to note those which implicitly contain cooccurring kinesic behaviors, for we know that each of them elicits a congruent facial expression and/or bodily articulation.

Primary qualities

Primary qualities, so essential on the stage, are: Timbre (permanent voice register, higher in women and children, but typically used by the less experienced acting amateurs of both sexes), resonance (oral—nasal), volume, tempo (often made faster by amateurs), pitch level (the tone of a portion of speech), pitch registers (during speech, from overlow to overhigh or falsetto), pitch interval or syllabic distance (from overnarrow in excitement to overspread from boredom), pitch range in one's speech (overnarrow—overwide), syllabic duration (drawled—clipped), intonation range (melodious—monotonous) and general rhythm of speech (regular and smooth—irregular and jerky). They are permanent features with which the cast must identify the individuals on the stage as well as certain situations (e.g., the slow tempo of superiority, the higher pitch of surprise, the lower one of confidentiality), yet playwrights rarely establish this character's 'voice set' when they give us their initial physical portraits. They only indicate volume (often confused with intensity of deliverance, and vice versa, due to the ambiguity of [!]), pitch (when the character speaks 'gaily', 'hysterically' or 'dully'), and sometimes drawling and clipping when depicting the vernacular speech (as in *Desire Under the Elms*).

Qualifiers

Qualifiers can be outlined again as: Respiratory control (usually exhaling air during speech, but ingressive in expressions of terror, fear, etc.), glottis control (from weak whispering and 'stage whispering' to murmured voice, and quavery voice), laryngeal control (creaky, whisper-creaky, breathy voice), velar control (very oral—very nasal), pharyngeal control (hollow, throaty or guttural, pharyngeal as in ventriloquism, snorting, husky, hoarse, the American hillbilly's nasal twang, etc.), articulatory tension (very lax—very tense), articulatory control (very clear—very slurred), labial control (which changes voice when the lips are pursed, rounded, spread, etc., in different degrees which typify specific emotional situations, age, sex, etc.), maxillary control (either anatomically conditioned or shaped for different real-life or performing purposes as when portraying an underworld character). Some of these may, of course, be also permanent qualities in one's voice set which must override the actor's deliverance while on stage.

Along with primary qualities, qualifiers constitute the bulk of the paralinguistic repertoires manipulated by actors, of which some examples of the playwright's labeling for stage directors will suffice to show how they mark the development of the characters:

In Chekhov's *The Cherry Orchard*'s (1904) first act, the old valet Firs, as he performs his duties faithfully, speaks "anxiously", "sternly" to the maid, "gleefully" to one of his young mistresses, mutters often, "reprovingly" in his concern for his master's appearance. In Ibsen's *Hedda Gabbler*'s (1890) third act, Mrs. Elvstead, Lovborg's mistress, betrayed by Hedda, speaks "terrified", "softly and piteously", "imploringly", "wringing her hands", "softly, in agony", "with a suppressed shriek", "trying to conceal her anxiety", "wandering restlessly about the room". In *Desire Under the Elms*' first scene of Part II, Abbie, who appears sitting in a rocker and enervated by the heat, speaks "triumphant", "softly", "murmurs languorously: Hain't the sun strong an' hot? . . . burning inside ye—makin' ye want t' grow—into somethin' else", "seductively", "trying to cancel a growing excitement", "excitedly", "weakly", "bursting out", "furiously", "savagely", "stung", "fiercely", "in a scream", "bitterly", "scornfully", "jeeringly", "crossly", "indifferently", "resentfully", "harshly", "remorselessly", "vengefully", "enraged", "beyond endurance", "wildly", "vindictively", "defiantly", "frightened", etc.

Differentiators

Differentiators have been identified earlier as laughter, crying, sighing, coughing, yawning, sneezing, belching, hiccoughing, snorting, snuffling, and different degrees of whispering and shouting, all while speaking. They differentiate physiological and psychological states and are intimately co-structured with kinesic behavior, while being modified by primary qualities and qualifiers.

Laughter has received the most attention for its many forms and functions in society (from affiliation, bond-forming, love, tension-relief, commicality, and happiness, to aggression, mocking, seduction, and deception, each with different phonetic and kinesic qualifiers). While the novel affords much more elaborate descriptions of their display and meanings, the dramaturgic definitions play also important functions in the script, and a detailed analysis by the performers of what, how and why they 'mean' by laughter should prove quite useful. In an emotional play like *Desire Under the Elms* laughter is carefully defined and even typifies the individual characters. The men: "half jocularly", "with a forced jocular heartiness", "beginning to laugh", "laughingly", "chuckling bitterly", "with a sardonic chuckle", "both roar with a sardonic laugh", "abrupt sardonic laughter", "with his sardonic burst of laughter", "holding their sides, rocking with wild laughter" (as certain other behaviors, a clear social identifier). Abbie, "with a cold laugh of confidence", "snickers contemptuously", "with a shrill laugh: Can't I?", "she laughts a crazy triumphant laugh". And the people gathered in the Cabots' home repeat Abbie's remark about Eben "with many a guffaw and titter, and a roar of laughter". *The Cherry Orchard*, on the other hand, is a story of quiet sadness caused by the sale of the orchard to a merchant, and its owner, Madame Ranevsky, "speaks softly through her tears", "weeping quietly", "weeping bitterly", while the old house-servant Firs "weeps with joy at seeing her again". But many other differentiators are used, as in real life, as modifiers of verbal language, as when Simeon, in *Desire Under the Elms*, retorts at his stepmother's sense of possession "with a snort: *Her* house!" A second look at the few differentiators just quoted suggests their cooccurrent kinesic behaviors, particularly facial expressions, which proves the integration of the Basic Triple Structure: language (*what* they say), paralanguage (*how* they say it), kinesics (how they move it).

Alternants

Alternants, finally, constitute the most numerous series of utterances which in fact form a true lexicon with almost as clear meanings as ethymologically derived words, and of which, in English, a recent 'College Edition' of the Webster Dictionary (1974) includes: *Aha, Ahem, Er, Ha, Ha-ha, Hem, Hum, H'm, Hep, Hip, Hist, Ho, Humph, Ooph, Poof, Pooh, Psst, Pugh, Shoo, Tsk, Ugh, Uh-huh, Oh-uh*. Many more, of course, can be classified and studied (Poyatos 1975e) as vocalic or consonantal, articulated or inarticulated, as they range from audible air ingressions (a gasp, or a cue to start talking) or an apico-alveolar click of the tongue (of content, hesitation, prespeech) to a subtle sniff of resignation (which characterized Julietta Massina in the film *La strada*), a sensual moan, a beckoning hiss in some cultures or any form of laughter, crying or sneezing (when not modifying speech as differentiators).

Alternants are so much a part of each culture and of the daily conversational lexicon that both novelists and playwrights—particularly the latter, who cannot indulge in detailed descriptions of otherwise meaningful alternants—should be able to resort to established written forms of utterances which must necessarily be used by their characters, as they are constantly in real life with as much lexical values as words in many instances. Thus, Shaw had to write in *Pygmalion* (1912): "MRS. EYNSFORD HILL *clicks her tongue sympathetically*!!!" As discussed in Chapter 5, the situation is absurd because we lack verbs, nouns and even labels for several varieties of, for instance, hissing, which have also different meanings. Many alternants, however, are so subtle acoustically that even if they occur 'naturally' on the stage (as part of an otherwise 'non-spontaneous' performance) they would not be perceived by the majority of the audience in the theater, as would happen with the very common prespeech, floor-claiming tongue click, audible air ingression, or a light snuffling laugh of contempt, or a repressed short and ingressive hissing of pain or fear. And yet, the use of alternants can certainly identify personality, status, sex, and situations, and their status runs high in the modern theater.

In *Desire Under the Elms*, Eben, "his hands on his hips, stares at the sky, sighs with a puzzled awe: God! Purty!", "sighs heavily and Abbie echoes him" (both in adjoining bedrooms), "violently speaking between sobs and gasps" after fighting with his father, "panting and sobbing" after Abbie has killed their child, "panting exhaustedly wild-eyed and mad-looking", and at the end "Sshh! Listen! They've come t' take us!" Abbie, "with a little cry she runs over to hug and kiss Eben", both then "panting like two animals", then "with an uncertained troubled laugh: Waal, I kissed you anyways—!", "with a stiffled cry" she runs toward the struggling father and son, and "sobs unrestrainedly", looks at Eben "with a cry of anguished joy" at being together. Simeon, Eben's brother, "smacks his lips: I air hungry!" "putting his muddy boots up on the table, tilting back his chair, and puffing defiantly", "they both sigh", "they drink—puff resolutely—sigh—take their feet down from the table".

In *The Glass Menagerie*, the characters display alternants very much in consonance with the personalities as the writer imagined them: Laura, crippled and moody, "draws a long breath" when her mother mentions her lost ambitions for her and "utters a startled, doubtful laugh" at the thought of marriage, "clears her throat" when embarrassed and when she is turning the broken unicorn in her hands; her bitter and dreaming brother "laughs wildly", utters "an outraged groan" when he struggles with his coat, "lies down groaning", sips, gasps, spits and blows in the already quoted scene with his mother, and uses 'Um-hum', 'Ugh', and 'Huh'; the mother, a nostalgic former Southern belle, "draws a long breath" and dabs her lips and nostrils with a handkerchief, laughs with "gay laughter", and "a peal of girlish laughter".

7. Kinesics in the Script: Stageable vs. Unstageable, Explicit and Implicit

I have mentioned how the fact that kinesic activities, if only a flitting gesture, are impossible to disassociate semantically and structurally from language and paralanguage when one of the two is active, prompted me to wonder whether the ancient pictographic representations called rebus, which depicted certain kinesic behaviors, could not have gradually developed to include some kinemes or kinemorphemes, just as it developed into the symbolization of phonemes and morphemes (Poyatos 1977b).

This thought would certainly apply much more to the theater, since the playwright might have welcomed the use of a few symbols to refer at least to some basic movements and postures. After all, mime and silent film are possible, but verbal theater without facial and body expression is inconceivable, and the decoding process at the spectator's end leans heavily on the kinetic-visual channel, at times the only one through which messages are being coded. While the novelist has at his disposal the whole gamut of kinesic expressions and can see and make his characters express themselves, or qualify their words with a twitch of the mouth or a tightening of a handshake, the playwright must realize that the subtleties of real-life kinesics, if produced on the stage, are lost beyond the first rows of the theater.

Someone like O'Neill can provide the script with all sorts of kinesic stage directions. He says that Abbie's body "squirms desirously", that old Cabot's "hard grim expression of his face has changed" and "seems . . . softened, mellowed", his eyes with "a strange, incongruous dreamy quality", and later "stares at Eben with a trace of grudging admiration", as in so many other instances of gaze behaviors, such as important research area today, applicable very particularly to the semiotics of the stage.

O'Neill also writes that Eben's face is "very pale", that Abbie's is "flushed", and that Simeon and Peter, whose boots are supposed to be "caked with earth", "smell of earth". In other words, to difficult kinesic behaviors he adds sensorial experiences which are impossible to convey on a stage, as they fall outside the dramaturgic world, unless the audience experiences, as happens in real life, a synesthesial visual interpretation of, for instance, the olfactory properties of the earth-stained bodies.

As for the subtle kinesic messages, such as the ones quoted, the actor must discern between what is utterly impossible and what is feasible only through sheer exaggeration and overacting. He must possess the ability to strike a balance between the perceptual capabilities of first-row spectators and gallery ones because, as he displays both paralinguistic and kinesic behaviors, the more at home he feels 'living' the character, the more likely his is to emit signs which will never be perceived, thus causing the zero-decoding situation mentioned when discussing the sign-meaning relationship

(Chapter 3). This situation, possible with subtle paralinguistic and kinesic activities, can be detrimental for the performance because in the costructuration of verbal and nonverbal behaviors those which are missed might not necessarily be *secondary* sign systems in a particular situation, but very much *primary* ones, conveying specific messages more accurately than words.

As with paralanguage, many kinesic behaviors are already implicit in the text as inherent in specific verbal and paralinguistic constructs, as when Higgings utters the last words in *Pygmalion*: "Pickering! Nonsense: she's going to marry Freddy. Ha ha! Freddy!! Freddy!! Ha ha ha ha ha!!!!! [*He roars with laughter as the play ends*]". Again, the performing tean director-cast must decide whether they are translating kinesics as well as language and paralanguage, for some cultures display different gestures in the same situation, and not rendering the play into the audience's own culture may conspicuously betray the actors' incongruent movements as they portray certain typical foreign characters. I have witnessed this particular problem while watching a supposedly very good Spanish production of John Patrick's *Teahouse of the August Moon* (1952) (with typical American G.I.s) and then an American one of Lorca's *The House of Bernarda Alba* (1936).

8. The Physico-psychological Portrait of the Character

As with the paralanguage attached to or alternating with verbal speech, both actor and director will complete the kinesic phraseology of the character, since the playwright does not even provide the key gestures and movements as the character is seen by each of his or her readers-actors.

An essential stage direction for establishing the nonverbal configuration of the character is, in my opinion, the initial physical or *physico-psychological portrait* provided by some playwrights but neglected by others. Chekhov and Strindberg, for instance, do not give an initial definition of their main characters. Neither does Ibsen in *Ghosts* (1881) or *The Wild Duck* (1884), although he describes them in *Hedda Gabbler*, a later play, saying of Hedda that "her steel-gray eyes express a cold, unruffled repose", that Mrs. Elvsted is of "fragile figure [. . .] with a startled, inquiring expression", and describing Brack's and Lovborg's features in detail, though without truly kinesic clues. Shaw describes Liza in *Pygmalion* only as "not at all a romantic figure [. . .] perhaps eighteen, perhaps twenty", yet in *Saint Joan* (1923) he draws the heroine's face with "eyes very wide apart and bulging as they often do in very imaginative people, a long well-shaped nose with wide nostrils, a short upper lip, resolute but full-lipped mouth, and handsome fighting chin". In *Juno and the Paycock* (1924), O'Casey's Mary Boyle is "a well-made and good-looking girl of twenty-two" and the "opposing forces" in her life (circumstances and the books she has read) "are apparent in her speech and manners", while the alcoholic and dissipated Captain Boyle's cheeks are "reddish-purple, are puffed out, as if he were always repressing an almost irresistible ejaculation", and he "carries himself with the upper part of his body slightly thrown back and his stomach slightly thrust forward. His walk is a slow, consequential strut".

With such initial definitions the sensitive actor can shape the nonverbal repertoire of his character without deviating much from his creator's conception. However, the discrepancy between minutely described settings and undefined characters occurs even in modern realistic American drama, in which the character's creator gives the performers total freedom to shape them on the basis of their development throughout the play, as happens in Williams' *The Glass Menagerie* (but not in *The Rose Tattoo*'s [1950] lively portrayal of Rosa, Assunta and Serafina). It is true that the subsequent behavior of characters like Abbie, in *Desire Under the Elms*, can be based on the initial presentation: "buxom, full of vitality. Her round face is pretty but marred by its rather gross sensuality. There is strength and obstinacy in her jaw, a hard determination in her eyes, and about her whole personality the same unsettled, untamed, desperate quality which is so apparent in Eben". However, others, such as Willy Loman in *Death of a Salesman*, though lacking an introductory portrayal, can also be shaped by carefully putting together all the verbal and nonverbal expressions and attitudes indicated as a progressive definition throughout the play, in such a way that we might feel we are getting to know him better and better every time we watch him as happens in real life.

9. A Note on Further Research

Intimately related to the study of sound (language-paralanguage) and movement (kinesics), in the theater are those of *silence* and *stillness*, the basic meaningful nonactivities, discussed in Chapter 6. It has been seen (a) that silence and stillness can act as signs proper ("He lapses into crushed silence", *Desire Under the Elms*, III, iv), as 'zero signs', which signify by the very absence of sound and movement, and more significantly, as 'carriers' of the activity just heard or seen, which they enlarge and make more meaningful, and (b) that they are costructured with preceding, simultaneous and succeeding activities, and qualified further by the intensity of the mental or sensible cooccurring activities and by their duration. Silence and stillness in the theater (the former studied by Hess-Lüttich [1979]) still awaits systematic treatment from the point of view of the various encoding-decoding processes discussed in this chapter.

Finally, apart from these considerations, with which I merely intend to incite others to pursue much needed studies in the area of nonverbal communication in the theater, I wish to mention three other interrelated aspects as the topic of my own future work: (a) an analysis of the different somatic and extrasomatic systems based on the classification of nonverbal categories discussed in Chapter 4, and (b) a study of what exactly goes on on the stage when the playwright's script is brought to life, and what exactly the theatrical interaction is made of, for it is not 'natural conversation'—with the spontaneity of its rules, counterrules, simultaneous behaviors, pauses, feedbacks and counterfeedbacks—but 'contrived conversation'. These topics can yield much theoretical background for the performers themselves if approached in terms of the various nonverbal categories, among them: 'emotional expressions', 'emblems' (which usually express kinesically what a word or phrase would), 'language markers' (which punctuate and emphasize them), different classes of sound and movement imitations, kinesic 'pictographs' that describe the shape of the referent, and above all, "identifiers" that give bodily form to abstract concepts and moral and physical qualities, 'ideographs' that trace the direction of one's unverbalized thoughts, and 'externalizers' with which in real life we react to what is being said or silenced (but nevertheless felt) and to experiences of the external world; in addition to a series of behaviors involving physical contact with ourselves, others (varying crossculturally) and objects, and the so-called interactive 'regulators', which include all bodily systems used in real life, fewer in the theater and in film, yet such an essential gauge for the evaluation of naturalness or lack of it in the performance.

Particularly the amateur company ought to be perfectly familiar with all the regulatory elements that operate on the stage, from the handling of silences and the desirable congruity among the various systems displayed by performers, to the use of paralinguistic alternants, and typical problems such as the aforementioned 'dropping out of character' during silences, before exits, and at other times through the performance.

Notes

1. [*Abbie enters. For a moment she stands looking at* Eben. *He does not notice her at first. Her eyes take him in penetratingly with a calculating appraisal of his strength as against hers. But under this her desire is dimly awakened by his youth and good looks. Suddenly he becomes conscious of her presence and looks up. Their eyes meet. He leaps to his feet, glowering at her speechlessly.*]

ABBIE [*in her most seductive tones which she uses all through this scene*]. Be you—Eben? I'm Abbie—[*She laughs.*] I mean, I'm yer new Maw.

EBEN [*viciously*]. No, damn ye!

ABBIE [*as if she hadn't heard—with a queer smile*]. Yer Paw's spoke a lot o' yew. . . .

EBEN. Ha!

ABBIE. Ye mustn't mind him. He's an old man. [*A long pause. They stare at each other.*] I don't want t' pretend playin' Maw t' ye, Eben. [*Admiringly.*] Ye're too big an' too strong fur that. I want t' be frens with ye. Mebbe with me fur a fren ye'd find ye'd like livin' here better. I kin make it easy fur ye with him, mebbe. [*With a scornful sense of power.*] I calc'late I kin git him t' do most anythin' fur me.

EBEN [*with bitter scorn*]. Ha! [*They stare again,* Eben *obscurely moved, physically attracted to her—in forced stilted tones.*] Yew kin go t' the devil!

ABBIE [*calmly*]. If cussin' me does ye good, cuss all ye've a mind t'. I'm all prepared t' have ye agin me—at fust. I don't blame ye nuther. I'd feel the same at any stranger comin' t' take my Maw's place. [*He shudders. She is watching him carefully.*] Yew must've cared a lot fur yewr Maw, didn't ye? My Maw died afore I'd growed. I don't remember her none. [*A pause.*] But yew won't hate me long, Eben. I'm not the wust in the world—an' yew an' me've got a lot in common. I kin tell that by lookin' at ye. Waal—I've had a hard life, too—oceans o' trouble an' nuthin' but wuk fur reward. I was a orphan early an' had t' wuk fur others in other folks' hums. Then I married an' he turned out a drunken spreer an' so he had to wuk for others an' me too agen in other folks' hums, an' the baby died, an' my husband got sick an' died too, an' I was glad sayin' now I'm free fur once, on'y I diskivered right away all I was free fur was t' wuk agen in other folks' hums, doin' other folks' wuk till I'd most give up hope o' ever doin' my own wuk in my own hum, an' then your Paw come. . . . [Cabot *appears returning from the barn. He comes to the gate and looks down the road the brothers have gone. A faint strain of their retreating voices is heard: "Oh, Californi-a! That's the place for me." He stands glowering, his first clenched, his face grim with rage.*]

EBEN [*fighting against his growing attraction and sympathy—harshly*]. An' bought yew—like a harlot! [*She is stung and flushes angrily. She has been sincerely moved by the recital of her troubles. He adds furiously.*] An' the price he's payin' ye—this farm—was my Maw's, damn ye!—an' mine now!

ABBIE [*with a cool laugh of confidence*]. Yewr'n? We'll see 'bout that! [*Then strongly.*] Waal—what if I did need a hum? What else'd I marry an old man like him fur?

EBEN [*maliciously*]. I'll tell him ye said that!

ABBIE [*smiling*]. I'll say ye're lyin' a-purpose—an' he'll drive ye off the place!

EBEN. Ye devil!

ABBIE [*defying him*]. This be my farm—this be my hum—this be my kitchen—!

EBEN [*furiously, as if he were going to attack her.*] Shut up, damn ye!

ABBIE [*walks up to him—a queer coarse expression of desire in her face and body—slowly*]. An' upstairs—that be my bedroom—an' my bed! [*He stares into her eyes, terribly confused and torn. She adds softly.*] I hain't bad nor mean—'ceptin' fur an enemy—but I got t' fight fur what's due me out o' life, if I ever 'spect t' git it. [*Then putting her hand on his arm—seductively.*] Let's yew 'n' me be frens, Eben.

EBEN [*stupidly—as if hypnotized*]. Ay-eh. [*Then furiously flinging off her arm.*] No, ye durned old witch! I hate ye! [*He rushes out the door.*]

ABBIE [*looks after him smiling satisfiedly—then half to herself, mouthing the word*]. Eben's nice. [*She looks at the table, proudly.*] I'll wash up *my* dishes now. [Eben *appears outside, slamming the door behind him. He comes around corner, stops on seeing his father, and stands staring at him with hate.*]

CABOT [*raising his arms to heaven in the fury he can no longer control*]. Lord God o' Hosts, smite the undutiful sons with Thy wust cuss!

EBEN [*breaking in violently*]. Yew 'n' yewr God! Allus cussin' folks—allus naggin' 'em!

CABOT [*oblivious to him—summoningly*]. God o' the old! God o' the lonesome!

EBEN [*mockingly*]. Naggin' His sheep t' sin! T' hell with yewr God! [Cabot *turns. He and* Eben *glower at each other.*]

CABOT [*harshly*]. So it's yew. I might've knowed it. [*Shaking his finger threateningly at him.*] Blasphemin' fool! [*Then quickly.*] Why hain't ye t' wuk?

EBEN. Why hain't yew? They've went. I can't wuk it all alone.

CABOT [*contemptuously*]. Nor noways! I'm wuth ten o' ye yit, old's I be! Ye'll never be more'n half a man! [*Then, matter-of-factly.*] Waal—let's git t' the barn. [*They go. A last faint note of the "Californi-a" song is heard from the distance. Abbie is washing her dishes.*]

2. In the book on paralanguage I have just completed (which must by necessity be on the Basic Triple Structure) I elaborate on the topic of laughter as a paralinguistic-kinesic construct of great importance along with crying. Two possible punctuation symbols for such basic emotional displays, and often language modifiers, have been suggested in Chapter 8. Without dwelling on other aspects of laughter at this point, the theatrical scripts offer a unique inventory of different types of *independent laughter*, as an alternant, and what we may call *bound laughter*, that is, as a differentiator overriding speech. Besides the many positive and negative social functions of laughter, which sometimes may be identified only by subtle costructurations of voice quality,

facial expression, posture, muscle tonus, etc., the actor, as much as the linguist or the student of nonverbal communication, must be aware of what exactly it is that makes 'that' particular form of laughter 'sound' and 'look' like what it expresses, e.g.: type of paralinguistic and kinesic onset and offset, volume, pitch, resonance, and articulatory characteristics, including its vowel type, the different facial cooccurring signs, and the basic facial anatomy.

11

Literary Anthropology: a new Interdisciplinary Perspective of Man Through His Narrative Literature

1. The Subject of Literary Anthropology[1*]

GIVEN the present-day proliferation of interdisciplinary and intercultural studies concerned with complementary perspectives of man's activities, whether in relation to his congeners (verbal and nonverbal systems of communication, ecological behaviors, etc.) or to the environment (landscaping, architecture, his built objectual world), the unquestionable yet unjustifiable gulf between the theory and practice of literature and the various areas subsumed under anthropology is becoming more and more conspicuous. This betrays some unfortunate limitations on the part of whoever deals with our life habits and our material or intellectual products. In fact, it even hinders the development of some amazingly rich but rather neglected perspectives in the realm of poetics and the general theory of literature, particularly the novel and other forms of narrative. On the other hand, as anthropology involves the greater number of approaches to man, it seems to be the responsibility of both the anthropologist and the literary theoretician to explore those new perspectives and open common avenues of research, which would ultimately result in a deeper and exhaustive knowledge of themselves as members of a culture and of the defining elements of each culture.

Their tool, narrative literature (and, in a lesser degree, dramaturgic literature), constitutes without doubt the richest source of documentation of human life styles, as well as the most advanced form of one's projection in time and space and of communicating with contemporary and future generations. Even if we should exploit narrative literature from the point of view of communication only, the research area whose main characteristics and objectives are outlined here would offer an abundant array of interdiscipli-

* Superscript numbers refer to Notes at end of chapter.

nary perspectives, since the very nature of communication is interdisciplinary.

I began to develop the idea of *literary anthropology*, as an independent but complementary domain, through the interdisciplinary study of the nonverbal repertoires of the characters in narrative literature, and the transmission process that takes place, aided by those nonverbal behaviors, between writer and reader (Poyatos 1977b). Soon, however, I faced the rich world of the written narrative and realized its interdisciplinary possibilities, be it a medieval poem or a modern novel, as a source of much documentation existing in many cultures—and conspicuously lacking in others—beyond its semiotic dimension. Precisely because of the many research possibilities afforded by the analysis of nonverbal systems of communication, particularly the paralinguistic and kinesic activities described in the text, it can be said that nonverbal communication systems constitute the basis of literary anthropology, for it is by and through the display of those behaviors that cultural patterns, as well as universal or anthroponemic ones, are perceived. As I taught novel courses to students from cultures other than those depicted or revealed in the worlds we were dealing with, it became apparent that nonverbal systems were always elements of literary realism. When dealing with works like Dickens' *Pickwick Papers*, full of nineteenth-century detailed descriptions of people's interactive behaviors and their environment, or in social-realistic ones such as Steinbeck's *Grapes of Wrath*, or its contemporary *Pather Panchali*, by Banerji, it would be shortsighted not to acknowledge the functions of the nonverbal repertoires of the characters in allowing the reader to reconstruct the sensible world, which was so important in the writer's mind, and dismiss them as elements foreign to the literary analysis itself. After all, the fact that authors like Fielding, Faulkner or Hemingway play no emphasis on nonverbal communication, while in the ones just mentioned, or in the *Poema del Cid*, Cervantes, Dostoevsky or Simenon it becomes so important, proves the necessity to analyze why nonverbal communication is or is not acknowledged.

On the other hand, even a purely literary interest in the novels I had to study (and I feel that 'literary' should, by nature, imply 'interdisciplinary') soon revealed the six types of realism discussed and illustrated in Chapter 9, namely, physical, distorting, individualizing, psychological, interactive, and documentary or historical. It was mainly this last type of realism, obviously susceptible of both a diachronic and synchronic analysis of man's ways in the various national literatures, that revealed in turn a possible *anthropological realism*, which would contain sensible systems (whether somatic, objectual, or environmental) and intelligible systems, as classified in Fig. 11.1 'Systems in Literary Anthropology'. As this disclosed the multifaceted subject of literary anthropology it became clear that the researcher would have to seek his material in the realistic forms of narrative literature, whether fictional

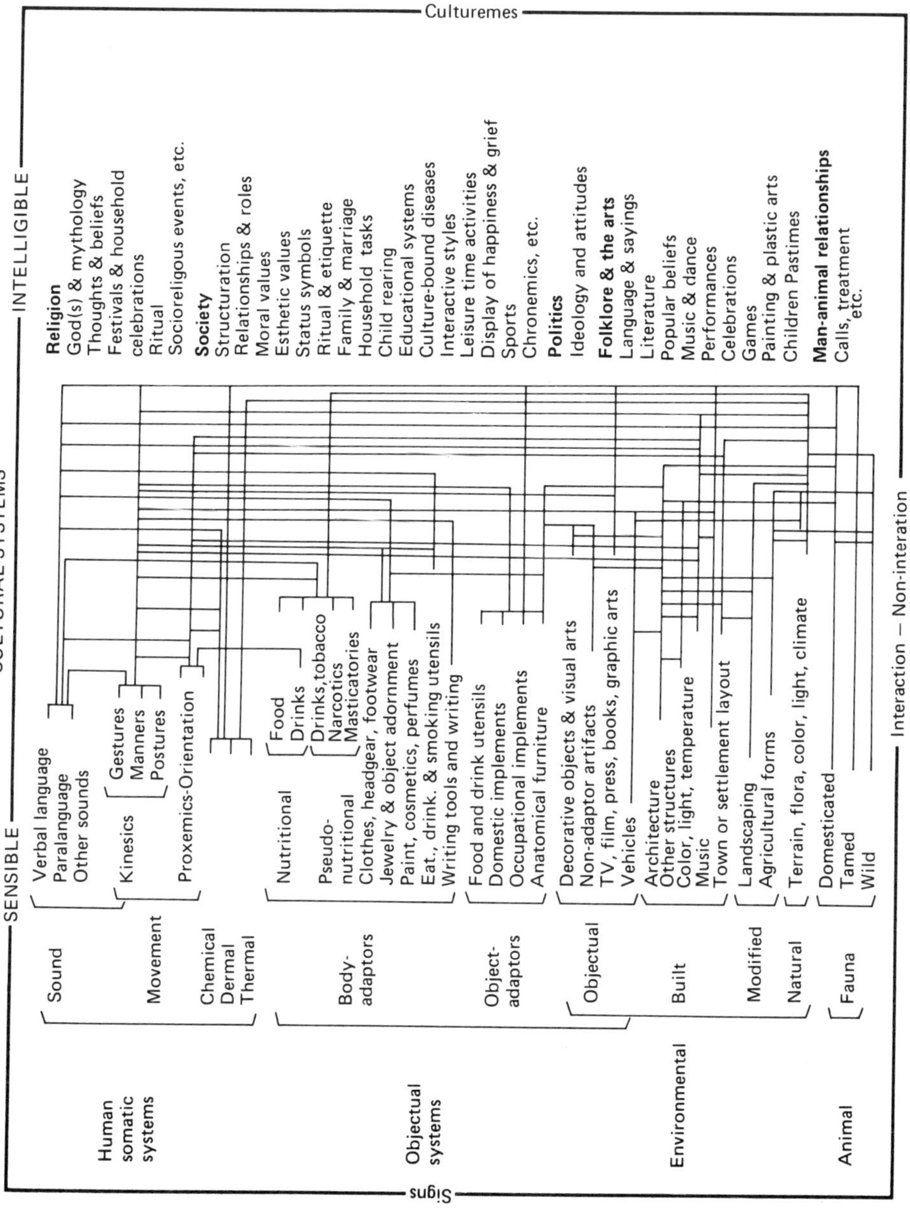

Fig. 11.1. Systems in Literary Anthropology.

(novels, short stories, epic poems) or nonfictional (chronicles, travel books, cultural accounts, biographies). Literary anthropology, then, in the light of the definition of culture offered in Chapter 1, seemed to become distinctly defined as: the study of people and their cultural manifestations through their literatures.

2. The Semiotic-Cultural Approach to Literary Anthropology

Whatever the discipline through which one may want to investigate the communicative elements of a narrative work, the researcher should seek the most systematic and, if so needed, exhaustive way of dealing with them. In this sense, only a semiotic classification of his corpus in terms of *signs* will yield a method based on an unfailing order.

A piece of narrative is made up of signs of many kinds that form the writer's fictional world, founded on his real-life one. Narrative literature, from the early national epics to the contemporary novel, shows, both universally and culture-specifically, what is probably the richest source of signs among man's intellectual achievements. Words evoke abstract concepts as well as elements of the surrounding objectual and environmental world. But, on a deeper level, we find that they may both evoke in turn whole cultural situations which contain a multitude of signs of virtually all types—whether described by the writer or implied between lines—precisely because of that sort of sign chain reaction whereby the visually present signs in the written text, sensorially and intelligibly perceived, elicit many more according to the conditioning background of each one of us. Those signs are originally of either sensory or intelligible nature, consequently this relative dichotomy makes the material under discussion clearly divisible into two principal *classes* of signs, that is, of things evoked by the writer: those which are perceived by the senses and those which are intellectually discerned, although in reality we, as readers, perceive only the printed narrative text, a crucial limitation in the interactive process between narrator and reader, as has been discussed.

Figure 11.2, 'Semiotics of Literary Anthropology', suggests the two classes of signs of which the world in a narrative work is formed. It is based on the classification of somatic signs I suggested in Chapter 2 and elsewhere (Poyatos 1981f), which can be applied to extrasomatic and intelligible ones as well, although the somatic and extrasomatic ones give concrete reality to all abstract systems.

Once the differentiation between directly perceived signs and those that are interpreted through a printed text is established—which for many would fall more within a strictly literary analysis—an anthropological criterion applied to a novel, an author, a tendency or a period would recognize, first of all, the existence of channels through which signs are conveyed, that is, sensory (e.g., visual) or intelligible (i.e., our intellect), and then:

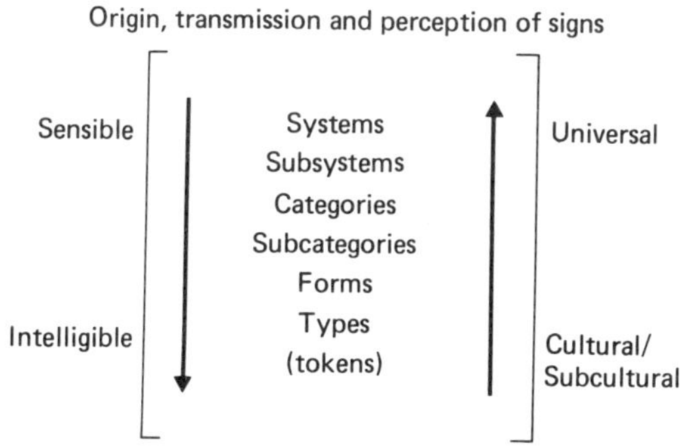

FIG. 11.2. Semiotics of Literary Anthropology.

(a) *systems* of signs, e.g.: the culture-specific kinesics displayed in *Pather Panchali*, or the widow's system of ritual behaviors when she remembers "They made me take the bangles off my arms, and the silver wristlets [. . .] and I had to rub the vermilion mark off my forehead and go and bathe in the river. I knew then I was a widow" (Banerji, *PP*, 37);[2] the series of brass and earthenware containers that constitute an important part of the household, etc.; systems, therefore, can be equated to the culturemes discussed in Chapter 2 and are, on a semiotic level, the first broad groupings of signs, whether universal or culture-specific;

(b) *subsystems* are, within systems, the various kinds of pots (clay, brass) observed in *Pather Panchali*, or the gestures, manners and postures in *Pickwick Papers*' rich kinesic repertoires;

(c) *categories* will further identify free and bound kinesics, with which Dickens definitely identifies the society of his period, and in *Pather Panchali*, the various kinds of clay or brass pots within the previously differentiated subsystem.

(d) *subcategories*, further refining our analysis, will differentiate various forms and functions of free or bound gestures, manners and postures separately, as well as the distinct functions of each of the categories of pots used;

(e) *forms*, which in somatic systems constitute the core of somatic behavior (the form of a wink in kinesics, for instance, varying across cultures, the forms of olfactory perception of perspiration as a chemical sign, etc.), define the specific use of each pot within each subcategory; which finally brings us, in this hierarchization that reveals the complexity of the deeper layers of sign processes, to

(f) *types* themselves, such as a slow 'type' of wink, and not just a wink (as different types of a wink can be recorded in different narratives), or a culture-bound, or subcultural, way of performing the use of each utensil.

The researcher may begin either by considering whole systems as they show themselves in the literary work (and perhaps completing the scale down to specific types) or work in the opposite direction by identifying single types and finding also forms, subcategories, categories, subsystems and systems. On the other hand, since the categories 'sensible' and 'intelligible' overlap, the literary anthropologist may discover 'intelligible' sociocultural systems through their sensory manifestations; or, being aware of those patterns, gradually discover their physical characteristics within a given culture.

At any rate, it should not be difficult to understand why an at least initial semiotic approach to the elements expected in a narrative work (or play, for that matter)—including the established pragmatic and semantic perspectives outlined in Chapter 2—can afford a systematic kind of study that may otherwise escape the researcher. Semiotics deals with signs, signs are what a culture, a society and its material and intellectual products are made of, and thus they constitute in a natural way the basis of literary anthropology as they do of any other subject that deals with man and his world. Furthermore, as one engages in a diachronic or synchronic study of the anthropological elements encountered in literature and, at the same time (or perhaps independently of it), in an analysis of 'culturemes'—both of which perspectives are outlined below—the necessity of using sign analysis becomes even more obvious.

Finally, the definition of literary anthropology given above makes it quite clear that the investigator is dealing with communicative signs, that is, with the many forms of communication, mostly nonverbal, that define individuals and cultures, conveyed in this case by the narrative literature of each culture, as a given culture is, in a greater or lesser degree, revealed by the literary work. This concept of communication goes, of course, way beyond that which considers only language, paralanguage, kinesics and, at the most somatic systems that may be wittingly employed to transmit messages. Any systems, whether bodily ones or cultural products, communicate as eloquently as those which develop directly between two or more people, therefore we must extend the semiotic study of signs to at least the basic cultural systems schematized in Fig. 11.1, which are always present in the narrative literature of a culture. Besides, this cultural-communicative approach is precisely what differentiates the literary anthropologist from the purely literary scholar, much too often uninterested in and unaware of a wealth of elements that happen to be inherent to his subject of study.

3. The Diachronic and Synchronic Approach as a Tool in Literary Anthropology

According to the discussion of *culturemes* in Chapter 2, it seems quite apparent that while an anthropologist might analyze a culture by breaking it down into discrete culturemes, and thus carry out a truly systematic and progressive study from broader areas or categories to the smaller culture-specific elements, the semiotician would perhaps use the sensory and intelligible sign analysis just outlined, reaching similar results. Each one would be valid in itself. However, I would say that the interdisciplinary principle that should characterize the work of the literary anthropologist ought to combine both approaches, the analysis of signs and the analysis of culturemes. A single sign, say a culturally differentiated wink, may constitute a cultureme, while a cultureme such as that formed by formal postures within a given culture or class will contain a number of sign systems, subsystems, categories, subcategories, forms and types. Both combined provide a solid method of analysis which allows not only for a much deeper treatment of the anthropological elements in a narrative work, but for a far-reaching literary analysis as well.

Just as in the social sciences we concern ourselves with a comparative synchronic study of certain habits, on the one hand, and a diachronic one on the other, the literary-anthropological approach becomes most fruitful when, instead of studying one single work in isolation, we seek both its spatial and temporal dimensions, the two basic dimensions of any human activity, that is, of those culturemes, their crosscultural similarities and differences as well as their historical permanence or evolution. The various possibilities could be diagrammed as in Fig. 11.3.

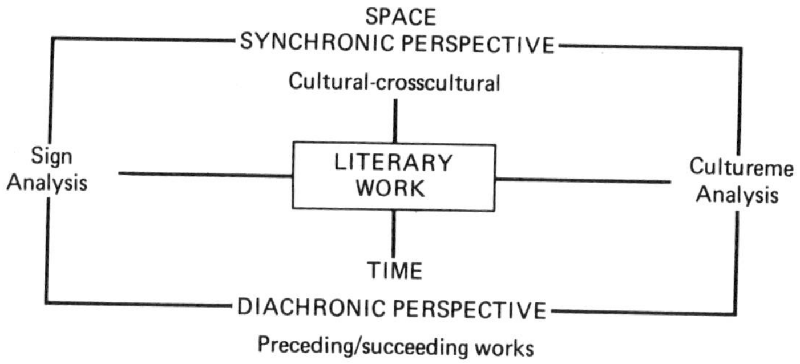

FIG. 11.3. The Synchronic-Diachronic Approach of Literary Anthropology.

The spatial or synchronic approach

By adopting a spatial or synchronic approach to a given culture in an attempt to develop a literary-anthropological description of it, the work we may use as our starting point, say *Pather Panchali* for India, would have to be related, for an intercultural or subcultural panorama, to contemporary novels like R. K. Narayan's *Mr. Sampath*, Mulk Raj Anand's *Coolie* or *Untouchable*, Raja Rao's *Kanthapura* or *The Serpent and the Rope*,

Khushwant Singh's *Train to Pakistan*, or Kamala Markandayas's *Nectar in a Sieve*. Only then would we be able to establish—and here is where the systematic cultureme approach proves useful—a system of descriptive data for that culture.

Now, why and when would one follow the literary-anthropological method, and would it replace the direct fieldwork approach. First of all, in approaching a culture it may happen that the anthropologist has as yet no direct access to it, or that, even if he does have access, he considers the narrative literature of that culture a first step that will provide a number of insights into the sensible and intelligible systems he might otherwise overlook. He may also gather the literary data simultaneously to his actual field work, as the narrative work will serve as an invaluable guide tool in the identification and building up of different culturemes.

On the other hand, the native researcher, that is, the one who is working on his culture, may investigate how it is depicted in and through its literature (both explicitly and implicitly), a research topic in itself.

But even the literary values of the works under study constitute a valid touchstone for the analysis of the esthetic and socioliterary values of a period. Witness the correlation of literary realism-naturalism and the industrial upsurge, the emergence of the middle class and the resulting literary and artistic realism. In other words, the social or cultural anthropologist would do well to use the narrative literature of the period to ascertain the cultural aspects he is studying, which are but complementary to the purely literary ones, giving him a broader and richer understanding of its subject (cf. Erickson 1983, on *Buddenbrooks*).

Finally, if we were to elaborate, as we ought to, cultural atlases, such as an analytical kinesic atlas of a culture—which would show, for instance, the distribution and adaptation of postural habits according to terrain, cultural or subcultural furniture, domestic architecture, moral values or role expectations—the national and regional narratives would supply the most eloquent documentation, a characteristic that becomes more conspicuous when we are engaged in a diachronic or historical approach.

The temporal or diachronic approach

As I indicated earlier, it was this documentary and historical aspect of narrative literature that showed me, more than anything else, the potential value of literary anthropology, as a temporal diachronic approach must observe the cultural habits in a historical, evolving perspective. This perspective will, at one point or another in time, draw from documents of the past, and narrative literature is definitely the richest source. In fact, it is the only one for the study of human somatic systems of communication besides verbal language, that is paralanguage and kinesics mainly, until the appearance of sound recording and film. Actually, the kinetic cultural repertoires revealed or depicted by painting and sculpture lack the description of their cooccurrent verbal, paralinguistic and, in general, contextual elements, such as dress and furniture, as well as the emotional factors involved (e.g., situations of bereavement, happiness, proxemic and chronemic attitudes, interactive patterns, etc.).

But painting, it must be emphasized, is also a powerful tool in the hands of the anthropologist or, better yet, literary anthropologist—actually as 'pictorial anthropology'—for systematic research by cultural anthropologists interested in the study of the anthropological values of the representing forms of art, since they record quite a few of the somatic, objectual and environmental systems, as well as many of the interrelationships shown in Fig. 11.1. For instance, the narrative or anecdotal painting of the nineteenth century, from Russia to the United States, constitutes a unique document (very often depicting scenes from narrative works of literature the literary anthropologist might be using too), say, for the study of posture, because of its static nature, but also of certain society manners, both conditioned in turn by dress, furniture, morals, etc. Gombrich (1972), in a paper totally in line with my thoughts on this subject, has practically set the basis for this type of research, precisely in a book about nonverbal communication (Hinde 1972).

A novel, however, in which both the author and his characters convey to us the spatial and temporal settings of the story, allows us to determine, when viewed side by side with preceding and succeeding works, how certain cultural habits appear, develop and even disappear, applied both to sensible and intelligible systems.

Furthermore, it can be combined with a crosscultural historical view in a given period, as what would be *comparative literary anthropology*, in which we would actually carry out a comparative crosscultural historical view of, for instance, a given period, such as the social novel of the thirties and forties in India, the United States and Southern Europe. The pertinent culturemes would be sought, but also discovered, in the comparative process.

At any rate, the historical approach to narrative literature seems, for all the descriptive passages it contains, an indispensable companion tool in direct field work as the only possible way for us to relate the present living culture to the sensible or intelligible forms of the past. I would also like to stress that the narrative literatures of the different cultures 'speak about', and not just describe, many of the behaviors and thought patterns typical of those cultures, thus rating high above any form of representation in the case of somatic systems, besides being an indispensable complement for the study of intelligible ones or any other sensible manifestations.

4. Forms and Functions of Somatic Systems in Narrative Literature

Having discussed the distinction between sensible elements or signs in man and his culture and intelligible ones—acknowledging the basic external first perception of the latter—I shall briefly identify the various systems. This in turn reveals, not only the highly interdisciplinary stand we must adopt when dealing with a culture in this way, but the richness of the anthropological study we should endeavor to analyze, through the culture's narrative works, the synchronic or diachronic dimensions of a cultureme or class of culturemes.

The average narrative writer, particularly the novelist, endows his characters with somatic characteristics which, consciously or unconsciously on his part, allow them to communicate with each other in the fictional world, as those characteristics constitute different systems that operate in real life according to the biophysico-psychological socioeconomic and cultural conditioning factors mentioned in Chapter 3. On the other hand, those descriptions communicate to us the readers, not just personalities and idiosyncrasies shaped in the author's mind, but a specific culture, whether the writer wants it or not. This, of course, applies to intelligible systems as well. The anthropologist, therefore, is in a position to perceive that culture even in the least conspicuously 'cultural' novels, for there are always some tacit or explicit clues, through the inevitable flesh-and-bone vitality of the character, to a cultural setting and to a temporal one.

Paralanguage

It has been established that the basic core of human communication, what truly differentiates somatic anthropocommunication from zoocommunication, is the Basic Triple Structure of human communication behavior, language-paralanguage-kinesics.

Apart from *verbal language*, which, if read in the original version—otherwise the problems inherent in 'interlinguistic' and 'intercultural' translation crop up—will require the literary anthropologist's discernment of the various socioeconomic strata, sex, age, levels of usage (as established in Chapter 5), etc., paralanguage offers a wealth of clues to culture-specific as well as cross-cultural features. It is not what the characters say, but 'how' they say it, the nonverbal voice qualities, voice modifiers, and independent sounds (alternants) with which, consciously or out of awareness, we support, emphasize or contradict the linguistic, kinesic and proxemic messages mainly.

> Indir Thakrum knew a number of old ballads by heart [. . .] She droned through them in a long sing-song chant. (intonation range) (Banerji, *PP*, 29)

> And Granma raised a shrill voice, "Preacher? You got a preacher? Go git him." (glottis control) (Steinbeck, *GW*, 70)

> "Go away", she cried through her tears, "go away". (differentiator) (Huxley, *PC*, 185)

The importance of 'alternants' must be emphasized once again, as they definitely form the most interesting group of paralinguistic features from both a cultural and crosscultural point of view, which would warrant extensive field work, as each language, each culture, possesses a great number of them encoded and decoded in daily interaction as systematically as dictionary entries, in fact, with perfectly lexical values. In literature many alternants are described, but only a few represented because of the spelling difficulties. Through their descriptions, however, we can gather data for a much needed in-depth cross-cultural study of alternants, as they perform important functions in such culture-bound situations as display of affects, man–animal interaction, etc.

> He cleared his throat, and coughed once or twice. He had not the courage to call out. (Banerji, *PP*, 284)

> Mr. Pickwick nodded assent, and coughed to attract the attention of the young gentleman [. . .] (Dickens, *PP*, 301)

> Arkady recalled his old nurse, Yegorovna, and sighed, and wished her "rest in peace". (Turgenev, *FS*, 178)

> the other shampoo'd Mr. Winkle with a heavy clothes-brush, indulging [. . .] in that hissing sound which hostlers are wont to produce when engaged in rubbing down a horse. (Dickens, *PP*, 104)

> "Sh!", said Tom. / Al whispered, "You awake? How'd you get wet?" / "Sh!", said Tom [. . .] / "What's the matter 'th him, Ma?" / "Hush!", Ma said. (Steinbeck, *GW*, 346–7)

> "Can you imagine it—a cross between a cobra and a guinea pig?" / "Ugh!" the other one shuddered. (Huxley, *PC*, 43)

By *other somatic sounds* I mostly mean certain physiological reflexes such as belching, sneezing or hiccoughing, whose occurrence is shown in narrative literature as conditioned by socioeconomic patterns of social interaction, thus providing additional insights for the anthropologist.

Kinesics

Since movement and sound are the two basic dimensions of human life, *kinesics* complete, with language and paralanguage, the Basic Triple Structure. Apart from its anthropological interest from a phylogenetic point of view—that is, its development from broader movements to subtle ones of the fingers, the eyelids, the eyes, etc.—the fact that cultural advancement and technology has enriched the repertoires of gestures, manners and postures through the evolution of dwellings, furniture, utensils, clothes, hairdo, etc., is illustrated in the narrative literature (and, as a source of comparison, in painting, mainly for postures) of the different cultures. The earlier distinction between *free* and *bound* movements, for instance, becomes particularly interesting for the study of affective behaviors (greetings, goodbyes, expressions of grief, aggression/affiliation, etc.) in the national narratives, from the epics on, as it reveals some long disappeared ritual patterns, cultural or class prejudices, higher-class and lower-class etiquette, etc. Beyond that basic formal differentiation, narrative literature also illustrates the following functional categories:

Functional categories

Further to the basic classification of kinesic forms, as outlined in Chapter 5, and equally applicable to paralanguage and even verbal language, the literary anthropologist must distinguish, in first-hand observation as well as in narrative literature, four main functional categories: *conversational*, as displayed mostly in everyday personal interaction, whether consciously or out of awareness; *ritualistic*, prescribed mainly by religious, military, protocolarian, sporting, ancestral (e.g., folk dances), and artistic (e.g., ballet) norms; *occupational*, typical of people in specific lines of work, such as policemen or sport players, whether or not in interaction; *task-performing*, as when kneading, grooming others, handling eating utensils or mating, not always performed in the same way in the various cultures; and *somatic and random*, culturally institutionalized as manners when in interaction, though aimed mostly at relieving physiological needs (getting up, sitting down, sneezing, coughing) or performing quite unconscious acts, such as preening oneself, taking off a hat or reacting to sudden pain.

The following are descriptions of kinesic behaviors in each category taken quite at random from narrative works in different cultures, showing by their self-explanatory characteristics the specific interests which I shall not comment upon for lack of space.

Conversational:

> And the maistri grew so fierce at this that he howled and spat at her and said his word was his word [. . .] (Rao, *K*, 46)
>
> he bent down respectfully to touch his mother-in-law's feet upon her arrival [. . .] (Banerji, *PP*, 47)
>
> And the stout gentleman playfully inserted his elbow between the ribs of Mr. Pickwick, and laughed heartily. (Dickens, *PP*, 89)

Pavel Piotrovich took his beautiful hand with his long, rosy nails [. . .] out of the pocket of his pantaloons and held it out to his nephew. Having accomplished this preliminary European handshake, he kissed him three times, Russian fashion; in other words, he touched his nephew's cheek three times [. . .] (Turgenev, *FS*, 176)

' "But Huzoor", said Hari, pushing forward his hands in abject humility, "you are the giver of food to the poor, Sahib" ' (Anand, *C*, 199)

[When El Cid and his men meet the King upon their return from exile] he fell to the ground on his hands and knees, / the grass of the fields he took with his teeth, / welling his eyes from the great happiness [. . .] (*Poema del Cid*, v. 3031, translation mine) (1)

When the rainy season comes and there's little rice to eat, she will pass by your door and spit three times at you in the name of her children. (Rao, *K*, 18)

' "But, Huzoor!" said Hari, touching the foreman's black boots with his and taking the touch of the beef hide to his forehead. "Be kind [. . .]" ' (Anand, *C*, 199)

Occupational:

Minnie or Susy or Mae any hamburger stand attendant in the U.S. middleaging behind the counter [. . .] Mopping the counter with circular motions. (Steinbeck, *GW*, 139)

The bearer [. . .] walked off with a swagger characteristic of the white man's servant (Anand, *C*, 205)

Task-performing:

Their voices were harsh and strident, and as they schoolboys at school sitting on grass mats recited they swung their bodies backwards and forwards [. . .] (Banerji, *PP*, 111)

'[. . .] we put the water jugs on our hips, and we rushed back home [. . .]' (Rao, *K*, 162)

Somatic and random:

Emile [. . .] stood at the cracked mirror with his face screwed up, fastening the buttons in the front of a clean boiled shirt. (Dos Passos, *MT*, 85)

he wiped his face with the end of his tunic and blew his nose by catching it between the thumb and forefinger of his right hand (Anand, *C*, 60)

Other somatic systems

Closely related to the Basic Triple Structure, and determined by kinesic behaviors in its daily interactional context, *proxemics* is also documented in literature and should be of paramount importance in literary-anthropological cultural and crosscultural studies of interaction in organized communities, including man's layout of his living spaces, of furniture and the rest of the human built environment.

In order to complete this panoramic view of external, sensorially apprehended human systems the literary anthropologist should of course consider the ones already outlined in Chapter 3 and their interactive or noninteractive costructuration with language, paralanguage and kinesics. While operating more efficiently in certain nonhuman species, chemical, dermal and thermal messages play also important functions as controllable or uncontrollable systems in humans, therefore being acknowledged in narrative literature in greater or lesser degree. In fact, they may document different culture-specific characteristics, say, the display rules concerning crying and tear-shedding in situations such as bereavement and as regards male–female differences, or the occurrence of blushing across cultures and according to evolving morals and relationships. Both reactions have been investigated before but without resorting to the more realistic narrative descriptions as a source of data which would most appropriately complement, for instance, Darwin's discussion of crying and blushing. In his own period one could resort to the very realistic documentation of contemporaries like Tolstoy, Dickens, Zola, Hardy, and the many lesser narrators who, despite their literary values, were faithfully documenting the behaviors of the people in many cultures. Those descriptions did not only depict various bodily activites and their direct perception in social interactions, but the synesthesial appreciation of others which due, for instance, to dress styles (due in turn to prevailing morals and rules of conduct) were not perceived directly but through clothes, gait and postures.

I would add to this cursory review of somatic systems, that, beyond the possibilities of written words, punctuation should be acknowledged as a very neglected expressive tool, whose evoking qualities reveal at times cultural characteristics such as voice volume, silences of varying duration and moments of stillness, as was illustrated in Chapter 7.

5. Objectual and Immediate Environmental Systems in Literature

If we imagine the various sensible systems of communication as concentric circles closer to or farther removed from the central one, that is, the body itself (the Basic Triple Structure being the core of its communicative capabilities), we find that in addition to his strictly bodily systems man has developed through the centuries—subject to cultural differences—other systems external but immediate to his body as a socializing organism. These systems, however, act as additions to or extensions of it in the sense that they may modify its appearance and convey cultural or personality-defining messages, thus constituting a wealth of information for the anthropologist. Narrative literature, by granting those systems their due importance as complementary to the Basic Triple Structure repertoires of the characters, acknowledges their mutual costructuration as well as their communicative functions in social interaction. I will illustrate some of them.

Body-adaptors: nutritional and pseudonutritional

Products, namely, food and drink, and tobacco and the various masticatories used in the different cultures; their adaptation to the body is a physiological one more than an external one, although they condition specific kinesic behaviors, as they become part of it modifying its appearance at times (according to nutritional habits) due to changes in body weight or to derived malfunction, and conditioning other somatic systems such as kinesics (e.g., in postural habits, or while intoxicated). Narrative literature offers cultural and crosscultural inventories of these body-adaptors.

As a foreign researcher in India, its narrative literature of the last fifty years provided me with inventories of body-adaptors before I would seek them in real life.

For the Bengal region of India, *Pather Panchali* documents the consumption of: rice, fried potatoes, fried *dhal* (up to nine kinds of pulses), bread, milk, curds, sugar cane, eggplant, khoya fish; sweets like *luchi* and *mohombhog*; fruits like mango and lichi; boiled neem tree bark; a meal consisting of "coarse rice with papaya, figs, banana shoots, prawns and other curries; and there were fried banana fritters and sweet creamed rice"; and the Indian masticatory, betel.

For the South of India, *Kanthapura* shows rice, rice-cake, puffed rice, paddy (unhusked rice), *chitranna* (rice), *dhal*-soup, curds, *ragi* (cereal), chillies, *paysam*; sweets like Bengal-gram, *khis*, *happallam*, fried *odé*, *laddu*, honey; *copra*, coconut rice, *phem*; chillies; drinks like toddy; and betel. *Nectar in a Sieve* records how for the feast on the tenth day from the birth of a first son, "we prepared mounds of rice, tinting it with saffron and frying it in butter; made hot curries from chillies and *dhal*; mixed sweet, spicy dishes of jaggery and fruit; broiled fish; roasted nuts over the fire; filled ten gourds with coconut milk; and cut plantain leaves on which to serve the food" (Markandaya, *NS*, 25).

The description of how betel is used (chewed actually from West Africa to Oceania) provides the anthropologist with an eloquent document of how a body-adaptor determines specific task-performing kinesic behaviors: "He opened his betel-bag and carefully taking a tobacco leaf, he seated himself, and wiping the tobacco leaf against his dhoti, he put it into his mouth, then put an areca nut with it and began to munch" (Rao, *K*: 13 and author's note on p. 201). Furthermore, the consumption of tobacco, for instance, affords a most interesting cross-cultural comparative study of certain social attitudes such as ritualized etiquette patterns like the offering of the cigarette pack to those present when one is going to smoke, as is invariably done in Spain.

On the other hand, not only could a *food atlas* be traced through the narrative literatures, but also the social, economic and even religious implications of the different products consumed, such as the intoxicating toddy or palm-wine of the countryside people, a state monopoly under the British, today prohibited as a drink in most Indian states (Rao, *K*: 213–14), the *paysam* and *chitrama* of certain religious festivals, the obsequial dinners of honey, curds and *khir* (Rao, *K*: 21), etc.

On the other hand, one of the comparative perspectives gained through the narrative sources of the different cultures is that of the so-called food cultures, a consequence of the soil and climate of the environment and the traditions and economic potential of the people involved, which in turn define a geography of disease related to those cultures and their maladjustment between society and its environment as evidenced, for instance, by diseases such as beriberi in the rice cultures, or pellegra in the corn culture (see the excellent work on the geography of diseases by Howe [1977]).

Body-adaptors: dress, jewelry, and chemical products

Wearing objects, jewelry, and chemical products form the second class of body-adaptors, with which the body can be emphasized, concealed, adorned, made smell, each with very different functions, each changing through centuries and years according to the evolution of taste, morals, social sophistication, ritual behaviors, etc. As with the previous categories, the fictional and nonfictional narrative literatures serve as a diachronic and synchronic tool for the study of those human habits, not only providing descriptive records of the gradual changes undergone by dress, jewels or cosmetics, but helping us to understand, for instance, the costructuration of clothes and kinesic behavior, mainly manners and postures, as in walking, sitting, standing or reclining positions, as well as their relationship with socioeconomic status and even political ideology.

> He [the gentleman] put his sword back in and fixed it in place, along with a string of large beads as belt. And with calm gait and erect, rocking his body and head very elegantly, throwing the end of his cloak over the shoulder, sometimes under his arm, and resting his right hand on his side, he left [. . .] (*Lazarillo de Tormes*, 99, translation mine) (2)

he wore a three-strand garland of basil plaited round his neck, as many Vaisnavas [Vishnu's worshippers] do. (Banerji, *PP*, 122)

the cheap glass bangles she [a poor Brahmin's daughter] was wearing on her arm. (Banerji, *PP*, 201)

he [a Gandhi man] had given up his boots and hat and suit and had taken to dhoti [loincloth fabric and loincloth itself] and khadi [homespun cotton as opposed to English-made fabric] (Rao, *K*, 5)

Pavel Piotrovich sat down at the table. He was wearing an elegant morning suit of English cut, and his head was adorned with a little tarboosh. This tarboosh and the small, negligently tied cravat suggested the freedom of country life; but the tight-fitting collar of the shirt, which, to be sure, was not white, but colored, as it should be for the morning toilet, dug with its customary inflexibility into his clean-shaven chin. (Turgenev, *FS*, 182)

In Banerji's *Pather Panchali*, for instance, we find several instances of the use of chemical body-adaptors and their various functions: "when he was eighteen months old [. . .] she recalled how she used to darken his eyes with collyrium and put a spot of it in the middle of his forehead" (98), "she had painted the edges of her feet red with *alta* dye" (101), "the oil he put on his hair" (113), "Nilmoni Mukherji was sitting at home massaging his body with oil before going down to the river for a bath" (249).

Object-adaptors

Farther detached from the body, between body-adaptors and the general objectual, built or modified environment, are object-adaptors, which we do not consume or wear but only touch and bring in contact with our bodies by handling them or by using them as resting artifacts: food and drink utensils, domestic implements, 'anatomical' furniture, occupational task-performing object, etc. They are, in other words, modifiers of somatic systems, mainly kinesics, by conditioning manners and postures. They are also described in narrative literature, from the national epics (arms, riding equipment) to nineteenth-century realism or the more realistic social type of novels in our days.

In Rao's *Kanthapura* we read: "we put the water jugs on our hips" (162), as they are handled in many other cultures, and learn about domestic artifacts like the spinning wheel (symbolic of Gandhi's ideology), the broom and the blowpipe (symbols of housewife authority), the *quern* (small household grinding mill), the hookah pipe and the lathi-ring (the manifold-purpose bamboo stick), etc., as well as musical instruments like bells, cymbals, sitars, drums and conches. In Banerji's *Pather Panchali* we see that "the schoolmaster usually sat on a palm-leaf mat", while the schoolboys were "sitting on grass mats" (113).

In Hawthorne's *The House of the Seven Gables* the New England fish-dealer blows a conch as he goes down the street "announcing his approach" (110).

6. Objectual, Built, and Modified Environments

Beyond body-adaptors, but overlapping object-adaptors, narrative literature depicts its characters in their total environment through the environmental systems we find in each culture, including: objectual, built or modified, and natural environments, the latter comprising also the various animal species, whose somatic systems are at times associated to man's systems, as discussed earlier. I would like to define *environment* at this point, according to the elements acknowledged as such in Fig. 11.1, as: the sensible and intelligible elements of man's world which exist beyond himself as a cognitive social organism, including objectual, built, modified, and natural (terrain, fauna and flora) surroundings as well as conceptualized patterns of thought, beliefs and attitudes. This realistic definition, on which I would elaborate at a later date, prompts the sort of interdisciplinary attitude any research area should adopt, while perhaps alleviating the definitory uncertainty referred to by Rapoport (1976: 17).

The objectual environment

The objectual environment is made of all the objects that surround us in our private or social life, such as household wares and artifacts that are not object-adaptors proper, decorative objects, 'nonanatomical' furniture, vehicles, etc.

In *Kanthapura* we learn about the itinerant monk's begging bowl, the festivals pots, the bamboo *pandal* raised for a cremation ceremony and other public gatherings, etc. In *Pather Panchali*, "the old woman had a jar too, made of sheet brass, an earthenware vessel for curds, and a few odd earthenware pots. The brass jar was full of baked rice, some of which she used to grind at night with pestle and mortar [. . .] In one of her earthenware pots she kept her oil, in another salt, and in a third some molasses." (28).

In Dickens, *Pickwick Papers* we see English interiors of that period like a clerk's office "dark, mouldy [. . .] a couple of old wooden chairs: a very loud-ticking clock: an almanack, an umbrella stand, a row of hat-pegs, and a few shelves [. . .] old deal boxes with paper labels, and sundry decayed stone ink bottles of various shapes and sizes" (298).

The built and modified environments

The built and modified environment, beyond but associated with the objectual one by way of cultural and socioeconomic patterns, includes, first of all, the architectural structures, their resulting spaces and their layout in the natural environment as compounds, villages and cities, any other built structure (bridges, wharves, scaffoldings, power lines, fences, etc.), and man-produced colors and light; secondly, the modified natural environment, that is, land and flora, as man-shaped landscaping and agricultural forms.

As with other sensible sign systems, the environmental ones—with which the literary characters live and interact—provide not only the adequate esthetic accompaniment and the desired realistic effect, but also an invaluable document; sometimes from the times when no other accounts exist, except perhaps the buildings and the modified natural elements themselves, yet without the social living context that completes their culture. Even in contemporary literature we can find the relationship between, for instance, domestic architecture and class identity, something equally defined by other communication systems, from language down to the object-adaptors and the built objectual environment. The most perceptive authors from nineteenth-century realism and naturalism on have acknowledged the relation between, for instance, the way a person dresses and his or her verbal and kinesic repertoires (what is actually 'standard' in that person), the chosen objectual environment and the house and the landscaping by which that person wishes to be surrounded and identified with (cf. Duncan 1973 on residential landscaping as a social identifier).

In *Kanthapura* we see the town layout: "Our village had a Pariah quarter too besides a Brahmin quarter, a Potters' quarter, a Weavers' quarter, and a Sudra quarter" (5) and that a well-off person "had a real *thothi* house, with a big veranda and a large roof, and there must have been a big granary somewhere inside" (5).

In *Pather Panchali*, the home of another well-off man had "apart from the kitchen-house, a variety of sheds and other auxiliary structures, consisted of two main buildings [. . .] The pillars and cross-beams [. . .] of *tal* palm wood, a timber which only a fairly rich man could afford [. . .] Inside there was so much furniture and so many chests and boxes [. . .]" (47).

The objectual, built and modified environments, being the subject of quite detailed descriptions in the more realistic authors, serve to identify whole cultures—or at least certain strata in those cultures—in past periods, such as England through Dickens, Trollope or Thackeray, France through Balzac, Maupassant or Zola, Russia through Tolstoy or Turgenev, Spain through Galdós, Alas or Blasco-Ibáñez, The United States' turn-of-the-century years through Howells or Dreiser. The literary anthropologist finds in them part of the history of even certain somatic signs conveyed by language, kinesics, body-adaptors, object-adaptors, and their environment.

7. Man–Animal Relationships

As indicated in Fig. 11.1 by the lines joining language, paralanguage and kinesics and the various kinds of animal species, each culture possesses a series of universal or specific interactive systems between man and domestic and tamed animals. It is a fact that those species become 'culturized' (so to speak, to differentiate it from acculturation), that many of their behaviors respond to human linguistic, paralinguistic and kinesic calls and gestures aimed at regulating their actions, either as part of their interactive relationships with us or for the performance of certain assigned tasks. The different cultures control their man-oriented activities by resorting to the objectual environment as well, either for the training of the working animals (sticks of varying length and thickness, whips and crops, leashes, bells, blinkers, etc.) or for the actual execution of their chores (saddles, ploughs, threshing boards, water-wheels, yokes, etc.). On the other hand, man–domestic animal relationships vary interculturally, and even socioeconomically, from sheer exploitation and selfish and cruel indifference to human concern and true affection, and animals react accordingly, more with fear than aggressiveness when being antagonized. Even wild species display man-conditioned behaviors of affiliation and trust or flight and mistrust, as happens with squirrels, rabbits and birds.

These relationships, about which zoology, ethology and, subsuming both, zoosemiotics teach us so much, are also depicted in narrative literature and descriptive nonnarrative works, which therefore provide a documentation on sometimes evolving attitudes on the part of man, linked to socioeconomic changes. Anthropology should make strides in this rather neglected area of study, and literary anthropology could certainly contribute its recorded confirmation of, or the only material about, a number of factors (geographical, social, religious, economic, nutritional, etc.).

> Dung is too useful in our homes to be given to the land, for it is fuel to us and protection against damp and heat and even ants and mice. (Markandaya, *NS*, 36)

Those factors determine the various types of man–animal relationships that affect in turn the layout of towns and homes in rural areas, the development of a number of artifacts, the growing or manufacturing of animal food, the shaping of dress, or the creation of certain status symbols represented by the ownership.

8. The Natural Environment

Finally, literature records the natural environment of its characters, both as a personality and circumstantial conditioning factor in the development of the story—emphasized, for instance, by naturalist writers—and as an esthetic complement.

The natural environment is understood here as comprising not only the terrain and the flora associated with a given culture—what we refer to as natural landscape (as opposed to built landscaping)—but the fauna as well, as elements that surround us either almost universally (dogs, horses, flies) or more culture-specifically (elephants, camels, storks), being, as indicated earlier, 'culturized' and conditioned with respect, for instance, to their territoriality according to our attitude toward them.

While the natural landscape serves in narrative fictional and nonfictional literature to provide a geographical background as well as a conditioning factor for the characters' personalities and emotional circumstances (witness the Nature–Man relationship in the romantic and naturalistic periods in different literatures), plants and animals perform more esthetic and stylistic functions besides providing a realistic background. For the literary anthropologist, however, both flora and fauna, as well as terrain and climate, document territorial patterns, nutritional habits, man–animal interaction, the general medical state and the environmentally-conditioned ailments, social and religious implications contained in those natural elements, etc.

In Turgenev's *Fathers and Sons*, "everywhere the skylarks poured out endless, ringing streams of song; the pewits called as they hovered about the low-lying meadows [. . .] beautifully black, the rooks wandered amid the tender green of [. . .] the crops [. . .]" (174).

Kanthapura opens with a description of the region, "a centre of cardamon and coffee, rice and sugar cane. Roads, narrow, dusty [. . .] through the forest of teak and jack, of sandal and of sal, and hanging over bellowing gorges and leaping over elephant-haunted valleys [. . .] into the great granaries of trade" (1). Throughout the novel of South India we identify the flora, made up of cardamon, coffee, rice, sugar cane, mango, lentils, dhal, lantana, pipal tree, neem tree, bel tree, tamarind tree, betel-nut tree, coconut tree, champak tree, toddy tree, etc., domestic species like the working bulls, buffaloes and elephants, and wild ones like six kinds of snakes, the cheetah, the tiger, the sacred eagle (vehicle of Vishnu), etc.

Pather Panchali shows a rich flora of dozens of trees (olive, bay, coconut, banyan, boku, chatim, kukshima, jagadumar, kunch, shondali, etc.) and plants (bamboo, gulancha, alkushi, jasmine, basil, etc.) as well as animal species such as the much appreciated khoya fish, the blue-throated jay, the cormorant, the kokil, etc.

In *Nectar in a Sieve* "The animals bullocks, refreshed, began stepping jauntily again, tossing their heads and jangling the bells that hung from their red-painted horns. The air was full of the sound of bells, and of birds, sparrows, and bulbuls mainly, and sometimes the cry of an eagle, but when we passed a grove, green and leafy, I could hear mynahs and parrots."

9. The Sensory Interaction Between People and Their Environment

Beyond the specific sensible systems apprehended through the various receptive channels (e.g., kinesics: visually-audibly, tactually; domestic animals: visually-audibly-dermally; cosmetics and lotions: olfactorily-visually; flora: visually-olfactorily, etc.), a culture communicates itself in a purely impressionistic fashion which truly confirms the varying sensory involvement to which either members of that particular culture or foreigners are exposed, the latter usually in a more conscious way. Those *cultural sensory signs* are of either chemical (olfactory) or physical (visual, tactile, audible, kinesthetic) origin and are not always easily isolatable but fused together in certain culture-identifying compounds that account for our appreciation of a culture and that are acknowledged in literature as definitely environmental and often conditioning factors.

The North American small town, for instance, offers few of those cultural sensible cues because it lacks, within its urban section, the integration of farming homes and farming tasks and working animals, of regular homes and craft shops; besides, apart from the smell of freshly-mowed grass or the sound of some public bells and carillons (rarely calling to or informing of different events and happenings), the town hardly 'smells' or 'sounds'. Its French, Spanish, Italian or Moroccan counterparts, for instance, are in themselves a different world of sensory involvement. They offer, to mention but a few characteristics, the kinesthetic and tactile perception of their narrow streets and alleys, the textures of the various architectural materials and of cobblestones, the changing smells of those materials when it rains, or in the summer heat. The olfactory perception of those cultures includes also the wet or dried-up mixture of cattle and domestic animal droppings, manure, straw and hay that fall while being transported, and then the many smells of open-door craft shops, bakeries, taverns and cafés, butcher shops, fish shops, fruit shops, or the weekly open-air market with all its smells. But, as we smell, we may also hear the sound of animals of various species, of craft tools, of heavy old doors that squeak, of human and animal steps on the rough pavement. And human everyday interaction takes place within, surrounded by and as part of that whole sensorial involvement, for its proxemics is, in comparison with that of an Anglo-Saxon culture, for example, a more intimate one, as people get closer to each other and touch each other more in the casual street encounters.

It should be of particular anthropological interest to establish the order in which the various sensorial perceptions impinge on a foreigner, or on the native entering a town, returning to his culture, or thinking about it as an informant or as his own conceptualization of it. There seems to be a definite hierarchization of sensory experiences to the extent that a Moroccan town, for instance, hits the eye right away (dress, architecture), but even more olfaction (that aura that envelops it, the mixture of odorous molecules from crafts, food, spices, people), while a Spanish village strikes the visual and auditory senses first, since smells, in comparison with Morocco, are in general more subdued.

Again, the realistic narrative works of the old days as those of today provide the complementary—if not the only one—documentation concerning a number of already disappeared sensible elements, which reveals important sociocultural changes like industrialization and mechanization, country-to-city migrations, middle-class dominance, and evolving status symbols of various sorts. Nineteenth-century and early twentieth-century realist and naturalist novelists have left the most vivid descriptions of the sensory involvement typical of their respective cultures, of places, of the food eaten on different occasions, of crafts, animals, and the fields. They did it with the same detail with which all the realistic school of painting depicted the visual qualities of their home cultures on canvases through which today the literary anthropologist can complete the literary-pictorial document.

In addition, cultural sensory cues constitute one more anthropological, sociological and psychological perspective, namely the definition of the perceptual world of so many impaired persons, particularly the deaf and the blind. As this chapter concerns itself solely with the definition of literary anthropology, it will suffice to say that the blind person can only perceive his or someone else's culture audibly, olfactorily, kinesthetically and by touch, while the deaf one will perceive signs through all those channels, except audibly. I would think that a blind Canadian novelist who is now living in the highly sensorial city of Marrakesh, surely possesses an infinitely richer source of sensible experiences than a comparable man of imagination in his own country or in the United States, as he perceives the Moroccan culture; not just in its purely sensory aspects, but in what is implied in those sensations that reveal, for instance, a particular chronemic attitude through the sounds and smells typical of each time of the day.

10. The Intelligible Cultural Systems in Literature

It has been sufficiently demonstrated in the preceding sections, I hope, that the study of either sensible or intelligible cultural systems is of necessity based on the former. Not only because the concepts 'sensible' and 'intelligible' overlap, but because any religious, social or economic culture-defining patterns we may study are always understood as such precisely through visual, audible, contactual, olfactory or gustatory signs; that is, mostly somatic signs—in a direct contact with a culture, of course, not if we are only basing that study on the written evocation of the literary sources—and their systematic occurrence reflect the concepts and values that constitute a culture. We may elaborate a kinesic inventory of a given culture or subculture, for instance, but in so doing we are going to deal with bound manners and postures, and those instances of physical contact in situations of happiness, bereavement, etc., will in turn define culture-specific forms of relationships at different personal levels (whom, when, and how to embrace, for instance), of affect-displays in different contexts, of etiquette patterns, or role expectations, of morals, etc. In the same manner, a systematic account of dress styles and their various social functions—particularly if done from both a synchronic and diachronic point of view, will reveal through visual perception the historical reasons for the changes they have undergone, as well as their socioeconomic or moral implications and the morphological relationship between dress and the evolution of other material systems such as furniture.

As for the methodology for the study of intelligible systems, if we regard a first-hand, field-work type of approach to a culture as a form of acculturation process in which there is a hierarchization of the perceptual possibilities, we realize that we can use two different and yet complementary ways of gathering our data: (a) to consider religious, socioeconomic, sexual or moral attitudes as they are perceived by the senses, that is, within each of the sensory categories outlined, in which case the sensible qualities of a culture are allowed to stand out and measure the degree of sensory involvement that exists in each society, in other words, the degree in which intelligible systems can be interpreted through sensory signs; (b) to start by establishing a classification of intelligible systems according to our specific strategy and in keeping with the characteristics of a given culture (e.g., not every culture contains mythological beliefs), and then perhaps differentiate the various sensible ways by which each system can be apprehended.

But, whatever the method employed, I believe that it is important to appreciate the sensory possibilities and manifestations that, ultimately, constitute live culture, as opposed to a series of passive cultural traits and written accounts. Interaction, whether among human congeners, betweeen man and God, man and animal, or man and his environment, is the foundation of our thought patterns, attitudes and actions, and it is an exchange that takes place between at least two participants, one of which at least encodes and decodes messages through somatic channels.

Both the sensible and the intelligible systems can be viewed through the sort of cultureme analysis outlined in Chapter 2, which allows us to conduct the most systematic and orderly study of the different aspects of a given culture and integrate it into a wider crosscultural perspective. However, the literary anthropologist who may not have been able to expose himself to a previous acculturation process—or simultaneously to his study of the literary sources—may simply combine both approaches and, based on an initial categorization of intelligible systems similar to the one roughly suggested in Fig. 11.1, decide which sensible manifestations each intelligible system is revealed through, or vice versa, which religious, economic, folkloric, etc., culture-defining elements and systems are perceived visually, audibly, tactually, kinesthetically, olfactorily or gustatorily, or in different combinations of the various output–input channels. The instances of sensible perception illustrated so far will have by now suggested, I trust, the two ways of dealing with intelligible systems as well as the inherent overlapping qualities of the two perceptual modes.

What follows, then, is obviously not intended as an exhaustive classification of intelligible systems, but simply as an indication of the basic areas of physical and mental cultural activities which narrative literature display explicitly or implicitly as part of its subject matter: religious, social, political, folkloric and artistic, and, in addition, those that involve human–animal relationships. What cannot escape anyone, of course, is that some of these areas, in greater or lesser degree according to the specific culture, are very difficult to delimit, since, for instance, some celebrations that are basically religious are also 'social', while certain social ritualistic behaviors may carry strong religious connotations in countries like India.

Religion

God(s) and Mythology: In *Kanthapura*, besides referring to Brahma and Siva, to mythological figures like Damayanthi, Sakuntala, Yashoda and Ravana, and to holy rivers like the Ganges, the Godavery and the Cauvery, we see how a country woman "tore a rag from her sari fringe, and put into it a three-pice bit and a little rice and an areca nut, and hung it securely to the roof. And, of course, she woke up the next morning to find no fever at all [. . .]" (52).

Thoughts and beliefs: in *Pather Panchali*, "I must have lived a very sinful life in my previous birth for all this sorrow to come upon me now" (54); in *Kanthapura*, "When the Pariahs will have worn out their karma [. . .] nobody will prevent them from becoming Brahmins, even sages, in their next lives" (90), "were he full of the radiance of ahimsa [Gandhi's non-cruelty] such things should never have happened" (61).

Festivals are mentioned or described in *Pather Panchali* (those of Lakshmi, Manasa, Chorok, Satyanarayan, Savitri, etc.), *Kanthapura* (those of Gauri, Rama, Kenchamma and Ganapati, and that of Dasara, etc.) and *Nectar in a Sieve* (Deepavali, etc.).

Religious rituals, which in India permeate so many forms of 'social' ritual, *Kanthapura* alone offers a wealth of information on different instances, like obsequial dinners with honey, curds and *khir*, the evening ablutions, the household's sacred flame, the drinking of Ganges water and *tirtham*, yoga, the holy fire to walk on, the camphor ceremonies, the holy ashes, etc., besides detailed situations: "O Kenchamma! Protect us [. . .] We shall offer you our first rice and our first fruit, and [. . .] saris and bodice-cloth for every birth and marriage [. . .]" (2), "People came [into the temple] and [. . .] banged the bell and touched the bull [. . .]" (218).

Socio-religious celebrations, as in *Kanthapura*, "[. . .] as the bridegroom's procession came along, and we all stood by the village gate, with coconuts and kumkum water to welcome him [. . .]" (80), "In the evening the invitation rice is sent." '[. . .] there will be a nuptial ceremony [. . .] You are all invited', and they offer kumkum to her silently in return" (114).

Society

Social structuration: in *Kanthapura* we find Brahmins, pariahs, peons, swamis, etc., while in *Fathers and Sons* someone decides "not to keep any freed servants or any of the former domestic serfs, or at least not to entrust them with any positions involving responsibility" (172).

Social relationships and role expectations: in *Kanthapura*, the maltreatment of the pariahs by the sahib (55), and that Moorthy "was a nice Brahmin boy—he neither smoked nor grew city-hair, nor put on suits and hats and shoes" (30), in *Pather Panchali* that "The wife of the family is supposed to look after the rice and do the housework" (120).

Evolution of the social structures and relationships: illustrated in *Fathers and Sons*: "And the flies, too, were a nuisance. In normal times a yard boy drove them off with a large green branch; but on this occasion Vasily Ivanovich sent him out, for fear of being condemned by the younger generation" (272).

Social ritual and etiquette: a particularly interesting area that awaits a crosscultural diachronic study of social manners (e.g., greetings and goodbyes) for which literature is the only record in the case of long-disappeared forms: "[When El Cid and his men meet the King upon their return from exile] he fell to the ground on his hands and knees, / the grass of the fields he took with his teeth" (*Poema del Cid*, v. 3031, translation mine) (3); in *Fathers and Sons*, "Arkady energetically turned to his father and kissed him vigorously on the cheek" (170); in *La Regenta* "he [the provincial city playboy] shook her hand with that firm pull he always used, in keeping with the fashion that was new then in Madrid" (347) (4); in the Hungarian novel

St. Peter's Umbrella, by Mikszáth, "the old gentleman took her small hand in his large one, and pinched her cheek in fatherly fashion" (263). Often, these social rituals have religious connotations, as in *Pather Panchali*, "she [the daughter of a rich family] would not drink water until her husband had touched it with his foot [. . .] a wife of the good old type" (38), "the bucket [for milking the cow] wasn't cleaned properly; and [. . .] it's been handled by a low-caste woman. Moreover, it's going to be taken into the kitchen [. . .] If I had [touched it] I should have had to go and bath all over gain! [. . .] do the kitchen floor with cow-dung, as always has to be done when a place has been defiled" (169), and in *Nectar in a Sieve*, "On the doorstep I traced out a *colam*, a pattern in white rice flour to welcome them [. . .] Ira [her daughter] knelt at my feet" (53).

The good manners of the upper classes constitute the prejudiced gauge by which we tend to judge people. However, not only can we behave more fluently when interacting with lower-status persons if we practice their well-defined etiquette norms (as it is easier for us to do so than it is for them to adopt ours), but, as researchers, we are offered a most detailed documentation on this fascinating subject by both the novel of different periods and the modern realistic theater, apart from a number of treatises written in different periods (see Wildeblood 1965).

Household chores like "the letting off of the morning cattle", in *Kanthapura* (119), or "how to milk the goat, how to plant seed, how to churn butter from milk, and how to mull rice", in *Nectar in a Sieve* (14).

Child-rearing: some ways common to other cultures, such as women who "had children at their hips" while carrying bundles of washing, in *Nectar in a Sieve* (11).

Culture-bound diseases: Smallpox and dysentery in *Kanthapura*, cholera in *Fathers and Sons*, etc.

Leisure time and games, such as dice (*Pather Panchali*).

Chronemic patterns, as the months of the Hindu calendar (Vaisakh, 1st; Sravan, 5th; Kartik, 7th; Pushya, 10th), or the eleventh day of the moon (Ekadashiday) and the Day of Brahma, in *Kanthapura*.

Emotional-displays, documented from the early narratives on, as when in the *Poema del Cid* "he saw Minaya [his nephew and a knight] appear on his galloping horse, he hastened to embrace, / he kissed him on his mouth and on his eyes" (v. 920, translation mine) (5); in *Fathers and Sons* "he leaned toward Arkady [his son's friend] and kissed him on the shoulder" (277); in Balzac's *La Cousine Bette* "the tears [. . .] returned in torrents. In an access of filial love [. . .] she fell on her knees in front of her [her mother], took the hem of her dress and kissed it" (293) (6); and in *Nectar in a Sieve*, after a damaging monsoon rain, "the drums of calamity began; their grave, throbbing rhythm [. . .] through the night" (46).

Political ideology and attitudes

In *Kanthapura* we witness India's struggle for independence from the British in a village: "The next morning after a confrontation with policemen on the toddy grove, with bell and camphor and trumpet, we planted our trophies before the temple. Five twigs of toddy trees [. . .] and a toddy pot [. . .] and she spat on us and called us toddy people. Yes, yes, sister, we are toddy people! But we don't marry our daughters to gap-toothed sons-in-law. Nor do we go on Kashi-pilgrimage with toddy contract money" (133).

Folklore and the arts

Popular language and sayings: in *Kanthapura*, 'Purnayya has a grown-up daughter, who will "come home soon" ' (she is pregnant with her first child) (208), Moorthy was 'as honest as an elephant' (9), and "Postman Subbayya [. . .] had no fire in his stomach and was red with red and blue with blue [no will of his own]" (113), besides the culture-defining popular or literary similes, a fascinating research topic in itself, as it offers, not only a historical record of their appearance, evolution, elaboration, and sometimes disappearance of similes, but a rich documentation of household chores and objects, domestic and wild animals (with whose qualities man is related), occupations, long forgotten figures and better known ones, the countryside and its products, and place names (see Poyatos 1973, from a doctoral dissertation); as in *Pather Panchali*: as pure as the goddess Jagaddhatri (26), "as beautiful as the goddess Jagaddhatri" (38), "as generous as Annapura" (38), "as pink as a *kunch* tree" (126), "as black as *jhinge* seeds" (159)); and in *Kanthapura*: "as honest as an elephant" (9), "as blue as a marriage shawl" (51), "as lean as an areca-nut tree" (181).

Popular or learned literature, as in *Pather Panchali*, "I am a Brahmin and a Sanskrit scholar. I sing the *Chandi* poems and the holy *Bhagavat* and the *Gita*" (253), "spread her sari around her, and began to chant part of the Mahabharat [. . .] the poem by Kasidas" (75), the *Ramayan* (151), the old narrative poems called panchalis (151), the *Poem of Brave Women* [an 1862 work]" (155), etc., and in *Kanthapura*, sastras (27), *Bhagavad Gita* (21), etc.

Popular beliefs: in *Fathers and Sons* "a hand mirror had [. . .] been shattered, and [the old woman] [. . .] regarded that as a bad sign" (343); in Mikszáth's *St. Peter's Umbrella* the Hungarian folk say: 'We wanted to kill [the dog] [. . .] but no one dared to, for they say that the spirit of his old master would come back and haunt us' (12).

Folk celebrations: as the small-town wedding described in Chapter 6 of *Nectar in a Sieve*.

Performances: *Pather Panchali*'s frequently mentioned jatras, during the Chorok season (chapters 21 and 22), or *Kanthapura*'s Sankara-jayanthi (7) and Harikatha (8).

Music, like the one played with "her bulbul tara [. . .] plucking at the strings [. . .] and singing", in *Nectar in a Sieve* (25).

Children's pastimes, such as the paper boats they sail down the river (to Benares, according to popular belief) when the rains come (*Kanthapura*, 109).

11. Cultural Styles of Interaction in Literature

Although I am sparing any sort of elaboration on the different intelligible systems that make up a culture, I feel I must emphasize the necessity for the literary anthropologist—or the average fieldworker for that matter—to seek in the narrative literature of a culture the characteristics of the interactive styles peculiar to that culture and perhaps its various subcultures, not only geographically but across society. It has been made clear that culture is communication. Communication, at least in its fullest and most real form, is personal interaction.

Personal interaction is today the subject of intensive research on the part of communicologists, psychologists and social psychologists, clinical psychiatrists, and semioticians, and within anthropological meetings, though not as intensively by fieldwork anthropologists as it should. Besides, while investigators focus most of the time on what is known as face-to-face interaction—no doubt the core of human communication and the basis of everyday conversational encounters—there are other forms of interaction that may also show certain cultural characteristics and that seem to be unduly neglected.

A novel, in general, presents a kind of conversation between two or more interlocutors which, from a realism-seeking point of view, or a sociological one, seems to flow precisely with unreal fluency, that is, the participants take turns in an orderly fashion, hardly ever interrupting each other in the middle of a sentence or before the speaker yields the floor, and never—due to the traditional limitations of the written narrative text—speaking simultaneously for a varying length of time, thus not reflecting a very conspicuous characteristic of some cultures. Only in some instances, and more often in the behavioristic type of novel (e.g., Dos Passos' 1925 *Manhattan Transfer*, Hortelano's 1962 *Summer Storm*) do we find attempts to get away from what is actually 'contrived conversation' as opposed to 'natural conversation' (as discussed in Chapter 7) by depicting the lack of fluency typical of a real-life encounter, simply because of the limitations of both the writer and the written text itself to convey the reality of a conversation.

At any rate, although the Basic Triple Structure, language-paralanguage-kinesics, constitutes the foundation of any conversational encounter, and these three costructures appear in the way I have illustrated earlier, we can also observe the functional characteristics of the rest of the somatic systems and their relationships with objectual and environmental forms of communication or sign production. These relationships are, again, suggested in Fig. 11.1 by the lines joining different systems. What must be emphasized is that we are not dealing simply with a one-to-one type of association, for any stretch of cultural interactive exchange may bring into play an incredibly complex mesh of signs of many kinds. Furthermore, that particular interactive event is invariably conditioned by a few, or many, of the factors included in the Total Conditioning Background discussed in Chapter 3. But even without considering their conditioning elements, the way the various systems are linked together in a given culture is something that the anthropologist must be sensitized to an investigate, for it is only then that one can fully appreciate the mutual intertwining of sensible and intelligible systems peculiar to a particular culture beyond any universal pattern.

Since the structure of conversation has been discussed in Chapter 7, I will simply refer the researcher, who might combine the cultural study of narrative literature with subsequent or simultaneous direct contact with the culture, to that discussion of the various interactive behaviors displayed in the course of a conversation by means of verbal, paralinguistic, kinesic and proxemic behaviors mainly, but also displayed in certain situations by dermal-thermal cues (e.g., blushing as a form of feedback), chemical cues (e.g., tears as feedback or an ending pause) or chronemic ones (the duration of a pause, of a laugh, of a gesture or a postural or proxemic change).

The literary documentation of intersystem relationships

As illustrating only the relationships indicated by lines in Fig. 11.1 could well occupy a whole volume, I will merely in this first exploration of literary anthropology differentiate between *direct* and *indirect* or complementary relationships. We know that proxemics, for instance, and language, paralanguage or kinesics are mutually conditioned in such a way that intimate distance will elicit equally intimate choice of words, intimate paralinguistic feature and intimate kinesic behavior.

That is a direct relationship or series of relationships. But, beyond that, we also know—perhaps within a single research area and without attempting an interdisciplinary approach—that proxemic and kinesic behaviors are conditioned by furniture arrangement and shape, and that this in turn depends on the interior architectural spaces. Therefore, through proxemic behavior we find a morphological and functional relationship between any of the components of the Basic Triple Structure and architecture, or between them and furniture. Clothes have always conditioned kinesic behavior, mainly manners and postures, in both men and women, while furniture has also conditioned postural habits, therefore we clearly see the not so indirect association of furniture and dress style. Furthermore, both dress and furniture—witness and ordinary man–woman's encounter across a small table in a bar or restaurant—may condition intimate language and paralanguage; cosmetics (olfactorily perceived as a chemical system) may determine language, paralanguage and kinesics, while being related to proxemics in such a situation; in addition, all three systems of the triple structure, plus proxemic, dermal (blushing) and thermal (a rise in body temperature) signs—to recall the semiotic perspective of sign production and mutual relationships—are also conditioned by alcohol consumption, in turn partly influenced in this context by the intimacy of the low lights perhaps, which is a conditioning factor for paralinguistic (e.g., low-pitch, breathy voice), kinesic (e.g., contact of hands and faces) and proxemic (intimate distance) behaviors.

One could keep enumerating the interrelationships of sensible systems in a particular situation, and then we would have to carry it further as these very relationships would reveal their own associations with certain intelligible systems, such as role expectations, moral values, leisure behavior, etc., thus disclosing certain patterns peculiar to a particular culture along with some universal ones.

On this occasion, however, I would invite the reader to trace the various intersystem relationships by following each horizontal line from each individual system towards the right where it joins a common vertical line which establishes one or several relationships. This purely visual exercise will reveal many different kinds of associations that will in turn suggest a great number of research topics within the realms of many different fields.

In the end we have established an intricate set of sensible and intelligible system interrelationships which would afford an exhaustive microanalysis of culturally-conditioned human behaviors in interaction, in itself the concern of anthropologists as much as social psychologists, clinical psychiatrists, architects, semioticians, philosophers or literature scholars. What each of those disciplines should do on its own is to emphasize certain aspects, but without neglecting the others, for that simply perpetuates the traditional gulf that exists among the various sciences devoted, paradoxically enough, to the study of people.

For the anthropologist, literary anthropology would prove to be the kind of tool that would undoubtedly contribute to the systematic and exhaustive approach to a culture one ought to pursue. I trust that the preceding pages will have shown with enough clarity, not only the theoretical foundation of the proposed research area, but the basic avenues of its methodology according to the specific strategies of the various disciplines. The 1983 Symposium on Literary Anthropology in Québec City will no doubt open many more perspectives generated by the different disciplines that will interact on that occasion.

Notes

1. I proposed 'Literary Anthropology' for the first time (apart from an occasional suggestion in earlier papers) at a post-congress conference I organized in Calcutta, sponsored by the Anthropology Department of Calcutta University, for the 1978 Xth International Congress of Anthropological and Ethnological Sciences. A reduced version of this paper appeared in *Man and Life*, 5: 3/4, 127–145 (Poyatos 1979c) and the longer one in *Versus: cuaderni di studi semiotici* (Poyatos 1981c). At this writing I am organizing a symposium on 'Theory and Applications in Literary Anthropology', as part of the XIth International Congress of Anthropological and Ethnological Sciences (Phase One), to be held in Quebec City in August 1983.

2. Literary works quoted. Original dates appear after the titles, which are shown by initials in the main text, and the original texts of translations from French, English and Spanish appear after the Notes, numbered as throughout the article.

Alas, Leopoldo, *La Regenta*, 1884–5 (Madrid: Alianza Editorial, 1966) *LR*.

Anand, Mulk Raj, *Coolie*, 1936 (New Delhi, Orient Paperbacks, 1972) *C*.

Anand, Mulk Raj, *Untouchable*, 1935 (New Delhi, Orient Paperbacks, 1970).

Balzac, Honoré de, *La Cousine Bette*, 1846 (Paris: Garnier-Flammarion, 1977) *CB*.

Banerji, Bibhutibhushan, *Pather Panchali*, 1929 (Bloomington/London: Indiana University Press, 1968) *PP*.

Cervantes, Miguel de, *Don Quijote de La Mancha*, 1605–15 (Barcelona: Editorial Juventud, 1965) *DQ*.

Dickens, Charles, *Pickwick Papers*, 1836–7 (New York: Dell Publishing Co., 1964) *PP*.

Dos Passos, *Manhattan Transfer*, 1925 (New York: Bantam Books, 1959) *MT*.

Dostoevsky, Feodor, *Crime and Punishment*, 1866 (New York: W. W. Norton, 1975) *CP*.

Hawthorne, Nathaniel, *The House of the Seven Gables*, 1851 (New York: Washington Square Press, 1960). Cited once by title.

Huxley, Aldous, *Point Counterpoint*, 1928 (New York: Avon Books) *PC*.

Lazarillo de Tormes (Anonymous), 1554, in *La novela picaresca española* (Madrid: Editorial Aguilar, 1956). Cited by title.

Markandaya, Kamala, *Nectar in a Sieve*, 1954 (New York: New American Library, 1954) *NS*.

Mikszáth, Kálmán, *St. Peter's Umbrella*, 1896 (New York: Harper, 1901) *SPU*.

Poema del Cid (Anonymous), 1140 (Madrid: Espasa-Calpe, 1951). Cited by title.

Rao, Raja, *Kanthapura*, 1938 (New York: New Directions, 1963) *K*.

Rao, Raja, *The Serpent and the Rope*, 1961 (New Delhi, Orient Paperbacks, 1961).

Steinbeck, *Grapes of Wrath*, 1939 (New York: Bantam Books, 1964) *GW*.

Turgenev, Ivan, *Fathers and Sons*, 1861 (New York: Vintage Books) *FS*.

(1) 'Cuando Sancho vió que no hallaba el libro, fuésele parando mortal el rostro; y tornándose a tentar todo el cuerpo muy apriesa, tornó a echar de ver que no le hallaba, y sin más, se echó etrambos puños a las barbas, y se arrancó la mitad de ellas, y luego, apriesa y sin cesar, se dio media de puñadas en el rostro y en las narices, que se las bañó todas en sangre'.

(2) 'Tornóla a meter [la espada] y ciñósela, y un sartal de cuentas gruesas de talabarte. Y con paso sosegado y el cuerpo derecho, haciendo con él y con la cabeza muy gentiles meneos, echando el cabo de la capa sobre el hombro y a veces so el brazo, y poniendo la mano derecha en el costado, salió [. . .]'.

(3) 'dio aquel tirón enérgico que él siempre daba, siguiendo la moda que en Madrid empezaba entonces'.

(4) 'los inojos e las manos en tierra los fincó,/las yerbas del campo a dientes las tomó [. . .]'.

(5) 'Quendo vido mio Cid asomar a Minaya,/el cavallo corriendo, valo abracar sin falla,/ besóle la boca e los ojos de la cara [. . .]'.

(6) 'les larmes [. . .] elles revinrent à torrents. Dans un accès de piété filiale [. . .] elle se mit à genoux devant elle, saisit le bas de sa robe et la baisa [. . .]'.

Appendix

Outlines (for 1982–83) of the three nonverbal communication courses offered at the University of New Brunswick's Departments of Anthropology, Sociology, and Psychology. "Fig." refers to figures and tables in class handouts; "VIDEO", to video-illustrations of topics.

Anthroplogy 3431

Nonverbal Communication I: Interdisciplinary Theory

Course Outline

1	SEP	13	INTRODUCTORY LECTURE1. Nonverbal Communication Studies today. Bodily, objectual, and environmental systems of communication. Figs. 1, 2.
2		15	INTRODUCTORY LECTURE 2. The application of NVC Studies in Anthropology, Sociology, Psychology, Nursing, Business, Media, Education, Linguistics, Film, Theater, Painting, Architecture, Semiotics, and Literature.
3		16	CULTURE AS COMMUNICATION. Basic forms of culture. Culture as a dynamic continuum. Inherited and learned habits. Spatial and temporal approach.
4		20	COMMUNICATION AND CULTURAL FLUENCY. The NV barriers of intra- and intercultural communication. Emitting and perceiving Cultural Fluency. The Fluency Quotient.
5		22	SENSIBLE AND INTELLIGIBLE SYSTEMS. Somatic, objectual, and environmental sign systems and their intelligible background. A culture's sensory world. Fig. 2.
6		24	ANALYSIS OF A CULTURE THROUGH ITS CULTUREMES. The theory of culturemes: the progressive and systematic study of a culture and its people. Fig. 3.
7		27	ENCODING AND DECODING IN SOCIAL INTERACTION. Input, sign-meaning relationship (arbitrary, iconic, intrinsic), and decoding. Behaviors as related to each other and to sender and receiver. Fig. 4.
8		29	THE SENSORY CHANNELS BETWEEN TWO BODIES 1. Direct perception and synesthesial assumption. Visual, audible, olfactory, gustatory, dermal, and kinesthetic receptors. The main human systems: sound and movement. Fig. 5.
9	OCT	1	THE SENSORY CHANNELS BETWEEN TWO BODIES 2. Chemical messages in humans as compared to animals: from pheromones to cosmetics. Thermal messages.
10		4	THE SENSORY CHANNELS BETWEEN TWO BODIES 3. Dermal messages. Direct and synesthesial perception of shape, size, consistency, and weight of another body. Contextual and situational hierarchization of sensory channels.

11		6	CATEGORIES OF INTERACTIVE NONVERBAL BEHAVIORS 1. Kinesic and paralinguistic emblems. The anthropology and sociology of hand emblems. Fig. 6.
12		8	CATEGORIES OF INTERACTIVE NONVERBAL BEHAVIORS 2. Language markers. Markers of stress, punctuation, pronouns, adverbs, etc. Markers of paralanguage. VIDEO.
13		13	CATEGORIES OF INTERACTIVE NONVERBAL BEHAVIORS 3. Illustrators of space and time: space markers and time markers. Deictics (pointers).
14		15	CATEGORIES OF INTERACTIVE NONVERBAL BEHAVIORS 4. The imitative series of discourse illustrators: pictographs, echoics, kinetographs, and kinephonographs.
15		18	CATEGORIES OF INTERACTIVE NONVERBAL BEHAVIORS 5. Ideographs and event tracers. Identifiers: illustrating abstractions and physical referents in conversation. VIDEO.
16		20	CATEGORIES OF INTERACTIVE NONVERBAL BEHAVIORS 6. Externalizers: our reactions to self, others, events, and the environment.
17		22	MID-TERM EXAM (lectures 3–16).
18		25	CATEGORIES OF INTERACTIVE NONVERBAL BEHAVIORS 7. Self-adaptors: forms and functions of contacts with ourselves.
19		27	CATEGORIES OF INTERACTIVE NONVERBAL BEHAVIORS 8. Alter-adaptors: forms and functions of contacts with others.
20		29	CATEGORIES OF INTERACTIVE NONVERBAL BEHAVIORS 9. The immediate extrasomatic systems: forms and functions of body-adaptors and object-adaptors.
21	NOV	1	THE BASIC TRIPLE STRUCTURE OF HUMAN COMMUNICATION. Language, paralanguage, and kinesics contrasted. The limitations of words and the lexicality and grammaticality of the three cosystems in discourse. Fig. 7.
22		3	PARALANGUAGE 1: PRIMARY QUALITIES. The identifying features of a person's voice: timbre, volume, resonance, tempo, pitch qualities, intonation range, syllabic length, and rhythm. Figs. 8, 9.
23		5	PARALANGUAGE 2: QUALIFIERS. Our biological, psychological and situational voice modifications: respiratory, glottis, laryngeal, velar, pharyngeal, articulatory, tension, labial, and maxillary controls. Social functions.
24		8	PARALANGUAGE 3: DIFFERENTIATORS. The anthropology and sociology of laughter, crying, sighing, coughing, hawking, spitting, nose-blowing, yawning, and sneezing
25		10	PARALANGUAGE 4: ALTERNANTS. The functions of tongue clicks, uh-hu's, m-hm's, moans, grunts, gasps, hisses, etc. Their lexicality. Problems of representation and labeling. Articulated, inarticulated, and pausal. Alternants cross-culturally.
26		12	VIDEO-ILLUSTRATION OF PARALANGUAGE IN REAL LIFE. VIDEO.
27		15	KINESICS: THE LANGUAGE OF BODY MOVEMENTS AND POSITIONS. Phylogeny, ontogeny, and cultural development of free and bound gestures, manners, and postures.
28		17	GESTURES. Free and bound gestures. Universal and culture-specific displays. Interactive and noninteractive facial gestures. Interdisciplinary research.

29 19 MANNERS. Free and bound manners. Culture, gender, age, and socioeconomic level. Gait. Posture-forming, body-adaptor, alter-adaptor, and object-adaptor manners.

---

30 22 POSTURES. The anthropology and sociology of posture: forms and functions. Interpersonal attitudes and personality. Cultural evolution and conditioning factors. Fig. 10.

31 24 VIDEO-ILLUSTRATION OF KINESICS IN REAL LIFE. VIDEO.

32 26 KINESICS CROSSCULTURALLY: INVITED INFORMANTS FROM FIVE CULTURES.

---

33 29 GAZE BEHAVIOR AS A RESEARCH AREA. Animal gaze behavior. Crosscultural differences. Applications in the social and behavioral sciences, nursing, business.

34 DEC 1 PROXEMICS: THE BEHAVIORS OF SPACE. Far, public, social, personal, intimate, and objectual distances. Intercultural problems of personal and intimate distances. Fig. 1.

35 3 THE COSTRUCTURATION OF SOMATIC AND EXTRASOMATIC SYSTEMS. The mutual conditioning of bodily systems, body- and object-adaptors, and environmental systems. Its effects on social interaction. Fig. 2.

---

36 6 INTRODUCTION TO THE MECHANISM OF CONVERSATION. Speaker's and Listener's behaviors. Rules and counterrules. Simultaneous behaviors. Forms of feedback. Pauses. Fig. 13.

37 8 LITERARY ANTHROPOLOGY. The use of the national narrative literatures as a research tool in anthropology, sociology, psychology, and other fields. Interdisciplinary crossfertilization through the study of the documented verbal and nonverbal systems. Fig. 2.

Sociology 3233

Nonverbal Communication II: Interdisciplinary Applications

Course Outline

1 JAN 7 INTRODUCTORY LECTURE: Review of 3431. Nonverbal Communication Studies. The Present Course. Figs. 1, 2.

---

2 10 THE TOTAL CONDITIONING BACKGROUND OF HUMAN BEHAVIOR. Biological, physiological, psychological, socioeducational, and environmental variables. Fig. 1.

2 12 USAGE AND FUNCTIONS OF BEHAVIORS. Forms of usage: standard, extrastandard, infrastandard, ultracorrectness, and group behavior. Functions: interactive, occupational, task-performing, ritualistic. Fig. 3.

4 14 PARALANGUAGE 1: FORMS AND SOCIAL FUNCTIONS OF CRYING. Paralinguistic-kinesic forms. Positive and negative functions. Grief and bereavement across cultures. Masculine crying.

---

5 17 PARALANGUAGE 2: SILENCE IN SOCIETY: FORMS AND FUNCTIONS. Interactive and non-interactive, and positive and negative silences. Qualifying features. Fig. 4.

6 19 GESTURES CROSSCULTURALLY (beyond 3431): INVITED INFORMANTS FROM FIVE CULTURES

7		21	GESTURES INVENTORIES. Interacting and noninteracting observation. Informants. Literary sources. Films. Illustration, classification, labeling, description, and context. The Morris-Collett kinesic-atlas inventory.
8		24	MANNERS 1: GREETING BEHAVIORS CROSSCULTURALLY. First encounters, acquaintances, close friends, relatives. Short and long absence. Age, sex, and social differences.
9		26	MANNERS 2: SOCIAL ETIQUETTE. Good and bad manners crossculturally. The need for low-class etiquette research and practice.
10		28	HUMAN TERRITORIALITY. Personal space crossculturally. Territorial definitions. Forms of privacy. Forms of privacy intrusion: physical, visual, acoustic, olfactory. The nonperson situation.
11		31	VERBAL-NONVERBAL BEHAVIORS IN PUBLIC PLACES. Travel conveyances. Bars. Terminals. Privacy in public. Hitchhiking as nonverbal communication.
12	FEB	2	VERBAL-NONVERBAL COMMUNICATION IN SHARED QUARTERS. Sommer's geriatric ward experiment. Roommates at UNB's Lady Dunn Residence (results of interviews).
13		4	VERBAL-NONVERBAL BEHAVIORS OF PEDESTRIANS. The rules of the street across cultures. Pedestrian routing, gaze and collision avoidance. Problem areas.
14		7	TOUCHING AND BEING TOUCHED. The physicopsychological experience of touch. Costructuration with other senses. Body-adaptors. The development of tactile experiences crossculturally.
15		9	CLOTHES, APPEARANCE, AND BODY ADORNMENT. Evolution and influence on kinesic behaviors. The three semiotic realizations of clothes. Self- and alter-interaction through clothes.
16		11	A PERSON'S OBJECTUAL ENVIRONMENT. Research on residential landscaping. The interior environments: spaces and spacing, materials and locations. Cross-cultural differences. The American 'living-room scale', then and now.
17		14	THE SENSORY INTERACTION OF PEOPLE AND THEIR CULTURAL ENVIRONMENT. Visual, acoustic, olfactory, kinesthetic and tactile involvement. The blind and the deaf. Crosscultural differences. SLIDES.
18		16	CHRONEMICS: THE BEHAVIOR OF TIME. Conceptualization of time. Social, interactive, and professional time. One's time in the helping professions.
19		18	MID-TERM EXAM (lectures 2–19).
20	MAR	2	FEMININE AND MASCULINE NONVERBAL BEHAVIORS. Paralanguage, gestures, manners, postures, and proxemics. 'Effeminate' and 'mannish'. The issue of male dominance and gender inequality: nonverbal aspects.
21		4	NONVERBAL COMMUNICATION IN NURSE–PATIENT RELATIONS 1. Language, paralanguage, kinesics, gaze, proxemics, and touch. Olfactory discrimination.
22		7	NONVERBAL COMMUNICATION IN NURSE–PATIENT RELATIONS 2. Experiences at the ECH (from student papers). Children. The aged. The terminally ill. The handicapped. The visitors. The patient's objectual environment. Review of the nursing literature on nonverbal behavior.
23		9	PERSPECTIVES IN DEVELOPMENTAL NONVERBAL COMMUNICATION. The parallel development of language-paralanguage-kinesics. The development of nonverbal categories: emblems, language, markers, identifiers, and externalizers.

24		11	NONVERBAL COMMUNICATION IN EDUCATION 1. The environment: the school, classroom layout, color, light and seating arrangement.
25		14	NONVERBAL COMMUNICATION IN EDUCATION 2. The nonverbal appearance and behaviors of teacher and student: paralanguage, kinesics, gaze proxemics, and touch.
26		16	NONVERBAL COMMUNICATION IN EDUCATION 3. Story-reading to children: the reader's nonverbal style (paralanguage, kinesics, gaze, and replay silences). The Canadian multicultural classroom: nonverbal issues and problems.
27		18	NONVERBAL COMMUNICATION IN BUSINESS 1. The person: sex, height, clothes, and other body-adaptors. Static and dynamic bodily characteristics. Culture.
28		21	NONVERBAL COMMUNICATION IN BUSINESS 2. The environment: the outside office, the office (location, layout, objectual identifiers). The dynamics of business meetings: location, time, and seating arrangements.
29		23	NONVERBAL COMMUNICATION IN BUSINESS 3. The interview: setting, the interviewer's style and structuration of the encounter, the interviewee's positive and negative nonverbal behaviors. Interviewing in the Oromocto's military.
30		25	NONVERBAL SYSTEMS IN MAGAZINE ADVERTISING 1. From the 20's to the 80's. The people, the setting, language and stilled kinesics. Direct and synesthesial perception. SLIDES.
31		28	NONVERBAL COMMUNICATION IN TV ADVERTISING. Still image vs. live paralanguage and kinesics. Primary message and supporting messages. The cultural commercial. Exploitative methods and consumer manipulation. VIDEO.
32		30	NONVERBAL COMMUNICATION IN PHOTOGRAPHY. Socio-anthropological and personal documentation. Photojournalism: testimony and manipulation. SLIDES.
33	APR	6	NONVERBAL COMMUNICATION IN PAINTING. From primitive conceptual style to physical and psychological nonverbal realistic tendencies. SLIDES.
34		8	NONVERBAL COMMUNICATION IN THE NOVEL. The individualization of characters. Stylistic and technical functions of nonverbal systems. Sociocultural documentation.
35		11	NONVERBAL COMMUNICATION IN THE THEATER. Script vs. novel. Development of nonverbal stage directions. The nonverbal playwright–director/actor–audience relationship. Stageable and unstageable systems.

Psychology 3012
Psychology of Nonverbal Communication

Course Outline

1	JAN	7	INTRODUCTORY LECTURE: NONVERBAL COMMUNICATION IN PSYCHOLOGY TODAY. The development of the field. Interdisciplinary trends. Research, literature, and meetings. New York's Inst. of NVC Res. The NATO institutes. Figs. 1, 2.

2		10	HUMAN ETHOLOGY AND NONVERBAL COMMUNICATION. Expressive behaviors and the culturalists-universalists controversy: Darwin, Eibl-Eibesfeldt, La Barre, Birdwhistell. Ekman's neurocultural theory of emotional expressions.
3		12	THE MECHANISMS OF INTERSOMATIC COMMUNICATION. Encoding-decoding of messages. Direct and synesthesial perception. Interrelationships of verbal and nonverbal behaviors. The Total Conditioning Background. Fig. 3.
3		14	THE REVISION OF THE REDUNDANCY AND FLUENCY CONCEPTS AND THE HIERARCHIZATION OF SIGN SYSTEMS. Redundancy vs. complementarity. Costructuration, intensity, and duration. Verbal-nonverbal fluency. Psychological implications.
5		17	THE BASIC TRIPLE STRUCTURE OF COMMUNICATION. Language-Paralanguage-Kinesics. The triple transcription. Fig. 4.
6		19	PARALANGUAGE 1: REVIEW OF PARALINGUISTIC PHENOMENA. Primary Qualities, Qualifiers, Differentiators, and Alternants. Fig. 5.
7		21	PARALANGUAGE 2: FORMS AND SOCIAL FUNCTIONS OF LAUGHTER. Verbal, paralinguistic, and kinesic components. Positive and negative functions. Fig. 6.
8		24	PARALANGUAGE 3: VIDEO-ILLUSTRATION OF FEATURES IN NATURAL SITUATIONS. VIDEO.
9		26	PSYCHOLOGICAL RESEARCH IN PARALANGUAGE SINCE THE 50s. Personality, attitudes, psychopathology, and interaction.
10		28	KINESICS: PSYCHOLOGICAL RESEARCH SINCE THE 50s. Birdwhistell's kinesic-linguistic analogy. Transcription systems. Fig. 7.
11		31	SCHEFLEN'S STRUCTURAL WORK ON SOCIAL AND CLINICAL KINESICS. Structure of the psychotherapy interview. Postural markers. Quasi-courtship behaviors.
12	FEB	2	SPEECH-AND-BODY MOTION RESEARCH. Self-synchrony and speaker-listener interactional synchrony. The work of Condon and Kendon.
13		4	EKMAN AND FRIESEN'S WORK IN PSYCHOPATHOLOGY. Nonverbal categories. Judgement and component approaches. Deception clues and information leakage.
14		7	THE FACE: THE TELLTALE SIGNS. Static, slow, and rapid signs. Identity, race, sex, age, kinship, beauty, sexual attractiveness, emotion, culture.
15		9	NONVERBAL BEHAVIORS OF THE FACE AND HANDS 1. Coding and crosscultural aspects of emblems. Coding and forms of language markers. Fig. 8.
16		11	NONVERBAL BEHAVIORS OF THE FACE AND HANDS 2. Identifiers of abstractions and sensible qualities. The person's articulateness. Externalizers: origin, elicitors, channels, and perception of reactions.
17		14	NONVERBAL BEHAVIORS OF THE FACE AND HANDS 3: VIDEO-ILLUSTRATION. VIDEO.
18		16	MEASURING FACE, BROWS, AND HAND MOVEMENTS. Ekman's Facial Action Code and Hand Movement Code. Fig. 9.
19		18	MID-TERM EXAM (lectures 2–18)
20	MAR	2	SILENCE AND STILLNESS AS MESSAGE-CONVEYING SYSTEMS. Costructuration with preceding, simultaneous and succeeding activities. Decoding in interaction. Fig. 10.

21		4	GAZE BEHAVIOR 1: THE MECHANISM OF VISION. Psychological and interactive aspects of macular and peripheral vision. Interactive and noninteractive functions of fixation, blank fixation, solo, personal and environmental scanning, long-range pursuit, pupil reactions, blinking, and gaze breaking.
22		7	GAZE BEHAVIOR 2: SOCIAL AND CLINICAL ASPECTS. Positive and negative functions of eye contact and gaze aversion. Costructuration with other systems. Research on gaze behavior. Crosscultural differences.
23		9	PROXEMICS: LIVING SPACES AND BEHAVIOR. Sociofugal-sociopetal and fixed-semifixed features. Personal space, territorial markers, an invasion. Sommer's work. Architectural psychology.
24		11	TOUCHING: THE SOCIOPSYCHOLOGY OF INTIMACY. Development of touch. Crosscultural differences: greetings and conversation. Touch in the helping professions. Research on interpersonal touch.
25		14	DEVELOPMENTAL NONVERBAL COMMUNICATION: NEW PERSPECTIVES. Language development vs. verbal-nonverbal development. The Basic Triple Structure and the interactive nonverbal categories. Research on developmental nonverbal communication.
26		16	INTERACTIVE RANDOM BEHAVIORS. Encoding and decoding. Cultural, social, and psychological aspects. The work of Krout and others. New perspectives.
27		18	THE STRUCTURAL NATURALISTIC STUDY OF INTERACTION. The principles. Scheflen's work. Kendon's and Poyatos' instructional examples. The cultural and multi-channel approach to the structure of interaction.
28		21	REDUCED INTERACTION: FORMS, FUNCTIONS, CHANNELS, AND CODING. Language-culture barrier, opaque obstacle, deafness, transparent obstacle, distance, noise, darkness, social situation, agreed-upon silence, blindness, deafness, anosmia, telephonic conversation, and medical forms.
29		23	THE STRUCTURE OF CONVERSATION 1: SPEAKER–LISTENER INITIAL AND TURN-CHANGE BEHAVIORS. Initial turn claim, spontaneous initial-turn taking, failed spontaneous initial turn taking, initial-turn offer, granted initial-turn taking. Turn claim, -offer, -preopening, -granting, -yielding, -taking. Fig. 11.
30		25	THE STRUCTURE OF CONVERSATION 2: SECONDARY TURN-CHANGE BEHAVIORS. Turn holding, turn-claim suppressing, turn suppressing, -relinquishing, -opening, absent turn claiming, failed turn claiming, absent turn taking. VIDEO.
31		28	THE STRUCTURE OF CONVERSATION 3: LISTENER–SPEAKER-DIRECTED BEHAVIORS. Forms of feedback, requests for clarification and volume, repetitions, restatement, simultaneous conclusion, sentence completion, interruptions, prompting signals.
32		30	THE STRUCTURE OF CONVERSATION 4: INTER-LISTENER BEHAVIORS. Feedback, turn offer, -claiming, granting, -suppressing, prompting signals. VIDEO.
33	APR	6	THE STRUCTURE OF CONVERSATION 5: SPEAKER'S SECONDARY BEHAVIOR. Counter-feedback, feedback request, turn preclosing, -closing, -resumption.
34		8	THE STRUCTURE OF CONVERSATION 6: SIMULTANEOUS BEHAVIORS. Simultaneous 'symmetrical' and 'multiple' acts. Turns, claims, taking, conclusions relinquishing, yielding, silences.
35		11	THE STRUCTURE OF CONVERSATION 7: ACOUSTIC AND VISUAL PAUSES. Absent-turn claim, absent turn taking, offering, opening, pre-ending, ending, relinquishing/yielding, transitional, hesitation, feedback-seeking, task-performing, somatic-function. VIDEO.

References

ABERCROMBIE, DAVID (1968) "Paralanguage", *British Journal of Disorders of Communication*, **3**, 55–59. Also in J. Laver and S. Hutcheson (Eds.), *Communication in Face-to-Face Interaction: Selected Readings*, 64–70. Penguin Books, Harmondsworth, 1972.

AESCHYLUS (458 B.C.) *Agamemnon*. In D. Grene and R. Lattimore (Eds.), *Greek Tragedies*, Vol. I. The University of Chicago Press, Phoenix Books, Chicago, 1960.

ALAS, LEOPOLDO (1884–5) *La Regenta*. Alianza Editorial, Madrid, 1967.

ALEMÁN, MATEO (1599–1604) S. Gil y Gaya (Ed.), *Guzmán de Alfarache*. Espasa-Calpe, Clásicos Castellanos. Madrid, 1963.

ALLPORT, GORDON W. and P. E. VERNON (1933) *Studies in Expressive Movement*. Macmillan, New York.

ANAND, MULK RAJ (1972) *Coolie*. Orient Paperbacks, New Delhi.

ANAND, MULK RAJ (1970) *Untouchable*. Orient Paperbacks, New Delhi.

ARISTOPHANES (411 B.C.) *Lysistrata*. In A. W. Allison, A. J. Carr and A. M. Eastman (Eds.), *Masterpieces of the Drama*. Macmillan Publishing Co., New York, 1974.

ARGYLE, MICHAEL (1967) *The Psychology of Interpersonal Behavior*. Penguin Books, Harmondsworth.

ARGYLE, MICHAEL (1969) *Social Interaction*. Methuen, London; Etherton, New York.

ARGYLE, MICHAEL (1972) "Non-Verbal Communication in Human Social Interaction'. In R. A. Hinde (Ed.), *Non-Verbal Communication*. Cambridge University Press, Cambridge, 243–269.

ARGYLE, MICHAEL (1975) *Bodily Communication*. Methuen, London.

ARGYLE, MICHAEL and ROGER INGHAM (1972) "Gaze, Mutual Gaze, and Proximity". *Semiotica*, **6**: 1, 32–49.

ASHCRAFT, NORMAN and ALBERT SCHEFLEN (1976) *People Space*. Anchor Books, Doubleday: Garden City, New York.

AUSTIN, WILLIAM (1965) "Some Social Aspects of Paralanguage". *The Canadian Journal of Linguistics*, **11**: 1, 31–35.

BAKER SIDNEY J. (1955) "The Theory of Silences". *The Journal of General Psychology*, **53**, 145–167.

BALZAC, HONORÉ (1833) *Eugénie Grandet*. Garnier, Paris.

BALZAC, HONORÉ DE (1846) *La Cousin Bette*. Garnier-Flammarion, Paris, 1977.

BANERJI, BIBHUTIBHUSHAN (1929) *Pather Panchali*. Indiana University Press, Bloomington/London, 1968.

BARAKAT, ROBERT A. (1973) "Arabic Gestures". *Journal of Popular Culture*, **6**, 749–893.

BASSO, K. H. (1972) "To Give Up On Words: Silence in Western Apache Culture". In P. P. Giglioli (Ed.), *Language and Social Context*. Penguin Books, Harmondsworth, 67–86.

BAUER, OLGA (1959) *Cortesía y etiqueta modernas*. Aguilar, Madrid, 3rd edition.

BELLOW, SAUL (1964) *Herzog*. Viking Press; Fawcett World Library, New York, 1965.

BEVANS, M. (1960) *McCall's Book of Everyday Etiquette*, Golden Press, New York.

BIRDWHISTELL, RAY L. (1952) *Introduction to Kinesics. An Annotated System for Analysis of Body Motion and Gesture*. Dept. of State, Foreign Service Institute, Washington, D.C.

BIRDWHISTELL, RAY, L. (1954) "Kinesics and Communication". *Explorations*, **3**, 31–41. Also in E. Carpenter (Ed.), *Explorations in Communications*. Beacon Press, Boston, 1960, 54–64.

BIRDWHISTELL, RAY L. (1961) "Paralanguage 25 Years After Sapir". In Henry W. Brosin (Ed.), *Lectures on Experimental Psychiatry*. University of Pittsburgh Press, Pittsburgh. Also in John Laver and Sandy Hutcheson (Eds.), *Communication in Face-to-Face Interaction: A Reader*. Penguin Books, Harmondsworth, 1972, 82–100.

BIRDWHISTELL, RAY L. (1968) "Kinesics". *Intl. Encyclopedia of Social Sciences.* Macmillan and The Free Press, **8**: 379–384.

BIRDWHISTELL, RAY L. (1970) *Kinesics and Context.* University of Philadelphia Press, Philadelphia; Ballantine Books, New York, 1972.

BOLINGER, DWIGHT (1968) *Aspects of Language.* Harcourt, Brace & World, New York.

BRUNEAU, THOMAS (1973) "Communicative Silences: Forms and Functions". *The Journal of Communication*, **23**: 117–46.

BRUNEAU, THOMAS J. (1979) "Silence, Mind-Time Relativity, and Interpersonal Communication". In *The Study of Time, III: Proceedings of the Third International Society for the Study of Time.* Alpbach, Austria.

BRUNEAU, THOMAS J. (1980) "Chronemics and the Verbal-Nonverbal Interface". In M. Key (Ed.), *The Relationship of Verbal and Nonverbal Communication.* Mouton, The Hague, 101–117.

BYNON, JAMES (1976) "Domestic Animal Calling in a Berber Tribe". In W. C. McCormack and S. A. Wurm (Eds.), *Language and Man: Anthropological Issues.* Mouton, The Hague, 39–65.

CABALLERO BONALD, JOSÉ (1962) *Dos días de setiembre.* Seix-Barral, Barcelona.

CALDWELL, E. (1958) *Claudell Inglis*, Little, Brown, Boston.

CATFORD, J. C. (1968) "The Articulatory Possibilities of Man". In B. Malmberg (Ed.), *Manual of Phonetics.* North-Holland Publishing Co., Amsterdam, 309–333.

CELA, CAMILO JOSÉ (1951) *La Colmena.* Editorial Noguer, Barcelona-México, 1962.

CELA, CAMILO JOSÉ (1942) *La familia de Pascual Duarte.* Ediciones Destino, Barcelona, 1968.

CERVANTES, MIGUEL DE (1605–15) *Don Quijote de la Mancha.* Editorial Juventud, Barcelona, 1965.

CHATHAM, S., U. ECO, and J.-M. KLINKENBERG (Eds.) (1979) *A Semiotic Landscape: Proceedings of the First International Congress of Semiotic Studies.* Mouton, The Hague.

CHEKHOV, ANTON (1904) *The Cherry Orchard.* In *Four Great Plays by Chekhov*, trans. by C. Garnett. Bantam Books, New York, 1958.

CHEKHOV, ANTON (1897) *Uncle Vanya.* In *Four Great Plays by Chekhov*, trans. by C. Garnett. Bantam Books, New York, 1958.

COLLETT, PETER, (1974) "Pattern of Public Behavior: Collision Avoidance on a Pedestrian Crossing". *Semiotica*, **12**: 4, 281–299.

CREIDER, C. (1977) "Toward a Description of African Gestures". *Sign Language Studies*, **14**: 1–20.

CRYSTAL, DAVID (1971) "Prosodic and Paralinguistic Correlates of Social Categories". In Edwin Ardener (Ed.), *Social Anthropology and Language.* Tavistock Publications, London, 185–206.

CRYSTAL, DAVID (1974) "Paralinguistics". In T. Sebeok *et al.* (Eds.), *Current Trends in Linguistics and Adjacent Arts and sciences*, Vol. 12. Mouton, The Hague, 265–295.

CRYSTAL, DAVID and RANDOLPH QUIRK (1964) *Systems of Prosodic and Paralinguistic Features in English.* Mouton, The Hague.

DARWIN, CHARLES (1972) *The Expression of the Emotions in Man and Animals.* University of Chicago Press, London/Chicago (orig. ed. 1872).

DICKENS, CHARLES (1836–7) *Pickwick Papers.* Dell Publishing Co., New York, 1964.

DITTMANN, ALLEN T. (1971) Review of *Kinesics and Context. Psychiatry*, **34**, 334–342.

DITTMANN, ALLEN T. (1963) "Kinesic Research and Therapeutic Process: Further Discussion". In Peter Knapp (Ed.), *Expression of the Emotions in Man.* International University Press, New York, 140–159.

DITTMANN, ALLEN T. (1972a) *Interpersonal Messages of Emotion.* Springer, New York.

DITTMANN, ALLEN T. (1972b) "Development Factors in Conversational Behavior". *The Journal of Communication*, **22**: 4 (special issue on nonverbal communication), 404–423.

DITTMANN, ALLEN T. (1973) "Style in Conversation" (review of Efrón's *Gesture, Race, and Culture*). *Semiotica*, **9**: 3, 241–251.

DOS PASSOS, JOHN (1925) *Manhattan Transfer.* Bantam Books, New York, 1959.

DOSTOEVSKY, FEODOR (1866) *Crime and Punishment* (Ed. by G. Gibian). W. W. Norton & Company, New York, 1975.

DREISER, THEODORE (1925) *An American Tragedy.* Dell Publishing Co., New York, 1960.

DREISER, THEODORE (1900) *Sister Carrie*. Charles Scribner's Sons, New York, 1953.

DUBOS, RICHARD (1970) *So Human an Animal*. Hart-Davis, London.

DUNCAN, JAMES S., Jr. (1973) "Landscape Taste as a Symbol of Group Identity: A Westchester County Village". *Geographical Review*, July, 334–355.

DUNCAN, STARKEY, Jr. (1969) "Nonverbal Communication". *Psychological Bulletin,* **72**: 2, 118–137.

DUNCAN, STARKEY, Jr. (1972a) "Some Signals and Rules for Taking Speaking Turns in Conversations". *Journal of Personality and Social Psychology*, **23**: 2, 283–292.

DUNCAN, STARKEY, Jr. (1972b) "Distribution of Auditor Back-Channel Behaviors in Dyadic Conversation" . *Journal of Psycholinguistic Research*.

DUNCAN, STARKEY, Jr. (1973) "Toward a Grammar for Dyadic Conversation". *Semiotica*, **11**: 1, 29–46.

DUNCAN, STARKEY, Jr. (1974a) "On the Structure of Speaker–Auditor Interaction During Speaking Turns". *Language in Society*, **2**, 161–180.

DUNCAN, STARKEY, Jr. (1974b) "On Signalling That It's Your Turn to Speak". *Journal of Experimental and Social Psychology*, **10**: 3, 234–247.

DUNCAN, STARKEY, Jr. (1975a) "Interaction Units During Speaking Turns in Dyadic, Face-to-Face Conversations". In A. Kendon, R. Harris, and M. Key (Eds.), *The Organization of Behavior in Face-to-Face Interaction*. Mouton, The Hague, 199–213.

DUNCAN, STARKEY, Jr. (1975b) "Language, Paralanguage, and Body Motion in the Structure of Conversation". In Thomas R. Williams (Ed.), *Socialization and Communication in Primary Groups*. Mouton, The Hague, 283–311. Also in William McCormack and Stephen A. Wurm (Eds.), *Language and Man: Anthropological Issues*. Mouton, The Hague, 239–267.

DUNCAN, STARKEY, Jr. and DONALD W. FISKE (1977) *Face-to-Face Interaction: Research, Methods, and Theories*. John Wiley & Sons, New York.

EAST REGINALD (1977) *Heal the Sick*. Bethany Fellowship, Minneapolis.

EFRÓN, DAVID (1941) *Gesture and Environment*. King's Crown, New York. Reprinted as *Gesture, Race, and Culture*. Mouton, The Hague, 1972.

EIBL-EIBESFELDT, IRÄNAUS (1972) "Similarities and Differences Between Cultures in Expressive Movements". In Robert A. Hinde (Ed.), *Non-Verbal Communication*. Cambridge University Press, Cambridge, 297–314.

EIBL-EIBESFELDT, IRÄNAUS (1979a) "Universals in Human Expressive Behavior". In Aaron Wolfgang (Ed.), *Nonverbal Behavior: Applications and Cultural Implications*. Academic Press, New York, 17–30.

EIBL-EIBESFELDT, IRÄNAUS (1979b) "Ritual and Ritualization from a Biological Perspective". In Mario von Cranach, K. Foppa and W. Lapenies (Eds.), *Human Ethology*, 3–55.

EIBL-EIBESFELDT, IRÄNAUS (1980) "Strategies of Social Interaction". In Walburga von Raffler-Engel (Ed.), *Aspects of Nonverbal Communication*. Swets and Zeitlinger, Lisse, 45–65. Also in *Emotion: Theory, Research, and Experience, Vol. I: Theories of Emotion*. Academic Press, New York, 57–80.

EKMAN, PAUL (1972) "Universals and Cultural Differences in Facial Expressions of Emotion". In J. Cole (Ed.), *Nebraska Symposium on Motivation*. University of Nebraska Press, Lincoln.

EKMAN, PAUL (1973) "Cross Cultural Studies of Facial Expression". In P. Ekman (Ed.), *Darwin and Facial Expression: A Century of Research in Review*. Academic Press, New York, 169–222.

EKMAN, PAUL (1976a) "Measuring Facial Movement". *Environmental Psychology and Nonverbal Behavior*, **1** :1, 56–75.

EKMAN, PAUL (1976b) "Movements With Precise Meanings". *Journal of Communication*, **26**: 3, 14–26.

EKMAN, PAUL (1977) "Biological and Cultural Contributions to Body and Facial Movement". In John Blacking (Ed.), *The Anthropology of the Body*. Academic Press, New York, 39–84.

EKMAN, PAUL (1978) "Facial Signs: Facts, Fantasies, and Possibilities". In T. Sebeok (Ed.), *Sight, Sound and Sense*. Indiana University Press, Bloomington, Indiana, 124–156.

EKMAN, PAUL (1979) "About Brows: Emotional and Conversational Signals". In Mario von Cranach, K. Foppa, W. Lepenies, and D. Ploog, (Eds.), *Human Ethology*. Cambridge University Press, Cambridge, 169–249.

EKMAN, PAUL (1980) *The Face of Man*. Garland STPM Press, New York.

EKMAN, PAUL (1982) "Methods for Measuring Facial Action". In Klaus R. Scherer and Paul Ekman (Eds.), *Handbook of Methods in Nonverbal Behavior Research*. Cambridge University Press, Cambridge; Editions de la Maison des Sciences de l'Homme, Paris, 45–90.

EKMAN, PAUL and WALLACE FRIESEN (1968) "Nonverbal behavior in psychotherapy research". In J. Shlien (Ed.), *Research in Psychotherapy*, Vol. 3. American Psychological Association, Washington, D.C., 179–216.

EKMAN, PAUL and WALLACE FRIESEN (1969) "The Repertoire of Nonverbal Behavior Categories: Origins, Usage, and Coding". *Semiotica*, **1**, 49–98. Reprinted in A. Kendon (Ed.), *Nonverbal Communication, Interaction, and Gesture*. Mouton, The Hague, 1981, 57–105.

EKMAN, PAUL and WALLACE FRIESEN (1972) "Hand Movements". *The Journal of Communication*, **22**, 353–374.

EKMAN, PAUL and WALLACE V. FRIESEN (1974) "Nonverbal Behavior and Psychopathology". In R. J. Friedman and M. M. Katz (Eds.), *The Psychology of Depression: Contemporary Theory and Research*. Winston & Sons, Washington, D.C., 203–232.

EKMAN, PAUL and WALLACE FRIESEN (1975) *Unmasking the Face*. Prentice-Hall, Englewood Cliffs.

EKMAN, PAUL and WALLACE FRIESEN (1976) "Measuring Facial Movement". *Environmental Psychology and Nonverbal Behavior*, **1**: 1, 56–75.

EKMAN, PAUL, WALLACE V. FRIESEN, PHOEBE ELLSWORTH (1972) *Emotion in the Human Face: Guidelines for Research and an Integration of Findings*. Pergamon Press, New York, 1972.

EKMAN, PAUL, W. V. FRIESEN, and KLAUS R. SCHERER (1976) "Body Movement and Voice Pitch in Deceptive Interaction". *Semiotica*, **16**: 1, 23–27.

ERICKSON, VINCENT (1983) "Buddenbrooks and the Study of 19th Century North German Social Class: Some Problems in the Utilization of Literary Anthropology" (Unpublished).

ETIEMBLE (1961) *Blason d'un corps*. Gallimard, Paris.

EURIPIDES (406 B.C.) *The Bacchae*. In A. W. Allison, A. J. Carr and A. M. Eastman (Eds.), *Masterpieces of the Drama*. Macmillan Publishing Co., New York, 1974.

FAULKNER, WILLIAM (1930) *As I Lay Dying*. Penguin Books, Harmondsworth, 1963.

FENWICK, M. (1948) *Vogue's Book of Etiquette*. Simon & Schuster, New York.

FIELDING, Henry (1749) *Tom Jones*. Washington Square Press, New York, 1963.

FITZGERALD, F. SCOTT (1925) *The Great Gatsby*. Charles Scribner's Sons, New York, 1953.

FLYNN, LESLIE B. (1977) *19 Gifts of the Spirit*. Victor Books, Wheaton, Illinois.

FREEDMAN, NORBERT (1972) "The Analysis of Movement Behavior During the Clinical Interview". In A. Siegman and B. Pope (Eds.), *Studies in Dyadic Communication*. Pergamon Press, Oxford, 153–175.

FREUD, SIGMUND (1901) *Psychopathology of Everyday Life*. Macmillan, New York.

FRIESEN, WALLACE V., PAUL EKMAN and HAROLD WALLBOTT (1979) "Measuring Hand Movements". *Journal of Nonverbal Behavior*, **4**, 2, 97–112.

GALLOIS, CYNTHIA and NORMAN N. MARKEL (1975) "Turn-Taking: Social Personality and Conversational Style". *Journal of Personality and Social Psychology*, **31**: 6, 1134–1140.

GIBIAN, GEORGE, (1970) Critical edition of Leo Tolstoy's *Anna Karenina*, translated by Louis and Aylmer Maude, 1918. W. W. Norton & Company, New York.

GIDE ANDRÉ (1919) *La symphonie pastorale*. Gallimard, Paris, 1966.

GOFFMAN, ERVIN (1963) *Behavior in Public Places*. The Free Press of Glencoe, New York; The Free Press of London: Collier-Macmillan, New York, 1966.

GIVENS, DAVID B. (1977) "Shoulder Shrugging: A Densely Communicative Expressive Behavior". *Semiotica*, **19**: 1/2, 13–28.

GOMBRICH, E. H. (1972) "Action and Expression in Western Art". In R. A. Hinde (Ed.), *Non-Verbal Communication*. Cambridge University Press, Cambridge, 373–94.

GOODALL, JAN VAN LAWICK (1971) *In the Shadow of Man*. William Collins, London; Fontana Books, 1973.

GREEN, JERALD R. (1968) *A Gesture Inventory for the Teaching of Spanish*. Chilton Books, Philadelphia, 1968.

HALL, EDWARD T. (1959) *The Silent Language*. Doubleday & Company, Inc., New York. Reprinted, Fawcett Publications, Greenwich, Conn., 1966.

HALL, EDWARD T. (1966) *The Hidden Dimension*. Doubleday, New York.

HALL, EDWARD T. (1974) *Handbook for Proxemic Research*. American Anthropological Association, Society for the Anthropology of Visual Communication.

HALL, EDWARD T. (1977) *Beyond Culture*. Anchor, New York.

HARDY, THOMAS (1895) *Jude the Obscure*. Dell Publishing Co., New York, 1960.

HARPER, ROBERT, G., ARTHUR N. WIENS and JOSEPH MATARAZZO (1978) *Nonverbal Communication: The State of the Art*. John Wiley & Sons, New York.

HAWTHORNE, NATHANIEL (1851) *The House of Seven Gables*. Washington Square Press, New York, 1960.

HAYES, ALFRED S. (1964) "Paralinguistics and Kinesics: Pedagogical Perspectives". In Thomas A. Sebeok, Alfred S. Hayes and Mary C. Bateson (Eds.), *Approaches to Semiotics: Cultural Anthropology, Education, Linguistics, Psychiatry, Psychology*. Mouton, The Hague, 145–172.

HENLEY, N. (1977) *Body Politics: Power, Sex and Nonverbal Communication*. Prentice-Hall, Englewood Cliffs.

HESS-LÜTTICH, ERNEST W. B. (1979) "Drama, Silence and Semiotics". *Kodikas/Code*, **1**: 2, 105–120.

HESS-LÜTTICH, ERNEST (1982) *Multimedial Communication II: Theatre Semiotics*. Gunter Narr Verlag, Tubingen.

HEWES, GORDON W. (1949) "Lateral Dominance, Culture, and Writing Systems". *Human Biology*, **21**, 233–245.

HEWES, GORDON W. (1955) "World Distribution of Certain Postural Habits". *American Anthropologist*, **57**: 2, 231–244. Also in L. Samovar and R. Porter (Eds.), *Intercultural Communication: A Reader*. Wadsworth Publishing, Belmont, California, 1972, 193–200.

HEWES, GORDON W. (1957) "The Anthropology of Posture". *Scientific American*, **196**, 123–130.

HEWES, GORDON W. (1973a) "Primate Communication and the Gestural Origin of Language". *Current Anthropology*, **14**: 1–2, 5–24.

HEWES, GORDON W. (1973b) "An Explicit Formulation of the Relationship Between Tool-Using, Tool-Making, and the Emergence of Language". *Visible Language*, **7**: 2, 101–127.

HILL, ARCHIBALD E. (1952) "A Note on Primitive Languages". *International Journal of Applied Linguistics*, **18**, 172–177.

HILL, ARCHIBALD E. (1958) *Introduction to Linguistic Structures*. Harcourt, Brace & World, New York.

HOCKETT, CHARLES F. (1960) "Logical Considerations in the Study of Animal Communication". In W. E. Lanyon and W. N. Tavolga (Eds.), *Animal Sounds and Communication*. American Institute of Biological Sciences, Washington, D.C., 392–430.

HOFFER, BATES and ROBERT ST. CLAIR (Eds.) (1981) *Developmental Kinesics*. University Park Press, Baltimore.

HORTELANO, JUAN GARCÍA (1962) *Tormenta de verano*. Seix Barral, Barcelona.

HOWE, G. MELVYN (1977) *A World Geography of Human Diseases*. Academic Press, New York.

HUSBAND, T. F. and M. F. A. HUSBAND (1905) *Punctuation: Its Principles and Practice*. George Routledge & Sons Ltd., London; E. P. Dutton & Co., New York.

HUXLEY, ALDOUS (1928) *Point Counterpoint*. Avon Books, New York.

IBSEN, HENRIK (1890) *Hedda Gabbler*. In *Four Great Plays by Ibsen*, trans. by J. Gassner. Bantam Books, New York, 1958.

IBSEN, HENRIK (1884) *The Wild Duck*. In E. Bradlee Watson and B. Pressey, (Eds.), *Contemporary Drama: 15 Plays*. Charles Scribner's Sons, New York, 1959.

JAMES, HENRY (1898) *The Turn of the Screw*. J. M. Dent & Sons, London, 1952.

JEFFERSON, GAIL (1973) "A Case of Precision Timing in Ordinary Conversation". *Semiotica*, **9**: 1, 47–96.

JESPERSEN, OTTO (1933) *Essentials of English Grammar*. George Allen & Unwin Ltd., London.

JOHANNESEN, RICHARD L. (1974) "The Functions of Silence: A Plea for Communication Research". *Western Speech*, Winter, 25–35.

JOHNSON, HAROLD G., PAUL EKMAN and WALLACE V. FRIESEN (1975) "Communicative Body Movements: American Emblems". *Semiotica*, **15**: 4, 335–353. Reprinted in A. Kendon (Ed.), *Nonverbal Communications, Interaction, and Gesture*. Mouton, The Hague.

JOHNSON, SAHNNY (1982) *A Handbook on Nonverbal Communication for Teachers of Foreign Languages*. Newbury House, Rowley, MA.

JOHNSON, SAHNNY (1983) *Japanese Nonverbal Communication*. Newbury House, Rowley, MA.

JOURARD, S. M. (1966) "An Exploratory Study of Body-Accessibility". *British Journal of Social and Clinical Psychology*, **5**, 221–231.

JOYCE, JAMES (1916) *A Portrait of the Artist as a Young Man*. Penguin Books, Harmondsworth, 1976.

JOYCE, JAMES (1922) *Ulysses*. Vintage Books, New York, 1961.

KAHN, JOAN Y. (1978) "A Diagnostic Semiotic". *Semiotica*, **22**: 1/2, 75–106.

KENDON, ADAM (1967) "Some Functions of Gaze-Direction in Social Interaction". *Acta Psychologica*, **26**, 22–63.

KENDON, ADAM (1969) "Progress Report on an Investigation Into Aspects of the Structure and Function of the Social Performance in Two-Person Encounters". In Michael Argyle (Ed.), *Social Interaction*. Methuen, London.

KENDON, ADAM (1970) "Movement Coordination in Social Interaction". *Acta Psychologica*, **32**, 1–25.

KENDON, ADAM (1972a) "Some Relations Between Body Motion and Speech: An Analysis of an Example". In Aaron Siegman and Benjamin Pope (Eds.), *Studies in Dyadic Communication*. Pergamon Press, Oxford, 177–210.

KENDON, ADAM (1972b) Birdwhistell's *Kinesics and Context* (Review). *American Journal of Psychology*, **85**: 3, 441–455.

KENDON, ADAM (1973a) "The Role of Visible Behavior in the Organization of Social Interaction". In Mario von Cranach and Ian Vine (Eds.), *Social Communication and Movement: Studies of Interaction and Expression in Man and Chimpanzee*. Academic Press, London/New York, 29–74.

KENDON, ADAM (1973b) "A Description of Some Human Greetings". In R. P. M. Michael and J. H. Crook (Eds.), *Comparative Ecology and Behavior of Primates*. Academic Press, London/New York. Also in Adam Kendon (Ed.), *Studies in the Behavior of Social Interaction*. Mouton, The Hague, 115–117.

KENDON, ADAM (1976) "Some Functions of the Face in a Kissing Round". *Semiotica*, **15**: 4, 299–334.

KENDON, ADAM (1977) *Studies in the Behavior of Face-to-Face Interaction*. Peter de Ridder Press, Lisse.

KENDON, ADAM (1980a) "Features of the Structural Analysis of Human Communication Behavior". In W. von Raffler-Engel (Ed.), *Aspects of Nonverbal Communication*. Swets and Zeitlinger B.V., Lisse, 29–43.

KENDON, ADAM (1980b) "Gesticulation and Speech: Two Aspects of the Process of Utterance". In M. Key (Ed.), *The Relationship of Verbal and Nonverbal Communication*. Mouton, The Hague, 207–227.

KENDON, ADAM (1981) *Nonverbal Communication, Interaction, and Gesture*. Mouton, The Hague.

KENDON, ADAM (1982a) "Some Uses of Gestures". 2nd Annual Conference on Conversation Analysis and Interaction. University of South Carolina, Columbia, S.C., April, 1980.

KENDON, ADAM (1982b) "The Organization of Behavior in Face-to-Face Interaction: Observations on the Development of a Methodology". In Klaus R. Scherer and Paul Ekman (Eds.), *Handbook of Methods in Nonverbal Behavior Research*. Cambridge University Press, Cambridge. Editions de la Maison des Sciences de l'Homme, Paris, 441–505.

KEROUAC, JACK (1958) *On the Road*. Signet Books, The New American Library, New York, 1960.

KEY, MARY R. (1974) "The Relationship of Verbal and Nonverbal Communication". In

Proceedings of the Eleventh International Congress of Linguists, edited by L. Heilman. Societa Editrici Il Mulino, Bologna.

KEY, MARY R. (1977) *Nonverbal Communication: A Research Guide and Bibliography*. Scarecrow Press, Metuchen, New Jersey.

KEY, MARY R. (1975) *Paralanguage and Kinesics*. Scarecrow Press, Metuchen, New Jersey.

KEY, MARY R. (1980) *The Relationship of Verbal and Nonverbal Communication*. Mouton, The Hague.

KEY, MARY R. (1982) *Nonverbal Communication Today: Current Research*. Mouton, The Hague.

KLUCKHOHN, CLYDE (1949) *Mirror for Man: The Relation of Anthropology to Modern Life*. Whittlesey House, New York.

KOCH, H. (1933) "An Analysis of So-called Nervous Habits in Young Children" (abstract). *Psychological Bulletin*, **30**, 683.

KRIEGER, DOLORES (1972) "The Response of In-Vivo Human Hemoglobin to an Active Healing Therapy by Direct Laying-On of Hands". *Human Dimensions*, **1**, 12–15.

KRIEGER, DOLORES (1974a) "The Relationship of Touch, With Intent to Help or to Heal, to Subjects' In-Vivo Hemoglobin Values: A Study in Personalized Interaction". *American Nurses' Association Ninth Nursing Research Conference*. American Nurses' Association, Kansas City.

KRIEGER, DOLORES (1974b) "Healing by the Laying-On of Hands as a Facilitator of Bioenergetic Change: The Response of In-Vivo Human Hemoglobin". *Psychoenergetic Systems*, **3**: 3.

KRIEGER, DOLORES (1975) "Therapeutic Touch: The Imprimatur of Nursing". *American Journal of Nursing*, **75**: 5, 784–787.

KROUT, MAURICE H. (1935) "Autistic Gestures". *Psychological Monographs*, **46**, 1–126.

LABARRE, WESTON (1947) "The Cultural Basis of Emotions and Gestures". *Journal of Personality*, **16**, 49–68. Also in John Laver and Sandy Hutcheson (Eds.), *Communication in Face-to-Face Interaction*. Penguin Books, Harmondsworth, 1972, 207–224.

LAVER, JOHN (1968) "Voice Quality and Indexical Information". *British Journal of Disorders of Communication*, **3**, 43–54. Also in John Laver and Sandy Hutcheson (Eds.), *Communication in Face-to-Face Interaction*. Penguin Books, Harmondsworth, 189–203.

LAVER, JOHN (1978) *The Phonetic Description of Voice Quality*. Cambridge University Press, Cambridge.

LAVER, JOHN and SANDY HUTCHESON (1972) *Communication in Face-to-Face Interaction: Selected Readings*. Penguin Books, Harmondsworth.

LAWRENCE, D. H. (1921) *Women in Love*. Modern Library, Random House, New York, 1950.

Lazarillo de Tormes (1554) Anonymous. In *La Novela Picaresca española*. Editorial Aguilar, Madrid, 1956.

LEACH, EDMUND (1972) "The Influence of Cultural Context on Non-Verbal Communication in Man". In R. Hinde (Ed.), *Non-Verbal Communication*. Cambridge University Press, Cambridge.

LENNEBERG, ERIC H. (Ed.) (1964) *New Directions in the Study of Language*. M.I.T., Boston.

LEVINE, ROBERT A. (1973) *Culture, Behavior, and Personality*. Aldine Publishing Company, Chicago.

LIEBERMAN, PHILIP (1975) "Linguistic and Paralinguistic Interchange". In A. Kendon, R. Harris and M. Key (Eds.), *The Organization of Behavior in Face-to-Face Interaction*. Mouton, The Hague, 277–284.

LINDENFELD, JACQUELINE (1971) "Verbal and Non-Verbal Elements in Discourse". *Semiotica*, **3**: 3, 224–233.

LINDENFELD, JACQUELINE (1973) "Affective States and the Syntactic Structure of Speech". *Semiotica*, **8**: 4, 368–376.

LINDENFELD, JACQUELINE (1974) "Syntactic Structure and Kinesic Phenomena in Communicative Events". *Semiotica*, **12**: 1, 61–73.

LORENZ, KONRAD Z. (1952) *King Solomon's Ring*. Thomas Y. Crowell, New York. Signet, 1972.

LURIA, A. (1932) *The Nature of Human Conflicts*. Liveright, New York.

LYONS, JOHN (1972) "Human Language". In Robert A. Hinde (Ed.), *Non-Verbal Communication*. Cambridge University Press, Cambridge, 49–85.

MACNUTT, FRANCIS (1974) *Healing*. Ave Maria Press, Notre Dame, Indiana. Bantam Books, New York.

MACNUTT, FRANCIS (1977) *The Power to Heal*. Ave Marie Press, Notre Dame, Indiana.

MALAMUD, BERNARD (1971) *The Tenants*. Pocket Books, New York, 1972.

MANN, THOMAS (1901) *Buddenbrooks*. Vintage Books, New York, 1952.

MAHL, GEORGE (1968) "Gestures and Body Movement". In John M. Shlein (Ed.), *Research in Psychotherapy*. American Psychological Association, 295–346.

MALINOWSKI, BRONISLAW (1923) "The Problem of Meaning in Primitive Languages". In C. K. Odgen and I. A. Richards (Eds.), *The Meaning of Meaning*. Routledge and Kegan Paul, London.

MARKANDAYA, KAMALA (1954) *Nectar in a Sieve*. New American Library, New York.

MARKEL, NORMAN (1975) "Coverbal Behavior Associated with Conversation Turns". In A. Kendon, R. Harris and M. Key (Eds.), *Organization of Behavior in Face-to-Face Interaction*. Mouton, The Hague, 189–197.

MAUGHAM, W. SOMERSET (1915) *Of Human Bondage*. Modern Library, Random House, New York, 1942.

MCBRIDE, GLENN (1973) Comments to and in Gordon W. Hewes, "Primate Communication and the Gestural Origin of Language". *Current Anthropology*, **141/2**, 5–24.

MCCORMACK, WILLIAM C. and STEPHEN A. WURM (Eds.) (1976) *Language and Man: Anthropological Issues*. Mouton, The Hague.

MCQUOWN, NORMAN (1957) "Linguistic Transcription and Specifications of Psychiatric Interview Materials". *Psychiatry*, **20**, 79–86.

MCQUOWN, NORMAN, MARY C. BATESON, R. BIRDWHISTELL, HENRY W. BROWIN, CHARLES F. HOCKETT (Eds.) (1971) *The Natural History of an Interview*. Microfilm Col. of Manuscripts on Cultural Anthropology, Fifteenth Series. The University of Chicago Joseph Regenstein Library, Dept. of Photoduplication, Chicago.

MENDILOW, A. A. (1965) *Time and the Novel*. Humanities Press, New York.

MEREZHKOVSKY, DIMITRI S. (1912) *L. Tolstoi i Dostoevsky: Zhizn', tvotchesvo, i religiia*. St. Petersburg-Moscow. M. O. Wolf Edition of Merezhkovsky's *Collected Works*, Vol. VII, pp. 154–157, 193–201, as cited (in the essay "Tolstoy's Physical Descriptions") by G. Gibian in his edition of *Anna Karenina*. W. W. Norton, New York, 1970.

MERRYTHEW, ANNE (1982) "What the Nurses Nose Should Know". Unpublished paper.

MIHAILA-COVA, RODICA (1977) "Le silence en tant qu'acte de langage". *Revue Roumaine de Linguistique*, **22**: 4, 417–421.

MIKSZÁTH, KÁLMÁN (1896) *St. Peter's Umbrella*. Harper, New York, 1901.

MILLER, ARTHUR (1949) *Death of a Salesman*. In A. W. Allison, A. J. Carr, and A. M. Eastman (Eds.), *Masterpieces of the Drama*. Macmillan Publishing Co., New York, 1974.

MILLER, JONATHAN (1972) "Plays and Players". In Robert A. Hinde (Ed.), *Nonverbal Communication*. Cambridge University Press, Cambridge, 359–372.

MONTAGUE, ASHLEY, (1971) *Touching: The Human Significance of the Skin*. Harper & Row Publishers, New York, 2nd ed., 1978.

MORRIS, DESMOND (1972) *Intimate Behavior*. Random House, Bantam Books, New York, 1973.

MORRIS, DESMOND, PETER COLLET, PETER MARSH and MARIE O'SHAUGHNESSY (1979) *Gestures: Their Origins and Distributions*. Stein and Day, New York.*

O'CASEY, SEAN (1924) *Juno and the Paycock*. In A. W. Allison, A. J. Carr, and A. M. Eastman (Eds.), *Masterpieces of the Drama*. Macmillan Publishing Co., New York, 1974.

OLIVER, DOUGLAS L. (1964) *Invitation to Anthropology*. Natural History Press, American Museum Science Books, New York.

OLIVER, ROBERT (1971) *Communication and Culture in Ancient India and China*. Syracuse University Press, Syracuse.

OLSON, W. C. (1931) "A Study of Classroom Behavior". *Journal of Educational Psychology*, **22**, 449–454.

O'NEILL, EUGENE (1924) *Desire Under the Elms*. In A. W. Allison, A. J. Carr and A. M. Eastman (Eds.), *Masterpieces of the Drama*. Macmillan Publishing Co., New York, 1974.

* Review article by Adam Kendon, *Semiotica*, **37**: 1/2, 1981, 129–163.

PAGE, A. (1961) *Etiquette for Gentlemen*. Ward Lock, London.

PARTRIDGE, ERIC (1953) *You have a Point There*. The English Language Book Society and Hamish Hamilton, London.

PARTRIDGE, ERIC (1966) "Punctuation". In James H. Campbell and Hal W. Hapler (Eds.), *Dimensions in Communication*. Wadsworth Publishing, Belmont, California, 199–207.

PATRICK, JOHN (1952) *The Teahouse of the August Moon*. Heinemann, London.

PIKE, KENNETH (1943) *Phonetics*. The University of Michigan Press, Ann Arbor, 1943.

PIKE, KENNETH (1954) *Language in Relation to a Unified Theory of the Structure of Human Behavior*. Summer Institute of Linguistics, Glendale, California.

PIKE, KENNETH L. (1964) "Towards a Theory of the Structure of Human Behavior". In Dell Hymes (Ed.), *Language in Culture and Society*. Harper & Row, New York, 54–62.

PIKE, KENNETH L. (1967) *Language in Relation to a Unified Theory of the Structure of Human Behavior*. Mouton, The Hague.

PIRANDELLO, LUIGI (1921) *Six Characters in Search of an Author*. In A. W. Allison, A. J. Carr and A. M. Eastman (Eds.), *Masterpieces of the Drama*. Macmillan Publishing Co., New York, 1974.

PITTENGER, ROBERT E. (1956) "Linguistic analysis of tone of voice in the communication of affect". *Psychiatric Research Reports*, **8**, 41–54.

PITTENGER, ROBERT E., CHARLES F. HOCKETT and JOHN DANEHY (1960) *The First Five Minutes: A Sample of Microscopic Interview Analysis*. Paul Martineau, Publisher, Ithaca.

PITTENGER, ROBERT E. and HENRY L. SMITH (1957) "A Basis for Some Contributions of Linguistics to Psychiatry". *Psychiatry*, **20**, 61–78. Also in A. Smith (Ed.), *Communication and Culture*. Holt, Rinehart & Winston, New York, 1966, 169–182.

Poema del Cid (1140) Anonymous. Edited by R. Menéndez-Pidal. *Clásicos Castellanos*, Espasa-Calpe, Madrid, 1951.

PORTER, RICHARD E. (1972) "An Overview of Intercultural Communication". In Larry A. Samovar and R. E. Porter (Eds.), *Intercultural Communication: A Reader*. Wadsworth Publishing Co., Belmont, California, 3–18.

POST, EMILY L. (1965) *Emily Post's Etiquette: The Blue Book of Social Usage*, 11th ed. Funk & Wagnall's, New York.

POYATOS, FERNANDO (1969) "Enfoque behaviorista del hablante como miembro de su cultura". *Filología Moderna*, **35/36**, 165–172.

POYATOS, FERNANDO (1970a) "Paralinguística y kinésica: para una teoría del sistema communicativo en el hablante español". In *Actas del Tercer Congreso Internacional de Hispanistas*. El Colegio de México, México, 725–738.

POYATOS, FERNANDO (1970b) "Lección de paralenguaje". *Filología Moderna*, **39**, 265–300.

POYATOS, FERNANDO (1970c) "Kinésica del español actual". *Hispania*, **53**: 3, 444–452.

POYATOS, FERNANDO (1971) "Sistemas comunicativos de una cultura: nuevo campo de investigación". *Yelmo*, **1**, 27–32.

POYATOS, FERNANDO (1972a) "The Communication System of the Speaker-Actor and His Culture". *Linguistics*, **32**, 64–86.

POYATOS, FERNANDO (1972b) "Paralenguaje y kinésica del personaje novelesco: nueva perspectiva en el análisis de la narración". *Revista de Occidente*, **113/114**, 148–170.

POYATOS, FERNANDO (1972c) "Paralenguaje y kinésica del personaje novelesco: nueva perspectiva en el análisis de la narración". *Prohemio*, **3**: 2, 291–307.

POYATOS, FERNANDO (1973) "La comparación inglesa con *as-as* en la lengua hablada". *Filología Moderna*, **46/47**, 31–61.

POYATOS, FERNANDO (1974a) "Del paralenguaje a la comunicación total". In *Doce ensayos sobre el lenguaje*. Fundación Juan March, Madrid, 159–171.

POYATOS, FERNANDO (1974b) "Cultura, comunicación e interacción: hacia el contexto total del lenguage y el hombre hispánicos, I". *Yelmo*, **19**, 23–26.

POYATOS, FERNANDO (1975a) "Cultura, comunicación e interacción: hacia el contexto total del lenguaje y el hombre hispánicos, II". *Yelmo*, **20**, 33–45.

POYATOS, FERNANDO (1975b) "Cultura, comunicación e interacción: hacia el contexto total del lenguaje y el hombre hispánicos, III". *Yelmo*, **21**, 14–16.

POYATOS, FERNANDO (1975c) "Cultura, comunicación e interacción: hacia el contexto total del lenguaje y el hombre hispánicos, IV". *Yelmo*, **22**, 27–29.

POYATOS, FERNANDO (1975d) "Gesture Inventories: Fieldwork Methodology and Problems". *Semiotica*, **13**: 2, 199–227. Reprinted in A. Kendon (Ed.), *Nonverbal Communication, Interaction, and Gesture.* Mouton, The Hague, 1981, 371–379.

POYATOS, FERNANDO (1975e) "Cross-Cultural Analysis of Paralinguistic 'Alternants' in Face-to-Face Interaction". In A. Kendon, R. Harris, and M. Key (Eds.), *Organization of Behavior in Face-to-Face Interaction*. World Anthropology Series. Mouton, The Hague, 285–314.

POYATOS, FERNANDO, (1976a) *Man Beyond Words: Theory and Methodology of Nonverbal Communication*. New York State English Council, Oswego.

POYATOS, FERNANDO (1976b) "Nueva perspectiva de la narración a través de los repertorios extraverbales del personaje". In S. Sanz-Villanueva and C. Barbachano (Eds.), *Teoría de la novela*. S.G.E.L., Madrid, 353–383.

POYATOS, FERNANDO (1976c) "Coding and Functions of Nonverbal Communication in the Novel". *The Canadian Journal of Research in Semiotics*, **3**: 2, 53–66.

POYATOS, FERNANDO (1976d) "Language in the Context of Total Body Communication". *Linguistics*, **168**, 49–62.

POYATOS, FERNANDO (1976e) "Analysis of a Culture Through Its Culturemes: Theory and Method". In A. Rapoport (Ed.), *The Mutual Interaction of People and Their Built Environment.* World Anthropology Series. Mouton, The Hague, 265–274.

POYATOS, FERNANDO, (1976f) "Analysis of Culture Through Its Culturemes: Theory and Method". In W. McCormack and S. Wurm (Eds.), *Language and Man: Anthropological Issues*. World Anthroplogy Series. Mouton, The Hague, 313–322.

POYATOS, FERNANDO (1976g) "Verbal and Nonverbal Expression in Interaction: Research and Pedagogical Perspectives". In G. Nickel (Ed.), *Proceedings of the Fourth International Congress of Applied Linguistics*, Vol. I. Hochschul Verlag, Stuttgart, 87–97.

POYATOS, FERNANDO (1976h) "Codificación y descodificación del personaje en la narrativa española: enfoque semiótico". *Papeles de Son Armadáns*, **82**: 245/246, 113–132.

POYATOS, FERNANDO (1977a) "The Morphological and Functional Approach to Kinesics in the Context of Interaction and Culture". *Semiotica*, **20**: 3/4, 197–228.

POYATOS, FERNANDO (1977b) "Forms and Functions of Nonverbal Communication in the Novel: A New Perspective of the Author–Character–Reader Relationship". *Semiotica*, **21**: 3/4, 295–337.

POYATOS, FERNANDO (1978a) "Ampliación interdisciplinar de los estudios hispánicos: temas y perspectivas". *Hispania*, **61**: 2, 254–269.

POYATOS, FERNANDO (1978b) "Kinesics in the Context of Culture and Interaction". In C. Pearson and H. Hamilton-Faria (Eds.), *Proceedings of the First Meeting of the Semiotic Society of America*. Georgia Institute of Technology, Atlanta, 192–199.

POYATOS, FERNANDO (1979a) "Phonetic and Interdisciplinary Perspectives in Paralinguistic Studies". In H. Hollien and P. Hollien (Eds.), *Current Issues in the Phonetic Sciences: Proceedings of the Eighth International Congress of Phonetic Sciences*. Amsterdam Studies in the Theory and History of Linguistic Science, IV; Current Issues in Linguistic Theory, 9. John Benjamins B.V., Amsterdam, 1105–1116.

POYATOS, FERNANDO, (1979b) "The Challenge of 'Total Body Communication' as an Interdisciplinary Field of Integrative Research". In S. Chatman, U. Eco and J.-M. Klinkenberg (Eds.), *A Semiotic Landscape: Proceedings of the First International Congress of Semiotic Studies*. Mouton, The Hague, 349–355.

POYATOS, FERNANDO (1979c) "Literary Anthroplogy: A New Interdisciplinary Perspective of Man". *Man and Life*, **5**: 3/4, 127–149.

POYATOS, FERNANDO (1980a) "Interactive Functions and Limitations of Verbal and Nonverbal Behaviors in Natural Conversation". *Semiotica*, **30**: 3/4, 211–244.

POYATOS, FERNANDO (1980b) "Man as a Socializing Being: New Integrative and Interdisciplinary Perspectives Through Cultural and Crosscultural Studies in Nonverbal Communication. In W. von Raffler-Engel (Ed.), *Aspects of Nonverbal Communication*. Swets & Zeitlinger, Lisse.

POYATOS, FERNANDO (1981a) "Forms and Functions of Nonverbal Communication in the Novel: The Author–Character–Reader Relationship". In A. Kendon (Ed.), *Nonverbal Communication, Interaction, and Gesture* (Approaches to Semiotics, 41). Mouton, The Hague, 107–149.

POYATOS, FERNANDO (1981b) "Gesture Inventories: Fieldwork Methodology and Problems". In A. Kendon (Ed.), *Nonverbal Communication, Interaction, and Gesture* (Approaches to Semiotics, 41). Mouton, The Hague, 371–399.

POYATOS, FERNANDO (1981c) "Literary Anthropology: A New Interdisciplinary Perspective of Man Through His Narrative Literature". *Versus: cuaderni di studi semiotici*, **28**, 3–28.

POYATOS, FERNANDO (1981d) "Punctuation as Nonverbal Communication: Toward an Interdisciplinary Approach to Writing". *Semiotica*, **34**, 1/2, 91–112.

POYATOS, FERNANDO (1981e) "Silence and Stillness: Toward a New Status of Non-Activity". *Kodikas/Code*, **3**: 1, 3–26.

POYATOS, FERNANDO (1981f) "Toward a Typology of Somatic Signs". *Semiotic Inquiry*, **1**: 2, 135–156.

POYATOS, FERNANDO (1981g) "Interactive Nonverbal Categories: A Reappraisal and Elaboration". In M. Herzfeld and M. Lenhart (Eds.), *Proceedings of the Fourth Meeting of the Semiotic Society of America*. Plenum Press, New York.

POYATOS, FERNANDO (1982a) "Nonverbal Communication in the Theater: The Playwright–Actor–Spectator Relationship". In E. Hess-Luttich (Ed.), *Multimedial Communication II: Theatre Semiotics*. Gunter Narr Verlag, Tubingen, 75–94.

POYATOS, FERNANDO (1982b) "New Perspectives for an Integrative Approach to Nonverbal Systems". In M. Key (Ed.), *Nonverbal Communication Today: Current Research*. Mouton, The Hague, 121–138.

POYATOS, FERNANDO (1982c) "Language and Nonverbal Behavior in the Structure of Social Conversation". *International Journal of the Language Sciences*, **4**: 2, 155–185.

POYATOS, FERNANDO (1983a) "Language and Nonverbal Systems in the Structure of Face-to-Face Interaction". *Language and Communication*, **3**: 2.

POYATOS, FERNANDO (1983b) "The Multichannel Reality of Discourse: Language-Paralanguage-Kinesics and the Totality of Communication Systems". In F. Peng (Ed.), Volume from the Second International Conference on the Language Sciences. In press, Tokyo, 1982.

POYATOS, FERNANDO (1983c) "Linguistic Fluency and Verbal-Nonverbal Cultural Fluency". In A. Wolfgang (Ed.), Volume from the Second International Conference on Nonverbal Behavior. In press, Toronto, 1983.

POYATOS, FERNANDO (1983d) *Paralanguage: Interdisciplinary Theory and Applications*. (Amsterdam Studies in the Theory and History of Linguistics; Current Issues in Linguistic Theory). John Benjamins B.V., Amsterdam. In press.

QUILIS, ANTONIO (1975) "Las unidades de entonación". *Revista de Linguistica Española*, **5**: 2, 261–280.

RAO, RAJA (1938) *Kanthapura*. New Directions, New York, 1963.

RAO, RAJA (1961) *The Serpent and the Rope*. Orient Paperbacks, New Delhi.

RAPOPORT, AMOS (Ed.) (1976) *The Mutual Interaction of People and Their Built Environment*. Mouton, The Hague.

REED, WILLIAM S. (1979) *Healing the Whole Man: Mind, Body, Spirit*. Fleming H. Revell Company, Old Tappan, New Jersey.

ROBBE-GRILLET, ALAIN (1963) *Pour un nouveau roman*. Gallimard, Paris.

ROCHESTER, SHERRY R. (1973) "The Significance of Pauses in Spontaneous Speech". *Journal of Psycholinguistic Research*, **2**: 1, 51–81.

ROSTAND, EDMOND (1897) *Cyrano de Bergerac*. Fasquelle Editeurs, Paris.

RUESCH, JURGEN and WELDON KEES (1956) *Nonverbal Communication: Notes on the Visual Perception of Human Relations*. University of California Press, Berkeley.

SACKS, HARVEY, EMMANUEL SCHEGLOFF and GAIL JEFFERSON (1974) "A Simplest Systematic for Turn-taking in Natural Conversation". *Language*, **50**: 4, 696–735.

SAGAN, FRANCOISE (1965) *La chamade*. Julliard, Paris.

SAITZ, ROBERT L. and EDWARD J. CERVENKA (1962) *Colombian and North American Gestures: A Contrastive Inventory*. Centro Colombo Americano, Bogotá. As *Handbook of Gestures: Colombia and the United States*. Approaches to Semiotics, 31. Mouton, The Hague, 1972.

SÁNCHEZ-FERLOSIO, RAFAEL (1958) *El Jarama*. Ediciones Destino, Barcelona.

SANFORD, AGNES (1966) *The Healing Gifts of the Spirit*. A. J. Holman Company, Trumpet Books Ed., 1976, Philadelphia and New York.

SANFORD, AGNES (1969) *The Healing Power of the Bible*. A. J. Holman Company, Pillar Books, Philadelphia and New York.

SANFORD, AGNES (1972) *Sealed Orders*. Logos International, Plainfield, New Jersey.

SAPIR, EDWARD (1929) *Language: An Introduction to the Study of Speech*. Harcourt Brace, New York.

SAPIR, EDWARD (1924) "Culture, Genuine and Spurious". *American Journal of Sociology*, **29**, 401–429. Also in E. Sapir, *Culture, Language and Personality*. University of California Press, Berkeley/Los Angeles, 78–119.

SARA, D. (1963) *Good Manners and Hospitality*. Collier, New York.

SCANLAN, MICHAEL (1979) *A Portion of My Spirit*. Carillon Books, St. Paul, Minnesota.

SCHEFLEN, ALBERT (1964) "Communication and Regulation in Psychotherapy". *Psychiatry*, **29**: 3, 126–136.

SCHEFLEN, ALBERT (1965) "Quasi-courtship behavior in psychotherapy". *Psychiatry*, **28**: 3, 245–257.

SCHEFLEN, ALBERT E. (1972) *Body Language and the Social Order*. Prentice-Hall, Englewood Cliffs, New Jersey.

SCHEFLEN, ALBERT (1973a) *Communicational Structure: Analysis of a Psychotherapy Transaction*. Indiana University Press, Bloomington and London.

SCHEFLEN, ALBERT (1973b) *How Behavior Means*. Gordon & Breach, Science Publishers, New York. Doubleday, Garden City, 1974.

SCHEGLOFF, EMANUEL (1972) "Sequencing in Conversational Openings". In J. Laver and S. Hutcheson (Eds.), *Communication in Face-to-Face Interaction*. Penguin Books, Harmondsworth, 374–405. Also in *American Anthropologist*, **70**, 1968, 1075–1095. Also in J. J. Gumperz and D. Hymes (Ed.), *Directions in Sociolinguistics*. Holt, Rinehart & Winston, New York, 1972.

SCHEGLOFF, EMANUEL A. and HARVEY SACKS (1973) "Opening Up Closings". *Semiotica*, **8**: 4, 289–327.

SCHERER, KLAUS (1979) "Personality markers in speech." In K. Scherer, H. Giles (Eds.), *Social Markers in Speech*. Cambridge University Press, London.

SCHERER, KLAUS R. (1982) "Methods of Research on Vocal Communication: Paradigms and Parameters". In Klaus R. Scherer and Paul Ekman (Eds.), *Handbook of Methods in Nonverbal Behaviour Research*. Cambridge University Press/Paris: Editions de la Maison des Sciences de l'Homme, 136–198.

SCHERER, KLAUS R. and PAUL EKMAN (Eds.) (1982) *Handbook of Methods in Nonverbal Behavior Research*. Cambridge University Press, Cambridge. Editions de la Maison des Sciences de l'Homme, Paris.

SCHIFFRIN, DEBORAH (1974) "Handwork as Ceremony: The Case of the Handshake". *Semiotica*, **12**: 3, 189–202.

SEBEOK, THOMAS A. (1972) *Perspectives in Zoosemiotics*. Mouton, The Hague.

SEBEOK, THOMAS A. (1974) "Semiotics: A Survey of the State of the Art". In T. Sebeok *et al.* (Eds.), *Current Trends in Linguistics, Vol. 12, Linguistics and Adjacent Arts and Sciences*. Mouton, The Hague, 211–264.

SEBEOK, THOMAS A. (1975) "The Semiotic Web: A Chronicle of Prejudices". *Bulletin of Literary Semiotics*, **2**, 1–63.

SEBEOK, THOMAS A. (1976) "Iconicity". *Modern Language Notes*, **91**, 1427–1456.

SEBEOK, THOMAS A. (1977a) "Six Species of Signs: Some Propositions and Strictures". In T. Sebeok (Ed.), *Contribution to the Doctrine of Signs*. The Peter de Ridder Press, Lisse, pp. 117–142.

SEBEOK, THOMAS A. (1977b) "Zoosemiotic Components of Human Communication". In T. Sebeok (Ed.), *How Animals Communicate*. Indiana University Press, Bloomington, 1056–1077.

SEBEOK, THOMAS A., ALFRED S. HAYES and MARY C. BATESON (Eds.) (1964) *Approaches to Semiotics: Cultural Anthropology, Education, Linguistics, Psychiatry, Psychology*. Mouton, The Hague.

SEBEOK, THOMAS, SAHNNY JOHNSON, and JULIE HENGST (1982) *A Handbook on Nonverbal Communication for Teachers of Arabic as Spoken in the Area of the Gulf of Arabia*. Newbury House, Rowley, MA.

SHAW, BERNARD (1912) *Pygmalion*. Penguin Books, Harmondsworth, 1941.
SHAW, BERNARD (1923) *Saint Joan*. Penguin Books, Harmondsworth.
SHERIDAN, RICHARD BRINSLEY (1775) *The Rivals*. In A. W. Allison, A. J. Carr, and A. M. Eastman (Eds.), *Masterpieces of the Drama*. Macmillan Publishing Co., New York, 1974.
SHLEMON, BARBARA (1976) *Healing Prayer*. Ave Maria Press, Notre Dame, Indiana.
SHLEMON, BARBARA, DENNIS LINN, and MATTHEW LINN (1978) *To Heal as Jesus Healed*. Ave Maria Press, Notre Dame, Indiana.
SINGH, KUSHWANT (1956) *Train to Pakistan*. India Book House PYT. Ltd., Bombay.
Sir Gawain and the Grene Knight (14th c.) Anonymous (Ed. by R. Waldron). Northwestern University Press, Medieval Texts Series, Evanston, Illinois, 1970.
Sir Orfeo (c. 1320) Anonymous. In Boris Ford (Ed.), *The Age of Chaucer* (*A Guide to English Literature*, Vol. I). Penguin Books, Harmondsworth.
SITARAM, K. S. (1972) "What is Intercultural Communication?" In Larry A. Samovar and Richard E. Porter (Eds.), *Intercultural Communication: A Reader*. Wadsworth Publishing Co., Belmont, California, 18–23.
SKELTON, REGINALD (1933) *Modern English Punctuation*. Sir Isaac Pitman & Sons, London.
SMITH, HENRY L. (1953) "The Communication Situation". Foreign Service, U.S. Department of State, Washington, D.C. (mineographed paper).
SOPHOCLES (430 B.C.) *Oedipus Rex*. In A. W. Allison, A. J. Carr, and A. M. Eastman (Eds.), *Masterpieces of the Theater*. Macmillan Publishing Co., New York, 1974.
SPARHAWK, CAROL M. (1978) "Contrastive Identificational Features of Persian Gesture". *Semiotica*. Reprinted in A. Kendon (Ed.), *Nonverbal Communication, Interaction, and Gesture*. Approaches to Semiotics, 41. Mouton, The Hague, 1981.
STEINBECK, JOHN (1931) *Grapes of Wrath*. Bantam Books, New York, 1964.
THORPE, W. H. (1972) "The Comparison of Vocal Communication in Animals and Man". In Robert A. Hinde (Ed.), *Non-Verbal Communication*. Cambridge University Press, Cambridge, 27–47.
THORPE, W. H. (1974) *Animal Nature and Human Nature*. Methuen, London.
TOLSTOY, LEO (1873–7) *Anna Karenina*. Edited by G. Gibian. W. W. Norton & Company, New York, 1970.
TOLSTOY, LEO (1889–99) *Resurrection*. Progress Publishers, Moscow, 1972.
TOURNIER, PAUL (1974) *A Doctor's Casebook in the Light of the Bible*. Harper & Row, San Francisco.
TRAGER, GEORGE L. (1955) "Language". *Encyclopedia Britannica*, vol. 13. 696–703.
TRAGER, GEORGE L. (1958) "Paralanguage: A First Approximation". *Studies in Linguistics*, **13**, 1–12. Also in Dell Hymes (Ed.), *Language in Culture and Society*. Harper & Row, New York.
TRAGER, GEORGE L. (1960) "Taos III, Paralanguage". *Anthropological Linguistics*, **2**, 2, 24–30.
TRAGER, GEORGE L. and HENRY L. SMITH, Jr. (1956) *An Outline of English Structure. Studies in Linguistics: Occasional Papers*, No. 31. Battenburg, Norman, Oklahoma, 2nd print. American Council of Learned Societies, Washington, D.C., 1956.
TURGENEV, IVAN (1861) *Fathers and Sons*. Vintage Books, New York, 1950.
TYLER, VERNON LYNN and JAMES S. TAYLOR (1978) *Reading Between the Lines: Language Indicators Project*. Eyring Research Institute, Provo, Utah.
VANDERBILT, AMY (1956) *Everyday Etiquette*. Bantam Books, New Jersey.
VON RAFFLER-ENGEL, WALBURGA (1978) "The Acquisition of Kinesics by the Child". In F. Peng and W. von Raffler-Engel (Eds.), *Language Acquisition and Developmental Kinesics*. Bunka Hyoron Publishing Co., Hiroshima, 140–149.
VON RAFFLER-ENGEL, WALBURGA (1980) "Developmental Kinesics: The Acquisition of Conversational Nonverbal Behavior". In W. von Raffler-Engel (Ed.), *Aspects of Nonverbal Communication*. Swets & Zeitlinger, Lisse, 133–159.
VON RAFFLER-ENGEL, WALBURGA (1981) "The Acquisition and Maturation of Conversational Nonverbal Behaviors". In B. Hoffer and R. St. Clair (Eds.), *Developmental Kinesics: The Emerging Paradigm*. University Park Press, Baltimore, 5–27.
WATSON, O. MICHAEL (1974) "Proxemics". In Thomas A. Sebeok (Ed.), *Current Trends in Linguistics*, Vol. 12: 1. Mouton, The Hague, 311–344.

WAXER, PETER (1978) *Nonverbal Communication in Psychotherapy*. Praeger Publishers, New York.

WIEMANN, JOHN M. and MARK L. KNAPP (1975) "Turn-taking in Conversations". *Journal of Communication*, **25**: 2, 75–92.

WIENER, H. (1966) "External Chemical Messengers: I, Emission and Reception in Man". *New York State Journal of Medicine*, **65**, 3153–3170.

WIENER, H. (1968a). "External Chemical Messengers: IV. Pineal Gland". *New York State Journal of Medicine*, **68**, 912–938.

WIENER, H. (1968b) "External Chemical Messengers: V. More Functions of the Pineal Gland". *New York State Journal of Medicine*, **68**, 1019–1038.

WILDEBLOOD, JANE P. (1965) *The Polite World*. Oxford University Press, London.

WILLIAMS, TENNESSEE (1945) *The Glass Menagerie*, New Directions Books, New York, 1966.

WILLIAMS, TENNESSEE (1950) *The Rose Tattoo*. In S. Clayes and D. Spencer (Eds.), *Contemporary Drama: 13 Plays*. Charles Scribner's Sons, New York, 1962.

WYCHERLEY, WILLIAM (1675) *The Country Wife*. In A. W. Allison, A. J. Carr, and A. M. Eastman (Eds.), *Masterpieces of the Drama*. Macmillan Publishing Co., New York, 1974.

WYLIE, LAURENCE (1977) *Beau Gestes: A Guide to French Body Talk*. The Undergraduate Press, Cambridge, Mass.

YNGVE, VICTOR H. (1970) "On Getting a Word in Edgewise". *Papers from the Sixth Regional Meeting of the Chicago Linguistic Society*. Chicago Linguistic Society, Chicago.

Author Index

Subject Index